HISTORY OF BRITISH INDIA

D1880411

Owing to the antiquity and rarity of this book, certain pages are regrettably absent, and readability is compromised due to the blurring of the original text. If you possess any insights regarding the availability of these missing sections, kindly inform us. Your assistance is crucial in ensuring the completion of this significant work for the benefit of future generations.

HISTORY OF BRITISH INDIA

UNDER THE COMPANY AND THE CROWN

P. E. ROBERTS

GYAN

Published by

GYAN

Gyan Publishing House
5, Ansari Road
Daryaganj, New Delhi-110002
Phone: 011-47034999, 9811692060
E-mail: books@gyanbooks.com

Distribution Network
gyanbooks.com
India, USA, Canada, UK, Australia

© Publisher

All rights reserved. No part of this work may be reproduced, stored, adapted, or transmitted in any form or by any means, electronic, mechanical, photocopying, micro-filming, recording or otherwise, or translated in any language, without the prior written permission of the copyright owner and the publisher.

ISBN: 978-93-7447-387-0 (PB)

First Published, 1945

2nd Impression 2025

Printed at: Gyan Press, Delhi.

The book is sold subject to the condition that it shall not, by way of trade or otherwise, be lent, resold, hired out, or otherwise circulated without the prior publisher's written consent.

HISTORY OF BRITISH INDIA

Author: P. E. ROBERTS

HISTORY OF BRITISH INDIA

UNDER THE COMPANY AND THE CROWN

BY

P. E. ROBERTS

FELLOW OF WORCESTER COLLEGE, OXFORD

SECOND EDITION

OXFORD UNIVERSITY PRESS
LONDON : HUMPHREY MILFORD

CONTENTS

LIST OF MAPS

HISTORICAL GEOGRAPHY OF INDIA

CHAPTER I

PHYSICAL AND GEOGRAPHICAL FEATURES

THE geography of India will be treated fully in a separate volume, and in this chapter only such broad aspects of the subject will be indicated as are absolutely necessary for a right understanding of the history.

The natural frontiers of India are mountains and sea, and this fact has had a preponderating influence upon her annals. From the mouth of the Indus on the west to the delta of the Ganges on the east the waters of the Arabian Sea and the Indian Ocean wash the shores of the great triangular peninsula of central and southern India. A vast irregular semicircle of mountains, with a few breaks in the line, extends from a point westward of the Indus to the shores of Arakan—the country on the eastern bend of the Bay of Bengal. This colossal natural rampart, if we trace its course from west to east, begins with the Kirtha range striking northward from Karachi, the seaport of Sind. At Quetta the mountains curve eastward for a time till the Sulaiman range again trends in a northerly direction. Sweeping round to the east are the Hindu Kush and the Karakoram mountains with their tremendous summits, some attaining an altitude of 28,000 feet. Thence the mighty double barrier of the Himalayas, including amongst its peaks Mount Everest, the loftiest elevation on the surface of the globe, stretches in a slightly concave south-eastern curve to the northern frontier of Assam. At the base of the central Himalayas runs a belt of malarial tiger-haunted jungle called Tarai or Duars, and beneath the forest overgrowth lie the buried remains of ancient cities famous in Buddhist history. At right angles to the eastern edge of the Himalayas, hill ranges of lesser but still considerable elevation run due south to the seaboard of Arakan. India is thus magnificently fortified by nature, for the lowest passes over the Himalayas to the barren highlands of Tibet are 17,000 feet up, and are therefore useless except for the purposes of a primitive form of trade. To land armies she is vulnerable only from the west and north-west region of the mountain barrier, where the passes of the Khyber, Kurram, and Bolan lead down from the eastern edge of the Iranian plateau into the wide plains of the Punjab. Through their grim and frowning valleys successive invading hosts of Aryans, Huns, Afghans, Persians, and Mughals have marched to the conquest or plunder of Hindustan.

The configuration of the territories within these boundaries of mountain and sea now demands our attention. India falls naturally into two great divisions. First, Hindustan, which consists of the Himalayan system, the great northern alluvial plains, and the broken central plateau of Malwa and Bundelkhand; secondly, the Deccan, the triangular shaped peninsula of the south.[1] The division is marked by a broad belt of hills, forest, and the course of two rivers; the Satpura mountains run due east from the Gulf of Cambay, and in a deep trench between them and the Vindhya range the Narbada, 800 miles in length, flows westward into the

[1] Both names 'Hindustan' and 'Deccan' have unfortunately a wider and narrower denotation. Hindustan in its wider sense means all India lying north of the Vindhya Mountains; in the narrower sense, the upper basin of the Ganges. In like manner the Deccan sometimes means all India south of the Narbada, sometimes only the territory lying between that river and the Kistna. Further the term Hindustan is sometimes loosely applied by modern writers to the whole of India.

Arabian Sea; in an opposite direction the Mahanadi, with a more winding course, flows eastward into the Bay of Bengal. The barrier between Hindustan and the Deccan has always been well defined, and till the days of British rule it prevented India from being brought successfully under one imperial sway.

The great plains of India are in Hindustan. From the southern bases of the Himalayas they stretch westward to Kathiawar and eastward to the northern coast line of the Bay of Bengal. They are almost entirely composed of alluvial soil, the drainage of the mountains, brought down by two great rivers, the Indus and the Ganges. The Indus, 1,800 miles long, rises north of the Himalayas, and after flowing north-west for about 500 miles in a deep trough at the back of the range, pierces the mountain wall and turns southward. Then, after receiving as affluents the combined waters of the other four great rivers of the Punjab, it makes its way with greatly increased volume but slackened stream through Sind and empties itself by a network of channels into the Arabian Sea. The Ganges, swollen by its great tributaries, the Jumna, the Gogra, and the Gandak, flows for 1,500 miles across northern India almost parallel with the line of the Himalayas and, after irrigating an immense basin, finds its way through many mouths into the Bay of Bengal. Just before it merges into the sea, it is joined at Goalundo by the Brahmaputra, which under its Tibetan name of Tsanpo rises north of the Himalayas a few miles only from the source of the Indus, and flowing in a directly opposite direction for more than a thousand miles turns the eastern flank of the mountains by a wide detour winding first west and then south through the valleys of Assam into the plains of lower Bengal. So great is the volume of water carried down by these two mighty rivers that their combined delta, interlaced with innumerable channels, covers a space of 50,000 square miles. The great river systems of

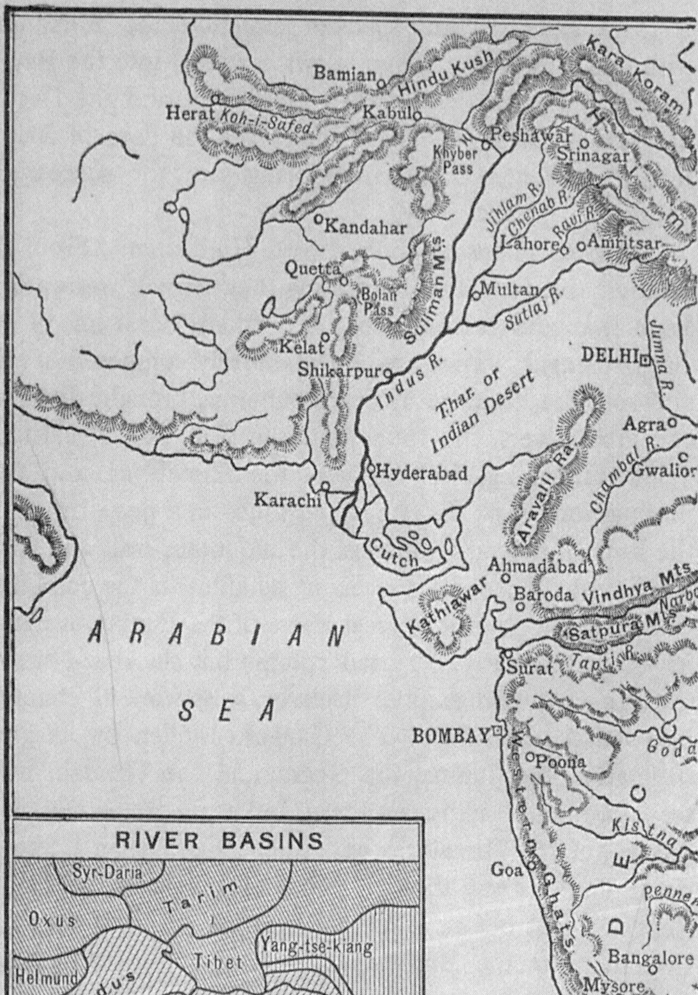
Hindu Kush
Kara Koram
Bamian
Herat
Koh-i-Safed
Kabul
Peshawar
Srinagar
Khyber Pass
Kandahar
Jihlam R.
Chenab R.
Ravi R.
Lahore
Amritsar
Quetta
Bolan Pass
Suliman Mts.
Multan
Sutlaj R.
Kelat
Shikarpur
Indus R.
DELHI
Jumna R.
Thar or Indian Desert
Agra
Chambal R.
Gwalior
Hyderabad
Aravalli Ra.
Karachi
Cutch
Ahmadabad
Kathiawar
Baroda
Vindhya Mts.
Satpura Mts.
Tapti R.
Surat
ARABIAN SEA
BOMBAY
Western Ghats
Poona
Kistna
Goa
Bangalore
Mysore
Nilgiri Hills
Calicut
Kaveri
Laccadive Is.
C.Comorin
Maldive Is.
RIVER BASINS
Syr-Daria
Oxus
Tarim
Tibet
Yang-tse-kiang
Helmund
Indus
Tharr
Brahmaputra
Ganges
Irawidi
Salween
Mekong
Mahanadi
Godavari
Kistna
Menam
Indian Ocean
China Sea
Inland Basins
WAXTYPE

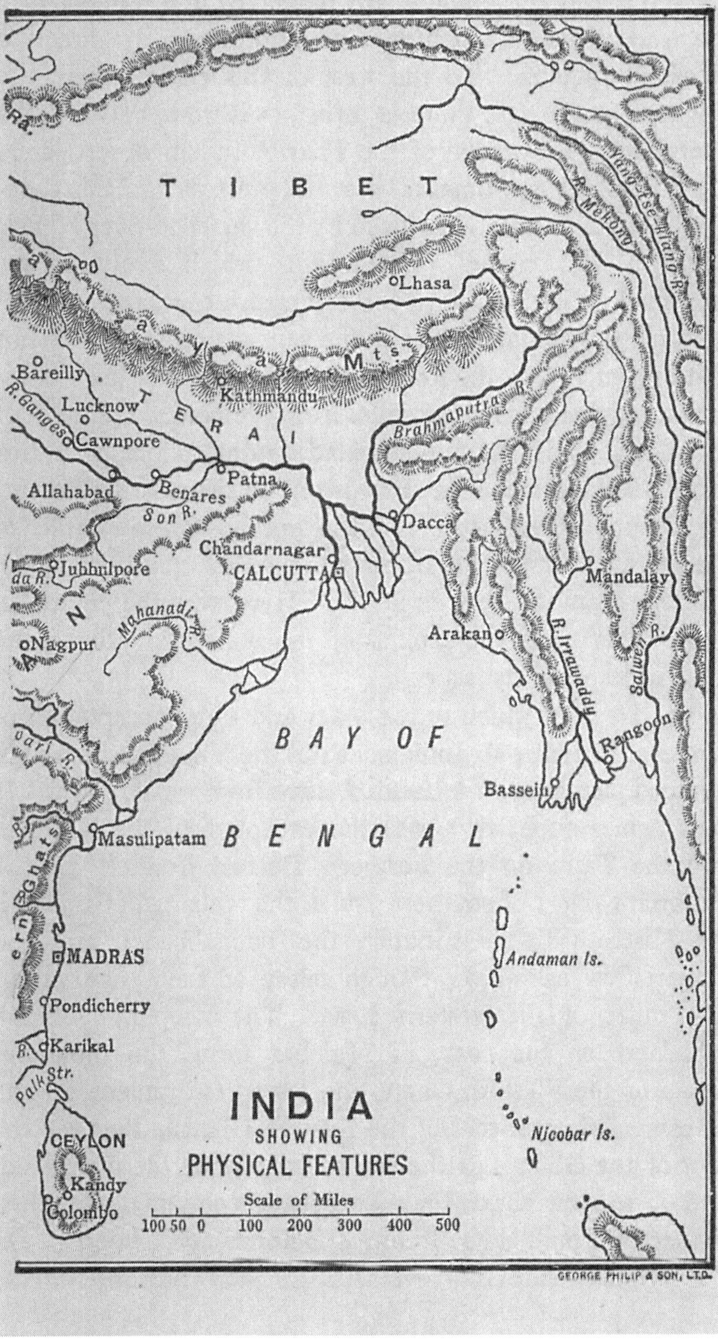

GEORGE PHILIP & SON, LTD.

the Indus and the Ganges are parted by the watershed of the Aravalli range which runs in a north-easterly direction across Rajputana. To the west of this chain, where the irrigating waters fail, there is thrust, as it were, between the river valleys the wedge of the Thar or Indian desert, once the floor of a vast primaeval sea. A great part of this desolate tract was formerly fertilized by the vanished river Hakra, flowing almost parallel with the Indus, which is said to have only finally disappeared in the eighteenth century.

While the climate of the Indus valley is on the whole hot and dry, and along the lower reaches of the river itself cultivation only extends a few miles from the banks, the plain of the Ganges with its moisture-laden atmosphere, rich rice fields, and luxuriant vegetation is one of the most fertile and thickly populated districts in the world. On the banks of the sacred river and its tributary the Jumna stand the fairest and most famous cities of India. Here were the centres of early civilizations, the capitals of the ancient kingdoms, the seats of imperial dynasties.

The Deccan, which in the older and wider acceptation of the term includes all India south of the Vindhyas, is a high terraced plateau with a decided slope from west to east. It thus comes about that with the exception of the Narbada and the Tapti on the northern Deccan frontier, all the important rivers of southern India, the Mahanadi, Godavari, the Kistna with its tributary the Tungabhadra, and the Kaveri flow eastwards, though many of them rise within fifty miles of the western coast. The steep wall of the tableland on the coast of Malabar forms the mountain range of the Western Ghats, the lower escarpment on the Coromandel coast that of the Eastern Ghats. Between the foot of the Ghats and the sea lie belts of fertile plain land, and it was on these that Europeans coming by sea first landed and built their primitive factories and stations. On the Bombay side the level strip is very narrow, for the mountains scarcely ever recede more than forty miles from the coast. On the Madras side it is much broader and the valleys of the Deccan rivers run far back among the hills. In the extreme south-east is the comparatively broad plain of Madura and Tinnevelly, for the Eastern Ghats, about two hundred miles from Cape Comorin, bend away to the west, and are linked up with the Western Ghats by the transverse range of the Nilgiris.

The coast line of India, which is about 3,000 miles in length, is singularly devoid of indentations, and the deltas of the rivers are difficult to navigate. On the western shore —the natural point of approach from Europe—Bombay is the only good unartificial harbour, and though it is one of the finest in the world, the city and its hinterland is so shut in by the Western Ghats, which extend from the Narbada to Cape Comorin with one break at Palghat, that till the development of railways it was a very poor centre for distribution. The eastern shore of the Deccan is a shallow, surf-beaten strand, and till the modern harbour of Madras was constructed landing could only be effected in small boats. Hence the unchallenged supremacy of Calcutta as a port for so many years. A glance at the physical map of India might suggest that the valley of the Indus was a more likely *point d'appui* from Europe. But the control of that waterway passed late into the hands of the British, and Karachi has only been made a tolerable port by artificial works. So, though the silt-laden channel of the Hughli is only kept open with difficulty, and its navigation is extremely dangerous, the delta of the Ganges has been till modern times the gate of India from the sea.[1]

[1] Of the physical and geographical features of Burma something will be said in chap. xiii.

CHAPTER II

SKETCH OF POLITICAL HISTORY TO THE APPEARANCE OF THE BRITISH IN INDIA

In this work we are not concerned with the ancient or mediaeval history of India. A few paragraphs must suffice to sum up the centuries that elapsed before India came into contact with European nations by sea. India has been called an 'ethnological museum'; it is a land with an infinite variety of races, religions, and languages. The original inhabitants seem to have been of a short, dark, and snub-nosed type, and their descendants now dwell mainly in southern India. The prevailing type in northern India is tall, fair-skinned, and long-nosed. They are almost certainly a branch of the great Aryan race which from about 1500 B.C. came thronging into Hindustan through the north-western passes in successive waves of immigration, driving back the aborigines into the fastnesses and tablelands of the Deccan. The Indo-Aryan invaders evolved their wonderful Vedic literature and the religion of Brahmanical Hinduism in the Punjab; and much later, about 500 B.C., in the upper Ganges valley, the religions of Buddhism and Jainism came into existence. Jainism never extended beyond India and is even there a declining faith. Buddhism has disappeared from the land of its birth, but its votaries outnumber those of any other creed upon the earth. There too was produced the unique caste system, which now holds all Hindu India in its deadening grip, segregating the population into thousands of non-associating groups parted from each other by immaterial yet adamantine barriers which forbid common intercourse and intermarriage.

Other invaders, Sakas, Kushans, and White Huns, followed in their train, some near akin to the Aryan stock, some (and these came probably through the north-eastern passes) of the yellow Mongolian type. In many cases the invading peoples intermarried with the aborigines, thus producing further varieties of races and languages. But on the whole the Aryan type prevailed in northern India and the pre-Aryan in the Deccan. The tribes of the south are conveniently but not very scientifically known as Dravidians, and the ancient tongues they speak, Tamil, Telugu, Kanarese, Malayalam, and Tulu, are classified as belonging to the Dravidian family of languages.

Under the humanizing influence of Buddhism, Jainism, and Hinduism, a comparatively high stage of civilization was attained. Many Hindu empires and kingdoms rose and flourished, an outline of whose history is now being painfully wrested by scholars mainly from epigraphic and numismatic sources. About 500 B.C. the Indus valley was subdued by the generals of Darius, son of Hystaspes, King of Persia, and became for a short time a province of the Persian Empire. Indian archers fought in 479 B.C. on the field of Plataea. In 326 B.C. Alexander the Great crossed the Indus in his triumphant march across Asia and subdued the north-western part of Hindustan. But on his death in 323 B.C. his empire rapidly dissolved. No lasting imperial dominion in India was ever established by a Hindu people, though on three occasions such an event appeared to come within the bounds of probability. The short-lived empire of Asoka (273 to 232 B.C.?) is supposed by some authorities to have extended from the Hindu Kush mountains to, approximately, the northern frontier of Mysore. Again, Samudragupta of Pataliputra (the modern Patna) A.D. 400, and Harsha of Kanauj about 200 years later, extended their suzerainty over a great part of northern India, but neither founded a lasting dynasty.

India was next destined to experience the conquering sword of Islam. In the beginning of the eighth century of the Christian era the Arabians conquered Sind, and two hundred and fifty years later Muhammadan Turks were gathering threateningly round the northern mountain walls. Ghazni in Afghanistan was occupied in A. D. 862, and the Sultan of that city, Mahmud, between A. D. 997 and 1026, made fifteen raids into northern India, though the province of Lahore was the one permanent possession that remained to his house. Muhammad of Ghor, having conquered Ghazni, led six invasions of India between 1175 and 1206, and one of his generals founded a Turkish dynasty which ruled at Delhi. The Muhammadans gradually acquired Bihar and Bengal and penetrated far into the Deccan. Four dynasties of Muhammadan kings succeeded each other on the throne of Delhi between A. D. 1206 and 1526. Meanwhile in central and southern India many ruling Muhammadan Houses established themselves, pre-eminent among them being the five Deccan kingdoms of Ahmadnagar, Bijapur, Golconda, Bidar, and Berar, which for about 150 years before A. D. 1565 maintained a desultory warfare with Vijayanagar, the chief Hindu state of southern India.

Finally, in the sixteenth century a new conqueror, Babar the Mughal, overthrew the other Muhammadan powers of northern India. Originally the chief of Farghana in modern Turkestan, he had made himself master of Kabul, and between A. D. 1505 and 1525 led four expeditions through the north-western passes. In his fifth expedition he defeated Sultan Ibrahim, the last of the Lodi kings of Delhi, on the field of Panipat (1526) and founded the Mughal Empire. But in 1530, before he could consolidate his power, he died. His dominions extended over part of northern India, roughly speaking from the Indus on the west to the frontier of Bengal. His son Humayun, after some troubled years of rule, was driven back to Afghanistan, but in 1555 partially recovered his father's conquests. He died in the moment of his triumph and left to his son Akbar in 1556 a kingdom consisting practically of the Punjab with the districts round Delhi and Agra. Akbar (1556–1605), almost exactly contemporary with Queen Elizabeth of England, was the greatest of the Mughal emperors. He subdued Rajputana, Gujarat, Sind, Malwa, Khandesh, Bengal, and Kashmir; recovered Kandahar, and Afghanistan, and, by making Ahmadnagar a dependency of the empire, extended his frontier in the Deccan roughly speaking to the line of the river Godavari. But Akbar did more than enlarge the boundaries of his dominions. He built up an administrative and financial system which gave a definite form and cohesion to Mughal sovereignty. The empire was divided into fifteen *subahs* or provinces, each under a governor or viceroy known as *Subadar*, *Nawab*, or *Nazim*, with a financial officer to assist him known as the *Diwan*. Muhammadan political terminology is not very scientific. Properly speaking the title *Subadar* would seem to be applied to the rulers of the great provinces, and that of *Nawab* to his subordinates, the governors of the lesser subdivisions. Thus the *Subadar* of the Deccan was the overlord of the *Nawab* of the Carnatic. Often, however, these titles seem to be interchangeable; Bengal was politically perhaps the most important province of all, but its ruler was more often styled *Nawab* than *Subadar*. In India the bulk of the state revenue has always been derived from the soil, and Akbar's great Hindu minister, Todar Mall, carried through the first great land settlement, i. e. he determined and placed on record the proportion of the produce that must be paid to the treasury by the cultivators, as Crown rent.

Up to this time the Mughal sway in Hindustan had been little more than a military occupation, but Akbar left to his son Jahangir (1605–27)—almost coeval with James I, to whom in character he has been compared—an empire strong and well administered. It was in the latter's reign that the English acquired their first factory on the Indian coast, and at his court that Sir Thomas Roe resided for three years as ambassador from the King of England. For about a hundred years from the accession of Jahangir, the Mughal Empire was governed by a line of able and powerful rulers, and the general peace they maintained throughout northern and central India was undoubtedly favourable to the growth and development of the European settlements. In the reign of Shah Jahan (1627–58) the southern Muhammadan kingdoms of Bijapur and Golconda acknowledged the suzerainty of Delhi, and though the control of the Mughals over the Deccan was never very effective, the states in that region were to some extent overawed and induced to maintain comparative peace amongst themselves by their dread of the great empire in the north. When after 1712 the mighty fabric fell into decay, the European settlers, though they had many difficulties and dangers still to face, were left strong enough to maintain their position in the era of confusion and political anarchy that ensued.

In the reign of Aurangzeb (1658–1707), by far the greatest event as regards the history of India was the gradual rise of the Marathas, a Hindu people whose original home was Maharashtra, the hilly territory of the Western Ghats lying east of Bombay and south of the Satpura mountains. This despised race of Deccan peasants was destined to be the most powerful solvent of the Mughal Empire and the most determined rival of British supremacy in India. The people themselves and their ruling house were of low caste origin, though many of their later political leaders were high caste Brahmans. They were physically a small, active, hardy tribe, famous as light horsemen and contemned as mere plunderers and brigands—the 'mountain rats of the Deccan', as Aurangzeb styled them. They were welded together as a nation by Sivaji (1627–80), who successfully resisted

Mughal efforts to crush him and gradually extended his sway over southern India wherever his neighbours were weak and their territories defenceless. Ranging over the Deccan he demanded *chauth* or blackmail, a tribute usually of one-fourth of the revenue, from the states not strong enough to withstand him, and if they refused to pay it he harried their lands with fire and sword. The descendants of Sivaji in the second generation reigned only as pageant kings at Satara, and the real sovereignty passed to their Brahman minister or *Peshwa*, Balaji Vishvanath, who founded a dynasty seated at Poona. But Maratha power still grew, and by the middle of the eighteenth century threatened every settled government from Cape Comorin to Bengal and Rajputana. A terrible defeat on the field of Panipat in the Punjab at the hands of the Afghan invader of India, Ahmad Shah Durrani, in 1761, drove them back for a time in headlong rout to the Deccan, but the conqueror returned to his own country and the Marathas soon recovered their position. It seems certain that but for the British challenge the whole inheritance of the Mughals would have passed into their hands, and, as we shall see in the course of this history, four hard-fought campaigns were necessary before the Maratha confederacy was shattered, subdivided, and subdued.

CHAPTER III

EUROPEAN COMMERCE WITH INDIA

AFTER the invasions of Alexander the Great and his successor Seleucus Nikator about 300 B.C., India, except for the travels of Marco Polo the Venetian in 1294–5, remained practically unvisited by Europeans till the end of the fifteenth century.

Even the genius of Imperial Rome had turned back from the thought of Indian conquest. The distances were appalling, the difficulties insuperable. Yet the products of Indian soil and craftsmanship were from time immemorial well known in western marts. They were brought by ancient trade routes to the shores of the Black Sea, to the Levant, or to Egypt. In classical times Tyre, Alexandria, and Constantinople became successively the chief *emporia* of eastern commerce, to be replaced in the Middle Ages by Venice and Genoa, whence merchants carried their wares to Antwerp, or Bruges in the Netherlands, and the cities of the Hanseatic league.

The conquest by the Turks of south-western Asia and south-eastern Europe did much to close the old channels of commercial intercommunication, and dealt a serious blow at the prosperity of the Italian republics and the marts in northern and central Europe with which they were connected. The onslaught of the Ottoman power, however, only hastened a movement that was in any case inevitable. The discovery of the ocean route to India could not be indefinitely postponed, though the barrier interposed across the ancient land paths stimulated the cause of maritime enterprise. The ancient fame of India and the desire for a share in her traditional wealth led indirectly to the discovery of a new world in the West, the tragedies of early Arctic exploration, and the full recognition by mankind of the spherical form of this planet.

In the opening up of new continents men of Latin race led the way. Christopher Columbus the Genoese, seeking to reach India by the western route, discovered the West Indies and South America for Spain in 1492. In 1497 John Cabot, also a Genoese by birth but a naturalized citizen of Venice, sailed from Bristol with an English crew and landed in Newfoundland. To Portugal belongs the glory of having realized the quest for India by sea after years of stubborn endeavour and heroic perseverance. From 1418 to 1460 a succession of Portuguese sea captains, inspired and trained by Prince Henry the Navigator, crept further and further down the western shore of Africa. In 1486 Bartholomew Diaz was carried by storm winds past the Cape of Good Hope. In the following year Pedro de Covilham, travelling overland, reached the coast of Malabar and explored the Indian Ocean from an eastern base. The south-eastern route to India was now definitely proved to be feasible, and Vasco da Gama safely rounded the Cape, crossed the Indian Ocean, and in May 1498 anchored off the coast of Calicut.

During the sixteenth century the Portuguese enjoyed a monopoly of the trade to the East—a monopoly formally granted to them by the *fiat* of the Papacy. By the Bull of Pope Alexander VI in 1493, as interpreted by the Treaty of Tordesillas in 1494, and ratified in further Bulls of Julius II and Leo X in 1506 and 1514, an imaginary line was drawn 370 leagues west and south of the Cape Verde Islands. All undiscovered countries east of that line were assigned to Portugal, and all lands on the west to Spain. The pronouncement of the Pope was universally regarded throughout Catholic Europe as the highest possible expression of international law, while the Protestant nations for nearly a hundred years did not feel themselves strong enough to defy it. Not till many hopes had been dashed and many lives lost in the attempt to force a route to India by a north-west or north-east passage (upon which no embargo was laid by the Bulls) did England and Holland nerve themselves to strike out to the south-east and south-west.

For a century, therefore, Portugal had a clear field. She held 'the gorgeous East in fee', at least so far as the Popes could enable her to do so. The sails of her swift caravels were seen henceforward from Ormuz in the Persian Gulf, as far eastward as Malacca and the Spice Islands. Goa, on the western coast of the Deccan, the capital of Portuguese India, was acquired in 1510 and fortified factories were established at Quiloa, Mombassa, and Melinde on the east coast of Africa, at Ormuz in the Persian Gulf, at Diu, Daman, and Cochin on the coast of Malabar, and at Malacca in Malaysia. The period of Portuguese supremacy produced some great names, especially those of Vasco da Gama, Almeida (1505–9), and Albuquerque (1509–15). It brought riches and fame to the Portuguese kings, and inspired the epic genius of the poet Camoens; but Portugal was not destined to win a permanent dominion in India. By the discovery or Brazil a great part of her colonizing energy was devoted to the West. Portugal, says Mr. Whiteway, was the earliest intruder into the East, and the East 'has resented' the intrusion 'by absorbing and degrading the intruder'.[1] The trading methods of Portuguese sea captains had more than a flavour of piracy about them. Profits were derived quite as much from plundering raids upon Arabian merchants as from legitimate commerce. Portuguese treatment of the natives often showed a cruelty lower than the standards of a cruel age. The eastern power

[1] *The Rise of Portuguese Power in India*, R. S. Whiteway, p. 2.

of the Catholic pioneer nation was destined to yield before the more vigorous methods and less romantic ideals of the commercial Protestant states of the North, but even had the field been left clear, it is very doubtful whether her power would not have slipped from her hands, either when the Mughal Empire conquered the southern Muhammadan kingdoms, or at the recrudescence of Hindu power under the Marathas.

Gradually, as the sixteenth century drew to an end, the conviction was reached that there was no feasible route to India by a north-west or north-east passage. The voyages of the Englishmen, Hore, Willoughby, Frobisher, Davis, and the Dutchman Barents, were not unfruitful either in the field of commerce or in that of geographical exploration. Hore reached Newfoundland in 1536, Sir Hugh Willoughby discovered Nova Zembla and explored the northern coast of Russia. His voyage resulted in the foundation of the Russia or Muscovy Company which opened to English merchants an overland trade with Persia. Frobisher (1575–8) and Davis (1585–7) traversed the fringe of the Arctic regions to the north-west, while the Dutchman Barents (1594–6) made desperate attempts to break through to the north-east, in the course of which he visited Staten Island and Spitzbergen. In 1519–21 a Spanish squadron accomplished the dream of Columbus in reaching the East Indies by the western route. It was commanded by Ferdinand Magellan, who, having served under and quarrelled with Albuquerque, offered his services to the Emperor Charles V. He coasted down the shores of South America, passed through the straits that have immortalized his name, and voyaged across the vast expanse of the Pacific to the Philippines. There he himself was killed, but the expedition reached the Moluccas and one ship returned to the port of embarkation, having thus completed the circumnavigation of the globe. This was a wonderful feat in view of the small vessels and rude nautical instruments of the time, and it clearly showed that of the possible southern routes the one to the south-west was so tedious and circuitous that it could never be commercially profitable.

Three causes, geographical, religious, and political, thus converged to make England and Holland openly refuse to obey any longer the Papal Bull. First, their despair of discovering the northern passage. Secondly, their rebellion from the Pope's spiritual authority. Thirdly, the forcible annexation by Spain of the kingdom of Portugal in 1580, which set a totally different aspect upon the question. England ever since 1386 (the Treaty of Westminster) had remained on friendly terms with Portugal, and the United Netherlands had traded freely with Lisbon, the commodities of eastern marts being shipped thence to Antwerp for distribution amidst the ports of northern Europe. After 1580 the port of Lisbon, now under the territorial sovereignty of Philip II, closed its gates to the rebels of the Low Countries, and Elizabeth of England was gradually driven by her people, by the merchants and the buccaneers, to make open war with Spain. In 1579 Sir Francis Drake on his way round the world visited the Moluccas, or Spice Islands, in the East Indies by the south-western route and is said to have entered into treaty relations with the chief of Ternate. From this date it was inevitable that England and Holland should openly challenge the supremacy of Portugal in the Indian Ocean. Spain even offered in 1607 to renounce her claim to sovereignty over the United Provinces if the Dutch would abandon the navigation of the Indies. The English and Dutch assault upon the Portuguese monopoly was contemporaneous, and it was quite an open question in the race for pre-eminence which nation would be the first to reach its goal. It is impossible here within the space at our disposal to describe in detail the fluctuations in fortune and the progressive steps by which now England, now Holland, pushed forward her pioneering flag. Broadly, and in outline, the course of events was as follows. The East India Companies of the two nations were founded within a few years of each other. The English Company was the first to be incorporated, but for many years it lagged behind the great Company of the United Netherlands in power and prosperity. For the first decades of the seventeenth century both nations were forced to make their way in the teeth of Portuguese resistance, but when that was surmounted, they turned jealously upon one another. Both coveted the Far East, the Malay Archipelago, rather than the mainland of India, as the fairer and more profitable inheritance, and there ultimately the Dutch secured their hold, driving out the English by their superior physical force, and keeping them out by the restrictive and monopolizing spirit that in the seventeenth century dominated the colonial policy of Holland. The English reluctantly and perforce were driven to develop their settlements on the mainland, little realizing at the time that India itself was destined to confer on its possessors the sovereignty of the East, while the attractive Spice Islands were in reality a seductive by-path leading those who followed it astray from the road to dominion. The Dutch had thus early in their eastern history been led into a cardinal error, but it was an error impossible for them or any other nation to avoid in the light of contemporary knowledge. Nor would it be fair to attribute wholly to this initial step the fact that the English and not the Dutch were ultimately to attain supremacy in the East. Dutch power in India was largely jeopardized on European battlefields. The eastern dominion of Holland, compact and profitable, is even now no mean inheritance, and is perhaps as great in extent and achievement as it ever could have been, in view of the endless political difficulties from European complications that beset the path of Dutch statesmen. It was on the Dutch pattern that the English of the seventeenth century consciously modelled their administrative system in India. 'Our design in the whole', wrote the Court in 1687, 'is to set up the Dutch government among the English in India (than which a better cannot be invented) for the good of posterity and to put us upon an equal foot of power with them to defend or offend or enlarge the English dominion, and unite the strength of our nation under one entire and absolute command subject to us as we are and ever shall be most dutiful to our sovereign, with this distinction that we will always observe our own old English terms, viz. Attorney General instead of Fiscal. . . . President and Agent instead of Commandore, Directore, or Commissaries.'[1]

Such is the barest outline of the course of events. The history of Holland in the East can only be dealt with in detail where it touches that of Great Britain, and even so the narrative must necessarily be summarized.

[1] India Office Records, Letter Book No. 8, Dispatch to Fort St. George, Sept. 28, 1687.

CHAPTER IV

THE BIRTH OF THE LONDON EAST INDIA COMPANY

The visit of Sir Francis Drake to the Moluccas in 1579 has already been noticed. It was prophetic of what was to come. The craving of adventurous Englishmen to sail southwards and eastwards could no longer be kept back by the calculating policy of the Queen, who, a slave now to the purely negative and dilatory policy that had served her so well at the opening of her reign, still blew hot and cold in her reluctance to come to an open breach with Philip of Spain. She braced herself in 1580 to declare to the Spanish ambassador that 'the ocean was free to all, for as much as neither nature nor regard of public use do permit the exclusive possession thereof'.[1] In 1582 England made the first direct attempt of any European power to break down the Portuguese monopoly by a voyage round the Cape. Edward Fenton sailed with four ships, but proved an unfortunate or incompetent captain, and the expedition ended disastrously.

The first Englishman known to have lived on the mainland of India was Thomas Stephens. He became in 1579 Rector of the Jesuit college in Goa. The letters he wrote to his father are said to have spread in England a wider desire for direct communication with the East. In 1583 two English merchants, Fitch and Newbery, accompanied by Leedes, a jeweller, and Story, a painter, journeyed overland to India. The Portuguese arrested them at Ormuz, and took them prisoners to Goa. After their release, Story

[1] *History of Elizabeth*, William Camden, 1675, p. 255.

became a monk, Leedes entered the Mughal service, Newbery died on the way home, but Fitch, after adventurous wanderings through Bengal, Burma, Malacca, and Ceylon, returned safely home in 1591, to inspire in his countrymen a keener desire for trade and exploration in the East.

The defeat of the Armada in 1588 impelled even the Queen to show her hand more boldly. Permission was granted to some merchants to attempt a voyage by the Cape route. In 1591 James Lancaster, in the *Edward Bonaventura*, reached Cape Comorin and the Malay Peninsula, though the commander of the expedition, George Raymond, went down with his ship. On his return voyage Lancaster was driven by storm winds to the coast of Brazil and the West Indies. There part of his crew mutinied and carried off the ship, and Lancaster sailed for England in a French vessel, arriving in May 1594. In 1596 a squadron of three vessels was dispatched by Sir Robert Dudley under the command of Benjamin Wood, but was never heard of again. In 1599 a London merchant adventurer, John Midnall or Mildenhall, reached India by the overland route. He was granted a passport by Elizabeth, and spent seven years in the East, during which time he visited the court of the Emperor Akbar at Agra, and procured from him certain privileges of very dubious value. These he afterwards attempted in vain to sell to the East India Company, which had been incorporated during his absence.

The old Turkey Company, founded in 1581, had been granted permission in 1593 to trade overland as far as the East Indies, and was renamed the Levant Company, but the difficulties of the trade route were such that little good came of it. Accordingly two prominent members of the Levant Company, moved no doubt by the fact that Cornelius Houtman, a Dutchman, had sailed to Sumatra and Bantam by the Cape route in 1596, came forward with a number of other merchants and raised a subscription for a voyage to India by way of the Cape. On September 24, 1599, they met together, subscribed a sum of £30,133 3*s*. 8*d*., and applied to Elizabeth for a charter. But in the realm of high politics negotiations were pending for a truce to end the long war with Spain, and the government were not inclined to imperil all chances of a settlement by granting the prayers of a few traders. The next year prospects were more favourable, for the peace proposals had been shipwrecked. Accordingly, a year later all but a day, September 23, 1600, the adventurers met again, in Founders' Hall, more than doubled the amount of their former subscription, raising it to £68,373, and purchased ships. They asked only for leave to trade in the East where Spaniards and Portuguese 'have not any castle, fort, blockhouse, or commandant'. They thus ignored the right founded on a Papal Bull, but recognized the doctrine of effective occupation. On the last day of the year 1600 the East India Company was incorporated by name of 'the Governor and Company of Merchants of London trading into the East Indies'.

The number of subscribers was 217. The first governor, Thomas Smythe, and twenty-four 'committees' (i.e. committee men) were nominated in the charter, and were afterwards to be annually elected. The exclusive trade with India was granted for fifteen years. Thus the first great step was taken on that path which was to lead Great Britain to the goal of her wonderful eastern empire. It is interesting to pause for a moment and attempt to estimate the magnitude of the task that lay before the stout-hearted body of merchant adventurers, to eliminate for a moment the facts of later history as we know them, and face the problem as they faced it. The preliminary step was one requiring no mean courage on the part of those who took it. They had no first-hand knowledge of the East; the reports of Fitch and Stephens and a translation of the works of the Dutch traveller, Linschoten, who had lived at Goa 1583–9, were almost all upon which they had to rely. Peace with Spain was not concluded till 1604, and they fully realized that they had to face the determined hostility of the Spaniards and Portuguese, the latter of whom had enjoyed for a century the prescriptive right to the Indian seas. The Dutch also were certain to prove formidable rivals. Though the great United Dutch Company was not founded till 1602, the numerous provincial companies of the Netherlands dispatched between 1595 and 1601 no less than fifteen expeditions to the East consisting of sixty-five ships.

The task before the London East India Company was therefore a hard one. It had to explore and map out the Indian seas and coasts, it had painfully to work out a system of commerce, to experiment with commodities and merchandise, to train and discipline a staff of servants. It had to brave or conciliate the hostility of England's hereditary Catholic enemy and her new Protestant rival. Further, it had to establish a position even at home. The English East India Company was the first organized attempt to trade with India based upon individual effort. Portugal's achievements in the East had been due mainly to the protecting care of her royal house. The Dutch Company was to be backed and defended by the states of the United Netherlands, which through its agency transferred to the Indian Ocean and there prosecuted with renewed vigour their undying quarrel with the Spaniard. Just as Elizabeth left the sporadic naval war with Spain, and even the defence of England against the Armada, mainly to private enterprise and patriotism, so there was no active state support given to England's first essays in the East. The East India Company was cradled in the chilly but invigorating atmosphere of individualism. It had to cope with the lingering mediaeval prejudice against the export of bullion and a fallacious theory of foreign trade. It had to depend altogether on mercantile initiative, and merchants desire a profitable and immediate return upon their outlay. Profitable the returns of an Indian voyage often were, though the margin of possible disaster was very wide; immediate, never. A period of two years was almost the least time that could elapse between the departure and the return of a ship, even if it survived the hazard of storm or the attack of an enemy. Under the early system of separate voyages, in which each fleet was dispatched to India by a particular group of subscribers, who on the return of their vessels wound up the venture and realized the profits, there was no averaging up the losses and gains, for each venture stood by itself. It was not till after more than half a century of trial that the Company was driven by various stages to adopt a permanent joint stock after the fashion of modern times.

Fortune smiled upon the Company's first voyage. It consisted of five vessels under the command of James Lancaster, who set sail on February 13, 1601, visited Achin in Sumatra, and delivered to the King a letter from Queen Elizabeth. Having captured a richly laden Portuguese carrack and left a factory at Bantam, Lancaster returned to England in September 1603. Middleton, the commander of the second voyage, visited Bantam and the Spice Islands, Amboyna, Ternate, and Tidore (1604–6). He encountered much opposition from the Dutch, who, since the coalition and federation of the provincial companies into the great United East India Company of the Netherlands, with a capital eight times as great as that of its English rival, were sedulously pushing forward their claim to monopolize the spice trade of the Archipelago. The third voyage was memorable from the fact that a landing was then first made on the mainland of India, Captain Hawkins disembarking at Surat in 1608 and visiting the court of Jahangir at Agra. The Emperor received him favourably and granted the English permission to settle in Surat, but the Portuguese were still strong enough in India to procure the revocation of the decree. Hawkins waited in vain for two and a half years at Agra, marrying an Armenian wife at Jahangir's suggestion, and hoping against hope, as he wrote to the Company, 'I should feather my nest and do you service'. Finally he made his way down to the coast, and embarked in an English ship in January 1612.

The year 1612 forms a convenient terminal date for the first chapter of the Company's history. It is the year of the ninth and last separate voyage,[1] and of Captain Best's naval victory over the Portuguese off Swally, which was not only the East India Company's first definite armed success over a European rival, but resulted, through the foresight and policy of Thomas Aldworth, in permission to build a factory at Surat. In the first twelve years of its existence the East India Company could claim only a moderate measure of success. Till 1612 the English had obtained no permanent establishment on the mainland of India, while their position in the eastern islands was weak as compared with that of the Dutch, and in the Red Sea they had seriously damaged their commercial reputation by the 'romaging'—that is, pillaging—of Indian vessels. On the other hand their profits, though irregular, had been large, and the approval of the Crown and the nation had been shown in the grant of the second charter, dated 1609, which re-endowed the Company, now reinforced by many members of the nobility, with the trade in perpetuity, unless it should prove unprofitable to the realm, when it could be revoked on three years' notice being given.

But the Company was about to enter another zone of troubles and hardships. It had still battles to fight with

[1] Between 1612, the date of the last separate voyage, and 1657, when the permanent joint stock was raised, there was an intermediate stage of transitory joint stocks and 'Particular' or 'General' voyages.

the Portuguese before it could secure a foot-hold on the mainland, and even fiercer combats to wage with the Dutch for what was universally regarded as the *El Dorado* of the East, the Spice Islands of the Malay Archipelago. Troubles from interlopers—that is, traders who infringed the monopoly—civil war, popular hatred, and the favours of fickle and embarrassed sovereigns were to beset it at home, and during the next hundred years the Company had many a struggle to maintain its corporate existence and the continuity of its trade.

CHAPTER V

THE ENGLISH, DUTCH, AND PORTUGUESE IN THE EAST

BEFORE dealing in detail with the early settlements of the Company, something may profitably be said of the international relations of the three European nations competing for the Indian trade, during the first half of the seventeenth century. Such a summary will inevitably pass beyond the period with which we are at present concerned, but it is convenient to group certain facts under definite headings and to dispose of them before resuming the main thread of the narrative.

The conflict was a threefold one. There was the struggle between the Portuguese and the Dutch, between the Portuguese and the English, and between the Dutch and the English. The first aspect of the conflict hardly concerns us here. It is enough to say that the Dutch captured Amboyna from the Portuguese in 1605 and gradually supplanted them in the Spice Islands. They blockaded Goa in 1639, seized Malacca in 1641, and took the last Portuguese stronghold in Ceylon in 1658. By 1664 they had ousted their rivals from most of their early settlements on the Malabar coast.

Peace between England and Spain was made in 1604, but it hardly extended to the Indies, though by the treaty and their charter the English were henceforward debarred from resorting to Portuguese possessions, since the Spanish and Portuguese Crowns were united from 1580 to 1640. In 1611 a Portuguese fleet prevented Sir Henry Middleton from entering the mouth of the Tapti river. But in

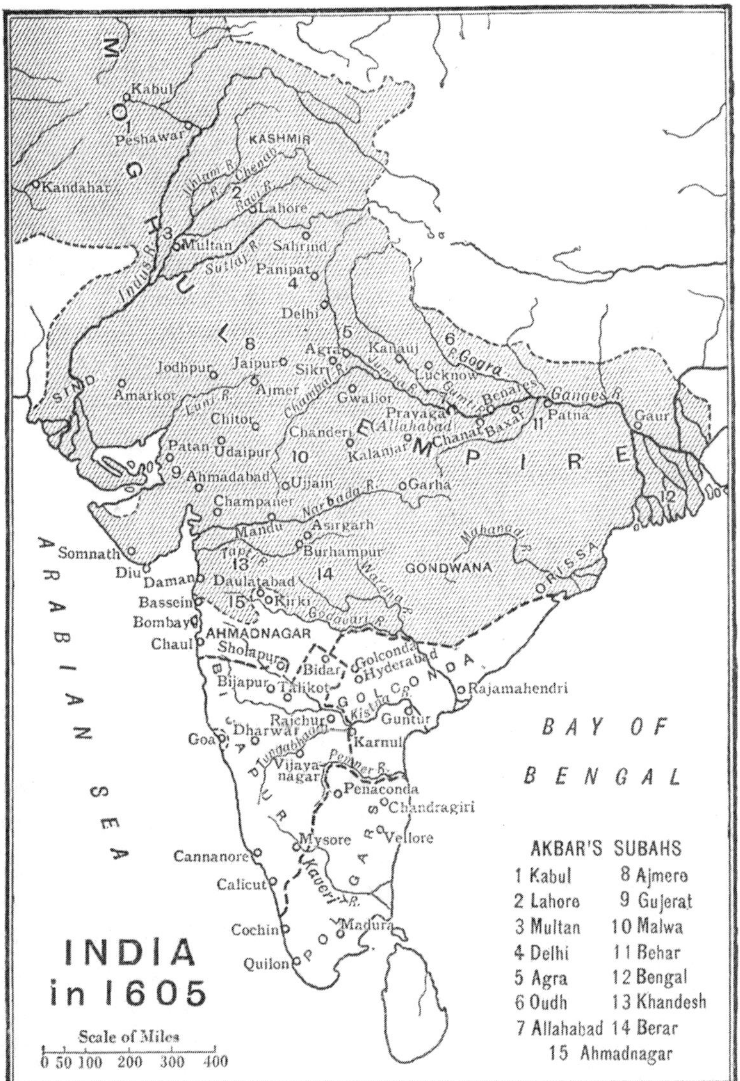

WAXTYPE GEORGE PHILIP & SON, LTD.

November and December of the following year Captain Thomas Best with two ships defeated them in several engagements. In December 1614 and January 1615 Captain Nicholas Downton, with a larger squadron of four vessels, won a still more decisive victory over the Portuguese viceroy in person. These defeats irretrievably damaged the credit of the Portuguese on the western shore of India, and in the eyes of the native powers the English were the natural successors to the prestige they had enjoyed. In 1622 the English allied themselves with the Shah of Persia and captured Ormuz in the Persian Gulf from the Portuguese, being rewarded by permission to settle in Gombroon and to receive half the customs dues. Henceforward Portugal ceased to be a dangerous rival to England. In 1630 the Treaty of Madrid declared that the two countries should abstain from hostilities in the East. But a convention signed by Methwold, the English President of Surat, and the Viceroy of Goa in 1634 was of much more practical importance, and actually guaranteed commercial inter-relations between the English and Portuguese in India. The recovery by Portugal of her independence from the yoke of Spain in 1640 further mitigated the hostility of the English, and recalled the old tradition of alliance and friendship with the Portuguese nation. In 1642 Charles I of England and John IV of Portugal concluded a treaty for freedom of trade between the two countries, and definitely accepted the Surat-Goa convention. Finally Cromwell, in his Treaty of July 1654, extorted from Portugal a full recognition of England's right to trade to the East Indies. The Treaty which brought Bombay to Charles II in 1661 as part of the dower of Catherine of Braganza, bound him to maintain the Portuguese possessions in India against the Dutch.

But the enmity between England and her hereditary foe the Catholic and Latin Spanish-Portuguese Empire was as nothing to that which existed in the eastern seas between herself and the Dutch, the northern Protestant power with whom, in Europe at any rate, she seemed to have so much in common. This was no doubt mainly due to the fact that at a comparatively early stage the Englishman realized that 'the Hollander' and not 'the Portugal' was the real enemy. The Dutch, on the other hand, were aggrieved by the mere appearance of the English in the East. Their assault on Portuguese possessions was a continuation of the struggle for freedom against the despotic power of Spain. 'Holland', says Sir William Hunter, 'turned her despairing land-revolt into a triumphant oceanic war';[1] she extended that war to the Far East and she wanted no third competitor for the prize of victory. In 1609 her proud enemy Spain, after vainly endeavouring in 1607 to purchase a Dutch withdrawal from India by conceding independence in Europe, was forced to agree to a twelve years truce. The Dutch were now free to display their enmity to the English and to develop their plan of campaign for acquiring a monopoly of the trade in the Moluccas, which they claimed by right of conquest from the Portuguese. On the high seas and in many an Indian port, collisions took place between hot-headed sea captains or jealous commercial rivals; a famous incident in this unofficial war was Nathaniel Courthope's defence of Pulo Run, one of the Banda Islands, with a tiny garrison for four years (1616–20) against frequent assaults from the Dutch. The representatives of both nations endeavoured to undersell one another and to form binding ties with the native powers. The Dutch asserted that they had linked to themselves by treaty almost all the petty rulers of the Moluccas; the English put forward a claim to priority of occupation dating from the famous voyage round the world of Sir Francis Drake, charging the Dutch with oppression and intimidation of the natives, while they zealously and with good reason combated the idea that a

[1] *A History of British India*, vol. i, p. 237.

few isolated and widely separated 'forts' amounted to genuine and effective occupation of the whole island group. Dutch power there was consolidated and regularized by the appointment of Pieter Both[1] (1609–14) as first Governor-General. The English Company in 1611, in a petition to the Earl of Salisbury (Lord High Treasurer), declared that they were 'enforced at last to break silence and complain their griefs'.[2] Continuous conferences in London and at the Hague (1611 and 1613–15) ended in failure to bring about a settlement, for though proposals for a union of the two companies were freely made, and it was even suggested that a joint subscription should be raised, the English looked with suspicion and dislike upon the heavy military expenditure of their rivals and, when called upon to share it, showed the strongest disinclination to do so. Meanwhile, open reprisals never ceased in eastern waters until, in July 1619, the English Company unwillingly came to terms with the Dutch, and entered into a union giving up their claims to compensation for past injuries. They engaged to share in the expenses of Dutch fortifications and to provide half of a fleet of defence of twenty ships which was to remain in the East for the purpose of patrolling the seas. In return for their acceptance of these onerous conditions, the English were grudgingly granted a certain proportion of the trade. The Company's assent to the treaty was largely due to the pressure put upon them by James I, who then, as always, was exceedingly ambitious of the renown of the peacemaker. The treaty was to be executed by a joint Council of Defence in the East, consisting of four members from each Company, with an appeal to the States-General of Holland and the King of England.

[1] This is the Dutchman who gave his name to the well-known rock in Mauritius. He was lost off that island in 1616. See vol. i of this series, 2nd edition, p. 146.

[2] *First Letter Book of the East India Company*, Sir G. Birdwood and W. Foster, p. 429.

The treaty was ill received by the Dutch in the East, who, under their able Governor-General Coen (the founder of Batavia in 1619), believed they had the English almost at their mercy. 'The English ought to be very thankful to you', wrote Coen, 'for they had worked themselves very nicely out of the Indies, and you have placed them again in the midst.'[1] Within two years the union had utterly broken down. The English were violently expelled from Lantor and Pulo Run (1621–2), and negotiations were resumed in London in 1621; but before the Dutch and English commissioners could come to any agreement, news arrived of the massacre of Amboyna in 1623, a bloody and brutal piece of work committed by a subordinate Dutch official, which put an end to all compromise and stirred up in England a deep and just resentment.

Van Speult, the Dutch Governor of Amboyna, arrested Towerson the English agent and eighteen other Englishmen besides several Japanese soldiers on a trumped-up charge of having conspired to seize the Dutch fort. There was no evidence against the prisoners at the time, except confessions drawn from them by fiendish torments and revoked immediately they were carried from the torture chamber. On the other hand there exists abundant proof in both the Dutch and English archives that the supposed plot was a mere figment of the imagination, if it were not a deliberate device to exterminate the English factory. Towerson and nine other Englishmen with nine Japanese were put to death; their papers and protestations of innocence were destroyed, but a few pathetic and broken sentences written on the leaves of Prayer Book or Bible or in the pages of a ledger escaped unnoticed, and served afterwards to inflame popular feeling in England to fury.

The action of Van Speult was not only a crime but a blunder, and the Prince of Orange openly declared that he

[1] *A History of British India*, Sir W. W. Hunter, vol. i, p. 384.

wished that 'when Speult began to spell this tragedy, he had been hung upon a gibbet, with his council about him'.[1] But in spite of intense popular excitement no real reparation was extorted from the Dutch till after the lapse of thirty-one years. James I, angered at the refusal of the Spanish court to favour his matrimonial plans for his son Charles, was inclining at this time for alliance with the Netherlands. Once again state policy was at variance with the aspirations of the Company, though at this time these aspirations were backed by the voice of the whole English people. Both James and his successor Charles I used brave words, but failed to follow them up with courageous action. The East India Company found a more worthy protector in Oliver Cromwell, who by the Treaty of Westminster in 1654 referred the question of claims and counter-claims to four commissioners, to be named on both sides, meeting in London, with an appeal on disagreement to the Swiss Cantons. The commissioners restored Pulo Run to the English, and awarded them a sum of £85,000 as indemnity for the Company, with £3,615 for the heirs of the sufferers at Amboyna.

In the East, Dutch sovereignty in the Spice Islands remained secure. Though the English continually reasserted down to 1667 a claim to Pulo Run, re-established a factory at Bantam in 1628 (which supported a troubled existence till 1682), and maintained a Presidency at Bencoolen in Sumatra till 1824, they never seriously challenged the position of the Dutch in the Malay Archipelago until Lord Minto's conquest of Java in 1811. Dominion in that region was denied them, but the door was opened thereby to a wider and more imperial destiny.

[1] *Calendar of State Papers, East Indies* (1622–4), ed. by W. N. Sainsbury, p. 331.

CHAPTER VI

EARLY SETTLEMENTS IN INDIA. THE COMPANY UNDER THE STUARTS, THE COMMONWEALTH, THE PROTECTORATE, AND RESTORATION

In the Spice Archipelago, as we have seen, the star of the English had waned before that of the Dutch. In the meantime the factors and agents of the East India Company in the face of many difficulties and discouragements were opening up trade with the ports of the mainland of India and endeavouring to obtain permission for the factories which their system of commerce rendered necessary. The failure of Captain Hawkins in 1608, through Portuguese opposition, to settle in Surat has been already mentioned. A different complexion was put upon matters by Best's victory in the sea fight off the mouth of the Tapti in 1612, and an English factory was permanently established there on a grant obtained from Jahangir by Thomas Aldworth, who pronounced it to be 'the only key to open all the rich and best trade of the Indies'.[1] A foothold once effected, commercial ties were gradually formed with the country inland, and subordinate agencies were established at Ahmadabad, Burhanpur, and, in the heart of the Mughal's dominions, at Ajmer and Agra.

The East India Company wisely determining to press home by all possible means the advantages they had gained, decided to send an ambassador 'of extraordinary countenance and respect' to reside at the court of the Emperor. Their

[1] *Letters received by the East India Company from its servants in the East*, vol. i, ed. by F. C. Danvers, p. 238.

choice fell upon Sir Thomas Roe as being 'of a pregnant understanding, well spoken, learned, industrious, and of a comelie personage'.[1] The sanction of James I for the appointment was then obtained—the more readily perhaps because the Company paid the ambassador's salary and allowances. Roe sailed in February 1615. On his arrival at Surat in September he discovered that Downton's victory over the Portuguese early in the year had only served to endanger the English cause in the eyes of the Mughal government. There was a strong party at the court of Jahangir, headed by Prince Khurram (afterwards the Emperor Shah Jahan), which favoured the Portuguese, and was now endeavouring to procure the expulsion of the English from Surat. Roe won the favour of Jahangir and lived at his court as accredited ambassador from the King of England for three years, at Ajmer, Mandu, or Ahmadabad. He failed to procure, as he had hoped to do, a formal and definite treaty, but he obtained permission for the establishment of factories at certain towns in the Mughal dominions, and did much, by his statesmanship and tact, to instil into the Mughal mind a respect for the English as a nation. Above all, he formulated a policy for the Company which they followed for seventy years, a policy which was to be unaggressive and wholly mercantile. Roe disliked the military-commercial policies of the Portuguese and Dutch, which he believed to consume all their profit. 'It is the beggaring of the Portugal, notwithstanding his many rich residences and territories, that he keeps soldiers that spend it, yet his garrisons are mean. He never profited by the Indies, since he defended them. Observe this well. It hath been also the error of the Dutch, who seek plantation here by the sword. They turn a wonderful stock, they prowl in all places, they possess some of the best; yet their dead payes consume all their

[1] *The Embassy of Sir Thomas Roe*, ed. by W. Foster [Hakluyt Society], vol. i, Introd., p. iv.

gain. Let this be received as a rule that if you will profit, seek it at sea, and in quiet trade; for without controversy, it is an error to affect garrisons and land wars in India.'[1] Roe served the Company well, claiming with truth 'my sincerity toward you in all actions is without spot; my neglect of private gain is without example, and my frugality beyond your expectation'.[2] He left India in February 1619.

The English factory at Surat henceforward became the chief English settlement in the East, even Bantam being made for a time subordinate to it in 1630. It was seriously affected by the depredations of Courten's association,[3] 1636–49, and by their rival factory at Rajapur, but recovered its position in 1657, remaining the headquarters of the Company in the East till its place was taken by Bombay in 1687.

On the eastern coast Captain Hippon in 1611 landed at Pettapoli in the Kistna delta, and proceeding northwards founded a factory at Masulipatam, a seaport of the Muhammadan kingdom of Golconda. For some years the factory flourished, but after 1624 declined before the opposition and 'foul injuries' of the Dutch. The English factors even abandoned the place in 1628, and, though they returned two years later, they cast about for another station where they might be unimpeded by European rivals. In 1640 Francis Day, a member of the Masulipatam council, procured from a petty Hindu raja a narrow strip of land about 230 miles south of Masulipatam with permission to build a fortified factory which he named Fort St. George. Round the guns of this protected factory grew up within a few years the town of Madras, divided into the White Town, or European settlement, and the Black Town, where the Indian merchants and weavers congregated. The Court of Committees at first looked askance at the expense involved in the new

[1] *The Embassy of Sir Thomas Roe*, ed. by W. Foster [Hakluyt Society], vol. ii, p. 344.

[2] Ibid., p. 343.

[3] See *infra*, p. 36.

settlement and entered the name of its founder in the Black Book which recorded the deeds of those servants who had incurred their displeasure. But Fort St. George soon justified its existence, and in 1642 it displaced Masulipatam as the chief settlement on the coast of Coromandel, though it remained subordinate to Bantam till 1653, when it was raised to the position of an independent agency.

In the meantime the English, striking northwards, had made their first settlements in Orissa and Bengal. In 1633, Ralph Cartwright, sailing from Masulipatam, established stations at Hariharpur in the Mahanadi delta and at Balasore on the boundary between Bengal proper and Orissa. For many years the English only maintained their hold upon these places with the greatest difficulty, being fiercely assailed by the Portuguese and Dutch and decimated by the deadly exhalations of the malarial swamps. Indeed, it was only the foresight of Francis Day, the founder of Madras, which prevented the total abandonment of the Bengal factories in 1642. English prospects were much improved by the efforts of Gabriel Boughton, surgeon of the Company's ship *Hopewell*, who since 1645 had lived as court physician with the Mughal Subadar, or viceroy, of Bengal. In 1650 he obtained from his patron a licence for the Company to trade in the province, and in the following year an English factory was established at Hughli, where the Portuguese and Dutch were already settled. But misfortunes still dogged the Bengal stations. They were too far from Madras to be effectively controlled. The factors sent there fell into irregular and dishonest courses. In 1656 the Madras Council had determined to withdraw from Bengal altogether, but the arrival of new supplies and men in 1658, after Cromwell's charter, made them alter their decision. In the same year all the settlements in Bengal and on the Coromandel coast were made subordinate to Fort St. George.

Meanwhile, at home the Company's fortunes were under

a cloud. As a monopoly their claims aroused much opposition from the growing popular party in England. Their practice of exporting bullion was regarded as ruinous to the country, for the political economy of that day, says Sir William Hunter, 'was a compound of mediaeval tradition and national prejudice'.[1] Based as the Company was upon a royal charter, it might be expected that their reliance would be mainly upon the throne, but a Stuart king was only a broken reed. In fact, as Charles and the Parliament were rapidly drifting into a life-and-death struggle, the East India Company was likely to fare ill in the capacity of third party. There is noticeable a distinct attempt, and complete failure on their part, to prevail upon the Commons to include their grievances amongst those preferred by the popular party against the throne, and at other times to coerce the King by the threat to appeal to Parliament. In 1628 they laid a formal Petition and Remonstrance before the Commons which was disregarded. The rebuff from Parliament was followed by a still severer blow from Charles. In 1635, on the ground that the Company 'had merely intended and pursued their own present profit and advantage without providing any safety or settledness for establishing of traffic in the said Indies for the good of posterity',[2] the King granted a licence for trade in the East Indies to a courtier, Endymion Porter, who was financed by Sir William Courten or Courteen, a great London merchant, son of a Protestant Flemish refugee. The monopoly of the Company was for a time at an end. Courten's association did their utmost to secure an immediate profit without a too scrupulous regard for the rights either of their fellow countrymen or of the Hindu and Mughal traders with whom they had dealings. The Company petitioned Parliament again in January, 1641, but Charles persuaded them to recall their petition, admitting

[1] *A History of British India*, vol. ii, p. 20.
[2] Grant to Sir W. Courten, Dec. 12, 1635.

that 'Mr. Porter had nothing to do in the business, his name only being used, and that what was done was His Majesty's act'.[1] Courten's association established a settlement at Assada in Madagascar, whence the name of 'Assada Merchants' by which they soon became known. Meanwhile a renewed petition of the East India Company to the Long Parliament in June 1641 had been unnoticed, and the only action of that famous assembly in relation to the Company was to force the officers of their ships to take the Solemn League and Covenant. The ruinous competition between the two bodies was brought to an end in 1649 by a 'union' to which both sides reluctantly consented. In 1654 the original members of the East India Company desired to raise another joint stock while the Assada Merchants were in favour of converting the Company into a 'Regulated' one, i. e. of allowing members to trade individually with their own capital and ships. Both sides appealed to the Council of State, but for three years nothing was done. Cromwell indeed was credibly said in 1657 to have contemplated declaring the trade to India open, and the Company in despair threatened to withdraw from India altogether.[2] Their threat seems at last to have turned Cromwell's attention to the grievances they had pressed upon him so long. He granted them a charter in 1657. Under its provisions they raised the first permanent joint stock and 'the Company passed from its mediaeval to its modern basis'.[3] Ninety-one new factors and merchants were dispatched to the East, and the settlements there entered upon a new lease of life.

Based as it was upon the constitutional exercise of the royal prerogative, the Company had always been ill at ease under the Commonwealth and Protectorate. It had indeed,

[1] India Office Records, Court Book No. 17, p. 385.
[2] Ibid., No. 23, pp. 546, 556.
[3] *A History of British India*, Sir W. W. Hunter, vol. ii, p. 103.

when ordered to do so, effaced the royal arms upon its ships, and even, as we have seen, attempted to identify its cause with the cause of the Parliamentary Party, but that was only when all other expedients had failed.

With the Restoration came a welcome change in its fortunes. The twenty years 1660–80 may be regarded as the golden age of the Company while still a non-political, non-territorial trading body. Its stock steadily rose in price. It stood at 130 in 1669, 245 in 1677, 280 in 1681, and 360 in 1683. Dividends between the years 1659 and 1691 averaged 25 per cent. per annum. The Company at home enjoyed royal patronage and support, for if Charles II, like his father, borrowed money of the Court of Committees, he was, unlike his father, punctual in paying it back. The charters granted between the years 1661 and 1683 strengthened the position of the Company in many ways, giving it the right to coin money, erect fortifications, exercise jurisdiction over English subjects residing in the East, make peace or war, and form alliances with non-Christian peoples. The Company acquired the town destined to be the seat of its western Presidency through the marriage of the King with a Portuguese princess, Catherine of Braganza. She brought Bombay with the best harbour in India to Charles II as part of her dowry in 1661, to the despair of the viceroy of Goa, who wrote, 'India will be lost on the same day on which the English nation is settled in Bombay'.[1] Charles found the place an exceedingly unprofitable possession, and was glad in 1668 to hand it over to the East India Company at a rent of ten pounds a year, to be held, in quaint legal phraseology, 'as of the manor of East Greenwich in the county of Kent in free and common soccage'. Bombay gradually grew in fame and prosperity and succeeded Surat as the chief settlement on the west coast in 1687.

The Company's success during the first twenty years of

[1] *The Rise of Bombay*, S. M. Edwardes, p. 91.

the Restoration period was largely due to the fact that they were practically unmolested by European rivals. Charles II did indeed wage two wars with Holland in 1665–7 and 1672–4, but there was hardly any collision of the hostile forces in the East that was worthy of notice. By the Treaty of Breda, 1667, Pulo Run and some other places were finally relinquished to the Dutch in return for the far more valuable colonial possession (though its worth was not recognized at the time) of New Amsterdam, renamed New York. In India proper the Dutch mainly directed their operations against France, and so, without intending it, conferred a service upon England by checking at a very critical time the growth of the French Company.

After 1685 the East India Company once more entered upon a period of stress and difficulty. The early essays of the English nation in India had fortunately coincided with the reigns of the Mughal emperors who for about a hundred and fifty years gave political cohesion at least to northern India. During the latter part of the reign of Aurangzeb, the last of those able sovereigns, the empire was politically amidst the breakers. The provincial viceroys were getting out of the control of the central government; Sivaji the great Maratha leader, up to his death in 1680, had raided and plundered in open defiance of the supreme power. The wide extent of country over which he ranged may be gauged from the fact that in 1664 and 1670 he was driven with difficulty from the walls of the English factory at Surat after he had pillaged the town, while in 1677 he passed close to Madras on his way to the capture of Jinji. The result was a breakdown of that internal order and good government which was absolutely essential to a profitable trade. The English in Bengal were oppressed by the Nawab Shaista Khan (1664–77 and 1679–89). 'The whole kingdom', said Job Charnock in 1678, 'is lying in a very miserable feeble condition, the great ones plundering and robbing the feebler'.[1] The change that had passed over the Indian scene is graphically described by Gerald Aungier in a striking dispatch, 'the state of India . . . is much altered of what it was; that justice and respect, wherewith strangers in general and especially those of our nation were wont to be treated with, is quite laid aside; the name of the honourable Company and the English nation through our long patient sufferings of wrong, is become slighted; our complaints, remonstrances, paper protests, and threatenings are laughed at, ... in violent distempers violent cures are only successful . . . the times now require you to manage your general commerce with your sword in your hands'.[2] To this general cause were added others more directly affecting the Company. A curious rebellion of Keigwin, the royalist commander of the garrison at Bombay, in 1683–4, and a rising in St. Helena, the 'Sea Inn' of East Indiamen (first occupied by the English in 1659 and finally taken from the Dutch in 1673), embarrassed the Company and brought their administration into evil odour at home as tyrannical. To meet these new conditions the Company, though with reluctance, determined to employ new methods. The advice of Gerald Aungier therefore fell on willing ears, and the Court of Committees groping in the dark and neither understanding the real weakness of the Mughal Empire nor the immense difficulties which as yet made their attempt hopelessly premature, resolved to declare war on Aurangzeb. Having definitely decided to break with the old traditions which had been laid down by Sir Thomas Roe and had served them since his time, their conversion was whole-hearted. They expressed a new-born admiration for the 'wise' Dutch who were concerned less with trade than 'their government, their civil and military policy, warfare

[1] *Diary of William Hedges*, ed. by Sir Henry Yule [Hakluyt Society], vol. ii, p. 46.

[2] India Office Records, O. C. 4258.

and the increase of their revenue'.[1] They realized that the inevitable question would be put, 'Why cannot the Company now subsist with as small duties as they levied formerly?' and their answer was: 'They may subsist as they did, having their factories generally at the mercy of the Heathens among whom they lived.'[2] But the Company since the charter granted them by James II was in 'the condition of a sovereign state in India',[3] and no longer chose to live from hand to mouth. It was at this time (1687) that one of their dispatches contained the famous sentence so often quoted as a prophecy—truer than they could ever have guessed—of British destiny in the East; they urged their President and Council to 'establish such a Politie of civil and military power and create and secure such a large Revenue . . . as may be the foundation of a large, well grounded sure English Dominion in India for all time to come'.[4]

Tradition has largely associated this new departure with the names of Sir Josia and Sir John Child. Recent research has disproved the belief that they were related. The former certainly wielded for many years an almost autocratic influence in the counsels of the Company at home, being four times governor between 1681 and 1687. Some letters of his still preserved in the Bodleian Library at Oxford[5] show clearly how all-powerful was his position in the Court of Committees, even at a later date than this (1692–4). Sir John Child was President of Surat and Governor of Bombay, that is, really chief of the Company in India from 1682–90.

The policy thus valiantly and grandiloquently formulated ended in bitter disappointment. Captain Nicholson was

[1] India Office Records, Letter Book No. 9, Dispatch to Bombay, Sept. 11, 1689.
[2] Ibid., No. 8, Dispatch to Fort St. George, Jan. 14, 1686.
[3] Ibid., Sept. 28, 1687.
[4] Ibid., Dec. 12, 1687.
[5] Bodleian Library, Rawlinson MSS. A. 303.

sent from England with a fleet of ten armed vessels and a force of 600 men, to be reinforced by 400 taken on board at Madras. He was ordered to capture and fortify Chittagong on the north-eastern shore of the Bay of Bengal (though the Court of Committees believed it to be somewhere 'up the great Ganges'), as the future seat of the Company in those regions, to go to war with the King of Siam, and to capture Salsette from the Portuguese. Not one of these ambitious aims was realized. When the expedition arrived at Hughli in October 1686, hostilities broke out prematurely, and after the town had been bombarded the English retired twenty-seven miles down the river to a village called Sutanati, the site of the modern Calcutta. The Emperor now gave orders for a general attack on the English settlements. The factories at Patna, Cossimbazar, Masulipatam, and Vizagapatam were seized, and Bombay was besieged. Captain Heath was sent out from England with reinforcements, and in 1688 took on board all the English in Bengal with the Company's goods, bombarded and burnt Balasore and sailed to effect the conquest of Chittagong. But he found the place strongly defended and after a month of futile negotiations, made his way to Madras. There he arrived in March 1689. And so the consequence of the Company's spirited war policy was the evacuation of Bengal and the loss of the results of half a century's painful toil and effort.

The position of the English in India was only saved by their sea power. Sir John Child on the western coast seized all the Mughal shipping he could lay his hands on, and sent his captains to the Red Sea and Persian Gulf to arrest the pilgrimage traffic to Mecca. This bold stroke induced Aurangzeb at last to listen to overtures for peace, though the terms he conceded were harsh and contemptuous. In February 1690 he granted the English pardon and a new licence for trade, provided they paid a fine of £17,000, engaged 'to behave themselves for the future no more in such a shameful manner', and that 'Mr. Child who did the disgrace, be turned out and expelled'. The English were spared this last humiliation, for Sir John Child, worn out with his exertions, had died earlier in the month, having, in the words of his employers, despite his final failure, 'done more for the Company and the honour of his country than ever any Englishman did in India'. The tale of disaster was relieved by one episode, the importance of which could not be realized at the time. Job Charnock, the English agent at Hughli, had twice since 1686 endeavoured to establish a settlement on the site of Calcutta, and had twice been forced to abandon it, when the open breach occurred with the viceroy of Bengal. At the conclusion of the peace the English were contemptuously granted permission to resume their settlements in the delta of the Ganges. And so after fifteen months' sojourn at Madras he made his way back almost unnoticed to his ruined settlement. The same year, therefore, which witnessed the abasement of the Company before Aurangzeb, also witnessed the humble foundation of a future capital of British India, the first step in the realization of the half unconscious prophecy of 1687.

CHAPTER VII

THE NEW EAST INDIA COMPANY

THE opponents of the Company in England inveighed against 'the unjust and wicked war with the Great Mogul',[1] and the news of the humiliating peace concluded in India gave them a welcome handle against the Court of Committees. Opposition to the East India monopoly had been growing for many years and took many forms. There was a considerable section which objected to the trade altogether for economic reasons that are not unknown at the present time. They disliked it because of the export of bullion which was its necessary concomitant, and because it imported manufactured goods and commodities which they supposed to be positively harmful, for instance coffee, which as a contemporary writer quaintly remarked was 'most useless since it serves neither for nourishment nor debauchery'.[2] Such opponents laid down the principle that no foreign trade was advantageous to the kingdom which did not export produce and manufactured goods and import raw materials. It is interesting to note that, if these specious arguments—which are often enunciated to-day—had prevailed, the incalculable advantage of the Indian trade would have been lost to England.

The Company's apologists in their attempts to answer these objections groped their way to a sounder economic theory which often anticipated the conclusions of Adam Smith and the Free Trade school. They declared stoutly that 'no

[1] *Some Remarks upon the present state of the East India Company's Affairs*, 1690.

[2] *Britannia Languens, or a Discourse of Trade*, 1680.

nation ever was or will be considerable in trade, that prohibits the exportation of bullion'.[1] It was a fallacy to regard bullion or specie as different from any other form of wealth, 'gold and silver and ... money are nothing but the weights and measures by which traffic is more conveniently carried on than could be done without them'.[2] These writers objected to the whole principle of state interference in commercial matters, 'Laws to hamper trade whether foreign or domestic relating to money or other merchandizes are not ingredients to make a people rich. . . . No people ever yet grew rich by policies.'[2] 'Few laws relating to trade', wrote Davenant, 'are the mark of a nation that thrives by traffic.'[3] But they based the main defence of the India trade on yet wider grounds: 'Since the discovery of the East Indies, the dominion of the sea depends much upon the wane or increase of that trade, and consequently the security of the liberty, property, and protestant religion of this kingdom.'[1]

A second party were opposed simply to the Joint Stock theory and clamoured for a company on a regulated basis, i. e. one in which merchants traded on their individual capital as members of a guild.

Thirdly, a large and increasing number objected to the existing Company as resting on a too narrow and exclusive basis. When these men urged the dissolution of the Company, they only meant the winding up of the particular group of subscribers who had monopolized the trade since 1657, and there was little doubt that the Company might well have increased its capital and admitted a greater number to share its high profits. This section inveighed fiercely against the autocratic power which Sir Josia Child wielded in the Courts of the Company. In 1681 a prominent member of

[1] *A Treatise wherein is demonstrated, that the East India Trade is the most national of all foreign trades*, by Φιλόπατρις, 1681.

[2] *Discourses upon Trade*, Sir Dudley North, London, 1691.

[3] *An Essay on the East India Trade*, 1696 [by Charles Davenant]

the Court, Thomas Papillon, foreseeing the tendency of affairs, suggested that the Company itself should take the initiative by admitting more outsiders to a share in its privileges. But Sir Josia Child refused to accept the proposal and hounded Papillon and his associates out of the Company. 'The great Ministers and chief men at court fell in with Sir Josia', and he and his supporters 'do tumble the members in and out of the Committee according as they serve their own terms'.[1]

For many years individual 'interlopers' in India had defied the Company's servants, or acted in collusion with them; one of the most famous of the interlopers was Thomas Pitt, grandfather of the Earl of Chatham, who made a large fortune by unlawful, or, at least, unauthorized trading, and purchased a large landed estate together with the pocket borough of Old Sarum. These men had in vain attempted to get a pronouncement that the monopoly of the Company was illegal, in the famous trial of Thomas Sandys in 1683, when Judge Jeffreys decided for the Company. The only result seems to have been the charter of 1686, which strengthened the Company's power against both native chiefs in India and contumacious Englishmen, 'forming us', as Sir Josia Child triumphantly wrote, 'into the condition of a sovereign state in India'.[2]

The fall of the Stuart dynasty was a serious blow to Child. 'The Revolution', says Sir William Hunter, 'brought the Company face to face with Parliament.'[3] The London Company's numerous enemies associated themselves with the Whig Party, and as early as 1690 succeeded in inducing a parliamentary committee to pass a resolution in favour of a new Company. About this time they banded them-

[1] *Some Remarks upon the present state of the East India Company's Affairs*, 1690.

[2] India Office Records, Letter Book No. 8, Dispatch to Fort St. George, Sept. 28, 1687.

[3] *A History of British India*, vol. ii, p. 275.

selves together in an informal kind of association meeting in the Hall of the Skinners' Company in Dowgate Street. Parliament and the King in vain endeavoured to persuade the old Company to admit new members, and finally the Commons petitioned the Crown to dissolve the defiant corporation. So far from being intimidated Sir Josia Child expended over £80,000 in bribery among ministers and actually thus procured a new charter for the old Company in 1693. The result was, as might be expected, an outburst of great anger in the country and in the Commons. An interloper, Gilbert Heathcote, whose ship was seized in the Thames, voiced the national feeling when he declared, before a committee of the House of Commons, that 'he did not think it any sin to trade to the East Indies, and would trade thither till there was an Act of Parliament to the contrary'.[1] Parliament itself subscribed to this view and resolved, in 1694, 'that all the subjects of England have equal right to trade to the East Indies, unless prohibited by Act of Parliament'.[2] This resolution, which was promptly acted upon by many daring spirits, seriously invalidated the Company's position. In 1695 an inquiry was held into the Company's corruption. It was found that £107,000 had been expended between 1688 and 1694. These revelations caused a great sensation and brought about the political ruin of a minister, the Duke of Leeds.

At the very time that the Company was incurring disgrace from these damaging disclosures, an attack on their privileged position was made from an unexpected quarter, in the attempt of Scotland, still legally a separate and independent kingdom, though united under one crown, to win a share in the Indian trade. Nearly ninety years before, in 1617, James I had granted letters patent to Sir James Cunningham, one of his northern subjects, to trade to the East Indies,

[1] *Journals of the House of Commons*, Jan. 8, 1694.
[2] Ibid., Jan. 16, 1694.

but the London Company warded off the danger by buying him out. In 1693 the Scottish Parliament legalized the formation of associations for over-sea trade, and followed this up in 1695 by establishing the Company of Scotland, trading to Africa and the Indies. One of the leaders of the movement was William Paterson, the founder of the Bank of England. The names of the subscribers to the capital of £400,000, and the representative classes from which they were drawn, prove that the undertaking was essentially a national one. A Scottish pamphleteer of the day declared that Scotland had 'been most unmercifully cramped and fettered in its national liberties . . . till the late providential and happy revolution', and prayed that the harmonious working together of the English and Scottish Companies might be an inducement to all men to 'lay aside misplaced passion, . . . obliterate and bury in oblivion the distinguishing names of Scotch and English, and then voluntarily list themselves under the united banner of undivided Britain'.[1] But this generous dream was soon dispelled, and the episode of the Scottish Company was destined rather to embitter for many years the feeling between the two countries. However divided the English people might be as to the domestic question between their own Old and New Companies, they were at one in their opposition to possible rivals from the north. William III, as sovereign of both nations, was in an unenviable position, being bound either to disappoint the legitimate aspirations of one kingdom or to fall foul of the strong prejudices of the other. Both the English Houses of Parliament presented to him an address against the Scottish Company, and he rather weakly temporized by replying, 'I have been ill-served in Scotland, but I hope some remedies may be found to prevent the inconveniences which may arise from

[1] *A letter from a member of the Parliament of Scotland to his friend at London.*

this Act'.[1] The English Parliament next passed a violent resolution that the Directors were guilty of a high crime and misdemeanour, and should be impeached. But, in the end, it was their own ill-advised action that ruined the Scottish Company and freed the King from an embarrassing predicament. They were debarred from settling on territory belonging to a friendly power, but in spite of this they established a settlement on the Isthmus of Darien, which was claimed by Spain. The Spaniards protested, and the English government left the settlers to their fate, warning the English colonists at New York, Barbados, and Jamaica not to render them any aid. Disease and famine, combined with Spanish hostility, completed the ruin of the colony and brought about the fall of the Company.

In 1698 the members of the Dowgate Association, on raising a loan of £2,000,000 at 8 per cent. for Montagu, the Chancellor of the Exchequer, were incorporated under the name of the General Society. To this Society was granted the exclusive trade to India, saving the rights of the Old Company, which would expire after three years' notice, and saving also the private rights of those traders who had embarked for India on the strength of the Resolution of the House of Commons in 1694. The Old or London Company, to safeguard some of their privileges in the East India trade, subscribed £315,000 in the name of their treasurer, John Du Bois. The General Society was, in deference to the critics of the Old Company, established upon a regulated basis, which meant that the subscribers might trade individually to India, but the King was empowered to incorporate as many of such members as desired it into a joint-stock company, and undoubtedly such a development was contemplated from the very first. By far the greater number at once took advantage of this provision,

[1] *A Comprehensive History of India*, Henry Beveridge, vol. i, p. 369.

and were incorporated on September 5, 1698, as 'The English Company trading to the East Indies', controlled by a court of twenty-four 'Directors'. It must clearly be understood that, for the next few years, there were four classes of traders who possessed a legal right to trade to the East Indies. (1) The New English Company. (2) The Old Company, trading on their full capital until 1701 and after that on their limited subscription of £315,000 to the General Society. (3) Subscribers to the General Society who had refused to incorporate themselves in the joint stock of the New Company, and it must be remembered that after 1701 the Old Company ranked under this category. The capital of the separate traders, apart from the Old Company, did not amount to more than £22,000. (4) A few private adventurers, who had embarked in the trade to India after the Commons' Resolution in 1694 and before the incorporation of the General Society in 1698.

The private traders under the last two heads had little importance, and the real struggle for supremacy lay between the English and the London Company. It may be asked, why did not the state give the Old Company the statutory notice, enjoin them to wind up their affairs, and then allow the New Company to begin trading with India? To permit both associations to co-exist for three years, and wage internecine warfare with one another, seems at first sight a most impolitic course. But the truth is that it was, from a practica point of view, most undesirable that there should be any breach in the continuity of the trade. If left to themselves, the Old Company might have wound up their affairs so effectually as to sever the British connexion with India altogether. With all its disadvantages, the method adopted ensured a certain dove-tailing of one Company into the other. As early as October 1698 the Old Company write that their rivals' 'principal reliance is upon a new-fashioned word now in vogue in all public places; they call it coalition, by which we think they mean that our stock should be joined to theirs, and we are so much for the public good of our country that probably it may come to that in due time, when their stock and ours meets about the same price'.[1] But in the meantime both parties manœuvred for position, and the struggle was fought out bitterly both at home and abroad before the stern logic of events drove them to amalgamate.

The Old Company at first staggered under the blow dealt them, but as 'veteran soldiers in this warfare'[2] they braced themselves bravely for the struggle. On taking stock of the position, they found it less desperate than they had supposed. They still had their forts and factories in the East, of which no Act of Parliament could deprive them, and the right for three years to carry on their business under the old conditions. After that date they could still, so they hoped, as members of the General Society, trade on the limited capital of £315,000 subscribed by them in the name of their treasurer. The only doubt was whether they could legally transfer to themselves as an association this sum, which still stood in the books of the General Society as contributed by John du Bois. To strengthen their position, they at once began to petition for an Act continuing them a corporation even after their existence as the 'London Company of Merchants trading to the East Indies' should be terminated.

On the other hand, the New Company, having begun by lending its capital to government, found considerable difficulty in raising new funds for commerce, and they were confronted with the arduous task of establishing themselves in the East in the presence of jealous rivals already in

[1] India Office Records, Letter Book No. 10, Dispatch to Madras, Oct. 28, 1698.

[2] Ibid., Dispatch to Bengal, Aug. 26, 1698.

possession. They decided to make their head-quarters in India at, or near, the chief seats of the Old Company, doubtless with the expectation of stepping into possession of their factories and buildings at the end of the three years' period. As their representatives, they sent out Sir Nicholas Waite to Bombay, Sir Edward Littleton to Bengal, and John Pitt to Madras, but they were unfortunate in their choice. All these men were dismissed servants of the Old Company, and they proved incompetent and faithless in their new service. The New Company, in opposition to the trade policy of fortified settlements, had deliberately adopted the plan of attempting to establish diplomatic relations with the Indian powers. They therefore not only selected Sir William Norris, member of Parliament for Liverpool, to go as ambassador to the Mughal Emperor, to win for them the same privileges from Aurangzeb that Sir Thomas Roe had procured from Jahangir for their predecessors, but they procured from the Crown commissions as King's Consuls for their Presidents. These commissions only helped to embroil the holders of them with the servants of the Old Company, who sturdily refused to recognize their validity, at any rate till the period of three years' grace had elapsed. The New Company's servants claimed that their credentials should be acknowledged from the outset, 'threatening imprisonment in irons and strange bugbear powers'[1] over those who refused to listen to them. 'All Englishmen whatsoever', wrote Norris, 'are under my care and protection',[2] a claim which his rivals treated with quiet contempt. They had no intention, they declared, 'of running under their consuls' wings for shelter and protection. We think our forts under the auspices of our sovereign, represented by His Majesty's flag flying upon

[1] India Office Records, Letter Book No. 10, Dispatch to Persia, Aug. 21, 1700.
[2] Ibid., Factory Records, Miscellaneous, No. XIX.

them, are much better securities than any pompous character of Consul, Deputy Consul, Vice-admiral, or the like titles.'[1]

On the whole, then, in India the Old Company, with its better equipped factories, longer experience, and more competent servants, proved superior in the struggle, though in Surat disaster overtook them. There, Sir Nicholas Waite, a headstrong and meddlesome man, only succeeded in ruining his rivals' business without furthering his own. He embroiled Sir John Gayer, the Old Company's President, with the Mughal government, with the result that the factory at Surat was seized, all trade stopped, and Gayer himself imprisoned. In the other two Presidencies everything went in favour of the Old Company. In Bengal, which had been constituted a separate Presidency in 1699, Sir Edward Littleton, a dishonest and incapable person, was successfully kept at bay by John Beard, while in Madras, Thomas Pitt, the ex-interloper, but since 1697 President of Fort St. George, a man of original character and great ability, completely out-manœuvred his passionate and conceited cousin, John Pitt. Most calamitous of all was the complete failure of the embassy from which so much had been expected. Sir William Norris was far the most estimable of the men sent out by the New Company; he was honest, industrious, and conscientious, but he had none of the patient diplomatic ability necessary for success in the very delicate and difficult task on which he had embarked. He succeeded, after ruinous expense and much delay, in gaining an audience of the Emperor Aurangzeb, who was conducting a campaign against the Marathas, at Panalla, a fortress near Bijapur, but he found it impossible to obtain a commercial treaty, owing to the mischievous interference of Sir Nicholas Waite. The latter had, without

[1] India Office Records, Letter Book No. 10, Dispatch to Fort St. George, June 18, 1700.

any authority to do so, promised the Emperor that the New Company would take upon themselves the burden of defending from the pirates the waters of the Arabian Sea and Persian Gulf along the route followed by the Mughal ships carrying Muhammadan pilgrims to the sacred shrine of Mecca. This duty had hitherto been shared by the English, French, and Dutch together, and it was impossible for the ambassador to place the whole burden on the shoulders of the New Company. The Emperor made the acceptance of the duty of patrolling the seas a necessary condition of the grant of any privileges, and Sir William Norris returned to the coast baffled and deeply chagrined, to die on his passage home, worn out by his physical exertions and mental anxieties. The ruin of the embassy was due to the injudicious interference of Sir Nicholas Waite, the intrigues of the Old Company's native agents, the unfamiliarity of Norris with the dilatory and tortuous methods of Oriental diplomacy, the disturbed condition of the Mughal Empire at the time, and the natural failure of Aurangzeb to comprehend the opposing claims of the two Companies.

Meanwhile, at home, events had been tending towards an amalgamation. The New Company had long given up all hope of beating down their adversaries by force, and a union on favourable terms was the most for which they now looked. This solution of the deadlock was, however, postponed for a time by the fact that early in 1700 the Old Company succeeded in obtaining the coveted Act of Parliament enacting that they should be continued as a corporation after 1701, to trade to India on their subscription of £315,000 to the General Society. They exultingly claimed that this, with their Indian possessions, gave them all they desired; 'as it will give new vigour to our people, so it will clip the wings of that assumed authority the new gentlemen pretend to, and wherewith being grown giddy they know not how to behave themselves'.[1] But the union was only postponed. The Directors of the New Company wrote in 1702, 'the loss we sustain by the India trade at present, and particularly from the coast (of Coromandel), has induced us not to decline entering into a treaty with the Old Company';[2] while their rivals, in spite of their Pyrrhic victory in the East, were driven to recognize that 'two sellers in India depreciate our Europe commodities, and two buyers there enhance India goods'.[3] Other causes contributed to the same end. War with France was impending—an obviously cogent reason for healing intestine strife in the East. The question of the Indian trade transcended for the time (especially during the elections of 1701) all other matters. Both sides intrigued, and spent money freely, scandalizing observers by the corruption they practised among the electors. The King and Parliament were anxious for a settlement, and put pressure on both Companies.

Accordingly a preliminary 'Instrument of Union' was signed in April 1702. The Old Company was ordered to purchase £673,000 additional stock in the General Society, to make its share equal to that of its rival. The houses, factories, and forts of the Old Company in India were valued at £330,000, those of the New at £70,000, and the New were called upon to pay £130,000 to the Old. The old twenty-four committees were superseded by twenty-four managers, twelve to be elected by each Company, who were to direct the trade from 1702. The factors of the two Companies in the East were directed henceforward to work together in unity, and in some cases presided over the settlements in rotation. A letter of the Old Company to their servants breathes the new spirit of hope and consolida-

[1] India Office Records, Letter Book No. 10, Dispatch to Persia, Aug. 21, 1700.

[2] Ibid., Letter Book No. 11, Dispatch to John Pitt, Jan. 8, 1702.

[3] Ibid., Letter Book No. 10, Dispatch to Madras, March 6, 1702.

tion: 'The present union having put a full stop to all your late competitions and struggles, and the trade to India being settled on the firm basis of an Act of Parliament and a large stock, we have a hopeful prospect that the same will in due time become more flourishing than ever, to the honour of our nation and the profit of the adventurers, and that we shall mutually concur to the retrieving the English reputation in India, which has severely suffered by the villainies of the pirates, the ill offices of our own countrymen, and the perfidiousness of the Moors (i. e. Muhammadans), who took advantage from both to oppress and lessen us.'[1] Naturally, however, there was still a good deal of friction among the English in India, and it was some time before the exhortations of the home authorities 'to bury all that is past in silence and forgetfulness'[2] were really carried out. Even at home the union was not finally completed till 1708, when all disputed points were finally settled by the award of the Earl of Godolphin. Henceforward there was but one Company, under the title of the 'United Company of Merchants of England trading to the East Indies'. This body received at intervals new charters prolonging the period of its monopoly, and though in time its sovereign powers were much curtailed, it continued its corporate existence till the cataclysm of the Mutiny brought about the abolition of its remaining privileges and the transference of its dominions and revenues to the Crown.

[1] India Office Records, Letter Book No. 10, Dispatch to Bombay July 26, 1702.

[2] Ibid., Dispatch to Madras, March 5, 1702.

CHAPTER VIII

GROWTH OF THE SETTLEMENTS, 1708–1746
THE OSTEND COMPANY

AFTER 1708 the position of the East India Company at home was secured for many years, and in India there ensued a period of peaceful commercial development. That period is almost ignored by historians, who are naturally eager to press on to 1746, when the Company is drawn into the vortex of a European war, embroiled in conflicts with native dynasties, and itself becomes a territorial power. But from the colonial aspect these years require a somewhat closer attention. The English had established themselves in India when the Mughal Empire, at the height of its greatness, imposed order and peace over Hindustan, and claimed suzerainty even over the Deccan. Aurangzeb, the last great Emperor, died in 1707, the year before Lord Godolphin's award united the warring Companies in England. His reign had been a long one, and he had reduced the Deccan nominally to dependence—thus realizing the aim of all previous sovereigns, but in the process he had fatally weakened his own dominions. When he died, the Rajputs (whom he had alienated by his Muhammadan bigotry) were in arms, the Sikhs were showing signs of activity, anarchy was rampant in southern India, for he had destroyed the kingdoms of Bijapur and Golconda without being able to put anything in their place, and the Marathas, vanquished in tactics but conquerors in strategy, were roaming throughout western and central India, on the eve of that great development which was, within the course of the next fifty years, to make them the most formidable military and political force in India, and to carry their arms to the banks of the Indus. Aurangzeb was succeeded on the throne of Delhi by a succession of rulers whose reigns were short and troubled. Henceforward, as the Frenchman Bussy, a keen observer, declared, the Mughal government was 'feeble with numerous forces badly led, and poverty-stricken with great wealth badly administered'.[1] The Viceroys or Subadars of the Empire for the most part left the capital to itself, and, when they were able to repel the Maratha onset, founded independent kingdoms for themselves out of the provinces they governed.

Though these political changes foreshadowed difficulties and dangers for the East India Company's settlements in the future, at this particular date they afforded conditions which were not altogether unfavourable. The English factories were already strong enough to maintain themselves against the local Muhammadan governors or coast rajas with whom they came in contact, and whereas they might have been exposed to the envy of a powerful emperor, the rulers of the newer semi-independent kingdoms set up in Bengal and southern India were less inclined to dread western influence, and often welcomed the resources they drew from their connexion with the traders from over the sea.

The English even took advantage of the now frequent revolutions at Delhi to legalize their *status* in India. In 1707, on the news of Aurangzeb's death, they hastened to strengthen Fort William in Bengal 'whilst there is an interregnum, and no one likely to take notice of what we are doing'.[2] In 1715 an embassy, under John Surman and Edward Stephenson, went from Calcutta to Delhi through country that was everywhere disturbed. There, after long

[1] *Mémoire pour le sieur de Bussy*, 1750, p. 17.

[2] C. R. Wilson's *Early Annals of the English in Bengal*, vol. i, p. 282.

delay and the exhibition of indomitable patience, they procured *Farmans* or signed privileges, which Orme afterwards described as the *Magna Charta* of the Company. Their success was largely due to the Emperor's gratitude to William Hamilton, surgeon to the embassy, who cured him of a dangerous illness. Certain villages near Calcutta and Madras were made over to the Company, and a formal recognition was given to the residence of its servants in India. The value of the concession was weakened by the fact that the Mughal authority itself was henceforward of little weight, except in northern India, but, as Burke afterwards declared, the East India Company in a legal sense now became an integral part of the empire of the Mughals. The embassy, at any rate, opened the eyes of the English to the hideous rottenness of the empire. The very present which they carried to the Emperor Farrukhsiyar had been prepared originally for Bahadur Shah, and was then destined for his successor, Jahandar Shah, but civil disorders had prevented any possibility of its being delivered to either. The envoys witnessed the revolt of a Mughal army in the streets of Delhi, they saw that the Emperor himself, whom they had addressed as 'absolute monarch and prop of the universe', to whom the Governor of Fort William was, in his own words, but as 'the smallest particle of sand . . . (with his forehead, at command, rubbed on the ground)',[1] was but a feeble *roi fainéant*, a mere tool in the hand of unscrupulous ministers.

The subject that bulks largest in the India Office records during the first thirty years of the eighteenth century is the struggle with the Ostend Company. After the revolt of the seven United Provinces of the Netherlands, the ten remaining ones had a very chequered history. They were alternately bandied to and fro between the power of Austria and

[1] *Early Annals of the English in Bengal*, C. R. Wilson, vol. ii, part I, p. iii.

that of Spain. At various crises in their fortunes they made attempts to procure a share of the trade to India. These attempts proved abortive, though one, in 1698, only seemed to fail of success through the death of Charles II of Spain and the outbreak of the war of the Spanish succession. For the next twelve years the Lowlands were converted into one vast battlefield, ever resounding with the tramp of European armies. The Peace of Utrecht in 1713 brought about a revival of commerce, and the subjection of the country to the house of Austria. In their new sovereign, Charles VI, the inhabitants of the Low Countries found a patron who was quite prepared, for reasons of his own, to support them in their efforts to obtain a share of the Eastern trade. The Emperor dreamt of establishing an Imperial mercantile marine on the profits of Indian commerce, which should form a counterpoise to the naval supremacy of the English and the Dutch.

The Ostend Company was not formally chartered, as we shall see, till 1722, but commissions for single vessels seem to have been granted as early as 1714, and in 1716 a proclamation was issued by the Prince of Wales, then acting as Regent in his father's absence, against the King's subjects trading to the East Indies under a foreign flag. Between 1718 and 1721, fifteen vessels sailed from Ostend to the East. Many renegade Dutch and English sea captains and factors, especially Jacobite exiles, took service with the Ostenders. For some time the trade continued under a kind of temporary association of merchants. Ships were fitted out at Lisbon and Leghorn as well as at Ostend, and, according to one authority, even cleared from British ports. The Emperor contemplated establishing stations for the Indian fleet also on the shores of the Adriatic at Fiume and Trieste, but this part of the scheme, at any rate, was not developed at this time.

Before long the Ostend merchants began to agitate for a

formal charter of incorporation. De Merveille, formerly a sea captain in the English service, is said to have been the first to present a scheme at the Imperial court. But the Emperor, on the advice of his ministers, and especially of Prince Eugene, Governor of the Netherlands from 1716–24, for a long time refused to entertain such a proposal, dreading the enmity of the maritime powers. England and Holland had indeed shown, in no uncertain manner, with what distrust they regarded the appearance of 'so ominous an invader'[1] as the new Company, in the Eastern world. It was found that Indian goods were being smuggled from Flanders into Great Britain. This contraband trade was carried on in large boats with ten or twelve oars, which rowed 'from Ostend to the river (Thames), and often at high water have run through bridge before the face of the custom-house officers'.[2] To prevent this, special Acts of Parliament were passed in 1719 and 1721, forbidding British subjects to trade to the Indies under commissions of a foreign state, and prohibiting any boat from rowing on the Thames, either above or below London Bridge, with more than four oars. This measure was followed by other Acts and proclamations threatening severe penalties against British subjects concerned in the Ostend ventures, and the letters of the Company for many years breathe stern denunciations against all who should be suspected of having any relations with the intruders.

But in 1722 the Emperor, against the advice of Prince Eugene and his ministers, decided to brave all opposition and grant a charter. An English merchant, Colebrook by name, is said to have been very prominent in procuring this important concession. The letters patent were issued December 22, 1722, though they were not published openly till the summer of the following year. The capital of the

[1] *Mr. Forman's letter to the Rt. Hon. Wm. Pulteney . . .*, 1725, p. 34.
[2] *The Importance of the Ostend Company considered*, 1726, p. 33.

Company was fixed at 6,000,000 florins. To attract foreign support, one clause in the charter provided that the shares of foreigners should not be liable to confiscation in the event of a war between Austria and their native country. Subscription books were opened at Antwerp on August 11, and by noon next day the capital was all subscribed, and at the end of the month the shares were up to twelve or fifteen per cent. premium.

So far the new Company had made a promising start, but the granting of the charter redoubled the opposition in Holland and England. The question of the Ostend Company became, for the next nine years, one of the thorniest of diplomatic problems. The charter was not publicly announced till August 1723, but the news had probably leaked out; in April, M. Bruyninx, the Dutch Minister at Brussels, presented a memorial of remonstrance to the Marquis de Prié, the Austrian Governor of the Netherlands. The protest of the Dutch was based upon the articles of the treaty of Munster (1648), by which Philip II, King of Spain, and at that time sovereign of the Netherlands, had practically renounced all part or lot in the Indian trade by the Cape route. The Dutch declared that the Austrian Netherlands continued under this prohibition by the terms of the Barrier treaty concluded at Antwerp in 1715. They had assisted Charles VI to claim the sovereignty over the southern Netherlands only on the footing of his right to the Spanish monarchy, and, therefore, he could hold these provinces no otherwise than the Kings of Spain had held them. It is clear that a somewhat subtle point of diplomacy was here raised; the clause of the treaty was in truth rather ambiguous, and, as a contemporary writer observes, 'it seems this treaty has two handles, and each (party) lays hold of that which is most for his purpose'.[1] The East India Company in England eagerly supported the Dutch;

[1] Boyer's *Political State of Great Britain*, vol. xxxi, p. 351.

they had the memorial translated and copies presented to the members at the door of the House of Commons. Pamphleteers of the day strove vigorously to raise the cry, even then losing much of its force, that Protestantism was in danger. If the Ostend Company succeeded, 'the commerce and riches of one of the bulwarks of the Protestant interest would be thereby transferred to augment the strength of a Roman Catholic state'.[1] Feeling in Holland had been so bitter that the States-General threatened the penalty of death against any Dutchman concerned in the Ostend trade. The prevalent opinion of the time certainly was that the question as between the Emperor and the Dutch could not be terminated without recourse to arms. But though the subject reappears in almost every European treaty for several years, and becomes a stock question of diplomacy, that pass was never reached. In 1725 the House of Commons resolved that the Treaty of Vienna, by which Spain, supporting Austria, opened her American ports to Ostend ships, was 'calculated for the entire destruction of the British trade', and a year later France and Holland joined England in a treaty denouncing the Company. The Emperor found the European opposition too strong, and the States of the Empire had little interest in the commerce of the Netherlands. Bavaria announced in 1726 that she would not regard as 'Imperial' any war waged for the Ostend Company. In the end, Charles sacrificed the Company and his own policy to his dynastic aims. To win the consent of the maritime powers to the Pragmatic Sanction conferring his hereditary possessions on his daughter, Maria Theresa, he agreed in 1727 to suspend the Company's privileges for seven years, and by another treaty with Great Britain, March 16, 1731, he bound himself to suppress the Company altogether, and promised never to

[1] *Mr. Forman's Letter*, p. 39.

permit vessels to sail to India from any country that had been subject to Spain in the reign of Charles II of England.

Attempts were made by the Company to re-establish itself on the Adriatic, at Trieste and Fiume, ports within the Empire which did not come under the prohibitory clauses of the treaty, but the scheme fell through. Failing this, recourse was had to other European powers. In 1728 Frederick IV of Denmark granted a special charter enabling many members of the suppressed Company to join his subjects in the Indian trade, and setting up an India House at Altona, a town belonging to the Danish Crown, but close to Hamburg, a free city of the Empire. Other members enrolled themselves under a new Swedish Company, chartered in 1731. The latter was left more or less undisturbed, because the commerce of the Swedes was rather with the further East, China and Japan, than with India. But in Denmark the British and the Dutch ambassadors were ordered to protest against the new association as being practically a revival of the Ostend Company, and, though Frederick denied their contention, the India House at Altona, after some delay, was closed.

The Ostend Company had always bulked more largely on the horizon of European politics than in the East itself; still, in spite of Carlyle's famous description of 'Karl VI's third shadow hunt, the mere paper Company which never sent ships, only produced diplomacies and had the honour to be', the Ostenders had not only traded in the Indian seas, but had founded two settlements, at 'Bankibazaar' [i.e. Bankipore] on the Hughli and Covelong or Coblon near Madras. The number of vessels sent out had been steadily increasing up to the suspension of the Company, and good dividends had been paid.

But in India the Company had to deal with implacable rivals. The English merchants in Bengal, spurred on by promises of indemnification at home, endeavoured, even before 1727, to seize and imprison Hume, the renegade Englishman who had been appointed Chief of Bankipore, and, as they afterwards admitted, 'had gone some lengths that are not so proper to be committed to Black and White'.[1] From the beginning the Dutch had not scrupled to capture Ostend ships, and after the Company was abandoned by the Emperor, its settlements soon came to ruin. The English seized a vessel in the Ganges in 1730, and a squadron commanded by Captain Gosfright blocked up two more 'so that they can never come away'.[2] Finally, in 1733, the Bengal Presidency stirred up a Muhammadan official to attack Bankibazaar, the isolated station, which was still garrisoned by fourteen persons. They made a despairing resistance, but were obliged to surrender, and were conveyed back to Europe. The Covelong factory existed some years longer. The Company was not legally defunct till 1793.

So ended the ill-fated Ostend Company. To contemporaries it seemed as though a formidable hydra had been slain. 'If one considers seriously', says an observer in 1731, 'the course of the many and various transactions of Europe for these eight or ten years past, it will appear a little strange, and yet very certain, that the charter granted by his Imperial Majesty to the Ostend Company has been the original cause of all the jumble that has ensued among the Princes of Europe, and the difficulties that have occurred in reconciling again their several jarring interests. After that obstacle was once removed, we see how soon the Public tranquillity has been restored.'[3] The crippling of the Company marked the triumph of the narrow policy of restriction and monopoly typical of the century, fortified, in this instance, by national jealousy. Within a few years, enlightened statesmen had begun to see that England's action

[1] Letter of Henry Frankland, Governor of Bengal, 1727.
[2] Boyer's *Political State of Great Britain*, vol. xl, p. 305.
[3] Ibid., vol. xlii, p. 143.

in the matter was not only selfish, but of doubtful expediency. 'The abolition of the Ostend Company', said Pitt in 1742, 'was a demand we had no right to make, nor was it essentially our interest to insist upon it, because that Company would have been more hostile to the interests both of the French and Dutch East India Companies than to our own.'[1]

The further history of the three Presidencies must be very briefly summarized until the outbreak of the war of the Austrian succession, when the French attack on Madras inaugurated a new era in the Company's history. The period was one of growth and consolidation. The Company drove a steady and prosperous trade, subject to normal fluctuations.

The war of the Spanish, unlike that of the Austrian, succession left the Indies almost untouched. Operations were confined wholly to the sea, and apart from uneasiness as to the fate of outgoing and incoming ships, nothing was feared from the French. In the whole course of the war, 1702–13, the Company do not seem to have lost more than seven ships. In March 1712, runners were posted on the road between Madras and Calcutta, and were kept in constant pay, that quick and speedy advices might reach Bengal of any French ships sailing up the coast. But how little the war affected the settlements themselves may be seen from the fact that in 1712 the English at Fort St. David, being at war with the Raja of Jinji, requested the mediation of M. Hébert, the French Governor of Pondicherry. The latter hesitated at first, the two nations being still at war, but finally he consented to act, and brought about a settlement.

In Bengal, the European settlers felt less than in either Bombay or Madras the effects of the failure of Mughal power. The Emperor exercised some sort of control over the Subadars or Nawabs of Bengal for a longer period than over his viceroys elsewhere, though at the end of the period they

[1] *Earl of Chatham's Speeches*, 1853.

too were practically independent. The Nawabs themselves were men of some ability, and under Murshid Kuli Khan 1713–25, Shuja Khan 1725–39, and Ali Vardi Khan 1741–56, the province enjoyed, according to native standards, good government and internal peace. The English in Calcutta, though they complained bitterly from time to time of the exactions levied on their trade by the Mughal officers, lived on good terms with the Nawabs. The building of Fort William, which was begun in 1696, was completed about 1715. After the end of the rotation government[1] in 1710, the trade of the settlement steadily grew. The commerce of Bengal, consisting of silks, muslins, saltpetre, sugar, opium, rice, jute, and oil, was the most valuable in India. Round the English factory, warehouses, godowns, and fort, there grew up a prosperous native town, with a population that was estimated at 100,000 by 1735, while the broad pool, almost deserted when Charnock first anchored there, was thronged with shipping.

On the western coast of India, Bombay felt more acutely the effects of the breakdown of Mughal rule. The Marathas were now steadily extending their power northwards from Maharashtra, the home of their origin, and occupying the hinterland of the Portuguese and English settlements. The descendants of Sivaji still ruled nominally at Satara, but their palace was practically a royal prison, for all real power had passed to their ministers, the Peshwas, who made their office hereditary and established their dynasty at Poona. The English and Portuguese on the western coast forgot their old enmity, and drew together in face of the common peril. In 1731 Bombay sent a reinforcement of 300 sepoys to Goa, but they found themselves unable to offer further help, since Portuguese affairs in India were 'in a very declining if not desperate and irretrievable condition'.[2] In

[1] See *supra*, p. 58.
[2] *Bombay Gazetteer*, vol. xxvi, part I, p. 194.

1738 the Marathas captured Bassein, twenty-eight miles north of Bombay. On the sea, the famous corsair chief, Kanhoji Angria, preyed on all the shipping of the coast from Bombay to Goa, darting forth from the creeks and harbours where he had established his strongholds, with his swift sailing ships and oared galleys, called *grabs* and *gallivats*. He had originally been the commander of the Maratha fleet, but, as generally happened with Maratha leaders, he soon made himself independent. At first he only attacked Mughal shipping, but later he ventured, sometimes in alliance with Taylor, England, and Plantain, the notorious pirates of Madagascar, to assail the largest East Indiamen. Attacks were made in vain on his chief stations in 1717, 1718, 1720, and 1737, but his capital at Gheria defied not only the Company's fleet, but (in 1720) a royal squadron, till it was finally captured by Clive and Watson in 1756. Angria himself died in 1728 or 1730 (the date is uncertain), but his sons continued his lawless sway, one at Kolaba and the other at Sevendrug. Bombay, thus fiercely assailed, remained weak for the first eighteen years of the eighteenth century, and her trade greatly suffered, but from that date a steady improvement set in. In 1744 her population was estimated at 70,000. Though unable to afford much help to the Portuguese, she developed, in the invigorating atmosphere of opposition, a strength to meet the attacks of her enemies, and by 1746 she was the strongest of the Presidency towns from a military point of view. 'It sadly concerns us', wrote the Court of Directors, 'to find you have such occasion for warlike forces by sea and land on your side of India.'[1] But Bombay, in spite of protests from home, developed her Indian navy, and in 1737 her land forces amounted to over 2,600 men, including 750 Europeans, a much larger garrison than was maintained at this time at

[1] India Office Records, Letter Book No. 16, Dispatch to Bombay, Feb. 27, 1719.

either Calcutta or Madras. Inch by inch the Company's servants resisted the danger; successively they had allied themselves with the *Sidi*, the Mughal admiral, against Angria, with one of Angria's sons against the other, and with the Portuguese against the Marathas; finally, in 1739, they concluded the first British treaty with the Marathas themselves, by which the Peshwa conceded free trade to the Company throughout his dominions.

Madras had been profoundly affected by the results of Aurangzeb's campaign in the Deccan, 1683–7. The last spasmodic efforts of the old Emperor brought to ruin the southern kingdoms of Golconda and Bijapur, but left nothing in their place. 'The governments which had in some degree kept up order in the Deccan being annihilated, the frame of society which depended upon them was dissolved, and the scattered materials remained as elements of discord.'[1] The disbanded armies of the two conquered kingdoms either joined the Maratha Sambhaji or wandered plundering in scattered bands. It is true that Sambhaji fell, and that from 1700–4 the Emperor gradually reduced the Maratha forts, but by that time his efforts were exhausted; with complete disorder in his finances, and his soldiers 'croaking like crows in an invaded rookery'[2] for pay, he made no further advance, and when he died, in 1707, the Deccan was still in a state of complete disorder. Thomas Pitt seized the opportunity in September 1708 to obtain from the Nawab of the Carnatic a grant of 'five towns' in the neighbourhood of Madras. But for some years the Company were unable to occupy them permanently, for the Nawab afterwards revoked his grant. The surrender of these five towns or villages was one of the results achieved by Surman's embassy, but even when the *farman* arrived at Madras in 1717, the English found it necessary to fight their way into one of them at the

[1] M. Elphinstone's *History of India*, 1866, p. 654.
[2] Ibid., p. 669.

point of the bayonet. This high-handed manner of carrying out the Emperor's grant contrasts strangely with the stately reception accorded to the actual *farmans*, the salute of 151 guns from the fort and the broadsides of every vessel lying in the roads.

All control over southern India soon passed out of the Mughal's hands. In 1713 Asaf Jah (afterwards known as Nizam-ul-Mulk) was appointed Subadar of the Deccan. Though recalled for a time, he re-established himself in 1723, and became independent of Delhi in all but name. There now ensued a long duel for power in the Deccan, between the Marathas and Nizam-ul-Mulk. The policy followed by the English during this troublous time was to keep on good terms with the Nizam, and slowly strengthen their fortifications. Various presents and complimentary letters were sent to Hyderabad during the struggle with the Marathas, as the issue swayed backwards and forwards. No doubt the even nature of the long conflict was a great gain to the English at Madras. Neither side had leisure to notice the quiet, imperceptible strengthening of the Company's settlement. On the Coromandel coast, a strong native dynasty established itself in the Carnatic, the broad strip of territory between the mountains and the sea, bounded by the Kistna on the north and Tanjore on the south. These rulers owed a submission that was little more than nominal to Nizam-ul-Mulk, himself in theory the representative of the Mughal in the Deccan, who reigned over what was practically an independent kingdom at Hyderabad. Sheltered, as it were, behind this double rampart of stable government, the English at Madras plied a peaceful commerce, remaining on excellent terms with both the ruler of the Carnatic and his overlord, the Subadar of the Deccan. But towards the end of the period, the political equilibrium of southern India was upset by the Marathas, who pressed hard against the Nizam, and in 1740 burst into the Carnatic, slaying the reigning Nawab, Dost Ali, in a pitched battle. The English at Fort St. George began to tremble for their safety, but could look with satisfaction on a stronghold which now mounted 193 guns. In 1741, while the main army was besieging Trichinopoly, straggling bands of Maratha horsemen plundered up to the very borders of Fort St. David. The success of the invaders was but temporary, and in 1743 the Nizam recovered control of the Carnatic. Four years before, Bombay had concluded a treaty with the Peshwa, and in 1742–3 the inhabitants of Calcutta hastily threw up the famous 'Ditch', on the news that the Marathas had defeated Ali Vardi Khan, the Subadar of Bengal, and plundered the outskirts of Murshidabad. The great Hindu confederacy of marauders was therefore, about the same time, approaching all the Presidency towns of the Company on the western, south-eastern, and north-eastern shores of India, a premonitory sign that the era of peaceful commerce was drawing to a close.

In the whole of this period, there were few men of striking personality among the English. During thirty-six years (1708–44) there were seven presidents of Bengal, seven presidents of Bombay, and twelve presidents of Fort St. George; yet out of this number only two men, both presidents of Madras, Thomas Pitt and the Scotsman, James Macrae (1725–30), have found a place in the *Dictionary of National Biography*. But if few of the Company's servants were distinguished, few perhaps were incapable. Surman's success at Delhi was the due reward of a dogged perseverance which refused to be discouraged by any check. The political situation which these men had to face was a terribly difficult one: an empire sinking into decrepitude, great nobles carving for themselves kingdoms out of the remnants, and, most formidable of all, the rise of the turbulent military state of the Marathas, with all its resources devoted to predatory war.

CHAPTER IX

THE LIFE OF THE ENGLISH IN THE EAST

Before passing on to the political history proper of the East India Company, it is desirable, in a narrative which regards the eastern empire in its colonial aspect, to say something of the daily life lived by our countrymen in India.

The Company's servants after 1676 passed through a regular gradation of rank as apprentices, writers, factors, merchants, and senior merchants. The factory was a compact little nest of buildings, consisting of the lodgings of the Chief or President and his subordinates, warehouses, godowns, and offices, the whole surrounded by the ramparts of the 'fort'. Originally no provision was made for family life. Even the chiefs were rarely accompanied by their wives, and the others were not expected to marry. This procedure directly contrasts with that of the French Company, which definitely from the first proposed to establish colonies. The factory was the commercial counterpart of a University college. Meals were taken in common till about 1720; there were daily prayers, and the gates were closed at stated hours. The President was given disciplinary control over the younger members, and fines were imposed for breaches of rules or misconduct, such as drunkenness, dicing, brawling, or insubordination. From the first, considerable state was kept up. The governors of the settlements only moved abroad with flags, trumpets, and the firing of salutes.

The common custom of speaking of the Company's settlements prior to 1746 as mere factories is erroneous. The

English had not yet acquired provinces, but they ruled over towns with heterogeneous populations, consisting of Muhammadans, Hindus, and Europeans trading under the Company's licence. As early as 1671 Bombay was definitely styled a 'colony' in a dispatch from India, and it was in regard to that settlement that the Company first consciously aimed at establishing something more than the factory with which they had been formerly content. Soon after its acquisition they sent out twenty single women of 'sober and civil lives', engaging to keep them for a year and provide them with one 'suit of wearing apparel'.[1] Unfortunately, we hear later that some of these women 'are grown scandalous to our nation, religion, and government'. The authorities at Bombay were bidden to 'give them all fair warning that they do apply themselves to a more sober and Christian conversation, otherwise the sentence is this, that they shall be confined totally of their liberty to go abroad, and fed with bread and water till they are embarked on board ship for England'.[2] From this time the Court began to allow and even to encourage Englishmen not of the Company's service to 'trade up and down in India', and they declared (in 1687) that their policy was to make 'our towns replete with people and marts for all nations'.[3] A contemporary tract (1681) speaks of many hundreds of families (though here there is probably some exaggeration) enjoying free liberty of trade to and from all ports and places in India.[4] This development brought with it dangers of its own, and the new heterogeneous populations were not so easily controlled as the old Factory house. Sir Edward Winter, a governor of Fort St. George, being reduced to

[1] India Office Records, Court Book No. 26, p. 183.
[2] Letter of Surat Council to Bombay, Dec., 1675.
[3] India Office Records, Letter Book No. 8, Dispatch to Fort St. George, Sept. 28, 1687.
[4] *A Treatise wherein is demonstrated that the East India trade is the most national of all foreign trades* . . . by Φιλόπατρις, 1681.

Second in Council by the Court in 1665, and having refused to vacate his office, seized and imprisoned Foxcroft, his successor designate, on the plea that he had betrayed Roundhead and Republican sympathies. He only submitted, and made a compromise with the Company, when they despatched five armed ships to blockade their own settlement in 1668.

The Court of Committees also began to perceive that the scope of their servants' energies in the East was widening. In 1687 they appointed a candidate, one of many aspirants, as member of Council, at Fort St. George, because he was 'a man of learning and competently well read in ancient histories of the Greeks and Latins, which with a good stock of natural parts only can render a man fit for government and political science, martial prudence and other requisites to rule over a great city'. 'For', as they added, '. . . its not being bred a boy in India, or staying long there and speaking the language or understanding critically the trade of the place, that is sufficient to fit a man for such a command as the Second of Fort St. George is, or may be, in time, though all these qualifications are very good in their kind'.[1]

The development of the Company's positions in India from the *status* of factories to that of quasi-colonies may be said to have gone on pretty continuously all this time, under the leadership of Sir George Oxenden (1662–9), Gerald Aungier (1669–77), and Sir John Child (1682–90), the representatives of the East India Company in western India, holding the two offices of the presidency of Surat and the governorship of Bombay; of Sir Streynsham Master (1677–81), and Elihu Yale (1687–92), Presidents of Madras; and of William Hedges (1681–84), Governor of the factories in Bengal, which from the date of his appointment were made independent of Madras. Aungier especially did much to enlarge the precincts of the old factory by the foundation of

[1] India Office Records, Letter Book No. 8, Dispatch to Fort St. George, Sept. 28, 1687.

a hospital, a church, a gaol, and courts of justice at Bombay. In 1688 the Directors ordered the establishment there of a Post Office. In the same year a municipal government consisting of a mayor and ten aldermen, three to be Company's servants, three Portuguese, and seven Indians, was established at Madras. This policy was carried further in 1726, when a royal charter provided for the establishment of a mayor's court at each of the Presidency towns for the trial of civil actions.

Colonel Yule, in his *Diary of William Hedges*, has thrown a flood of light upon the social life of the first century of the Company's history. A few later extracts from the records may here be given to show the condition of the settlements from 1700 to 1750. In 1711, rumours had reached Leadenhall Street that there had been much insubordination among the junior factors at Fort St. George, and that recourse had been had to the most drastic measures for maintaining order. 'We are sorry to hear that of late there has not been a sufficient decorum kept up among our people, and particularly among the young writers and factors, that there has (*sic*) been files of musketeers sent for to keep the peace at dinner time.' The theory of the factory always presupposed that the Head of it should exercise a kind of paternal control over the younger members, and the Directors went on to suggest a system of discipline: 'We direct that you the President and Council, do at certain stated seasons set apart a time to enquire into the behaviour of all our factors and writers, . . . and calling them severally before you, let them know the account you have of them, and as they deserve either admonish or commend them . . . It lies very much in your power to form their minds to virtue.'[1]

At a time (1714) when in England any gentleman might be called on to defend his life against every swaggering

[1] India Office Records, Letter Book No. 14, Dispatch to Fort St. George, Jan., 1711

bravo who chose to insult him, the Court were stringent in their prohibition of the practice of duelling. 'You have done exceeding well', runs a letter to Bencoolen, 'in discountenancing that intolerable practice of Inferiors challenging their Superiors, or others their Equals; howsoever that practice is winked at in the camp, it must never be cherished or connived at in the factory or Counting House, and on the other hand to prevent the temptation, if any person abuses or affronts another let it be made a standing rule, and Public notice given that it is so, that you will do the complainant justice'.[1]

Intemperance in the East brings a swift and terrible retribution with it. The Directors are never tired of dwelling on its evil effects. The settlement at Bencoolen in Java seems to have been notorious for drunkenness. We find the following counsel given in 1717:—

'Could we once hear Sobriety was become as fashionable on the West Coast as hard drinking hath been, we should entertain strong hopes that your new settlement at Marlborough . . . would give a better reputation to the West Coast than it hath hitherto had on account of health . . . it is positively affirmed you have good water, if you will be at the pains of fetching what is so; it is further said that a little tea boiled in the water doth admirably correct it, and that water kept till cold and so drank as water would contribute to the health of those who used it'.[2]

But apparently this excellent suggestion to substitute cold tea for more generous potations had not the effect desired, for the next year the Directors, in commenting on the accounts of the steward of the factory, indite the following scathing passage:—

'It is a wonder to us that any of you live six months to

[1] India Office Records, Letter Book No. 15, Dispatch to Bencoolen, Oct. 27, 1714.

[2] Ibid., Letter Book No. 16, Dispatch to Bencoolen, Feb. 6, 1717.

an end, or that there are not more quarrellings and duellings among you, if half the liquors he charges were really guzzled down.' Reference is then made to that 'monstrous expense of July . . . we find the amount to be seventy-four dozen and a half of wine, of which 8 dozen and 5 were double bottles, and 50 dozen and 5 single bottles of French claret, 24½ dozen of Burton Ale and Pale Beer, two pipes and 42 gallons of Madeira wine, six flasks of Shyrash (Shiraz), 274 bottles of Toddy, three leagers (i. e. casks) and ¾ of Batavia Arrack, and 164 gallons of Goa'. They go on to state that this amount was consumed *among nineteen persons*, of whom some had diet money besides; 'you tell us . . . that all are now diligent, no drunkenness or revelling are permitted, all the candles are out and all gone to rest before ten at night, good order and economy kept up, and as few disorders as can be expected, and no other contentions among you but who shall excel—we suppose you mean in serving us best—and . . . you say none of the covenant servants are out of order, which is owing to the regular living and good table you keep. Doth the above expense and these fine characters agree? Be yourselves, when sober, the judges.'[1]

Another grievance of the authorities at home was the amount of powder sometimes wasted in salutes. It is said that a Portuguese ship once emptied her magazine in complimentary salvoes, and when war broke out and she met an enemy on the open seas, her guns were of necessity silent. Among the French Company's servants the practice of saluting was carried to an almost grotesque extent, and every movement of the governor was accompanied by the roar of artillery. In like manner, we find the settlers of St. Helena not proof against this weakness; they expended their masters' powder not only on every public occasion, but on festivals of a purely private and domestic nature.

[1] India Office Records, Letter Book No. 16, Dispatch to Bencoolen, March 14, 1718.

'We directed for every ship of ours that comes in or departs, generally seven or nine guns, and (yet) when the fleet went away in July 1712, there is 385 pounds weight of powder charged as expended, and 134 guns fired, of which six and twenty of your greatest guns on the place. These, we think, too much, and for the future expect better husbandry. . . . We allow the number of guns fired on the days of public solemnity, such as the Queen's birthday, coronation day, etc., but can't do so for others, such as twenty guns for Mrs. Mashborne's, the same at Mr. Hoskinson's funeral, one and twenty guns at Mr. Mashborne's wedding, and the same at the governor's landing, these are too many, a smaller number ought to serve.'[1] In addition to drunkenness and wastefulness, gambling was a besetting sin of the English in India, both men and women. In 1721 a letter to Madras ran as follows:—

'It is with great concern we hear the Itch of gaming hath spread itself over Madras, that even the gentle-women play for great sums, and that Capt. Seaton makes a trade of it to the stripping several of the young men there. We earnestly recommend to you to check as far as you can that mischievous evil. Let Capt. Seaton know if he continues that vicious practice he shall not stay but be removed, and do you take care he be sent off the shore, . . . and civilly acquaint the gentle-women that we desire they will put a stop to all high gaming, because first or last it will be prejudicial and ruinous to them or theirs.'[2]

Thirty years later we find the Court still complaining that 'the pernicious vice of gambling has spread like a contagion among all ranks and degrees of our servants',[3]

[1] India Office Records, Letter Book No. 15, Dispatch to St. Helena, March 5, 1714.
[2] Ibid., No. 17, Dispatch to Fort St. George, April 26, 1721.
[3] Ibid., No. 27, Dispatch to Fort St. David, Jan. 12, 1750.

and dismissing two men in high office (one, Governor of Fort St. David) for their indulgence in the practice.

From the beginning of the Company's history the Directors had to exercise vigilance against the private trading of their servants in India, and they were especially severe on the Presidency of Bengal, always the richest, and therefore the most suspected, settlement. They refer to 'the old Bengal doctrine to amuse us with good words',[1] and again, to 'the Bay Proverb, "Self and then Company"'.[2] But the ingenuity of some men, especially those in high places, found means to keep within the letter of the law and yet defraud the Company. A governor of St. Helena took the Company's slaves from their work on the plantations, to mend the paths over the rocks to his house, and carry himself and his friends up and down in sedan chairs. Further, he 'has built a shed of 400 feet long, for no other use than that he may ride therein on his asses, and be covered from the weather . . . and he has wasted a great deal of our timber therein'. Again, 'the charge of the new path hath and will cost us £1,000 . . . a banqueting house is to be made, half-way up, and a place for nine-pins'; he had also employed labour for months to build a 'tomb of ten foot high and seven foot broad of cut stone . . . for his wife'. The Directors had perhaps a right to feel annoyed, for the governor had charged this to the Company as fortifications.[3]

The East India Company, during the first half of the eighteenth century, employed slave labour on a large scale. For instance, in 1735, at St. Helena, it possessed 180 slaves, and the free planters, 458. In 1735, orders were given to provide 250 for Bombay, while in 1751 the Direc-

[1] India Office Records, Letter Book No. 19, Dispatch to Bengal, Jan. 29, 1742.

[2] Ibid., No. 15, Dispatch to Bengal, Jan. 12, 1715.

[3] Ibid., No. 15 and No. 16, Dispatches to St. Helena, March 5, 1714, and Feb. 22, 1717.

tors wished to buy 600 for Fort St. George. At the small settlement of Bencoolen, in 1712–13, there were 189 slaves. Most of them came from Madagascar. There was a regular tariff for luckless humanity in that island, perhaps the scene of greater continuous misery than any other spot on the surface of the globe. The price of a man was 'one Buckaneer (a kind of primitive cannon), one trading gun, one large bamboo of powder of between four and five pounds weight, fifty shot and fifty flints'. A woman was worth 'two trading guns, two small bamboos of powder, thirty shot and thirty flints'.[1]

Regulations were drawn up for the transport and care of the slaves. On arrival from Madagascar at Fort St. George, the President of that place was to pay the Company's agents twenty shillings a head, and the surgeon five shillings a head for every slave delivered alive. A committee was to be appointed to consider 'of the properest measures for rendering them (the slaves) most useful to us, as likewise to regulate their habitation, diet and clothing, in such a manner as may best contribute to their health, and make their servitude easy to them. What occurs to us as necessary on this occasion are, that they be lodged together in a convenient place, under the particular inspection of some trusty person or persons; . . . that the soldiery and others be not permitted to have any intercourse with them; . . . that their diet and clothing be ascertained which is to be reasonable and fully sufficient for them; that the slaves be acquainted with the particulars of their said diet and clothing; that if they are not duly supplied therewith, they may on complaining to you have justice done them; that they be attended when sick, by our surgeons, with as much care as the soldiers.'[2]

A proclamation was issued at St. Helena that the gover-

[1] India Office Records, Letter Book No. 23, p. 20.
[2] Ibid., No. 28, Dispatch to St. Helena, Nov. 14, 1751.

nor and council would 'let out any of our black children to such as would keep them for their labour till they were ten years old'. The Directors at home gave this scheme their approval, and added a suggestion, 'You should enter in consultation, what children were so put out, to whom, and for how long time; by this means there would be a register and remembrance when to call for them again.'[1] When grown up they were to be taught a trade: 'Remember that Mr. Pyke's Blacks were so well bred up to work and skilful, that you paid him for one £80, for three each £60, and all the rest of the one and forty from £30 to £40 a head, except three at £25.'[2]

In the instructions of the Directors there is often evident a collision of ideas, inevitable when a people otherwise civilized bring themselves to tolerate the essentially barbarous institution of slavery. Slaves were human beings, and yet they were chattels. The Court was occasionally shocked at the callousness of its servants. 'We cannot approve', they wrote to St. Helena in 1749, 'of putting any of the slaves to death.'[3] When they indulge in the luxury of humanitarian feelings, we have passages like the following:—

'Remember they are men and women, though slaves, and therefore are to be used humanely, according to their circumstances, and not treated as bad or worse than brutes.'[4] Again (1717), 'Touching the slaves ... we need not repeat the directions given you. The short of all which you must take continued care of, is to treat them humanely, ... to apply them to such works of ours as they are or can be severally made fittest for, to breed them up, especially the younger,

[1] India Office Records, Letter Book No. 15, Dispatch to St. Helena, March 20, 1713.
[2] Ibid., No. 17, Dispatch to St. Helena, May 31, 1721.
[3] Ibid., No. 27, Dispatch to St. Helena, Feb. 15, 1749.
[4] Ibid., No. 15, Dispatch to Bencoolen, March 20, 1713.

to all sorts of handicraft trades, . . . to keep them to constant hours of labour, allowing them leisure on all Sundays, except in cases of present real necessity, and on some particular festivals. To suffer none to insult them, or even to strike them, but their own immediate officers, the guardians, and not to suffer *them* to tyrannize over them. This will make them love and fear you, for they are endued with reason as well as you, and their own minds can discern the difference between right and wrong, and if only punished when they deserve it, they will stand self-condemned in their own consciences, and that is the first step to reformation.'[1]

As is well known, books were occasionally sent out to the factories, and the nucleus of a public library was thus formed. In early days a Puritan Court of Committees dispatched the works of that 'worthy servant of Christ, Mr. William Perkins'; in 1686 Purchas's *Pilgrims* was sent, 'a book', ran the Company's letter, 'very necessary for you thoroughly to peruse at all leisure times, and for all men that would arrive at any maturity of understanding in the affairs of India, and of the Dutch wiles and former abuses of our nation'.[2] In 1715 the Directors ordered the chaplains of Fort St. George to sort the volumes there into their proper classes, and draw up a catalogue.[3] A copy of the latter had to be sent to Leadenhall Street, but was not approved of, for we find this stimulating piece of criticism on the performance of the reverend gentlemen :—

'A great part of the titles of the books are false spelt or wrong copied or named; if the books are arranged in the order taken in the catalogue, they are so confused there is no likelihood of finding any of them out but by looking them

[1] India Office Records, Letter Book No. 16, Dispatch to Bencoolen, March 14, 1718.
[2] Ibid., No. 8, Dispatch to Bengal, Jan. 14, 1686.
[3] Ibid., No. 15, Dispatch to Fort St. George, Jan. 12, 1715.

all over till they come to what they want. We wonder they (i. e. the Company's ministers) should expose themselves to sign such a list, surely they never made use of any part of that library for their own studies, if they did, they would put them in better order.'[1]

The common theory that the Directors cared nothing except for their profits, gives only one side of their policy. They were certainly, first of all, traders: 'Our business is not to increase our settlements or territories, but to be content with the peaceable enjoyment of what we have, unless a lucky hit be afforded to obtain an addition at little charge.'[2] But a keen desire for gain was tempered with the sense that the Company represented a national force. The United Company began the first of its dispatches with a dignified exordium: 'Now we are established by a Parliamentary authority, we esteem it a duty incumbent upon us, to England and our posterity, to propagate the future interest of our nation in India.'[3] Reprisals were indeed 'like extreme unction, never to be used unless in the last extremity',[4] but a certain limit must not be passed. In 1719 the Directors, driven out of all patience by the depredations of Angria and other marauders on the Bombay coast, write, 'We say you must do all you can to frustrate their attempts, and make them feel your power. . . . Choose the fittest opportunity to chastise these Pickeroons. We should think it best . . . that when you do strike, you strike home.'[5] On the whole, a study of the records reveals the fact that the Directors always kept to some extent before them their famous resolution to establish a 'well-grounded sure English dominion in India for all time to come' (see *supra*, p. 44). They aimed

[1] India Office Records, Letter Book No. 16, Dispatch to Fort St. George, Jan. 25, 1717.
[2] Ibid., No. 15, Dispatch to Fort St. George, Jan. 13, 1714.
[3] Ibid., No. 12, Dispatch to Bengal, March 2, 1703.
[4] Ibid., No. 16, Dispatch to Bengal, Jan. 8, 1718.
[5] Ibid., No. 16, Dispatch to Bombay, Feb. 27, 1719.

at increasing the population of their towns, not indeed by conquest, but by allowing freedom of trade and administering a just government, and their advance was not quite the unconscious lapse into dominion that it is sometimes represented to be.

Especially excellent are their instructions as to our first attempts in the task of governing eastern peoples. In 1714 they write, 'We have always recommended to you to see justice administered impartially to all and speedily, to govern mildly and yet preserve authority. We have reason to add it here again for your remembrance, and earnestly to desire you will take care none under you be suffered to insult the natives, and that no voice of oppression be heard in your streets, this is the best method to enlarge our towns and increase our revenues.'[1] It would be difficult to draw up better general maxims for guidance in the administration of justice than the following: 'Never do an act of arbitrary power to hurt anybody. Let your determinations be always just, not rigorous but inclining to the merciful side. Always try the cause, never the Party. Don't let passion overcloud your reason. This will make the people respect you whereas one violent sentence or action will sully the reputation of ten good ones.'[2] 'Remember and always religiously perform that maxim in Magna Charta, *Nulli Vendemus, Nulli Deferemus, Nulli Negabimus justiciam.*'[3] In 1719, alluding to complaints they have received from natives as to some alleged extortion, the Directors order a strict inquiry to be made, and conclude with a passage through which breathes an altogether admirable spirit of dignity and power. 'Remember whoever is specially authorised thereunto and doth not act uprightly and heartily in relieving the oppressed,

[1] India Office Records, Letter Book No. 15, Dispatch to Bengal, Jan. 13, 1714.
[2] Ibid., No. 16, Dispatch to St. Helena, Feb. 22, 1717.
[3] Ibid., Dispatch to Bombay, Feb. 27, 1719.

brings upon himself the guilt of that oppression which will prove a load too heavy to bear perhaps in this life when his conscience is awake, but to be sure in that day when the secrets of all hearts shall be laid open and all the actions of men's lives accounted for at an unerring and just tribunal.'[1] In 1721, in a letter to Bengal, they thus sum up their doctrine of free commerce and equity in India: 'We have always built upon' this 'as a fundamental maxim that security of Protection and freedom in liberty and property with a due administration of justice must of necessity people your territories, considering the country all about you is under a despotic government.'[2]

If the problem before the English in India was one requiring greater qualities than those of merchants only, that which confronted the Court of Directors was perhaps even more formidable. For their knowledge of the East they had mainly to rely upon information from men whose interests did not always lie in telling them the truth. For some reason difficult to understand, the practice of electing to the directorate those who had served the Company in India was not popular. It had worked well in the case of William Methwold, but his case never became a precedent. For forty years after 1700, the lists of directors reveal, as far as I can find, the names of only two men, Captain Matthew Martin and Alexander Hume, who had lived in India, and the latter of these two men had been in the service of the Ostend Company.

The powers of the Governor and Council, and their relations to each other, are thus clearly set forth in a dispatch to St. Helena: 'We will . . . tell you the authority we invest you and the Council with, as that each may know how far he ought to go. The Governor is entrusted by us, in the first place, to see all our orders are obeyed; we appoint a

[1] India Office Records, Letter Book No. 17, Dispatch to Fort St. George, Dec. 19, 1719. [2] Ibid., Dispatch to Bengal, April 26, 1721.

Council to join with him therein, and to give their opinion each of them in all matters that come before them; the Majority of votes are to determine every question. If any one or more of the Council think the determination wrong, they must enter their dissent in consultation with their reasons, or else we take it for granted they agreed thereto, and shall censure them as we think they deserve. The whole Council when assembled are to judge of the management of each member, the Governor as well as the rest, for he is but one though chief, and if they find anything done or intended against our interests or orders, they are to remedy or prevent it, or else must bear the blame. In the absence of Councils, the Governor is to have the general care of all things, but as Councils must frequently meet and all the members are to be present when health will permit, we direct positively that the Council do meet once a week, and oftener, if occasion. We will never allow the Governor to prevent anyone of the Council's entering in the consultations the proposal they make, which they think for our service though rejected, if they shall desire such entry. If he doth, let them give us notice, and then they clear themselves of imputation on that account.' [1]

The Council was thus to be a real check upon the Governor; in another dispatch, to Fort St. George, this feature is emphasized. 'We appoint them (the Council) to their stations not to sit as Cyphers, but to have each his Negative whenever they believe they have a just reason.' [2] Again, in a similar letter to Bombay, 'No person of the Council shall be brow-beaten or intimidated on account of making exceptions.'

This system of check and counter-check has been much criticized, and in after years, when wider opportunities and

[1] India Office Records, Letter Book No. 16, Dispatch to St. Helena, March 21, 1718.

[2] Ibid., Dispatch to Fort St. George, Oct. 17, 1718.

deeper responsibilities crowded upon the Company's servants, it proved a source of great danger. But it must in fairness be remembered, that if a President or Commander in the East chose to defy his masters, it was extremely difficult to bring him to account. We have seen how Keigwin and Winter rebelled with impunity, and a curious instance occurred at Fort St. David in 1713, where Robert Raworth, the Deputy Governor, who had gallantly defended the town against the raja of Jinji the year before, revolted from Edward Harrison, the Governor of Madras. After holding out for some time, and firing on the envoys from Fort St. George sent to bring him to terms, he finally surrendered to the President in December, and retired to Pondicherry. Thence he set sail for France, and died in Paris, just as the Directors of the Company were preparing to prosecute him in England. A very vivid dread of such outbreaks impelled the Directors to crush with a heavy hand all symptoms of disloyalty, and explains the promptness with which (to take an instance) they dismissed the Governor and some members of Council at Fort St. George in 1721, for neglecting to obey their orders. The vigour of their language is typical of their fears: 'had this been only the hair-brained (*sic*) notions of a giddy-headed youngster we could have slighted and pitied it, but when we find the Council in the General letter patronizing it and referring us thereto to justify their proceedings, it is time for us to look about us, and crush this cockatrice of rebellion in the egg. We have often found fault with some instances of mismanagement, and generally in an expostulatory mild manner, hoping thereby to bring our affairs into a faithful, frugal and regular method of administration, as being unwilling to proceed to rougher methods of cure. But since Lenitives will not do, and the infectious gangrene spreads so fast, we must though with regret apply the last remedy.'[1]

[1] India Office Records, Letter Book No. 17, Dispatch to Fort St. George, April 26, 1721.

CHAPTER X

THE ENGLISH AND FRENCH IN INDIA TO THE PEACE OF AIX-LA-CHAPELLE

In the middle of the eighteenth century a change came over the destinies of the European settlements in India. The English and French Companies began to be embroiled in the international conflicts of their respective countries. The war of the Spanish succession, as we have seen, had run its course without any open conflicts between the belligerent nations in the East; the war of the Austrian succession was destined to have a different issue. Henceforward, European conflicts were to have their echoes in distant climes, and, in the words of Voltaire, 'the first cannon shot fired in our lands was to set the match to all the batteries in America and in Asia'.[1]

A few preliminary words must be said about the position of the French. The history of eastern exploration records some very early French attempts to reach India by the Cape route; for instance, that of Jean Parmentier, poet and scholar, who, with his brother Raoul, visited Madagascar and the Moluccas in 1529, and died in Sumatra. Henry IV chartered two companies for the Indian trade, but they failed for want of money and popular support. In 1642 Richelieu founded the 'Société de l'Orient', which dissipated its energies in the colonization of Madagascar, under the leadership of Pronis and Flacourt.

The first French East India Company that succeeded in establishing permanent trade relations with India was that

[1] *Fragments sur l'Inde*, 1773, p. 5.

of 1664, which owed its inception and most of its early success to the fostering care of the great French minister, Colbert, and Louis XIV himself. The first expeditions of the Company were wasted in attempts to revive the Madagascar colonies. A factory was founded at Surat in 1668 by Caron, a Dutchman in the French service, and another was established at Masulipatam in 1669. In 1674 François Martin founded Pondicherry, the future capital of French India, on a small piece of territory ceded by a native ruler, eighty-five miles south of Madras. In Bengal, 1690–2, a factory was built at Chandarnagar[1] on the Hughli, sixteen miles above Calcutta, on a site given to the French by the Nawab in 1674. In the seventeenth century the European wars of Louis XIV reacted adversely upon the East India Company. France was at war with Holland, except for short intervals, from 1672 to 1713, and though for the first two years of that period she was allied with England, even then the fighting in the East fell mainly to her share. In 1672 the French occupied St. Thomé on the coast of Coromandel, but in the following year de la Haye, their admiral, was driven from Trincomali in Ceylon, and in 1674 the Dutch captured St. Thomé. In 1693, after a short siege, the Dutch inflicted a decisive blow by the capture of Pondicherry itself. For six years the town remained in their hands, and they constructed there fortifications which long ranked as the finest in India. It was restored to the French with defences intact by the Peace of Ryswick in 1697, but was not actually handed over till 1699. Under the care of Martin, its founder, though he received hardly any help from home, Pondicherry grew into a flourishing town of 40,000 inhabitants. But elsewhere French influence in India decayed. The factories at Surat, Bantam, and Masulipatam were abandoned. The Company in

[1] *La Compagnie des Indes Orientales*, P. Kaeppelin, 1908, p. 301.

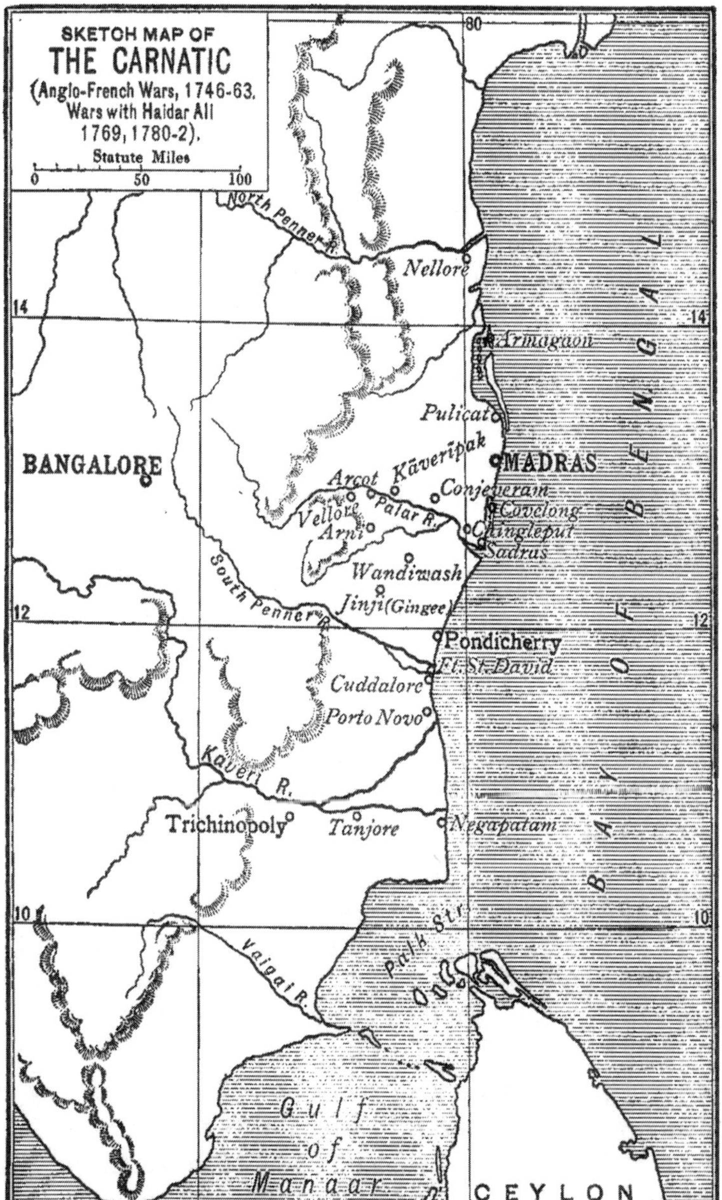
SKETCH MAP OF
THE CARNATIC
(Anglo-French Wars, 1746-63.
Wars with Haidar Ali
1769, 1780-2).
Statute Miles
0
50
100
North Penner R.
Nellore
Armagaon
Pulicat
BANGALORE
MADRAS
Kāveripak
Arcot
Conjeveram
Vellore
Palar R.
Covelong
Arni
Chingleput
Sadras
Wandiwash
South Penner R.
Jinji (Gingee)
Pondicherry
Ft. St. David
Cuddalore
Porto Novo
Kaveri R.
Trichinopoly
Tanjore
Negapatam
Palk Str.
Vaigai R.
Gulf of Manaar
CEYLON
C. Comorin
BAY OF BENGAL
80
78
14
12
10
8
WAXTYPE
GEORGE PHILIP & SON, LTD.

France was practically moribund, and, from 1708 to its reorganization in 1720, sublet its privileges of trading to India to some merchants of St. Malo.

When the Scotsman, John Law of Lauriston, began his amazing career as controller of the French finances, the East India Company was soon involved in his famous 'system'. It was incorporated with the Canada Company, the Mississippi Company, or Company of the West, the Senegal Company, the China Company, and the Companies of Domingo and Guinea, and this mammoth association, known as the 'Company of the Indies', was also granted the right of issuing the coinage, the monopoly of tobacco, and the control of the public debt. When the crash came in 1720, the East India Company was reconstituted as the 'Perpetual Company of the Indies', and the monopoly of tobacco was the only one of the special privileges granted by Law that was left to it. From this date the fortunes of the French East India Company greatly improved. In 1721 its servants finally took possession of Mauritius (Isle of France), whither they had first gone in 1715. In the Isle of Bourbon they had probably settled as early as 1657, seven years before the founding of Colbert's company.[1] In 1725 they acquired Mahé in Malabar, and in 1739 Karikal on the coast of Coromandel.

The relative positions of the English and French in 1744 were as follows:—The English Company was by far the wealthier body, and drove the more vigorous trade. Its fleets of merchantmen were larger, and more regular in their voyages to and fro. It had a longer, more continuous and less chequered history in the East. The Presidency of Bombay was far superior in strength to any French settlement on the west coast, Calcutta quite dwarfed Chandarnagar in the Gangetic delta, and Madras was at least equal

[1] For the dates of the settlements in these islands, see vol. i of this series, 2nd edition, p. 134.

to Pondicherry in size and strength, and, on the testimony of the Frenchmen Dupleix and Labourdonnais, greatly excelled the French settlement in the extent and variety of its commerce.[1] Finally, and this is perhaps the most important point of all, the English Company was a great private corporation, founded and maintained by individual enterprise, supported by the profits drawn from the trade with India, not dependent in any way on the state, but rather having the state itself considerably in its debt; unconnected officially with the government by any legal tie, but able, by the presence of many of its Directors in Parliament and by its wealth and interest, to exercise no slight influence upon national policy.

As for the French Company, their settlements on the western shore and in Bengal could not claim, as we have seen, to rival those of the English, though in Pondicherry (their chief station) they possessed a fine and well-fortified town. In the Isles of France and Bourbon they had a *point d'appui* to India, on the value of which contemporary critics were not agreed, some holding these possessions to be of great value as a refuge for French fleets when driven by the autumn monsoons or a European enemy from the exposed sea-board of Coromandel, others considering that as a base of operations they were too far from the mainland of India, and therefore a source of weakness.

Viewed from the home aspect, the French Company differed strikingly from its rival. It had always been more the offspring of state patronage than the outcome of spontaneous mercantile activity,[2] and by 1744 it had sunk to the position of a subordinate department of state. From the very beginning the Company had never been in a position to dispense with royal subsidies and royal interference.

[1] *Mémoire pour le sieur de la Bourdonnais, Pièces Justificatives*, 1750, pp. 83, 98 seq.

[2] Compare vol. v, part I, of this series, pp. 79–80, 94, &c.

The King had often intervened drastically in its administration, as, for instance, in 1684, when he appointed Seignelay Perpetual Chief, President and Director. Its shareholders were a body of *rentiers*, with no lively personal interest in the Indian trade. Its revenue was largely drawn from the monopoly of tobacco, the one special privilege conferred upon it by Law which it had been able to retain. The Directors and Inspectors, who managed the most important affairs of the Company, were nominated by the Crown, and all real control passed into the hands of the King's Commissaries. The Crown was again and again obliged to come to the aid of the Company. From 1725 to 1765 no meeting of shareholders was ever called, and after 1733 the state even guaranteed dividends at a fixed rate. The most prosperous period of the French Company financially was probably from 1731 to 1738, and on the eve of the war of the Austrian succession their fortunes had already begun to wane.[1] As a consequence of the state's bureaucratic control a certain lethargy crept into all the Company's business, and was reflected in their Indian settlements. Trade flagged, or at least remained stationary. There was little enterprise or growth. Pondicherry had been developed by the energy of its founder, François Martin, who died in 1706, and later by Lenoir and Dumas. But Chandarnagar in Bengal, which province was commercially and politically the key of India, made little progress till it came under the control of Joseph François Dupleix, 1731–41. Captain Alexander Hamilton says contemptuously, 'for want of money they are not in a capacity to trade. They have a few private families dwelling near the factory, and a pretty little church to hear Mass in, which is the chief business of the French in Bengal'.[2] The perusal of the

[1] *Mémoire sur la situation actuelle de la Compagnie des Indes*, M. l'Abbé Morellet, Paris, 1769, pp. 43 seq.

[2] *A New Account of the East Indies*, Capt. Alexander Hamilton, 1744.

records in the India Office gives the same impression. It is extraordinary how few references there are to the French in the Company's *Letter Books* down, at any rate, to 1720. As late as 1718 the Dutch are still considered the strongest European nation in the Indies: 'Their strength', wrote the Court, 'is greatly superior to ours and all other Europeans joined together, and nothing but the Powers in Europe makes them afraid to prove it against any or all of their competitors in the trade of India'.[1] Just as the English failed to realize how near the influence of Holland in India proper was to decay, so they failed at first to foresee how soon the French were to exhibit a brilliant revival. It was the news of the union of the Company of the West and the Company of the Indies that first made the Court of Directors in London uneasy. In 1719 they communicated to their servants in the East the details of Law's great scheme, and referred to a rumour that ten or twelve ships were building in England for the French Company. They added, 'what the issue of this mighty project will prove, which at present appears like a blazing comet, time only can ascertain. Our eye is upon that part of it which relates to the East Indies'.[2]

The more clearly it is understood that the revival of the French power only dates from about 1728, the greater is the testimony to the ability of men like Dumas and Dupleix, who in the short space of twenty years could lift the fortunes of their country to something like an apparent equality with that of their longer established rivals. But at the same time the reflection is suggested that the roots of the English Company must have struck far deeper into the Indian soil. No French ships at all sailed from France in 1721 and 1722. In October 1727 and January 1728 the imports

[1] India Office Records, Letter Book No. 16, Dispatch to Bombay, Feb. 21, 1718.

[2] Ibid., No. 17, Dispatch to Fort St. George, Dec. 19, 1719.

were only valued at 2,234,385 francs; in September 1729 and January 1730 at 5,404,290 francs. In 1734 the sales of the Company realized 18,000,000 francs, and in 1740 22,000,000. But even these totals are easily surpassed by the value of the English imports, which in the two later years were respectively £1,372,215 and £1,795,584.[1] The era of prosperity enjoyed by the French Company in great measure coincided with the accession to power of Cardinal Fleury (1726), and the peaceful policy which he inaugurated. M. Orry, Minister of Finance, appointed his brother to direct the Company's affairs, and under his able guidance the Indian trade for a time flourished.

At the outbreak of the war, therefore, though to a superficial view the English and French seemed about equally matched in strength and extent of possessions, it cannot be doubted that in financial power, in commercial wealth, and in material resources the advantage lay considerably on the side of the English. For all that, the French, partly through the genius of their governors and commanders, partly through the blunders of their opponents, were able to launch a formidable and brilliant attack upon the English Company. Whether they ever came within a measurable distance of ultimate success is exceedingly doubtful. Their triumph was in reality short-lived; it lasted but from 1746 to 1754, and seven years after that date their defeat was complete.

For some years before 1744 hostilities between England and France were seen to be in prospect. Both nations had taken part in the war of the Austrian succession which began in 1740, and had met face to face on European battlefields, but only as auxiliaries to the main combatants. In 1742 the French government, foreseeing the inevitable issue, made overtures to the English East India Company with a view to

[1] *Reports of the House of Commons*, vol. iv, p. 75. Third Report from the Committee of Secrecy, Feb. 9, 1773.

neutralizing the Indian settlements of both nations, but failed to come to a definite agreement.

Meanwhile, plans of a very different nature were maturing in the ingenious mind of Mahé de la Bourdonnais, an adventurous sea captain who, after many years under the French East India Company, broken by two years' service with the Portuguese, had been appointed Governor of the Isles of France and Bourbon in 1734, and in the course of five years, by his energetic administration, had done wonders for the prosperity of those colonies.[1] Returning to France in 1740 and anticipating a speedy declaration of war, he determined to fit out a privateering fleet to attack English shipping in India. The French government gave their assent to his schemes when laid before them, and coerced the East India Company into providing part of the fleet. La Bourdonnais sailed from home in 1741, boasting that he would carry out the greatest *coup* ever achieved upon the sea.[2] His plan was to await in Mauritius the declaration of war. But events moved much slower than he had expected. No declaration of war came, and so in 1742 the Company, who had never approved of his plan and still hoped for neutrality in the eastern seas, ordered him to send his ships back to France. La Bourdonnais, though bitterly disappointed, obeyed, and shortly afterwards was exasperated at receiving a second dispatch which cancelled the order and expressed the hope that he would have taken upon himself the responsibility of disregarding it. Shortly afterwards war was declared, and La Bourdonnais had the intense mortification of seeing the opportunity, for which he had waited so long, present itself when he had momentarily lost all chance of profiting by it. Not only that, but the English, having received intimations of his designs, had put forth great efforts, and a royal fleet under Commodore Barnet

[1] See vol. i of this series, 2nd edition, p. 135.

[2] *Mémoire pour le sieur de la Bourdonnais*, 1750, p. 22.

appeared on the Coromandel coast (1745) and threatened Pondicherry. The French Governor-General, Dupleix, who assumed office in January 1742, promptly appealed to the Nawab of the Carnatic, and the latter forbade the English to violate the neutrality of the Mughal Empire. Having thus secured himself from attack, Dupleix carried the war into the enemy's country. He planned with La Bourdonnais, who had equipped a new fleet in the Isles and also received reinforcements from France, to sail to the Indian coast and attempt the siege of Madras. La Bourdonnais reached Pondicherry at the beginning of July 1746, after fighting a drawn battle with Peyton, a very incompetent officer, Barnet's successor in the command of the English fleet.

But La Bourdonnais and Dupleix were not destined to act in unity. La Bourdonnais's original intention had apparently been to prey on British shipping, and as soon as he arrived at Pondicherry he seems to have shrunk from the attempt on Madras. He had at first some reason for hesitation, for he certainly could not have anticipated that Peyton would so pusillanimously have left the town to its fate. For six weeks he refused to set sail, unless he received from Dupleix and the Pondicherry Council a signed order to assault the town and a definite promise on their part to take all responsibility, for he feared the English fleet would attack him in the rear when engaged in the blockade. Dupleix in reply insisted that La Bourdonnais should either assault Madras or fight the English on the high seas, but he refused to relieve La Bourdonnais of the responsibility of deciding between these two courses.

In September La Bourdonnais was finally prevailed upon to commence operations. Madras, under its governor, Nicholas Morse, made a very feeble resistance, and surrendered on September 21, after a bombardment of a few days, during which not a man was touched on either side by the shot of the other, the only loss of life being caused by the accidental explosion of a shell in the English ranks. Among the prisoners of war surrendered was Robert Clive, then a young writer in the Company's service, a youth of twenty-one with a melancholic temperament, high ambitions, and great, though as yet unsuspected, powers.

When Dupleix received La Bourdonnais's first dispatch announcing that Madras was in his hands and that he had the English at discretion, his satisfaction was complete, and he prepared to press his advantage to the full. To his intense disgust he received letters from La Bourdonnais proposing that the English Company should be allowed to ransom their settlement. Dupleix flatly refused to be a party to any such proceeding, claimed the right as Governor-General to adjudicate on the fate of the town, and implored La Bourdonnais not to lose the advantage of so unexpected a success. But La Bourdonnais, declaring that his word was already pledged to the English in Madras, hastily concluded the negotiations, and, influenced—in all probability—by a handsome bribe or *douceur* promised him by Morse,[1] signed a Convention engaging to restore Madras for £400,000. The conduct of La Bourdonnais was obviously disingenuous, for in his first dispatch he declared that the English had surrendered at discretion, and he had, since the capitulation discussed with Dupleix, as though the matter were still open, the various possibilities of ransoming the settlement, demolishing it, or retaining it as a French possession. Dupleix, putting a strong curb upon his natural feelings of resentment, had exhausted every means, reason, persuasion, and even entreaty, to prevent La Bourdonnais from taking the final step; but all in vain. 'The anger and vexation of the Governor,' says a native observer, 'when he heard the convention was signed, cannot be adequately described.'[2] His

[1] For the evidence of this see *History of the French in India*, by G. B. Malleson, Appendix A. Also *Dupleix*, by Prosper Cultru, pp. 217–19.

[2] *The Private Diary of Ananda Ranga Pillai*, ed. by Sir J. F. Price, K.C.S.I., vol. ii, p. 345.

bitter chagrin was natural enough, for he had from the first, since 1741, taken the chief part in preparing for the attack upon Madras, and it was mainly at his expense that the expedition was fitted out. An unedifying personal quarrel was soon raging between the two men; the writer quoted above noted in his diary that 'the ways of Europeans, who used always to act in union, have apparently now become like those of natives and Muhammadans'.[1]

La Bourdonnais refused to communicate with the officials whom Dupleix sent to take over possession of the town, and Dupleix called upon the officers of the army and the fleet to disregard the orders of La Bourdonnais as a rebel. There can be little doubt that in the main dispute Dupleix was in the right and La Bourdonnais in the wrong. The French in Pondicherry for the most part supported the Governor-General, and regarded his adversary as the victim of an incomprehensible infatuation. The legal point at issue was somewhat technical. In the ordinary course of events the final arbitrament as to the disposal of Madras would rest with Dupleix as Governor-General of the French possessions in the East. La Bourdonnais, however, constantly maintained that he had been given independent powers by the Minister of Marine, and had received orders not to retain any place he should capture. But this commission dated back to 1741, when only a privateering cruise against British shipping was in contemplation. The minister, in laying an injunction upon him not to retain any conquests, had not foreseen that he would co-operate with Dupleix in an attack upon an English Presidency town, and, as the Pondicherry Council pointed out, the alleged 'independent powers' were no more than those granted to any admiral of a squadron over his subordinate captains.[2] In truth, when La Bourdonnais

[1] *The Private Diary of Ananda Ranga Pillai*, ed. by Sir J. F. Price, K.C.S.I., vol. ii, p. 395.

[2] *Mémoires historiques de B. F. Mahé de la Bourdonnais*, Paris, 1828, pp. 288–9.

demanded an Order in Council before he would move to the siege of Madras, he virtually acknowledged the authority of the Governor-General, and condemned by anticipation the attitude he adopted after the surrender of Madras.

The course of events played into the hands of Dupleix. The break-up of the monsoons in October 1746, which began with a gale of unusual severity, drove La Bourdonnais back to the Isles with shattered ships. As soon as he had departed, Dupleix seized Madras, repudiated the Convention on the ground that the action of La Bourdonnais in concluding it had been *ultra vires*, and marched the English into Pondicherry as his prisoners of war. There, however, his success ended. The attack on Fort St. David, where the refugees from Madras had congregated, was repelled by Stringer Lawrence, a brave officer and sound tactician, who was destined to play a long and honourable part in the Anglo-French conflict in India. A formidable English fleet with thirteen ships of the line now appeared off the Coromandel coast and subjected Pondicherry to a severe siege. The French defence was ably directed, though the enemy's conduct of the operations is said to have been very incapable, and Dupleix had the satisfaction of seeing the English abandon their trenches, after losing one thousand men, a week before the Peace was proclaimed in India. During the war the English and French had been fighting in the far West as well as in the East, and diplomatists in Europe made success in one hemisphere balance defeat in the other. The Peace of Aix-la-Chapelle in 1748 restored Madras to the English and Louisbourg in North America to the French.

Thus ended the first round of the Anglo-French conflict. It has often been said that the quarrel between the two French commanders saved the English in India from ruin. But there is no real ground for such a statement, which magnifies the incident out of all proportion to its real import. As the French historian Cultru points out, the most the French could have achieved at this time was to take Madras, and they took it; had there been no quarrel, they would merely have kept the town till the Peace, and they kept it, in spite of the quarrel. They retained, and could have retained it, no longer, simply because the matter was settled over their heads by statesmen in Europe. It may be added that the fall of Madras was a serious enough disaster for the English and a sufficiently great achievement of the French, without its being exaggerated to imply that the total ruin of the English settlements was threatened. The war on the Coromandel coast affected a single English Presidency town, and that one probably the weakest of the three. Calcutta and Bombay, the latter at this time the strongest European settlement in India, still remained. It may be argued that, had Dupleix and La Bourdonnais been united, they might have followed up their success against Madras by an attack on Bengal. But though Dupleix with characteristic daring suggested this course, it was scouted by La Bourdonnais on the ground that to violate the neutrality of the Mughal Emperor in Hindustan would have meant the expulsion of the French from his dominions. Dupleix failed even to reduce Fort St. David, a few miles south of Pondicherry. Calcutta was hardly likely to have surrendered as weakly as Madras, and Peyton's squadron was still cruising in the Bay of Bengal. In 1747 Boscawen was already on his way from England with the most powerful armament that had yet appeared in the East. Had the French been engaged before Calcutta when he arrived, they would have been easily blocked up in the Hughli, and Pondicherry itself would have been in imminent danger.

CHAPTER XI

THE ENGLISH AND FRENCH ON THE COROMANDEL COAST, TO THE RECALL OF DUPLEIX

AFTER the treaty of Aix-la-Chapelle, to all outward appearances the *status quo* on the coast of Coromandel was restored, though the French were left with a sense of being unfairly robbed of victory and the English of having fortunately avoided defeat. Besides this, the servants of the two Companies had openly confronted each other sword in hand, and the old peaceful relations could never be completely re-established. The war had changed their whole point of view: it had taught them, says a contemporary writer, for the first time 'the geography of the country a hundred miles round their settlements'.[1] It had also taught them incidentally their own strength in relation to the native powers. In 1746 an open collision had taken place between the French and An-waru-din, the Nawab of the Carnatic, under whose protection the English and French had long dwelt secure. Dupleix had only won his countenance to the French attack on Madras by promising to surrender the place to him after its capture from the English, a promise he had no intention of fulfilling. When the Nawab attempted to enforce his claims, a mere handful of French troops had defeated An-waru-din's army in a battle rather absurdly said by Voltaire to exceed in fame the feat of the Spartans at Thermopylae.[2] The victory, however, was extremely significant, and the lesson it conveyed was not

[1] *An Account of the War in India*, R. O. Cambridge, 1761, p. vi.
[2] *Précis du siècle de Louis XV*, p. 599.

lost upon Dupleix, who henceforward assumed, and rightly assumed, that the unwieldy, ill-disciplined, and badly led armies of the Muhammadan powers in southern India could not stand for a moment against troops trained by Europeans. After 1748 Dupleix was strongly disinclined to resume the rôle of the peaceful trader. He was, indeed, little fitted to be the chief of a trading-company's settlement in time of peace. He disliked the drudgery, and despised the monotony of a commercial life, and it was his firm conviction that in trade, at any rate, his nation could never hope to rival the English settlements. His bent lay rather in the direction of diplomacy and intrigue. Like all able men, he loved power, and both from policy and inclination was not adverse to a certain theatrical pomp and display. He had studied sedulously the complicated native politics of southern India, and soon found in them a promising field for the exercise of his peculiar talents. But it is an error to suppose that he began with such a comprehensive scheme as has often been attributed to him for the acquisition of dominion in India. He was, like most successful politicians (and this is said in no disparaging sense), an adventurer and an opportunist. His ideas widened and developed as he advanced from success to success. He hardly realized himself till the end of his Indian career whither his course was leading him, and, as we shall see, he afforded little opportunity to the authorities of the French East India Company or the French ministry to appreciate his position. Further, his fall was largely due to two other causes—the recklessness of his financial methods and his lack of restraint.

The English themselves had afforded Dupleix a precedent for his excursions into native politics. In return for the cession of a port at the mouth of the Coleroon river, they had supported the pretensions of a claimant to the throne of Tanjore. The Frenchman gave the policy a wider extension and a more daring application. In 1748 the aged ruler of southern India, Asaf Jah, the famous Nizam-ul-Mulk, died, and his sons and grandsons immediately commenced to fight with one another for the succession. Dupleix had already begun to favour the claims of a native prince known as Chanda Sahib, whom all contemporary writers describe as a man of exceptional ability, against An-waru-din, the ruling Nawab of the Carnatic, and as this man united his forces with those of Mozaffar Jang, one of the claimants to the inheritance of Nizam-ul-Mulk, he had good hopes that in the future both the ruler of the Carnatic and his overlord the Subadar of the Deccan would owe their thrones to French arms. It is fairly obvious that if the design had succeeded, the resulting advantages to the French would have been very great. Dupleix played for a high stake and came within a measurable distance of success.

Mozaffar Jang and Chanda Sahib, supported by French troops, defeated and killed An-waru-din at Ambur in 1749. Muhammad Ali, the illegitimate son of the late ruler, fled to Trichinopoly, but the rest of the Carnatic passed under the dominion of Chanda Sahib, who liberally rewarded his benefactors, the French, by grants of land consisting of eighty villages round Pondicherry. Dupleix was eager to follow up the great initial success thus secured by a concentrated attack on Trichinopoly, and an advance in force against Nasir Jang, the *de facto* Subadar of the Deccan, but he could not prevail on his native allies to act as vigorously as he wished. Chanda Sahib wasted time in a fruitless attack on Tanjore, and in the meantime Nasir Jang marched into the province with a huge and unwieldy army, it being recorded that the circuit of his camp was twenty miles in circumference. He was joined by a British contingent of 600 under Major Lawrence, for the English, much against their will, had been driven to the conclusion that they must take up arms to prevent the native powers falling completely under the influence of the French. They had therefore reluctantly sent a small reinforcement to the fugitive Muhammad Ali at Trichinopoly, though they foolishly declined Boscawen's offer to remain with his fleet on the Coromandel coast. Owing to the desertion of thirteen French officers, Mozaffar Jang surrendered himself to Nasir Jang, and Chanda Sahib was obliged to fall back upon Pondicherry. But the check to the French was only momentary, for Dupleix met the crisis with great coolness and resource. He intrigued first with Nasir Jang, then with disaffected individuals in his camp. His officers captured Masulipatam and Trivadi, and Bussy took Jinji, a position which had hitherto been considered invincible. Nasir Jang was soon afterwards assassinated, in December 1750, and Mozaffar Jang was released and installed as Subadar of the Deccan at Pondicherry. There he made over to the French the towns of Divi and Masulipatam, and added large pecuniary grants. A sum of £50,000 was given to the Company and a like amount to the troops, while Dupleix it is said received £200,000 and a *jagir* consisting of the village Valdavur with £10,000 a year. The new Subadar hailed Dupleix as suzerain of southern India from the Kistna to Cape Comorin. This 'vague and magnificent'[1] title, as it has been described, by no means meant, as Macaulay and many other writers have supposed, that Dupleix henceforward 'ruled thirty millions of people with almost absolute power'. It gave him no direct right of administration over the region indicated, which embraced the territories of Tanjore, Madura, and Mysore. These kingdoms had never even acknowledged the suzerainty of the Subadar of the Deccan, and that ruler had no power to delegate sovereignty over them. Even in the Carnatic, as we know, Chanda Sahib was Nawab till his death. When that event took place, Dupleix seems to have contemplated assuming the title himself, but was dissuaded from doing so by Bussy, who saw that it would exasperate

[1] *Dupleix*, Prosper Cultru, pp. 257–8.

the English irreconcilably, and Chanda Sahib's son was allowed to succeed. The title conferred merely an 'honorary suzerainty', but it no doubt added greatly to the prestige of the recipient in the eyes of the native powers, and enabled him to assume the state and even the dress of an Indian prince.

After Mozaffar Jang's enthronement at Pondicherry, the new Subadar set out in January 1751, accompanied by Bussy, the ablest of the French commanders, for Aurungabad. The original intention was that Bussy should return as soon as he had escorted the new ruler to his capital, but Mozaffar Jang was killed in a chance skirmish a few days after the march had begun. For a moment it seemed as though the wonderful success of the French was in jeopardy, but Bussy proved equal to the occasion. He boldly set aside Mozaffar Jang's infant sons, on the plea that it was impossible for a minor to succeed to so troubled an inheritance, elevated to the throne Salabat Jang, the third son of the late Nizam-ul-Mulk, who happened to be a prisoner in the camp, and conducted him safely to Hyderabad. Bussy stayed on to buoy up the power of his *protégé*, and for seven years he maintained his position with wonderful skill and address, guiding the policy of Salabat Jang, protecting him against his numerous enemies at home and defeating the foreign powers that invaded his territory.

Meanwhile in the Carnatic Dupleix reached the apogee of his fortunes in 1751. From that year his influence began to wane. Hitherto the English, reluctant to enter into the dynastic wars, had given but feeble assistance to those candidates for the thrones of the Deccan and the Carnatic who were supposed to favour their cause, and at one time had withdrawn all support from Muhammad Ali. But realizing at last that they could not afford to see him captured in Trichinopoly, they determined to help him effectually with money and men. Above all it was essential that the important strategic position of Trichinopoly should not fall into the hands of the French. English trade would be ruined if all the hinterland of the seaports were to pass into the power of their European rivals. Hence followed the confused struggle known as the war in the Carnatic. The whole position was anomalous in the extreme. England and France were at peace in Europe, and therefore the representatives of the two Companies could not attack each other directly, nor, of course, assail each other's settlements. They waged war nominally as the allies of belligerent native powers, and at first some attempt was made, though it was soon abandoned, to maintain the legal fiction of Anglo-French peace, by a mutual understanding that the European forces should not fire upon each other. The whole of the Carnatic became the theatre of the war, and suffered terribly The Rajas of Tanjore and Mysore were drawn into the conflict, and the Marathas were always at hand, ready and eager to fish in the troubled waters.

In the spring of 1751 it looked as though Trichinopoly must inevitably fall, but the genius of Clive evolved a scheme for its relief. By a daring expedition, in August 1751, he seized upon the fort at Arcot, the political capital of the Carnatic, and thus, as he intended, obliged Chanda Sahib to send half his army from Trichinopoly to attempt its recapture. Clive sustained the famous siege of fifty days immortalized and somewhat exaggerated in the glowing periods of Macaulay, and in the end beat off his assailants; he followed up this success by victories at Arni and Coveripak. Trichinopoly was relieved and reprovisioned by Lawrence and Clive; Jacques François Law, the French commander, nephew of the famous financier, John Law of Lauriston, was forced to capitulate with his army, and Chanda Sahib driven to surrender to the general of the Raja of Tanjore, who was then allied with Muhammad Ali. He was treacherously put to death, somewhat to the discredit of the English, who might have exerted themselves to save him, and henceforward Muhammad Ali was *de facto* Nawab of the Carnatic. Dupleix always showed his greatest side in adversity, and he met these disasters with his usual intrepid resourcefulness, summoning to his aid the forces of the Marathas and intriguing incessantly with the native allies of the English. But Lawrence completely defeated de Kerjean at Bahour, and though there was still much hard fighting in the neighbourhood of Trichinopoly and many isolated French successes, the opponents of Dupleix slowly and steadily gained ground. Even Bussy began to urge the Governor-General to make the best peace he could. His own influence at the court of the Subadar of the Deccan had been eclipsed for a time, though he soon re-established his position, and in the autumn of 1753 obtained the cession of 'the Northern Circars', that is, the valuable districts south of Orissa and north of the Carnatic extending for about six hundred miles along the coast. This was, however, no unconditional grant of territory, as is sometimes supposed, but the allocation of the land revenue of the provinces for the support of his troops as long as they were in the service of the Subadar. As a matter of fact, southern India had been so desolated by the long war that for some years but little revenue from them was forthcoming.

'Mr. Dupleix', wrote the English at Madras in 1753, 'has by repeated strokes been reduced very low.'[1] At the end of that year he was driven to make overtures for peace. His generals had been defeated, his allies were discontented, and he was in sore need of money. His representatives met the English authorities in conference at Sadras, a Dutch settlement between Madras and Pondicherry. He there produced patents from Salabat Jang and the Mughal Emperor himself, appointing him Nawab of the Carnatic.

[1] India Office Records, French in India, vol. ii. p. 103, Letter from Fort St. George, Oct. 29, 1753.

The English pronounced the invalidity of the document purporting to come from the Emperor to be 'as clear as the sun at noon', and themselves produced other patents in favour of Muhammad Ali. The conference proved abortive, Dupleix refusing to moderate any of his demands, and the English indignantly declaring that they were not 'begging a peace'.[1]

In the meantime the Directors of the Companies in both London and Paris were growing dissatisfied with the too vigorous part played by their servants in these dynastic wars. Duvelaer, a Director of the French Company, finding it necessary to go to London on private business at the end of 1753, was authorized to discuss matters informally with the representatives of the English Company. Several conferences were held by him and the Duc de Mirepoix, the French ambassador, with the Duke of Newcastle and the Earl of Holdernesse, but though negotiations were spun out till 1755 no agreement was reached. A study of original documents[2] has revealed the fact that there is no truth in the traditional story that the English demanded the recall of Dupleix in return for that of Saunders, the President of Fort St. George, and then, in spite of their proposal being accepted, unfairly retained the latter in office. There was no such reciprocal agreement. As a matter of fact, in the negotiations of 1753 the name of Dupleix does not seem to have been mentioned. His recall had been determined upon before the conference began. Silhouette, the King's Commissary, had always been opposed to his policy. The news of Law's surrender at Trichinopoly had caused great uneasiness in France, and seemed fatally to corroborate the charges contained in the memoirs of La Bourdonnais which were published in 1750.

[1] *An Account of the War in India*, R. O. Cambridge, 1761, Appendix.

[2] By Prosper Cultru, in his *Dupleix*, pp. 359 seqq.

Godeheu, a Director of the Company, was sent out at the beginning of 1754 with plenary powers to supersede Dupleix and hold a searching inquiry into the state of affairs in India. He was also given sealed orders, which were quite unnecessary and might well have been dispensed with, to arrest the ex-Governor-General if he proved contumacious. The loyalty and patriotism of Dupleix were never in question; so far as he had erred, it was only in the means by which he had sought to promote the glory and honour of his country. Godeheu landed at Pondicherry in August 1754. In October he brought about a suspension of arms for three months, and followed this up in January 1755 by a provisional treaty which was not to be valid unless it were accepted by the two Companies at home. By its terms, both nations agreed to interfere no further in the quarrels of native princes, and to renounce all Muhammadan offices and dignities. The right of either party to various possessions was guaranteed, the only territorial concession contemplated being that the English should receive either Masulipatam or Divi in the Northern Circars, of part of which region they were already in effective occupation.

Dupleix afterwards protested that Godeheu had 'signed the ruin of the country and the dishonour of the nation'. His contention was that when his successor arrived in India, French affairs had already taken a turn for the better, and with the reinforcements which he brought with him Godeheu might have captured Trichinopoly and defeated the English. This judgement has passed into a verdict of history. Even Cultru—the brilliant French historian who, from an exhaustive study of the records, has taught us so much of the life and policy of Dupleix and exploded so many fallacies—seems to lapse back to the old view that Godeheu, out of pure 'baseness of soul', laboured to undo the work of his predecessor just as the tide was turning and success had come within the range of practical politics.[1] Apart from the fact that this judgement seems to run counter to the conclusions of three-quarters of Cultru's book, I do not believe that there is a particle of evidence for it except in the biassed statements of Dupleix and his supporters. There appears no reason to postulate malevolence on Godeheu's part to explain why he acted as he did. He declares that he went out with an open mind, or even with predispositions in favour of the man he was to succeed; that he found the greatest confusion, the army clamouring for pay, and the treasury empty. To continue the war would have been the height of folly. He states that the troops he brought with him were almost worthless for fighting purposes. All this is absolutely corroborated by the Pondicherry Council, who wrote to the Directors that nothing more fortunate than the Peace could have happened to the Company, and that they had always doubted that the English would have been willing to accede to it in view of the advantageous position they occupied.[2] The Council added that the English had 2,500 men, including 1,150 soldiers of a King's regiment, many allies and plenty of money, while the French possessed but 1,150 troops—'God knows what sort of troops'—and were almost without allies and in sore straits for gold. The English in India unanimously took the same view. They held that the Peace was unduly favourable to the enemy. They had at the time 900 French prisoners of war in their hands as against 200 held by their opponents. Edward Ives, who arrived in India with Watson's fleet in 1754, says 'the Peace was by all deemed to have been a masterly stroke of French politics: on the contrary, the advantages resulting from this treaty to the English East India Company were beyond every one's comprehension, for it was by everybody known that at this time, exclusive of our naval force, our troops on the coast exceeded

[1] Prosper Cultru, *Dupleix*, p. 355.

[2] *Mémoire à consulter pour le sieur Godeheu*, 1760, pp. 85-6.

those of the French in number one thousand'.[1] Admirals Watson and Pocock loudly lamented that the Peace had tied their hands and robbed them of an assured success. With these views, the historian Orme, at that time resident in Madras—a man who never underrates the power of the French—thoroughly agrees. The truth is that the over-sanguine temperament of Dupleix, which carried him so far on the road to victory when fortune was kind, rendered him constitutionally unable to recognize the fact of failure. His own officers were well aware of this trait. 'He has always persisted', said Law, 'in refusing to believe anything as to the superiority of the army of the enemy over ours';[2] 'I see with sorrow', wrote Bussy, 'that events alone can convince you, and that you will only recognize the value of my advice when it is too late to profit by it.'[3]

It is to be noted, too, that Godeheu at first held out for higher terms, and it was only the arrival of Watson's fleet with a strong force on board, which threatened, in alliance with the Marathas, to launch a formidable attack from Bombay on Bussy in the Deccan under the leadership of Clive, that forced him to moderate his demands. It is indeed a mistake to represent the Peace as in any sense humiliating to the French. The territories guaranteed to them were assessed at an annual revenue of £800,000, those guaranteed to the English at £100,000. Godeheu fully appreciated the work of Bussy, who himself had no illusions as to the critical position of affairs, and in spite of the clause against interference in native politics the latter was left undisturbed at Hyderabad. Finally, the Peace was only provisional and required ratification by both Companies at home. Till then everything was to remain on the footing of *uti possidetis*. That ratification never came, for the outbreak of the Seven

[1] *A Voyage from England to India . . .*, Edw. Ives, 1773, p. 46.
[2] *Plainte du Chevalier Law*, p. 28.
[3] *Mémoire pour le sieur de Bussy*, Paris, 1764, p. 38.

Years' War occurred before the decision of the home authorities was known. Therefore even the slight territorial changes suggested in the draft treaty were never made, and, as two recent French historians, Cultru and Weber, admit, it was the outbreak of hostilities in 1756 and not Godeheu's treaty which ruined the French settlements in India. The plain truth is that the schemes of Dupleix, bold, ingenious, and far-reaching as they were, had broken down. It was Godeheu's task to save what he could from the wreck. He succeeded to a greater extent than might have been expected, and afforded his countrymen an opportunity to recuperate—an opportunity of which they were unable to avail themselves to the full because a European war occurred before they had consolidated their strength.

When Godeheu arrived, the financial position was desperate. Dupleix had exhausted the treasury and anticipated his revenues in subsidies to his native allies and in the heavy expenses of the war. Had his plans succeeded, he would no doubt have been able to recover his loans and realize a surplus for the Company, but success had not come to him. Not only was the treasury empty, but Dupleix claimed that the Company owed him an immense sum advanced to them from his private purse. Godeheu has been freely blamed because he refused to admit this debt or give Dupleix assignments on future revenue. Such censure is unjust and beside the mark. Many of the ex-Governor-General's statements cannot be accepted without reservation. He declared in his *Memoirs* that he acquired an immense private fortune at Chandarnagar, and the implication is that it was this money he used in the Company's service. But his own letters, recently brought to light, prove conclusively that he had lost almost all the wealth he had amassed before he went to Pondicherry; his savings in 1741, on his own admission, were not large enough to enable him to retire in comfort to France. The sums he had spent had been derived from the gifts and *jagirs* made over to him by native princes, which he was actually forbidden by a royal ordinance to accept. The Company's answer therefore, with some reason, was that he had squandered what was not his to spend, that he had used his position to acquire revenues without their permission, and had spent them in furthering a policy on which they had not been consulted. Godeheu's action seems to have been unimpeachable; he made him a generous grant for the expenses of his journey home, allowed him to retain the revenues from Valdavur, which produced about £10,000 a year, and referred the whole matter for final settlement to the Company. The Company and not Godeheu were responsible if any injury was done to Dupleix. The whole question is involved in considerable difficulty. However obtained, Dupleix had certainly spent his wealth from generous and patriotic motives in the public service, and the Company should at least have seen to it that their brilliant servant had a respectable pension, and this, if the traditional account is to be trusted, they do not seem to have done. But Dupleix did not die till 1763, and it seems only to have been in his latter days that he fell into poverty. With the loss of the French dominions his revenues from Valdavur came to an end, and the Company itself was then naturally in the greatest difficulties. Dupleix seems constitutionally to have had little sense of the value of money, and Godeheu says that he practised the most profuse expenditure on his return to France.

Many facts have recently come to light which explain, if indeed they do not altogether justify, the apparent failure of the Company and the home government to support Dupleix. He had treated them in a very cavalier fashion, informing them of his victories but concealing his defeats. His dispatches never even mentioned Clive's capture of Arcot.

The news of these disasters ultimately reached the Directors through Dutch or English news-sheets or private letters, and naturally aroused in them the greatest distrust. When Godeheu sailed from France, the Company, partly in this case through the delay of a ship, had received no news for a year, that is since the tidings of the surrender of Law at Trichinopoly. Dupleix had gradually, as we have seen, formulated a definite policy of building up French influence and dominion by a calculated interference in native politics, but he had failed to keep the authorities informed of his proceedings and the reasons for them. The Company only received a full and detailed account six months after he was recalled, and when they received it they cancelled his supercession, but, as it happened, too late, for he had already sailed for home.

We can accept no longer the character of Dupleix as depicted by Colonel Malleson, which was based too exclusively on the former's own memoirs, and did less than justice to his subordinates and colleagues. There is something rhetorical and artificial about the 'memoirs' of all the great Frenchmen in India at this time. Voltaire, with a characteristic sneer, declared they were large enough to chronicle the conquests of an Alexander. They were indeed not memoirs in the ordinary sense of the word, but manifestoes and protests, panegyrics of the writer's own career, and invectives against his rivals. They were usually drawn up or edited by advocates, and the same lawyer was responsible for the final form of the memoirs of La Bourdonnais and Dupleix. Thus the violent animosities engendered in the East were transferred to French soil, and there burned themselves out with fierce splutterings and fitful explosions, till they were finally quenched by the death of the disputants. But in spite of his final failure, Dupleix is a striking and brilliant figure in Indian history. For even if we give up the old uncritical estimate, we need not deny his real claims to greatness. His political conceptions were daring and imaginative. He raised the prestige of France in the East for some years to an amazing height, he won a reputation among Indian princes and leaders that has never been surpassed, and he aroused a dread in his English contemporaries which is at once a tribute to his personal power and a testimony to their sagacity.

CHAPTER XII

ENGLISH AND FRENCH IN INDIA, TO THE PEACE OF PARIS. REASONS FOR THE FRENCH DEFEAT

AFTER the departure of Dupleix, the English and the French in the Carnatic enjoyed a four years' breathing space—the neutrality of mutual exhaustion. In that interval Siraj-ud-daula captured Calcutta, and Clive with the best troops on the Coromandel coast sailed away to restore British authority in Bengal. When the Seven Years' War broke out, the time seemed peculiarly opportune to the French government for an attack on the English settlements in southern India. Count de Lally, son of an Irish refugee, who had fought at Fontenoy, and at Falkirk in the Jacobite rising of 1745–6, was sent out to achieve this object. He landed in April 1758, after an unusually protracted voyage, by which time the English had recaptured Calcutta. Fort St. David was bombarded and taken by the French, much to the anger of Clive, who characterized the surrender as 'infamous'. There, however, Lally's success stopped. He had many virtues, for he was brave, conscientious, incorruptible—a somewhat rare virtue in India and at that time—and no mean tactician; but he was hot-headed and intolerant of advice, even from those better acquainted than himself with the conditions of Indian warfare.

The Governor of Pondicherry would not, and probably could not, furnish the money necessary for the pay of the troops; and Lally was driven to march against the Raja of Tanjore to exact payment of a bond of fifty-six lakhs of rupees that had come into the hands of the French. This expedition, which was declared by Bussy to be 'equally unjustified in its motive and its execution',[1] was a lamentable failure and seriously damaged the already waning prestige of the French. D'Aché, the French admiral, who had fought two drawn battles with the British fleet in April and August, now sailed for the Isles of France and Bourbon in spite of Lally's protests.

Though it was an almost hopeless project to besiege an open port when his naval coadjutor had thus left the command of the sea to the British fleet, Lally now marshalled his forces for the attack on Madras. He summoned Bussy, who had all this time, in spite of great difficulties and some vicissitudes of fortune, kept his position at the court of Hyderabad, to come to his aid. Bussy obeyed, but with extreme reluctance, knowing all too well that he could never recover his influence there. His forebodings were soon justified. Clive, in spite of his critical position in Bengal, was watching events in southern India with a general's eye, and 'thought it was his duty to contribute his mite towards the destruction of the French'.[2] Accordingly, in October 1758, contrary to the inclinations of his whole council, he sent Forde, an officer of great ability, to intervene in the Northern Circars. Forde defeated Bussy's successor at Condore in December 1758, and stormed Masulipatam in the following April. French influence at the Court of Hyderabad was gone for ever. Salabat Jang ceded Masulipatam with territory of eighty miles long and twenty wide to the British, and engaged to have no more dealings with the French.

In the meantime Bussy's presence had been of little support to Lally. The two men differed fundamentally in policy. Bussy believed in a French dominion dependent upon a system of treaties and alliances, with himself, the keystone of the arch, residing at the court of Hyderabad

[1] *Lettres de messieurs de Bussy, de Lally et autres. Mémoire pour le sieur de Bussy*, p. 16.
[2] *Reports of the House of Commons*, vol. iii, p. 156.

and commanding an army of picked men; Lally's object was to expend all his energies and concentrate all his forces in attacks on the English settlements one by one. 'The King and the Company', he said, 'have sent me to India to chase the (English) Company out of it. . . . It doesn't concern me that such and such rajas dispute for such and such a nawabship.'[1]

The siege of Madras began in December 1758, but was abandoned in February, when the town was relieved from the sea. Henceforward the English were the aggressors, and Lally stood on the defensive. His troops were in a constant state of mutiny. He had absolutely no money, and his relations with the Governor of Pondicherry and his own officers were deplorable. D'Aché returned to the Coromandel coast in September 1759, and fought a third indecisive battle with Pocock. But, though his fleet was considerably the more powerful, he yielded the fruits of victory to the English, and retreated to the Isles in October, abandoning Pondicherry to its fate. For all that, Lally held out desperately for two years. In January 1760, however, he was severely defeated by Sir Eyre Coote at Wandiwash, where Bussy was taken prisoner. He was driven into Pondicherry, and there forced to surrender in January 1761. To such an extent had he made himself hated that, had it not been for a British escort, he would probably have been torn to pieces by the infuriated mob when he was leaving the city. He was conveyed to England as a prisoner of war, but obtained release on parole and returned to France in order to face the charges there preferred against him. After a two years' trial he was most iniquitously condemned to death and executed, though only errors of judgement could be proved against him.

The fall of Pondicherry sounded the knell of French dominion in India, for though the town was restored to

[1] *Lettres de messieurs de Bussy, de Lally et autres. Mémoire de Bussy*, p. 3, Letter of Lally to Bussy, June 13, 1758.

France by the Peace of Paris in February 1763, the fortifications had been demolished, and the treaty, in accordance with Clive's suggestion to the Marquis of Bute, limited the number of armed men which the French might maintain on the Coromandel coast, and excluded them altogether from Bengal except in a purely commercial capacity. Muhammad Ali, the English candidate, was recognized as Nawab of the Carnatic; and, though Salabat Jang's title to the Subadarship of the Deccan was acknowledged, French influence at his court was now a thing of the past. Moreover, the recognition was valueless, for Salabat Jang had been deposed by his brother Nizam Ali in 1761, and was murdered by him six months after the signature of the treaty. The Northern Circars had passed under the sway of the English, and in 1765 Clive procured an imperial decree ratifying and regularizing the English title.

Henceforward Pondicherry was always occupied by English troops on the outbreak of war with France. France did indeed make one formidable attempt to re-establish her power in 1781–3, an attempt which will be described in its proper place; but her attack on that occasion was directed from the sea, and the want of a regular base on land caused it to fail. The privileges of the French Company were suspended by a royal decree in 1769, Morellet, one of the ablest of the Physiocrats (the famous school of French economists who advocated a single tax on agricultural rents), having passed a severe condemnation on its past financial history.[1] In April 1785. the French Company was re-established, but only as 'a simple commercial house fortified by a monopoly, and no longer the sovereign mistress of a mighty empire'.[2]

Many causes contributed to the final victory of the English

[1] *Mémoire sur la situation actuelle de la Compagnie des Indes*, M. l'abbé Morellet, Paris, 1769.

[2] *La Compagnie française des Indes*, Henry Weber, p. 635.

Company, and not the least of them were its commercial superiority and better financial position. Morellet gives the value of the sale of Indian goods in France from 1736 to 1756 as, in round numbers, £11,450,000,[1] but the total of the sales of the English Company during the same period was more than three and a half times greater, amounting to £41,200,000.[2] After all, a flourishing business is essential to the prosperity of a trading company, whatever its administrative or military success. As Bussy—himself the most brilliant representative of the Political Resident—declared, 'laurels and conquests are for a commercial company a matter of simple calculation, always bad when the expense exceeds the receipts, or even when the produce is not at least on an equality with the outgoings'.[3] This principle certainly governed the destiny of the nation that proved the successful rival of the French. The English did, on the whole, make their conquests pay. They observed the law which Dupleix endeavoured to override. All through the war, the English busily transacted their ordinary commercial affairs and increased the value of their exports, as the records of their trade and shipping prove. The French figures, on the other hand, show a serious falling-off for some years after 1746. Later on, the territorial acquisitions in Bengal filled the English coffers. The English never forgot that they were primarily a trading body. Dupleix, on the other hand, deliberately came to the conclusion that for France, at any rate, the Indian trade was a failure, and that a career of military conquest opened up a more attractive prospect. But, under the circumstances that determined the fates of Europeans in the East, this was a cardinal error. India was too far distant from Europe, and France was too much involved in western continental politics to conquer an eastern empire

[1] These figures are derived from Morellet, pp. 86, 87.
[2] *Reports of the House of Commons*, vol. iv.
[3] *Mémoire pour le sieur de Bussy*, p. 23.

by the sword alone. The policy of Dupleix, wrote the English at Madras in 1753, 'seems to require National, and not a Company's support.'[1] No power could attempt to hold India from a distant base over sea unless its occupancy was based on sound commercial and financial lines. When Dupleix consciously inaugurated a different policy, he had already taken the first step in the decline of French power in India.

The English Company was still a vigorous, self-reliant, commercial body, managed by a private corporation, so far from being dependent upon state support that it had long been a creditor of the government for large sums. Its constitution enabled it to wield no inconsiderable influence in matters of public policy, while at the same time it escaped the deadening effects of detailed state interference.

The French Company had in reality long ceased to be anything but a subordinate department of government. All power was in the hands of the royal commissary. The Proprietors of the Company took no interest in its fortunes provided they could draw the interest on their capital, and this interest had since 1733 been guaranteed them by the state. The ministers of Louis XV were no doubt lethargic and unenterprising, but it must in fairness be remembered that European complications necessarily limited the amount of attention they could devote to eastern affairs; also, it is quite clear from the early history of the French Company that individual initiative in France was sadly lacking in matters of foreign trade. The state, under Louis XIV and Colbert, had galvanized the French Company into life, and when the vigorous hands of its patrons were withdrawn its energy evaporated. The state could not continue to subsidise the Company indefinitely. Morellet, in the course of his inquiry into the history of the Company's finances, lays

[1] India Office Records, French in India, vol. ii. p. 103, Letter from Madras, Oct. 29, 1753.

down two canons, the truth of which no economist will be inclined to deny. First, that there are infinitely more legitimate and more important uses to which the public revenue can be put than in maintaining a company which is bankrupt when left to itself; secondly, a commercial enterprise which is not self-supporting ought to be abandoned.[1] There is much truth in the judgement of an English observer in 1744, who commented even thus early upon 'the lamentable condition of the French East India Company's affairs'. Their attempts, he argues, have miscarried 'notwithstanding all the pains and assistance the government has bestowed upon them. In all other countries, but particularly [in] Great Britain and Holland, undertakings of this sort have been the work of private men in the beginning and have never claimed the aid or even the protection of the state till they were in some degree of forwardness, and then only from the apprehension of this difficulty, that the desire of gain might engage such numbers of adventurers in the same branch of commerce as might prove prejudicial to the public and to themselves. But in France it has been quite otherwise; private people never did anything till excited and encouraged by the government, and then were able to do little more than ruin themselves by launching out into enterprises beyond their abilities.'[2]

In the grim hand-to-hand fighting in southern India that went on almost uninterruptedly from 1746 to 1753, the English remained on the whole victorious, largely owing to the indomitable efforts and talent for leadership of Lawrence and Clive. Success on the mainland was seconded by success at sea. During all this period England was gradually building up her ascendancy on the waterways of the world,

[1] *Mémoire sur la situation actuelle de la Compagnie des Indes*, M. l'abbé Morellet, 1769, p. 253.

[2] *An Account of the French East India Company*, 1744, printed at end of vol. i of J. Harris's *Navigantium atque Itinerantium Bibliotheca*, London, 1744.

and after the beginning of the Seven Years' War, when France became more and more involved in central European entanglements, her predominant position became relatively greater. Indeed, British naval superiority would probably in any case have rendered the ultimate success of Dupleix impossible. Clive's capture of Chandarnagar robbed France of her chief settlement in the province that was in more respects than one the key of India. Even through the war of the Austrian succession, 1744–8, the English had succeeded in increasing their trade and so supporting the charges of war. After 1757, they could draw upon a new source of wealth—the revenues and resources of Bengal, which they administered for the Nawab.

None of these causes should rightly be emphasized to the exclusion of the others. Too close an attention directed to the long, tedious, and uninteresting military operations in India itself produces the frame of mind which seems to hold that the mutual squabbles of two commanders and the success or failure of a few subordinate officers determined the future of a great empire. But India was not won by the English and lost by the French because in one battle a commander marched up a hill when he should have marched down, or marched down when he should have marched up. The causes of great historical events are wrought deeper into the woof of things. A later and truer view relegates the land campaigns (though here there is some exaggeration in the contrary direction) to the domain of 'obscure operations' and believes that the control of the sea was all-important. Captain Mahan, the chief exponent of this theory, has made a very weighty contribution to naval history, but as the history of Europeans in India was not his main subject he has been inclined to underrate other factors contributing to this particular question.[1]

[1] Captain Mahan, in *The Influence of Sea Power upon History*, p. 254, says: 'The movement toward colonial extension by France is

A wide and impartial survey will give to each and all of them their proper place, and will attribute a full share of credit to the masterful genius displayed alike in peace and war by Robert Clive.

wholly popular, though illustrated by a few great names; the attitude of the rulers is cold and mistrustful.' This is certainly not true of French history in India. The Company was almost wholly the creature of the Crown and the ministers; state patronage and assistance in this case may have been a mistake but they were necessary, if there was to be any French trade with India, for want of popular enterprise and enthusiasm.

CHAPTER XIII

THE REVOLUTION IN BENGAL. PLASSEY, AND CLIVE'S FIRST GOVERNORSHIP OF BENGAL

IN southern India, as we have seen, the Anglo-French conflict was fought out in about twenty years. The main *motif* there was the rivalry of the two European powers and the native states were dragged almost against their will into the arena of the strife. In Bengal, on the other hand, three European nations, the English, the French, and the Dutch, had long been accustomed to live together peaceably; the outbreak of hostilities came as a mere incident in the open war that broke out between the English East India Company and the native powers. The chief stations of all these nations were built upon the Hughli, the English at Calcutta, the French at Chandarnagar, and the Dutch at Chinsura; and a glance at the map will show that the English, as nearest the mouth of that river, held the key of Bengal, for in order to reach the wharves of their respective ports it was necessary for French and Dutch ships to sail past the batteries of Fort William. But unlike the settlements in southern India, Calcutta and Chandarnagar had observed a strict neutrality during the war of the Austrian succession, under the protection of Ali Vardi Khan, the Subadar or Nawab of Bengal, who ruled from 1741 to 1756. He was a man of considerable ability and great natural shrewdness. He seems to have clearly foreseen that with an incapable ruler of Bengal the country would soon pass under the sway of the western nations, and he compared Calcutta to a hive of bees that was a source of profit to its owner when undisturbed, but a cause of danger and embarrassment if rashly interfered with. Ali Vardi Khan was succeeded by his grandson and grandnephew, Mirza Muhammad, generally known by his title Siraj-ud-daula, a youth of barely twenty years of age, with all the weaknesses and vices so often met with in the harem-reared princes of the East. During the reign of Ali Vardi Khan the Europeans in Bengal had been forbidden to fortify their settlements except as a defensive precaution against Maratha raids. But just before his death, both English and French, foreseeing that war in Europe was inevitable, and possibly reckoning on the fact that the change in the succession would weaken the native power, began to erect fortifications. Siraj-ud-daula ordered them to desist. The French made their peace with him, but the English were less fortunate. They failed to convince him that they intended to observe his command, and offended him by refusing to yield up a fugitive from his tyranny who had taken refuge in Calcutta. They had also undoubtedly given Siraj-ud-daula some ground for complaint by abusing the trade privileges granted them by the *farman* of 1717.

These questions were, however, but the occasion and pretexts for the outbreak of the war. The general causes lay deeper and were closely connected with the political and economic condition of Bengal. The revolution of 1756–7 was not primarily or solely the conquest of an Indian province by a European trading settlement. It was rather the overthrow of a foreign (Muhammadan) government by the trading and financial classes, native (Hindu) and British; both the latter gained commercially, though the British took the predominant part in the actual events, and alone succeeded to the political sovereignty. The fall of the Muhammadan power was precipitated by its internal dissensions.

The great province which included Bengal proper, Bihar,

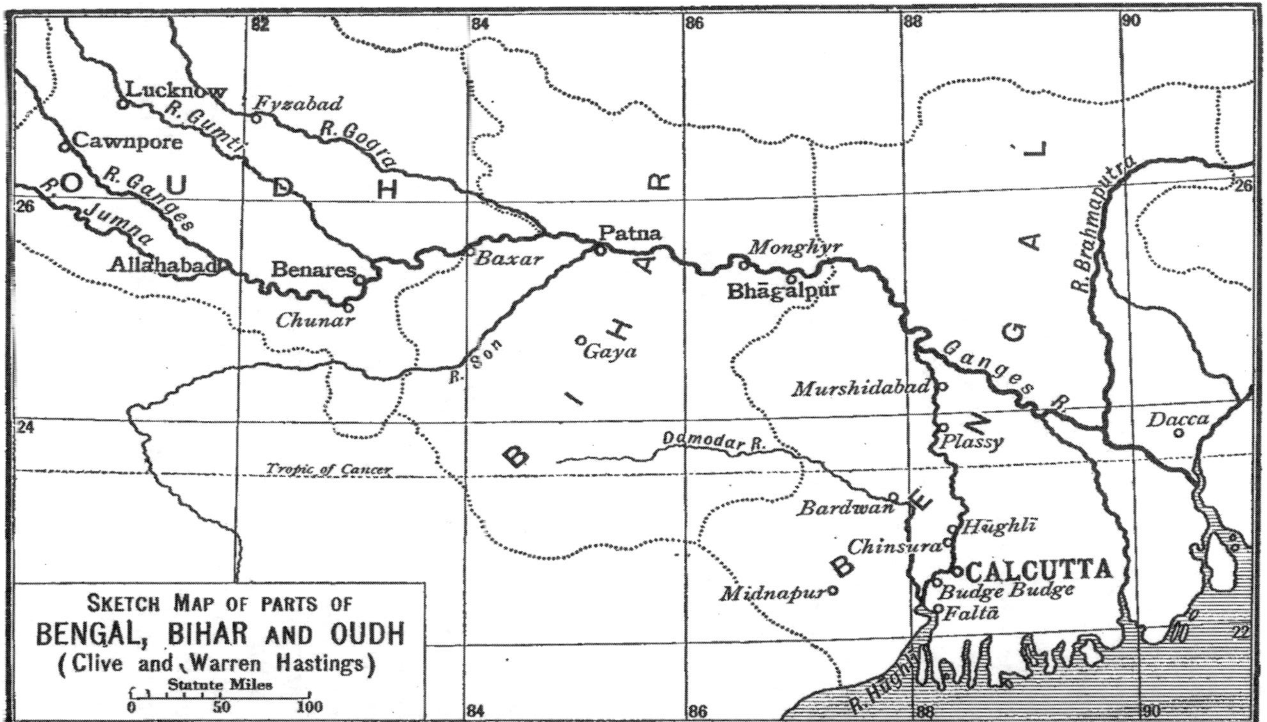

WATTYPE GEORGE PHILIP & SON, LTD.

and Orissa was governed, as we have seen, by Nawabs owning nominally the suzerainty of the Emperor of Delhi. But for many years now they had been practically independent and strove to make their office hereditary. They were men of Mughal, Persian, or Afghan race ruling over a Hindu people. Most of the wealth of the country was in the hands of the latter, and a certain community of interest existed between them and the western settlers with whom they drove so prosperous a trade. It was noticed about 1750 that the Hindus were less tolerant than they had once been of the rule of the Muhammadan minority, and were casting about for some opportunity for freeing themselves from the yoke. Even before the death of Ali Vardi Khan, it was clear to keen observers that a collision could not long be avoided. The Nawab was strict and repressive rather than unjust, but the English were becoming restive under the many vexatious restrictions on their trade. ''Twould be a good deed', wrote Orme to Clive in 1752, 'to swinge the old dog. I don't speak at random when I say that the Company must think seriously of it, or 'twill not be worth their while to trade in Bengal.'[1] As long as Ali Vardi Khan lived, discontent only smouldered, but when he was succeeded by a headstrong, weak, and vicious youth, who pressed equally hard upon the European traders and his Hindu subjects, and insulted the great native financial house of the Seths, events hastened to the catastrophe. Siraj-ud-daula determined to drive the English from his dominions, and in directing his attack upon them rather than upon the French or the Dutch he was guided, from his own point of view, by a right instinct. Their settlement was the largest and the richest, their trade under Surman's *farman* was the greatest, and they were most closely connected with the Hindu merchant class.

[1] *The Indian Records Series. Bengal in 1756–7*, S. C. Hill, 1895, vol. i, Introduction, p. xxxiii.

If the English were expelled, the Nawab could deal at his leisure with the other European settlements. Accordingly, having seized the factory of Cossimbazar and ill-treated his prisoners, he marched upon Calcutta with an army of 50,000. The regular European garrison was under 300 men, and at that particular time it was much reduced beneath its ordinary strength, owing to the wars in southern India, but including volunteers and native troops a force of 515 was finally mustered, about 230 of whom were Europeans. The fort was in disrepair, the guns old, the powder deficient. The Company's servants in Calcutta seem to have been taken absolutely by surprise, and made frantic appeals for aid to the French and the Dutch, who, however, were in a still weaker position than themselves. The Nawab advanced to the attack on June 16, and two days later the women and children were put on board the ships in the river; at the last moment the Governor (Drake) and the commander of the garrison (Minchin), two most incompetent men, joined them. The fleet dropped down the river a short distance below the town and shamefully left the rest of the garrison to its fate, though Orme believed that a single sloop with fifteen brave men on board might have rescued the whole party. The fugitives landed at Fulta, twenty miles lower down the river. After the flight of the Governor and Commandant, the besieged garrison elected to the command Holwell, an ex-surgeon, under whom they held out for two days longer. They surrendered on June 20, being then reduced to 170 men. There followed the horrors of the 'Black Hole of Calcutta'—an oft-told tale. A hundred and forty-six English prisoners, one of them a woman, were forced to spend the night of an Indian summer in the military punishment cell of the fortress, a room of about eighteen feet square. One hundred and twenty-three perished in the inferno so vividly portrayed by Holwell, himself one of the survivors.

The Nawab does not appear to have been personally responsible for this ghastly deed, which was due partly to the stupidity, partly to the savagery, of subordinates, but he never attempted to punish the perpetrators, and treated the survivors with callous severity. Terrible, indeed, was the disaster that had fallen upon the flourishing English settlement. Within a few days the up-country factories and agencies had fallen into the hands of Siraj-ud-daula, Calcutta itself was in his grip, and a few fugitives huddled together in misery and privation at Fulta—where the refugees from the fleet were joined by the survivors of the Black Hole—now represented the British occupation of Bengal. There for the time they were contemptuously left unmolested by their cruel enemy.

When the news of this appalling disaster reached Madras, anxious consultations took place. War with France was known to be imminent, and at first it was seriously doubted whether the English could afford to denude the Coromandel coast of troops. But in the end it was decided to make the recovery of Calcutta the first care. Orme, the historian, who was then one of the council at Fort St. George, eagerly advocated this course, and it was he who suggested that Clive, lately returned from England to be Governor of Fort St. David, should command the main relief expedition, rather than Pigot, the Governor of Madras, or Colonel Aldercron, an officer in the King's service. A small advance-guard reinforcement was at once dispatched under Major Kilpatrick, which arrived at Fulta at the end of July.

The selection of Clive in preference to officers of senior standing was a master-stroke of policy. The enterprise appeared to his colleagues difficult and dangerous, but he had no doubts and no tremors. He turned with delight from the work 'of improving and increasing the investment at Fort St. David' to his warlike and more congenial mission. 'The capture of Calcutta', he wrote, 'appears no very difficult task.' He was buoyed up with the conviction that a great opportunity had come to him, and wrote to his father in an exultant strain: 'It is by far the grandest of my undertakings, I go with great forces and great authority.'[1] His supreme self-confidence was fully justified. He commanded a force of about 900 Europeans and 1,500 natives, while the fleet, consisting of five men-of-war and five transports, was under the command of Admiral Watson. The expedition, starting October 16, reached the mouth of the Hughli after an unfavourable voyage, and relieved the fugitives at Fulta in December. On January 2, 1757, Calcutta fell, and within a few days Hughli also surrendered to the British. Siraj-ud-daula once more led his army against Calcutta, and a sharp engagement was fought, which appears to have disheartened the enemy though it was by no means decisive. On February 9 an offensive and defensive alliance was concluded between the English and the Nawab. The Company's fort and all their former privileges and rights were restored to them, compensation was to be paid for losses, and permission was given to coin money and fortify Calcutta.

Within a few weeks of their appearance in Bengal, Clive and Watson had thus restored the English to their old position and wrested from Siraj-ud-daula the concession, the withholding of which had been the main cause of the outbreak. But it may appear strange that any alliance at all should have been entered into with the author of the Black Hole atrocity, and that the treaty should have contained no provision for the punishment of the guilty. The truth is, that Clive found himself in a very dangerous and critical condition, and he was forced to take many things into consideration besides the English quarrel with Siraj-ud-daula; his main reason, stated by himself, was that

[1] *The Indian Records Series. Bengal in 1756–7*, S. C. Hill, 1895 vol. i, p. 227.

'the delay of a day or two might have ruined the Company's affairs by the junction of the French with the Nawab'. His relations with the commander of the fleet were often strained. Clive was not only a soldier but a servant of the Company. Watson, as a King's officer, openly showed his contempt for all civil and commercial affairs, and in one moment of anger, according to Clive, he went so far as to threaten to open fire upon him with the guns of the fleet. Besides this, the Calcutta council claimed authority over Clive himself, and strongly objected to the special powers given to him by the authorities at Madras. Clive had, therefore, to steer his way with the greatest caution; the commercial interests of the Company required peace; and so he compounded with the Nawab when he could, realizing, in all probability, that he was but postponing an inevitable conflict. He took upon himself the responsibility of refusing a summons from Madras to return thither. He held that to leave Bengal at that time was to imperil the whole of his work there, and he judged—and judged rightly—that Madras with its own resources was capable of warding off any attack from the French. There was, however, a very real fear of effective French intervention in Bengal now that war was openly declared. Bussy was in the Northern Circars within 200 miles of Calcutta. Siraj-ud-daula, smarting from his humiliation at British hands, was strongly suspected of leanings towards a French alliance, and accordingly Clive and Watson turned their attention to Chandarnagar. There had already been some futile negotiations to maintain the neutrality that had hitherto been characteristic of European settlements in Bengal, and neither side had played a very ingenuous part therein. The British now felt themselves strong enough to assail Chandarnagar, and dispatches were received from England enjoining hostilities with the French. Admiral Watson sailed up the river and bombarded the enemy's forts on

March 23, 'as daring and meritorious an attempt', in Clive's words, 'as ever was made in His Majesty's sea service',[1] while Clive himself on the land side drove in the pickets and attacked the garrison at all points. The French fought gallantly, and inflicted severe loss upon the fleet, but, after having nearly 200 of their small force put out of action, surrendered. Part of the garrison made their escape to Cossimbazar, where Jean Law, brother of Jacques-François Law, was in command of the French forces.[2] Clive had extracted from the Nawab some reluctant and ambiguous words which he construed into permission to attack the French, but it required great tact to keep Siraj-ud-daula from intervening. About this time, we are told, Clive received from him as many as ten letters in one day, and answered every one 'with all the calmness and complaisance imaginable'. The Nawab's hesitation, so fortunate for the British, was partly due to the fact that a terrible blow had just fallen upon the Mughal Emperor, whose vassal he nominally was. In January 1757 Ahmad Shah Durrani had sacked Delhi. For the moment, the Nawab, uncertain what enemies might assail him from northern India, was anxious to maintain his alliance with the British, and was therefore disinclined to save the French.

The danger from the French removed, Clive had won a breathing-space and could reconsider his attitude to the native powers. It must have been clear to all that a recrudescence of hostilities with the Nawab was only a question of time. Subsequent events were to show that the huge army of Siraj-ud-daula was no match for the British forces, and if Clive had declared open war upon him success

[1] *Reports of the House of Commons*, vol. iii, p. 146.

[2] After Plassey, Law was chased by Coote over the Oudh frontier. Within the next two years Law pursued the career of a military adventurer, marching to Lucknow and Delhi, and twice assisting the rebel son of the Mughal Emperor to invade Bengal. He finally surrendered to the English with the honours of war in 1761.

would probably have been his. Unfortunately, this was not, and perhaps could not have been, understood at the time, and the English chose to fight the Nawab with the weapon of political intrigue. A revolution was in progress at the court of Siraj-ud-daula, and a conspiracy to dethrone him had been formed by disaffected nobles in favour of Mir Jafar, brother-in-law of Ali Vardi Khan. These men made overtures to the British, and Clive, feeling that 'there can be neither peace nor security while such a monster reigns', took the questionable course of supporting the plot against the ruler who was legally the ally of the Company. This first false step led almost inevitably to others. The negotiations were conducted by Aminchand (Omichand), a wealthy Sikh financier, who demanded a large commission on the money that might be found in the Nawab's treasury, and threatened unless this was guaranteed to him to divulge the whole plot to the Nawab. The threat of the blackmailer placed the Bengal council in a most unenviable position. They were at the mercy of Aminchand, and probably the least objectionable course would have been, as Orme declared, to pay him his commission, excessive as it was, and leave him to enjoy it 'in oblivion and contempt'. Clive thought otherwise. He afterwards declared that 'art and policy were warrantable in defeating the purpose of such a villain', and he won the consent of the Secret Committee of the council, who were entrusted with the negotiations, to a scheme to outwit Aminchand. Two drafts of the treaty with Mir Jafar were prepared; one authorized the commission demanded by Aminchand and was shown to him; the other, the real document, did not. The fictitious treaty was signed by Clive and the Secret Committee. Watson refused to meddle in the transaction, and Clive ordered his signature to be counterfeited and appended to the sham treaty.

Clive always consistently defended this episode, and

modern casuists have sometimes composed a laboured apology. But it was really indefensible. The critical position of affairs at the time affords a palliative but not an adequate justification. Clive's action no doubt suggested Horace Walpole's reflection that 'our governors there [in India], I think, have learned more of their treachery and injustice, than they have taught them of our discipline'.[1] In the treaty, Mir Jafar promised, when he became Nawab, to confirm all privileges allowed by Siraj-ud-daula, to make an offensive and defensive alliance with the British, exclude the French from Bengal, guarantee the Company a million sterling as compensation for the loss of Calcutta, and pay half that amount besides to the European inhabitants. By a private arrangement, not divulged to the Company at home, large gratuities were promised to the army and navy and members of the council.

These preliminaries settled, Clive now showed his hand to Siraj-ud-daula. He sent a letter taxing him with having evaded the provisions of the treaty of February 9 and corresponded with the French. He further proposed to refer the dispute to the Nawab's own council. Receiving no reply, he marched northwards from Chandarnagar, at the head of about 3,200 troops, for the famous grove of Plassey, twenty-three miles south of Murshidabad, where the Nawab was already stationed with an army of about 50,000 men. At Katwa, on the bank of the river within fifteen miles of Plassey, he halted for four days. It was still uncertain which side Mir Jafar would choose in the end to betray, and Clive's anxiety was great. The eve of his great victory was, curiously enough, almost the only occasion on which he seems to have shown any sign of indecision. He called a council of war and gave his own vote against advancing; twelve officers supported him in the majority, but seven led by Eyre Coote voted in opposition. Clive, after the

[1] *Letters of Horace Walpole*, P. Toynbee, vol. vi, p. 28.

council had broken up, meditated for an hour in solitude, and then announced that he would, in spite of its decision, continue to advance. He crossed the river on the 22nd, and reached Plassey shortly after midnight.

The battle was fought on June 23, 1757. There was a large disparity of numbers against the British, but a great part of the Nawab's forces were commanded by the traitor Mir Jafar, and never properly came into action. At the same time Mir Jafar himself, possibly moved by a last piteous appeal of the deluded Nawab to his honour, did not take that prominent part against his fellow-countrymen that the English had expected, and his conduct caused Clive the greatest uneasiness. Indeed, he only moved forward to join Clive when the issue was already determined. A long cannonade in the morning was followed by a British attack in the afternoon. The only resistance worthy the name came from a handful of Frenchmen in the Nawab's service. It was a mere rout rather than a battle. Clive had twenty-three men killed and forty-nine wounded, and the enemy not more than five hundred killed and the same number wounded out of his large army.

After the battle, Mir Jafar, conscious of the sorry part he had played, advanced with obvious diffidence and mistrust, but he was saluted by Clive as Nawab of the province and enthroned at the capital, Murshidabad. When the treasury there was entered it was found to contain not more than one and a half millions sterling, instead of the forty millions which popular rumour supposed, or the twenty-four millions estimated by the Company's agent at Cossimbazar. The total sum to be paid over to the English amounted to nearly two and three-quarter millions; it was therefore arranged that the debt should be discharged in instalments. The deluded Aminchand was informed that he was to get nothing; the wretched fugitive Siraj-ud-daula, abandoned by all his servants, fell into the hands of Mir Jafar's troops a few days later, as he fled up the Ganges, and was put to death by order of the son of his supplanter.

Mir Jafar might be the nominal head of the government, but the real power behind the throne was Clive, and such success as the new régime at first met with was almost entirely due to his inexhaustible energy. After he had been appointed Governor of Bengal he quelled several insurrections against Mir Jafar's authority and defended him against his external foes—the eldest son of the Emperor who was in rebellion against his father, and the ruler of Oudh. Besides protecting the *roi fainéant* that he had set up, Clive used his position to strike down Great Britain's remaining European rival in Bengal. The Dutch at Chinsura looked with undisguised dislike on the sudden aggrandizement of Calcutta, and were enraged by the grant to their rivals of liberty to search all vessels in the Hughli. Accordingly they entered into communications with the Nawab, who was already growing restive under Clive's domination. A fleet of seven ships appeared in the Ganges from Batavia, and assumed a threatening demeanour. The two nations were at peace in Europe, but Clive with calculated audacity took the law into his own hands. The Dutch gave him a handle by laying hands on some British shipping. He launched all his available force against them, captured their fleet, and defeated them on land through the agency of Forde, in November 1759. The Dutch made a complete submission, disavowed the acts of their naval commanders, acknowledged themselves to be the aggressors, and paid damages. From this date, though they preserved their commercial *status*, they abandoned all attempts to rival the British in the wider field of Indian politics.

In February 1760 Clive sailed for England, at the zenith of his fame while only thirty-five. In the position of the British in India he had wrought a truly marvellous transformation. Writing to the historian Orme in 1757 he said: 'I am possessed of volumes of materials for the continuance of your history, in which will appear fighting, tricks, chicanery, intrigues, politics, and the Lord knows what.' The boast was true, and with characteristic frankness Clive did not disguise the large part played by stratagem and finesse in his policy.

A comparison of the position in 1756 with that in 1760 reveals beyond all possibility of cavil the magnitude of his achievement. In 1756 the British in Bengal, though the most prosperous European community in that province of the empire, were regarded merely as a body of merchants with one rich settlement, a few territorial rights in the villages round Calcutta, and some up-country agencies or factories at Cossimbazar, Dacca, Balasore, Jagdea, and Patna. Though shrewd observers, such as Bernier the French physician at the end of the seventeenth century, and Colonel Mill about ten years before Plassey, had seen and recorded their opinions that Indian armies would be helpless before trained European troops, the British had never yet dreamt of challenging the power of the Nawab of Bengal. They had submitted with occasional protests to Ali Vardi Khan's strict and irksome control. It was necessary to keep on good terms with him, for the up-country factories were quite unfortified, and it was the practice of the Nawabs in any serious dispute to blockade them and stop all trade till submission was made. By 1760 the position was entirely altered. The British were supreme in Bengal. The French and Dutch were impoverished and reduced; their military and political power was gone. The titular Nawab of the province was little more than the creature and protégé of the Company. British influence extended outwards from Calcutta through Bengal and Bihar to the southern boundary of Oudh. The possession of this rich country also completely altered the English position in Madras.

This tremendous change was almost entirely the work of Clive. He was throughout the moving spirit. The more closely the contemporary records are examined, the more clearly his immense energy, masterful will, and dominating influence over his colleagues stand out.

But when every tribute has been paid to the intellectual quality of Clive's achievement, certain moral limitations must be noted, for they reacted on the permanence and value of his results. Recent writers on Indian history do not err on the side of hostile criticism of eighteenth-century empire-builders, but if James Mill and his school were over-harsh in their judgements, the pendulum has now perhaps swung too far in the other direction. By certain of his actions Clive had marred both the glory and the usefulness of his work. Like the great Duke of Marlborough, he was over-fond of money, and he had unequalled opportunities of amassing it. Like Marlborough too, he did not make it dishonestly, nor was anything he did, perhaps, at variance with the deplorably low standard of his age; but it is difficult to combat the verdict of Macaulay that he cannot be acquitted 'of having done what, if not in itself evil, was yet of evil example'. The facts are not in dispute. By a private arrangement made with Mir Jafar before Plassey it was stipulated that £400,000 should be given to the army and navy and £120,000 (afterwards apparently increased to £150,000) to the Select Committee of six persons. Additional presents were afterwards received. Clive's share in all amounted to £234,000, and other members of the Council received from £50,000 to £80,000. A sinister fact was that Mir Jafar, as subsequently appeared, imagined that in paying these additional sums he was purchasing immunity from his obligations to the Company. Clive's defence was that at this time there was no regulation of the Company forbidding the receipt of presents; and when presents were not exacted by compulsion, when they were given by a prince in a state of independence, they were not dishonourable.[1] The defence was legally sound, but in the first place Clive must have known that Mir Jafar was hardly a free agent. These sums, says Sir Edward Colebrooke, were not really presents in any sense of the word; 'they were moneys bargained for the sale of a province under a transaction stained with falsehood and treachery throughout'[2]—a judgement which, though perhaps over-severe, is hardly untrue. Secondly, Clive, as a practical politician, should have recognized that he was creating a very dangerous precedent, and, as we know, after his departure the Bengal Council, within the space of five years, engineered three more revolutions without any of the strong reasons which palliated, if they did not excuse, Clive's action, and on each occasion dipped their hands deep into the treasury of the Nawab.

Burgoyne's doctrine, afterwards laid down in the House of Commons, is unimpeachable: 'that it was impossible that any civil or military servant in treating with a foreign prince or state could, while doing so, lawfully bargain for or acquire property for himself'. That Clive had an uneasy sense of the truth of this is proved by the fact that in a long dispatch to the Secret Committee of the Court of Directors, written four weeks after he entered Murshidabad, he gave full details as to the compensation to the Company and inhabitants of Calcutta that Mir Jafar had stipulated to pay in the public treaty, and described the deficit in the treasury, but he made no allusion to the private agreement, the large sums paid to the services and the Committee, or to the huge amount afterwards received as presents. He did indeed, later on, allude to the fact that the generosity of the Nawab had made his fortune easy, but the Directors, when

[1] *Reports of the House of Commons*, vol. iii, p. 148.

[2] *Rise of the British Power in the East*, M. Elphinstone, ed. by Sir E. Colebrooke, p. 315.

they wrote, 'we do not intend to break in upon any sums of money which have been given by the Nabob [Nawab] to particular persons by way of free gift',[1] could hardly have realized what large amounts were in question. An excuse is often found for Clive in the parsimonious conduct of the Directors, who still insisted on paying low official salaries to their servants in India. But though the salaries were nominally meagre enough, there were recognized ways of increasing them by the right of private trade. Clive himself, on his first return to England in 1753, at the age of twenty-eight, after but nine years' service, brought back a fair fortune, which enabled him to pay off his father's debts, make considerable display as a man of fashion, and win a Parliamentary election after a lavish expenditure of money.

Finally, by the acceptance of these presents, Clive, though perhaps unconsciously, imperilled the permanence of his settlement of Bengal, and so infringed his own canon that presents must not be received to the disadvantage of the Company. Before Plassey, the British seem really to have believed that the treasury at Murshidabad contained as much as forty millions sterling, and, in the light of this belief, the sums accepted as presents may have appeared comparatively small. The real value, as has been said, was discovered to be £1,500,000, while the British claims under the public and private treaty amounted to over two and three-quarter millions. The obviously right course was to surrender the sums promised by the Nawab as gratuities, but it was not taken. The new government of Mir Jafar was saddled with the obligation of discharging the debt, and so started on its difficult and dangerous path already heavily handicapped. Clive's famous exclamation is well known, that, when he remembered the gold, silver, and jewels in the treasury of Murshidabad, he was astonished at his own moderation. But when he made this statement in 1773 he must have

[1] *Reports of the House of Commons*, vol. iii, p. 149.

forgotten, or ignored, the fact that at the time he was obliged to make arrangements with the Nawab to have the sums due to the British paid by instalments, for the reason that the deposits in the treasury were insufficient to discharge the debt.

But Clive was to receive still more. Mir Jafar had procured for him from the Emperor the title of *Omrah*, or noble. It was customary, when this rank was conferred on native subjects, for a *jagir*, or revenue derived from land, to be given them to support their rank. In Clive's case, of course, the title was merely honorary, but thinking apparently that a quarter of a million was not a sufficient reward for his services to Mir Jafar, he wrote, on his own admission,[1] to the financial minister of the Nawab, informing him that he had been made an *Omrah* without a *jagir*. The hint was taken, and a little later Mir Jafar, partly out of gratitude for the driving away from Bengal of the Emperor's rebellious son, partly, as was suggested at the time, for fear that his intrigues with the Dutch would be punished, granted to Clive the huge sum of £30,000 a year, being the quit rent paid to himself by the Company for lands south of Calcutta. There was nothing technically illegal here, but the want of delicacy shown by Clive was surely amazing. We have to remember that he had already received £234,000 from the man to whom he made this further application—an application that, in the relations in which they stood to one another, was almost a demand. The acceptance of the *jagir* made him, the servant of the Company, also its landlord—a position which, as the Court of Directors afterwards maintained, was, even if legal, highly improper. It has been well said that 'however great Clive's services may have been, they were really the services of those who employed him, and therefore, if the Nawab was in a position to renounce the quit rent, the renunciation ought to have

[1] *Reports of the House of Commons*, vol. iii, p. 154.

been made in the Company's favour'.[1] But there was at any rate here no concealment, and the Company deserve little sympathy, for instead of objecting at once, as they should have done, to the position 'of being tributary to their own servants', they allowed the payments to be made for some years, and then withheld them on purely personal grounds, 'all cordiality with Lord Clive being at an end'. The Company, therefore, must share the responsibility, though it must be admitted that Clive was in a position to know, and they were not, how straitened at this time were the means of the Nawab. He was asked at the Parliamentary inquiry of 1772 whether, at the time the *jagir* was granted, he knew that the troops of the Nawab were mutinous and clamouring for pay, and he answered that he did, adding, as a kind of justification, that it was the custom of the country never to pay the army a fourth part of what was promised them. He was then asked whether he was aware that before the grant was offered to him the Nawab's jewels, goods, and furniture were publicly sold to pay the Company the sums stipulated in the treaty, and again he was forced to answer 'Yes'.[2]

Clive, therefore, by crippling the resources of Mir Jafar at the beginning of his administration, cannot be exonerated from some share of the blame for the notorious misgovernment in Bengal that followed. Full allowances must be made on the score of the lower public morality current at the time in all matters of finance. It was the rule and not the exception for statesmen in the eighteenth century to make large personal profits out of their official positions. The whole doctrine of prize money governed not only military but civil life as well. At the capture of Gheria from the pirate chief Angria in 1756 the English troops divided £120,000 amongst themselves, reserving not one penny for

[1] *A Comprehensive History of India*, by H. Beveridge, vol. i, p. 659.
[2] *Reports of the House of Commons*, vol. iii, p. 155.

the East India Company. Lecky has recorded the fact that the Duke of Marlborough received from the state no less a sum than £64,000 per annum. The truth is that everywhere at this time, and especially in India, as Sir John Malcolm, Clive's biographer, admits, a 'spirit of plunder' and a 'passion for the rapid accumulation of wealth' actuated all ranks. The whole atmosphere was corrupt from a modern point of view. The older school of historians were apt to judge men like Clive and Warren Hastings too severely by the standards of a later age, but it is not less absurd to assume that all their financial transactions were worthy of praise. To do so is unjust to men who were capable of rising to greater heights. The Governors-General appointed from the ranks of English statesmen after 1785 excelled even the best of the Company's servants in their attitude to such questions. The historian Thornton with justice remarks that the views and actions of Indian officials at this time present a very discreditable contrast to the conduct of Lord Wellesley in refusing the sum of £100,000 tendered to him without solicitation by the Court of Directors from the spoils of Seringapatam.

CHAPTER XIV

MISGOVERNMENT IN BENGAL. REFORMS AND CLIVE'S SECOND GOVERNORSHIP

On Clive's departure for Europe there ensued, in the words of Sir Alfred Lyall, 'the only period of Anglo-Indian history which throws grave and unpardonable discredit on the English name'. The fact was more lamentable than surprising. A little body of Englishmen engaged in commercial pursuits had, within a few years, been raised from the control of a single town and some up-country stations to a real, though as yet unacknowledged, authority throughout a wide province. Theirs was the power of the sword that upheld the native ruler whose sway was acknowledged throughout Bengal, Bihar, and Orissa. This man, their tool and nominee, was himself in theory the deputy of a *roi fainéant*, the Mughal Emperor. The divorce of the *de facto* power from the *de jure* sovereignty was at this time the political fashion throughout India, and it appeared in the greatest Hindu state as well as in the Mughal Empire, for the actual authority in the Maratha confederacy had already passed from the successor of Sivaji, seated on his prison throne at Satara, to the Peshwa, or Mayor of the Palace, and was soon to be transferred from the Peshwa to the Peshwa's Brahman minister, and from the minister to the hereditary generals of the confederate armies. These political shams inevitably had a demoralizing effect upon the trend of British policy, for which great allowance must therefore be made. For the British in Bengal to have accepted the native political claims at their face value would have meant that the burden of the administration and of warlike operations would have fallen on their shoulders, while the profits of power would have been paid into the exchequer of worthless and helpless native rulers. The practice generally adopted by the British was to concede the native political claims as far as possible, at the same time taking care that their own services should not go unrewarded. When this course led them to an *impasse*, as it ultimately did through the anarchical condition of native jurisdictions, they were apt themselves to solve the difficulty by some rather transparent political fiction, when it would have perhaps been better openly to acknowledge that their own interest and the cause of humane government required the drastic sweeping away of the cobwebs of outworn political systems.

On Clive's departure, Vansittart, the new Governor, and the Council were confronted with some special difficulties. The Company's treasury was exhausted. The Nawab was in arrears with the subsidy for their troops, and, worst of all, no remittances were sent from home, the Directors believing that vast wealth had been acquired in Bengal, and expecting that Presidency to supply money for Bombay and Madras. 'It is a most amazing thing to consider,' wrote the Directors in 1758, 'that a settlement so abounding with industrious inhabitants, and flourishing in its trade . . . should produce so little profit to the Company. This cannot be easily accounted for other ways than from the luxurious, expensive, and idle manner of life . . . among all ranks of our servants.'[1]

Foreign difficulties were added to internal complications. The new Mughal Emperor, Shah Alam, nominal suzerain of Mir Jafar—the theoretical overlord of the Company—invaded Bengal. He was defeated by a British force, but entered into friendly relations with his conquerors. At the same time the Bengal Council, at the instigation of Holwell, find-

[1] Letter to Calcutta, March 3, 1758.

ing that Mir Jafar was hopelessly weak, deposed him in favour of his son-in-law, Mir Kasim. It is only fair to state that many members of the Council protested strongly against the decision 'to dethrone a man we were bound to support by the most solemn ties, divine and human', and stigmatized it as 'an indelible stain upon our national character'.[1] Vansittart and Holwell hoped to regularize this second revolution by using the power they had so suddenly gained over the Emperor. Nothing could have shed a clearer light upon the whole situation. Mir Kasim, the nominee of the East India Company's servants, sitting on a throne erected within the English factory at Patna, was endowed with the viceroyalty of Bengal, Bihar, and Orissa, by a sovereign who had just been defeated and taken prisoner by British troops. The British had far more real power than Mir Kasim, and Mir Kasim than the Emperor, who was in fact a homeless fugitive; and yet in theory these positions were exactly reversed.

The British obtained from Mir Kasim, as the price of their support, the cession of the districts of Burdwan, Midnapur, and Chittagong, which gave them valuable territory to the west, north-west, and east of Calcutta, and the Council followed Clive's unfortunate precedent by receiving for themselves gratuities to the amount of £200,000. A sidelight is thrown upon the rapacity of the Company's servants at this time by the simple fact that Vansittart, the Governor, whose character stood higher than that of the average civil servant at this time, received more than £50,000, though he had an allowance from the Company of £18,000 a year, and carried on trade on his own account besides.

Mir Kasim was a ruler of considerable administrative ability, and in many ways improved the position of his province, but he soon came into collision with the British in

[1] *Reports of the House of Commons*, vol. iii, pp. 252, 254.

Calcutta. Ever since 1717 the Company had been allowed to conduct its export trade from Bengal free of duty. After 1756 its servants began illegally to claim exemption on their private trade, which they carried on in the province and in which they competed with the Nawab's subjects. It therefore happened that, while the Company was demanding heavy subsidies from that unfortunate ruler for the support of the troops that defended his dominions, its servants, by claiming an illegal monopoly, were lessening his revenues and impoverishing his people. The evidence of the wrong thus done to the natives of the province is indisputable. Verelst, afterwards Governor of Bengal, admitted that 'a trade was carried on without payment of duties, in the prosecution of which infinite oppressions were committed'; and the young Warren Hastings warned his fellow-countrymen that they were 'erecting themselves into lords and oppressors of the country'. It is quite impossible, in a short history, to enter into the details of the struggle. It must be enough to say that Mir Kasim was gradually driven to the conviction that he could get neither justice nor a fair hearing from the Bengal Council, who, in their attitude towards their oriental suzerain, displayed, as Macaulay says, 'the strength of civilization without its mercy'. Finally, all the hidden ferocity and brutality of the Nawab's nature flared out; he seized the servants of the Company, was defeated in two fiercely-contested engagements, and massacred two hundred of his prisoners. Throughout this discreditable episode, only two Englishmen played an honourable part, Vansittart and Hastings, who resisted their fellows at the Council board, and supported the Nawab until his acts of violence and treachery made it impossible for them to do so any longer. The conduct of Hastings was especially commendable, for he did not stand high in order of seniority; he seems to have successfully resisted the many strong temptations of wrongly acquiring wealth that beset him, and he was perhaps the only Englishman in Bengal who emerged from the business with clean hands and unsullied honour.

Mir Kasim was deposed, July 1763, and Mir Jafar once more placed upon the throne. He was forced to grant the English the privilege of internal trade, and indemnify the Company for their losses at the hands of Mir Kasim, who by British aid had usurped his throne. Mir Kasim fled across the frontiers of Oudh. The rulers of that country enjoyed the title of Nawab Wazir, i.e. First Minister of the Mughal Empire, though they had long been practically independent, and were often at variance with their suzerain. The then holder of the title, Shuja-ud-daula, was however for the moment supporting the Emperor, Shah Alam, and it was over their combined forces that Major Munro, who had just quelled the first sepoy mutiny in the Company's army by stern measures, won a great victory at the Battle of Baxar in 1764.

Baxar, as Sir James Stephen says, deserves far more than Plassey to be considered as the origin of the British power in India. It was a fiercely-contested battle, and the troops of Mir Kasim offered a determined resistance. The English lost 847 killed and wounded, while the enemy left behind them 2,000 dead. It was not merely the Nawab of Bengal, as at Plassey, but the Emperor of all India and his titular Prime Minister who were defeated. The Emperor at once made his submission, but the Nawab Wazir refused to come to terms till British forces had marched into Lucknow and Allahabad, and all Oudh was at their mercy.

Meanwhile Mir Jafar, the puppet Nawab of Bengal, had died in February 1765, and the Bengal Council raised to his throne the second son in preference to a grandson. They seized the opportunity to strengthen their own control over the country, for the real administration was to be henceforward in the hands of a deputy Nawab (Muhammad

Raza Khan), to be appointed on their advice and not to be dismissed without their sanction. The Court of Directors had again and again condemned the private trading rights claimed by their servants, and had sent the strictest orders against the taking of presents. In face of this the Bengal Council forced the new ruler to leave their trading rights untouched, and compelled him to make handsome presents to the Governor and his colleagues of £139,357. Corruption had done its work, and the moral fibre of the whole settlement was rotten. 'There was', says Verelst, 'a general contempt of superiors . . . a total contempt of public orders whenever obedience was found incompatible with private interest.' Such was the state of affairs when Clive arrived to take up his second governorship, after a five years' residence in England. He had been given an Irish peerage, a reward deemed by himself inadequate. He entered Parliament, purchased a great English estate and several rotten boroughs, so that he was soon at the head of a little coterie of followers in the Commons. He also plunged into the politics of the India House, where he encountered considerable opposition, probably due to his famous letter to Pitt, written from India in January 1759 and advocating that the Crown should take over the East India Company's territorial acquisitions. The party hostile to Clive (led by the Director Sulivan—once his friend but now a bitter opponent), having gained the ascendancy in the Court of Directors, ordered the authorities in Calcutta to cease paying to him the revenues of the *jagir*, whereupon Clive instituted against them a suit in chancery.

In February 1764 news arrived of the deplorable position of affairs in Bengal, and these disastrous tidings enabled Clive to win a complete victory over his enemies in the Directorate. The Court of Proprietors insisted that he should be sent out to restore the fortunes of the Company and overrode all objections. He was appointed Governor of Bengal and Commander-in-Chief. The enjoyment of the *jagir*, on his own proposal, was guaranteed to him for ten years, or till his death, if he died before that period had elapsed. His chief partisan, Rous, was elected Chairman of the Court of Directors. On arriving in India he was to work with the existing Bengal Council, if possible; if not, he was empowered to form a Select Committee of four, presided over by himself, to whom all the functions of government were to pass. Two of the Committee, Colonel Carnac and Verelst, were already in Bengal. The others, Sumner and Sykes, sailed with him. Clive arrived in May 1765, to find the external position completely retrieved, the Company's arms everywhere victorious, and the highest political authority of all India a suppliant for British charity. In internal affairs the Calcutta government had openly defied all the regulations for reform put forth by the Directors, had thrice set their own candidate upon the *masnad* (or throne) of Bengal, and had turned each occasion shamelessly to their own profit. Finally, owing to their policy towards Mir Kasim, they had plunged into a war on a question that did not concern their employers' interest in the least, for the East India Company was only concerned with the oversea trade.

Clive acted with his usual decisive promptitude. His work may be classified under three heads; first, his reform of the Company's civil and military services; secondly, the acquisition of the *Diwani* (or revenue administration) of Bengal; and thirdly, his external policy. It will be convenient to summarize as clearly as possible his acts under these separate designations, and then to add a few words of comment on his achievements as a whole.

Clive soon made up his mind that to stem the tide of corruption with the existing Council would be a hopeless task. He therefore nominated his Select Committee two days after his landing. The Company's servants were forced to subscribe the covenants against the receipt of presents, and the system by which they had been enabled to escape the regular internal imposts on their private trade was abolished. Clive himself was in favour of the total abolition of licensed private trading, and advocated a large increase in official salaries; but he could not win the Court of Directors to his views. As an alternative, he attempted to regularize and limit the existing practice by granting a monopoly of the trade in salt to the superior servants of the Company in graduated shares, so that the Governor received £17,500 per annum; a Colonel in the army or a member of Council, £7,000; and lower ranks, lesser amounts in a descending scale. Clive was afterwards severely censured for this arrangement, which was said to run counter to the orders of the Directors against allowing their servants to trade in certain commodities, of which salt was one. This was no doubt technically true, but every one at the time considered it essential to augment the official salaries in some way, and since, as we shall see, a fixed allowance was henceforward to be made to the Nawab by the Company and his income was no longer to be derived from internal dues, many of the former objections against private trade in salt were removed. Two years later the Directors abolished his system and substituted for it commissions on the revenues of the province, which gave to the Governor about £18,500 a year in addition to his salary of £4,800, and to other ranks emoluments in proportion.[1]

Naturally these drastic reforms were not carried through without the most determined resistance from the original Council, of whom Spencer, the Governor, and several other leading officials were expelled or forced to resign. When Clive thundered against 'the rapacity and oppression'

[1] *Reports of the House of Commons*, vol. iv, p. 460. It was sometimes even more. The amount paid to the Governor Verelst for the year ending Aug. 31, 1768, was £27,093, ibid., p. 162.

universally prevalent and declared that 'every spark of sentiment and public spirit was lost and extinguished in the inordinate lust of unmerited wealth', the men who were trounced in this heated language naturally recalled the huge sums amassed by their censor in his first period of office. To them it appeared that Clive, having then secured a colossal fortune, was apprehensive that, if similar methods were not checked in Bengal, Parliament would direct its attention to the matter and his own conduct in the past would not escape investigation. To this feeling they attributed the fury of his onslaught. Plausible as all this must have sounded at the time, it was almost certainly untrue. That Clive's action in the past was injudicious and that it involved a most unfortunate precedent we have shown. But, too apt as he was to shelter himself behind technicalities and the letter of the law, he was honestly convinced of his integrity and the purity of his motives. He would have answered that in 1757 there was no order of the Court of Directors against the receipt of presents, and that the change of succession brought about in that year was a genuine revolution. The very strength and violence of his language in describing the corruption in Bengal, though it was perhaps partly due to natural irritation at the attacks of which he was made the object, shows that he really considered his own conduct in the past to have been on quite a different level from that of Spencer and his colleagues. It *is* true, therefore, to say that during his second governorship he cleansed the Augean stables of the Bengal establishment, that he acted throughout with a single-eyed aim for the good of the Company, that he took, as he frequently boasted, no profit to himself and received no emolument from the Court of Directors. On the other hand, it is equally true that, when Clive arrived in India and heard at Madras that the Company's affairs were far more prosperous than had been supposed, he wrote post haste in cipher to his agents in London to invest all his available funds in the purchase of East India stock—a not very reputable use of knowledge gained in his official capacity. Though he did not take for himself the huge profits (£17,500) allocated to the Governor from the salt monopoly, he yet distributed his share among his relatives and dependents, and though he repeated with unnecessary iteration that he would receive no profit of any kind from his second governorship, yet he was afterwards granted by the Company on his return another ten years' enjoyment of the *jagir*, and had he lived this would have amounted to £300,000—not an insufficient emolument for a period of office of two years.

By his reforms Clive alienated the whole of the civil service in Bengal, and by abolishing, as he had been required to do, the custom of extra pay or 'double batta' in the army, which, properly only granted on active service, had been continued by Mir Jafar since Plassey in time of peace, he incurred the relentless enmity of the officers. A dangerous mutiny was organized, and Clive at one time stood almost alone in Bengal, against a combination of very sinister forces. His commanding genius was never more in evidence. He determined 'to put all to the risk rather than suffer the authority of the Council to be insulted'. By promptitude and daring he crushed the mutinous spirit and completely cowed the rebellious factions.

The famous acquisition of the *Diwani* of Bengal was the first great step by the Company towards territorial dominion. Before he reached Bengal, Clive had come to the conclusion that some such responsibility must be incurred. He wrote from Madras, 'we must become Nabobs in fact if not in name, perhaps totally so, without disguise'. The *Diwani* conferred upon its holder the right to collect and administer all the revenues of the province, and Clive prevailed upon the Emperor Shah Alam to confer this momentous power upon the East India Company. Henceforward its servants were to collect the revenues and defray the charges of government, to pay to the Nawab a fixed sum of 53 lakhs of rupees (reduced to 41 lakhs in 1766 and to 32 in 1769), and to the Emperor 26 lakhs.

The constitutional relations between the Nawab of Bengal and the East India Company are very complicated and difficult to understand. Perhaps the clearest explanation that can be given of them is as follows. The Nawab or Subadar of Bengal, as Viceroy of the Mughal Emperor, exercised two functions: (1) the *Diwani*, i. e. revenue and civil justice, (2) the *Nizamat*, i. e. military power and criminal justice. Now, as Sir James Stephen points out, in February 1765 the Nawab practically had granted the *Nizamat* to the Company, and in August 1765 the Emperor ceded to them the *Diwani*; 'the Company thus held the *Diwani* from the Emperor and the *Nizamat* from the Subadar'. So far the position, though highly technical and intricate, is not difficult to grasp. It was further complicated by the fact that the servants of the East India Company as yet did not undertake their duties as Diwan or Nazim in their own persons. The nominal head of the administration was a Deputy Naib or Nawab (the words are practically identical), whom the Nawab bound himself to appoint with their sanction. A similar Deputy was appointed for Bihar. The whole administration was for many years conducted almost entirely through native agency, though in 1769 English supervisors (afterwards called collectors) were appointed to control the native revenue officers. But according to the testimony of Kaye, they only 'made confusion more confounded and corruption more corrupt'. Such was Clive's famous 'dual system'. It was easy even at that date to point out its defects. The unfortunate divorce of power from responsibility soon caused a recrudescence of the old abuses. The policy indeed can only merit approval in so far as it led up to the more open assumption of responsibility by the Company under Warren Hastings and Lord Cornwallis. But Clive could not afford to indulge in counsels of perfection; he had to deal with actualities. He admitted that the Nawab had only 'the name and shadow of authority', yet 'this name . . . this shadow it is indispensably necessary that we should venerate'. As Verelst—an acute observer—noted, it was almost impossible at first to have taken over the full management, because of the limited number of the Company's servants and their ignorance of the task of administration. There was finally the consideration that openly to have assumed the government of Bengal would have caused a breach with other European powers, and Clive was supported in this by the almost universal opinion of the statesmen of his day.

So much for the internal administration. Clive had next to deal with the foreign relations. It was expected, when he left England, that he would be called upon to conclude the war raging between the Company and Mir Kasim. But he found the work of conquest completed by the victories of Adams and Munro, and it is probable enough, as was hinted at the time, that he felt a little natural disappointment when he discovered nothing to do in the field. There was, however, abundance to satisfy the most insatiable diplomatist. The whole political system of northern India was in the melting-pot. The Mughal Emperor and his chief minister were in the Company's power and suppliants for their bounty. Oudh lay defenceless before British armies. Clive determined to confine the territorial influence of the Company to Bengal, Bihar, and Orissa; to restore his forfeited dominions to the ruler of Oudh; to recognize the title and, as far as possible, support the power of Shah Alam. Shuja-ud-daula was called upon to pay fifty lakhs of rupees as a war indemnity, and was reinstated in his possessions with the exception of the districts of Kora and Allahabad. A defensive alliance was concluded whereby the Company engaged to provide him with troops for the defence of his frontiers if he needed them and consented to furnish the cost of maintenance. The settlement with Oudh was destined to be the most lasting of Clive's political acts, and it remained in the condition of a 'buffer' state till its annexation by Lord Dalhousie on the eve of the Mutiny.

It was necessary next to deal with the fugitive Emperor, Shah Alam, who with his high claims and feeble resources presented a political problem of a peculiarly delicate and embarrassing nature. Clive made over to him the districts of Kora and Allahabad which had been withheld from the Nawab of Oudh, for the support of his imperial dignity, together with an annual subsidy of twenty-six lakhs. He also obtained from the Emperor the reversion of his *jagir* to the Company, when his own ten years' enjoyment of its revenues should be terminated.

The settlement with the Emperor was an adroit compromise and easily laid itself open to attack from political theorists. Clive was at once accused of being quixotically generous to a political fugitive and of having treated cavalierly a monarch in distress. Men were found (of whom Eyre Coote was one) to advocate a British march to Delhi and the conquest of all India in the name of Shah Alam. But Clive, though he recognized that 'It is scarcely hyperbole to say that to-morrow the whole Mughal Empire is in our power', was not to be dazzled by these brilliant prospects. It was a great step in advance to extend British sway over the three provinces of Bengal, Bihar, and Orissa, and even so he begged the Court 'not to be staggered at the Magnitude of their possessions'. He knew as well as any one that, from a purely military point of view, there was nothing to stop British troops from advancing on Delhi; but he was a statesman as well as a soldier, and deliberately recorded his opinion that 'to go further . . . is a scheme so extravagantly ambitious and absurd that no governor and council in their senses can even adopt it unless the whole scheme of the Company's interest be first entirely new modelled'. How right was Clive's judgement was proved by the fact that during the next twenty years the frontier of British dominions was only defended with difficulty from external enemies. The Maratha onset was repelled, but had the British lines been thrown further forward, it is possible that in the troublous times ahead they could not have been held.

Clive left India January 1767, shattered in health and spirits. He had carried considerable reforms, though the partiality of biographers has sometimes exaggerated them. The Company's civil service was not thoroughly purified till the time of Cornwallis, but Clive had done more than any one man at the time could have hoped to accomplish. He had made many enemies, who returned to England vowing vengeance against him. They effected an alliance with a party whose motives were far more worthy of respect—men genuinely desirous that a stricter control should be established in financial matters over the Company's servants. A feeling of alarm was springing up at home at the temptations of the East and the fatal facility with which great fortunes were acquired. 'Those men', says a contemporary writer in 1772, 'must have more than a moderate share of virtue, who, considering the universal veneration in this country paid to men of wealth, will return with a moderate fortune after being several years entrusted with the government of India',[1] and two years before, Lord Chatham from his place in Parliament declared, 'For some years past there has been an influx of wealth into this country, which has been attended with many fatal consequences, because it has not been the regular natural produce of labour and industry. The riches of

[1] *Considerations on a pamphlet entitled Thoughts on our Acquisitions in the East Indies*, 1772.

Asia have been poured in upon us, and have brought with them not only Asiatic luxury but, I fear, Asiatic principles of government. Without connexions, without any natural interest in the soil, the importers of foreign gold have forced their way into Parliament by such a torrent of corruption as no private hereditary fortune could resist'.[1] In 1772 it became apparent that Clive's measures had not availed to ward off a serious economic crisis, and Parliament found that the Company was in danger of insolvency, unless the Treasury or the Bank came to its aid. This was the one unpardonable sin. 'If . . . sovereignty and law are not separated from trade', said Burgoyne, the leader of the Company's critics, 'India and Great Britain will be sunk and overwhelmed, never to rise again'.[2] In that year a Select Committee of thirty-one members and a Secret Committee of thirteen inquired into Indian affairs. The first *Reports* of the former dealt with the revolutions in Bengal, 1757–60, the presents granted to the Company's servants, and Clive's *jagir*. It is usually said by Clive's biographers that these Committees were inspired solely by animus against him, and Clive himself indignantly declared that they questioned him as though he were a sheep-stealer; but there is little evidence of any unnecessary bias in the *Reports* themselves, and they are a valuable storehouse of facts for the history of the East India Company. It was inevitable that Clive should be the chief person examined, for he had played the predominant part during those years on the Indian stage; and it was inevitable also, though most unfortunate, that his earlier acts in Bengal, the deception of Aminchand and the taking of presents, should be severely criticized. In the meantime, it is true, Clive had performed great services, and stemmed the tide of corruption in Bengal; but this was almost forgotten for the moment

[1] Chatham's speech, Jan. 22, 1770, Hansard.

[2] *The Parliamentary History of England*, vol. xvii, p. 458.

in the excitement caused by the revelations of the two Committees.

On May 10, 1773, Colonel Burgoyne moved three resolutions of importance: '(1) That all acquisitions made under the influence of a military force or by treaty with foreign princes do of right belong to the state. (2) That to appropriate acquisitions so made to the private emolument of persons intrusted with any civil or military power is illegal. (3) That very great sums of money and other valuable property have been acquired in Bengal from princes and others of that country, by persons intrusted with the civil and military powers of the state; which sums of money and valuable property have been appropriated to the private use of such persons.' These resolutions were carried, as they were almost bound to be, for they merely stated incontrovertible facts. On May 17, Colonel Burgoyne abandoned general and abstract resolutions for a specific attack on Clive. He moved that Clive 'through the influence of the powers with which he was intrusted as a member of the Select Committee and commander-in-chief of the British forces did obtain and possess himself of the sum of £234,000; and that in so doing the said Robert Clive abused the power with which he was intrusted to the evil example of the servants of the public and to the dishonour and detriment of the state'. This resolution as drafted would have blasted Clive's reputation. Brought face to face with his enemies, Clive defended himself passionately and with striking ability. His speech ended with the famous words, 'Before I sit down I have one request to the House, and it is that when they come to decide upon my honour they will not forget their own.'

In the House itself there was a great revulsion of feeling. It was strongly felt that Clive had nobly atoned by his subsequent career for the errors of taste and judgement in 1757. The original motion was discarded. The mere statement that £234,000 had been received was carried, but the words of reflection on Clive's honour were negatived without a division. Finally, after a whole night's debate, at five o'clock in the morning, the famous resolution was carried unanimously, 'That Robert Lord Clive at the same time rendered great and meritorious services to his country.'

But Clive's wounded feelings were only partly salved by this honourable acquittal. He had always been rather melancholic in temperament, and brooding thoughts over the attacks upon his name, together with the agonies of a painful disease, drove him to take his own life on November 2, 1774, in his fiftieth year. Thus in physical misery and with somewhat tarnished fame perished the real founder of British dominion in India. Clive's qualities peculiarly fitted him for the rôle on the Indian stage that he was destined to fill. He had a certain rough-hewn, almost elemental force and a tireless energy which made him a true pioneer of empire. 'He settled great foundations', said Burke; and again in another passage, 'When Lord Clive forded a deep water with an unknown bottom, he left a bridge for his successors over which the lame might hobble and the blind might grope their way.'[1] The note of his character was decision and an iron will. He diagnosed a situation quickly, knew exactly what he wished to attain, and directed his course thither relentlessly. As a soldier he was a great leader of men, but Pitt's famous description of him as a heaven-born general is hardly appropriate. 'There is little trace', says Sir Charles Wilson truly, 'of skilful combination in his plans, and on some occasions he appears to have neglected the most obvious military precautions. To seek the enemy and, on finding him, to attack with headlong valour seems to have been

[1] *Speeches in the Trial of Warren Hastings*, ed. by E. A. Bond, vol. iv, pp. 329, 348.

his guiding principle, and his successes were due rather to his personal intrepidity, and to his power of inspiring large masses of men with confidence, than to studied plans or dexterous manœuvres.'[1] All his contemporaries in India, even when they hated and feared him, seem to have acknowledged his personal force. Early in his career he was led into courses that a strict morality or the standard of a later age would condemn, but Clive, like his great successor, Warren Hastings, was convinced of his own integrity. He never ceased to defend and even claim merit for the actions that were impugned. This aspect of his character is portrayed by Horace Walpole with a characteristic jibe, when he writes of Clive's great speech in his own defence: 'Though Lord Clive was so frank and high-spirited as to confess a whole folio of his Machiavellism, they were so ungenerous as to have a mind to punish him for assassination, forgery, treachery, and plunder, and it makes him very indignant.'[2] In spite of some faults, there is the stamp of grandeur on all Clive's words and actions. His last sad act showed that, though he valued overmuch the material things of this world, they counted as nothing with him in comparison with what he reckoned to be the loss of his honour. His headlong valour on the battlefield, his splendid daring and audacity in a political crisis, his moral courage in facing disaffected and mutinous subordinates, his force and fire in debate, all justify the lofty verdict of Lord Macaulay that our island 'has scarcely ever produced a man more truly great, either in arms or in council'.

[1] *Lord Clive* (English Men of Action Series), p. 57.
[2] *Letters of Horace Walpole*, P. Toynbee, vol. xiii, p. 277.

CHAPTER XV

THE ADMINISTRATION OF WARREN HASTINGS TO THE END OF THE ROHILLA WAR

A PERIOD of five years elapsed between the final departure of Clive from India and the appointment to the governorship of Bengal of Warren Hastings. Two men of mediocre ability, Verelst (1767–9) and Cartier (1770–2), bridged over the interval. Their periods of office were signally uneventful, and only revealed the administrative failure of Clive's scheme for a double government. The puppet Nawab and his officers proved quite unable to repress the private trading and extortion of the Company's servants; many of the abuses which had been temporarily checked by the reforming hand of Clive once more made their appearance. In 1769–70 a terrible famine visited Bengal. It has been estimated that one-third of the population, that is, about ten million souls, perished of starvation and disease, and one-third of the cultivated land became waste. 'The scene of misery that intervened', wrote one of the Company's servants in 1770, 'and still continues, shocks humanity too much to bear description. Certain it is, that in several parts the living have fed on the dead.'[1] Many of the Company's servants were accused, with too much reason, of making large profits by buying up rice and retailing it at high prices. The revenue, as Warren Hastings admitted, was collected with cruel severity; less than five per cent. of the land tax was remitted at the time of greatest distress, and ten per cent. was actually added to it in the

[1] *The Annals of Rural Bengal*, Sir W. W. Hunter, p. 410.

following year. This terrible calamity, 'whose ravages two generations failed to repair',[1] had far-reaching social and economic effects. Many of the farmers of the revenue and the old aristocratic families were ruined. Bengal scarcely began to recover its former prosperity till after the Permanent Settlement of 1793. While the Company's servants made large private fortunes, the profits of the Company itself from this time steadily decreased till, as we shall see, its credit became so impaired that the state was forced to step in and regulate its affairs.

In southern India an era of troubles began. The relations of the Presidency of Madras with Muhammad Ali, the Nawab of the Carnatic, were necessarily very difficult. Indeed, the double government of Madras, though it has attracted less attention, produced perhaps even more discredit and corruption than that of Bengal. Outside the frontiers of the Carnatic, three native powers—Mysore under Haidar Ali, an extremely able and ruthless usurper who had dispossessed the old royal house; the Maratha confederacy; and the Nizam of Hyderabad—were striving for supremacy, and they alternately courted the British power or combined together to threaten its existence. Cool heads and a consistent policy were necessary, if the Presidency were to escape the pitfalls on every side. Unfortunately the Madras Council embarked on a course of war and diplomacy which ended in discredit and disaster. Their position was much weaker than that of Bengal in regard to the native powers. Their nominal ally, the Nizam, only acquiesced in the surrender of the Northern Circars (for which Clive had procured an imperial grant) on promise of a yearly tribute. In 1765 the Council made an alliance with the Nizam, which involved their supporting him against Haidar Ali and the Marathas. The Nizam was, from the

[1] *The Annals of Rural Bengal*, Sir W. W. Hunter, p. 19.

first, intriguing with the enemy, though with extraordinary obstinacy the Madras Council refused to recognize a fact that was plain enough to their officers in the field. The British troops, however, even after the Nizam had openly thrown in his lot with Mysore and the Marathas, proved strong enough, under the leadership of Colonel Smith, to defeat the combined forces at the Pass of Changama and Trinomali in 1767. In spite of these victories, the Presidency, by the treaty of Masulipatam in 1768, concluded a humiliating and ill-advised peace with the Nizam, involving terms that needlessly invited the hostility of Haidar Ali. 'You have brought us into such a labyrinth of difficulties', wrote the Court of Directors, 'that we do not see how we shall be extricated from them.'[1] The Court had just previously stated their considered policy as to their Indian dominions in these words: 'The *Diwani* of Bengal, Bihar, and Orissa, with the possessions we hold in those provinces, are the utmost limits of our views on that side of India: on the Coast, the protection of the Carnatic and the possession of the Circars, free from all engagements to support the Subah of the Deccan, or even with the Circars, preserving only influence enough over any country power who may hold them, to keep the French from settling in them; and on the Bombay side the dependencies thereon, the possessions of Salsette, Bassein, and the castle of Surat. . . . Much has been wrote from you and our servants in Bengal on the necessity of checking the Marathas, which may in some degree be proper; but it is not for the Company to take the part of umpires of Hindustan . . . we wish to see the present Indian powers remain as a check one upon another without our interfering.'[2]

Though the Nizam took no further part in the war,

[1] *Rise and Progress of the British Power in India*, P. Auber, vol. i, p. 233.

[2] *A Comprehensive History of India*, H. Beveridge, vol. ii, p. 261.

hostilities continued with Haidar Ali; and after a lamentable series of blunders on the part of the English, the ruler of Mysore practically dictated peace on his own terms almost under the walls of Madras in 1769. All conquests made by either side were restored, and the British, with criminal folly, undertook to aid the ruler of Mysore if he were attacked by another power. This calamitous clause only plunged them into fresh difficulties. In 1771 a Maratha army invaded Mysore, and Haidar Ali applied for British help: that help was not forthcoming; the Madras Presidency earned at once the bitter animosity of a relentless foe, and incurred the discredit of repudiating their treaty obligations.

The administration of Warren Hastings falls into two unequal divisions—the first from April 13, 1772, to October 19, 1774, when he was Governor of Fort William in Bengal; and the second from October 20, 1774, to February 8, 1785, when he became 'Governor-General of the Presidency of Fort William in Bengal', under the constitution set up by the Regulating Act. The title was a cumbrous one, and the wording of it emphasizes the fact that he was by no means supreme over Madras and Bombay. There was as yet no 'Governor-General of India'.

The career of Warren Hastings has always been, and probably always will be, a subject of controversy. His enemies in his lifetime were fierce, unscrupulous, and relentless. They transcended all reason and decorum in their attacks upon his name and fame. Many of his actions were grotesquely misrepresented, and unworthy motives were freely imputed. Where criticism was permissible, and temperate disapproval would not have been out of place, the wildest invective was indulged in. Hence came a natural reaction. Of late years, the apologists of Hastings have held the field. It may be admitted at once that in most cases the charges of his adversaries have been completely disproved. In some, alleged crimes and misdemeanours have been shown conclusively to be mere errors of judgement, venial and excusable in the difficult position in which Hastings found himself. But the zeal of Hastings's supporters has sometimes outrun their discretion. There remain some few incidents which it is only possible to justify entirely by a rather desperate casuistry. It is the fashion sometimes to speak as though the only censures on Warren Hastings came from Burke, Macaulay, and James Mill; but almost all the older school of Indian historians, Thornton, Marshman, and H. Beveridge, condemn in temperate language some parts of his policy, and in the case of Thornton and Marshman there was assuredly no natural bias against the great Governor-General. Their sympathies were always naturally with the men on the spot, the representatives of the Company in India, rather than with the home government.

In the present work it would be impossible to enter into details of these great controversies. The writer's conclusions have been based on a careful review of the evidence, and when he dissents from the judgement of modern biographers of Hastings it must be understood that he has given their arguments the most careful consideration.

Immediately on his succession Warren Hastings introduced important administrative reforms. The subject is severely technical, and only the barest outlines can be given here. Clive's dual system was now thoroughly discredited, and the Court of Directors decided to 'stand forth as Diwan', i. e. collect the revenues of the provinces of Bengal, Bihar, and Orissa through the agency of their own servants. Hastings, at their orders, removed from office the Deputy Nawabs of Bengal and Bihar. These men were prosecuted for peculations, but were honourably acquitted. Their offices were abolished, a Board of Revenue was established, and the treasury was transferred from Murshidabad to Calcutta. Great gains were at once apparent; for though Hastings, taking advantage of a fresh succession, cut down the Nawab's allowance from 32 to 16 lakhs of rupees, he was able, through economies in details and the abolition of sinecure offices, to hand over to the Company's pensioner a larger net sum. In 1772, in the face of many difficulties, he carried out a quinquennial settlement of the land revenues, and appointed English officials, now first called 'collectors', aided by native assistants, to superintend the districts. It may be admitted that this settlement was only a qualified success, but that was solely due to the inherent difficulties of the problem, and the criticisms passed on Hastings were factious and ungenerous. At the end of five years (1777) annual settlements were substituted, and continued till the Permanent Settlement of Cornwallis. The collectors dispensed civil law, but natives still presided over the criminal courts of the districts. Hastings set up two Courts of Appeal in Calcutta—the *Sadr Diwani Adalat* (supreme civil court), presided over by the Governor-General and two members of Council; and the *Sadr Nizamat Adalat* (supreme criminal court), the president of which was an Indian judge. All these reforms were logical steps to those of a more fundamental nature introduced by Cornwallis; and Hastings, had he been given free scope, would have gone farther than the home authorities, and placed the administration of criminal affairs also in British hands. The changes were carried through with conspicuous ability, and Warren Hastings well and firmly laid (in the words of Sir William Hunter) 'the foundations of the system of civil administration' on which 'the superstructure was raised by Cornwallis'.[1]

Hastings had next to turn his attention to foreign policy. Clive's scheme for protecting the Bengal frontiers, after working well for five years, was in danger of collapsing. The Marathas, recovering from their terrible defeat in 1761 at Panipat, had crossed the Narbada again in 1769, raided through Rajputana and Rohilkhand, and were now threaten-

[1] *The Imperial Gazetteer of India*, vol. ii, p. 486.

ing danger to British territories. They began to intrigue with the puppet Emperor, that 'wretched king of shreds and patches', as Hastings called him, who had been subsisting at Allahabad on the revenues paid to him by the East India Company. The Marathas offered to place the Emperor on the throne of Delhi, and, in spite of the earnest expostulations of the British that he should not entrust himself to the hands of the hereditary rebels against the Mughal throne, he accepted their proposal. Sindhia, in December, 1771, escorted him into his capital. He at once found, as the British had predicted, that he was a mere state prisoner in the hands of his nominal protectors, and he was forced to hand over to the Marathas the districts of Kora and Allahabad, which had been given to him as an act of grace by Clive. It was impossible to imagine a more awkward and critical position for the Governor-General. To permit Maratha hordes to occupy the districts was to surrender the outworks of Bengal to the enemy; to continue paying the Emperor's subsidy was really to replenish their treasury. Both courses were impossible to a practical politician, and yet probably no other was free from legal and technical objections. Hastings adopted a bold policy. He decided to discontinue the tribute to Shah Alam, which as a matter of fact had not been paid since the Bengal famine of 1769–70; by the Treaty of Benares he restored Kora and Allahabad to the ruler of Oudh for fifty lakhs of rupees in addition to a subsidy for the maintenance of a garrison of the Company's troops. For this drastic solution of the difficulty Hastings has been roundly attacked, but he seems to have been abundantly justified. He held that Clive surrendered these districts to the Emperor as living under British protection. The Emperor had forfeited them morally, if not legally, when he parted with them to the Company's potential enemics. There are political situations where ordinary formulae and rules seem hopelessly to break down, and this was one of them. All temperate and responsible opinion has supported Hastings's conduct in a most difficult crisis.

The sale of Kora and Allahabad to the Nawab of Oudh was ratified by the Treaty of Benares, September 1773, and Hastings, in personal interviews with Shuja-ud-daula, was led into the policy which ended in the Rohilla war. The facts are briefly as follows. Rohilkhand was a fertile belt of country with an area of 12,000 square miles and a population of about 6,000,000, skirting the base of the Himalayas to the north-west of Oudh. The bulk of the population were Hindus, but the ruling race were Rohillas and Pathans—Muhammadans coming originally from Afghanistan. The government was a loose and ill-defined confederacy of chiefs, presided over by Hafiz Rahmat Khan, the ablest and strongest of their number. From about the year 1770 the Marathas hung threateningly on the frontiers of Rohilkhand and Oudh. A tortuous scene of intrigue and negotiation followed. The Nawab of Oudh and Hafiz Rahmat Khan at one time meditated a coalition for mutual defence against the Marathas; at another time each ruler contemplated joining the Marathas against the other. The three parties were, as Sir John Strachey says, 'all utterly unscrupulous, and each knew that no trust could be placed in either of the others'.[1] Finally, however, in June 1772, a treaty was concluded between the Rohillas and Oudh, by which it was agreed that, if the Marathas invaded Rohilkhand, the Nawab Wazir should come to the rescue of the invaded country; and if he were successful in obliging the Marathas to retire by peace or war, he should receive a sum of 40 lakhs from the Rohillas. The treaty was signed in the presence of Sir Robert Barker, who witnessed the signatures of the contracting parties. In 1773 the Marathas invaded Rohilkhand; a demonstration was made against them by the Nawab of

[1] *Hastings and the Rohilla War*, Sir John Strachey, p. 49.

Oudh supported by a British contingent, and they retired. Shuja-ud-daula promptly demanded the stipulated sum of 40 lakhs, and Hafiz evaded payment.

At Benares Shuja-ud-daula proposed that the English, in return for a large subsidy, should lend him a brigade to conquer the Rohillas, as a penalty for their breach of the treaty. Hastings was attracted to the proposal, partly from the strategical advantage that would be gained 'by extending the boundary of Oudh to the natural barrier formed by the chain of hills and the Ganges and their junction', partly from the opportunity of replenishing the coffers of the Company in a time of need. But he recognized at this time, at any rate, that there were other objections to the scheme, and he gave a rather reluctant assent, apparently hoping that the need for sending British troops would never arise. However, in January 1774, the Nawab of Oudh demanded the promised aid. A British brigade under Colonel Champion joined him, and their united forces invaded Rohilkhand on April 17. The decisive battle was fought at Miranpur Katra six days later, and Hafiz Rahmat Khan, who had shown considerable strategic skill, was killed fighting bravely. About 20,000 Rohillas were banished from the country, which was incorporated with the dominions of Shuja-ud-daula of Oudh.

Endless controversy has raged round the policy of the Rohilla war. It formed one of the main counts for the attacks on Hastings in Parliament, and it has been severely condemned, not only by Macaulay and Mill, but by most of the older school of Anglo-Indian historians. The case against Hastings was grotesquely exaggerated by the venom of Francis, the eloquence of Burke, the prejudice of Mill, and the over-charged metaphors and similes of Macaulay. Hastings was depicted as an unscrupulous schemer, who had sold the lives and liberties of a free people for filthy lucre, and stood callously by while nameless atrocities were perpetrated. The Rohillas were described as a simple pastoral people, patterns of antique virtue, and their adversary, Shuja-ud-daula, as a monster of depravity and cruelty.

Modern criticism dispenses altogether with this kind of invective. The question of the origin of the Rohilla race is really quite irrelevant to the point at issue. Burke and his followers were mistaken in supposing that they had any long prescriptive right to the territories they ruled. They were a plundering tribe, who had only established their power over the Hindu population of Rohilkhand for about twenty-five years. On the other hand, their claim was quite as good as that of most of the Indian states of the day, who had risen on the ruins of Mughal power. If the war were wicked, it was not less so because the Rohillas had not long established their sovereignty in the country.

But it can certainly be established that the Nawab had a legal and technical case against his enemies for infringing a treaty, which will pass muster. Military operations were probably not attended with any worse excesses than were common in India at this period, though it is perhaps going a little too far to say that the campaign 'had been carried on with an absence of violence and bloodshed and generally with a degree of humanity altogether unusual in Indian warfare'.[1] Though Champion's criticisms of his native allies were coloured by dissatisfaction at his position in regard to them, and jealousy of the booty they acquired, yet he undoubtedly committed himself to the assertions that he had been obliged to shut his eyes 'against a wanton display of violence and oppression, of inhumanity and cruelty', and that 'the whole army were witnesses of scenes that cannot be described'. These positive assertions made at the time must have contained some basis of fact, and we can hardly regard them as completely discredited by the halting statements of Champion himself, made twelve years later at the Parliamentary inquiry, or the evidence of other officers

[1] *Hastings and the Rohilla War*, Sir John Strachey, p. 233.

on the same occasion, who may have had reasons for minimizing the facts. But they were undoubtedly exaggerated, and Macaulay and Mill were, to some extent naturally, misled by them. The question matters the less because it is quite certain that Hastings did his best, by strong and dignified protests, to check any brutalities the moment his attention was called to them, and there is no truth at all in the insinuation that he connived at them.

From all the graver charges, then, Hastings may be fully acquitted; but it does not really follow, as many of his modern defenders seem to suppose, that his policy was above reasonable criticism any more than that of other statesmen, however supremely able they might be. And first of all, exception may, perhaps, be taken to it even from the point of view of expediency. We have seen that the Governor-General himself, at the time of the Treaty of Benares, seriously doubted the wisdom of acceding to the Nawab Wazir's request for aid. He felt the time was unfavourable, since 'the Company at home was exposed to popular clamour, all its measures liable to be canvassed in Parliament, their charter drawing to a close, and His Majesty's Ministers unquestionably ready to take advantage of every unfavourable circumstance in the negotiations for its renewal'.[1] The reasons for letting the whole business alone could hardly have been better stated. The best course probably would have been to tell the Nawab Wazir that he must settle his differences with the Rohillas as he best could. Hastings afterwards declared that the Company were bound to intervene as having guaranteed the treaty; but this was an afterthought, and Sir Robert Barker had merely witnessed the signatures of both sides. To suggest that his doing so committed the Company to seeing that the treaty was fulfilled was disingenuous. Hastings showed throughout the early stages of the business a vacillation that was

[1] *Hastings and the Rohilla War*, Sir John Strachey, p. 121.

unusual with him, and he failed to handle the situation with his usual firmness. To give a reluctant assent in a matter of such importance, with the lame half hope, half belief, that the occasion contemplated would never arise, is not impressive as statesmanship. There were other objections to the policy. It obviously broke the rule of the Directors against engaging in Indian warfare, and it is difficult to dissent from the judgement of Sir Alfred Lyall that an unfortunate precedent was created when British troops were lent to be employed against a people with whom the Company had no quarrel. Though the Hindus were not driven out of the country with the Rohillas, they can hardly have gained by the change of masters. The rule of Hafiz Rahmat had been mild and popular; we have Sir John Strachey's high authority for the statement that, under his strong personal control, the Hindu population was treated with greater consideration and received better protection than in any of the neighbouring provinces, with one exception.[1] The régime of Shuja-ud-daula proved weak and bad, and we know that under his successor Rohilkhand was shamefully misgoverned. The utmost, however, that can fairly be said against Hastings from the moral aspect, and it is not a very serious charge, is that his view of the business was, as Sir John Strachey admits, 'somewhat cynical', and that in his dispatches and minutes the financial advantages of the agreement with the Nawab appear unduly prominent.[2]

[1] *Hastings and the Rohilla War*, Sir John Strachey, p. 30.
[2] Ibid., pp. 113, 263.

CHAPTER XVI

WARREN HASTINGS. THE REGULATING ACT AND THE TRIAL OF NANDKUMAR

THE Rohilla war was the last important event of Hastings's first period of administration. His powers were considerably modified by the Regulating Act of Lord North, and it is necessary for a moment to retrace our steps, and examine the causes responsible for that measure.

Through the latter half of the eighteenth century we may trace the gradual growth of a feeling that the nation itself, through Parliament, rather than through a private trading company, however powerful and wealthy, must ultimately be responsible for British rule in India. Clive had himself, in 1759, suggested in a letter to Pitt that 'so large a sovereignty' as the *diwani* of Bengal, and the power that went with it, 'may possibly be an object too extensive for a mercantile company: and it is to be feared that they are not of themselves able, without the nation's assistance, to maintain so wide a dominion'. He went on to suggest that if the state were to take over Bengal, Indian revenues might go towards easing the burden of English taxpayers at home. But Pitt was not prepared at the moment to raise so serious a question, and gave an evasive reply, declaring that the affair was 'of a very nice nature'. During the fifteen years that followed the battle of Plassey, immense wealth was brought back from India by retired servants of the East India Company, who bought estates and rotten boroughs, and expected to be received on terms of social equality with the old landed aristocracy. The 'Nabobs', with their orientalized ways and ostentatious expenditure, figure largely in the caricature and satire of the age.

Two important events sprang from their incursion: politicians conceived the idea of converting to the Exchequer some portion of this wealth, and the Proprietors of East India stock clamoured that a greater share of the profits of the trade should come to them, and less be intercepted by their servants in the East. After the news reached England of the acquisition of the *Diwani*, the Proprietors could no longer be restrained, and in spite of the opposition of the Court of Directors, who knew their real position was not as prosperous as it appeared, they raised the dividends on their stock in 1766 from six to ten per cent., and the next year to twelve and a half. From 1766 Parliament began to take —from the point of view of the Directors—an embarrassing interest in Indian affairs; and an active little band of members, prominent amongst whom were Beckford, Barré, and Nugent, constantly urged that the Company's Indian possessions belonged of right to the Crown, though, as was contended at the time, the Company had legally no such 'possessions', being technically a mere Zamindar for Shah Alam, the Mughal Emperor. The ministry, however, clearly shrank from any heroic solution of this problem, and avoided raising it in its full sense. They were quite ready to make so much use of the agitation as that a part of the Company's alleged wealth might be diverted to the depleted coffers of the state. But some form of compromise was the course that most commended itself to them. Accordingly Parliament, in 1767, declined to pass any sweeping measure, though it interfered openly and drastically in the affairs of the Company. It modified their internal constitution, limited the rate of dividend to be declared, and obliged them to pay to the Exchequer an annual sum of £400,000, in return for which they were allowed to retain their territorial acquisitions and revenues. This originally held good for only two years, but subsequent Acts extended the period till 1772. One measure for the relief of the Company is interesting, not for its intrinsic importance, but for the momentous and unforeseen consequences that followed it. The Company's teas exported to Ireland and the North American colonies were entitled to draw back the whole duty. It was a consignment of this tea that the Boston 'rebels', in 1773, threw into the sea. Thus curiously for a moment were the destinies of England's oversea dominions in two hemispheres linked together.

Neither the Court of Directors nor Parliament was yet satisfied, and in 1769 the former sent out three of their old servants, Vansittart, Colonel Forde, and Scrafton, as 'supervisors', with instructions to investigate every branch of the administration in India, and full powers to suspend, if necessary, even the Presidents and Councils. But this commission, which might have revolutionized the Company's government in the East, met with a tragic fate. The ship in which they sailed was never heard of again after leaving the Cape of Good Hope. Meanwhile, the hostile interest of the nation in the affairs of the Company had not diminished. A great outcry was raised when, after loans from the Bank had failed to buoy up their sinking credit, the Directors were forced to inform Lord North in 1772 that, unless they could obtain a loan of one million pounds from the state, they could not carry on their business. In that year, both a Select and a Secret Parliamentary Committee, of thirty-one and thirteen members respectively, were appointed, and began to publish those exhaustive reports which led incidentally to the attacks on Lord Clive already described. These reports showed that within nine years, that is, from 1757 to 1766, £2,169,665 had been distributed by natives of Bengal as presents to the Company's servants; and this sum did not include Clive's *jagir*, which capitalized would have represented a further sum of £600,000. Besides this,

£3,770,833 had been paid in compensation for losses incurred.[1] The reports of the two committees drove home the conviction that the independence of the Company must yield to the supremacy of Parliament.

Two Acts were passed in 1773, one of which granted a state loan to the Company, limited their dividends, and obliged them to submit their accounts to the Treasury; the second and more important, known as the Regulating Act, gave the Company a new constitution. The Directors were henceforth to be elected for four years, and one-fourth of their number were to retire every year, remaining at least one year out of office. There was to be a Governor-General of Bengal, assisted and controlled by four Councillors (for the voice of the majority was to bind the whole), the Governor-General being merely allowed a casting vote when there was an equal division of opinion. The Governor-General and Council were to have power to superintend and check the subordinate presidencies in their relations with native powers. The Directors were to lay before the Treasury all correspondence from India dealing with the revenues; and before a Secretary of State everything dealing with civil or military affairs and government. The first Governor-General and Councillors, Warren Hastings, Lieutenant-General Clavering, Monson, Barwell, and Philip Francis, were named in the Act. They were to hold office for five years, and future appointments were to be made by the Company. A Supreme Court of Judicature was set up at Calcutta, consisting of a Chief Justice (Sir Elijah Impey) and three puisne judges. Liberal salaries were granted, £25,000 to the Governor-General, £10,000 to each Councillor, and £8,000 to the Chief Justice.

The Regulating Act was a half-measure, and disastrously vague in many points. The titular authority of the Nawab of Bengal was left by implication intact, and no assertion

[1] *Reports of the House of Commons*, vol. iii, pp. 311–12.

was made of the sovereignty of the Crown or Company in India. The Council had the power to bring about a deadlock in the executive by overruling the Governor-General. The control of the supreme government at Calcutta over the other presidencies only applied to their powers of making war on, or concluding peace with, Indian states, and was qualified by the provision that, in the event of having received special orders from home or in the case of urgent necessity (of which they themselves could be the only judges) the subordinate governments could act without leave being first obtained from Bengal. Finally, and this was destined to have calamitous consequences, neither the field of jurisdiction of the Supreme Court nor the law it had to administer, nor its relations to the Council, were defined with sufficient accuracy. Some of the particular appointments made by Parliament were very unfortunate. Francis (identified by general consent with the author of the letters of Junius) and Clavering had no Indian experience, and they seem to have sailed for India with the idea deeply rooted in their minds that the government was corrupt and tyrannous. Francis, moreover, believed himself to be 'on the road to the governorship of Bengal', which he described as 'the first situation in the world attainable by a subject'.

The new Councillors (with the exception of Barwell, who was resident in India) arrived on October 19, 1774. The judges had landed two days before, and the new régime was formally inaugurated on the 20th. There ensued a six years' struggle which is probably unique in the history of administration. The Councillors began badly by quarrelling with the Governor-General on some petty point of ceremonial in his reception of them, and they proceeded to make an acrimonious attack on his whole policy and method of government. Any other man but Hastings would have been hounded from office. In the course of the next few years he was often out-voted, and, though nominally at the head of the administration, had frequently to carry out a policy of which he disapproved. It was no ordinary opposition that he had to meet, for Francis was no ordinary man. Facing his chief across the council table, he criticized with a plausible, subtle, and vindictive ingenuity almost everything the latter suggested. Hastings could not rely upon support at home; he was ultimately censured by the Directors, and his recall more than once demanded by Resolutions of Parliament. There is something almost superhuman in the way he faced his enemies. From 1774 to 1776 he was generally overruled. Monson died in September 1776, and by the use of his casting vote Hastings regained control in the Council. In 1777, however, his rather ambiguous and ill-advised instructions to an agent in London resulted in the latter tendering the Governor-General's resignation. But Hastings, declaring his agent had exceeded his powers, refused to make way for Clavering; the Supreme Court upheld his decision, though they immediately afterwards rightly prevented a very ill-judged and high-handed attempt on his part to declare that Clavering had, by his action in the matter, forfeited his offices of Councillor and Commander-in-Chief. In 1777 Clavering also died, and in 1780 Hastings disabled Francis in a duel. His great enemy left India later in the same year. 'My antagonists', he wrote triumphantly, 'sickened, died, and fled', and from that time onward his position was established. He had charge of the government of India at the most critical and perilous period of British Indian history, but the struggle with his Council alone would have exhausted the powers of any but a very strong man. He was enveloped, as he said himself, in an atmosphere of 'dark allusions, mysterious insinuations, bitter invective, and ironical reflections'.

The first action of the new Councillors was to condemn

the Rohilla war. They recalled Middleton, the British Resident at Lucknow, and made a most unreasonable demand that the whole of his correspondence with the Governor-General, part of which was confidential, should be submitted to their inspection. They ordered Colonel Champion to make a peremptory demand on the Nawab of Oudh for the forty lakhs he had promised to the Company for the expulsion of the Marathas. They 'denounced', it has been said with truth, 'the Rohilla war as an abomination, and yet their great anxiety now was to pocket the wages of it'.[1] In reply to all this, Hastings with excellent reason contended that, whatever the rights of the case, the Rohilla affair belonged to the past administration and was on the point of being concluded, and therefore that the new government might have been satisfied with recording their disapproval of the enterprise. The real value of the new Councillors' sympathy with the native powers was seen by their treatment of Oudh. The Nawab Wazir died in January 1775, and they seized the occasion to force upon his successor a new treaty, increasing the subsidies to be paid by him for the use of British troops, and obliging him to surrender to the Company the sovereignty of the district of Benares. Hastings eloquently exposed the injustice and impolicy of this proceeding, in vain pointing out that it was a complete reversal of the Company's traditional friendship with Oudh.

The whole position of Hastings was undermined in the public eye by the procedure of the Council, and many of his enemies in Calcutta thought they saw an opportunity to bring about his ruin. Several charges of defalcations were produced against him by native informers, and in March 1775 Raja Nandkumar (Nuncomar), a Brahman of high rank, laid a letter before the Council charging him with having received, amongst other bribes, one of three and a

[1] *A Comprehensive History of India*, H. Beveridge, vol. ii, p. 365.

half lakhs of rupees from the widow of the old Nawab, Mir Jafar. The accusation was welcomed with indecent haste by Francis, Monson, and Clavering, who, without waiting for proof, recorded their opinion that 'there is no species of peculation from which the Governor-General has thought it reasonable to abstain'. Hastings absolutely declined to be arraigned at the Council board by 'so notoriously infamous' a man as Nandkumar. When the majority persisted in summoning the accuser, the Governor-General refused to meet him, declared the Council dissolved, and left the room. It has been pointed out that Hastings's case would have stood better had he courted inquiry and openly denied the truth of the accusation against him, which he never seems to have done. But he had good cause to object to the high-handed and insulting attitude of his colleagues on the Council, and he may have thought it would be difficult to prove his innocence before so openly prejudiced a court. There was further the fact that Hastings actually had received 150,000 rupees from the princess as entertainment money, when he visited Murshidabad, 'a transaction', as his strenuous defender Sir James Stephen[1] admits, 'which, if not positively illegal, was at least questionable', and which certainly ran counter to all the Company's instructions as to the acceptance of presents.

On the withdrawal of Hastings, the majority of the Council resolved that the sums in question had been received by the Governor-General, and required him to repay the amount into the Company's treasury. Hastings treated this resolution with disdain, and a few days later lodged a charge of conspiracy against Nandkumar and his accomplices. While this matter was still pending, Nandkumar himself was suddenly arrested, at the instance of a Calcutta merchant, on a charge of forgery unconnected with either

[1] *The Story of Nuncomar and the Impeachment of Sir Elijah Impey*, Sir J. F. Stephen, vol. i, p. 72.

his insinuations against Hastings or the latter's action for conspiracy. He was put on his trial before the Supreme Court, condemned to death, and executed. The charges against Hastings were dropped, and never proceeded with.

Men will probably never agree as to the meaning of this somewhat mysterious sequence of events, for the key to them lies in the ambiguous and doubtful region of secret motives and desires. The incident created an extraordinary impression, and it was naturally believed for a long time that Nandkumar had paid the penalty of death, nominally for forgery, but really for having dared to accuse the Governor-General. The matter, however, is one rather of biographical than of historical interest, and can only be very briefly dealt with here. Modern research regards the suggestion that Hastings and Impey deliberately schemed together to remove Nandkumar by a judicial murder as baseless.[1] There is certainly, as Pitt saw, not a vestige of solid proof for it. There are indeed many reasons against it. Hastings and Impey by no means always saw eye to eye with one another, as their quarrel in regard to the respective jurisdictions of the Supreme Court and the Council proved. At the trial Impey was only one of four judges, and therefore, unless the other three were either in the conspiracy or so hopelessly incompetent that they followed the Chief Justice blindly, the insinuation falls to the ground. The charge of forgery had originated in a natural way from long-standing litigation months before Nandkumar accused the Governor-General, and in the words of an authority, by no means excessively favourable to Hastings, 'That charge would, in the natural course of law, have been made at the

[1] Sir James Stephen's *Story of Nuncomar and Impey*, though a very able defence, is not quite the last word on the controversy that it is sometimes represented to be, as Sir Alfred Lyall—himself very favourable to Hastings—recognized. Those who wish to pursue the matter further should also read *The Trial of Maharaja Nanda Kumar*, by Mr. H. Beveridge.

very time when it was made, though Nandkumar had never become a willing tool in the hands of Messrs. Clavering, Monson, and Francis.'[1] Sir James Stephen claims to show that Impey tried the case fairly and patiently; that in his summing up he gave full weight to anything that could tell in favour of the prisoner; and that, though the evidence was not overwhelming, the verdict cannot be said to have gone against it. On the other hand, it was certainly unfortunate that the judges themselves cross-examined, and that somewhat severely, the prisoner's witnesses, on the alleged ground that counsel for the prosecution was incompetent, and that Sir Elijah Impey in his summing up laid it down that, if Nandkumar's defence was not believed, it must prove fatal to him. Impey no doubt spoke in good faith, but more Indian experience would have taught him that in the East, as Sir James Stephen admits, a good case is often bolstered up by perjury.

But even if we hold it established that there was no judicial murder, there was certainly something equivalent to a miscarriage of justice. For that, however, the Supreme Court in the first instance, and Hastings's opponents on the Council subsequently, were mainly responsible. However guilty Nandkumar may have been, the punishment of death was far too severe, and fine or imprisonment, as Sir James Stephen allows, would have been the appropriate penalty. It is very doubtful whether the Supreme Court had any jurisdiction over natives, and there is practically no doubt at all (though the point has been contested) that the English law making forgery a capital crime was not operative in India till many years after Nandkumar's alleged forgery had been committed.[2] Apart from all this, the Supreme Court had

[1] *A Comprehensive History of India*, H. Beveridge, vol. ii, p. 378.

[2] The judges no doubt acted in good faith, but Sir James Stephen admits that their view was 'opposed to an opinion which is so firmly established in India, and has been so often acted upon by the courts and the legislature that it can hardly be disputed'. See his *The Story of Nuncomar*, vol. ii, pp. 27–34. Also H. Beveridge, *The Trial of Maharaja Nanda Kumar*, pp. 210–12.

authority 'to reprieve and suspend the execution of any capital sentence, whenever there shall appear in their judgement a proper occasion for mercy'. Since the natives universally regarded forgery as a mere misdemeanour, this was just the occasion for the exercise of such discretionary power. But though the judges made an error of judgement and callously upheld the extreme letter of the law, it is unnecessary to impute to them corrupt motives. They appear to have been exceedingly jealous of their rights and privileges. They had not been long enough in India to adapt their legal theories to eastern ideas, and their attitude in this case is only consonant with their conduct throughout, which was one ill-judged attempt to apply the methods of English courts to the whole native population of Bengal. Impey especially seems to have held that a severe example was necessary to check the frequent occurrence of crimes of forgery in Bengal: in view of Nandkumar's widespread influence and great wealth he considered that any remission of his sentence would have suggested to the native mind that the Supreme Court had been corrupted. 'I had', he said, 'the dignity, integrity, independence, and utility of that court to maintain.'

One of the most difficult things to understand about this sinister business is why the majority of the Council, at any rate, did not petition the Supreme Court in Nandkumar's favour. Hastings perhaps could hardly have been expected to intercede for his adversary, though his admirers could wish he had shown such a noble magnanimity.[1] But Francis, Clavering, and Monson had every apparent reason, as Sir James Stephen shows, to petition for a reprieve on the ground that Nandkumar's execution would prevent the charges against Hastings from being properly investigated,

[1] It should be noted that Mr. H. Beveridge, in *The Trial of Maharaja Nanda Kumar*, claims to have shown (and gives some evidence for his contention) that a private secretary and dependent of Hastings exerted himself to prevent a respite being granted to the condemned man.

and that the execution of an accuser of the Governor-General might well be misconstrued by the Indian population. They refused to have anything to do with such a petition, and Nandkumar went to his doom without a protest from them. Almost the only theory that will explain their conduct is that they had ceased themselves to believe in his charges, and were relieved to see him put out of the way. Francis may even have thought that Nandkumar dead would be a more potent weapon against the Governor-General than Nandkumar living, and may have foreseen the use that might afterwards be made of his execution. At the time he himself described as 'wholly unsupported and libellous' the suggestion made in a final petition of Nandkumar that there was a conspiracy between the judges and the Governor-General, though a few weeks afterwards we find him adopting the suggestion and giving it his approval.

CHAPTER XVII

WARREN HASTINGS. WARS IN WESTERN AND SOUTHERN INDIA

WE must now turn from Bengal to western and southern India. Over Bombay and Madras the Regulating Act, as we have seen, had given the Bengal government a control that was none too definite. The subordinate Presidencies at this time, especially Madras, were administered by very incapable men, and their history is complicated and confused. Broadly speaking, it may be said that they succeeded in embroiling themselves in wars with almost all the native powers of southern and central India, till in 178c the foundations of British rule were shaken to their base The control of Hastings over the policy of Bombay and Madras at the beginning was almost non-existent, for either he could not impose his will upon them, or he was outvoted in his own Council; and thus it was often the opinions of the recalcitrant triumvirate, Francis, Monson, and Clavering, rather than those of the Governor-General, that were ultimately forced upon the provincial governments. Hastings was frequently left the dismal choice between wresting what success he could from a plan of action of which he had disapproved, or disowning and cashiering his subordinates. He cannot fairly, except perhaps in one instance, be blamed for the welter of 'unjust and rather disreputable wars', bad diplomacy, and general mismanagement which made up the history of the Deccan under his governor-generalship. As briefly as possible the course of events must now be summarized. In March 1775 the Bombay authorities, ignoring the claim of the Regulating Act in regard to the inter-relations of the supreme and subordinate governments, pledged themselves by the Treaty of Surat to support a pretender to the Peshwaship in return for the cession to themselves of Bassein and the island of Salsette, which they had already, by a high-handed action, occupied. They announced the *fait accompli* to their superiors at Bengal. The Governor-General concurred with his Council in stigmatizing their proceedings as 'impolitic, dangerous, unauthorized, and unjust', but there his agreement with the majority at his Council board ended. Since the Bombay administration had already commenced hostilities and won some success, though at a heavy cost, he argued that they must be supported in continuing the war till peace could be made on advantageous terms. But he was overruled, and Colonel Upton was sent direct from Calcutta to Poona to conclude the Treaty of Purandhar in March 1776, by which the English abandoned the cause of Raghunath Rao the Pretender, usually known as Raghoba, on condition of being allowed to retain Salsette. The Court of Directors unexpectedly and rather inconsistently—in view of their decided opinion against entanglements with native powers—disapproved of this treaty, and in 1778 Hastings with their full consent renewed the alliance with Raghoba. On this occasion Francis seems decidedly to have been for once on the right, and Hastings and the Court on the wrong, side. The able minutes and protests of the former repay the most careful study. But Hastings by the exercise of his casting vote committed himself and the Company to a long and costly war against the Maratha confederacy, with whom in time, as we shall see, all the powerful native states of southern India became allied. It would be difficult to exaggerate the sinister effect of this unhappy decision upon the career of Hastings. Owing to this war and its complement, the war with Haidar Ali, added to it by the folly of the Madras government, his resources were exhausted and he was driven to those questionable expedients for raising money which brought about his impeachment. The most cogent argument put forward by Hastings for a renewal of hostilities was the arrival at Poona in 1777 of a French agent, and the consequent fear of 'a repetition of the scene of wars and intrigues formerly acted on the coast of Coromandel'. This man, however, proved to be an impostor unauthorized by the French government. It was during the debates on the Maratha war that news arrived in India of the great disaster to British arms in North America—Burgoyne's surrender to General Gates at Saratoga (1777). Francis made the news an argument against 'hazarding offensive operations'. Hastings with his usual indomitable spirit replied: 'I hope that our affairs in America are not in the desperate situation in which they are described to be; but . . . if it be really true that the British arms and influence have suffered so severe a check in the western world, it is the more incumbent upon those who are charged with the interest of Great Britain in the East to exert themselves for the retrieval of the national loss.'[1]

We may here conclude the tale of events as they concerned western India. An expedition from Bombay, wretchedly led, concluded the disastrous convention of Wargaon in January 1779 (afterwards disowned by the civil authorities), by which all territorial possessions obtained by Bombay since 1773 were given up. Such successes as were gained by British arms were due to what his enemies styled 'the frantic military exploits' of the Governor-General. Goddard completed a brilliant march across India from the Jumna, took Ahmadabad, and, having crossed the Narbada, captured Bassein in 1780; while in the same year

[1] *Selections from the Letters, Despatches and other State Papers in the Foreign Department of the Government of India, 1772–1785*, G. W. Forrest, vol. ii, p. 402.

Popham caused a thrill throughout India by his escalade of Gwalior, a fortress universally deemed impregnable. But subsequent operations were less successful; Goddard made the one mistake of his career in April 1781 in a premature advance on Poona, and Hastings concluded a separate peace with Sindhia by skilful diplomacy, detached the Raja of Berar from the Maratha confederacy, and was glad to conclude the Treaty of Salbai in May 1782, by which all territory west of the Jumna was restored to Sindhia, Raghoba pensioned off by the Peshwa, and the *status quo* before the war re-established at Bombay. Since the British only retained Salsette—the exact position at the Treaty of Purandhar—the material gains of a costly and harassing four years' war were not, it must be confessed, very impressive. But the treaty at least secured peace with the Maratha powers for twenty years.

The Presidency of Madras during the decade 1770-80 was passing through a dismal epoch in its history. Its relation to Muhammad Ali, the titular Nawab of the Carnatic, in some way resembled that of Calcutta to the Subadar of Bengal. Muhammad depended just as much on British bayonets as his northern counterpart, but since Madras did not possess anything equivalent to the *Diwani* giving them executive and financial control over the Carnatic, a perilous amount of responsibility was left in the hands of their nominal suzerain. In 1770 and 1771 the British government tried the experiment of maintaining at his court, as plenipotentiaries independent of the Company, Sir John Lindsay and Sir Robert Harland, but the result was not successful and hopelessly compromised the Company with the Nawab. In 1773, just before Hastings conquered Rohilkhand for the Nawab of Oudh, the Madras authorities subdued and deposed the Raja of Tanjore, with whom they had no quarrel, in order to oblige Muhammad Ali. The latter demoralized and corrupted the whole administration of the Presidency by his collusive financial dealings with the notorious Paul Benfield and other junior servants of the Company. From Muhammad Ali's transactions with these men sprang the huge scandal known as the Nawab of Arcot's debts. The historian Thornton hardly speaks too strongly when he says, 'the moral atmosphere of Madras appears at this time to have been pestilential'.[1] Within seven years two governors were dismissed from office by the Court of Directors and a third suspended by the Governor-General; while Lord Pigot, who had been sent out to restore the Raja of Tanjore, was actually deposed and imprisoned by his subordinates for the necessary though rather tactless opposition he had made to their dishonest dealings. The unhappy man died in prison in 1777, Hastings showing a strange lack of sympathy in his case, though, as Sir Alfred Lyall notes, he might have been expected to exhibit some fellow-feeling towards a governor in difficulties with his council. These open scandals and constant changes in the government naturally resulted in an inconsistent and chaotic policy which soon entangled the Presidency in the war already raging on the western side of India. The Nizam had long looked with growing disfavour on our alliance with Raghoba, but he made no movement till the Madras government tactlessly offended him. He then built up a terrible confederacy of practically all the native states whose power was worth anything. Mysore, Hyderabad, and Poona, supported by all the Maratha chieftains except the Gaikwar of Baroda, joined together for one desperate attack upon British rule in India. In July 1780 Haidar Ali poured his swarms of horsemen through the pass of Changama down upon the plains of the Carnatic, till the citizens of Madras could see from their walls the smoke of burning villages rolling skywards.

[1] *History of the British Empire in India*, vol. ii, p. 247.

The government of Madras had shown an absolute want of forethought and preparation in meeting this terrible invasion, thus described by Burke in a famous passage: 'He (Haidar Ali) became at length so confident of his force, so collected in his might, that he made no secret whatsoever of his dreadful resolution. . . . He drew from every quarter whatsoever a savage ferocity could add to his new rudiments in the art of destruction; and compounding all the materials of fury, havoc, and desolation into one black cloud, he hung for a while on the declivities of the mountains. Whilst the authors of all these evils were idly and stupidly gazing on this menacing meteor, which blackened all their horizon, it suddenly burst, and poured down the whole of its contents upon the plains of the Carnatic. Then ensued a scene of woe, the like of which no eye had seen, no heart conceived, and which no tongue can adequately tell. All the horrors of war before known or heard of were mercy to that new havoc. A storm of universal fire blasted every field, consumed every house, destroyed every temple. The miserable inhabitants fleeing from their flaming villages, in part were slaughtered; others, without regard to sex, to age, to the respect of rank, or sacredness of function—fathers torn from children, husbands from wives—enveloped in a whirlwind of cavalry, and amidst the goading spears of drivers, and the trampling of pursuing horses, were swept into captivity in an unknown and hostile land. Those who were able to evade this tempest, fled to the walled cities; but escaping from fire, sword, and exile they fell into the jaws of famine.' Overcharged by the orator's genius as this purple passage undoubtedly is, the position was serious enough. An English brigade under Baillie was surrounded and cut up after a gallant resistance. Munro, the victor of Baxar, smirched his reputation by flinging his artillery into the tank at Conjeveram, and retreating in panic to Madras, where he was hooted in the streets by the indignant inhabitants. In October 1780 the capital of the Carnatic, Arcot, fell before Haidar Ali.

It is well to pause for a moment at this date, 1780–1, and examine the position as Hastings had to face it—in his own words, a 'war either actual or impending in every quarter and with every power in Hindustan'. 'The fortunes of the English in India', says Sir Alfred Lyall, 'had fallen to their lowest water-mark.' Nor were the dangers from Indian powers the only ones: France had declared war in 1778, and though Chandarnagar and Pondicherry, the latter gallantly defended by Bellecombe, had been captured in October, the French were known to be preparing a formidable expedition from home, hoping to recover their old prestige by fishing in the troubled Deccan waters. There could be little hope of help from England, now standing desperately at bay and confronting a coalition of France, Spain, Holland, and the revolting North American States.

Though Hastings had in some measure brought these troubles upon himself—for the Indian complications sprang mainly from the ill-judged renewal of the alliance with Raghoba in 1778, which he had only succeeded in carrying by the exercise of his casting vote—yet the dauntless demeanour with which he faced them extorts our fullest admiration. He interfered vigorously in the affairs of the Madras Presidency, suspended the Governor and sent the old veteran Sir Eyre Coote from Bengal, with all possible reinforcements and supplies, 'as the only possible instrument to retrieve our past disgraces'. He followed this up by dispatching Pearce in January 1781 to make his famous overland march from Bengal to Madras. He seconded the efforts of his captains in the field by his indefatigable diplomacy. He detached two of the most formidable members of the hostile coalition, winning over early in 1781 the Raja of Berar, who had for some time threatened an invasion of Bengal from the south, and concluding a treaty with Sindhia in October of the same year, by which the Maratha chief engaged to negotiate a peace between the other belligerents and the British. The result was the Treaty of Salbai in May 1782 (see supra, p. 194), which isolated Haidar Ali by withdrawing from him the aid of all the Maratha powers.

Meanwhile, in southern India, Eyre Coote, revisiting the scenes of his former fame twenty years before, defeated Haidar Ali with the loss of ten thousand men at Porto Novo on July 1, 1781. He next effected a junction with Pearce, who, having reached Pulicat, forty miles north of Madras, was threatened by Tipu, son of Haidar Ali; their combined forces fought a rather indecisive engagement in August at Pollilore. A month later Coote won a complete victory over Haidar Ali at Solingar. War had now been declared with the Dutch. In November 1781 Negapatam was taken, and in January 1782 the splendid harbour of Trincomali passed to the English. Here, however, came a check to their good fortune. Braithwaite, with a considerable force, after a desperate resistance lasting two days, was cut up in Tanjore by Tipu; and de Suffrein, the great French admiral, having first fought an indecisive engagement with Sir Edward Hughes on February 17 off Pulicat, landed more than two thousand French troops. Haidar Ali, forming a junction with them, captured Cuddalore from the British. Fortunately the French had strict orders to do nothing of importance till the arrival of Bussy, who, like Coote, was returning to the arena of his early exploits. But Bussy's arrival was long delayed owing to the increasing power of Great Britain on the seas. Though he started from Cadiz in November 1781, he found such difficulty in evading British squadrons that he was only able to join de Suffrein at Trincomali in March 1783, after long detentions at the Cape and the Isle of France. Moreover, he was unlucky in the hour of his coming. He landed at Cuddalore in April 1783, only to find that Haidar Ali had died in December of the preceding year, and that Tipu, with whom he wished to co-operate, had departed to the Malabar coast, where things were not going too well for him. Coote and Bussy were not destined to renew their battles, for the brave old English general died on April 26. The command lapsed into the hands of General Stuart, an incapable man, who invested Cuddalore in a dilatory manner. Before anything effective could be done, news arrived of peace between England and France, and Tipu thus lost his last ally. The chief interest of the years 1782 and 1783 lies in the naval operations of the French and British fleets off the coasts of Coromandel and Ceylon. Between February 1782 and June 1783 de Suffrein and Hughes fought five severe engagements, all of them so stubbornly contested that they were regarded as drawn battles. De Suffrein's greatest success was the recapture of Trincomali in August 1782, after he had cleverly outwitted his opponent. Up to that date the French had, on the whole, the superiority in naval matters, though they had been greatly hampered for want of a base on land. But reinforcements sent from France were constantly intercepted in European waters, and the arrival of a new fleet under Sir R. Bickerton in October gave the preponderance to the British. After Haidar Ali's death operations were chiefly confined to the western theatre of the war. In May 1783 Tipu captured Bednore; but when he proceeded to the investment of Mangalore on the coast, Fullarton made a brilliant raid into Mysore from the south-west. In November 1783 he captured Palghat and occupied Coimbatore; he was advancing on Tipu's capital, Seringapatam, hoping to end the war with one daring stroke, when to his bitter chagrin he was recalled by the Madras authorities, who had already begun to negotiate for peace. The Governor there was now Lord Macartney, who had arrived in June 1781. He was an energetic man of considerable force of character, and his internal administration, where he showed himself straightforward and incorruptible, was a great improvement on that of his predecessors; but he had no experience of the tortuous path of Indian diplomacy, and in the negotiations which ended the war he was no match for the wily Tipu, who succeeded in delaying matters till Mangalore had fallen. The Sultan treated the English envoys with studied disrespect, making it appear that the English had begged a peace, and that he had graciously granted it in the hour of victory. The Treaty of Mangalore, on the basis of *uti possidetis*, was signed in March 1784. Though Hastings strongly disapproved of its terms and tried in vain to amend them, the treaty at least enabled him, when he laid down his office a year later, to leave the British dominions at peace with all the native powers.

CHAPTER XVIII

CHAIT SINGH AND THE BEGAMS OF OUDH. THE IMPEACHMENT OF WARREN HASTINGS

THE wars described in the last chapter had been a very heavy drain on the Company's treasury, and Hastings, whose administration hitherto had been financially successful, had now to face something very like bankruptcy. In this period of difficulty and embarrassment he was led into those dealings with Chait Singh, the Raja of Benares, and the 'Begams', or Princesses, of Oudh, which furnished the most damaging counts at his trial, and have to some extent inevitably dimmed his reputation. The facts were briefly as follows: The Raja of Benares had formerly owed allegiance to Oudh, but by the treaty of 1775 he henceforward held his lands from the Company as overlord. In 1778, on the outbreak of hostilities with the French, Hastings considered that he was justified in demanding, over and above the ordinary tribute of 22½ lakhs (£225,000), a special sum of 5 lakhs (£50,000) as a contribution for war expenses. The Council rather demurred to the right to 'demand', and preferred the word 'request'; but the Governor-General carried his point by suggesting that the question of right should be reserved for the Directors. The Raja asked that the exaction should be limited to a single year, and was punished for his 'contumacy' by being ordered to pay the whole forthwith instead of by instalments. Chait Singh then asked for six or seven months' indulgence, whereupon payment was demanded within five days, and he was told that if he failed to comply he would be treated as though he had refused absolutely.

In 1779 the demand was repeated. The Raja remonstrated submissively enough, and objected that his agreement with the Company exempted him from all contributions beyond the tribute; but when British troops were ordered to march against him, he yielded, and paid the £50,000 and an additional fine of £2,000 for the expenses of the troops employed to coerce him.

In 1780 the demand for five lakhs was repeated; Chait Singh sent a confidential agent to Calcutta, and offered the Governor-General a present of two lakhs (about £20,000). Hastings at first refused, but finally accepted it. He was accused at the trial of having intended to appropriate this money, but this charge may be dismissed as groundless. The money was spent in the Company's service in equipping an expedition against Sindhia. At the same time, it is only fair to say that Hastings's critics had some reason to be led astray by the mystery in which he involved the matter at the time. Not wishing the rest of his Council to have control over the money or to know the source from which it was derived (and this was natural enough, for the only really upright course would have been to refuse it), he first spoke of it as a contribution from his own private estate, though, to safeguard himself, he revealed all the circumstances to the Director Sulivan as well as to the Accountant-General of the Company's treasury in Calcutta, and five months later informed the Directors that the money was not his own. But the five lakhs were exacted as before from Chait Singh, and apparently (though this is not certain) an additional fine was imposed for the effort to evade payment.

Attempts to gloss over this transaction had better be left to the thick-and-thin apologists of Hastings. It leaves upon the mind a most unpleasant impression of his attitude towards the unfortunate Raja. Hastings knew that the money was only offered as a bribe, and would certainly not have been paid except to relieve Chait Singh of the larger contribution. There was some justice in the stinging comment of the eleventh Report of the Select Committee of 1783: 'The complication of cruelty and fraud in the transaction admits of few parallels. Mr. Hastings ... displays himself as a zealous servant of the Company, bountifully giving from his own fortune ... on the credit of supplies, derived from the gift of a man whom he treats with the utmost severity, and whom he accuses in this particular of disaffection to the Company's cause and interests. With £23,000 of the raja's money in his pocket, he persecutes him to his destruction.'[1]

Chait Singh was not yet free of requisitions. He was next required to furnish 2,000 cavalry—a demand, on his protests, reduced to 1,000. The Raja ultimately got together 500, with 500 matchlock men as substitutes, and sent word to the Governor-General that they were ready to obey his orders. But he received no answer,[2] for Hastings had determined to impose upon him an immense fine of fifty lakhs (£500,000). 'I was resolved', he said, 'to draw from his guilt the means of relief to the Company's distresses. In a word, I had determined to make him pay largely for his pardon or to exact a severe vengeance for his past delinquency.'

Hastings left Calcutta in July. Chait Singh hastened to Baxar, and abjectly humbled himself before the Governor-General, who, however, declined to give him an answer till he arrived at Benares. There, Hastings refused another personal interview, and submitted his demands in writing. In answer he received a letter from the Raja in self-defence, which an impartial judge can only regard as perfectly respectful, and, considering the way he had been treated,

[1] *Reports of the House of Commons*, vol. vi, p. 582. The rupee was then reckoned at a little over 2*s*. 3*d*.

[2] Hastings himself admits that Chait Singh probably received no reply. See his *Narrative of the Insurrection which happened in the Zemeendary of Benares.*

extraordinarily moderate. Hastings, however, pronounced it to be 'not only unsatisfactory in substance but offensive in style', and though he had only a weak escort he had Chait Singh put under arrest. But though the Raja quietly submitted, this indignity placed upon him in his own capital was more than his troops could stand. They rose suddenly, without his connivance, and massacred the English sepoys with three officers. Chait Singh himself, fearing the consequences, made his escape in the general confusion. Hastings was in great peril, and was forced to fly for safety to Chunar. The rising became very serious, but the Governor-General showed his customary coolness and resource, and, summoning all available forces to his aid, defeated his enemies. Chait Singh, protesting his innocence of the massacre, was driven out of the country and found an asylum at Gwalior. His domains were declared forfeit and were conferred upon his nephew, who had henceforth to pay a tribute of forty lakhs, instead of twenty-two and a half, to Calcutta.

On this transaction some brief comments must be made. Modern apologists of Hastings either defend it by understating the facts, or find it convenient to slur it over. The whole proceeding was really indefensible. It is true that the Managers of the Impeachment overstated their case, confused the issues by lack of legal training, and used the most unwarrantable language. Hastings's defenders have a right to say that he had no thought of private gain, that his action was not perhaps more high-handed than many of those of Lord Wellesley, nor more unrighteous than Sir Charles Napier's treatment of the Amirs of Sind, and to point out that neither of these eminent men was impeached. But it does not follow that the episode was above criticism. Much time and trouble were expended at the trial in discussing the question whether Chait Singh was a Raja or a mere Zamindar. This point is really immaterial. A more important one is whether the Company had not definitely engaged in 1775 to levy no further contributions from Chait Singh as long as he paid his stipulated tribute. Wilson, in his notes on Mill, maintains that there was only a resolution of the Council to that effect, but no treaty. We now know, however, that there was a definite agreement with Chait Singh of July 5, 1775, that while he paid his contribution 'no demands shall be made upon him by the Honble Company, of any kind, or on any pretence whatsoever, nor shall any person be allowed to interfere with his authority, or to disturb the peace of his country'.[1] Wilson further states that a later *Sunnad* or grant of 1776 declared all former *Sunnads* to become null and void. He mentions that the prosecutors of Hastings affirmed that the *Sunnad* was altered in compliance with the representations of Chait Singh, but replies that they could not prove that any other *Sunnad* was ever executed.[2] But again, we now know that

[1] *Selections from the Letters, Despatches and other State Papers in the Foreign Department of the Government of India, 1772–1785.* Ed. by G. W. Forrest, vol. ii, p. 402. The extract consists of the draft agreement with Chait Singh produced by Warren Hastings at the secret consultations of the Bengal Council, June 12, 1775. Sir George Forrest prints less than half of the proceedings of that day, without any marks of omission to show that the entry is incomplete. The full account may be read in *Reports from Committees of the House of Commons* (1804), vol. v, pp. 618–19. The portion omitted, though no doubt this is accidental, contains statements of Warren Hastings which tell strongly against Sir George Forrest's view of the Chait Singh incident. Hastings says, almost prophetically, that without some such an arrangement Chait Singh 'will expect from every change of government, additional demands to be made upon him, and will of course descend to all the arts of intrigue and concealment practised by other dependent Rajahs. Hastings actually proposed that Chait Singh should pay his revenue at Patna and not at Benares, 'because it would not frustrate the intention of rendering the Rajah independent,' and for fear lest the influence of a Resident at the latter place 'might eventually draw on him severe restrictions, and end in reducing him to the mean and depraved state of a mere zamindar.' Sir George Forrest also omits all record of the fact that the agreement was reconsidered on July 5, and, with some modifications in detail, was agreed to by the whole Council. The terms of the agreement were communicated to Chait Singh by the instructions of the Council to Fowke. August 24, 1775, *Reports from Committees of the House of Commons*, vol. v, p. 466.

[2] *History of British India*, vol. iv, p. 256 (ed. 1858).

the prosecutors were right, that the words objected to were altered, a revised *Sunnad* given to Chait Singh, and the original draft recalled.[1] Therefore the agreement of 1775 was the one still regulating the relations between the Raja and the Company. The Council at Calcutta, though now consisting only of two persons very friendly disposed to Hastings, were obviously much embarrassed by the escapades of the Governor-General, and asked themselves three questions: '*Firstly*, Where were the Governor-General's particular instructions for such extraordinary demands on Chait Singh? *Secondly*, Why was that chief put in arrest when he offered to make every concession? *Thirdly*, Whether there was not a compact between him and the Company which specified that he was only to pay them a certain annual tribute?'[2] Their answers to these questions show more desire than ability to support the Governor-General. It is noticeable that in dealing with the third, which, as they naïvely admit, 'involves much argument', the theory that the *Sunnad* of 1776 had contravened the agreement of 1775 plainly never occurred to them. Neither did it occur to the Court of Directors, who in their judgement on the transaction concluded that the compact of 1775 pledged the Company to make no further demands upon Chait Singh beyond the stipulated tribute. But, waiving the question of the prior agreement and assuming that Hastings had the right in emergencies to revise the Company's treaty obligations, the question still remains whether he did not act in a harsh and precipitate manner towards a dependent. Here the facts speak for themselves to all those who are not obsessed with the conviction that Hastings was faultless. Many modern writers seem to have persuaded themselves that he was justified; but the late Sir Alfred Lyall, not only

[1] *Selections from the Letters, Despatches*, &c., vol. ii, pp. 512, 549, 557. I am at a loss to understand Sir G. Forrest's comments on this point in his Introduction, vol. i, p. lxviii.

[2] *Selections from the Letters, Despatches*, &c., vol. iii, p. 831.

an historian but a man of affairs, who did not even in the capacity of biographer lose all critical sense, admits in his masterly little *Life* that 'Hastings must bear the blame of having provoked the insurrection at Benares. . . . He followed the recognized custom of needy Indian potentates . . . and whenever the English in India descend to the ordinary level of political morality among Asiatic potentates they lose all the advantages of the contrast'. All those who have studied the records at first hand will also assent to Lyall's declaration that there was 'a touch of impolitic severity and precipitation about his proceedings against Chait Singh', suggesting that 'he was actuated by a certain degree of vindictiveness and private irritation' against him.[1]

One final line of defence should be noticed, namely that the political position in India was so serious as to justify almost any means of obtaining money; and that Hastings made, and rightly made, expediency the sole criterion here. Then it can only be said that, moral considerations apart, the whole proceeding was a sorry failure; and, if utility is the sole test, the Governor-General's action stands condemned. He set forth to get money from the guilt of the Raja; he got nothing. He jeopardized his own safety in a manner which earned the criticism of Sir Eyre Coote, and was stigmatized by the Court of Directors as 'unwarrantable and impolitic'. By his precipitate act in arresting Chait Singh in his own capital amid 200,000 of his own countrymen, 420 miles from Calcutta, he brought a hornet's nest about his ears, and the Raja escaped with part of his wealth. Further, through his injudicious letter encouraging the army in the hope of plunder, all the rest of the treasure found (twenty-three lakhs of rupees) was divided up amongst the troops, and the total financial result to the Company was the cost of the hostilities that ensued. In the future, no doubt,

[1] *Warren Hastings*, by Sir Alfred Lyall (English Men of Action Series), pp. 126, 127.

the Company gained by the larger tribute exacted from the Raja of Benares, but at a great cost to the unhappy country. Hastings himself had declared in 1775 that the province of Chait Singh was 'as rich and well cultivated a territory as any district, perhaps, of the same extent in India'. In 1784, when he visited the country, he records that he 'was followed and fatigued by the clamours of the discontented inhabitants', and he declares that 'the cause existed principally in a defective if not a corrupt and oppressive administration'.[1]

The second incident was the famous case of the Begams, or Princesses, of Oudh. The Nawab Wazir of Oudh, Asaf-ud-daula, had for some years fallen into arrears with his subsidy to the Company. His mother and grandmother, the Begams, held large *jagirs* or landed estates and had inherited, though there was some doubt of the authenticity of the will, a valuable treasure from the late Nawab. The Nawab Wazir had long desired to obtain part of this wealth, which he claimed was unjustly withheld from him. However this might be, in 1775 the widow of Shuja-ud-daula on the representations of the British Resident agreed to pay her son £300,000, in addition to £260,000 already given to him, on condition that he and the Company guaranteed that he should make no further demands upon her. Hastings at the time was opposed to such a pledge being given, but he was outvoted in the Council and the agreement was made. In 1781 Asaf-ud-daula asked that the treaty with the Begams should no longer be considered valid, and that he might seize their treasure to pay his debt to the Company, and Hastings, badly in need of money, consented. The Governor-General justified this abrogation of treaty rights on the ground that the rebellious conduct of the Begams was a reason for withdrawing from them British protection. At

[1] *Selections from the Letters, Despatches, &c.*, G. W. Forrest, vol. iii, p. 1082.

this point, however, the Nawab Wazir, who was thoroughly afraid of the 'uncommonly violent temper of his female relations', began to hang back, and he had to be screwed up by Hastings to the attempt to resume the *jagirs* and seize the treasure. 'You must not allow any negotiations or forbearance,' wrote the Governor-General to his agent in Oudh, 'but must prosecute both services until the Begams are at the entire mercy of the Nabob.'[1] British detachments were marched to Fyzabad to support the Nawab's troops, and the eunuchs who acted as stewards for the Begams were forced by imprisonment, fetters, starvation, and the threat, if not the actual infliction, of the lash to part with the hoarded treasure. Making every allowance for the difficulties of Hastings, it is impossible not to regret and condemn this proceeding. Even if we grant that the Begams were unjustly withholding state property from its rightful owner, and that the Company was not bound to maintain its deliberately given guarantee, yet the temperately worded verdict of Sir Alfred Lyall is the mildest form of censure that meets the case: 'The employment of personal severities, under the superintendence of British officers, in order to extract money from women and eunuchs, is an ignoble kind of undertaking; . . . to cancel the guarantee and leave the Nawab to deal with the recalcitrant princesses was justifiable; to push him on and actively assist in measures of coercion against women and eunuchs was conduct unworthy and indefensible.'[2] This point is of some importance, for a rather ill-judged attempt has lately been made to save Hastings's reputation. 'The cruelty', says Sir G. W. Forrest, 'practised by the Nawab and his servants has been greatly exaggerated, but it was sufficient to have justified the interference of the Resident. To have countenanced it by transmitting the orders of the Vizier

[1] Idem, vol. iii, p. 950.
[2] *Warren Hastings*, Sir A. Lyall, pp. 136, 137.

was a grave offence. But for what took place Hastings at Calcutta cannot be held responsible. He ordered the Resident not to permit any negotiation or forbearance, but there is a wide gulf between legitimate severity and cruelty.'[1]

Unfortunately for this comfortable doctrine it is quite clear from the extracts that Sir G. Forrest is editing that Hastings was the moving spirit throughout. He goaded on the reluctant Nawab, who protested that he was acting under compulsion, and we find two successive Residents informing the Governor-General, in answer to letters upbraiding them with being too mild, that they had gone as far as they deemed possible. Middleton writes in February 1782 apologizing for having admitted a 'temporary forbearance': 'I must also observe that no further rigour than that which I exerted could have been used against females in this country';[2] and Bristow in June quotes the opinion of the officer who commanded the troops, that 'all that force could do has been done'.[3] The eunuchs were seized in January and not released till December, and all this time the Residents were in constant communication with the Governor-General. It is quite obvious that they did not relish the work thrust upon them; that they could not satisfy Hastings's desire for coercion, and pleaded for gentler methods. The Governor-General himself, when Asaf-ud-daula repented of coercing the Begams, declared that the Nawab had been influenced by his minister to assume 'a very unbecoming tone of refusal, reproach, and resentment; in opposition to measures recommended by me, and even to acts done by my authority'.[4]

One other point must be briefly noticed. The defenders of Hastings maintain that the Begams were acting in

[1] *Selections from the State Papers of the Governors-General*, vol. i, p. 251.
[2] *Selections from the Letters, Despatches*, &c., vol. iii, p. 960.
[3] Idem, p. 969.
[4] Idem, p. 982.

complicity with Chait Singh, and that the Governor-General was convinced of the fact. To this it may be replied firstly, that if his treatment of the Raja of Benares was high-handed and oppressive—and it must certainly have appeared to be so at the time—it was sufficient to arouse the instincts of self-preservation in the hearts of any native rulers. The Court of Directors themselves declared, 'it nowhere appears from the papers at present in our possession that the Begams excited any commotions previous to the imprisonment of Chait Singh, and only armed themselves in consequence of that transaction, and it is probable that such conduct proceeded from motives of self-defence under an apprehension that they themselves might likewise be laid under unwarrantable accusations'. Secondly, the testimony to the fact is almost worthless, consisting of vague *ex post facto* statements of interested parties and hearsay evidence. Thirdly, were it true and Hastings convinced of it, the right and straightforward course would have been to produce the evidence at the time and openly to have demanded satisfaction from the Begams.

When all deductions are made for the great difficulties that beset him, it seems impossible altogether to acquit Hastings in these two famous cases. It is probable enough that, had it not been for the unexpected rising of Chait Singh's troops, which put everything to the test of the sword, Hastings would have lessened the fine he intended to inflict. But the point is that his harsh and precipitate attitude, culminating in the arrest of the Raja after the latter's abject submission, could have left no hope in the breast of that unfortunate man. The massacre of British troops (for which Chait Singh was not personally responsible) most disastrously embittered the whole question. But for that untoward incident, the Court of Directors might merely have reversed the Governor-General's action as impolitic and restored the Raja to his former position—a solution actually suggested at the time by the Bengal Council[1]—and the affair would only have been remembered as one of a few errors of judgement in a long and otherwise glorious period of office. In the case of the Begams of Oudh, Hastings himself at the order of the Directors made partial restitution. He was naturally the kindest of men, but there was a note of relentlessness in his character when he was in difficulties, and it is clear that he had steeled himself in this instance to measures of unjust severity. He would have been glad to thrust the responsibility on his agents, and he wished his purpose to be carried out without knowing too accurately how it was affected.

To pass so much of censure on the Governor-General's conduct is not for one moment to condone the proceedings of the managers in the impeachment. They grossly exaggerated and distorted the facts, and used language which could only have applied to the worst excesses of the worst of tyrants. Above all, they assumed that Hastings's motives throughout were based on self-aggrandizement and corruption. This at any rate was absolutely untrue. His aim was the security and welfare of the Company and British dominion in India. But until we hold that mere expediency may override all considerations of ethical and political right, we must continue to regard his conduct on these occasions as a serious departure from the best traditions of British statesmanship in the East.

By the end of 1779 the quarrel between the executive and the judicature, the Council and the Supreme Court—those 'ermined interlopers', as they were called—to which we have already alluded, became an open scandal. The Council ordered the zamindars not to acknowledge the jurisdiction of the judges, and the judges declared the Governor-General and Council guilty of contempt of court.

[1] *Selections from the Letters, Despatches*, &c., G. W. Forrest, vol. iii, p. 795.

But the tension was suddenly ended. In 1780 Hastings conferred upon Sir Elijah Impey the Presidency of the *Sadr Diwani Adalat*, or Company's Court of Appeal, with a salary of £6,500 revocable at the will of the Governor-General and Council—an office which he was to hold in addition to his Chief Justiceship of the Supreme Court and salary of £8,000. Impey, although he accepted the salary, declared himself prepared to refund it if his appointment were not approved at home. From the point of view of Hastings this adroit solution of the problem had many advantages. It put an end to an intolerable situation, conciliated Impey, and anticipated by many years the policy which extended the appellate jurisdiction of the Supreme Court over the provincial courts of the province. But at home there was a vehement outcry on the ground that his action violated the spirit of the Regulating Act, the chief object of which was to render the Supreme Court independent of the Executive. The law officers of the Crown afterwards gave their opinion that there was nothing illegal in the appointment, but Parliament was not satisfied; it passed an Act in 1781 exempting the Governor-General and Council from the jurisdiction of the Supreme Court, and a year later recalled Impey, though the subsequent attempt to impeach him broke down. Sir James Stephen has ably defended Impey from the charge of having acted from corrupt motives, but he admits that the Chief Justice after his fierce conflicts with the Council was not well advised in accepting an arrangement, which at any rate gave the impression that he had compromised his independence. It certainly seems impossible to deny that Impey had an evil reputation in India. Cornwallis, who was not naturally censorious and would never say a word against Hastings, wrote in 1786 in alarm to Dundas, 'I trust you will not send out Sir Elijah Impey. All parties and descriptions of men agree about him'; and again in 1788, 'If you are in the hanging mood, you may tuck up Sir Elijah Impey, without giving anybody the smallest concern'.[1]

Hastings spent eight months of 1784 in Benares and Oudh reorganizing the internal affairs and finances of the provinces, which were in the greatest distress partly through famine and partly through misgovernment. In Benares the rule of the new Raja had proved a poor substitute for the mild and comparatively equable sway of Chait Singh. On his return to Calcutta Hastings received the news of Pitt's India Act, and declaring that 'fifty Burkes, Foxes and Francises' could not have planned a worse measure, he acted on the resignation of his office which he had tendered early in the year, and left the shores of India in February 1785.

Pitt's famous statute was the culminating point of one of the recurrent periods of state inspection into East Indian affairs. For seven years after the passing of the Regulating Act (1773) popular attention had been mainly occupied with the rebellion of the North American Colonies and the war with France, but from 1780 India again attracted the notice of politicians. In 1781 a new Charter Act prolonged the Company's privileges for ten years and still further extended the control of the state over it in two directions: in the first place, three-quarters of any surplus, after a dividend of eight per cent. had been paid, was to go to the Treasury; secondly, as the Regulating Act had obliged the Court to communicate to ministers all dispatches received *from* India relative to revenue, civil, and military affairs, so they were now compelled to submit for inspection all such dispatches sent *to* India. In the same year Parliament appointed two committees, the first 'Select' and the second 'Secret', to inquire into the administration of justice in Bengal, and to investigate the causes of the war in the

[1] *Correspondence of . . . Marquess Cornwallis*, Charles Ross, vol. i, pp. 238, 310.

Carnatic. These committees presented voluminous reports, and in May 1782 the House of Commons resolved that Hastings and the President of Bombay should be recalled from office. The Proprietors of the East India Company sturdily refused to ratify this resolution, merely in accordance with a vote of the House of Commons', and the fall of Rockingham's ministry saved the Governor-General. The coalition government of Fox and North took office in 1783, and Fox brought forward his India Bills. The main provisions of the most important were that for four years all political and military power should be transferred to seven Directors or Commissioners, to be appointed at first by Parliament and afterwards by the Crown: all commercial business was to be controlled by nine 'assistant directors', also to be nominated in the first instance by Parliament but afterwards by the Court of Proprietors. Pitt, in his fierce opposition to the Bills, seized upon the fact that the immensely valuable patronage of India would practically pass into the hands of the government, and to play upon the ever-present fear that the corrupting power of ministers would be extended was, in the eighteenth century, the surest method of rousing popular feeling. This, however, in face of the great Parliamentary preponderance of the coalition, would have been of little avail had not George III through his influence over the Lords been able to force a dissolution. The Bill passed the Commons by ample majorities, but was thrown out in the upper house by what Fox described as 'an infamous string of bed-chamber janissaries'. The coalition were promptly dismissed from office by the king, and on the appeal to the country a few months later were utterly defeated. The Whig Party was ruined. Pitt came into power for twenty years and carried his India Act in 1784. This measure practically made the East India Company, in everything except its patronage and commerce (now rapidly dwindling), a subordinate department of state. Civil and military matters were to be controlled by six 'Commissioners for the affairs of India', popularly known as the 'Board of Control', consisting of the Chancellor of the Exchequer, one of the principal Secretaries of State, and four Privy Councillors. In practice the commission soon became a phantom body and all real power passed into the hands of the senior commissioner (other than the Chancellor of the Exchequer and the Secretary of State), who was known as the President of the Board of Control. The orders of the commissioners were to be transmitted to India through a secret committee of the Directors, and the Court of Proprietors was deprived of any right to annul or suspend any resolution of the Directors approved of by the Board. The government of India was placed in the hands of a Governor-General and Council of three, and the subordinate Presidencies were made definitely subject to Bengal in all questions of war, revenue, and diplomacy.

In the meantime the enemies of the late Governor-General were preparing an elaborate assault on his whole career, and in this work the generous humanitarian sympathies and lofty, though often misdirected, indignation of Burke were reinforced by the thwarted ambition and bitter enmity of Philip Francis. Hastings arrived in England in June 1785, and it seemed for a time as though the storm that threatened him would pass over. But in 1786 Burke, on an unwise challenge from Hastings's agent, moved in Parliament for papers dealing with various points in his administration. The attack, at first repelled, gathered in intensity and effectiveness. The House acquitted Hastings on the question of the wars against the Marathas and the Rohillas, but passed condemnatory resolutions on his dealings with Chait Singh and the Begams of Oudh. Pitt, who had hitherto supported Hastings, felt bound to vote against him on the two latter counts. An amazing amount of misplaced ingenuity has been expended in the endeavour to find some motive more or less unworthy for this action. The simple truth appears to be that he and Dundas felt there was too much evidence, at least for a prima facie case, for them to hold out any longer; and it must be admitted that before the full defence was made, which could only be done at the trial, the facts at the very least called for criticism and an explanation. The following passage in the letter of Dundas to Cornwallis of March 21, 1787, should put this controversy finally to rest: 'The proceeding (i.e. the impeachment) is not pleasant to many of our friends; and of course from that and many other circumstances, not pleasing to us; but the truth is, when we examined the various articles of charges against him with his defences, they were so strong, and the defences so perfectly unsupported, it was impossible not to concur.'[1]

The trial began in Westminster Hall on February 13, 1788. The articles of impeachment as finally presented were twenty in number. Most of them dealt with Hastings's relations with Oudh. He was charged with the violation of treaties made with the Nawab, unnecessary interference in his internal affairs, compulsion put upon him to maintain an excessive number of troops, with oppression in the case of the Raja of Benares, with the arbitrary settlement of the land revenues of Bengal, the removal of the treasury from Murshidabad to Calcutta, with fraudulent dealings in contracts, and the acceptance of presents and bribes. The chief managers of the impeachment were Burke, Fox, and Sheridan, and they were helped and prompted throughout by Francis. Largely through interminable wrangling over the admissibility of evidence the trial was spun out to an inordinate length. As it dragged on its slow course the growing violence and irritability of Burke, whose mind became

[1] *Correspondence of . . . Marquess Cornwallis*, Charles Ross, vol. i, p. 281.

almost unbalanced by the strain, gradually alienated all popular sympathy from his cause. It was strongly felt that, whatever Hastings's faults and errors might have been, they were more than adequately requited by the long-drawn-out agony of the trial. In 1791 it was decided to drop all the articles of charge except those dealing with the case of Chait Singh and the Begams of Oudh, fraudulent contracts, presents and bribes. The verdict was only given in the eighth year of the impeachment, on April 23, 1795. Hastings was acquitted on all the articles. In the voting the highest minorities were recorded in the charges relating to the rulers of Benares and Oudh, which were defeated by majorities of 23 to 6.

The pity is that the matter ever went any further than the Parliamentary inquiry. Hastings's critics might well have been content with the censure then passed on these two points, the least defensible of his acts. Following the precedent created in Clive's case, the Commons should at the same time have carried a rider recognizing the exceptional difficulties under which the late Governor-General laboured, and recording a generous appreciation of his long and splendid services to Great Britain in the East. Thus the justice of the case would have been met and the procedure in Parliament might well have been supplemented in due time by the grant of some high honour from the Crown. Unfortunately this course was not followed, and year after year the unedifying spectacle was presented of Hastings, still patient, imperturbable, and courageous, standing at the bar of the Lords, a target for the terrible invectives launched against him by the three greatest orators of the day.

Yet perhaps we may say that the impeachment had its uses, for while it ended in the acquittal of the accused, it brought about the condemnation of the system under which he had been called upon to govern ; and even if it revealed on his part some acts of impolitic and unjust severity and some instances of lax financial control, it also made known, as perhaps nothing else could have done, his splendid administrative abilities, his cool and dauntless courage, his marvellous equanimity under cruel provocation, and, finally, his untiring efforts, at last crowned with success, to wrest victory from defeat, and, in a time of world-wide disaster elsewhere, to leave the British inheritance in the East in extent and resources not less than he found it.

CHAPTER XIX

INTERNAL REFORMS. THE GREAT LAND SETTLEMENT. LORD CORNWALLIS AND SIR JOHN SHORE

WHEN Hastings left India, John Macpherson, the senior member of Council, succeeded him as temporary Governor-General. He was not above the average type of the Company's servants in their worst epoch. Concerned in some discreditable intrigues with the Nawab of the Carnatic both before and after he had entered the Company's service, he had been cashiered by Lord Pigot but reinstated by the Court of Directors. During his year and a half of office he only succeeded in making some ill-advised overtures to the Maratha government at Poona which afterwards embarrassed his successor, and in carrying through some reductions in expenditure. His administration, though approved by the Court of Directors and rewarded with a baronetcy, was declared by Lord Cornwallis, a man not given to exaggeration, to be a 'system of the dirtiest jobbing'.[1]

The feeling was now widely prevalent in England that a Governor-General should be appointed who had not spent his official career in the corrupt atmosphere of the covenanted service. The choice of the Court fell first upon Lord Macartney, who, without having passed through the subordinate ranks of the Company's service, had enjoyed as Governor of Madras considerable Indian experience. He was, however, passed over when he made

[1] *Correspondence of Charles, first Marquess Cornwallis*, Charles Ross, 3 vols., 1859, vol. i, p. 371

WAXTYPE

GEORGE PHILIP & SON, LTD.

his acceptance conditional on his elevation to an English peerage, and the office was conferred upon Lord Cornwallis, who on two former occasions, in 1782 and 1785, had declined it. A Bill was carried through Parliament (1786) legalizing his appointment both as Governor-General and Commander-in-Chief, and permitting him in emergencies to override a majority in his Council.

Lord Cornwallis was a man of high character, who in spite of his surrender to Washington at Yorktown—the reverse that ended the American War of Independence—retained the trust and respect of his countrymen. He was the personal friend of Henry Dundas, for sixteen years President of the Board of Control, and of Pitt, the Prime Minister, and had perhaps more than any other Governor-General the support of the Court of Directors. These circumstances, together with the extraordinary legal powers granted to him by the Act of 1786—a tribute at once to his personal integrity and a proof that the nation believed drastic reforms in Indian administration to be necessary—gave him far greater authority than any servant of the Company, however able, could have obtained. Yet it would hardly be fair to attribute the whole of Cornwallis's success to these advantages of position, conspicuous though they were. His standard of probity in financial matters was exceptionally high, and probably transcended that of all other politicians of his day. He seems almost to have been without personal ambition. His sole aim was to do what he conceived to be his duty adequately and without parade, and he was as phlegmatically calm in his triumphs as he was stoically unmoved in his defeats. There was abundant need for his reforming hand. It is perhaps somewhat necessary to emphasize this fact. Modern writers on Warren Hastings go so far in their defence of his policy that they sometimes leave the impression that there was nothing for Cornwallis to amend. But this was certainly not the case. Hastings, as we have shown, cared little for money himself, and his faults where it was concerned were carelessness and extravagance rather than avarice, but he hardly seems to have been revolted by the vitiated atmosphere in which he moved, and he freely used means, which a later age and a higher standard can only regard as questionable, to bind men to his interests and win their support. Sir John Malcolm says with truth that 'his most strenuous advocates . . . while they defend his personal integrity, are forced to acknowledge, that the whole system of the government over which he presided was corrupt and full of abuses'.[1]

In his assault on this system Cornwallis was in great measure single-handed. It was hopeless to expect the Court of Directors to take any clear and consistent line on the question of financial reform. We are apt to regard the Directors in England and their servants in India as two distinct bodies with very divergent interests, but though this is true to a certain extent, in some respects they were wont to act rather in collusion than in opposition. The position of Director at this time was chiefly valued for the patronage in Indian appointments and the opportunities for securing lucrative contracts which it conferred. There are many indications of a questionable co-operation between the Company's servants abroad and their nominal masters at home. The payment to Clive of his huge *jagir* was readily acquiesced in by the Court till they began to quarrel with him on other grounds. Johnstone, member of the Bengal Council in 1765, and other delinquents who had received valuable presents against the direct prohibition of the Directors, had influence enough in Leadenhall Street to quash the suits that were instituted against them for restitution of their ill-gotten gains. The notorious Paul Benfield wielded such influence both in the Court of Directors

[1] *Sketch of the Political History of India*, John Malcolm, 1811, p. 40.

and in Parliament as to prevent for many years all inquiry into the scandal of the Nawab of Arcot's debts—debts of millions of pounds 'in favour', as Burke declared, 'of a set of men whose names with few exceptions are either buried in the obscurity of their origin and talents or dragged into light by the enormity of their crimes'.[1] In spite of characteristic exaggeration there is some truth in the same orator's paradox: 'The servants in India are not appointed by the Directors, but the Directors are chosen by them. The trade is carried on with their capitals. To them the revenues of the country are mortgaged. The seat of the supreme government is in Calcutta. The house in Leadenhall is nothing more than a 'change for their agents, factors, and deputies to meet in.'[2] How else but by the existence of collusion between the Directors and their servants in the East can we account for the fact that the Resident of Benares, one of the posts in the gift of the Governor-General, was allowed to make an annual income of £40,000 a year besides his official salary of £1,350? When Cornwallis had cleansed the Augean stables he wrote, 'the splendid and corrupting objects of Lucknow and Benares are removed; and here I must look back to the conduct of former Directors, who knew that these shocking evils existed, but instead of attempting to suppress them, were quarrelling whether their friends, or those of Mr. Hastings, should enjoy the plunder'.[3]

Such was the state of things with which Cornwallis had to deal. Nor must it be supposed that any mere extension of state control over the East India Company would necessarily have done away with the corrupt atmosphere. Parliamentary government at this time was still hopelessly venal. Cornwallis himself was pestered by men of high rank in

[1] Burke's *Speeches*, vol. iii, p. 109.
[2] Idem, vol. ii, p. 473.
[3] *Correspondence of . . . Cornwallis*, Charles Ross vol. i, p. 306.

England, including the Prince of Wales, to perpetrate 'some infamous and unjustifiable job',[1] and when the question of the renewal of the Company's charter came to the fore in 1793, he declared he feared the 'furious clamour' that would be raised against 'annexing the patronage of India to the influence of the Crown', and he still thought a Court of Directors, though its constitution might be improved, could 'prove a useful check on the ambitious or corrupt designs of some future minister'.[2]

In a history like the present it is impossible to deal adequately with the work of each Governor-General in every field; but it is important to gain a clear idea of each man's most characteristic contribution to the building up of British dominion in India. Few were destined to do more permanent work than Lord Cornwallis, especially in the department of internal affairs. Externally the interest of his rule is almost confined to his war with Tipu Sultan of Mysore, and his success there, though considerable, was not of the nature of a complete triumph. In internal affairs his governor-generalship is one of the most notable, and his achievements in order of importance are the reform of the covenanted service, the permanent settlement of the land revenues of Bengal, and the reorganization of the Bengal courts of law.

The emolument of Englishmen who spend the best part of their lives in the East has always been fixed on a higher scale than that of their fellow-countrymen in temperate climates. Modern practice, the outcome of much experience and many mistakes in the past, has solved the question by the payment of adequate salaries during the working period of the civil servant's career, and retirement with a generous pension at a comparatively early age. The plan adopted by the Court of Directors, which they only

[1] Idem, vol. ii, p. 51.

[2] *Marquess Cornwallis*, W. S. Seton-Karr, p. 76.

abandoned reluctantly at Cornwallis's earnest solicitation, was small nominal salaries with large commissions at a fixed rate on the collection of revenues. The meagreness of the salaries is often greatly exaggerated, and if they were too small, the commissions and perquisites were a great deal too large. The Resident at Benares at this time, as we have seen, had a salary of 1,000 rupees a month or, at the current value of the rupee, £1,350 a year, which would now be considered fair remuneration for the position; but he made besides in indirect ways the huge amount of £40,000 a year and, if we are to believe Cornwallis, other perquisites besides. The truth seems to be that, as there was no pension awaiting the Company's servant on his retirement, it was considered absolutely necessary that in fifteen to twenty years' service each man should have accumulated a fortune upon which to retire in comfort. At this period we find that the Company's servants in Bengal (1) received a fixed salary from the Court of Directors, (2) received also commissions on the revenues of Bengal, (3) engaged in the forbidden private trade. 'I am sorry to say', wrote Cornwallis, 'that I have every reason to believe that at present almost all the collectors are, under the name of some relation or friend, deeply engaged in commerce, and by their influence as collectors and judges of Adalat become the most dangerous enemies to the Company's interest.'[1] The reforms effected by Cornwallis were wide and sweeping. He proved the stern foe of every kind of job, sinecure, or dubious contract. For the vicious system of commissions he substituted generous salaries at a fixed amount, and he separated the executive and judicial powers of the Company's servants. He thus left the functions and position of the collector very much what we know them to be to-day.[2] The covenanted service of the

[1] *A Comprehensive History of India*, H. Beveridge, vol. ii, p. 575.

[2] It must be noted however that the absolute separation between executive and judicial powers has not been maintained. See *infra* p. 289.

Company from that date assumed a new aspect, and grew by natural development into the imperial civil service of the Indian Empire.

In India the great bulk of public revenue has always been raised from the land. When the British in Bengal were granted the *diwani* in 1765, they found a system in vogue by which the 'ryot' or peasant cultivator paid a fixed share of the produce of his land either in cash or kind to the 'zamindars'. The 'zamindars' were at first mere collectors of the revenue. But the office gradually tended to become hereditary in the families of the original holders. Thus the 'zamindari', which was originally, as it has been described, an hereditary contract agency, became something resembling a landed estate. The zamindar received the territorial revenues of the state from the ryots and paid the Mughal sovereign or his Viceroy nine-tenths of what he received, retaining the remaining tenth for himself. He succeeded to his zamindari by inheritance, but was expected to pay a fine on his succession. He could sell or give away his office on obtaining permission, but if deprived of it by the state, he became entitled to compensation. Over the lands in his zamindari he had a right to regulate the incidence of the cesses (or taxes) imposed by the ruler of Bengal, and he was responsible for the keeping of the peace within his jurisdiction. On the acquisition of the *diwani* in 1765 the collection of the revenue was left in the hands of natives, though in 1769 with dubious success British 'supervisors' were appointed to control them.

In 1772, as we have seen, Hastings, on taking over the management of the *diwani* from Indian agents, leased the right to collect the revenues to the highest bidders for five years. This quinquennial settlement however proved a failure. The farmers of the revenue offered more than they could pay, and at the end of the period they were

2½ millions in arrears. Hastings, following instructions from home, returned to the system of annual leases. This precarious tenure by universal consent was a mistake. The flow of capital to the land was checked. The revenue steadily diminished. Cornwallis reported that on his arrival in India he found agriculture and trade decaying, ryots and zamindars sinking into poverty, and money-lenders the only flourishing class in the community. The annual tenure was not regarded favourably by the British Parliament of landlords, who looked upon the zamindars as landholders in the ordinary sense of the word. An Act of Parliament was passed in 1784 directing the Court of Directors to abandon the annual system and frame 'permanent rules' for the raising of the land revenues.

Nearly two years later the Court of Directors tardily urged Cornwallis to make a ten-years' settlement with the zamindars, which was eventually to be declared permanent, if it proved satisfactory. From that date, 1786, to 1789 Cornwallis with the aid of John Shore, a Bengal civilian whose knowledge of land tenures was wide and profound, studied the question, and in 1789 a settlement for ten years was made. In 1793 Cornwallis urged upon Dundas, against the advice of Shore, that the existing settlement should be made permanent. Dundas eagerly welcomed the suggestion, and shut himself up for ten days at Wimbledon with Pitt, the Prime Minister, that they might study the question without interruption. At the end of that time they decided for Cornwallis against Shore, and on March 22, 1793, the settlement was fixed in perpetuity.

Upon this famous Permanent Settlement historians have passed diametrically opposite judgements. 'It was', says Marshman, 'a bold, brave, and wise measure. Under the genial influence of this territorial charter, which for the first time created indefeasible rights and interests in the soil, population has increased, cultivation has been extended, and a gradual improvement has become visible in the habits and comfort of the people.'[1] On the other hand, Holmes says: 'The Permanent Settlement was a sad blunder . . . The inferior tenants derived from it no benefit whatever. The zamindars again and again failed to pay their rent charges, and their estates were sold for the benefit of the government.'[2]

The views quoted are typical of two opposing schools, and are not so irreconcilable as may at first sight appear. The Permanent Settlement, in contrast to the chaotic system which it supplanted, had many fairly obvious advantages. It ultimately improved the position of the zamindar, who was secured in his zamindari as long as he paid the state revenues. He henceforth appropriated to his own benefit the difference between the rents he received from the ryots and the claim of the state. He had no longer to pay fines on succession or obtain permission before effecting a sale, and he was relieved from the burden of maintaining order in his district. The Permanent Settlement gave popularity and stability to the British government, and has helped to make the province the wealthiest and most flourishing in India. It has avoided the evils of periodical assessments which, at however long intervals, produce economic dislocation, evasion, the concealment of wealth, and the deliberate throwing of land out of cultivation. Even though the state sacrificed much future revenue, it gained indirectly through the general increase in prosperity and the abolition of those checks to industry and improvements which must always appear when the government bears away part of the profit.

On the other hand, the immediate effect, even upon the zamindars, was disastrous. Many of them, being unable to recover the rent from the cultivators, could not pay the

[1] *The History of India*, J. C. Marshman (1871), vol. ii, p. 35.
[2] *History of the Indian Mutiny*, T. R. E. Holmes, p. 12

state dues and were forced to part with their ancient rights to new proprietors. To such of them as were able to withstand the first strain and to the new owners of zamindaris the Permanent Settlement ultimately gave an enormous increase in rent at the expense of the state and the ryots, while the hope that they would invest much capital in improving and developing their 'estates' was doomed to disappointment. The amount to be paid by the zamindars was fixed at three and three-quarter millions sterling, while the rents received by them now exceed thirteen millions. The state once and for all parted with the power to divert a portion of this unearned increment, and the rest of India has to be taxed more heavily that Bengal landlords may enjoy a position of especial emolument. Though Cornwallis endeavoured to some extent to mitigate, in the interests of the ryots, the hardships of an economic rent, it cannot be said that he was very successful. Their status was undoubtedly impaired, and it was not until 1859 that the Bengal Land Act afforded them real relief. This feature of the Permanent Settlement is its greatest blot in the eyes of those who regard the zamindar as originally the headman of the free village, representing the cultivators and nominated by the government to collect and pay over the state revenues. According to this view, though he tended as time went on to be looked upon as the landlord of his zamindari, the peasants who paid the dues 'were neither his tenants nor his vassals. . . . A very great blunder as well as gross injustice was committed when a settlement was made with zamindars alone, and rights of property every whit as good as theirs were completely ignored.'[1]

Summing up therefore, it may be said that most of the advantages of the Permanent Settlement might equally well have been obtained by a settlement for a long term of years. The state would not then have parted for ever with all power

[1] *A Comprehensive History of India*, H. Beveridge, vol. ii, p. 631.

to derive an increased revenue from the unearned increment of the land. 'The land revenue', throughout the Permanent Settlement area, says Mr. E. D. Maclagan, 'has now, like the English land tax, none of the characteristics of taxation, and may be said to be at the present day nothing more than a rent charge, the burden of which has long ago been discounted by the reduced selling price of the land which it affects.'[1] Had the Permanent Settlement but been postponed for another ten or twenty years, the capacities of the land would have been better ascertained. Many mistakes and anomalies would have been avoided, and the reforms brought about by Cornwallis himself in the civil service would have trained up a class of officials far more competent to deal with so vast and intricate a subject.

In the organization of the judicial courts, civil and criminal, Cornwallis completed the work begun by Warren Hastings. Briefly to summarize a very technical and difficult subject, he vested the collection of the revenues and the administration of justice in separate officers, though this principle was afterwards departed from in the governor-generalship of Lord Hastings. An ascending hierarchy of civil courts was established, consisting of (1) small courts for the recovery of petty debts, presided over by native commissioners; (2) *Zillah*, or District, and City Courts under a British judge with native assessors; (3) four Provincial Courts, each under three European judges, also with native assessors; (4) the Court of Appeal, or *Sadr Diwani Adalat*, consisting of the Governor-General and members of Council in Calcutta. A parallel organization of criminal courts was set up—the judges being practically the same and those of the provincial civil courts going on circuit—surmounted by the Court of Appeal, the *Sadr Nizamat Adalat*. The criminal jurisdiction of the native Deputy Nawab, or Naib Nazim, was thus finally abolished, and an elaborate new

[1] *The Imperial Gazetteer of India*, vol. iv, p. 220.

Code of Regulations, drawn up by George Barlow, was printed and published to guide the officials of the new judicial system.

In these three fields, then, the status of the covenanted civil service, the collection of the land revenues, and the organization of the judicature, lay the real and important work of Cornwallis. 'He gathered up the scattered fragments of government which he found and reduced them to one comprehensive system. He gave substance and permanency to what had before been light and transient. He laid the foundation of the present Indian constitution.'

In his foreign policy Cornwallis was anxious above all to maintain the neutrality and peace which was consonant with the declaration of Parliament made in Pitt's Act of 1784 and repeated in 1793, that 'to pursue schemes of conquest and extension of dominion in India are measures repugnant to the wish, the honour, and policy of this nation'.

He refused in 1788 to assist the son of Shah Alam, then residing at Benares, to recover his throne at Delhi, and he succeeded with some adroitness in extricating himself from the agreement which Macpherson had injudiciously made with the Peshwa—'a very awkward, foolish scrape',[1] but he was not able to avoid hostilities with the ruler of Mysore, the most formidable and relentless of the Company's adversaries. The path of the Governor-General was entangled with former ill-advised treaties made by the muddle-headed governments of Madras, and by the habitual treachery of the native powers. A very involved story must here be briefly told. The Nizam of Hyderabad, always the ally and generally the embarrassment of the Company, appealing to the Treaty of Masulipatam (1768), called for the aid of British troops to recover certain of his former territories from Tipu, while at the same time, as was afterwards discovered, he

[1] *Correspondence of . . . Marquess Cornwallis*, Charles Ross, vol. i, p. 219.

intrigued with the latter for a coalition against the English. When Lord Cornwallis looked into the diplomatic history of the point, he discovered that in 1769 a treaty had been made with Haider Ali explicitly recognizing his claims to the territories of which the Treaty of Masulipatam professed to deprive him. Further, the treaty of 1784, concluded with Tipu himself, also acknowledged these rights. On the other hand, it was clear that Tipu was meditating war against the Company's dominions, and Cornwallis was anxious before embarking on it to secure the alliance of the Nizam, but a clause in Pitt's Act of 1784 prevented the Governor-General without the consent of the home authorities from declaring war on native princes or entering into a treaty with that object, unless previously attacked. Cornwallis, by a rather desperate piece of casuistry, determined to accept the Nizam's appeal to the treaty of 1768, though his action in doing so violated the two subsequent treaties of 1769 and 1784. He adopted the extraordinary expedient of writing a letter to the Nizam, explanatory of the treaty of 1768, which declared that, if the districts claimed by the Nizam should ever come into the possession of the British, they should be handed over to him; troops were to be supplied to the Nizam but were not to be employed against any powers in alliance with the British; a list of these powers was added and the name of Tipu was deliberately excluded. The war with Mysore was in all probability, as Cornwallis said, 'an absolute and cruel necessity', but that so naturally open and frank a man should be driven to such expedients to range the Nizam on his side, illustrates the difficulties of the neutral course imposed by resolutions of Parliament and the precepts of the Court of Directors upon the Indian government, and, it must be confessed, lent some support to those who argued that Tipu was almost forced henceforward to take up arms in self-defence. Little wonder that even the peace-loving Cornwallis spoke feelingly of the 'unavoidable inconvenience of our being constantly exposed to the necessity of commencing a war, without having previously secured the assistance of efficient allies'.[1]

Tipu himself forced on the war. In 1787 he had sent envoys as far as Constantinople and Paris to seek allies against the British, and he was buoyed up by many deluding hopes. In December 1789 he attacked Travancore, a small state in the extreme south-west of the Peninsula, whose Raja was an ally of the Company, and in the following year he devastated the country with his usual wantonness and cruelty. Cornwallis succeeded in forming a triple league against him by agreements with the Peshwa and the Nizam in June and July 1790, each of whom was to provide a contingent of troops and share in the profits of the conquest. Both were unwilling allies and rendered no useful aid, but at least they were prevented from joining Mysore.

The campaign of 1790 conducted by General Medows was unsatisfactory. Accordingly in December 1790 the Governor-General himself assumed the command, captured Bangalore in March of the following year, and advanced on the capital, Seringapatam; but though he defeated Tipu in a pitched battle in May, he was forced through a shortage of supplies to spike his heavy guns and retreat. The third campaign in the late summer of 1791 was more successful. Tipu's mountain fastnesses were reduced, and in January 1792 a second advance was made with an imposing force on Seringapatam, and the outworks of the town were captured. Tipu then made his submission, which was accepted by the Governor-General. Some critics have supposed that Cornwallis had it then in his power to complete the work which he left to Wellesley, but there were many good reasons for stopping short of the storm of Seringapatam. Sickness was spreading in the British camps; treachery, and with good reason, was suspected in the Nizam and the Marathas. War

[1] *A Comprehensive History of India*, H. Beveridge, vol. ii, p. 582.

with France was evidently imminent, and the Directors were clamouring for peace. Further, the Governor-General was not eager to take over the management of the whole country of Mysore, and so deliberately stayed his hand. By the treaty of March 1792, Tipu was forced to cede half his dominions, pay an indemnity of more than £3,000,000, and surrender two of his sons as hostages.

The war brought the Company their first really important accession of territory since 1765. On the west of Mysore they obtained Malabar and the sovereignty over Coorg, whose Raja had supported their cause; on the south, Dindigul with the surrounding districts; on the east, the Baramahal and the command of the famous passes through which Haider Ali used to make his devastating incursions. The general result was that the British had cut off the Sultan of Mysore from approach to the sea on the west, and commanded the defiles giving access to the table-land of his country. The Marathas gained territory on the north-west and the Nizam on the north-east of Mysore. Each of the confederates got one-third of the indemnity. Cornwallis summed up the results of the war by saying, 'We have effectually crippled our enemy, without making our friends too formidable'.[1]

There was a pause for the moment, but the omens were not favourable for a lasting peace. Tipu was humiliated and cowed, but in his diminished kingdom he nursed an implacable resentment against the power that had vanquished him, and he had already begun to meditate busy intrigues with the French, the Amir of Afghanistan, and the native states of southern India. The Peshwa and the Nizam eyed each other jealously, and even during the campaign the Marathas were only kept from falling on the plains of Mysore by their fear of the British forces. In the meantime, while Corn-

[1] *Correspondence of . . . Marquess Cornwallis*, Charles Ross, vol. ii, p. 154.

wallis allied with the Peshwa was defeating Tipu, Sindhia and Holkar, the nominal generals of the Maratha confederacy, were fighting one another in northern India—a rivalry presaging trouble for the head of the nation at Poona and for the tranquillity of all India.

Still, on the whole, Cornwallis, now created a marquis, could leave India in October 1793 with the feeling that no immediate disturbance was imminent. Just before his departure, on the declaration of the Revolutionary war with France, the helpless French possessions were occupied by British troops.

The retirement of Cornwallis coincided with the renewal of the Company's charter in 1793. Had the period of their privileges chanced to lapse ten years earlier, it is likely that popular feeling would have gone hard against any extension of the monopoly. But the reforms of Cornwallis enabled a highly favourable balance-sheet to be set forth. The great seaports and manufacturing towns, Liverpool, Bristol, Glasgow, Manchester, Norwich, Paisley, and Exeter, petitioned against the exclusion of the country in general from a share in the Indian trade, and the whole question of Free Trade or Restriction was raised; but ministers supported the Directors, and the Company's privileges were extended for another twenty-four years, with the small concession that 3,000 tons of shipping should be provided annually for the use of private shippers. One of the main arguments of Dundas was that, if the trade to India were thrown open, the colonization of the country would follow, and India be lost to Great Britain.

Lord Cornwallis had once expressed a hope that he would never again see the supreme government in the hands of a Company's servant. He was, however, himself succeeded by such a one, Sir John Shore, his colleague and adviser in forming the land settlement in Bengal. The appointment was due to the failure to find in England what King

George III described as 'a very proper man of distinction'—a failure that caused Dundas, the famous President of the Board of Control, to entertain for a time the idea of himself proceeding to India. Since the governor-generalship of Cornwallis, only three of the Company's servants were promoted to the highest place, namely Sir John Shore, Sir George Barlow, and Sir John Lawrence, and in each case, it is interesting to note, their period of office was marked by a policy of peace and non-interference.

Certainly in the administration of Sir John Shore the neutral policy laid down by Parliament and the Court of Directors received a fair trial. The Indian government showed its genuine desire to allow the native powers to manage their own affairs. British dominion remained stationary, and Sir John Shore preserved neutrality even up to a pitch which, in the opinion of some, jeopardized the national honour of Great Britain. 'It was proved', wrote Sir John Malcolm, 'from the events of this administration, that no ground of political advantage could be abandoned, without being instantly occupied by an enemy; and that to resign influence, was not merely to resign power, but to allow that power to pass into hands hostile to the British government.'[1] Shore's period of office proved the lull before the storm. For five years a precarious peace was preserved, while the ominous clouds were gathering that resulted in the wars and annexations of Lord Wellesley. When the time for British interference came, it was all the more drastic for having been so long delayed.

The two native powers that most gladly submitted to British protection, the Muhammadan governments of Oudh and Hyderabad, were willing to do so because of their very weakness. The Company's alliance with them, especially with the Nizam, by the mere logic of events was destined

[1] *Sketch of the Political History of India*, John Malcolm, 1811, p. 225.

to carry the British far on the way to dominion in India; but at present the government hardly realized the lengths to which such engagements would lead them, and, in so far as they did realize them, shrank from the responsibilities involved. At the end of the Mysorean war, Cornwallis tried to persuade the Marathas and the Nizam to enter upon a mutual guarantee to protect each other's territories against Tipu Sultan. The Nizam, as the weaker party, had been willing to accede to this request, but the Marathas had refused, with the intention, no doubt, of making the Nizam their prey in the future as they had so frequently done in the past. The Nizam then endeavoured to obtain such a guarantee from the East India Company, but Cornwallis hesitated to give him more than a vague assurance of support. Sir John Shore firmly refused to do more than his predecessor, and the Nizam therefore turned to other aid. He employed a distinguished French officer, Raymond, to train and discipline his troops.

In the meantime the Maratha states were making their plans for the plunder of Hyderabad. Something must be said here of the power of their confederacy. A glance at the map will show the dominating position they held in central India. The territories of the Peshwa formed a broad belt of country, running down the western shore of the Deccan between the Nizam's dominions and the sea to the northern frontier of Mysore. The boundaries between the districts controlled by the Gaikwar, Holkar, and Sindhia were very wavering and ill defined, but roughly we may say that the Gaikwar held Kathiawar and Gujarat; Holkar, the south-western part of Malwa; Sindhia, north-eastern Malwa, the territory west of the Jumna, and the upper Ganges and Jumna Doab. The lands of the Raja of Berar extended in a broad belt from his capital, Nagpur, to the sea at Cuttack on the Bay of Bengal. Thus the Marathas commanded the wide centre of the peninsula, and stretched from Gujarat in the west to Orissa in the east, their territory reaching up northwards to the confines of the Punjab, and on its southern frontiers enveloping on three sides the dominions of the Nizam.

The constitutional position of the Maratha confederacy at this time forms a curious and baffling political puzzle, but for the understanding of what follows it is essential that an outline of the main features should be grasped. The nominal head of the whole, the descendant of Sivaji, still dwelt in his palace prison at Satara in the original Maharashtra. All real power in western India had long passed to the Peshwa (Prime Minister) at Poona, but he too had now become almost a *roi fainéant* in the hands of his minister, the able Nana Farnavis. The nominally subordinate members of the confederacy had in the meantime passed beyond the control of Poona in all but name. The Bhonsla Raja of Berar claiming kinship with Sivaji, Holkar of Indore, and Sindhia of Gwalior, hereditary generals of the Peshwa, who were originally given their lands as a reward for military service, and the Gaikwar of Baroda, were all practically independent princes. Between Sindhia and Holkar there was a family feud. The Raja of Berar was rather isolated by position from Poona intrigues, and the Gaikwar alone of Maratha powers never challenged British suzerainty, but maintained treaty relations of some kind or another from the date of Warren Hastings's Maratha war.

The greatest Maratha chieftain, in personal ability and in extent of his dominions, was Mahadji Sindhia, who since 1784 controlled Hindustan from the Sutlaj to Agra, held valuable territories in Malwa and the Deccan, and possessed a fine army disciplined and recruited by De Boigne, a brilliant Savoyard soldier of fortune. The old Emperor Shah Alam had been forced to put himself under Sindhia's protection, and, at the peremptory request of his protector, had issued patents appointing the Peshwa supreme Viccgerent of the Empire, and Sindhia himself the Peshwa's Deputy. So by an extraordinary series of political fictions and a curious turn of the political wheel, the Mughal emperor had now passed under the control of a general of the Hindu confederacy, which was swayed by the minister of the Peshwa—himself the Mayor of the Palace of the Raja of Satara, whose claims were historically based upon a rebellion against Mughal sovereignty. It is true that Sindhia for a time suffered vicissitudes of fortune. He was defeated by a Rajput coalition in 1786, and in 1788 he temporarily lost his hold on Delhi, when a savage Rohilla chief imprisoned and blinded the miserable Shah Alam. But by 1792 he had recovered his position, had rescued and restored the emperor, and again stood forth, in Sir John Malcolm's striking words, 'the nominal slave, but the rigid master of Shah Alam, Emperor of Delhi; the pretended friend but the designing rival of the house of Holkar . . . the oppressor of the Rajput princes . . . and the proclaimed soldier but the actual plunderer of the family of the Peshwa'.[1] In 1792 he obtained new patents from the emperor, making the titles Vicegerent and Deputy hereditary and perpetual. With these he marched to Poona and held a solemn investiture. He persuaded the Peshwa that a serious mistake had been made in the late war in supporting the British power against Mysore, and urged a closer connexion with Tipu. Before any definite action could be taken, Mahadji Sindhia died suddenly in 1794; his successor, Daulat Rao Sindhia, was a youth in his teens, and for a time the control of Maratha affairs passed again into the hands of Nana Farnavis. There was, however, no change in the hostility displayed to the Nizam, who appealed to Sir John Shore for support. The Governor-General, dreading to be dragged into a war with the whole Maratha confederacy,

[1] Quoted by H. Beveridge in his *Comprehensive History of India*, vol. ii, p. 661.

refused to intervene, though the Nizam was undoubtedly as much an ally of the Company as the Raja of Travancore had been in 1790. This policy has been universally condemned as a slavish observance of neutrality. British good faith was tarnished in the eyes of native powers. In fact, had it not been for the 'incapacity of Indians for acting together' which has so often saved the British position in India, serious consequences might have been the result of Sir John Shore's timidity. The Nizam was defeated at Kharda (Kardla) in March 1795—the last occasion, as Marshman notes, when all the Maratha powers mustered together—and forced to submit to humiliating terms. But dissensions broke out at Poona on a change in succession to the Peshwaship, and there ensued such a tangled skein of treachery and intrigue as to be almost unparalleled even in eastern history. As a result, the Marathas forfeited in great measure the prizes of their victory. Nana Farnavis, to gain the Nizam's support against the opposite party, surrendered most of the advantages gained at Kharda.

In northern India, Shore acted with more vigour than he had done in the south. The Nawab of Oudh died in 1797, and was succeeded by a reputed son of ignoble birth and utterly worthless character. The Governor-General interposed, and raised the brother of the late Nawab to the throne, taking the opportunity to conclude a treaty with him which made the Company responsible for the whole defence of Oudh, in return for an annual subsidy of seventy-six lakhs of rupees, and the cession of the fort of Allahabad; he also bound the Nawab to hold no communications with any foreign state. The motive impelling Sir John Shore to this unwonted attitude was probably the recent presence at Lahore (1796) of the last of the invaders of India from the north-west, Zeman Shah of Kabul, who aroused for a moment in Hindustan hopes and fears that he would repeat the career of his grandfather, Ahmad Shah Durrani. But he was recalled to deal with troubles in Afghanistan. The days of invasions by Asiatic conquerors from the mountains of the north-west were over.

Sir John Shore's integrity was undoubted, but the serious mutiny of the Bengal officers at the end of his governor-generalship went far to prove the wisdom of Cornwallis's warning, 'Such is the present temper of the British part of the community in India . . . that nobody but a person who has never been in the service can be competent to govern our possessions with that energy and vigour which is essential to our political safety and internal prosperity.' The mutiny was due to dissatisfaction with the economical reforms of Cornwallis and jealousy between the King's and the Company's services, and so threatening was the position that the Governor-General was driven to make many concessions to the disaffected. He was thereupon superseded and, after Dundas had again dallied with the idea of going to India, Cornwallis was appointed Governor-General in February 1797. But so many points were yielded to the mutineers even by the Court of Directors that Cornwallis resigned office before leaving England, and Shore, who was created Lord Teignmouth on his retirement, was succeeded in 1798 by the Earl of Mornington.

CHAPTER XX

EXPANSION. LORD WELLESLEY. SUBSIDIARY ALLIANCES AND ANNEXATIONS

RICHARD COLLEY WELLESLEY, Earl of Mornington (in the peerage of Ireland), had held office as a Lord of the Treasury and Commissioner of the Board of Control. He was in the prime of life, thirty-seven years of age, a great classical scholar, a master of stately if rather grandiloquent English, of brilliant and ardent temperament, and endowed with greater genius though less solidity of character than his more famous younger brother. He was one of the greatest of British rulers of India. Only Clive, Warren Hastings, and Dalhousie can challenge comparison with him, and in actual achievement he outdistanced them all. He came to India at an auspicious time for one who wished to play a great part, when the policy of non-interference and neutrality was on the point of breaking down, and he seized the tide of his opportunity at the flood. He had great chances and made the most of them—brilliant military commanders, governors of the subordinate Presidencies who did not dream of opposition, and, for the first few years at any rate, the active sympathy of Dundas and Pitt. But above all his own imperious will, wide and bold political grasp of facts, and gorgeous imagination swept onward to a more ambitious view of British Dominion than had hitherto been entertained. It was afterwards realized that the change he inaugurated was in any case inevitable. But while others shrank from it even when they saw it coming, Wellesley went boldly forth to anticipate and to meet it.

He saw that Great Britain could no longer play any but the predominant part in India. A balançe of power among the native states was impossible, however conscientiously the East India Company might strive to support it. When the armies of the Nizam and the Peshwa fought at Kharda, British representatives were with the sovereigns in either camp, and all the efforts of Sir John Shore were directed to isolating the conflict and preserving a benevolent neutrality. To Wellesley such an attitude was impossible, and in seven years' time he wrought a marvellous transformation; he crushed the power of Mysore, extended British control, protective but dictatorial, over the great Muhammadan states of Hyderabad and Oudh, took over the administration of Tanjore, Surat, and the Carnatic—that running sore of administration—struck boldly at the seat of Maratha power, left the Peshwa a mere dependent on British support, robbed Sindhia of Delhi and his royal prisoner, and was only prevented from anticipating the work of one of his successors, Lord Hastings, by the fact that his generals for the first time blundered in their tactics, and that his brilliant but somewhat breathless progress had long alienated the panic-stricken Court of Directors, and was now beginning to alarm even the ministers of the Crown.

Wellesley's first problem was Mysore. In his search for allies against the power that had humiliated him, Tipu had sent his emissaries to Arabia, Kabul, Constantinople, and Mauritius. The Governor of the Isles of France incautiously blazoned abroad the alliance between the French Republic and the tyrant of Mysore. Tipu with his own hand planted the tree of Liberty at Seringapatam—never surely before or since planted in such uncongenial soil—and was elected a member of a Jacobin Club. A few French troops (under a hundred in number) landed on the west coast of southern India at Mangalore almost at the same time as Lord Mornington stepped ashore at Madras. The Governor-General promptly determined on war. He would have launched against Mysore a military expedition at once, but he found the unprepared state of the military forces at Madras rendered this impossible, and altered his method though not his intention. He postponed operations for a year and made preparations with characteristic thoroughness. He endeavoured to revive the tripartite treaty of 1790 with the Nizam and the Marathas. The influence of Sindhia and the distracted state of the Maratha confederacy kept the Peshwa aloof, but he bound the ruler of Hyderabad to the British cause by the first of his famous 'subsidiary' alliances, September 1, 1798, that is, an alliance which implied the subordination of the allied Prince to the British government in external policy and foreign relations, the maintenance and payment of a contingent of the Company's troops, and the expulsion of the officers of other European nations. The Madras government with characteristic timidity opposed this measure, but Lord Mornington bore down their feeble opposition. This disbandment of the Nizam's formidable French force was carried out with great coolness and adroitness by Malcolm and Kirkpatrick, and an intercepted letter from Bonaparte at Cairo proved, at least to Wellesley, that action had not been taken a moment too soon. The Governor-General demanded absolute submission from Tipu, and, sweeping aside the latter's temporizing letters as insolent evasions, set his forces in motion. Simultaneously the main army under General Harris and the Nizam's contingent controlled by Arthur Wellesley, the Governor-General's younger brother, afterwards Duke of Wellington, invaded Mysore from the east, while a Bombay force made its way through the Western Ghats. Tipu was first defeated by the western invading force, then routed at Malavalli by Harris, and driven within the walls of his capital, Seringapatam. The city was carried by assault on May 4, 1799, after Tipu had refused to accept the hard terms of giving up £2,000,000 and half his remaining lands. The Sultan himself was killed in the breach. Mornington's success was greater than he had expected. He thought to have crippled Tipu permanently, not to have had his kingdom at disposal. He annexed to the Company's dominions large and important territories: Kanara on the west, Coimbatore on the south, and some districts on the east, together with the fortress of Seringapatam. The general result was that Mysore was surrounded on all sides except the north by the British frontier, and the Company held now continuous territory in the south from the coast of Coromandel to Malabar. To the Nizam were assigned certain lands on the north-east, while to the Peshwa, who may be said at least to have observed neutrality, some districts were offered on certain conditions, which he refused. Upon this they were divided between the Nizam and the East India Company. A child of the Hindu royal family dispossessed by Haider Ali was raised to the throne of Mysore, which, in spite of its diminished territories, was larger than the hereditary dominions of his house before the annexations of the last two Muhammadan usurpers. Tipu's sons were provided for with 'disproportionate magnificence'. The conquest was loudly acclaimed in England. General Harris was raised to the Baronage and the Governor-General was made Marquis Wellesley in the peerage of Ireland—an honour which he considered inadequate and describes bitterly as a 'double-gilt potato'. Sir Arthur Wellesley succinctly thus summed up the first year's work of the Governor-General: 'Our principal ally the Nizam was restored to us, the French state growing in the peninsula of India was destroyed, our formidable native enemy Tipu, the certain ally of the French in India, was subdued . . .'[1]

The history of the first and second wars with Mysore

[1] *A Selection from the Wellington Dispatches*, S. J. Owen, p. 10.

throws into relief the greatness of Wellesley's achievement. The ruler who had defied the arms of Hastings and prolonged the war of Cornwallis to three campaigns was vanquished in two months. Tipu was a savage and cruel despot, but his implacable enmity to the British claims the respect due to consistency. He, like his father, understood that Great Britain rather than any native power was the enemy, and he never leagued himself with her against his neighbours. It must be admitted that Wellesley, when he had once obtained incriminating evidence against Tipu, gave him little opportunity to recant or explain, but ruthlessly swept aside his letters as evasive and unsatisfactory. The allies Tipu sent so far to seek failed him in the hour of need, and he had to face unaided the whirlwind he had raised. Had the Maratha chieftains, sinking their internal differences, possessed his singleness of purpose and all-consuming hate, the final advance of British supremacy might have been long delayed.

Elsewhere Lord Wellesley extended the Company's sway by more peaceful means in accordance with the principle that he boldly enunciated a few years later: 'The Company with relation to its territory in India must be viewed in the capacity of a sovereign power.' In October 1799 he made a subsidiary treaty with the Raja of Tanjore, who practically resigned the whole administration in return for an annuity of £40,000. He took advantage of a change of succession at Surat to abolish the double government, pension off the Nawab, and assume supreme control. He then applied the same policy in more important fields. The government of the Carnatic had long been an open scandal. The dual control had debased the Nawab, ruined his people, and so corrupted the settlement of Madras that the civil servants of that Presidency possessed the worst reputation of all the Company's representatives. By a treaty made with Cornwallis the Governor-General had been empowered to assume the whole administration in time of war. This Wellesley had refrained from doing, but at the capture of Seringapatam he found evidence that the Nawab and his son had entered into some sort of correspondence with Tipu. This evidence, it must be confessed, was not very conclusive or convincing, but the evils of the Nawab's government were undeniable, and it afforded Wellesley the pretext he desired. On the death in July 1801 of the Nawab (son of that Muhammad Ali to establish whom so much British and French blood had been shed in the wars of 1746–63), Wellesley used this evidence to assume the whole civil and military government of the Carnatic, 'perhaps', as he himself declared, 'the most salutary and useful measure which has been adopted since the acquisition of the *diwani* of Bengal'. One-fifth of the revenue was paid to the new Nawab, who was allowed to retain the title.

Wellesley next turned his attention to his northern frontier. He held that the buffer-state of Oudh formed but a weak defence on the north-western boundary of Bengal, and he called upon the Nawab to disband a portion of his own ineffective army and receive a larger subsidiary force. The Nawab resisted till, wearied by the importunity of the British Resident, he expressed a wish to abdicate. Wellesley eagerly welcomed such a solution, and declared that the Nawab's intention could 'not be too much encouraged'.

But the proposal had not been seriously meant, and in any case the Nawab had only contemplated it on condition that his son should succeed him; when he found that Wellesley objected to this stipulation, he withdrew his offer. Wellesley's indignation knew no bounds, and, expressing himself 'extremely disgusted at the duplicity and insincerity of his conduct', he presented the Nawab with a draft treaty, which greatly increased the number of the subsidiary force and raised the subsidy payable to one and a quarter million sterling. The Nawab's protest, which showed some ability and appealed effectively to former treaties, was arbitrarily ignored by the Governor-General as containing 'unfounded calumnies and gross misrepresentations both of facts and arguments'. The Nawab submissively gave way. But new demands were made upon him. Wellesley had lately developed his favourite instrument of the subsidiary treaty in a new direction. By a revised agreement in 1800 the Nizam of Hyderabad, instead of guaranteeing an annual subsidy, handed over for the upkeep of the subsidiary force the territory acquired in the Mysorean wars of 1792 and 1799 (which brought the British frontier to the river Kistna), and was formally granted protection against all external enemies. Wellesley determined to adopt the same expedient in the case of Oudh, and though the Nawab had not failed with his subsidy, he demanded and extorted the surrender of Rohilkhand and the northern districts between the Ganges and Jumna, amounting roughly to one-half of his dominions. The settlement of the ceded districts was handed over to a commission presided over by Henry Wellesley, the Governor-General's brother. Thus trenchantly Lord Wellesley dealt with what he called 'the corruption, imbecility, and abuse of that vicious and incorrigible system of vexation and misrule'—the government of Oudh. Whatever may be thought of the means employed, the practical results were all-important. Oudh was now surrounded by a belt of British territory which abutted on the Himalayas and marched with the ill-defined frontiers of Sindhia's dominions in northern India.

Naturally the voice of criticism was raised on many of these transactions. The conduct of the Governor-General was sufficiently high-handed, especially in his dealings with the Nawabs of Surat and Oudh. An effective case was made out against him in the polemics of the day, and on paper it was sometimes unanswerable. In fact, no one who studies impartially the records of this period can deny that Wellesley was impatient of opposition, too regardless of the feelings of native rulers, often unjustified in the interpretation he chose to put upon treaties, and somewhat unscrupulous in the diplomatic pressure he exerted against those who dared to resist his designs. Even a favourable critic, for instance, has to admit that in the case of Oudh he 'subordinated the feelings and interests of his ally to paramount considerations of British policy in a manner that showed very little patience, forbearance, or generosity'.[1] His course has been justified on the ground merely of political exigency, and the measure of his success in extending the bounds of British dominion has been held a sufficient defence of the means he employed. But the political justification was assuredly not the only one. The sweeping and somewhat ruthless changes he made in the political map of India did undoubtedly on the whole make not only for the stability of British rule but for the amelioration of the lot of millions; there is apparent through all the Governor-General's speeches and dispatches a burning indignation at the wrongs and miseries inflicted by incompetent native governments on their hapless subjects, and a determination to wage a relentless war against the forces of anarchy and misrule. On that broad and general plea it is perhaps necessary, and it is certainly prudent, to rest Lord Wellesley's case, though to do so is frankly to abandon the outposts of a technical and legal defence.

As at this time most of the energies of the government at home were bent on combating the insatiable ambition of Bonaparte in the Revolutionary war with France, so Wellesley shared their cares in his distant outpost of empire, and his survey ranged even beyond the wide limits of his immediate charge. He has indeed been accused of exaggerating the French peril, partly because he counteracted it so thoroughly

[1] *British Dominion in India*, Sir A. Lyall, p. 246.

that men forgot its magnitude. Indeed, when he assumed office the growth of French influence in the courts and camps of native rulers was a serious menace to British power. No one could then know how quickly this menace would vanish before the Governor-General's vigorous treatment. Tipu was negotiating with the Governor of the Isles, and French officers were preparing to drill his troops. A French general commanded an army of 15,000 men in the Nizam's dominions, and Sindhia had 40,000 trained men under a French commander, so that Wellesley without much exaggeration could speak of 'the French state erected by M. Perron on the banks of the Jumna'.

The danger from French ambition Wellesley removed step by step, but he was not content with defensive strategy only. He projected an expedition against Mauritius, from which as a base French privateers preyed upon the shipping of the Indian Ocean, but was baulked by the refusal of Admiral Rainier to co-operate with him without authorization from home. He urged the ministry to take the Cape from the Dutch, now in alliance with France. He contemplated an attack upon Batavia, and in 1800 eagerly obeyed orders from England to send an Indian army to Egypt, which under General Baird landed at Cosseir on the Red Sea and marched across the desert and down the Nile to the shores of the Mediterranean at Rosetta, only to find the French force at Alexandria had capitulated, and that Bonaparte had abandoned his designs of direct eastern conquest. At the peace of Amiens, March 1802, which afforded but a thirteen-months' breathing space in the war with France, Wellesley on his own responsibility suspended the restoration of the French settlements—an action afterwards approved by the home government.

So far Lord Wellesley had carried with him in his policy the support of Pitt's ministry, though he had already alienated the sympathies of the Directors, who showed growing uneasiness at the constant extension of their territorial possessions. There were other causes of dissatisfaction. Wellesley was one of the first statesmen to appreciate the teaching of Adam Smith, and his leanings towards the principles of Free Trade were not popular in Leadenhall Street. The appointments conferred upon his brothers Henry and Arthur, and even the salaries paid to them, were criticized in a manner that roused the fury of the high-minded though autocratic Governor-General, who stigmatized the comments of the Court as a 'direct, marked, and disgusting personal indignity' to himself. His far-sighted efforts to secure a better training and education for the civil servants of the Company by establishing the college of Fort William were neutralized, and, finally, the wide sweep of his political outlook which caused him to dispatch John Malcolm in 1799 on a commercial and political mission to Persia, aroused nothing but distrust and dislike in what the Governor-General afterwards allowed himself in a letter to Dundas to style 'the most loathsome den of the India House'. In January 1802 he therefore announced his approaching resignation, but the Directors, though as yet willing to wound, were still afraid to strike, and they asked him to retain office for at least another year. Wellesley, foreseeing trouble from the Maratha confederacy, acceded to their request.

Wellesley's Maratha policy was destined to plunge him into a war which at its early stages proved to be the most successful and glorious ever waged by British arms in India, but later on was clouded by some unfortunate blunders and defeats. The fame of his governor-generalship was temporarily dimmed; the Directors clamoured for his recall; he lost for the first time the support of the ministry, and resigned before he could gather up the broken threads of his policy and complete his work.

The Maratha powers had regarded with great uneasiness

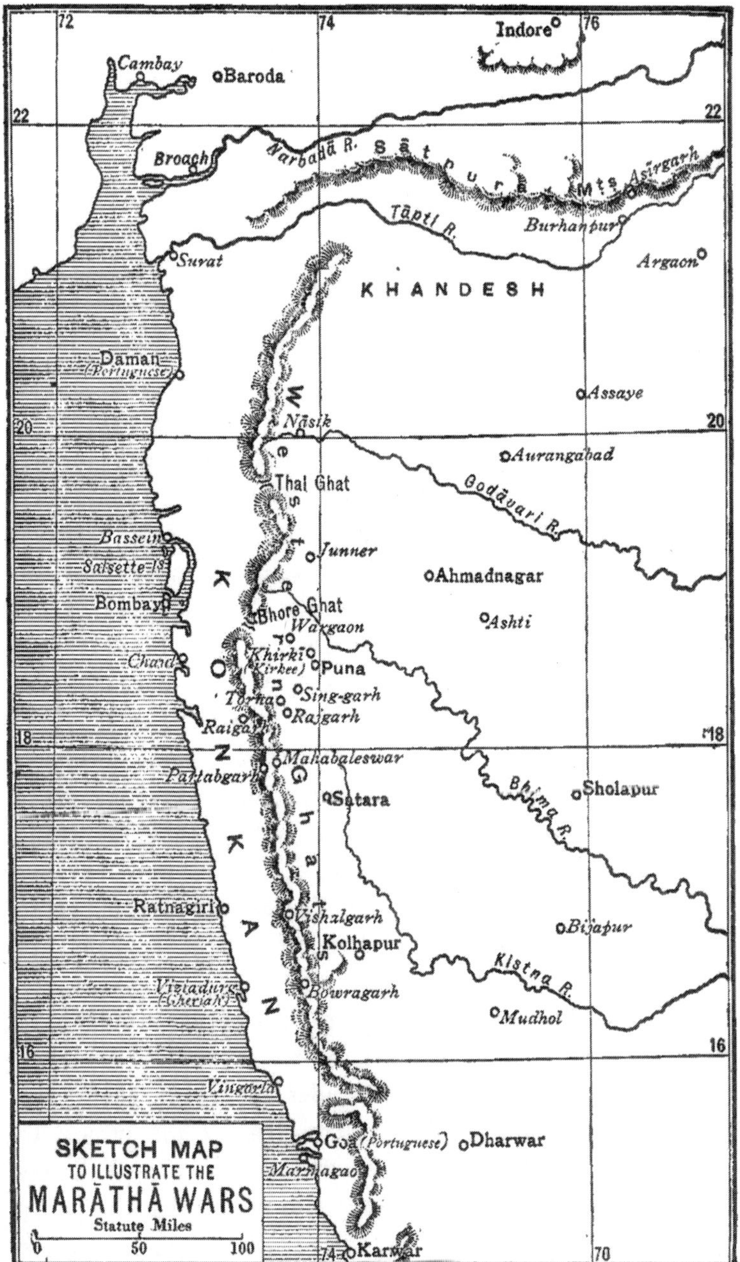

WATTYPE

GEORGE PHILIP & SON, LTD.

the revised subsidiary treaty with the Nizam, by the terms of which the East India Company engaged to protect his ill-defended territories against all enemies. They thus saw one of their most fertile plundering preserves withdrawn from them, and they greatly dreaded this thrusting of the wedge of British influence into their own territories; but had they remained united among themselves, they would have had little need for fear. All British statesmen had a salutary dread of stirring up the enmity of that hardy race of warriors, and Dundas in 1788 thought that an alliance with them, and the resulting combination of British infantry and Maratha cavalry, was 'all that is wanting to make our power complete'. The Marathas' own internal dissensions brought on them the fate they feared.

In March 1800 the shrewd old statesman Nana Farnavis died at Poona, and with him departed, in the words of the British Resident, 'all the wisdom and moderation of the Maratha government'. Both Daulat Rao Sindhia and Jaswant Rao Holkar at once endeavoured to obtain the upper hand at Poona, and went to war with each other. The harassed Peshwa, Baji Rao II, at first submitted, though with extreme reluctance, to the control of Sindhia, but at the moment Holkar was the strongest and most enterprising of the Maratha chieftains. He defeated their united armies at Poona in October 1802, the Peshwa fled for refuge to Bassein, and, being now in desperate plight, appealed for help to the British government.

There is not much doubt of the policy that would have been pursued by Lord Cornwallis or Sir John Shore. They would have left the Maratha rulers to settle their own disputes and have confined themselves at the utmost to protecting the frontiers of Hyderabad. Lord Wellesley decided otherwise. He believed with reason that the policy of non-intervention would only have meant postponing the evil day. He shrank from the ungenerous task of meeting the fugitive's request for aid with a refusal, and vividly foresaw the danger that the Peshwa might, if rebuffed, throw himself into the hands of the French as the Nizam had done in 1795—though it may be noted that his brother Arthur did not believe in the possibility of a Maratha-French alliance. Accordingly, by the Treaty of Bassein, December 31, 1802, he entered into a subsidiary alliance with the nominal head of the Maratha confederacy, involving the usual terms, the permanent stationing of the Company's troops at Poona, the control of the allied state's foreign policy, the cession of territory to meet the charges of the army of occupation, and a stipulation particularly humiliating to Sindhia and Holkar that the claims of the Peshwa upon the Nizam and the Gaikwar of Baroda should be subject to British arbitration. British troops reinstated the Peshwa in his capital in May 1803, and Holkar's troops precipitately retired.

This treaty is rightly regarded as one of the most important landmarks of British dominion in India. 'Wellesley's subsidiary troops', says Sir Alfred Lyall, 'were encamped at the capitals of the four great Indian powers . . ., at Mysore, Hyderabad, Lucknow, and Poona'. But the Treaty of Bassein was far more momentous than former subsidiary alliances. Henceforward the Company had either to control the greatest Indian power, or was committed to hostilities with it. The ministry at home, which had hitherto upheld the Governor-General, began to utter its misgivings. Lord Castlereagh, President of the Board of Control, characterized the policy as 'critical and delicate', and laid his finger correctly enough on its weakest aspect. To enter into treaty relations with the Marathas 'assumes that the genius of their government is industrious and pacific instead of being predatory and warlike'. He believed that it made war inevitable, and he hinted at the desirability of abandoning the connexion or modifying it. Wellesley replied that he had good hope of peace, but if war must come the treaty would enable the British to meet it under the most favourable circumstances.

On this point there was soon very little doubt; as Arthur Wellesley acutely observed, the treaty was made 'with a cypher'. The alarm and anger of the other Maratha leaders was soon manifest. Though they were often at variance with their titular chief, they willed that none should lower his prestige but themselves, and they rightly regarded the Treaty of Bassein as equivalent to an open surrender of national independence. They therefore began to compose their differences. The Peshwa himself secretly approved their action. Sindhia and the Bhonsla Raja of Berar, who was, according to Arthur Wellesley, the chief mover in the business, at once combined. Fortunately the recent devastating war between Sindhia and Holkar was too fresh in the memories of both these chieftains for a cordial co-operation at present, but at least they made peace with each other, and Holkar withdrew his forces to watch events; the Gaikwar held aloof.

Sindhia and the Bhonsla remaining south of the Narbada were requested, if their intentions were peaceable, to separate their forces and recross the river. They refused to do so, and war was the only alternative. The British had never been called upon in India to meet a more formidable enemy. Their forces during the war at no time exceeded 55,000 men; the Maratha armies were estimated at 250,000, besides 40,000 troops organized into brigades trained and disciplined by Frenchmen. Wellesley mapped out a comprehensive plan of campaign. The enemy was to be assailed at all points. The two main theatres of the war were to be the Deccan under Colonel Arthur Wellesley, and Hindustan under General Lake. But operations were to be conducted simultaneously in Gujarat and Orissa, where the territory of the Raja of Berar ran down to the sea and thrust a barrier between the southern districts of Bengal and the northern possessions of Madras.

The blows dealt at the enemy were swift and terrible. Arthur Wellesley captured Ahmadnagar in August 1803, and, forestalling the combined armies of Sindhia and the Bhonsla in an attempted dash on Hyderabad, brought them to action on September 23, 1803, at Assaye, a village about forty-five miles north of Aurangabad. Though he had under 5,000 men and the enemy over 50,000, Wellesley won a 'transcendent victory', as the Governor-General exultingly described it, and utterly shattered the Maratha army in a fiercely fought battle, the British loss in killed and wounded amounting to over 1,500. The remaining strongholds of Sindhia in the Deccan were speedily captured, and he was forced to make a truce on November 23 which dissolved the confederacy. Sindhia, in spite of this, had been secretly supporting the Bhonsla again, but Wellesley pursued them into Berar, defeated them at Argaon November 29, and captured the great fortress of Gawilgarh in December 1803.

The campaign in Hindustan was perhaps even more important. There the Frenchman Perron, acting as Regent for Sindhia, had founded an almost independent power in the Doab, the land lying between the Jumna and the Ganges. Lake, marching from Cawnpore, captured Aligarh at the end of August, and so disheartened Perron that he left Sindhia's service. Lake defeated his successor at the battle of Delhi in September, marched into the city, and took under British protection Shah Alam, now a miserable, blind old man of eighty-three, 'seated under a small tattered canopy'. Lake made a treaty in October with the Raja of Bharatpur, occupied Agra on October 18, and vanquished Sindhia's remaining army at Laswari in November. In the minor theatres of war everything had happened as Wellesley had planned. In Gujarat, Broach was captured and all

Sindhia's territories taken from him. In Orissa, Cuttack had been occupied and the Bhonsla's forces defeated. Four months' campaigning had seen the utter defeat of the whole Maratha confederacy. It was a wonderful result of a campaign wonderfully organized, and unstinted praise has been rightly given to the master mind which willed and planned the whole.

Nor was the victory won over a despicable foe. The fighting was severe and the battles were fiercely and stubbornly contested. For all that, the enemy partly owed their defeat to their abandonment of the old traditional Maratha tactics of wild, plundering raids, a swift retreat, and harassing guerrilla warfare. The true fortune of Maratha armies, as Holkar, more successful than his rivals, contended, was on their saddle-bow. The trained battalions and batteries of Sindhia could crush other native powers; they could only offer a fierce resistance to the Company's forces. De Boigne, the able Savoyard adventurer, who had trained these troops, had always foretold that they would never conquer British armies. Sir Thomas Munro, an acute observer, wrote of the Maratha army, 'its discipline, its arms, and uniform clothing, I regard merely as the means of dressing it out for the sacrifice.'

The results of the campaigns were consolidated in two treaties, that of Deogaon with the Raja of Berar, and that of Surji-arjangaon with Sindhia. Negotiations were entrusted to Sir Arthur Wellesley, who added the laurels of a diplomatist to those of a soldier, claiming with truth that he had 'made two very good treaties of peace'. The territorial dominions of the East India Company were widely extended. Their power henceforward shadowed and protected the descendants of Akbar on the throne of the Mughals. The annexation of the Doab and the overlordship of the cities of Agra and Delhi carried the British frontier to the upper course of the Jumna and the barrier of the Himalayas.

The acquisition of Cuttack and Balasore linked up the Presidencies of Bengal and Madras, and all the eastern seaboard now passed under British control. Valuable districts were ceded in Bundelkhand and Gujarat. All Sindhia's possessions in the Deccan were forfeited, and a great part of Rajputana was freed from his sway. In addition both Sindhia and the Bhonsla recognized the Treaty of Bassein, admitted British Residents to their courts, definitely surrendered their claims on the Nizam, and engaged to take no Europeans other than British into their service. The Raja of Berar relinquished to the Nizam districts in Berar west of the Warda river, and received a British Resident at Nagpur, while Sindhia, in February 1804, entered into a defensive alliance with the East India Company.

Wellesley triumphantly declared that the Peace 'comprehends every object of the war', as indeed it did, but he added, and here events proved him wrong, that it contained also 'every practicable security for the continuance of tranquillity'. Indeed Wellesley was curiously blind to the real feelings of the Maratha powers after the war, which were sullen resentment, bitter humiliation, and smouldering enmity. To the Governor-General in the enthusiasm of his victory, swayed no doubt by a half unconscious desire to win the approval of the ministry at home, it appeared that 'the influence and ascendancy of the British government in the councils of Hyderabad and Poona have been increased and permanently established, not by limiting the authority, controlling the independence, or reducing the power of these states, but by the operation of arrangements which have confirmed and corroborated their respective rights, authorities, and independence, extended their dominion, consolidated their power, and augmented their resources; secured them from the vexatious claims and litigious and violent interference of other powers, and established the resources of permanent tranquillity and prosperity within the limits of their respective dominions. Our influence and ascendancy in the Councils of those allies are now founded on the solid basis of their entire confidence in the equity and moderation of our views and in their just reliance on our protecting power.'[1]

No doubt it was provokingly perverse of the native powers not to adopt these enlightened views, but their real feelings could hardly have been more widely different from this stately presentation of them. Nor did the Governor-General's eloquent arguments altogether carry conviction to the ministry in England. Lord Castlereagh, in a dispatch which crossed that from which the foregoing passage is quoted, hinted a doubt whether the recent acquisitions did not contravene (as they most certainly did) the policy upon which Parliament had hitherto professed to act, and render 'the frame of our government complicated and unwieldly in such a degree as to hazard its becoming enfeebled and embarrassed in ordinary hands', when the directing mind of Lord Wellesley was in due course removed from the supreme control.

The peace indeed was soon endangered. For this Wellesley, even in the opinion of his brother, was partly responsible by pressing upon Sindhia and the Bhonsla a too stringent interpretation of the treaties. These chiefs rapidly became disaffected, but war broke out actually with Holkar, who had taken no part in the recent fighting. On his plundering the territory of the Raja of Jaipur, Wellesley ordered operations to be commenced. For the first time his generals made mistakes. Colonel Monson, advancing too far into the plains of Rajputana, was forced into a disastrous retreat, losing five battalions and six companies. Sindhia soon rose in arms, but the Maratha cause again waned. Holkar failed to take Delhi, ably defended by Ochterlony; one

[1] *A Selection from Wellesley's Dispatches*, S. J. Owen, p. 439.

army was defeated at Dig, November 12, and Holkar was himself routed by Lake at Farruckhabad, November 17, 1804. Then followed a serious error on the part of the British commander. The Ṛaja of Bharatpur had abandoned the British side, and Lake determined to capture his famous fortress and capital. He was essentially a field officer with no experience of sieges, and he was hot-tempered and impetuous. He launched four successive assaults on Bharatpur, all of which were beaten back, with a loss in killed and wounded of 3,203 men, and he was driven to make a peace with the Raja in April 1805, leaving him in possession of the fortress he had defended—a serious blow to British prestige.

The disaster was far from irreparable. Holkar's power had received some shattering blows, and in all probability another campaign would have seen him vanquished, but Lake's failure seemed to justify all the warnings and premonitions of the Governor-General's opponents. Lord Cornwallis, now in his sixty-seventh year, was appointed to supersede Wellesley. He arrived in India in July 1805, and Wellesley left in August.

It is easy to inveigh against the Directors for not appreciating the late Governor-General's brilliant services, but there was something to be said for their point of view. The debt of the Company had rapidly increased under stress of the constant military operations from 17 millions in 1797, to 31 millions in 1806. Wellesley's attitude to the Court was marked by a hauteur and contempt that he did not trouble to conceal. A widespread belief was gaining ground in England that our Indian conquests were getting larger than we could profitably or even safely manage. We have seen that even in the hour of victory the ministry had faltered in their usual approval of Wellesley's actions, and in the shadow of defeat they withdrew their support. Pitt expressed the opinion that the Governor-General 'had acted most imprudently and illegally, and that he could not be suffered to remain in the government '.[1]

There was a curious contrast in the treatment at home meted out to Lord Wellesley and his great predecessor, Warren Hastings. The Court of Directors on the whole, and the Court of Proprietors without any qualification, had steadily supported Hastings, and it was Parliament that had brought him to trial and striven for seven years to procure his condemnation. In the case of Wellesley Parliament promptly voted down two attempts of a private member to carry an impeachment, and passed a resolution eulogizing his ardent zeal for the public service. The Courts of Directors and Proprietors, on the other hand, pursued the late Governor-General with unrelenting opposition, and voted for his condemnation by an overwhelming majority. It was not till after the lapse of thirty years that they made their recantation by assuring him that they could now look back with feelings common to their countrymen to the eventful and brilliant period of his government in India.

[1] *Correspondence of . . . Marquess Cornwallis*, Charles Ross, vol iii, p. 522.

CHAPTER XXI

REACTION FROM THE POLICY OF ANNEXATION. LORD CORNWALLIS, SIR GEORGE BARLOW, LORD MINTO

THE aim of Lord Wellesley had been, as we have seen, to build up and consolidate British dominion in India, partly by absorbing those decadent, dependent rulerships such as Surat and the Carnatic, the administration of which had long been an eyesore to those imbued with western ideas, partly by securing a general control over all native states from Cape Comorin to the Sutlaj, maintaining in their territories subsidiary forces, and regulating their foreign policy.

An attempt was now to be made to withdraw from such wide responsibilities, limit the Company's sphere within a well-defined area, and leave the native powers outside the pale either to make their own peace or prey upon each other in intestine strife.

It may be noted that both Cornwallis and Barlow shrank from applying this policy with logical consistency. It was impossible now to denounce the subsidiary treaties with Hyderabád or Oudh, or even with Poona. The efforts of Wellesley's immediate successors were therefore confined to casting off embarrassing ties with Sindhia and Holkar, and sacrificing the subsidiary relation with those powers which Wellesley had contemplated. Even so, they went too far in the opinion of an acute observer, Metcalfe, afterwards acting Governor-General, who epigrammatically but rather unfairly described their policy as 'disgrace without compensation, treaties without security, and peace without tranquillity.' The British, he held, could no longer hope to 'insulate themselves', and to meet Maratha ambition and enterprise with the language of peace would be to 'preach to the roaring ocean to be still'.

It is easy to pour contempt on such a policy, which in the retrospect of the historian compares unfavourably with the long views and masterly schemes of Lord Wellesley, but it must be remembered that, for the moment, the financial position was desperate. The treasury was empty. Expenditure was annually exceeding revenue, and the export trade was practically at a standstill. The preceding years, said Cornwallis, called annually for 'reinforcements of men and remittances of money', which yielded 'little other profit except brilliant gazettes . . . We literally have not the means of carrying on the ordinary business of government'. For this reason the veteran statesman, though he recognized that it was 'a desperate act to embark for India at the age of sixty-six', sailed at what he believed to be the call of duty to carry out an unpopular policy.

He entered upon office again as Governor-General and Commander-in-Chief in July 1805, and soon after proceeded to the Upper Provinces to pacify if possible the restive Sindhia, and put an end to the war with Holkar. Cornwallis desired to conciliate Sindhia by the restoration of Gwalior and Gohad, and to relinquish all territory west of the Jumna with the exception of Agra. But he undoubtedly went too far in his desire for peace. To limit British responsibilities to the line of the river unfortunately implied removing British protection from several Rajput chieftains who had rendered loyal service in the late war. Cornwallis contemplated the surrender of Delhi to Sindhia and the removal of the king to some point within British territory, and he was even disposed to abandon the demand for the release of the British Resident imprisoned by

Sindhia 'as a mere point of honour'. He exaggerated the danger of a renewed war, and altogether failed to apprehend how near the power of Holkar was to collapse. But it is ill criticizing the work of a dying man, and Cornwallis was dying by inches. Sending forward his instructions to the horrified Lake, who protested vigorously against them, he was carried up the Ganges. At the end of September one of his staff wrote, 'the powers of his mind are unfortunately failing him fast, he dozes away the remnant of life that is left him'. On October 5 he died at Ghazipur, having won, even from those whose policy he was opposing, the respect due to his sterling honesty and noble simplicity of character. He was succeeded provisionally by Sir George Barlow, senior member of Council, a man of mediocre abilities and unpopular manners, but a conscientious administrator, with the civil servant's characteristic virtues of a regard for economy and of loyally carrying out the policy of his superiors, whatever his own feelings might be. He had proved a zealous subordinate to Lord Wellesley, but he did not hesitate to follow on the lines that Cornwallis had indicated.

A new treaty was made with Sindhia in November 1805, by which some of the clauses of the Treaty of Surji-arjangaon were modified. The defensive alliance was not renewed. Gwalior and Gohad were given back to him 'out of considerations of friendship'. The East India Company were to claim nothing to the south, and Sindhia nothing to the north, of the river Chambal, but the British withdrew their protection (and this was the discreditable point in the agreement) from the chieftains of Rajputana who had supported their cause.

In the meantime Lake had advanced as far as Amritsar, having hunted Holkar northwards till he appealed, but appealed in vain, for assistance to Ranjit Singh, then founding his Sikh kingdom. The Maratha chief received far better terms than he could have hoped for. Though he was called upon to renounce his claims north of the Chambal, he was promised the restoration of his forts in the Deccan after eighteen months. The Governor-General, dreading that the treaties with Sindhia and Holkar might imply that the Company was under an obligation to defend the trans-Chambal states, published declaratory articles surrendering Tonk and Rampur to Holkar, and withdrawing British protection from the rest, with the result that in a short time several of them felt the devastating hand of the Maratha leaders, and amongst others the Raja of Jaipur, to whom we were under special obligations.

Against these consequences Lord Lake bitterly protested, but Barlow had certainly carried out the will of the home government, and his policy held the field for ten years. With more political good sense than consistency he sharply recalled to his duty the Nizam, who was beginning to intrigue with the Maratha powers as though the subsidiary treaty no longer existed, and he successfully resisted the orders of the Directors to denounce the Treaty of Bassein. In internal affairs his considerable administrative talents enabled him to carry some drastic economies and to produce equilibrium in the finances.

A dangerous mutiny of sepoys at Vellore in the Madras Presidency afforded curious premonitory symptoms of the revolt of 1857. Some injudicious changes in military dress and new regulations in regard to the fashion of wearing the hair, like the famous order to use the greased cartridges, were taken to imply an attack upon caste and religion. As in the great Mutiny, the movement was fostered by the princes of a dethroned dynasty, the heirs of Tipu of Mysore, and was attended by the massacre of British officers. It caused the recall of Lord William Bentinck, the future Governor-General, from the governorship of Madras.

In 1807 Lord Minto, President of the Board of Control

in the new Whig ministry of 1806, exchanged that office for the governor-generalship. This step was the outcome of a curious deadlock. Barlow's appointment, at first avowedly provisional, had been made permanent with the consent of ministers. Ten days later Lord Minto announced to the Court the pending nomination of the Earl of Lauderdale. The Directors refused to acquiesce, on the ground that Barlow had been properly appointed and that Lauderdale was a free-trader, i.e. an opponent of the Company's monopoly, and a former supporter of the principles of the French Revolution. The ministry, exercising for the first time a right vested in them by Pitt's Act of 1784, recalled Barlow over the heads of the Directors without being able to give any convincing reasons for their sudden change of mind, which was strongly suspected to be nothing more than the desire to exercise a valuable piece of patronage. The constitutional question was raised in both Houses of Parliament, and produced a vehement though short-lived controversy. The Directors were unwilling to force a conflict with the Cabinet, and a compromise was effected by the withdrawal of Lord Lauderdale and the appointment of Lord Minto.

The new Governor-General, as Sir Gilbert Elliot, had been one of the managers for the impeachment of Warren Hastings and of Sir Elijah Impey, and his sympathies were therefore supposed to be against the expansion of British dominion.

Lord Minto went to India believing in the policy of non-intervention, and on the whole, in his dealings with the native powers, he did not depart from it. But though he waged no important wars on the soil of India, and maintained the settlement effected by Cornwallis and Barlow with the Marathas, he found himself obliged from time to time to abandon the strictest interpretation of a *laisser faire* attitude. To some extent as Governor-General he was forced to unlearn the lessons he had inculcated as President of the Board of Control, and when he laid down his office British power was obviously on the eve of another great forward step. But it did not come in his time, and therefore for just a decade after the retirement of Lord Wellesley the Company's dominions may be said to have remained on the whole stationary. It is true the surface of Indian politics was not unruffled, but the greater Maratha powers had received such severe blows in the late wars that the disturbances which occurred were local and temporary, and the wide and interconnected movements of Lord Wellesley's time were totally absent. In addition Holkar became insane, and the most formidable enemy of British rule was thus impotent for harm. There were disturbances in Bundelkhand, now under the Company's control, having been exchanged for districts near Poona which the Peshwa had originally ceded in the Treaty of Bassein, and thus again recovered. The country was settled after several turbulent chieftains had been defeated and their strongholds captured, including the famous fortresses of Ajaigarh and Kalinjar. The Governor-General was forced to arbitrate between the Peshwa and some of his discontented feudatories. But the most striking instances of Lord Minto's divergence from a strict non-interference policy were in regard to the Raja of Berar and the Sikhs, the formidable people of the Punjab with whom the British now for the first time came into contact.

In 1809 a turbulent Pathan chieftain named Amir Khan, at the head of 40,000 horsemen and more than 20,000 Pindaris or robber bands, claiming to be in alliance with Holkar, invaded Berar. The British government had no obligation to assist Berar, for the Raja had always refused to conclude a subsidiary alliance; indeed, if Amir Khan were, as he claimed to be, really one of Holkar's generals, to interfere would be an actual violation of the treaty by which the Company had engaged not to interfere in Holkar's affairs or with any wars he should wage with states not having treaty relations with the Company. Nevertheless Lord Minto decided he could not permit the forces of anarchy to be let loose in a country so near the frontiers of the Nizam as Berar, and he dispatched a force to aid the Raja of Berar merely on the grounds of preserving order, without exacting any subsidy or treaty in return. This act of moderation on his part, together with the fact that Holkar disowned Amir Khan, prevented his action from bringing on a general Maratha war, as it so easily might have done. Amir Khan was repulsed from Berar, and the peace of India was preserved.

The Sikhs are, properly speaking, not a race but a sect, and the name itself means 'disciples'. The religion was founded by a Guru, or Prophet, named Nanak (1469–1538), and developed by a line of successors, especially by Guru Govind Singh, who met his death at Naderah in 1708. Sikhism inculcates belief in one God; it denounces idolatry, caste distinctions, and the claims of Brahmanism. Its adherents, who were mostly of Jat origin, dwelt in the upper Punjab—in the troubled region which was so often the battle-ground of the Mughals and Afghans. Muhammadan persecution transformed a peaceful sect into a military theocracy, or commonwealth of the elect, known as the 'Khalsa', organized loosely into twelve 'misls' or confederacies. All true Sikhs took the surname of 'Singh', or 'the lion', and first as horsemen, then as infantry, they formed the finest native fighting force that ever took the field. They seized the opportunity of the anarchy in northern India, brought about by the invasions of Nadir Shah of Persia (1739) and Ahmad Shah Durrani (1756), to extend their hold over the Punjab. Though Ahmad Shah inflicted a severe defeat upon a great Sikh army in 1761, he returned to Afghanistan.

The greatest Sikh chieftain, Ranjit Singh, born in 1780, became a soldier, like Mithridates of Pontus, at the age of twelve, made Lahore his capital in 1799, and gradually subdued all the other misls west of the Sutlaj. In 1805 Holkar, then flying before Lord Lake, begged for his aid; but Ranjit Singh, having no wish to quarrel with the British on his account, declined to afford him protection.

Ranjit Singh had long cast covetous eyes on the territory of the Sikh chieftains who dwelt east of the Sutlaj in the country lying between that river and the Jumna, sometimes known as Sirhind. These states had acknowledged the supremacy of the Marathas, and when Sindhia had been driven out by the British they had informally been taken under the protection of the Company. In 1806 some of the chiefs quarrelling amongst themselves called in Ranjit Singh, who, eager to extend his influence, crossed the river both in that year and in the following one. Some of the Sikh chiefs, taking alarm, applied in 1808 to the British Resident at Delhi for protection, and the Governor-General was called upon for a momentous decision. Ranjit Singh clearly set forth his view in the words 'The country on this side of the Jumna except the stations occupied by the English is subject to my authority. Let it remain so.' Were he left to himself, he would undoubtedly in a few years have brought the Cis-Sutlej Sikhs to subjection. Was he to be allowed to advance to the Jumna? To resist him might mean war, and indeed few at the time could have expected the conciliatory shrewdness actually displayed by the Sikh ruler. Nevertheless Lord Minto risked the consequences. He did more; it was decided not only to confine Ranjit Singh to the line west of the Sutlaj, but to suggest to him an offensive and defensive alliance against the French, if they should ever march on India through Persia. Metcalfe, a promising young civilian, was sent to negotiate this difficult business. Ranjit Singh astutely made non-interference in his designs east of the Sutlaj the price of an alliance against the French; but in the meantime the fear of a French invasion had vanished, since Napoleon had embarked upon the Peninsular War. This completely altered the position of affairs, and the British envoy was now merely required to state that all Sikh states east of the Sutlaj had passed with the defeat of Sindhia under British protection, and to demand the withdrawal of the Sikh army. At first Ranjit Singh was obstinate. War was on the eve of breaking out when the Maharaja, conquered at last by Metcalfe's indomitable patience, yielded, and concluded at Amritsar, in April 1809, a treaty which guaranteed him from molestation west of the Sutlaj, provided he confined himself to that bank of the river.

Ranjit Singh is one of the great personalities of Indian history. A born leader of men, gifted with an iron will, selfish, treacherous, crafty, persevering, brave, and avaricious, he possessed just that combination of virtues and vices which is best adapted for building up an Oriental empire. Where he differed from many other great eastern potentates was in his statesmanlike recognition of the strength of the East India Company, the reliance he placed on British promises, and his loyalty to his plighted word. And so the Treaty of Amritsar was never broken while the Maharaja lived. The British frontier to the north-west, with its outpost garrison at Ludhiana, followed an unusually well-defined line, the course of the Sutlaj, and a powerful and friendly native state lay between the Company's dominions and any possible invasion from the mountains.

As we have seen, the mission to Ranjit Singh was partly due to fear of French designs; the same cause produced three other famous embassies by which, under Lord Minto's rule, the Indian government widely extended the sphere of its foreign relations. In the light of later knowledge, both geographical and historical, the fear of a Franco-Russian invasion through the north-western passes may seem almost grotesque, and in fact it was probably never within the bounds of possibility. But no one, in those days when ancient kingdoms in Europe were falling like ninepins, could set a limit to the power and ambition of Napoleon. As far back as 1801 a joint expedition had been proposed to proceed by way of Astrakhan, Bokhara, Khiva, Herat, and Kandahar. The Battle of Copenhagen and the assassination of the Tsar gave Napoleon other work to do. Russia and Great Britain made a treaty in 1805.

Napoleon's eager brain next turned to an alliance with Persia. The king of that country, being at war with Russia, appealed to the Indian government for help on the strength of Malcolm's treaty of 1800, an appeal which was necessarily disregarded since Russia was allied to Great Britain. The King of Persia then made application to Napoleon, who sent General Gardanne as his ambassador to Teheran. A treaty was concluded by which the French agreed to aid Persia against Russia, and Persia undertook to provision and reinforce any French army marching through their country to invade India. But another rapid change in the European political situation followed. In 1807 Napoleon defeated the Russians at Friedland, and the treaty of Tilsit bound the Tsar Alexander to an alliance with France. Schemes were revived for a Franco-Russian expedition against India through Asia Minor and Persia, now to be reconciled to Russia by French intervention. Alexander, however, passively opposed the plan, perceiving that all the advantages would go to his ally, and having a better knowledge than Napoleon of the appalling difficulties of the route. Within a year Napoleon again had other work upon his hands, and the vision of a French empire in the East faded away. Indeed, as far as India was concerned, Napoleon's devastating career only served to generate the expansive force which brought about Lord Wellesley's great wars, to justify them in the eyes of reluctant British statesmen, and to force Lord Minto to embark on an Asiatic rather than a purely Indian policy; while Napoleon himself, as events were to prove, was destined to spend his last years in the narrow prison of an island belonging to the East India Company.

Before the danger was recognized as over, John Malcolm, who had been sent to Persia by Lord Wellesley in 1799, was dispatched to Teheran by the Governor-General, while Sir Harford Jones was sent independently by the home government. A good deal of natural confusion and unseemly wrangling followed; but ultimately the Indian government accepted the treaty concluded by the Crown envoy, which bound the Shah to dismiss the French ambassador and resist the passage through his dominions of a European force marching on India, in return for a promise of assistance in men or money if his country were attacked by Europeans.

Mountstuart Elphinstone was sent with an embassy to Kabul on a similar errand. He did not, however, enter Afghanistan proper, for the King, Shah Shuja, met him at Peshawar and agreed to oppose the French and Persians in any attempt to march through his country; but before Elphinstone had returned, Shah Shuja was driven from his throne by intestine rebellion, and was clamouring in vain for British support in his dynastic troubles. Thirty years later he was to be restored with consequences equally disastrous to himself and those who reimposed his hated rule upon his subjects. The third treaty was concluded with the Amirs of Sind, who promised to exclude the French from their territory.

All these alliances were inoperative, for by 1810 France and Russia were at war again and the French peril passed away. The armies that Napoleon had dreamed of marching through the East were lost amidst the Russian snows. The Indian government, indeed, was able to turn from defensive diplomacy to offensive warfare. Successful expeditions were undertaken, not only against French possessions in the East, but also against those of other nations forced into unwilling alliance with Napoleon. When Portugal passed under French control, Goa was occupied; and in 1809 Macao, a Portuguese station in China, was seized, a proceeding which nearly plunged the Company into a war with the Chinese Empire. The French frigates and privateers that made their headquarters at the Isles of France and Bourbon had done brilliant service for their country and inflicted terrible damage on British shipping. In 1810, however, strong naval expeditions were sent against them by the Indian government. Bourbon (restored in 1815) and Mauritius (permanently retained) were captured. From the Dutch, whose country now lay at the mercy of Napoleon, the Cape of Good Hope had been finally taken in 1806. Amboyna and the Spice Islands were conquered in 1810, and in the following year Lord Minto won the consent of the home government for an attack on Java, the last Dutch eastern possession. A formidable fleet of ninety sail, carrying 12,000 troops under Sir Samuel Auchmuty as Commander-in-Chief, assembled at Malacca in June. Lord Minto himself accompanied the expedition, nominally as a volunteer, but really to organize the civil administration after the conquest. Napoleon had spared no pains to have the defences of the island strengthened, and had sent General Jansens, who had surrendered the Cape to the English, to command the 17,000 troops in Java, with the significant warning that 'a French General does not allow himself to be taken a second time'. The English expedition arrived early in August and promptly occupied Batavia. The main French army was lying behind strong entrenchments and redoubts at Cornelis, eight miles distant. The position was brilliantly stormed by Colonel Gillespie, and the broken ranks of the enemy were relentlessly pursued for ten miles. The French lost 6,000 prisoners, mostly Europeans, and 300 guns. They left 1,500 dead within their lines or along the route of their flight. The English had 900 put out of action, including 85 officers. General Jansens retired to the eastern part of the island, but was soon forced to capitulate. Thus Holland lost the whole of her eastern empire. The Directors had ordered that if the expedition were successful, the Dutch fortifications were to be levelled and the troops withdrawn; but Minto, seeing that it would be an inhuman act to abandon the Dutch colonists to the mercies of an exasperated native population, had the courage and independence to disregard these instructions. Having crushed the dangerous revolt of a native chief, he entrusted the government of the island to Sir Stamford Raffles, whose administration forms a brilliant chapter in the history of British colonization. In 1814 their eastern possessions, with the exception of the Cape, were restored to the Dutch, Java being actually handed over in 1816.

These notable achievements added military glory to the rule of Lord Minto, who was created an Earl and sailed for England in 1813, to die within a few months of his return. When he surrendered his charge he could claim that, with the exception of the minor operations in Bundelkhand, he had kept an honourable peace in India without drawing sword against the native powers. But signs were not wanting that there was trouble in store for his successor. The outrages of the Pindaris, roving free lances and robber bands, in central India, the encroachments of the Gurkhas of Nepal, and the insolent defiance of the Burmese indicated that a period of unrest and disturbance was again approaching.

CHAPTER XXII

FINAL DEFEAT OF THE MARATHA CONFEDERACY. LORD HASTINGS

THE year in which the Earl of Moira (afterwards Marquis of Hastings) began his long and notable period of office marked a new stage in the history of the East India Company. Since 1808 the question of the renewal of their charter (which was to expire on April 10, 1814) had been to the fore, and a Parliamentary Committee was engaged in inquiring into every branch of their administration. Two great questions were involved, the commercial monopoly, and the political or territorial rights of the Company. It was fairly plain that neither Parliament nor public opinion would tolerate a further grant of the full monopoly of the Indian trade. On the other hand, there was practically no desire to oust the Company from its political position, and that for two reasons. The people felt that the immense patronage of the Indian services would be less corruptly administered by the Court of Directors, standing apart as it did from the Party system, than by ministers obsessed with the idea of purchasing the votes and allegiance of their followers; while politicians themselves were disposed to be well content with a constitution which gave them a very real control over Indian affairs, and yet enabled them, if anything went wrong, to shift a good deal of the responsibility upon the shoulders of the Company.

The Directors fought stubbornly for every inch of their ground, and even when they were plainly told that the free export of goods to India from the 'outports', i.e. Liverpool,

Bristol, Hull, &c., would have to be conceded, they contended fiercely that all imports from India should be brought to the London docks. But petitions against this restriction poured in from the great provincial ports and manufacturing towns; and finally, though they were allowed to retain the profitable monopoly of the China trade, the commerce of India was thrown open. The whole question was thoroughly sifted in both Houses of Parliament, and Warren Hastings, an old man of eighty-one, was summoned to give evidence. As that venerable figure appeared for the last time before the bar of the House where more than a quarter of a century before he had stood for so many weary years to hear his whole career arraigned and held up to scorn and obloquy, members of the House, obeying a spontaneous impulse, rose and uncovered, an act of respect they repeated when Hastings, having given his evidence, withdrew. His testimony was all against change and therefore, though listened to with deference, weighed little with his hearers. The whole inquiry, indeed, proved but a dismal tribute to the value of expert evidence. All the greatest Indian authorities, Lord Teignmouth, Munro, and Malcolm were opposed to the abolition of the monopoly, and even Lord Wellesley appeared in the unexpected rôle of the Company's panegyrist. The dangerous pitfalls that beset political prophecy are well exemplified in the solemn warning of the Court of Directors that, if the trade to India were thrown open, it would prove their own utter ruin, involve a breakdown in the civil and military services, endanger the tranquillity and happiness of the people of India, imperil British interests in Asia, and even, as they declared by a fine effort of imagination, overthrow the constitution at home. One point raised in the controversy must not be omitted in a volume of this series. As a last resort the Directors painted in vivid colours the perils of a European colonization of India. Merchants and agents, artisans and labourers would flock to the East and settle in the country. These colonists, following the example of the North American states, would eventually achieve independence, and India would be lost to Great Britain. Such a danger only existed in the heated imaginations of interested controversialists, and, as a matter of fact, the immigration of Europeans into the country was still severely limited by statute. No person could proceed to India without a licence either from the Company or the Board of Control; they could be sent home by the government of India if it were deemed desirable, and they were made subject to the Regulation that forbade to Europeans the holding of lands. So little was actually done in the way of colonization that, in a period of eighteen years after 1814, the total number of persons not in the Company's service proceeding under licence to India was only 1,324. The ablest speech in the Commons was made by Canning, who shed the dry light of reason and the gleams of his mordant humour upon the overcharged statements of either side. The immigrants under the Act would probably be a few pedlars in hardware or needy knife-grinders, and they were hardly likely to project a colonial rebellion after the American pattern on the background of the immemorial East. In the Lords, Earl Grenville went much further than the government in his attack upon the Company, and in a speech of remarkable prescience advocated a scheme that would have antedated by many years the solution of succeeding generations. He held that twenty years, the term for which the Company's privileges were to be prolonged, was too long a period to farm out the commerce of half the globe and the sovereignty over sixty millions of people, particularly at a time when the whole fortune of the British Empire was at stake owing to the Napoleonic wars. Any plan adopted should be limited in duration to the restoration of peace. He believed that the Crown should definitely take over the political and territorial rights of the

Company, for 'no sovereign ever traded for a profit; no trading Company ever yet administered government for the happiness of its subjects.' The highest offices in India were already practically in the gift of the Crown, and appointments to the civil service should be made by competition from the great public schools and universities. The Company's military forces should be absorbed into the King's service, and the Indian markets should be thrown open to British capital and enterprise in the most unrestricted way. But Lord Grenville was half a century before his time. The Charter Act, as eventually passed, confirmed the Company in the government of India for twenty years from April 1814, and threw open the trade to India, but left them the monopoly of the profitable commerce with China. A small sum annually (£10,000) was allotted for the encouragement of education, literature, and science. For many years this fund was badly administered, but the clause marked the first open recognition by the government of the duty of ameliorating the moral and intellectual condition of the peoples of India.

The Earl of Moira, who came out to India in his sixtieth year, had been an opponent of Lord Wellesley's policy, and yet he was destined to complete the fabric of British dominion in India almost exactly as his great predecessor had planned it.

He was first called upon to deal with Nepal, the country lying along the northern frontiers of Bengal and Oudh for about seven hundred miles from the Sutlaj to Sikkim, and running back with an average breadth of about a hundred and thirty miles up the snow-clad slopes of the Himalayas. A Hindu race claiming Rajput origin had conquered the original inhabitants of Mongolian stock in the fourteenth century, and to some extent intermarried with them. The tribe of the Gurkhas under a powerful raja had, about ten years after Plassey, subdued the other ruling clans and given its name to the whole race. The Gurkhas were a very hardy, warlike stock, and they soon found their narrow mountain home too confined for them. Checked in their northern raids by the colossal power of the Chinese empire, they had since the beginning of the nineteenth century pressed hard on the ill-defined frontiers of Bengal and Oudh, and about this time they seized some districts in the southern lowlands claimed by the East India Company. They refused to withdraw and hostilities began in November 1814.

The first war waged by the Earl of Moira presents a curious contrast to his great series of operations against the Maratha powers. He has been accused of a failure to appreciate or provide for the peculiar difficulties of the campaign. But it must be remembered that Nepal is one of the most difficult countries in the world for military operations; the gallant little Gurkhas are the best fighting race, with the possible exception of the Sikhs, that India produces; the forces employed had no past experience that could aid them to contend with the tactical and strategical difficulties of the hill country, while the generals, with the exception of Ochterlony, showed great incapacity. In spite of the fact that the army of invasion numbered 34,000, while the Gurkhas could muster no more than 12,000, the first campaign of 1814–15 was perilously near being a failure. General Gillespie, the hero of the fighting in Java, was repulsed and killed in a premature assault upon a mountain fort. General Martindale was checked at Jytak, the central attacks on Palpa and Katmandu, the capital, were driven back and only General Ochterlony in the extreme west of Nepal succeeded in holding his own. Later in the year more success was achieved, and in December 1815 the envoys of the ruling chiefs accepted a treaty involving the cession of certain territories and the residence of a British representative at Katmandu. The central government however disowned the action of their plenipotentiaries and, though Lord Moira offered to moderate his terms, hostilities had to be resumed. Ochterlony, now in supreme command, advanced after hard fighting to within fifty miles of the capital, when the Gurkha chieftains announced their acceptance of the Treaty of Sagauli, March 1816. The Governor-General was only too pleased to accept the settlement, and no attempt was made to inflict a severer penalty. Both sides had learnt to respect each other's fighting qualities. The gains to British dominion were not unimportant. The Gurkhas abandoned most of their claims in the Tarai, or lowlands, along their southern border. The provinces of Kumaon and Garhwal at the extreme west of Nepal were surrendered, and the site of Simla, the future hot weather capital of British India, was thus acquired; the north-west frontier of the Company's possessions was carried right up to the mountains. A pathway was opened up to the regions of central Asia; 'countries before unknown have been added to geography; and nature has been explored by science in some of her most inaccessible retreats, and most rare and majestic developments. . . . Roads have been cut along the sides of precipices; bridges constructed over mountain torrents; stations have been formed which have grown into towns; and the stir and activity of human life have disturbed the silence of the lonely forests, and broken the slumber of the eternal snows.'[1] A protective treaty with the Raja of Sikkim drove a barrier between the eastern frontier of Nepal and Bhutan. Unlike some native states, the Nepalese were content with having once defied the British power, and have never since that date departed from an attitude of friendly independence.

The war was over, and the Governor-General, now Marquis of Hastings, whose equanimity and patience had sometimes failed him during its course, could afford to draw breath.

[1] *The History of British India*, H. H. Wilson, vol. ii, p. 59.

At one time the danger of a wide-reaching combination of Indian powers against the British had seemed very imminent. The Gurkhas had sent their emissaries far and wide to Sindhia, Ranjit Singh, the Pindari chieftains, and even to the capitals of the Burmese and Chinese empires. After the first unsatisfactory campaigns, when the British forces were locked up in the hill country, the Maratha states and Amir Khan, the Pathan leader of free companies, were obviously making ready to fish in troubled waters; even our great Sikh ally, perhaps doubting for once of British invulnerability, had moved 20,000 men to the banks of the Sutlaj.

The government, with the approval of George Canning, the new President of the Board of Control, now turned to deal with the Pathan and Pindari hordes, who had made central India outside the ring fence of British dominion a hell upon earth for the cultivators of the soil, and had lately even extended their raids into British territory.

The Pindaris were first heard of during the wars waged in the Deccan between Aurangzeb and Sivaji. They followed the Maratha armies, as irregulars and skirmishers without pay, subsisting on the plunder of the enemy's territory. Some of them were of Pathan origin, but broken and desperate men of all races joined their ranks; since the beginning of the nineteenth century Sindhia had granted their leaders settlements in Malwa near the Narbada. After 1805, the Maratha powers, cowed by Lord Wellesley's wars, were mainly at peace. The Pindaris, without having the excuse of warfare, extended their raids far and wide in central India—mere plundering and looting expeditions attended by every form of infamy, torture, and outrage upon the wretched peasants.

The ravages of the Pindaris had done more than anything else to discredit the policy of non-intervention. Their expeditions grew more and more daring and ferocious. In 1812 they broke into Bundelkhand, and for some time an attempt to keep them out was made by maintaining a line of fortified posts reaching from that district to the gulf of Cambay. The expedient proved neither economical nor effective. In 1815 and 1816 they plundered the Nizam's dominions, and in the latter year cruelly and wantonly ravaged the Northern Circars. This was the final blow that broke down the patience of the home authorities and the Calcutta Council. The Governor-General had long been urging war. Given a free hand at last, he made far-sighted and comprehensive preparations. To surround the Pindaris in Malwa, he gathered together a huge army of 113,000 men and 300 guns, subdivided into the army of Hindustan (four divisions) which he himself commanded, and the army of the Deccan (five divisions) under Sir Thomas Hislop. Such a force might seem excessive for the task of rounding up and exterminating an army of brigands; but the Governor-General realized that since the *laisser-faire* policy of the Cornwallis school was now being definitely reversed, he would have in every Maratha power a potential enemy eagerly waiting for any failure or faltering on the part of his generals. While one cordon of his army facing inwards had to encircle the robber bands, a wider ring facing outwards had to check the attempts of the Maratha states to break through to their assistance. His prescience was fully justified; 'the hunt of the Pindaris became merged in the third Maratha war'[1] and, though the campaign was brilliantly and finally successful, he had not a gun nor a man too many. The words above quoted give the key to the complicated operations which follow, and two main movements must be distinguished, the converging of forces upon the Pindari bands in central India

[1] *The Oxford Student's History of India*, by Vincent A. Smith, p. 204

and the defeat or neutralization of Sindhia, Holkar, the Bhonsla, and the Peshwa.

Serious trouble for the past two years had been threatening from Poona. The Peshwa, one of the most treacherous and cowardly of his line, had fallen under the influence of an unscrupulous minister, Trimbakji, and was intriguing once more to place himself at the head of the Maratha confederacy. In July 1815 the minister of the Gaikwar of Baroda was basely murdered, when visiting Poona under a British safe conduct to settle some disputed claims and counterclaims between the two Maratha governments. Trimbakji's guilt was certain, and the Peshwa's complicity strongly suspected. Fortunately at this crisis the Resident at Poona was Mountstuart Elphinstone, who happily combined the qualities of a scholar, diplomatist, and man of action. He promptly demanded the arrest of Trimbakji, and the Peshwa, after prevaricating as long as he dared, delivered him up to the British authorities in September 1815. A year later Trimbakji made a romantic escape from his prison and could not be found, though it was strongly suspected that the Peshwa was in communication with him. The Peshwa was meanwhile mustering his forces; his whole demeanour was so shifty that Elphinstone threatened him with open war and forced him on June 13, 1817, to sign a more rigorous subsidiary treaty involving the cession of territory and an explicit renunciation of all claims to the supreme place among the Maratha powers. 'We had no choice', wrote Hastings, 'consistently with our own security but to cripple him if we left him on his throne.' A year before (May 1816) a subsidiary alliance at his own request had been made with Apa Sahib, the regent for the imbecile Raja of Nagpur, who was so dependent for his position on British bayonets that he left his capital to live under the protection of the camp of his auxiliaries.

The Governor-General therefore could feel, when he left Calcutta in July 1817 to begin his great enveloping movement, that two of the Maratha powers had no excuse for not recognizing the determination of the British to be supreme in India south of the Sutlaj and to crush the forces of anarchy. Sindhia remained, and his attitude was not encouraging, for he was obviously very uneasy as to the fate of the ruffians whom he partly protected. Lord Hastings gave him little scope for ambiguity. Having crossed the Jumna he marched towards Gwalior. He made it clear to Sindhia that the days of non-intervention were over, and that the British government intended to cast its protection over the states of Malwa and Rajputana. On November 5, 1817, Sindhia, practically under compulsion, signed a treaty which bound him to give assistance against the Pindaris, and abrogated the clause in the Treaty of Surji-arjangaon debarring the British from making treaties with the Rajput chieftains. The latter gladly and eagerly welcomed the sheltering arm of British protection, and treaties were concluded by Metcalfe at Delhi with nineteen Rajput states, including Jaipur, Udaipur, Jodhpur, and Bundi.

On the very day that Sindhia was coerced into signing the revised subsidiary treaty, the Peshwa rose in final rebellion, expecting that his example would be followed by all the Maratha powers. The British residency was sacked and burnt. Elphinstone made his escape, marshalled his forces, and, though fearfully outnumbered, brilliantly defeated the enemy at Kirki. The Peshwa fled southwards, and as he went possessed himself of the person of his titular suzerain, Sivaji's descendant, the Raja of Satara. He was pursued and defeated in several engagements, but for many months eluded capture, doubling and twisting on his course in the vain attempt to break through to Berar. The Maratha states of central India were themselves in sore straits. At Nagpur, Apa Sahib, who had mounted the throne on the murder of the Raja, and at Indore, Holkar, or rather his government for he was still a minor, by a strange infatuation revolted just as the cordon of British armies was closing round them. They struggled desperately but fruitlessly in the toils. The forces of the Nagpur residency won a brilliant victory against terrible odds on the Sitabaldi hills on November 27. Holkar's forces were utterly crushed at Mehidpur on December 21. Both states were forced to accept treaties which greatly curtailed their territories and practically reduced them to vassalage.

Meanwhile, in spite of a serious outbreak of cholera in the British camp and the diversions created by the Maratha risings, the ring of fire and steel was closing round the Pindaris. They first darted northward, but were headed off from Gwalior and hemmed in on the south and east. Many of them were cut up and dispersed, but their wonderful mobility rendered it exceedingly difficult to prevent a certain number from making their escape. Very early in the campaign the Pathan leader, Amir Khan, who possessed a regular army with 150 guns, was persuaded to disband his forces on condition of being recognized as Nawab of Tonk. One Pindari leader was given lands at Gorakhpur, but many refused submission. Chitu, the most wicked and desperate of all, was hunted into the jungle and devoured by a tiger.

The final operations of the war were directed against the fugitive rulers of the defeated Maratha states. The Peshwa, after two more pitched battles at Koregaon and Ashti, bravely fought by his general Gokla, having over and over again baffled and eluded his pursuers, finally surrendered to Sir John Malcolm on June 18, when that distinguished officer with excessive generosity, to the great chagrin of the Governor-General, guaranteed the fugitive a pension of £80,000 a year. The ex-Peshwa resided henceforward at Bithur, twelve miles north-west of Cawnpore, the city that his infamous adopted son, Nana Sahib, was destined to desecrate with one of the most revolting of human crimes. Two hundred miles away, his confederate Trimbakji expiated his guilt by a lifelong imprisonment in the fort of Chunar near Benares.

In the long pursuit of the Peshwa the *fainéant* Raja of Satara had luckily fallen into British hands, and the Indian government, adopting the precedent followed by Wellesley in the case of Mysore, decided to confer upon him, as the representative of the line of Sivaji, a small principality carved out of Baji Rao's forfeited domains. He was accordingly solemnly enthroned as Raja of Satara on April 11, 1818. This policy was hardly justified by its results; the rule of the restored dynasty proved an evil and incompetent one, and Satara was one of the states to which subsequently the doctrine of Lapse was applied by Dalhousie: but the Indian government erred, if at all, on the side of generosity. An interesting alternative to the restoration of the old line was the suggestion of Sir Thomas Munro that the Company itself should assume the office of Peshwa, as in Bengal it had stood forth as Diwan.

Apa Sahib, the Bhonsla Raja of Berar, who had been pardoned and restored after Sitabaldi, proved a traitor, and his depleted dominions were given to another member of his house. He escaped from British custody and gathered together the remnants of defeated armies in the Mahadeo hills among the aboriginal tribes of the Gonds. After winning some preliminary successes, his bands were broken up; he fled to the Raja of Jodhpur and thence to Ranjit Singh, who was allowed by the British government to give him an asylum which was practically a prison. With the fall of Asirgarh in March 1819, the commandant of which had afforded help to Apa Sahib, the military operations of the war were concluded.

A great revolution had been effected in the political states of India. To sum up very briefly the results of this most complicated and intricate of campaigns :—

The Pindaris ceased to exist. Sindhia without having stirred in his own defence was humbled and rendered impotent for harm. Holkar was left with but half of his original possessions. Nagpur was mulcted in territory and reduced to the condition of a vassal state. The Peshwa was dethroned and his hereditary office abolished. His dominions with the exception of the districts granted to the Raja of Satara presently became part of the Presidency of Bombay. Some of Great Britain's bitterest enemies were settled as pensioners or prisoners within easy distance of Calcutta. Her protection now shadowed the ancient houses of the Rajput states, and her dominion extended from Cape Comorin to the banks of the Sutlaj, across which the military commonwealth of the Sikhs, at the zenith of its prosperity, still wielded and disciplined by its able ruler, stood firm in friendship and alliance. Such peace and order as had not been known since the greatest days of the Mughal Empire extended through central India.

Full justice has not perhaps always been done to the moderation of British policy throughout this epoch. Seldom have forbearance and firmness been more happily combined. Those bad rulers, the Peshwa and Apa Sahib, were again and again given chances to reform. The terms offered to the ruffian leaders of the Pindaris might be described as excessively generous. The fall of Asirgarh revealed deliberate treachery on the part of Sindhia which might have justified his deposition, and had Lord Wellesley been Governor-General, we may conjecture that his days of political independence would have been numbered, but Hastings passed him over in contemptuous silence.

In spite of the warlike nature of Lord Hastings's administration, some most important civil and administrative reforms were carried through. No Governor-General ever had four more brilliant subordinates than Sir John Malcolm, Sir Thomas Munro, Mountstuart Elphinstone, and Sir Charles Metcalfe, and all these men left the impress of their characters upon Indian history. Elphinstone's pacification of the provinces conquered from the Peshwa, and Munro's *ryotwari* settlement of the land revenues of Madras, i.e. a settlement made directly with the cultivators and dispensing with middlemen, are two of the abiding memorials of British administration. Elphinstone at Poona was ably seconded by Grant Duff, the Resident at Satara; and so by a curious coincidence two of the greatest historians of India were engaged at the same time in administrative duties in the same province.

In Bengal some legal reforms were found necessary owing to the congested state of the law courts. In civil actions the procedure was curtailed and simplified, while an important change was made in the administration of criminal justice. The rule laid down by Lord Cornwallis that the offices of collector and magistrate were never to be united, though in theory unimpeachable, had some practical disadvantages. A complete separation of the executive and judicial power implies a highly organized state. Among primitive civilizations there is much practical advantage, provided officials can be trusted, in uniting both functions in the same hands. Henceforward Lord Cornwallis's prohibition was removed. Lord Hastings probably felt, and with reason, that the newer generation of the Company's servants with their higher traditions would prove superior to temptations to which their predecessors had succumbed. Measures were also taken to protect the rights of the ryots as against the zamindars where experience showed that the working of the Permanent Settlement pressed too hardly on the cultivators of the soil. They were given a certain prescriptive right of occupancy as long as they paid their customary rents, and these rents could no longer be arbitrarily increased.

A beginning was made, on humble lines, with the education of the natives by the establishment of vernacular schools near Calcutta, and the first vernacular newspaper was published by the missionaries of Serampore. The finances of India were prosperous, and the only shadow on the administration was caused by the rather doubtful transactions of the firm of William Palmer & Co. with the government of the Nizam. Their loans to the Nizam had received the sanction of the Governor-General, but there was some question whether they did not infringe an Act of Parliament against the financial dealings of Europeans with native states. The only charge that could with justice be brought against Lord Hastings was that he had failed to exercise due caution in examining the details of the case, and out of excessive good nature had suffered his confidence to be abused. The Directors had already voted him a grant of £60,000 after the completion of the Nepalese war, but henceforward their relations with him were strained, though they admitted the purity of his motives. He resigned office in 1821, but did not actually lay down his functions till January 1, 1823.

Lord Hastings had carried through a great and necessary work. His material achievements challenge comparison with those of Lord Wellesley, but he was of course not so great or commanding a figure. He owed much of the success of his administration to a brilliant band of subordinates, men who had been trained and inspired by his great predecessor. Hastings did not possess Wellesley's dignity, eloquence, or originality; there was an element of vanity in his otherwise estimable character, and signs are not lacking that he would hardly have shown Wellesley's equanimity in the face of reverses or his noble consideration of defeated generals. On the other hand, he conceived and carried through the grandest strategical operation ever undertaken in India, in the course of which twenty-eight actions were fought and a hundred and twenty fortresses taken without a single reverse. He was less precipitate than Lord Wellesley, less harsh to errant native rulers, and he did not proceed against them till his case was very strong. He was an able administrator, a hard and conscientious worker, a good judge of men, and his name and fame deservedly rank only just below the greatest in the roll of Governors-General.

CHAPTER XXIII

THE FIRST BURMESE WAR. LORD AMHERST

On Lord Hastings's resignation, the brilliant orator and statesman, George Canning, was appointed Governor-General; but before he could sail for India the suicide of the Marquis of Londonderry (better known as Lord Castlereagh) opened to him the office of Foreign Secretary and the leadership of the House of Commons, whereupon he resigned his Indian appointment. The Directors, after considering the claims of Lord William Bentinck, nominated Lord Amherst, who had shown firmness and restraint on an abortive mission to China. In the seven months' interval which elapsed before Amherst's arrival in India the reins of government were held rather uneasily by John Adam, senior member of Council. A capable official in a subordinate capacity, he was hardly fitted for the head of the government and attempted with unhappy results, as we shall see later, to check the free discussion of political affairs in the press. The fabric of British dominion in India having been completed by Lord Hastings as far north as the Sutlaj River, at last it might seem to those who desired peace and the maintenance of equilibrium that a period of quiescence had arrived. But again such hopes were doomed to disappointment. The frontier to the north-west was to remain unviolated for another twenty years, but to the north-eastward the boundary line was still perilously indefinite.

The vast Bay of Bengal forms a great irregularly shaped horseshoe, starting from Cape Comorin in the south-west to the Malay Peninsula in the south-east. British dominion

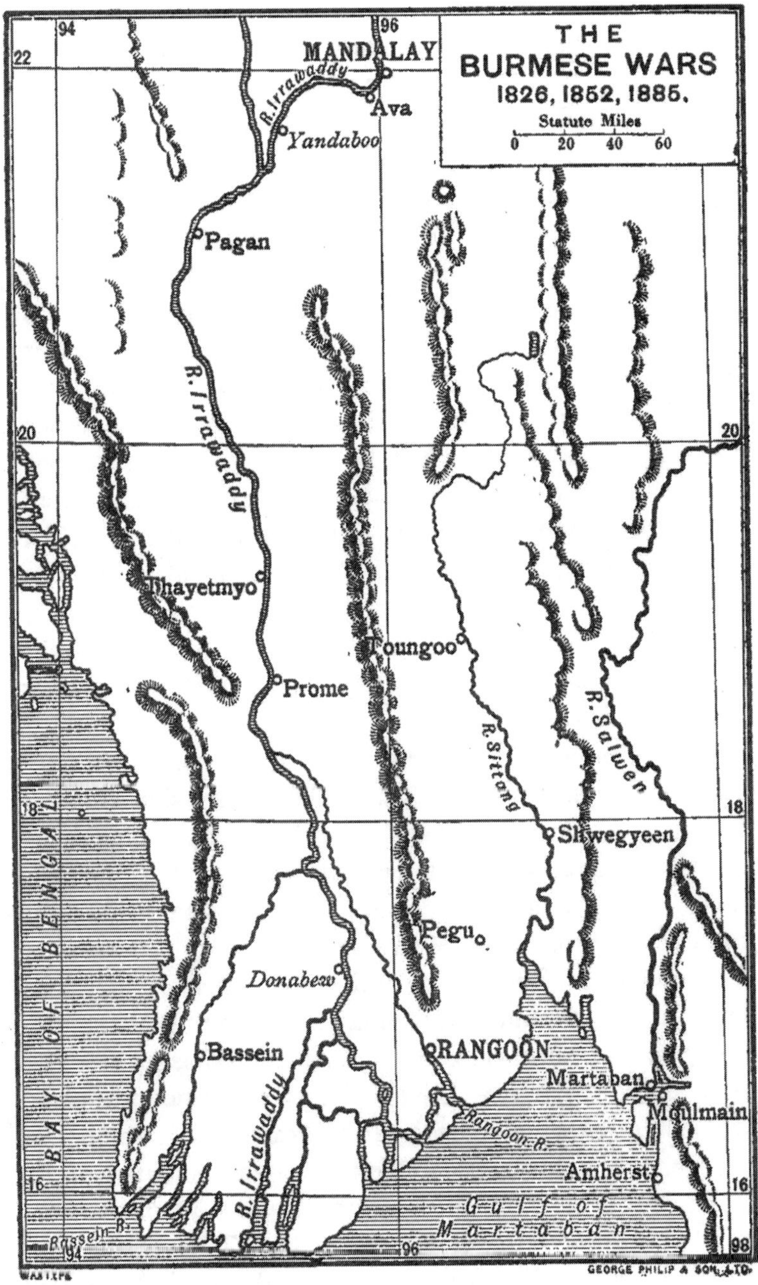

GEORGE PHILIP & SON, LTD.

now extended continuously all up the western side, round the northern bend, and as the district of Chittagong bounded by the river Naaf formed part of the province of Bengal, it stretched for about a hundred miles down the eastern side of the bay. The eastern boundary line of Bengal, roughly speaking, might have been found by drawing a line from Chittagong northward to the hills; but it was very ill-defined and variable. Immediately to the east of this line lay the kingdom of Assam with various little independent or semi-independent states. Neither the Company nor its servants in India had any desire to increase their responsibilities or their territory south and east of their outpost Chittagong, and it may safely be said that not even the most aggressive of the Governors-General had foreseen that, within thirty years from this date, the red line of British dominion would have crept without a break down the eastern side of the bay to a point on the same parallel of latitude as Madura in the extreme south of India. But since there was no natural barrier of mountain or river to the province of Bengal upon the east, the same law of development which had governed British expansion in the past again became operative. The British dominion in India there came into collision with a people of Tibeto-Chinese origin, who spreading outwards from the fertile valley of the mighty Irrawaddy had conquered down the coast southwards to the Malay peninsula and northwards to the confines of Chittagong, and was seeking to extend its sway further inland over Assam and the Brahmaputra valley to the north-eastern bend of the Himalayas. The same decade that saw Clive's victory at Plassey witnessed the first great step taken by the Burman chief Alompra in the founding of his considerable power—the conquest of the province of Pegu from the Talaings in the delta of the Irrawaddy. In 1766 the Burmese wrested Tenasserim from Siam; in 1784 they annexed the hitherto independent kingdom of Arakan, and by 1793 they had absorbed Upper and Lower Burma and were close to Chittagong. Fugitives flying from territories occupied by Burmese armies frequently took refuge over the British border, and sometimes, from a base established there, made retaliatory raids back upon the conquered provinces. The Burmese frequently demanded the surrender of the fugitives, and though, whenever they were clearly criminals, the British at Chittagong were willing to hand them over, they were naturally reluctant to refuse all right of asylum to defeated belligerents, especially in view of the cruelty of their enemies. In 1817–18 the Burmese forces were threatening Assam, and in the latter year they sent an insolent letter to the Indian government, laying claim to Chittagong, Dacca, Murshidabad and Cossimbazar. The letter was carefully timed, for the Burmese believed that the British were hard pressed in the Pindari war. Before it arrived, however, the danger had passed, and Lord Hastings with great forbearance chose to treat the dispatch as a forgery. The Burmese having in the meantime been defeated by the Siamese were, as the Governor-General had foreseen, 'thoroughly glad of the excuse to remain quiet'. The respite was only temporary; in 1822 the Burmese subjugated Assam and now confronted the British all along their ill-defined north-eastern frontier.

Their hitherto almost unbroken success had filled the Burmese with an overweening sense of their own prowess in war. They believed that no troops could stand against them, and 'from the king to the beggar they were hot for a war with the English'. Indeed, no conflict in which we engaged in the East was so wantonly provoked. In September 1823 they made an attack upon Shahpuri, a small island off Chittagong belonging to the Company, and commenced hostilities on the Assam frontier. British demands for satisfaction having been absolutely ignored, Lord

Amherst declared war on February 24, 1824. The campaign that followed was, considering the fighting qualities of the enemy, one of the most prolonged and least successful in the Company's history. The best defence of the Burmese lay in the natural features of the country, which was one vast expanse of forest and morass, laced longitudinally by mountain ranges and the valleys of the Irrawaddy, Sittang, and Salween. The central plain of Burma proper was regularly flooded in the period of the rains and clouded by steaming, noxious exhalations deadly to the health of European troops. As a fighting force in the open the Burmese army was a negligible quantity, but the Burmese soldier, each man carrying his mattock, was extraordinarily skilled at throwing up earthworks and sinking rifle-pits, or in building with great rapidity stout stockades of timber.

The British plan of campaign was to approach from the sea, capture Rangoon, and send an armed flotilla up the Irrawaddy to the capital; but the wrong season had been selected for such strategy. Rangoon was occupied in May by Sir Archibald Campbell, and then the rains, which transformed the Irrawaddy from a navigable channel into a rushing torrent, prevented for six months the advance up country. The Burmese had abandoned the town at the first appearance of the enemy and driven off all their flocks and herds into the jungles of Pegu. The British forces had thus to depend on rotting provisions provided by fraudulent Calcutta contractors, and amidst the fever-laden mists of the drenched country round Rangoon were soon decimated by disease.

In the meantime Bandula, the ablest Burmese general and the conqueror of Assam, was sent to attempt the invasion of Bengal from the north-east. He cut up an isolated British detachment at Ramu that had advanced too far from the base at Chittagong, but he was then recalled to march to the relief of Rangoon. In December he arrived before the town with 60,000 men, but he was driven back and retreated to Donabew, forty miles up the river.

Elsewhere, when it was found that Campbell was cooped up in Rangoon, the Indian government attempted to advance on Ava by two expeditions, one marching southwards through Cachar and Manipur, the other through Arakan and up the higher valley of the Irrawaddy. Both were failures. The first expedition was baffled by the difficulties of the country between Cachar and Manipur, and effected a retreat to Bengal; the second occupied Arakan without much difficulty but made very slow progress through inefficient leadership, and was so terribly reduced by fever that it had ultimately to be withdrawn.

Though the main force was almost inactive at Rangoon or engaged on minor operations, Campbell, in the autumn of 1824, had employed the fleet to transport troops to Tenasserim, and the province was quickly reduced. From it he drew large supplies of fresh provisions and cattle for the suffering army at Rangoon. Thus in February 1825, though he had wasted valuable time on dilatory preparations, he was able to resume his long interrupted advance up the Irrawaddy both in the flotilla and on land. Bandula in April was defeated and killed at Donabew after holding out bravely for a month, and three weeks later Campbell occupied Prome, the capital of Lower Burma, where he spent the rainy season. In August negotiations for peace were begun but terms were rejected by the Burmese, who had not even yet learnt their lesson. Fighting began again in November, and the British forces, having routed the enemy's forlorn hope at Pagan, advanced to Yandaboo within sixty miles of the capital. There, on February 24, 1826, peace was concluded. The King of Ava agreed to cede the provinces of Arakan and Tenasserim absolutely, to withdraw from Assam and Cachar, to recognize the independence of Manipur, enter into a commercial treaty, admit a British

Resident at Ava, and pay an indemnity of a million sterling. A glance at the map will show the importance of these results. The Burmese empire had been shorn of most of its sea frontage by the surrender of two long narrow provinces. Tenasserim extends southwards almost as far as does Cape Comorin on the other side of the Bay of Bengal, parted from it by fourteen hundred miles of sea. Assam, Cachar, and Manipur could henceforward be reckoned as British protectorates, for the Burmese were debarred from interference in that quarter. But they were left in possession of the whole basin of the Irrawaddy, and they had access to the sea by its mouths and the coast of the broad wedge of territory that parted the two provinces ceded to the British from one another.

The war had been for those days enormously expensive, for it had cost thirteen millions sterling, or more than twelve times the charges for the Pindari and Maratha campaigns. It had lasted two years, and, when every allowance has been made for the great difficulties to be faced, it must be admitted that the conduct of it reflected little credit either on the Indian government or the generals in the field. The latter were far too deliberate and leisurely in their movements, and showed great lack of initiative. The Governor-General and his Council had no clear and consistent policy. Many of the difficulties of commissariat and transport could have been provided for, and throughout there was a lamentable failure to concentrate and economize the forces employed. Had it not been for the splendid work of Sir Thomas Munro, the Governor of Madras, in sending reinforcements and supplies, that failure would have been still more marked. At the conclusion of the war Lord Amherst was given an earldom—a distinction he can hardly be said to have earned. He was a man of very mediocre abilities, and never showed any real grasp of the Indian problems of his day.

In the meantime various minor disturbances had been caused throughout India by the conviction that the British would be defeated in Burma. Above all, a usurper at Bharatpur, the famous stronghold that had resisted the desperate assaults of Lord Lake, defied the British power by keeping the rightful heir, a minor, from his inheritance. Sir David Ochterlony, starting with some precipitancy to Bharatpur, was promptly recalled by the Governor-General, and soon afterwards died of an illness partly, it is supposed, brought on by vexation and chagrin. There were ominous signs of unrest in Malwa, Bundelkhand, and Maratha territory, especially after the recall of Ochterlony, which was attributed to British fear of attacking an impregnable stronghold. Sir Charles Metcalfe in a famous minute maintained that 'our influence is too pervading to admit of neutrality'. He won over the government to his view, and in January 1826 Lord Combermere took the great fortress by storm.

A more sinister fact was the Sepoy mutiny at Barrackpore near Calcutta in 1824. The native soldiers feared the Burmese as magicians, and also held they would lose caste if required to go on shipboard. Besides these reasons, the officers with criminal folly had refused to redress, or even inquire into, some very real grievances respectfully put before them by the troops. The mutiny was only quelled after the mutinous regiments had been fired upon by British artillery, and the parade ground made a shambles. The name of the 47th Bengal Native Infantry was erased from the army list.

CHAPTER XXIV

LORD WILLIAM BENTINCK AND INTERNAL REFORMS

WITH the retirement of Lord Amherst there ensued a ten years' respite from major military operations. The new Governor-General, Lord William Bentinck, was happy in his date. He could hardly have found a more favourable opportunity to carry out the liberal and humanizing policy to which he was devoted. At the end of the decade India was destined again to enter upon a troubled epoch; it proved fortunate indeed that, in the interval, measures for the improvement of the country and the amelioration of the people were pressed on. The reform movement, interrupted for a time by the campaigns that followed the governor-generalship of Lord Auckland, never altogether lost its impetus, and was resumed with fresh vigour at the close of the war period by Lord Dalhousie. At first sight, perhaps, the omens for Bentinck's success were not very propitious. He had been deprived of the governorship of Madras in 1807 for an alleged failure to cope with the mutiny at Vellore. As a soldier he had at least enjoyed the opportunity of seeing operations on the grand scale, for he was present at Marengo; but his own military career had been undistinguished, and in the Peninsular campaign he had not impressed the Duke of Wellington as possessing pre-eminent qualities either for war or diplomacy. He was a true Liberal of his day, thoroughly in accord with the ideals that inspired the era of Catholic emancipation and Parliamentary reform. His personal habits were simple, and he intensely disliked the state that is generally considered necessary for the position he occupied. In this respect, as well as in his philanthropic care for the peoples of India, economy in administration and earnest desire to preserve peace, he may be compared with that other essentially Liberal Governor-General among his successors, the Marquis of Ripon. Bentinck's character to a certain extent lacks warmth and picturesqueness. Many were repelled by his chilling manner and somewhat cold benevolence. Yet he was undoubtedly the first Governor-General openly to act on the theory that the welfare of the subject peoples was a main, perhaps the primary, duty of the British in India, though this conception had already inspired the work of many great administrators, such as Elphinstone and Munro. Making every allowance for the warmth of personal friendship, and the eulogistic phraseology proper to the epigraphic style, it remains broadly true in the stately language of Macaulay's inscription that Lord William Bentinck ruled India 'with prudence, integrity, and benevolence . . . never forgot that the end of government is the welfare of the governed . . . abolished cruel rites . . . effaced humiliating distinctions . . . (and) allowed liberty to the expansion of public opinion'. The famous statement that he 'infused into Oriental despotism the spirit of British freedom' represents rather the pious aspirations of the Governor-General and the ultimate tendency of his policy, than anything actually achieved.

His internal policy may be briefly considered under the three heads of economical, administrative, and social reform. His first duty was retrenchment, rendered necessary by the wasteful extravagance of the Burmese war. Bentinck faced this task with his usual moral courage and noble disregard of personal unpopularity. A saving of one and a half millions was made by economies in the civil and military services. How necessary the reform was in the former case is seen from the fact that, even after the change, the average income of a civilian, ranging from member of Council to writer (the lowest grade), was still as high as £2,000 a year. The scale of remuneration in the army had never been so high as in the civil service. We have seen how Clive, in 1765, abolished the custom of double 'batta' (extra allowances made to officers in addition to their pay) in the teeth of disaffection and mutiny. By enforcing the new rule that, in the case of troops stationed within 400 miles of Calcutta, only half 'batta' was to be allowed, Bentinck earned much unmerited odium—unmerited because he was merely carrying out imperative orders from home. Further, part of the land revenue of Bengal, which, through the indulgence of the government and the ingenuity of native forgers of documents had been fraudulently alienated, was recovered for the state. By these and other financial reforms, though he succeeded to a depleted treasury and a deficit of a million, he left behind him a surplus of a million and a half.

Secondly, in the domain of administrative reform, Bentinck abolished the provincial courts of appeal and circuit set up by Cornwallis, which by their dilatory procedure had blocked the course of justice and merely afforded 'resting places for those members of the service who were deemed unfit for higher responsibilities'. The judicial reforms of Lord Cornwallis had found no place for the employment of native Indian ability except in the lowest grades; and though this defect had largely been remedied since that time by the appointment of many native judges, the home authorities and the most enlightened of the civil servants in India were in favour of extending the principle. Measures were now taken, therefore, to enlarge the jurisdiction of the native judges and increase their salaries. At the same time a great boon was conferred upon the suitors by permission to use the vernacular tongue instead of Persian, which had hitherto by an absurd legal convention been the language of the courts. Under Lord William Bentinck the great revenue settlement of the North-west Provinces, which took ten years to complete, was begun by Robert Bird. It was made for thirty years, and, according to the locality, either with the tillers of the soil, the landowners, or in some cases the village community, and it affected territory populated by 23,000,000 people.

Thirdly, there were the social reforms that have immortalized his name. He abolished, in 1829, the Hindu practice of *Sati*, or Suttee—the immolation of widows on the funeral pyres of their husbands. By this inhuman rite no fewer than 700 women were said to have been burnt alive in 1817 in Bengal alone. The prohibition of *Sati* had been urged by the Court of Directors upon Lord Amherst, but he shrank from interfering with a custom sanctioned by Brahman approval. Even men like Elphinstone, whose humanity was beyond question, seem to have dreaded the change, on the ground that it would violate the Company's traditional policy of toleration, and there were many dismal prophecies of disturbances if the custom were prohibited. But Bentinck, who had the courage of the genuine reformer, gladly took full responsibility upon himself, and, as so often happens, none of the gloomy prognostications of the prophets of evil were fulfilled. In 1830 there began, through the instrumentality of Colonel Sleeman, the breaking up of the Thugs (Thags), brotherhoods of hereditary assassins who, formed into a caste and worshipping the goddess Kali, went about the country strangling and robbing peaceful travellers. By such means Bentinck showed his care for the moral and material welfare of the people. Their intellectual development was affected by a change which had far-reaching consequences. It was decided in 1833 that the funds granted by government for education should be henceforward devoted, not to the fostering of Oriental learning, but to the instruction of the natives of India in the English language and in western science. There were many opponents of this change, ably led by H. H. Wilson, the historian; but the question was really settled by a famous minute of Lord Macaulay, at the time a member of the Governor-General's Council, who trenchantly routed the Orientalists. Macaulay characteristically saw only one aspect of the question. Subsequent experience has shown that there was more to be said on the other side than he was prepared to admit. But actual trial alone could reveal the fact that many of the extravagant hopes based upon the change were doomed to disappointment. Further, it was not so much the fact that English was established as the official and literary language that was unfortunate, as the choice of models and text-books afterwards made. It would have been prudent to train the subject races for self-government by inculcating obedience to law and a sense of discipline. The whole trend of English ideas for the next fifty years lay in the direction of a pronounced individualism and freedom from restrictive bonds of every kind. Englishmen with law-abiding habits and phlegmatic temperaments could indulge in revolutionary theories without any noticeable effect upon their practice. But the quicker and subtler brain of the Oriental is not so apt to keep speculation and action apart. The prose models, on which for many years Indian education was based, consisted of Burke, Bentham, Mill, and the philosophical Radicals. Absurdly enough, our Eastern subjects were prepared for taking their part in the government of the country by the study of writers who taught that government itself was at best a necessary evil. We attempted to raise a race of administrators on the literature of Revolt. This unfortunate feature affected one department of knowledge only. In other fields, in the domain of science, law, and letters, the results were all to the good.

In foreign affairs and in his relations with the native powers, Bentinck sedulously upheld the doctrine of non-intervention pressed upon him by the authorities at home.

In this aspect his administration has won less favour with historians. It is undoubtedly true that non-interference necessarily involved to some extent condoning evils in states bordering upon British dominion. Native princes were left a free hand as long as they discharged their treaty obligations to the Company; 'the character', says Wilson, 'of an importunate and self-interested creditor was to be substituted for that of a benevolent and powerful protector'.[1] But it was worth while to give the principle an extended trial, and Bentinck's defenders may justly claim that the great benefits which the period of peace enabled him to confer upon British India proper, should be set against any evils that he was forced to tolerate in native states. In necessary cases he did not even shrink from intervention. But his motive was always hatred of misgovernment, not extension of British influence or acquisition of territory. Three cases may be especially noticed: in one he took over the whole administration of a feudatory state, in the other two he made his only annexations to British dominion. In Mysore the Raja set up by Lord Wellesley, when he came of age, proved utterly unworthy of the trust conferred upon him. But Wellesley had explicitly reserved the right of resuming the government of the state in the event of mal-administration, and therefore Bentinck in 1831, though he is afterwards said to have regretted doing so, pensioned off the Raja, and for fifty years the country was administered entirely by British officials. In 1832 the small principality of Cachar on the north-east frontier of Bengal, from which the Burmese had withdrawn by the Treaty of Yandaboo, was annexed at the request of the inhabitants. A high forest-clad district, it has since been cleared and covered with tea plantations. In 1834 he deposed the Raja of Coorg, a monster of cruelty, and incorporated the country in British dominion, 'in consideration of the unanimous wish

[1] *The History of India*, H. H. Wilson, vol. iii, p. 365.

of the people'. Coorg lies between Mysore and the ocean on the western coast of southern India, and, standing 3,000 feet above sea-level, it has been found to possess a healthy climate and to be especially adapted for the cultivation of the coffee plant.

Disturbances appeared in Bhopal, Gwalior, and Jaipur, embarrassing to the Governor-General, who, however, steadily refused to swerve from his considered policy of neutrality. But all indications go to show that before very long even he would have been compelled to enter on a more active foreign policy. In 1835, on the eve of his departure, he recorded his conviction that the advance of Russia towards the Indian frontier was the greatest danger to which our empire in the East was exposed, and it has been well noticed by Sir Alfred Lyall that his commercial treaty with Ranjit Singh, and the agreement with the Amirs of Sind (to be dealt with later), were but preliminary steps that led to the Afghan war. But that forward movement, had Bentinck remained to direct it, would never have taken so violent and fatal a course as it did.

This peaceful and financially prosperous administration undoubtedly did the East India Company a great service, for any disastrous war or pecuniary deficit would have been promptly driven home when the question of the renewal of the charter, which expired in 1834, again came to the fore.

The monopoly of the Indian trade had gone in 1813. It soon became clear in the long debates in Parliament, and negotiations between the Court and the Board of Control, that the Company could not hope to save its monopoly of the China trade. Ideas of Reform and Free Trade were everywhere triumphant, and Huskisson himself led the attack upon the Company. It was not even permitted to compete in the China trade on level terms with private traders, but was forced to divest itself of its commercial character altogether, and to part with its assets at a valuation. At one time it hardly appeared probable that it would retain its existence as a governing body, but ministers shrank from taking over the whole administration of India, and the Company remained in an anomalous position, half a private corporation, half a government department, its dividends now fixed at 10½%, a charge upon the revenues of India—in Lord Ellenborough's striking phrase, 'in the very undignified and not very popular position of the mortgagees in possession'. The Charter Act further constituted a fourth Presidency of Agra (soon afterwards, 1835, reduced to the lieutenant-governorship of the North-west Provinces), conferred on the government of India the power of passing Acts instead of Regulations, added a fourth (legal) member to the Council of the Governor-General (Macaulay being the first to hold the office), gave the head of the supreme government for the first time the title of Governor-General of India (instead of Governor-General of the Presidency of Fort William in Bengal), and definitely and finally subordinated the Presidencies of Bombay and Madras to his control. The Act further gave the stamp of national and Parliamentary approval to the liberal policy of the reigning Governor-General in laying down the famous principle, a full realization of which is only becoming possible in our own time, 'that no native of India, nor any natural-born subject of his Majesty, should be disabled from holding any place, office, or employment, by reason of his religion, place of birth, descent or colour'.

Finally, every British subject was to enjoy the right of proceeding to the principal seats of government in India without licence, and of purchasing and holding lands. Henceforward, therefore, there was no legal barrier to the colonization, in the ordinary sense of the word, of the Presidency towns. On Lord William Bentinck's resignation in 1835, Sir Charles T. Metcalfe, one of the ablest of the

Company's servants in India, who had just been appointed Governor of the new Presidency of Agra, was made provisional Governor-General. The Court of Directors at first desired that his appointment should be permanent, till he completely forfeited their favour by carrying in September his famous Act, freeing the Press in India from all restrictions. The previous history of Press regulations in India is complicated and not very easy to summarize. The censorship had been originally established by Lord Wellesley in 1801, for military reasons during the war with France. A government official was charged with the duty of reading all journals before publication, and striking out anything he deemed inadvisable. This censorship was nominally abolished by Lord Hastings seventeen years later—nominally, because, though he did away with the name of an invidious office, he issued a comprehensive set of rules, very strictly limiting the topics with which Indian papers might deal, and practically prohibiting all criticism of the Executive under penalty of deportation from India. John Adam in 1823 sent back to England an editor who, in spite of having received many warnings from Lord Hastings himself, had infringed these restrictions. In the same year new regulations were made obliging every printer in Bengal to obtain a licence before he could publish a newspaper; four years later a similar rule was adopted in Bombay. These regulations remained in force till they were repealed by Metcalfe.

The governor-generalship was offered to Mountstuart Elphinstone, but declined by him owing to feeble health. The Tory government then nominated Lord Heytesbury, formerly ambassador to St. Petersburg, but before he could sail, the Ministry fell and the Whigs cancelled the appointment—an action which naturally exposed them to a storm of criticism. In an evil hour for India and Great Britain, they entrusted the governor-generalship to Lord Auckland. Metcalfe agreed to accept the lieutenant-governorship of the North-west Provinces, but found he had completely lost the confidence of the Court of Directors, and, on being passed over for the governorship of Madras, resigned the service. The Directors thus allowed one of their ablest servants to leave India. Metcalfe lived to earn further distinction under the Crown; he became successively Governor of Jamaica in 1839, and Governor-General of Canada in 1842. His later career will be found described in other volumes of this series.

CHAPTER XXV

THE FIRST AFGHAN WAR. LORD AUCKLAND AND LORD ELLENBOROUGH

WITH the accession of Lord Auckland to office the chief centre of political interest shifts to the north-west frontier of India, and it will be necessary briefly to sum up the course of events in that quarter since the famous treaty with Ranjit Singh in 1809. That treaty extended the British sphere of influence in the form of protectorates over the Rajputs and the Sikhs of Sirhind to the banks of the Sutlaj. Beyond that river, Ranjit Singh had been left a free hand to continue his career of conquest. The whole of the Punjab soon acknowledged his sway. The army of the Khalsa, originally composed almost entirely of horsemen armed with matchlocks, was transformed mainly into infantry battalions and artillery brigades. Having subdued the other Sikh chieftains Ranjit Singh came into collision with the eastern outposts of Afghanistan. He seized Attock on the Indus, took Multan in 1818, conquered Kashmir in 1819, and during the next two years subdued the Derajat—the long strip of plain country between the Indus and the hills. In 1822 he took into his service two of Napoleon's officers who had fought at Waterloo, Allard and Ventura, and these men with Court and Avitabile, who followed them, made the Sikh armies a still more formidable fighting force. Though twice defeated by the Afghans, Ranjit Singh ultimately made himself master of Peshawar, and forced the Afghan governor to pay him tribute. He had now welded together a compact kingdom embracing the Punjab and Kashmir and running up on the north-west to the base of the Afghan hills.

The conquests of the Sikh chief drew the attention of the Indian government to the north-west. They had long desired to obtain some influence in the valley of the Indus, and in 1831 Captain Alexander Burnes, a brilliant young linguist and traveller, under the thinly veiled pretext of conveying a present of English cart-horses to Ranjit Singh from Lord Ellenborough, President of the Board of Control, was sent up the Indus and the Chenab to Lahore. Later in the year Lord William Bentinck, conquering for political reasons his innate dislike of pageantry, met Ranjit Singh in great state on the banks of the Sutlaj, and renewed the treaty of alliance.

Beyond the north-western frontier of the Sikh dominions lay Afghanistan, a bleak tableland sloping gently from north-east to south-west, intersected by deep ravines and surrounded by steep mountain ranges. It contained three important cities—Kabul, nearly 6,000 feet above sea-level, in the north-east, Kandahar in the south-east, and Herat to the north-west. The political state of Afghanistan had long been one of anarchy. It is impossible here to unravel the tangled skein of intrigue and dynastic revolution. In 1836 Shah Shuja Abdali or Durrani, the Amir, to whom Lord Minto had sent Mountstuart Elphinstone in 1809, was living at Ludhiana, a pensioner of the British government. Dost Muhammad of the Barakzai clan was established at Kabul, and three of his brothers, who hardly pretended to acknowledge his authority, were lords of Kandahar. Herat was still ruled by a prince of the Durrani dynasty which Dost Muhammad had displaced in Kabul. Afghanistan was beset on the east by the Sikhs, and on the north and west by Persia. Just as Ranjit Singh, debarred by Lord Minto's Treaty of 1809 from expansion eastwards, was eager for aggrandizement at the expense of his northern neighbours, so the Shah of Persia, who had been forced to yield part of his northern territory to the Russians, was determined, if possible, to compensate himself towards the south-east. Afghanistan seemed thus in imminent danger of being squeezed out of existence between the two powers. In 1833 Shah Shuja had sought alliance with Ranjit Singh in an abortive attempt to recover his throne, and the Sikh monarch had seized the opportunity to occupy Peshawar. Four years later the Persian armies, trained and officered by Russians, were gathering round the walls of Herat.

The Afghan policy of Lord Auckland has met with practically universal condemnation at the hands of historians, and every re-reading of the evidence deepens and strengthens the conviction that the war was politically one of the most disastrous, and, morally, one of the least justifiable ever waged by the British in India. Of that verdict there can be no reversal. Yet it is at least possible to recognize that there were many difficulties confronting Lord Auckland in 1837. It is far easier to understand how the policy was initiated than to conceive why it was persisted in, when many of these difficulties had solved themselves, and every voice of weight and experience was raised in protest against it. The chief motive in the whole business was perhaps the dread of Russian influence in Asia. We have seen that by the Treaty of Teheran, concluded in 1809 and revised in 1814, Great Britain had agreed to help Persia with men or money against any European invader. The only result of that not very prudent engagement was to place us in an embarrassing and slightly ridiculous position. When Persia and Russia were at war in 1826 the Shah appealed to his ally, and the folly of contracting such obligations to a distant central Asian power was at once apparent. The British lamely excused themselves from rendering aid on the plea that the Persians were the aggressors, though it was perfectly clear that they had only declared war after frequent and repeated provocation from the Russians. When the war was over and the Persians severely defeated, the British government attempted to salve their political conscience by paying their ally a large indemnity to cancel the clause in the treaty of 1814 which bound them to aid Persia.

This not very impressive stampede from their treaty obligations left British statesmen with an uneasy sense of danger from Russian power, which indeed during the preceding fifty years had grown at an amazing rate. McNeill, British Minister to Persia in 1836, pointed out that a Russian regiment 'at her farthest frontier post, on the western shore of the Caspian, has as great a distance to march back to Moscow as onward to Attock on the Indus, and is actually farther from St. Petersburg than from Lahore, the capital of the Sikhs'. With excessive political prevision, Englishmen looked forward to the time when the Russian frontier should be conterminous with our own on the north-western frontier. They hardly seem to have realized that these vast distances were as much a source of weakness as an evidence of strength. Russia's outposts were still at least a thousand miles away from the Indian boundary and a corresponding distance from their base. The alarm of the ministry seems now excessive, for we appreciate better the difficulties of the approach from central Asia to the north-western ramparts of India. But it was at any rate obvious that Russian agents were encouraging the Persian advance on Afghanistan, and it was considered prudent to check this advance as far from the British frontier as possible.

Dost Muhammad was eager for an alliance with the British government. The chief difficulty in the way of accepting his proposal was that he made it a condition of his friendship that British diplomacy should be exerted to prevail on Ranjit Singh to restore Peshawar to him. Now Lord Auckland was undoubtedly right in deciding at all hazards to retain the friendship of the Sikh ruler, who was one of the most remarkable characters in Indian history. Illiterate, a drunkard, cruel, despotic, and unscrupulous, he realized, as no other eastern potentate ever did, the value to himself of our friendship, and he was absolutely loyal to his treaty obligations. It was certainly not worth while to jeopardize that alliance for the support of Dost Muhammad, who, though an able ruler and, as events were to prove, really desirous of a treaty with the British, was less known to us at the time. As it happened, the difficulty was by no means as formidable as it appeared: Burnes himself considered, and many others have since held, that the Peshawar question could have been solved by diplomatic treatment, and that it would have been perfectly possible to win the friendship of Dost Muhammad, of whose ability he warned Lord Auckland, without losing that of Ranjit Singh.

Were that idea abandoned, the wise course would now seem to have been to withdraw from all interference with Afghanistan, leaving Dost Muhammad to defend himself, rest the British line of defence on the Sutlaj, and support Ranjit Singh, if possible, with men and money against all aggressors. Then, before the Persian and Russian armies could have reached our frontier, they would first have had to conquer and traverse the terrible plateau of Afghanistan and defeat the powerful army of the Khalsa trained and led by Napoleon's generals. It is only fair, however, to note that one objection to this policy was that there was a deeply ingrained conviction in the minds of all politicians of the day that the mere fall of Herat, both for political and geographical reasons, would irretrievably damage British prestige in India itself. 'Near Herat', says Sir T. H. Holdich, 'there exists the only break in the otherwise continuous and formidable wall of mountains which traverse Asia from the Bering Strait to the Caspian Sea. Near Herat it is possible to pass from the Russian outposts . . .

to India without encountering any formidable altitude—and this is possible nowhere else.'[1]

Before describing Lord Auckland's own policy, it is necessary to narrate briefly the course of events. Immediately on his arrival in India, Dost Muhammad appealed to him for support against Persia and Ranjit Singh, and received an answer to the effect that it was not the practice of the British government to interfere in the affairs of other independent states. Dost Muhammad either at the same time or soon after made overtures to Persia and Russia, probably with the idea only of exerting diplomatic pressure on the British. But Lord Auckland, in spite of his pretence of non-interference, could not bring himself to let Dost Muhammad go his own way.

Captain Burnes was sent to Kabul, nominally on a commercial mission. The Persians, with Russian support, were already marching on Herat, and two months after Burnes's arrival in Kabul the siege began. Had the town fallen, the seriousness of the position as regards Afghanistan would have been intensified a thousand times. But a young British officer, Eldred Pottinger, who was travelling in Afghanistan, entered the town disguised as a Muhammadan devotee, and organized a gallant defence.

Two months after Burnes's arrival a Russian emissary entered Kabul, but for a time Dost Muhammad kept him at arm's length. It was quite obvious that the Amir would have preferred an English to a Russian alliance, and Burnes himself wrote to Lord Auckland that it was a pity we could not act with him. But the Governor-General and his advisers seem to have conceived a most unreasonable prejudice against this able ruler. They required him in a supercilious dispatch to break with Russia, but would not engage to protect him from the result of such an action, promising merely to use their good offices with Ranjit Singh

[1] *The Imperial Gazetteer of India*, vol. i, p. 14.

for the restoration of Peshawar. Dost Muhammad naturally swung over to the Russo-Persian side. The Russian envoy, hitherto treated with coolness, was received with marked favour, and Burnes left Kabul five days later.

Then Lord Auckland took the fatal plunge. He determined, with the aid of Ranjit Singh, 'the old man of Lahore', to depose Dost Muhammad, and place once more upon the throne Shah Shuja, the discredited pensionary of Ludhiana, who had failed in an attempt to recover his kingdom only four years before. In this he acted without consulting his Council, against the advice of his Commander-in-Chief, and in opposition to the Board of Directors. The ministry in England must share the blame, for a letter from Sir John Hobhouse, President of the Board of Control, approving of the policy, crossed the dispatch of the Governor-General announcing its adoption. Macnaghten, secretary to the government, a man of the highest intellectual attainments, like Burnes a brilliant linguist and a high authority on Indian law, was sent to Lahore, and the famous Tripartite Treaty between the Sikhs, Shah Shuja, and the East India Company was signed June 26, 1838. The treaty itself laid no obligation on the British even to cross the Indus. Auckland's first idea was to make a demonstration in force at Shikarpur, while Shah Shuja was replaced on his throne by his own adherents and his Sikh allies. It was soon ascertained, however, that unless he received more effective help he would never be restored at all. When Macnaghten returned from Lahore he found that the Governor-General had already committed himself to an invasion of Afghanistan. The objections to this policy were in truth overwhelming. It was morally unjustifiable. However much it might be opposed to British interests, Dost Muhammad had a perfect right as an independent sovereign to ally himself with Persia or Russia. It was politically inexpedient, for Dost Muhammad was an able ruler and had won the rarely yielded allegiance of his Afghan subjects. Though Shah Shuja was by no means lacking in capacity, his career had been one long failure. Expelled from the throne in 1809, his two attempts to return had ended in complete disaster. He was distrusted and disliked in Afghanistan, and his cause there never aroused one spark of enthusiasm. It was proposed, too, by an amazing perverseness to make him ruler over a fanatical Muhammadan people by the aid of Hindu Sikhs, between whom and his future subjects there had raged, only five years before, a *jehad* or holy war. Every one whose judgement was worth anything condemned the policy. Bentinck, Elphinstone, Wellesley were unanimous against it, and the Duke of Wellington in prophetic words declared that the consequence of crossing the Indus to settle a government in Afghanistan would be a 'perennial march into that country'. Finally, even such poor excuse as the framers of the policy originally had was swept away by the course of events before they were finally committed to it. The Russian government, under pressure from London, disowned and recalled its agents. Their emissary at Kabul returned to St. Petersburg and shot himself in chagrin and despair. The Shah of Persia, alarmed by a British expedition to Karrack in the Persian Gulf, raised the siege of Herat September 9, 1838, and withdrew to his own country. The danger from Russian intrigues had thus completely passed away, and a golden bridge was built for a retreat from an untenable position. But the Governor-General and his supporters were now infatuated with their scheme, and talked glibly of the proposed invasion of one of the most difficult countries in the world for military operations as a *promenade militaire*. On October 1, 1838, Lord Auckland issued a minute justifying his policy, in which, according to the severe but not unmerited verdict of Sir Herbert Edwardes, 'the views and conduct of Dost Muhammad Khan were misrepresented with a hardihood which a Russian statesman might have envied'

The history of the campaign must be briefly told. The 'Army of the Indus' mobilized at Ferozepore. Ranjit Singh objected to the passage of the British force through his territories. It was therefore decided that the Sikh expedition, accompanied by Shah Shuja's son, should invade Afghanistan from the Punjab through the Khyber Pass, while the main British army under Sir John Keane and Sir Willoughby Cotton, accompanied by Shah Shuja himself, entered by the Bolan Pass after traversing Sind. Macnaghten, as envoy and minister to Shah Shuja's court, had political charge of the expedition with Captain, now Sir Alexander, Burnes, as his chief lieutenant. One political crime leads inevitably to others, and the passage through Sind was in flagrant violation of a treaty lately made with the Amirs of that country, but our relations with those unfortunate chieftains will be dealt with later. After much difficulty and loss of baggage animals through the failure of fodder, the army emerged from the Bolan Pass in March. Kandahar was occupied in April, and Ghazni taken by storm in July. Dost Muhammad evacuated Kabul, and in August 1839 Shah Shuja was triumphantly conducted into his capital. So far success had attended the expedition, and a shower of honours fell upon the civil and military services. Auckland received an earldom, Sir John Keane, the Commander-in-Chief, a peerage, and Macnaghten a baronetcy. But this fair prospect was soon overclouded. Ranjit Singh died in June, before the object of the expedition was attained. It was only his iron hand and strong personality that had kept the Sikh misls united, and his death seriously endangered the British communications, for the Sikhs were soon in a state of disaffection. Later in the same year (November) the complete failure of a Russian expedition to Khiva showed how exaggerated had been the dread of Russia that inspired the policy of the war.

It soon became apparent that Shah Shuja depended

entirely on the support of British bayonets. The mere fact that he was imposed on the country from outside had alienated all popular support. The cost of the English army of occupation was excessive, and a serious dilemma presented itself. The British must either withdraw, when Shah Shuja's power would collapse like a house of cards, or, if he were to be maintained upon his throne, they must remain permanently in the country at a ruinous cost to the Indian treasury. So hostile was the feeling of the people that it was found impossible to evacuate the country, even after Dost Muhammad had surrendered himself in 1840 and been sent an honoured prisoner to Calcutta.

Probably the best way out of a bad business would have been to withdraw with Shah Shuja on the ground that he was found unacceptable to his subjects; but this would have been tantamount to a confession that the whole policy was a failure. The result was the adoption of an unfortunate half-way course. It was decided for the time to leave the troops quartered in Afghanistan, and to economize as much as possible by cutting down the stipends paid to the chiefs of eastern Afghanistan by the government to maintain communications with India. The natural result followed that the chiefs became contumacious and closed the passes.

Constant outbreaks all over the country showed that the situation was growing rapidly worse. The loose morals of some of the British officers quartered at Kabul stirred up a fierce and abiding resentment in the minds of the townsmen. Two fatal mistakes were committed by the British: the first was the appointment of General Elphinstone, a brave but old and incapable officer in bad health, to the command of the troops in Kabul. For this most calamitous step Lord Auckland was directly responsible, for he acted in opposition to the advice of the Commander-in-Chief, who wished to appoint General Nott, the commander at Kandahar, a vigorous soldier. Secondly, by an act of supreme folly, the palace-citadel of Kabul known as the Bala Hissar was given up to Shah Shuja for his seraglio, and the troops were cantoned in a plain exposed to attack on every side and separated from their provisions and stores. By the autumn of 1841 the country was seething with rebellion and intrigue, but the leaders remained blind to what was patent to many of their subordinates. The fertile brain of Macnaghten had been busy with schemes to acquire Herat and even to send expeditions against the Sikhs. In November he was preparing to leave Afghanistan to take up the government of Bombay, and Burnes, who was to succeed him as envoy at Kabul, congratulated him on leaving the country 'in a state of profound tranquillity'. The next day Burnes's house was surrounded by a howling mob, and he was dragged out and cut to pieces, while the British forces a mile and a half away, under the inefficient leadership of Elphinstone, made no attempt to interfere till too late. Then follows a miserable and almost incredible record of British incapacity and Afghan treachery. The military leaders were at variance with each other and with Macnaghten. Appeals were sent to General Sale at Gandamak and General Nott at Kandahar to come to the rescue. But Sale, finding he had not sufficient transport, preferred to fall back on Jalalabad to keep open communications with India, and Nott declared, with apparently good reason, that the march to Kabul through the snow was impossible. The British force abandoned at Kabul committed every conceivable blunder. Elphinstone allowed his stores to be captured without striking a blow, and Macnaghten, fearing starvation, concluded a humiliating treaty on December 11. He engaged that the British should evacuate Afghanistan, that Dost Muhammad should be set free, and Shah Shuja be given the choice of accompanying the British or remaining in Afghanistan with a pension. Akbar Khan, son of Dost Muhammad, was to escort the army to the frontiers. A few days later Macnaghten, distrusting Akbar Khan, was drawn into some questionable negotiations with rival chiefs. He was betrayed by them, enticed to an interview with Akbar Khan, and assassinated.

In spite of this a renewed treaty for withdrawal was made with the Afghan chiefs, though Major Eldred Pottinger earnestly pleaded that all negotiations with them should be abandoned, and that the army should either seize the Bala Hissar and hold out till succour came, or cut their way through, sword in hand, to Jalalabad where Sale was gallantly holding out. But neither of these, the only possible or even honourable courses, was adopted. On January 6, after giving up many of their stores and guns, the British forces and camp followers, in all 16,000 men, began their retreat, relying on the assistance of Akbar Khan, who proved quite unwilling or unable to protect them from the attacks of the Ghilzais and other tribesmen who swarmed round the line of route. From the beginning there was a complete failure to take the most ordinary precautions to maintain order or discipline. The generals lost their heads and the troops their *moral.* After a time the women and children and many of the officers, including Pottinger and Elphinstone himself, were surrendered as hostages to Akbar Khan. The rest struggled on in misery and privation through snow-storms and a constant hail of bullets. The retreat became a rout, the rout a massacre. No pen can do justice to the ghastly horrors of the final struggle. The last despairing stand was made at the Pass of Jagdalak, when twelve officers laid down their lives. One man, Dr. Brydon, half dead with wounds and exhaustion, staggered into Jalalabad—with the exception of about 120 prisoners in the hands of Akbar Khan, the sole survivor of 16,000 men who had set out from Kabul a week before.

It is not surprising that Lord Auckland, the man mainly responsible, was shattered and unnerved by this appalling calamity. He steeled himself to speak of it in a proclamation as a 'partial reverse', and as affording 'a new occasion for displaying the stability and vigour of the British power'; but in fact he could only suggest the withdrawal of Sale to Peshawar. His subordinates did what they could for the restoration of British prestige. The first relief force under Wyld, after entering the Khyber and capturing the fort of Ali Musjid, was forced to fall back. General Pollock, an able officer, was sent to Peshawar, but had not started on his quest to relieve Jalalabad when Auckland laid down the reins of office. Lord Ellenborough, the new Governor-General, came to India with a considerable reputation, and was undoubtedly a much abler man than his predecessor. As President of the Board of Control, an office he held on three occasions, he had shown vigour and decision of character. He was a ready and eloquent speaker of a somewhat florid type, self-confident, impulsive, and rather headstrong, so that even his friend the Duke of Wellington found it necessary to warn him of the need of 'caution and temper'.

As soon as he arrived in India he announced that the British government would no longer 'peril its armies, and with its armies the Indian Empire', to support the Tripartite Treaty. Its aim rather was now to save the troops in Afghanistan and inflict 'some signal and decisive blow' on the enemy. But within a month the defeat of General England at Hakalzai and Palmer's surrender of Ghazni caused him to falter in his resolution. Impulsively he determined on immediate evacuation without any attempt at reprisals or even the rescue of the prisoners still in the hands of the Afghans. Nott was ordered to abandon Kandahar, Pollock to withdraw to Peshawar. The order fell upon the army, as Outram said, 'like a thunderclap', for the position in Afghanistan had greatly improved. Pollock had marched through the Khyber on April 5, the same day on which the wretched Shah Shuja fell by the hand of an assassin; he reached Jalalabad ten days later to find that the 'illustrious garrison', as Ellenborough named it, had already sallied forth and defeated the besieging army in a pitched battle, while Nott had more than held his own at Kandahar. Neither Pollock nor Nott made any movement to obey the order for retirement, but pleaded lack of transport as a pretext for delay. In India there was an outburst of indignation, and Ellenborough saw he had made a mistake. Too much has perhaps been made of an error of judgement on the part of a Governor-General who had to decide a most difficult question before he had been a month in the country or had mastered the facts. But Ellenborough had ostentatiously refused to listen to the advice of experts, and he made things worse by his ill-advised endeavours to reverse the order while maintaining a verbal consistency. In July he repeated the order for a withdrawal from Afghanistan, but suggested to Nott that if he considered it feasible he was to 'retreat' to India, not by the Bolan Pass, but by Ghazni and Kabul through the Khyber, while Pollock was given leave to co-operate with him. A glance at the map reveals the rather puerile equivocation of the Governor-General's phraseology, and his critics were quick to note that the responsibility of making the decision was ungenerously thrown upon the shoulders of the generals. They, however, were glad enough to bear it. Pollock marched out of Jalalabad on August 20, defeated the Afghans at Jagdalak and Tezin, and planted the British flag once more on the Bala Hissar on September 16. The next day he was joined by Nott, who on his route had destroyed the fortifications at Ghazni, and brought away by Ellenborough's express orders the gates of the tomb of Mahmud of Ghazni which the conqueror was supposed to have carried off from the famous temple of Somnath in Gujarat in A.D. 1024. The European prisoners, who had been hurried by their guards from place to place, were rescued: by an inexcusable act of vandalism the great Bazaar of Kabul was blown up, and the city, after being sacked, was evacuated on October 12. The Governor-General met the returning troops in a great camp at Ferozepore with triumphal arches and histrionic paeans of victory. In a bombastic proclamation he announced to the Princes of India that 'our victorious army bears the gates of the temple of Somnath in triumph from Afghanistan and the despoiled tomb of Mahmud looks on the ruins of Ghazni. The insult of 800 years is avenged'. But the Muhammadans were only offended by this amazing fustian, and the Hindus had forgotten their ancient history, while antiquarians unkindly pointed out that the gates were much later in date than the eleventh century. In the end 'this glorious trophy of successful war', to quote the famous proclamation, was consigned to a lumber-room in the fort at Agra, and the British in India were left with the exasperating conviction that the Governor-General had only made himself and them slightly ridiculous in the eyes of the world. Dost Muhammad was released, and, making his way back to Afghanistan, soon re-established his power. His subsequent career was destined to show how futile had been the sacrifice of 20,000 lives and the waste of fifteen millions sterling.

CHAPTER XXVI

THE ANNEXATION OF SIND UNDER LORD ELLENBOROUGH

THE conquest of Sind followed in the wake of the Afghan war and was morally and politically its sequel.

Sind is the name given to the country lying on both sides of the Indus south of the Punjab and extending to the sea. The river gives it life and fertility, but it is surrounded on both sides to the east and west by barren and arid deserts. Sind had successively acknowledged the sway of the Mughals, made submission to Persia under Nadir Shah, and after his death owed for a time allegiance to Afghanistan.

Since the end of the eighteenth century the country was ruled by a number of chieftains or Amirs, of the Talpura tribe, coming originally from Baluchistan. The most important were seated at Khairpur, Mirpur, and Hyderabad; and the first of these claimed a vague suzerainty over the others.

The British in India had for many years looked with longing eyes on the Indus river, but an early factory established at Tatta had been abandoned. A treaty was made with the Amirs in 1809 (renewed in 1820) that they should not permit any settlement of 'the tribe of the French' in their country. But Sind remained practically unexplored by Europeans till Burnes in 1831, as already mentioned, made his way up the Indus on his passage to Lahore. 'Alas', said a Seiad, 'Sind is now gone since the English have seen the river'. The foreboding proved all too true. In 1831 Ranjit Singh proposed to Lord William Bentinck the partition of Sind between himself and the Company, a suggestion which the Governor-General of course refused even to discuss. Instead, in 1832, the Amirs very reluctantly agreed to a treaty (renewed in 1834) that the rivers and roads of Sind should be open to 'the merchants and traders' of Hindustan, but that no armed vessels or military stores should pass through the country. Another article, which showed the vivid fear of British absorption felt by the Amirs, ran, 'that the two contracting parties bound themselves never to look with the eye of covetousness on the possessions of each other'.

During the years 1834 to 1836 Ranjit Singh was again contemplating the conquest of Sind, which obviously lay at his mercy. The Indian government practically took the Amirs under its protection by warning the Sikh ruler that he could not be allowed to seize the country. In return for this service the British considered, perhaps fairly, that they had a right to make conditions with the Amirs favourable to themselves, and they wrested a very reluctant consent from them in 1838 to the admission of a British Resident at Hyderabad. Unfortunately they did not stop there: under Auckland and his cabinet of secretaries British policy in India had fallen to a lower level of unscrupulousness than ever before; and the plain fact is that the treatment of Sind from this time onward, however expedient politically, was morally indefensible.

On the outbreak of the Afghan war it was determined, in flagrant violation of the treaty of 1832, that the British forces should march through Sind. The Indian government appear to have held that they could legally amend a treaty by the formal announcement to the weaker party that they intended to violate one of its provisions. Accordingly the Amirs were informed that 'while the present exigency lasts . . . the article of the treaty prohibiting the use of the Indus for the conveyance of military stores must necessarily be suspended'. Further, a demand was made for a large sum in commutation of Shah Shuja's claims for tribute, which the Amirs had naturally ceased to pay during his thirty years exile from Kabul. Upon this the Amirs produced signed and sealed releases from all further claims given them by Shah Shuja himself in 1833. 'How this is to be got over', said the British Resident, 'I do not myself see'; but Auckland was not so easily baffled; the money was exacted and the unfortunate Amirs under threat of an advance upon Hyderabad were forced to enter into a new treaty in February 1839, by which they were required to pay three lakhs a year for a subsidiary force to be kept in their country; they were also informed that 'neither the ready power to crush and annihilate them nor the will to call it into action were wanting, if it appeared requisite however remotely for the safety and integrity of the Anglo-Indian Empire or frontier'. Such a brutal assertion of the doctrine that might is right is, fortunately for our national credit, unique in the annals of British administration in India. Even this treaty, however, after being accepted by the Amirs, was arbitrarily revised by Auckland and his advisers in their own favour, and returned to the Sind chieftains for signature, who 'objected, implored, and finally gave way'.[1]

During the Afghan war Sind was the British base of operations both for the original invasion and the reconquest of the country. The Amirs on the whole faithfully kept their agreements with us, and the fearful disasters that fell upon our army did not tempt them to any acts of hostility. Certain vague charges of disaffection were however made, based on evidence now generally recognized to have been unsatisfactory. Even if true, it would have been in accordance with the traditions of British rule in India to condone them, for the Amirs had received considerable provocation,

[1] *The History of the British Empire in India.* By Edward Thornton, vol. vi, p. 411.

and Lord Ellenborough himself declared that it was impossible to believe they could entertain friendly feelings towards us. Unfortunately, the settlement was not left to Outram, the Resident at Hyderabad, who thoroughly knew the Amirs and was personally liked by them, but to Sir Charles Napier, who was sent to Sind with full civil and military powers in September 1842. Napier was a brilliant general, happily combining the virtues of daring and caution, but he was impulsive, hot-headed, and extremely combative. He promptly announced to the Amirs that he considered the charges made against them had been substantiated and that he was authorized to revise the subsidiary treaty of 1839. The new terms submitted, or rather forced upon them, were that cessions of territory should be made in place of the tribute of three lakhs to maintain the subsidiary force, that the Amirs should provide fuel for British steamers navigating the Indus and should cease to exercise the privilege of coining. Money was henceforward to be issued by the British government and to bear on one side the 'effigy of the sovereign of England'. This last provision was naturally looked upon by the Amirs as a complete surrender of their national rights, and it is probable enough that from this time onward they only prolonged negotiations with a view to taking up arms at a favourable time. Before, however, the Amirs had accepted the treaty, Napier sequestrated the territory in question, and by his proclamations acted as though Sind had passed under his jurisdiction. To intimidate the Amirs, he took the amazing course of marching, without any declaration of war, upon Imangarh, a famous desert fortress, and razing it to the ground. The Amirs were induced by Outram to sign the treaties lest worse should befall them. They did so, but earnestly warned him to leave Hyderabad, as they would not be answerable for the temper of their countrymen. Their warning was fulfilled three days later, when a fierce mob attacked the Residency and compelled Outram after a gallant defence to take refuge on a steamer. Open war now ensued, and on February 17, at Miani, Napier by brilliant generalship utterly defeated an army of 30,000 men with a force of less than 3,000, inflicting on them a loss of 5,000 in killed and wounded. Hyderabad fell, and a month later another victory was won at Daba over the Amir of Khaipur. Though there was still fighting to be done, the war was now practically over. No one has ever successfully defended on moral grounds British policy in regard to Sind. It is difficult to believe, as Mr. Innes says, 'that the case for annexation was not more or less deliberately manufactured'.[1] An able and ambitious general, eager for distinction, and impatiently believing that the undoubted benefits of British rule justified almost any means of extending it, brought the rough-hewn ready-made solution of the soldier to bear on an intricate administrative problem. He was allowed to dictate the policy and was supported by the Governor-General against the high authority and considered protests of one of the most capable and best informed of the Company's servants. Sir James Outram remonstrated against the whole business as unjustifiable, and refused to touch a single rupee of the plunder of Hyderabad, which brought Sir Charles Napier £70,000. The Court of Directors condemned the policy, and Sir John Hobhouse, President of the Board of Control, afterwards declared that Ellenborough himself would not have given his approval had he known all the facts. Nor indeed is there need to seek laboriously for an ethical justification, since the author of the policy cynically abandoned the defensive position. Sir Charles Napier only saw that the government of the Amirs was weak and inefficient. He conscientiously believed that British administration would confer incalculable blessings on the country and was really

[1] *A Short History of the British in India.* By A. D. Innes.

indifferent how many legal, technical, and even moral considerations he swept away in benefiting the people of Sind against their will. He was gifted with a grim humour which disdained to employ political euphemisms for this drastic benevolence. Besides his sardonic pun in announcing his victory to Ellenborough ('peccavi', i.e. 'I have Sind'), we have the admissions in his Diary, 'We have no right to seize Sind, yet we shall do so, and a very advantageous, useful, humane piece of rascality it will be. . . . My present position is not however to my liking: we had no right to come here, and are tarred with the Afghan brush.'[1] Sind was annexed in August 1843 and the Amirs were sent into exile. The country was pacified and settled by Sir Charles Napier, who in this field for his talents displayed an energy and ability that were altogether admirable.

Ellenborough's action in Gwalior, though it did not err on the side of indulgence to the susceptibilities of a feudatory chief, is far more capable of justification. At least there he sought no territory and was confronted with a grave menace to British sovereignty. At the end of the Maratha war of 1818, Sindhia had been left the most powerful of the Maratha chiefs; he possessed from that time the only really formidable native army south of the Sutlaj. Daulat Rao Sindhia had died in 1827, and in 1843 a minor was on the throne; the Regent, approved by Lord Ellenborough, was dismissed from office by the youthful widow of the late ruler, and a characteristic scene of intrigue and counter-intrigue followed, which seemed only too likely to end in civil war. The great danger lay in the condition of the army; it consisted of over 40,000 men, a force far too large for the needs of a feudatory state, and in the strife of factions its influence was plainly increasing and becoming predominant in the government. Formidable as it was,

[1] *The Life and Opinions of General Sir C. J. Napier.* Ed. by Sir W. Napier, vol. ii, pp. 218, 290.

Ellenborough would not have interfered had he not clearly foreseen that a Sikh war was imminent. In September 1843 the Sikh Maharaja was assassinated. Palace revolutions quickly followed; there too the army of the Khalsa was obviously calling the policy of the state, and was on the verge of an outbreak. Ellenborough decided that he could not run the risk of these two disorderly armies fraternizing in the future. He proclaimed that the Company could not permit 'the existence within the territories of Sindhia of an unfriendly government nor that those territories should be without a government willing and able to maintain order'. The British, who had held themselves so lightly bound by treaty obligations in the business of Sind, suddenly developed an extreme punctiliousness even in regard to obsolete conventions. Ellenborough unexpectedly appealed to Lord Wellesley's treaty with Sindhia of 1804 establishing a subsidiary force, which had remained a dead letter from the day it was signed and been ignored in subsequent diplomatic relations. Two British armies advanced on the Chambal, though Ellenborough assumed that peaceful negotiations could still settle the question at issue. But the Gwalior army took matters into its own hands. It prevented a meeting between the Governor-General and the rulers of the state, and fought two battles with the British forces on December 29, 1843. At Maharajpur, north of Gwalior, Sir Hugh Gough, not anticipating resistance, came upon the enemy unexpectedly. There was no room for generalship, but by sheer hard fighting the victory was won. The enemy lost 3,000 killed and wounded, but the British losses also were severe, amounting to 797; on the same day a second and less costly victory was won by General Grey at Paniar.

The results were important. For though the dominions of Sindhia were left entire, Gwalior was now definitely made a protected state, and as the ruler at the time was a minor, this practically meant that for the next ten years the country was under British administration, the native council of regency being bound to follow the advice of the Resident. The army, thoroughly cowed by its two severe defeats, was cut down to 9,000 men, and a British contingent of 10,000 was enlisted. Thus by Lord Ellenborough's foresight all danger of a union between disaffected armies from Gwalior and Lahore was at an end. Strangely enough, in the days of the Mutiny, while Sindhia and the native army under the guidance of his famous minister Dinkar Rao remained loyal, the British contingent mutinied, murdered its officers, and inflicted a severe defeat on General Windham at Cawnpore in November 1857. Lord Ellenborough returning in triumph to Calcutta was astounded to receive the news that the Directors, exercising their constitutional right for the first time, had ordered his recall. They thoroughly distrusted his erratic genius: the tone of his dispatches had offended them: they most justly disapproved of the policy in Sind, and they accused him of systematically subordinating the interests of the civil to those of the military service. On his return he was elevated to an earldom.

CHAPTER XXVII

THE FIRST AND SECOND SIKH WARS AND THE CONQUEST OF THE PUNJAB. LORD HARDINGE AND LORD DALHOUSIE

LORD ELLENBOROUGH, who could at least take long views, had foreseen that a Sikh war was inevitable in the near future, and the Directors, though they did not desire that he should wage it, probably recognized that hostilities could not long be postponed, for on the suggestion of the Duke of Wellington they appointed to succeed him Sir Henry Hardinge, a Peninsular veteran in his sixtieth year.

Since the death of Ranjit Singh in June 1839, the state of the Punjab had been one of chronic revolution; all real power was in the hands of the Khalsa army, which over-awed the nominal rulers at Lahore through its delegates the *Panchayats* or Committees of five, who somewhat resembled the 'Agitators' of the Roundhead army in the English Civil War. A dismal series of revolutions and assassinations followed, the army in turn setting up and deposing those members of the royal house who bid highest for its favour. So helpless were these puppet princes that in 1841 Sher Singh, who was then seated on the unsteady Sikh throne, implored the help of Lord Auckland against his seditious soldiery. Rajas and ministers were murdered in quick succession. The army even drove away over the frontier Court and Avitabile, the European captains who had given them their wonderful coherence and discipline. Finally, in 1845, the army acknowledged the claims of Dulip Singh, a reputed son of their great chieftain, a child of five, whose mother the Rani, an able, intriguing, and licentious woman—the Messalina of the North, as Hardinge called her—acted nominally as regent, aided by her favourite minister and paramour, Lall Singh. Though she courted and fawned upon the army, she dreaded its absolute and capricious power, and found her only hope of security in urging it on to challenge British supremacy. Either it would spend its superabundant energies in a career of conquest and the sovereignty of Hindustan would pass to the Sikhs, or it would be shattered in the conflict and she could then make her own peace with the offended British nation. Her position could hardly be worse and might conceivably be bettered. This—the main feature of the first Sikh war—must constantly be borne in mind. The leaders were half-hearted or even treacherous, fearing victory almost as much as defeat. We were fighting against a fine army without a general, or, at any rate, without one supreme controlling mind.

On December 13, 1845, the Sikhs began to cross the Sutlaj. The British commander at Ferozepore made no attempt to dispute the passage, for which at that particular time and place we were inevitably to some extent unprepared. This involves no reflection on British policy. For some years, through the foresight of Ellenborough and Hardinge the frontier had been quietly and gradually strengthened, the army being increased to 40,000 men and 100 guns. Even as it was, some critics were found to aver that the massing and movements of these troops had provoked the war; and yet, had less been done, the opposite accusation of negligence would have been loudly made. To such a dilemma statesmen are always liable to be exposed, when a war long foreshadowed finally breaks out. Strategic counsels of perfection must sometimes be relaxed for political reasons. It was undoubtedly worth while to take some risks and so avoid jeopardizing all chances of peace;

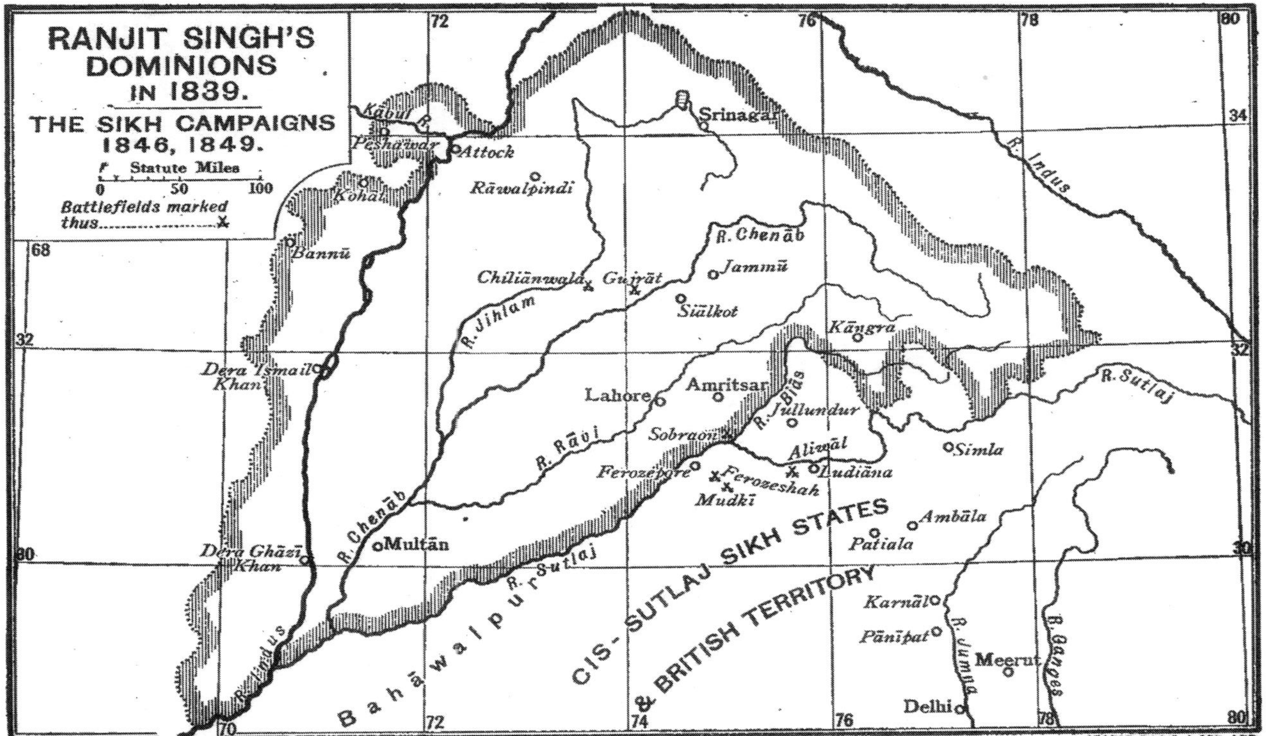
RANJIT SINGH'S DOMINIONS IN 1839.
THE SIKH CAMPAIGNS 1846, 1849.
Statute Miles
0 50 100
Battlefields marked thus........x
Kābul R.
Peshāwar
Attock
Kohāt
Bannū
Rāwalpindi
Srinagar
R. Indus
R. Chenāb
Jammū
Chiliānwala
Gujrāt
Siālkot
R. Jihlam
Kāngra
Dera Ismail Khan
Lahore
Amritsar
R. Biās
Jullundur
R. Sutlaj
Sobraon
R. Rāvi
Aliwāl
Simla
Ferozepore
Ferozeshah
Ludiāna
Mudkī
CIS-SUTLAJ SIKH STATES
Ambāla
Patiala
R. Chenāb
Multān
Dera Ghāzī Khan
R. Sutlaj
& BRITISH TERRITORY
Karnāl
Pānīpat
R. Jumna
R. Ganges
Meerut
Delhi
R. Indus
Bahāwalpur
WAXTYPE
GEORGE PHILIP & SON, LTD.

for peace need never be despaired of till the first shot is fired in anger.

On the news of the Sikh advance the Governor-General issued a proclamation, declaring all Sikh possessions east of the Sutlaj forfeit, and hurried his forces from Ambala and Ludhiana to save Ferozepore. The first battle was fought at Mudki, December 18, the British under Sir Hugh Gough coming in touch with the enemy somewhat unexpectedly after a march of twenty-two miles. There 'in a stout conflict' during 'an hour and a half of dim starlight' the Sikhs were defeated with the loss of seventeen guns, but the British casualties were very heavy, amounting to 872 killed and wounded. Among the dead was General Sir Robert Sale, the defender of Jalalabad. The victorious army then advanced on Ferozeshah, where 35,000 Sikhs under Lall Singh were awaiting them behind strong entrenchments. Though after the battle of Mudki the Governor-General had rather quixotically taken the office of second-in-command under Sir Hugh Gough, he now obliged the latter to delay the attack till Sir John Littler had arrived with reinforcements from Ferozepore—an act of very doubtful wisdom, for the gain in numbers was more than counteracted by the serious loss of time. The battle therefore did not begin till four o'clock of a short winter's day (December 21). A fierce frontal attack was made by the British troops, but two divisions were temporarily repulsed and the entrenchments were only partly carried when it became too dark to continue the fight. The British troops bivouacked on the battlefield, having lost touch with one another and being still exposed to a spasmodic and harassing fire from the enemy's batteries. During that 'night of horrors', as the Commander-in-Chief acknowledged, 'we were in a critical and perilous state', and there is no doubt that the British army came within an ace of a ruinous defeat. But fortunately there was dissension in the Sikh ranks through the treacherous conduct of their leader, and when the dawn of December 22 came a determined rush finally carried the entrenchments. Even so the danger was not past, for a fresh Sikh army under Tej Singh appeared, but after making a reconnaissance in force he retired, not realizing that the British soldiers were fasting, worn out with fatigue, and almost destitute of ammunition. The British losses amounted to 694 killed, including 103 officers, and 1,721 wounded. The Sikhs were estimated to have lost 8,000 men, and seventy-three guns were taken.

After this severe defeat the Sikhs retreated across the Sutlaj, but finding that the British, who were waiting for heavy guns and ammunition to be brought up from Delhi, did not follow them, they recrossed the river, and one of their divisions made a dash on Ludhiana. Sir Harry Smith (afterwards Governor of Cape Colony) was sent to intercept them, and, after suffering a check at Buddewal, brilliantly defeated them at the battle of Aliwal on January 28, 1846. He captured sixty-seven guns and drove the Sikhs in full rout back across the Sutlaj.

The final battle was fought on February 10 at Soḅraon, a village on the British bank of the river. The Sikhs had constructed a position of extraordinary strength, and hoped to secure a retreat, if necessary, by a bridge of boats in their rear. After a fierce artillery duel lasting two hours, the Sikh position was carried by storm, though only through fighting of the most desperate description. The bridge of boats collapsed under the weight of the flying Sikh regiments, and a fearful scene of slaughter and vengeance ensued; nearly ten thousand of the enemy were shot down by grape and shrapnel in the bed of the river, which ran red with blood, the British soldiers, infuriated by the mutilation of their dead in former battles, refusing to heed the cries for quarter. Our own losses were again very severe, amounting to 2,383 killed and wounded.

The army of the Khalsa was now vanquished, but the campaign had been a revelation. The magnificent fighting qualities of the Sikhs, and their skill as gunners and engineers, were for the first time appreciated. The war had lasted but fifty-four days, but during that time there had been four pitched battles—the fiercest and most desperately contested that British troops in India had ever been called upon to fight. Criticisms were, perhaps inevitably, passed on British strategy in the campaign. Gough was said to have been too fond of frontal attacks and not to have reconnoitred sufficiently the Sikh positions; but if British losses were heavy, the battles were proportionately decisive, and the Indian army, with rather a low proportion of European troops, was meeting the finest fighting force it had ever encountered.

Hardinge entered the capital, Lahore. The Sikhs by their absolutely unprovoked violation of British territory could have looked for little else than the complete loss of their independence. But Hardinge stopped short of the annexation of the Punjab for two reasons; in the first place respect was paid to the memory of Ranjit Singh, the old and faithful ally of Great Britain; and secondly, the Governor-General doubted whether he was strong enough to occupy the whole country. Shorn of some of their territory, and limited as to the size of the regular army they might maintain, the Sikhs were given one more chance to preserve their national existence. By the treaty of peace concluded in March 1846, all Sikh territories to the left of the Sutlaj, with the Jullundur Doab (the land between the Sutlaj and the Bias), were given up. An indemnity of one and a half millions was to be paid, or Kashmir ceded with half a million, and the latter alternative was the one actually accepted by the Sikhs. Kashmir was then handed over to Golab Singh,

Raja of Jammu, a chieftain who had been neutral in the war, for one million sterling. The army was henceforward to be limited to 20,000 infantry and 12,000 cavalry. Such were the penal clauses of the treaty. An attempt had now to be made to support the government of the little Maharaja, and it was agreed that a British force should occupy the capital, Lahore, till the close of the year, during the reconstruction of the government. Colonel Henry Lawrence was left behind as Resident, with Lall Singh as first minister. The Governor-General, now Viscount Hardinge, and the Commander-in-Chief, now Lord Gough, marched back in triumph to Calcutta with 250 captured Sikh guns to impress upon the peoples of India how severe had been the defeats inflicted upon the army of the Khalsa.

But the political position in the Punjab was still critical. Fortunately, Henry Lawrence by his sympathetic administration and personality won a wonderful influence over many of the Sirdars, or chieftains, though he was from the first opposed and thwarted by the court party headed and instigated by the Queen Mother. Lall Singh was soon found to have been concerned in a treacherous attack on the Raja of Kashmir, and his dismissal was found necessary. The friendly Sirdars themselves petitioned that the British garrison should not be removed at the end of the year, or the army of the Khalsa would again assert itself.

As a result, a new treaty was signed in December 1846 setting up a Regency Council of eight Sirdars, and maintaining British garrisons in the country for eight years till the Maharaja came of age. Henry Lawrence was to preside over the Council, and therefore was in fact the ruler of the Punjab, a position of magnificent responsibility. He gathered under him a famous staff of frontier officers, his brothers George and John Lawrence, Abbott, Edwardes, Hodson, Nicholson, and Lumsden, and entered upon that wonderful work of civilizing the Punjab, which was to be finally completed under British sway. A crusade was made against *Sati*, female infanticide, punishment by mutilation, and all the other abuses of Sikh rule. The burden of the land revenue was lightened and vexatious customs dues were abolished. But though these reforms brought relief to the common people, they were unpopular with the Sirdars. The Queen Mother supported the national and anti-foreign party with intrigues and plots, and it was found necessary in August 1847 to remove her from Lahore. The remnant of the Khalsa army looked sullenly on, still unconvinced of its inferiority to British troops and attributing its late defeats to the treachery of its leaders. Revolt would probably have come sooner or later in any case; it was possibly hastened by the temporary withdrawal of Lawrence, who returned to England for a hard-won holiday in January 1848. Lord Hardinge returned with him. His short administration had been almost wholly concerned with affairs in the Punjab. But he had won laurels not only as a conqueror but as an economist, and after the war he had carried out bold reductions in the army, 50,000 infantry being disbanded on the ground that the formidable forces of Gwalior and the Punjab had been vanquished and broken.

The Earl of Dalhousie landed at Calcutta in January 1848. He was in his thirty-sixth year, the youngest Governor-General that had hitherto held office. He had won a considerable reputation as President of the Board of Trade, but his great mental qualities were as yet known to few. Whether for good or ill, he was destined to leave a deeper personal impress on the destinies of India than any of his predecessors since Lord Wellesley. At the very beginning he was highly tried, for within three months of his arrival Hardinge's policy of 'experimental forbearance' in leaving the Sikhs a partial autonomy had broken down, and the Punjab was aflame with rebellion. The national party among the Sikh chieftains, as we have seen, had long been viewing with impatient and ill-concealed distrust the beneficent—but to them unpalatable—results of British influence. The first outbreak occurred at Multan in the south-west of the Punjab, where the Governor, Mulraj, took up arms, after his followers, probably with his complicity, had barbarously murdered two young British officers. Although Mulraj proclaimed a religious war and summoned all true Sikhs to flock to his banner, Dalhousie decided on the advice of Lord Gough, who was in this case unusually cautious, that operations must be postponed till the cold weather. Most authorities have held that, had Henry Lawrence been at Lahore and Lord Hardinge at Calcutta, troops would have been moved up at once and the insurrection would probably have spread no further. It was, however, a very difficult point for a Governor-General to decide, who had only been three months in the country, and had not yet made himself so absolutely conversant with Indian affairs as he afterwards became. It is permissible to surmise that a year later Dalhousie, with his prompt and masterful will, would have overruled the Commander-in-Chief instead of supporting him. There was, however, a good political reason for inaction, which is sometimes forgotten; it was theoretically the duty of the Sikh government at Lahore to punish Mulraj, who had risen against their authority, and, at any rate, till they proved unable or unwilling to demand reparation for the outrage on British subjects, the British government would legally have no right to interfere.

Though the supreme government therefore rightly for the time withheld its hand, a young lieutenant, Herbert Edwardes, employed under the Sikh Council of Regency, who was engaged in settling some districts beyond the Indus, hastily gathered together what levies he could, and attacked Mulraj, being, as he said himself, 'very like a Scotch terrier barking at a tiger'. He defeated the Sikh rebel in two engagements and drove him into Multan in July. Dalhousie supported these operations as far as he could, though he had not authorized them. General Whish and Edwardes began a regular siege of Multan, a very strong fortress, on September 7. Meanwhile the revolt throughout the Punjab was gradually spreading. The Maharani was found to be in correspondence with Mulraj and was removed to Benares. The British Resident at Lahore sent Sher Singh with a large force to assist the besieging army, but it went over bodily to the enemy on September 14. The blockading forces were at once withdrawn from the trenches, and the siege was not resumed for three months. At Lahore the Resident maintained his position with difficulty. The old soldiers of the Khalsa flocked everywhere to join Sher Singh, and the Sikh leaders entered into alliance with Dost Muhammad, the Amir of Afghanistan, once their bitterest foe, buying his aid by the surrender of Peshawar.

The rising had now become a national one, and the British government were warranted in meeting it with all their power. On October 10 the Governor-General made his famous declaration that, 'unwarned by precedent, uninfluenced by example, the Sikh nation has called for war, and on my word, Sirs, they shall have it with a vengeance'. For the moment however, of necessity action lagged behind these brave words. It was not till November 16 that Lord Gough crossed the Ravi. Six days later, having attacked Sher Singh at Ramnagar on the Chenab with characteristic impetuosity, he fought a drawn battle. In January he advanced to the River Jihlam, and on the 13th attacked the Sikh army, 30,000 in number, entrenched in a magnificent position where our cavalry had little room to manœuvre. The battle of Chilianwala has been graphically, if somewhat unfairly, described as 'an evening battle fought by a brave old man in a passion'. It was long believed that the Commander-in-Chief, angered at being fired upon by the Sikh gunners, gave up his original intention of a reconnaissance and a flank movement on the morrow, and ordered a frontal attack. His tactics were almost unanimously condemned at the time, and Dalhousie in a private letter to the President of the Board of Control wrote, 'the conduct of this action is beneath the criticism even of a militiaman like myself'.[1] Mr. R. S. Rait, in his recent biography of Lord Gough, claims to have shown on the evidence of his subject's diary and correspondence that there was no sudden change of plan, and that the story of his 'Irish blood' being roused by bullets falling near him is apocryphal. He also contends, though here no doubt his defence is more open to question, that the alteration in the Sikh formation made it impossible to retreat and unsafe to encamp, and that the mistakes in the battle were due to subordinates.[2] Wherever the responsibility lay, mistakes were undoubtedly made. The result of the battle was that, though the Sikhs after a desperate resistance abandoned their lines, they only retreated three miles in good order with the loss of twelve guns; on the other hand, a British brigade was repulsed with fearful loss, four guns captured, the colours of three regiments taken, and some cavalry squadrons disgracefully routed. British losses in killed and wounded amounted to 2,357 men and eighty-nine officers.

The account of the battle made a painful impression at home, and Sir Charles Napier was hurried out to supersede Lord Gough as Commander-in-Chief; but before he could arrive the latter rehabilitated his reputation and ended the war by a brilliant stroke. The battle of Gujrat, 'the battle of the guns', was fought on February 22. The Sikh army

[1] *The Life of the Marquis of Dalhousie.* By Sir William Lee-Warner, vol. i, p. 188.

[2] *The Life and Campaigns of Hugh, first Viscount Gough,* vol. ii, pp. 211–44.

was 50,000 strong, but this time the position was carefully reconnoitred, and Gough was prevailed upon to make proper use of his artillery. The infantry attack was not delivered till a tremendous bombardment had silenced the Sikh batteries. The enemy was put to flight and a brilliant and relentless pursuit made the battle completely decisive. Meanwhile after a desperate resistance the town of Multan was stormed, and Mulraj, who had retreated to the citadel, was finally forced to surrender at discretion. On March 12 Sher Singh and the remnant of the Khalsa army laid down their arms, and the Afghan forces of Dost Muhammad, which had taken no effective part in the war, were chased back to their hills.

Dalhousie, who received a Marquisate, had next to settle the future of the country. The practical courses of action were first, the re-establishment of the *status quo* before the rising, with possibly the annexation of the province of Multan; secondly, the permanent administration of the country by British officials, the Maharaja maintaining the titular sovereignty only; thirdly, the incorporation of the whole of the Punjab into British dominion. Sir Henry Lawrence and Lord Ellenborough were strongly opposed to annexation, and the Cabinet inclined to their way of thinking, though Dalhousie could get no very clear lead from them. Dalhousie considered that the first course would have given the Sikh nation better terms than they had any right to expect, and would have savoured of weakness on the part of Great Britain. As regards the second, he had no love for those titular pageantries and shadowy sovereignties which had done so much in the past to embarrass British statesmanship; accordingly, on his own responsibility he annexed the whole of the Punjab by proclamation on March 29, 1849—a momentous step which finally carried the frontiers of British India to their natural limits, the base of the mountains of Afghanistan. He endeavoured to meet the argument that Dulip Singh, being a minor, could not justly be held responsible for the misdeeds of his subjects, by granting him a generous pension of £50,000 a year. The child was given an English education, ultimately embraced Christianity, and lived the life of an English landlord on an estate in Norfolk. The Sikhs submitted to their lot more quietly than any one had anticipated, and as regards the material result the policy of the annexation was abundantly justified.

To settle the new province a Board of three commissioners was set up, consisting of Sir Henry Lawrence as President, his brother John, and Charles Mansel, who was replaced in 1851 by Robert Montgomery. Dalhousie would have preferred a single head, but he felt himself bound not to pass over Sir Henry Lawrence, and though he appreciated his fine and chivalrous character he did not consider him competent to take sole charge. To him was especially entrusted the 'political' work, i.e. negotiations with the chiefs, the disarming of the country, and the levying of the new Sikh regiment. To his brother John was given the settlement of the land revenue, while the third commissioner was mainly concerned with judicial matters. Fifty-six subordinates, the pick of the services, civil and military, formed the staff of the new province, and helped to carry out the settlement of the Punjab, which was destined to be one of the most brilliant administrative achievements of Englishmen in the East. The people were disarmed. A line of fortresses was carried along the north-west frontier. Roads were constructed throughout the province, the most notable being that which connected Lahore with Peshawar—a triumph of engineering skill. Canals were made both for transport and irrigation. The land tax was reduced from a half of the value of the produce to about a quarter. All internal imposts on the transport of goods were swept away. Slavery, thuggee, and dacoity were finally stamped out, and a clear and simple code of criminal and civil procedure, suited to a primitive political organization, instead of the cumbrous and complicated regulations of the older provinces, was drawn up. The most wonderful tribute to the success of these measures was the material prosperity and the contentment of the people. Within three years of the desperate valour and grim carnage of Chilianwala, Sikh soldiers were fighting for the Company in Burma of their own free will, and, when a little later the Mutiny threatened the existence of British dominions in India and offered to all subject peoples an unequalled opportunity for vengeance on their conquerors, the Punjab never faltered in its loyalty.

The credit for these splendid results must be shared between Lord Dalhousie and his subordinates, but the Governor-General played perhaps the predominant part. Though the plan of a Board was not adopted for that purpose, as was once erroneously supposed, it yet enabled him to inspire the policy of the commissioners and control their work. This was especially the case since there early appeared a cleavage of opinion between the brothers Lawrence. The elder was inclined to favour the Sirdars, or Sikh aristocracy, who were devoted to him personally, and to press on with material improvements regardless of the cost to the revenue. John Lawrence had more sympathy with the peasants than the chieftains, and as guardian of the public purse brought forward many practical objections to his brother's pet schemes. Not till nearly three years had elapsed did these differences prove a serious bar to administration. But early in 1853 the two brothers mutually agreed that it would be better for one of them to go. Dalhousie believing, in spite of Henry's many fine qualities, that John, 'take him all in all', was 'the better man', removed the elder brother, to his deep chagrin, to Rajputana as agent for the Governor-General, abolished the Board that had served its purpose, and made John Lawrence Chief Commissioner of the Punjab.

CHAPTER XXVIII

THE SECOND BURMESE WAR. LORD DALHOUSIE. THE DOCTRINE OF LAPSE

THE second war of Dalhousie's administration was waged on the far eastern frontier. It arose out of his determination to protect the interests of the merchants who, trusting to the Treaty of 1826, had settled on the southern coast of Burma. For some time they had been subject to petty persecutions at the hands of the Governor of Rangoon, who did everything possible to impede their trade, and in 1851 they applied for redress to Calcutta. Dalhousie sent a frigate to Rangoon to demand compensation. Many considered this action needlessly provocative, and even John Lawrence wrote meaningly, 'Why did you send a commodore to Burma if you wanted peace?' while Dalhousie himself afterwards admitted 'these commodores are too combustible for negotiations'.[1] But since the British government had long ceased to maintain a Resident at the court of Ava, owing to the insults to which they were subjected, there was perhaps no other means of showing the Burmese authorities that the matter was one of urgency. Even as it was, they ignored the representations of the commodore and his demands for compensation and fired upon him, when he rather injudiciously detained a royal vessel and proclaimed the blockade of the ports. They thus brought upon themselves the vigorous action of the Governor-General; an

[1] *Life of the Marquis of Dalhousie*, Sir William Lee-Warner, vol. i, pp. 417–18.

ultimatum was sent to the Court of Ava, demanding compensation and an indemnity of £100,000 under threat of war. The home authorities considered the tone of this dispatch too peremptory; but Dalhousie defended it on the ground that 'no Indian potentate would attend to any command conveyed as a European power would word it', and there seems little doubt that he would gladly have avoided what he called the 'mortification of war'. At the same time he was determined, if war should come, that it should be waged before the rains set in. No answer having been vouchsafed to the British ultimatum, Dalhousie pressed on preparations for war with extraordinary energy and thoroughness. He superintended nearly every detail himself, for he was determined that the mistakes and blunders of the first war should not be repeated. The commissariat and transport were thoroughly well organized. Every precaution to ensure the comfort and health of the troops was elaborately thought out. Within eight weeks from the commencement of warlike preparations, the flotilla appeared off Rangoon. Martaban was quickly captured. The great pagoda of Rangoon was stormed on April 14: Bassein fell a month later. The Commander-in-Chief, General Godwin, sent a force to reconnoitre Prome but did not advance thither, fearing to endanger his communications. The Governor-General himself proceeded to Rangoon in September, and determined that Prome should be taken. It was occupied in October; Pegu, already captured but besieged by the Burmese, was finally relieved in November, and military operations were thus concluded. Dalhousie pressed upon the Court of Directors the necessity of annexing the province of Pegu, partly because we could hardly abandon those of the inhabitants of that province, who had gladly welcomed British protection, to the fiendish cruelties of the Burmese. The Court accepted this suggestion, but put him in a difficulty by requiring either that the cession of Pegu should be regularly made in a treaty, or else that an advance should be made to Ava and the whole country subjugated.

Dalhousie realized that an advance to Ava 600 miles from our base was a chimerical scheme, even had the requisite transport and supplies been forthcoming, which they were not. On the other hand, any treaty with the barbaric court of Ava would be as 'flimsy as the paper on which it is traced'; he therefore took his own strong line, and when his overtures for a treaty produced no response, proclaimed the annexation of Pegu, or Lower Burma, on December 20, 1852. The results completely justified his bold action. Though the Burmese never formally recognized the cession of territory, they were too cowed to resent it in arms. The administration of the new province under Major Arthur Phayre was highly successful; but it was clearly proved that the ceded territory was large enough to tax his energies fully for many years. Granted that Burma was destined ultimately to pass under British sway, it was better, as Dalhousie declared, to take a second bite of the cherry. Dalhousie indeed experienced the usual fate of statesmen in being attacked from either side; for while some thought he had not gone far enough, others considered he had gone much too far; and he and the Court of Directors were roundly trounced for their love of territorial aggrandizement; but all the evidence goes to show that neither the Governor-General nor the home authorities desired annexation for its own sake. The new province extended as far north as Myede fifty miles beyond Prome. Westward it was bounded by the hills of Arakan and eastward roughly by the river Salwen. Independent Burma was now shut off altogether from the sea, and the whole coast-line of the Bay of Bengal from Cape Comorin to the Malay Peninsula passed under British control.

Sir William Lee-Warner has noticed three epochs in British relations with native states, first that of the 'ring fence' down to 1813, when native states were treated as really foreign and not interfered with; secondly, that of 'subordinate isolation' from 1813 to 1857, when the states were protected but their internal affairs were left entirely to themselves; and thirdly, that of 'subordinate union' from 1857 to the present day, when none are permitted to suffer from the misrule of their chiefs. Now in the first stage the oppressed subjects had at least the remedy of rebellion, in the last they can appeal to the strong arm of the suzerain. In the middle stage they had no redress. The British government often found itself confronted by the unpleasant dilemma of either breaking its agreements with native rulers or allowing their subjects to be down-trodden.

Dalhousie, girding against this state of things, sought a way out and found it in the famous doctrine of 'lapse', the principle of which had been distinctly recognized before his time. It was that in dependent states or those that owed their very existence to British power, the sovereignty, when the natural heirs of the royal line came to an end, passed back or 'lapsed' to the supreme power. The question, however, was complicated by that of adoption. All childless Hindus were accustomed to adopt sons whose main duty it was to perform those funeral rites without which the dead man would find no rest in the hereafter. Dalhousie claimed, undoubtedly with perfect correctness, that the sovereignty of a ruler could not pass to a son adopted without the consent of the suzerain. He held that, in view of the abuses to which native rule was so fatally liable, 'the British government in the exercise of a wise and sound policy is bound not to put aside or neglect such rightful opportunities of acquiring territory or revenue as may from time to time present themselves, whether they arise from the lapse of subordinate states by the failure of all heirs of every description whatsoever, or from the failure of heirs natural where the succession can be sustained only by the sanction of the government being given to the ceremony of adoption, according to Hindu law. The government is bound, in duty as well as in policy, to act on every such occasion with the purest integrity, and in the most scrupulous observance of good faith. When even a shadow of doubt can be shown, the claim should at once be abandoned.'[1] It must be remembered in the first place that the doctrine was not invented by Dalhousie; the principle at any rate had been recognized as early as 1834: secondly, that he applied it only to dependent states—those which had been avowedly dependencies of some suzerain conquered by Great Britain or had been actually established by her: thirdly, that in applying the doctrine he was animated by compassion for the peoples of the feudatory states as well as by a desire for territorial aggrandizement. It is not true, as has been so often said, that all native states were in danger of falling under British sway; for Dalhousie clearly recognized the right of those rulers, whose sovereignty dated back before the British régime, to adopt heirs freely.

On the other hand it is equally to be remembered that there was some technical difficulty in deciding which states were dependent and which were not, and the Governor-General's decision was sometimes overruled, as in the case of Karauli; secondly, that whatever may have been the facts, the natives did undoubtedly believe that the existence of all native principalities was threatened. As Mr. Innes well says, 'there was fully adequate precedent for every one of his annexations. But his predecessors had acted on the general principle of avoiding annexation if it could be avoided; Dalhousie acted on the general principle of annexing if he could do so legitimately.'[2] It was accidental, no doubt, that just at this time so many native rulers died

[1] *The Life of the Marquis of Dalhousie*, Sir W. Lee-Warner, vol. ii, p. 116.

[2] *A Short History of the British in India*, A. D. Innes, p. 279.

without heirs, but that being so, it would have been more expedient sometimes for the paramount power not to have exerted its full rights. It must be remembered also that 'lapse' was not the only means by which Dalhousie increased British dominion; opponents might say with some plausibility that, if the doctrine of lapse did not apply to all states, other principles, as in the case of Oudh, could readily be appealed to when Great Britain desired a pretext. An impartial critic, while fully recognizing the high and pure motives of the Governor-General, will not deny that there was abundant reason for uneasiness in the minds of native rulers, and there is much evidence to show that such uneasiness did, as a matter of fact, exist. Finally, as his latest biographer admits, Lord Dalhousie was sometimes rather unguarded and injudicious in the language he employed. The states that actually passed under British sway by lapse were Satara in 1848, Jaitpur and Sambalpur in 1849, Baghat in 1850, Udaipur in 1852, Jhansi in 1853, and Nagpur in 1854. In the case of three at least, and these the most important, no valid objection could be taken to Lord Dalhousie's policy either on the score of expediency or legal right. Satara was purely the creation of the British government. It had been bestowed as a principality on the representative of the house of Sivaji by Lord Hastings in 1819 after the overthrow of the Peshwa, and its existence had always been an embarrassment to the Presidency of Bombay, with which it was now incorporated. Jhansi was a tributary and dependent state in Bundelkhand which had also passed under British sway among Baji Rao's other dominions. It had been revived more than once, but on this occasion the belated adoption of the last Raja was set aside. The widowed Rani was pensioned, but in the Mutiny took a dreadful revenge for the loss of her throne by the massacre of every European who fell into her hands. Nagpur was by far the most important of all the lapsed states.

Conquered in 1818, Hastings had given back the forfeited kingdom to a prince of the royal house. The last Raja died in 1853, leaving neither collateral heirs nor adopted son. There was no need assuredly for the British government to grant away the sovereignty again. Of the political advantage to Great Britain of the annexation there could be no doubt. Nagpur comprised territory of 80,000 square miles with a population of 4,000,000; its possession gave us the finest cotton lands in India, and complete control of the land route from Calcutta to Bombay. On the other hand it might be pleaded that, as one of the great states of the Maratha confederacy, its annexation was bound to prompt misgivings in the hearts of other native rulers, who might not appreciate the subtle distinction—not always clear even to western minds—between 'dependent' states and 'protected allies'. Yet, on the whole, it may be concluded that the advantages of annexation in this case outweighed the disadvantages. The public auction of the jewels and furniture of the royal house, which made such an unfortunate impression, was a tactless blunder and one that might well have been avoided. In the other four cases mentioned there was some legitimate doubt as to whether they, properly speaking, fell under the definition of dependent states, and in regard to Udaipur in the Central Provinces it was fairly clear that, if heirs failed, the sovereignty lapsed to the Raja of Sarguja, not to the Company. In any event the states were small, and the gain of subjecting them to British rule hardly compensated for the uneasiness caused to surrounding chiefs. In the case of Baghat, a Cis-Sutlaj hill state, and Udaipur, Dalhousie's decision was afterwards reversed by Lord Canning. Finally the home government refused to approve of Dalhousie's tentative proposal to annex the little Rajput state of Karauli, on the ground that it was 'a protected ally' and not 'dependent'. They were undoubtedly right, and Dalhousie at once accepted their decision; on higher political grounds it would have been extremely impolitic to annex these ancient Rajput states, and it is perhaps surprising that the Governor-General ever suggested it.

Besides these actual acquisitions of new territory, Lord Dalhousie swept away certain titular sovereignties which had long ceased to have any real meaning, on the ground that they might at any time become a nucleus and rallying-ground for seditious agitation. Since 1801 the Nawab of the Carnatic had been avowedly a *roi fainéant*; in 1853, on the death of a holder of the title, Dalhousie supported the contention of the Madras government, that no successor should be recognized. He maintained that the treaty of 1801 created merely a personal, and not a hereditary title, which had only been re-granted in 1819 and 1825 by the indulgence of the British government. This decision was partially reversed in 1867, when the claimant to the Nawabship was pensioned and allowed to adopt the semi-royal style of Prince of Arcot. The regal title was also abolished in the case of Tanjore, whose last Raja died in 1855 leaving only daughters. Dalhousie would gladly have arranged for the abolition of the Mughal's title at Delhi, but in this respect he was overruled by the Court. Finally, on the death of Baji Rao, the ex-Peshwa, in 1853, Dalhousie refused to continue to an adopted son, afterwards known as the notorious Nana Sahib, the huge pension of £80,000 which Sir John Malcolm had unwisely granted.

The annexation of Oudh falls under the head neither of conquest, lapse, nor abolition of purely titular sovereignties. Since Lord Wellesley's famous treaty of 1801, Oudh had been a protected feudatory state with full internal independence. Power without responsibility was thus given to the ruler of Oudh (on whom the title of King was conferred by Lord Hastings in 1819), and the degeneration of the native administration followed its dreary and normal course in such cases. The court was given up to vicious luxury and puerile amusements. The people were oppressed; a special feature of misgovernment in Oudh was that many of the landowners, or 'talukdars', who were mainly Rajput in origin, resisted in their fortified strongholds the officers and disorderly armies of the King, and preyed on the hapless peasantry and weaker members of their own class. For many years the disorder had been going from bad to worse. Successive Governors-General had given solemn warning to the ruling house, especially Lord William Bentinck in 1831 and Lord Hardinge in 1847. But all without the least effect. Of the need of drastic intervention on behalf of a down-trodden people there can be no doubt. Colonel Sleeman in 1851 (though Dalhousie's critics declared he was sent forth as the 'missionary of a foregone conclusion') and Colonel Outram in 1854, both as a rule supporters of native dynasties and opposed to the policy of lapse, reported that the condition of Oudh was deplorable and could hardly be worse. Lord Dalhousie himself was in favour of taking over the administration and leaving to the King his nominal sovereignty with his palace, rank, and titles. But the home authorities overruled him and decided on annexation. In this particular case they were undoubtedly wrong and the Governor-General right. Lord Dalhousie would never have suggested the recognition of a titular sovereignty, to which as we have seen he was generally much opposed, had it not been for strong countervailing reasons. These were first, the unswerving loyalty of the Oudh dynasty to British rule ever since the treaty of 1801: secondly, the fact that the King of Oudh could with some reason maintain that annexation involved the repudiation of treaty obligations. The facts are involved and obscure, but may briefly be stated thus:—In 1837 Lord Auckland had concluded a treaty with the King of Oudh binding him *either* to introduce reforms *or* to hand over the administration to the British government while retaining the sovereignty. Now the Court of Directors disallowed this treaty, but Lord Auckland only informed the King of the disallowance of one clause, and by an inexcusable piece of carelessness the treaty was actually included in a subsequent government publication and was referred to as still in force by succeeding Governors-General. Upon Lord Dalhousie was thrust the invidious task of explaining to the King that the treaty, which he and former Governors-General had believed to be in force since 1837, had really been abrogated two years after that date, and of expressing a tardy regret that the communication of this fact had been inadvertently neglected. Such miserable and unpardonable mismanagement obviously gave too much ground to those who held that the annexation of Oudh was 'a gross breach of national faith'. But for this the home authorities, and not Lord Dalhousie, were responsible. He would gladly have avoided the necessity of carrying out the annexation, but nobly volunteered to settle the question with all the weight his eight years' rule had given him rather than leave the task to a successor newly arrived in India. Outram in vain attempted to induce the King to abdicate; the annexation was proclaimed on February 13, 1856, and a generous pension was settled on the deposed monarch.

Only the briefest mention can be made of the great internal reforms initiated and developed by Lord Dalhousie. He opened the first Indian railway, planned under Lord Hardinge, and set up the first telegraph wire—'the accursed string that strangled us', as one of the mutineers called it. He set up the Public Works Department, and established a cheap and uniform postage service over the length and breadth of India; he was called upon to carry out the famous educational dispatch of July 1854, which 'sketched in outline a complete scheme of public education controlled and aided, and in part directly managed by the state'.

When Lord Dalhousie left India his health was obviously shattered by his unsparing labours, and he died in 1860 after four years of physical pain and distress. These years were saddened by the apparent overthrow of his life work in the Mutiny. Naturally, though in great measure unjustly, his great annexations of territory, his innovations and reforms, were held to be the main cause of the revolt. He was accused of roughly overriding native feeling and native susceptibilities, of blindness to signs of unrest in the sepoy army, and of allowing the proportion of European to native troops to sink to too low a point. He refused to speak out in his own defence, partly because he proudly trusted to the verdict of posterity, partly from a noble resolve not to embarrass his successor or the home government by opening the floodgates of controversy. His private papers were left under seal for fifty years, and it is only within the last decade that they have been given to the world.[1] Their publication has cleared up many doubtful points, but his reputation had long been rehabilitated. Most of the charges against him were found to have been grossly exaggerated and some absolutely disproved: it was known, for instance, that he had urgently impressed upon the Cabinet that more European regiments should be sent to India, but his warnings had been disregarded. The great traits of his character are no longer in dispute. He was inspired with a noble and vivid ideal of duty, which drove him on to sacrifice his health and comfort recklessly. His powers of work were colossal, and, though he came to India with practically no previous experience of Indian problems, he mastered them in a remarkably short space of time. His minutes and dispatches are masterpieces of eloquent English, lucid statement, and merciless logic. He was a supremely able judge of character. 'As an imperial administrator', says Sir Richard Temple, one of his subordinates, 'he has never been surpassed and seldom equalled by any of the illustrious men whom England has sent forth to govern

[1] By Sir William Lee-Warner in his *Life of the Marquis of Dalhousie*.

India.' On the other hand, to use a hackneyed yet useful phrase, he had the defects of his qualities. He possibly attempted to do more than any one man, however able, could do. There was not much field left to his subordinates except to carry out his rather imperious will. Though he freely supported men with whom he was in complete agreement, he was somewhat intolerant of original ideas. It is only fair to remember that there was an opposition in India to many tendencies of his policy, and not a factious opposition only, but one based on reasoned principles. Men like Henry Lawrence, Low, Sleeman, and Outram, while freely admitting his splendid qualities, considered that he would have done better to pay more heed to native feelings and prejudices even at the cost of sacrificing some of his most valuable reforms. He had more downright opponents. The letters and diaries of Sir Charles Napier show to what a pitch enmity between able and high-minded men can be carried. In the controversy between them few doubt that on the whole Dalhousie was right, and Napier wrong. The latter, as we have seen in the case of Sind, had an almost limitless capacity for seeing only the right on his own side, and only the wrong on that of his opponents. But the collision between these two strong men, due to the fact that Napier altered the pay of the troops and disbanded regiments without consulting the Governor-General and Council, was doubly unfortunate. It seems undoubtedly true that Sir Charles Napier had some premonitory warnings of mutinous discontent in the sepoy armies. He was not consistent in his statements on the point, and greatly exaggerated them for controversial reasons. For the same reasons Dalhousie refused even to consider them. Had Napier been more temperate in his warnings and Dalhousie more ready to listen to advice, the whole question might have been opened and settled instead of being obscured by heated manifestoes, slashing minutes, and bitter enmities.

CHAPTER XXIX

THE CAUSES OF THE MUTINY. LORD CANNING

LORD CANNING, who succeeded the Marquis of Dalhousie in February 1856, had won a reputation for scholarship at Oxford and for statesmanlike ability as Postmaster-General. He was capable and industrious but somewhat diffident of his own powers, and not personally ambitious. Slow in making up his mind to any particular course of action, and conscientious almost to a fault, when he had once chosen his ground he defended it skilfully and held it with tenacity. Seeing many sides to every question and an adept at weighing evidence, he possessed the judicial rather than the administrative temperament. He hid a warm heart under a reserved and cold manner. Had his lot been cast in peaceful times he would have been an ideal head for the Indian government, but he was called upon to deal with one of the most terrible crises that ever confronted a statesman. Some of his actions were open to criticism, and have been freely criticized: but on the whole he emerged nobly from the appalling ordeal to which he was subjected. If he lacked the daring resolution, imperious will, and personal force of Dalhousie, he displayed a splendid constancy under taunts and misrepresentation, and he possessed a curious power of detaching himself from the influences and passions of the moment in solving intricate problems.

It appeared at first as though a central Asian question might chiefly engage the new Governor-General's attention. In 1855 the British minister at Teheran had been driven away by insulting treatment. In the following year Persian forces occupied Herat—a breach of the treaty of 1814. Canning was ordered by the home government to declare war in the name of the Company. A British expedition was sent to the Persian Gulf, captured Bushire and inflicted several defeats on the enemy. Finally a peace was made in May by which Persia agreed to evacuate Herat and interfere no more in Afghan affairs. This short war, and two treaties made in 1855 and 1857 with Dost Muhammad (signed by Sir John Lawrence but really due to Herbert Edwardes), were of importance as winning the favour of the Afghan chief and preventing him from embarrassing us during the Mutiny. The victorious troops on their return found work to do on a grimmer field, for the sepoys had broken out in the meantime.

There are two main views of the origin and meaning of the Indian Mutiny: one, that it was a mere military rising: the other, that it was a widespread conspiracy carefully organized for the overthrow of British power. The men with the best opportunity of judging came to diametrically opposite views on this point. Sir John Lawrence held that the Mutiny had its origin in the army and that its proximate cause was the cartridge affair and nothing else. It was not attributable to any antecedent conspiracy whatever, although it was afterwards taken advantage of by disaffected persons to compass their own ends. The view of Sir James Outram is almost the exact antithesis of this: he believed that it was the result of a Muhammadan conspiracy making capital of Hindu grievances. The cartridge incident merely 'precipitated the Mutiny before it had been thoroughly organized and before adequate arrangements had been made for making the Mutiny a first step to a popular insurrection'.

On the whole, in spite of the fact that in some districts the people seem to have risen before the sepoys, Lawrence's view seems most nearly to approximate to the truth. We may assume, therefore, that the rising was mainly military in origin, but that it occurred at a time when, for various reasons, there was much social and political discontent, and that the mutineers were promptly joined by interested adventurers, who tried to give it a particular direction to suit their own schemes. Fortunately for British dominion in India there was no single national cause to which the agitators could appeal. The fabric of British power was built over the ashes of warring factions and race enmities. The Mutiny was exploited alike to revive the vanished glories of the Mughal Empire—the foe of all Hindu principalities—and to re-establish the power of the Maratha Peshwa—the hereditary rebel against Mughal authority. The fact that the political direction of the Mutiny first fell into the hands of men who replaced Bahadur Shah upon his imperial throne, was enough in itself to alienate the sympathies of all Hindu states. The attempt to summon back the ghost of Maratha supremacy was, as it were, only the political second thought of the Mutiny, and came too late for success, when the back of the rebellion was broken and the cause of the insurgents was obviously waning.

The causes of the Mutiny may be summed up under the headings, political, social, religious, and military, but if the view adopted above is the right one, it is obvious that the latter alone can properly be considered to have brought about the actual outbreak; the other headings apply rather to the general unrest of the time which afforded so favourable a field for that movement to develop and spread.

To deal with the political causes first. There can be no doubt that Dalhousie's annexations and the doctrine of lapse had caused a thrill of uneasiness and suspicion throughout India. This fact does not necessarily involve any condemnation of the late Governor-General's policy. In all great reforms some vested interests must be alienated, and it is arguable that, but for the blunder of the greased cartridges, the political discontent would have been allayed by time and never have passed beyond the stage of a vague unrest. But some Englishmen in India had uttered warnings of the dangers ahead. Colonel Sleeman in 1853 had written words that future events made prophetic: 'The native states I consider to be breakwaters, and when they are all swept away we shall be left to the mercy of our native army, which may not always be sufficiently under our control.' Since Lord Dalhousie entered upon office, the great Sikh power had finally fallen; Oudh, the premier Muhammadan state, had been annexed; Satara, the original seat of the Sivaji, and Nagpur, one of the greatest states of the Maratha 'pentarchy', had been absorbed. Little indeed was left of the majesty of the Mughal Empire, but even that was diminished, for it had been ordained that on the death of the titular King of Delhi his successor was to leave his ancestral palace and eschew something of his royal splendour. In private unguarded words were often used which might well lead to the conviction that British policy had embarked on an unscrupulous course of aggrandizement. This, as we have seen, was far from the truth, but native hearers could hardly be expected to discriminate between authoritative statements and such language, half jest half earnest, as that used for instance by Sir Charles Napier in his private correspondence: 'Were I Emperor of India for twelve years, she should be traversed by railways and have her rivers bridged. . . . No Indian Prince should exist. The Nizam should be no more heard of. . . . Nepal would be ours. . . .'[1] We have seen that Dalhousie had refused to continue to Nana Sahib, the adopted son of the ex-Peshwa, the huge pension that had been granted to the latter by Sir John Malcolm. In this he was perfectly justified, for the

[1] *The Life and Opinions of General Sir C. J. Napier.* Ed. by Sir W. Napier, vol. iv, p. 188.

grant was only made to Baji Rao for life, and in the course of the thirty-five years during which he enjoyed the pension, he had accumulated a large fortune which Nana Sahib inherited. But, in the eyes of Hindus, Nana Sahib had succeeded to the office and privileges of the Peshwaship; the withdrawal of the pension made him the bitter and relentless foe of British rule, and was widely resented by his countrymen as an act of injustice. During the early months of 1857 Nana Sahib was moving to and fro from Delhi to Lucknow, a sinister figure, weaving a web of intrigue and sending his emissaries far and wide to enlist support and foster every movement of revolt.

Secondly, from the social aspect, every annexation of a native state not only deposed a reigning house but still further limited the rapidly narrowing field in which men of Indian race could display their political and administrative talents. In the pacification of conquered territories, and in the land settlements carried out in recent years, the claims of native aristocracies had been severely scrutinized by zealous officials, whose aim, in many ways laudable, was to protect the ryot, or peasant, from exaction and deal with him directly instead of through hereditary revenue collectors and middlemen. Bentinck's resumption of rent-free tenures had regained for the state much revenue that had been fraudulently withheld, but it had also reduced to poverty many landowners whose title-deeds had been lost or who had held their estates by long prescriptive right. In the five years preceding the Mutiny the famous *Inam* commission at Bombay (i. e. a commission to inquire into rent-free tenures) had confiscated 20,000 estates. In Oudh, above all, serious social unrest had been caused by the changes, many of them inevitable, that followed on annexation. Unfortunately, Sir James Outram, under whom the transformation was being smoothly worked, left Oudh in April 1856, and was succeeded by an energetic, just, but unsympathetic officer, Coverly Jackson, as Chief Commissioner. The native royal army was disbanded and the soldiers lost their livelihood. A too strict inquiry was made into the titles of the 'Talukdars' of Oudh, the hereditary revenue collectors, whose office had given them almost feudal rights over the soil and its cultivators. The recall of Jackson and the appointment of Sir Henry Lawrence did much to mend matters, and, in spite of the fact that Oudh became the chief theatre of the war, the 'Talukdars' did not as a body support the rebels till Havelock in his first advance was forced to turn back from Lucknow, nor did they themselves rise till Lord Canning's injudicious proclamation, which will be mentioned later, drove them to desperation.

Thirdly, to the devout Hindu, and especially to the priesthood, the hated and iconoclastic power of the British seemed to have invaded even the immaterial realms of faith and caste. There was a widespread belief that Lord Canning had been commissioned to convert India to Christianity. Hindu mythology had been disparaged in a brilliant essay by Macaulay, at one time member of the Governor-General's Council. *Sati* and infanticide had been prohibited. European science, astronomy, and surgery were all opposed to the teaching of the Brahmans. The mysticism and symbolism of the East were fading before the cold light of western materialism. The telegraph and railway were looked upon askance as magical and diabolical agencies. Recent laws had been passed that Hindu widows were free to marry a second time, and that a change of religion should not debar the convert from inheriting property. 'It must be admitted', says Sir William Lee-Warner, 'that even the most ignorant and apathetic Hindu was brought into more conscious touch with the spirit of the West during the eight years preceding 1857 than at any other period in the history of India.'[1]

[1] *The Life of the Marquis of Dalhousie.* By Sir William Lee-Warner, vol. ii, p. 379.

Lastly, we must take into account the condition of the sepoy army. The disparity in numbers between European and Indian troops had lately been growing greater; when Lord Dalhousie left India the army consisted of 233,000 natives and 45,322 British soldiers. For this, as we have seen, Dalhousie was not to blame: he had in vain endeavoured to get drafts from home to replace the regiments taken away from India for service in the Crimea. The disproportion was rendered more serious by the growing deficiency of officers, and of officers of the best type, who had been employed by Dalhousie in increasing numbers for administrative posts upon the frontier. The distribution of the troops was also very faulty. Delhi and Allahabad were wholly held by native levies and, except for one regiment at Dinapore, there were no British soldiers between Allahabad and Calcutta.

The Bengal army, as distinct from those of Madras and Bombay, had always been more difficult to handle from the great number of high caste men, Brahmans and Rajputs, in its ranks. Their discipline had been lately impaired. They had intensely disliked service in Afghanistan, and the men who returned were taunted by their fellows with having forfeited their caste. There had been some sinister outbreaks of insubordination in recent years. In 1824, as already mentioned, the 47th regiment was disbanded for refusing to serve in Burma. In 1844 four Bengal regiments declined to serve in Sind till extra allowances were made to them. The 66th native infantry mutinied at Govindgarh in 1849, and the 38th Bengal native infantry, who were acting within their rights, refused to serve in Burma in 1852. Great uneasiness was caused to the Bengal army in July 1856 by the passing of the General Service Enlistment Act, which forbade henceforward the enlisting of any recruit, who would not march whithersoever his services should be required. Hitherto, the scruples of the high caste sepoy as to crossing the sea, or serving out of India, had been respected, but with the rapid growth of the empire this limitation had been found irksome. The Act only applied of course to the future, but the sepoy was now practically the member of an hereditary military caste, and it meant to him either that his sons must be debarred from following his own profession or that they must run the risk of being outcasted.

The terrible blunder of the 'greased cartridges' fanned into a fierce and devouring flame all this smouldering discontent. The facts are well known. A rumour pervaded the sepoy army that the cartridges to be used with the new Enfield rifle had been greased with the fat of cows and pigs with the deliberate intention to outcast and defile both the Hindu, to whom the cow was sacred, and the Muhammadan, to whom swine were unclean. The story was everywhere received with an eager credulity which defied explanation, argument, remonstrance, and denial. Most unfortunately there was a certain amount of truth in the charge. Through carelessness or ignorance animal fat had actually been used in the ammunition factories at Woolwich. This was not discovered at once and was denied by the officers in good faith. The sepoys knowing the fact to be true, when they heard the denial, naturally imagined that they were being wilfully misled, and their worst suspicions were confirmed. Even when the mistake was rectified, no protestations of their officers, no proclamations or orders had any effect in restoring confidence.

Through the first four months of 1857 the whole native army of Bengal was in a state of sullen, brooding unrest. Outbreaks of incendiarism—a sure sign of sepoy discontent—occurred at Barrackpore in March, and a native regiment was disbanded. In April at the great military station of Meerut in the North-West Provinces some troopers of a native cavalry regiment, in spite of the explanations and appeals of their Colonel, refused on parade to use the cartridges supplied to them. After trial by court martial they were sentenced to ten years' imprisonment. On May 9 they were publicly degraded, stripped of their uniforms, and manacled. The assembled troops, overawed by loaded field guns and the drawn swords of an English dragoon regiment, made no sign, but the mutineers, as they were marched off to jail, shouted back reproaches on their comrades and curses on their commanding officer.

CHAPTER XXX

THE MUTINY

At Meerut on May 10, 1857, when the station was plunged in the calm of a Sunday evening, three native regiments rose, shot down their officers, broke open the prisons, released their comrades, and marched off to Delhi. Had they been vigorously pursued and cut down, it is more than likely that the Mutiny would have spread no further; but through the fatal inaction of the commanding officer of the station they were allowed to escape undisturbed. On the morning of the next day the outposts of the mutineers galloped into Delhi and called upon the troops there to revolt. Not a single British regiment was quartered at that time in Delhi, and in a few hours the city was in the hands of the rebels. The British officers of the sepoy battalions were murdered, every European found met the same fate, and the telegraph operator had only time to flash his alarming messages to the chief stations in the Punjab when he was cut down at his post. Finding resistance hopeless, the British defenders of the great magazine with splendid gallantry blew it and a thousand mutineers into the air. The rebels bursting into the Palace proclaimed Bahadur Shah, the old King of Delhi, once more Mughal Emperor of India.

Fortunately a short respite was given to the British authorities reeling under this shattering blow. No further mutinies, except in small and isolated stations, occurred for about three weeks, and though the space of time was all too short for what had to be done, it was something gained.

The most vigorous action came from the Punjab, in spite of the fact that a threefold peril had to be faced in that province—disaffection in the sepoy regiments, the risk of an Afghan invasion, and that of a rising of the Sikhs. Happily Dost Muhammad remained splendidly loyal to the treaties of 1855 and 1857, and the army of the Khalsa made no attempt to profit by the disasters of their recent conquerors. The sepoy regiments at Lahore were promptly disbanded, and a movable column was formed under John Nicholson to attack and destroy any mutinous bodies.

The most pressing need for the restoration of British prestige was the recapture of Delhi. Both Canning and Sir John Lawrence vehemently urged this upon Anson, the Commander-in-Chief, who, for the moment however, found it impossible to advance for lack of transport and supplies. Before the expedition could start, mutiny became general over Oudh, Rohilkhand, and many parts of central India. Between May 29 and June 5 the sepoys rose at Nasirabad in Rajputana, at Nimach in the Gwalior state, at Bareilly in Rohilkhand, and at Lucknow, Benares, and Cawnpore in Oudh, while the Rani of Jhansi headed the revolt in Bundelkhand and massacred every European that fell into her hands. In almost every case the mutineers after the outbreak set their faces towards Delhi: many murdered their officers before doing so; some, with a curious remnant of fidelity, escorted them first to positions of safety and then after saluting them marched off to join their comrades. In Oudh alone was this movement checked. The mutineers at Cawnpore had actually started along the Delhi road on June 5 when they were headed off by Nana Sahib the next day and brought back to besiege the British garrison weakly entrenched there. The rebels of Lucknow also remained to besiege the Residency, well provisioned and fortified by Sir Henry Lawrence, who alone of men in high positions seems to have realized from the beginning of the year the true nature of the peril that was approaching. For the moment, however, we must disregard the course of events in Oudh and return to the movements converging on Delhi.

Anson, marching from Ambala, died of cholera on May 27 at Karnal, less than half-way on the road to Delhi. He was succeeded by Sir Henry Barnard, who on June 4 was joined by Archdale Wilson from Meerut. Their combined forces defeated a rebel army at Badli Sarai on June 8, dislodged the enemy from the famous Ridge overlooking the city of Delhi, and made their camp there. Nominally the besieging force, they were themselves in reality besieged. Their number at first was under 5,000. That of the enemy was about 30,000, and reinforcements were constantly thronging into Delhi by the southern and eastern roads, which were completely open. All through June and July the English force maintained its position on the Ridge with difficulty, having constantly to beat back fierce attacks from the mutineers in the city.

Meanwhile Sir John Lawrence and his able coadjutors, Herbert Edwardes, John Nicholson, and Sydney Cotton, having crushed down mutiny in their own province, were straining every nerve to reinforce the army before Delhi and taking a splendid risk in denuding the Punjab of troops. To many the policy must have seemed hazardous in the extreme. There could be no certainty then that Dost Muhammad would remain faithful to his treaties, or, even if he did, that he could restrain his turbulent countrymen from raids upon our frontier. It must have appeared very doubtful whether the Sikhs could permanently resist the temptation to recover their independence. Little wonder that Lawrence, upon whom responsibility for failure would have fallen, often lagged behind the eager promptings of Edwardes or Nicholson. In his proposal, however, to surrender Peshawar to the Afghans and withdraw to the

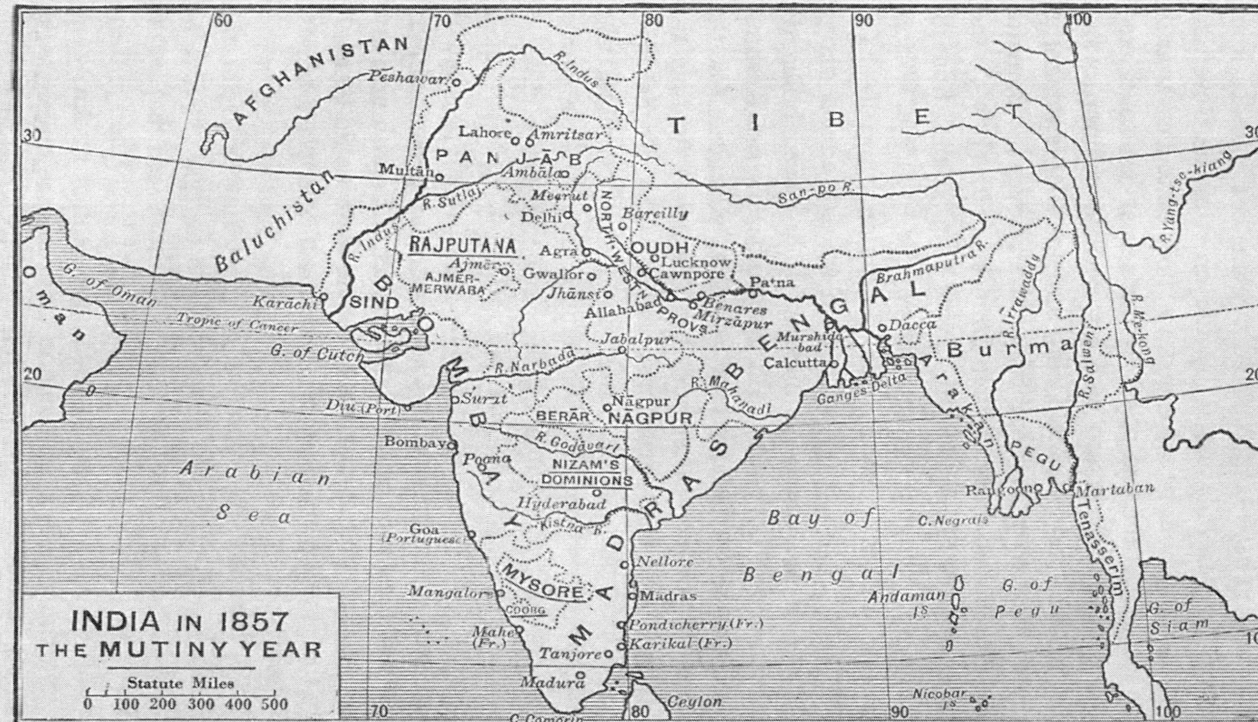
INDIA IN 1857
THE MUTINY YEAR
Statute Miles
0 100 200 300 400 500
AFGHANISTAN
Peshawar
Baluchistan
Oman
G. of Oman
Tropic of Cancer
Karachi
SIND
G. of Cutch
Diu (Port)
Lahore
Amritsar
PANJĀB
Multān
Ambāla
R. Sutlaj
R. Indus
Meerut
Delhi
NORTH-WESTN PROVS
Bareilly
OUDH
Lucknow
Cawnpore
RAJPUTANA
Agra
Ajmēr
AJMER-MERWARA
Gwalior
Jhānsi
Allahabad
Benares
Mirzāpur
Patna
Jabalpur
R. Narbada
Surat
Bombay
Poona
BERĀR
Nāgpur
NAGPUR
R. Godāvari
NIZAM'S DOMINIONS
Hyderabad
Kistna R.
Goa (Portuguese)
Nellore
Madras
MYSORE
COORG
Mangalore
Mahe (Fr.)
Pondicherry (Fr.)
Karikal (Fr.)
Tanjore
Madura
C. Comorin
Ceylon
BOMBAY
MADRAS
BENGAL
R. Mahanadi
Murshidabad
Calcutta
Ganges Delta
Dacca
Brahmaputra R.
TIBET
San-po R.
Arakan
Burma
R. Irrawaddy
PEGU
Rangoon
Martaban
R. Salween
R. Me-kong
R. Yang-tse-kiang
Tenasserim
Arabian Sea
Bay of Bengal
C. Negrais
Andaman Is.
G. of Pegu
Nicobar Is.
G. of Siam
60
70
80
90
100
30
20
10
WAKTYPE
GEORGE PHILIP & SON, LTD.

line of the Indus, he seems in the face of Edwardes's fervent entreaties to have contemplated a calamitous blunder from which he was only saved by the order of the Governor-General, to whom he appealed, to 'hold on to Peshawar to the last'. At the end of July Lawrence at last considered it safe to send Nicholson with his splendid column to join the British forces before Delhi, and the latter's wonderful vigour inspired a new spirit into the besiegers. Barnard, like Anson, had been smitten down by death (July 5), and his successor, General Reed, having soon resigned from ill-health, the nominal commander was Sir Archdale Wilson, though the real leader was Nicholson himself. On September 6 the heavy siege train arrived, after a daring attempt of the enemy to intercept it had been brilliantly defeated by Nicholson. On September 14 the Kashmir Gate was blown in and four columns advanced for the storm of Delhi. After six days' desperate fighting the city fell and the palace was taken. The English had 1,450 men put out of action, including Nicholson, who was mortally wounded as he stepped forward in a narrow lane swept by a withering fire to encourage a division that had momentarily wavered. The King was taken prisoner with his two sons, and the Princes were pistolled by Hodson, a brilliant cavalry leader, who had persuaded himself that they were guilty of the murder of English men and women, and that an attempt to rescue them would be made by the mob before he could take them to a place of safe custody.

To complete the narrative of the taking of Delhi the chronological order of events has been disregarded, and we must now retrace our footsteps. We have seen that by the first week in June Oudh was seething with rebellion and the mutineers were converging round two centres, Lucknow and Cawnpore. While the rising in that province threatened to cut all communications between Calcutta and the Punjab, it, at any rate, kept large bodies of rebels occupied who would otherwise have flocked to Delhi. The siege of the entrenchments at Cawnpore began on June 6 and lasted till the 26th; that of the Residency at Lucknow began on July 1 and continued till its final relief on November 16. The most strenuous efforts were made to relieve these two towns, and it was round them that the fiercest fighting of the whole war took place. On June 11 Neill by a bold and fortunate stroke secured the great fortress of Allahabad, valiantly held by an English officer with a small Sikh force but in imminent danger of falling into the hands of the enemy. This town was destined henceforward to be the base of operations for the relief of the beleaguered garrisons in Oudh and the ultimate reconquest of the province. Twelve days later Neill was joined by General Havelock just returned from the Persian expedition, an officer grown grey in the service in subordinate positions, to whom the task of relieving Lucknow and Cawnpore had been committed. On July 7 Havelock marched out of Allahabad with a little army of 2,000 men for what was to prove, considering the appalling difficulties that faced him, perhaps the most glorious campaign of the Mutiny. His meagre force was decimated by cholera and dysentery. The fierce rays of the Indian sun beat unmercifully on the exhausted ranks; and the enemy fought desperately and determinedly. Havelock was outnumbered ten to one. Yet between July 12 and September 25 he fought twelve pitched battles and accomplished his task. He knew even before he left Allahabad that, though the garrison at Lucknow was holding out, the end had come to the heroic defence at Cawnpore, and all he could hope to do there was to save, if possible, the lives of the women and children who were in the hands of Nana Sahib. The facts of the surrender are well known and can be only briefly summarized here. The garrison, through terrible misery and suffering, held out till June 26, and then, as the only hope of saving the non-combatants, surrendered on promise of honourable treatment to Nana Sahib, who from his estate at Bithur, granted him by the Company, was directing the operations of the mutineers. The British left their entrenchments and were conducted to boats on the river, but even before they had pushed off from the bank a hail of bullets and grape-shot from the banks overwhelmed them and a hideous carnage began. Four men only made their escape, the rest were massacred, and about 125 women and children were dragged ashore and reserved for a yet more dreadful fate.

After four fierce conflicts Havelock entered Cawnpore only to find that the day before his entry the captives, with some others brought in from other stations to the number of two hundred and eleven, had been foully murdered and their bodies flung into the famous well of Cawnpore. Leaving Neill, who had followed him from Allahabad, to take a grim vengeance for this ghastly deed, Havelock marched out on July 25 to cover the forty-two miles that separated him from Lucknow. There Sir Henry Lawrence had died on July 4 from a shell wound, but his work and influence lived on after him and inspired the defence which was splendidly maintained by Inglis. After winning two victories Havelock's little army was so shattered by cholera, sunstroke, and losses in action that he was forced for the moment to fall back on Cawnpore. There he defeated a large force of the enemy who were pressing Neill hard, and recruited his strength. He crossed the Ganges once more on September 19 with Outram, who had come out to supersede him, but who nobly volunteered to serve under his leadership till Lucknow was relieved. He routed the enemy in three more battles and fought his way at the point of the bayonet into Lucknow on September 25, just five days after Delhi had been finally occupied. As John Nicholson was mortally wounded in the storm of Delhi, so Neill, who so much resembled him in impetuous valour and force of character, met his death in the narrow streets of Lucknow.

These two events, the fall of Delhi and the relief of Lucknow, mark the end of the first stage of the Mutiny—the first desperate fight for very existence that had to be waged by men standing despairingly at bay without help from England. The back of the Mutiny was broken. From henceforward begins the second stage of reconquest. There was indeed yet much to be done; Lucknow itself had to be relieved a second time, for Havelock and Outram were not strong enough to remove the garrison and were themselves besieged; but the tension of the situation was lessened; there was time to draw breath; reinforcements were steadily pouring in from England, and two Generals of great experience, Sir Colin Campbell, Commander-in-Chief (afterwards Lord Clyde), and Sir Hugh Rose (afterwards Lord Strathnairn), were, the one on his way, and the other already landed in India. The operations that remained were briefly the reconquest of Oudh and Rohilkhand by Sir Colin Campbell, the brilliant campaign of Sir Hugh Rose in central India, starting from Bombay through districts where the rebels had hitherto been left almost undisturbed, and the final breaking up and pursuit of fugitive bands.

On November 9 Sir Colin Campbell advanced with 5,000 men for the second relief of Lucknow, and entered the city after a desperate conflict on the 16th. The non-combatants were removed, and Campbell began his return march to Cawnpore on the 27th, leaving Outram strongly posted with 4,000 men at the Alam Bagh, a large walled garden about four miles from the city. There the brave old hero Havelock, who died on November 24, worn out by his exertions and privations, was fittingly buried near the city he had saved. Sir Colin Campbell on his return was only just in time to avert a serious disaster, for the mutinous Gwalior contingent, 20,000 strong, under Tantia Topi, a Maratha Brahman, had suddenly advanced from Kalpi and repulsed General Windham, left in charge at Cawnpore. These troops had mutinied in June, but this was the first effective move they had made. Campbell severely defeated them on December 6, and proceeded to a regular campaign in Oudh and Rohilkhand. He was joined before Lucknow by a force of Gurkhas under Jang Bahadur, the able minister of the Raja of Nepal, who never lost faith in the British cause. Lucknow was finally captured and cleared of rebels by March 1, though Campbell's dread of losing men enabled large bodies of the enemy to make their escape. The resistance in Oudh was unfortunately prolonged by Canning's injudicious proclamation at the end of March, which declared the lands of all Talukdars forfeit to Government except those of six specifically mentioned and of others who could prove their loyalty. Canning's intention undoubtedly was to restore most of these estates after careful inquiry, but this was naturally not understood by the Talukdars, who in large numbers abandoned the attitude they had hitherto adopted of neutrality or mere passive support of the rebels for one of active participation, maintaining a harassing guerilla warfare till the end of the year. In May Campbell captured Bareilly in Rohilkhand, and this practically concluded operations on a large scale in the north.

Meanwhile Sir Hugh Rose had conducted a brilliant and decisive campaign in Bundelkhand, the southernmost theatre of the Mutiny. Advancing from Mhow, his base of operations, on January 8, 1858, he captured Ratgarh, and relieved Saugor in February. In March he invested Jhansi, and, after utterly defeating a great relieving army under Tantia Topi at the battle of the Betwa, he carried the fortress by storm. In May he routed a large army at Kunch. The campaign seemed over and he had just laid aside his command when he was startled by news of the deepest import.

The Rani of Jhansi and Tantia Topi, round whom the pursuers were closing, had conceived the brilliant design of marching to Gwalior on the desperate chance that Sindhia's army would come over to them. The Gwalior contingent or subsidiary force, as we have seen, had long joined the rebels, but Sindhia had hitherto kept his own army loyal. The daring scheme succeeded. When Sindhia marched forth to encounter the enemy his whole army deserted him; he himself barely escaped with his personal bodyguard to Agra. The rebels occupied Gwalior, seized the arsenal and the treasury, and proclaimed Nana Sahib as Peshwa. Rose recognized at once the terrible danger that Tantia Topi might now strike southwards into the Deccan and, with all the prestige that the possession of Sindhia's capital gave him, blow into flame the disaffection which, though as yet kept under, was known to exist south of the Narbada. With a supreme effort he flung his wearied troops on Gwalior and defeated the rebels in two battles, in one of which the Rani of Jhansi, clad in male attire, met a soldier's death. He recaptured the city on June 20.

Though it still smouldered in outlying districts, the great conflagration of the Mutiny had now been stamped out, and Canning felt himself justified in proclaiming peace on July 8. Some of the leaders still eluded their pursuers. But Nana Sahib was eventually driven into the pestilential jungles of the Tarai on the borders of Nepal and probably perished there miserably, for he was never seen again. Tantia Topi escaped southwards and was hunted up and down Bundelkhand and Malwa till he was betrayed into the hands of the British in April 1859 and hanged for complicity in the massacre of Cawnpore.

CHAPTER XXXI

THE END OF THE EAST INDIA COMPANY

THE Mutiny was over. Some reasons for the final English victory may here be considered. First, widespread and formidable though the revolt was, it was yet to some extent localized. The area affected was the Punjab, the United Provinces, Rohilkhand, Oudh, the territory between the Narbada and the Chambal, and the western part of Bihar and Bengal. On the north-west Afghanistan remained friendly under Dost Muhammad, Sind was quiet, Rajputana was loyal under the tactful guidance of George Lawrence, a third member of that family the value of whose services to England in the Mutiny was incalculable. India south of the Narbada made no movement of importance, though a native regiment mutinied at Kolhapur in the southern Maratha country, and there were very dangerous ebullitions of feeling at Hyderabad, the Nizam's capital. Central and eastern Bengal were undisturbed, and Nepal rendered the British valuable assistance in putting down the revolt.

Secondly, with the exception of the Rani of Jhansi, the Begam of Oudh, and some minor chiefs, none of the feudatory princes threw in their lot with the rebels. Sindhia and Holkar remained loyal, though their armies rose. The chieftains of Sirhind, prominent among whom were the Rajas of Patiala and Jind, repaid with a splendid devotion the protection granted to their ancestors against the aggression of Ranjit Singh. It would not be easy to estimate how much Great Britain owes to two great Indian statesmen, Sir Dinkar Rao of Gwalior and Sir Salar Jang of Hyderabad, for the retention of her Indian Empire. Sir Dinkar Rao, the minister of the young Sindhia, did much to keep his master loyal, and the importance of this can hardly be overstated. Had Sindhia raised the standard of revolt, every Maratha state would have joined him. 'His loyalty', says General Innes, 'saved India for the British.'[1] Again, the peril of an outbreak at Hyderabad, with its large and turbulent Muhammadan population, was at one time very great, and it was only warded off by the extraordinarily prompt and energetic conduct of Sir Salar Jang, 'a man', says Mr. Rice Holmes, 'whose name deserves to be ever mentioned by Englishmen with gratitude and admiration'.[2] Thirdly, it may be said that the mutiny which called forth so much ability on the British side produced no leader amongst the rebels; perhaps the most capable was a woman, the Rani of Jhansi. Sir John Lawrence used to dwell on the many errors of judgement committed by the mutineers and to declare that after they had revolted they seemed to become demented in their manner of conducting the rebellion, and often took the one course that was foredoomed to failure.

Fourthly, there were the exceptional characters of the men who were called upon to grapple with the Mutiny at the outset—the Lawrences, Outram, Havelock, Nicholson, Neill, and Edwardes. Had they proved weak, or even men of ordinary ability, none could have foretold the issue. The hardest fighting fell to their share. It is noticeable that the mutineers were far more formidable as a fighting force in the earlier months. The battles were more stubbornly contested, and the losses inflicted on the British far greater in the fighting round Delhi and in Havelock's and Outram's campaigns than they were in the operations of Sir Colin Campbell and Sir Hugh Rose. After the fall of Delhi and

[1] *The Sepoy Revolt*. By Lieut.-General McLeod Innes, p. 301.
[2] *History of the Indian Mutiny*. By T. R. E. Holmes, 1898, p. 499.

the first relief of Lucknow the resistance of the mutineers sensibly weakened. Sir Hugh Rose conducted a brilliant campaign, but he had the advantage of leisurely preparation and a good and efficient cavalry force, while the armies he met were dispirited and badly led.

Fifthly, there were the noble efforts of Lord Canning and Sir John Lawrence at an early stage to check the outcry both in England and India for a ruthless and indiscriminate policy of vengeance. That outcry was natural enough, for the provocation had been terrible. Many excesses could be forgiven to the men who had gazed with starting eyes and quivering lips on the horrors of the shambles of Cawnpore. Even Nicholson clamoured that 'the flaying alive, impalement, or burning of the murderers of the women and children at Delhi'[1] should be legalized. But Canning, though ready to exact the sternest penalties from the guilty, insisted that no mistake should be made as to their guilt. He passed regulations to check the excesses of self-appointed tribunals and to ensure proper trial and inquiry in all cases. He was loudly and bitterly assailed at the time, but maintained his view with a noble disdain of popular clamour. He was nicknamed 'Clemency Canning' in derision, but it was afterwards recognized that his clemency was not only morally splendid but politically expedient, for nothing could have been more dangerous than to embitter irretrievably our relations with the subject peoples.

The suppression of the Mutiny was deemed a fitting time for the Crown finally to take over the control of the Indian government. Against this decision the Company protested in a dignified and weighty petition drawn up by John Stuart Mill. They proudly claimed that the foundations of the Indian Empire had been laid by themselves 'at the same period at which a succession of administrations under the

[1] *History of the Indian Mutiny*, Kaye and Malleson, vol. ii, p. 301.

control of Parliament were losing to the Crown of Great Britain another great empire on the opposite side of the Atlantic'. They challenged the most searching investigation into the causes of the Mutiny, and pointed out with much force that in Indian affairs the government of the Crown had long possessed the deciding voice, and was thus 'in the fullest sense accountable for all that has been done, and for all that has been forborne or omitted to be done'. It was unreasonable to seek a remedy by 'annihilating the branch of the ruling authority which could not be the one principally in fault, and might be altogether blameless, in order to concentrate all powers in the branch which had necessarily the decisive share in every error, real or supposed'. But the Company did not seek to vindicate themselves at the expense of any other authority: 'They claim their full share of the responsibility of the manner in which India has practically been governed. That responsibility is to them not a subject of humiliation, but of pride. They are conscious that their advice and initiative have been, and have deserved to be, a great and potent element in the conduct of affairs in India, and they feel complete assurance that the more attention is bestowed and the more light thrown upon India and its administration, the more evident it will become that the government in which they have borne a part has been not only one of the purest in intention, but one of the most beneficent in act, ever known among mankind . . . and they are satisfied that whatever further improvements may be hereafter effected in India can only consist in the development of germs already planted, and in building on foundations already laid, under their authority, and in great measure by their express instructions.' In a further paper the Company pointed out the essential difference between the government of India and that of other colonies of the empire, 'the government of dependencies by a Minister and his subordinates, under the sole control of Parliament, is not a new experiment in England. That form of colonial government lost the United States, and had nearly lost all the colonies of any considerable population and importance. The colonial administration of this country has only ceased to be a subject of general condemnation since the principle has been adopted of leaving all the important colonies to manage their own affairs, a course which cannot be followed with the people of India.' All governments require constitutional checks, and in the case of India, since representative institutions were, at the time at any rate, impracticable, the constitutional security must lie in the construction of the administrative system itself; 'the forms of business are the real constitution of India'.

These dignified protests did not avail to avert the change, though, as the Court of Directors acknowledged, the 'clamour which represented the government of India by the Company as characterized by nearly every fault of which a civilized government can be accused' was succeeded by 'an almost universal acknowledgement that the rule of the Company has been honourable to themselves and beneficial to India'.[1] The assumption of the government of India by the Crown was indeed, as Sir H. S. Cunningham wrote, 'rather a formal than a substantial change'.[2] All real power had long passed to the President of the Board of Control, and the Directors had been for some time in the position of an advisory council, though with considerable powers of initiative. The last Charter Act of 1853, by throwing open the civil service to competition, had deprived the Directors of their most valued privilege, the patronage of India: it had also reduced their numbers from twenty-four to eighteen, and made six of them nominees of the Crown. This enabled the Government to appoint to the Court retired servants of the Company,

[1] *Report to the General Court of Proprietors*, 1858, p. 2.

[2] *Earl Canning*. By Sir H. S. Cunningham [Rulers of India Series], p. 170.

men who had little chance of being elected under the old system, and thus to leaven the directorate with first-hand Indian experience. The Act was obviously preparing the way for the assumption by the Crown of the government of India in name as well as in fact, for it gave no definite renewal of the charter for a term of years, as former measures had done, but merely provided that the Indian territories should remain under the administration of the Company in trust for the Crown until Parliament should determine otherwise. The Act of 1858 completed the process thus begun. A Secretary of State for India was to take the place of the President of the Board of Control. He was to be advised by a Council of fifteen appointed in the first instance for life, afterwards for ten to fifteen years; eight members were selected by the Crown, seven by the Court of Directors, subsequent vacancies in these seven places being filled by the Council itself. Though some of the old powers of the Court of Directors passed to the Secretary of State, its influence mainly lingered on in the Council. One of the chief advantages of the transfer of government from the Company to the Crown, though it caused at the time serious disaffection among the white troops, and especially among the officers, lay in the end of the awkward dualism of the Company's and the Queen's army, the Indian and the Royal navy.

On November 1, 1858, the new government was proclaimed by Lord Canning at Allahabad as first Viceroy and Governor-General for the Crown. The Queen, who had rejected the first proclamation submitted to her and requested that the revised draft 'should breathe feelings of generosity, benevolence, and religious toleration', disclaimed, as the Company had so often done, all desire for an extension of territory, promised to respect 'the rights, dignity, and honour' of native Princes and to uphold religious toleration, and declared it to be her will 'that so far as may be, our subjects, of whatever race or creed, be freely and impartially admitted to offices in our service, the duties of which they may be qualified by their education, ability, and integrity, duly to discharge'. Pardon and amnesty were offered to all those still in arms against the British government who had not been guilty of the murder of British subjects. The proclamation ended with a promise of measures for the material and moral improvement of the Indian peoples in whose 'prosperity will be our strength, in their contentment our security, and in their gratitude our best reward'.

The government now deliberately and openly renounced the policy of lapse, and the feudatory chiefs were granted *sunnads* or charters empowering them to adopt heirs. Henceforward the continual existence of native states was guaranteed, but their rights were limited and defined. They could have no relations with foreign powers, nor with each other, except through British mediation. Their military forces were to be strictly limited. Over internal affairs they had full control, except that in his minute of April 30, 1860, Lord Canning affirmed the principle that the government of India is not precluded 'from stepping in to set right such serious abuses in a native government as may threaten any part of the country with anarchy or disturbance, nor from assuming temporary charge of a native state when there shall be sufficient reason to do so'.

The change from Company to Crown government made few changes in the Indian administration. The Charter Act of 1853 had already enlarged the Governor-General's Executive Council for legislative purposes to twelve members, namely the Governor-General and Commander-in-Chief, the four ordinary members of the Executive Council, two judges, and four representative members nominated by the government of Bengal, Madras, Bombay, and the North-West Provinces. The Indian Councils Act of 1861, which completed the change, added a fifth member to the Executive Council, and to the Legislative Council not less than six or more than twelve additional members, at least one-half non-official, to be nominated by the Governor-General. Legislative Councils were also established in the other provinces and Lieutenant-Governorships.

Thus ended the Honourable East India Company,[1] not so much from any special responsibility for the Mutiny, for in political matters it had been for many years absolutely controlled by the state, but because it was felt to be an anachronism that a private corporation should, even though it were only in name, administer so vast a dominion. 'It was created by the Crown, two hundred and fifty years before', says Marshman, 'for the purpose of extending British commerce to the East: and it transferred to the Crown on relinquishing its functions an empire more magnificent than that of Rome.'[2] This great work was not accomplished, as we have seen, without some blunders and political crimes. To disguise them and to maintain that British administrators were always swayed by impeccable motives and unerring statesmanship is to produce an unreal and impossible picture, for we are dealing after all with human agency. But when all necessary qualifications are made the annals of the Company form one of the most fascinating and illustrious pages in history. There were grave mistakes, but they were rectified, great abuses, but they were swept away. If territories were sometimes questionably acquired, they were honestly and capably administered. Of the Company's servants, Clive, Warren Hastings, Wellesley, and Dalhousie were amongst the greatest Englishmen of their day as conquerors or statesmen; others, such as Cornwallis, Bentinck, Munro, Thomason, and Metcalfe,

[1] The Company for purposes of liquidation and legal requirements maintained a formal existence until 1874.

[2] *The History of India*, J. C. Marshman, 1874, vol. iii, p. 457.

evolved in an uncongenial atmosphere a high standard of humanitarian administration.

The closer India was brought to Great Britain by improvements in communication, the steamship, the railway, and the telegraph, the more possible and the more expedient became the control of the Imperial government. In spite of his vice-regal title the head of the Indian administration after 1858 was more dependent on the Secretary of State than his predecessors had been on the Board of Control and the Court of Directors, whom an adroit Governor-General could often play off one against the other. No Governor-General under the Crown has defied the home authorities like Warren Hastings, or overridden them like Wellesley. Though it might be undoubtedly better that the state in the nineteenth century should take over the government of the Indian Empire, it is certain that only an association based on individual effort and drawing its profits from commerce could in the beginning have acquired it from so distant a base, and have toiled so patiently for results so long deferred. Gradually the political and territorial displaced the mercantile and economic character of the Company. Leadenhall Street gave place to Whitehall. The East India Company, founded by a little body of pioneer traders in the reign of Queen Elizabeth, under whom our colonial dominions had their small beginnings, ended its career in the time of Queen Victoria, under whom grew up the British Empire of to-day.

PART II

HISTORY UNDER THE GOVERNMENT OF THE CROWN

HISTORICAL GEOGRAPHY OF INDIA

PART II

CHAPTER I

INDIA UNDER THE CROWN. SETTLEMENT AND PACIFICATION. THE END OF LORD CANNING'S ADMINISTRATION

AFTER the great events, fierce passions, and tremendous problems of the Mutiny, we pass into a comparatively mild and humdrum atmosphere. As government becomes better, history, it is to be feared, grows duller. The victories of the administrator and reformer over their immaterial enemies, corruption, vice, and ignorance, are less apt to strike the imagination than the triumphs of warring armies. Such victories are only won slowly and step by step; there are no stricken fields and few epoch-making dates. Except for the Second Afghan War 1878–80, the Third Burmese War 1885, and the Tirah campaigns 1897–8, there have been only minor military operations in India since 1858. The age has been one of material, moral, and intellectual progress, of improvements in communication, of commercial development, of administrative and legal reforms, and of constitutional experiment. The full effects of these changes it is as yet too early to gauge, and it is fatally easy to fall into an attitude, on the one hand of uncritical admiration, and on the other of captious criticism. Indian officials conscious of the rectitude of their intentions are sometimes apt to write as though British rule in India is, and should be, above criticism; while on the other hand we find so normally sane a statesman as John Bright committing himself to the monstrous statement that the history of Great Britain in India prior to 1862 was 'a hundred years of crime against the docile natives of our Indian empire'.[1] Between these partisan judgements truth somewhere resides, and the historian must walk warily in quest of her. Further, many of those who played the chief part on the Indian stage are either still living, or have passed away too recently for their work to be finally appraised, and, for the latter part of the period at any rate, to pass non-committal verdicts is not only the fairest and safest but often the only possible course.

The conquest of India within its own natural frontiers was now over. The status of the protected princes was settled and defined. They had rendered valuable services in the Mutiny and were described by Canning as 'breakwaters to the storm which would otherwise have swept over us in one great wave'. To preserve them as bulwarks of the empire has been ever since a main principle of British policy. Henceforward with the integrity of their territories guaranteed and the coveted right of adoption conceded, they had no need to fear incorporation in British dominion through the natural decay of their dynasties. Thus their relations with their suzerain entered on a new phase. They were brought into closer connexion partly by the confidence sprung from their now more assured position, partly by the material links of railways, canals, posts, and telegraphs. The supreme government became at once more sensitive to maladministration in a native state and more loth to impair the position of Indian princes. One instinct often warred with the other. The practical solution gradually worked out was that the Governors-General did everything in their power, by the early education of the chiefs, if possible when the occurrence of minorities gave them the opportunity, by

[1] Speech at Birmingham, December 18, 1862.

advice and exhortation in all cases, to guide Indian princes in the path of righteous dealing, and, if they strayed from it, exhausted all the resources of remonstrance and protest before employing drastic measures. If moral suasion finally failed, regency councils were appointed or the administration was temporarily entrusted to a British Resident, or again in extreme cases the reigning monarch was deposed and another member of the dynasty placed upon the throne.

Lord Canning, who had been the last Governor-General appointed by the Company, retained office as the first Viceroy and Governor-General under the Crown. In 1859 he was raised to the rank of an earldom. In completing the work of pacification he reaped the reward of his firm stand for mercy and moderation during the Mutiny. His successor, Lord Elgin, afterwards recorded his opinion that the fact that Canning had refused to listen to the clamour for indiscriminate vengeance, and the abuse in consequence poured upon him, imparted in the eyes of Indians 'to acts which carried justice to the verge of severity the grace of clemency'.[1]

Many of the chiefs and protected princes, who had proved faithful in the Mutiny, received honorary titles and gifts of money or lands. To the Nizam were restored some of the districts yielded up to British control in 1853, and his debts of £500,000 to the British government were remitted. Some tracts of forest-clad land on the frontiers of Oudh were given up to Nepal; Sindhia, the Begam of Bhopal, the Gaikwar of Baroda, and many of the Rajput princes were rewarded by territorial concessions or reductions of tribute, and upon many Indian princes and statesmen were conferred in 1861 knighthoods in the newly instituted order of the Star of India.

An important constitutional change in the working of the

[1] *Letters and Journals of Lord Elgin*, by T. Walrond, C.B., London, 1872, pp. 420-1.

Governor-General's executive council was carried out under Lord Canning. Hitherto the council had acted mainly as a consultative body, every question coming before the whole board and being decided by a majority of votes. One exception had been already made by the appointment of a member of council to deal especially with legal matters, and the principle of differentiation of functions was carried farther by the appointment of two successive financial members of council from England. The Indian Councils Act of 1861 empowered the Governor-General to delegate special business to individual councillors, and henceforward, although at this date[1] the separation of departments was less marked than in the Cabinet at home, the various members of council had each his own portfolio and dealt on his own initiative with all but the most important matters. These were placed before the Governor-General and, if any difference of opinion appeared, were considered by the whole council. The decentralization of business undoubtedly made for efficiency and dispatch, and was described by John Stuart Mill 'as one of the most successful instances of the adaptation of means to ends which political history . . . has yet to show'.

The most pressing problem to be faced after the suppression of the Mutiny was naturally that of the Exchequer. For the years 1857–61 there were deficits realized or anticipated amounting to thirty-six millions—a sum that about equalled the normal annual revenue. To reorganize the Indian finances, James Wilson, formerly Secretary to the Treasury and Vice-President of the Board of Trade, was sent out from England in 1859. He was one of the leading economists of the day, and happily combined wide theoretical knowledge with great practical and administrative ability. Unfortunately he died after holding office for eight months, but his work with some modifications was carried on by

[1] Of late years this separation has been carried very much farther.

Samuel Laing, a member of Parliament, who was sent out to succeed him. Wilson proposed three new taxes, an income tax, a licence duty on trades and professions, and an excise on home-grown tobacco. Only the first of these was ultimately adopted, and that after a heated controversy, which brought about the recall of Sir Charles Trevelyan, a very able administrator, who went somewhat beyond official lengths in his opposition to the supreme government. Wilson established a uniform import tariff of ten per cent., worked out a plan for a government convertible paper currency, and outlined drastic economies in both civil and military expenditure—reforms which were carried to completion by his successor. By means of the saving thus effected and by raising the salt duties Wilson and Laing were enabled to bring about an equilibrium in the finances by 1862—a fine administrative achievement on the part of two men who came to a strange country to meet, under unfamiliar conditions, a position of great difficulty.

Under Lord Canning the Indian government had to deal with certain questions which have some importance from the colonial aspect. About 1850 it was found that Assam and the slopes of the Himalayas were suitable for the cultivation of tea and the Nilgiri Hills for producing coffee. The result was an immigration into India of European planters, and the raising of the question as to the tenure of land in these regions. The land required by the planters was technically 'waste' and belonged to the state. The 'Waste Land Rules' were issued, which legalized the grant to Europeans or others of tracts up to 3,000 acres as freehold property exempt from land-tax on the payment of fixed sums.

Some other internal reforms were carried. The strength of the British army in India was reduced in 1861 to 76,000 men and that of the native army to 120,000. In 1857 universities were established at Calcutta, Bombay, and

Madras on the model of the University of London. The provinces of British Burma, Tenasserim, Pegu, and Arakan were consolidated under one Chief Commissioner, the first to hold the office being Sir Arthur Phayre, whose settlement of the country is one of the most famous chapters in the history of British administration in the East. His early efforts after Dalhousie's conquest of the country had been so successful that during the Mutiny it had been found possible to withdraw British troops from Burma. The old dualism of the Supreme and the *Sadr* courts, representing respectively the jurisdiction of the Crown and the Company, was abolished by the establishment of a High Court in each Presidency. Macaulay's penal code, originally drafted in 1837 and revised by Sir Barnes Peacocke, was finally adopted in 1860.

It has been already shown[1] that the permanent settlement of the land revenues of Bengal carried out by Lord Cornwallis was found to have insufficiently safeguarded the rights of the ryots, or peasant cultivators. The Court of Directors declared in 1858 that 'the rights of the Bengal ryots had passed away *sub silentio*, and they had become, to all intents and purposes, tenants-at-will'. But though a clause in the Regulations of 1793 had empowered the government to take measures to protect the peasants, it was not till 1859 that the Bengal Rent Act—applying also to Agra and the Central Provinces—was passed, which gave a right of occupancy to all cultivators who had possessed certain fields for more than twelve years, and forbade their rents being raised except on definite grounds specified in the Act itself. Ryots in the permanently settled districts, who had held their lands since 1793, were exempted from any increase in their rental for ever. The Act unfortunately resulted in a great increase of litigation in the courts.

At one time a far more epoch-making change was in

[1] *Historical Geography of India*, Part I, p. 230.

prospect which would have amounted to an agrarian revolution throughout the whole of India. In nearly the whole of Bengal, in a part (about one-fourth) of the Madras Presidency, and in a small portion of the United Provinces the land revenue is permanently settled. In the rest of India, or four-fifths of the country, settlements, that is the determination of the annual amount of land-tax or state rent to be paid to government, are revised at various periods—generally of twenty or thirty years. Perpetual controversy has centred round the merits and demerits of these systems. The arguments for and against a permanent settlement have been dealt with in vol. i in the chapter on the administration of Lord Cornwallis. The advantages of periodical settlements are obvious from the point of view of the state, which thereby retains the power of continually intercepting part of the 'unearned increment', and it is maintained that if the settlements are made carefully and for sufficiently long periods, they need not check the development of the land or the prosperity of the people. On the other hand, if a permanent settlement were made universal throughout India, the expense and trouble of continual assessments (which occupy about four to five years in the average province) would be avoided. Further, many high authorities have held that thrift and the sinking of capital in land would be encouraged, and that the evil custom of reducing cultivation, as the settlement periods end, in order to avoid enhancement of the revenue, would cease, and that the greater prosperity of the country and the proportionate increase of wealth taxable in other ways would more than compensate the state for some immediate sacrifice of revenue.

Some even go farther and believe that the terrible mortality in the famines of the last forty years is largely due to the fact that the periodical reassessments, which have in most provinces steadily increased the land revenue, have left the people too impoverished and weak to tide over the time of scarcity. Now it is undeniable that there have been many instances of over-assessment in the past. This fact rests not only on the assertion of Indian critics of the government but on the considered statements of British administrators who carefully weighed their words. Men like Charles Elliott, Charles Grant, A. Russell, and Colonel Maclean protested against the enhancement of the land revenues in the first settlements of the Central Provinces. Sir Auckland Colvin condemned in 1875 the over-assessments in Bombay, and Sir William Hunter in 1879 said bluntly in the Governor-General's Council that 'the fundamental difficulty of bringing relief to the Deccan peasantry is that the Government assessment does not leave enough food to the cultivator to support himself and his family throughout the year'.

But though we must admit that in some cases over-assessments may have intensified the effects of drought and scarcity, there is no justification for the statement sometimes made that they have caused the famines of recent years. Such an assertion is a grotesque perversion of the truth; it utterly ignores the operation of great natural causes and the fact that in many cases famines have been most severe in districts where assessments have been light, and but lightly felt in districts heavily assessed.

In 1861, however, Colonel Baird Smith, believing that there was a vital connexion between mortality in the case of famines and the settlement system under which the people lived, suggested that the principles of the permanent settlement of Bengal should be extended throughout the whole of India. The proposal was accepted by a majority of the Indian statesmen of the day; Sir William Muir, Sir Bartle Frere, Sir Richard Temple, Samuel Laing, and the Lieutenant-Governors of Bengal and the North-west Provinces were among those who gave their approval. This was an impressive consensus of expert opinion, and without necessarily admitting that it should have been conclusive, it must be acknowledged that the leaders of the modern Reform Party in India have every right to make it a prominent point in their case. Further, at home the proposed change was earnestly supported by Sir John Lawrence, and in July 1862 the Secretary of State, Sir Charles Wood, made the momentous announcement to the Indian government that the Cabinet had resolved to sanction a permanent settlement of the land revenues in all the provinces of British India. This decision was reaffirmed five years later by another Secretary of State, Sir Stafford Northcote, who declared that the government was prepared to make some sacrifice in regard to revenue 'in consideration of the great importance of connecting the interest of the proprietors of the land with the stability of the British Government'. A lengthy correspondence ensued but nothing was ever done, and the proposal was practically shelved—a result said to have been largely due to Lord Mayo's opposition to the policy. In 1883 the resolution was definitely and formally abandoned.

To complete the history of this proposal of 1862 we have had to overpass for the moment our chronological limits and must now retrace our steps. Lord Canning, whose health had completely broken down owing to his immense exertions in the Mutiny and grief at the death of his wife, resigned office in 1862. He returned to England to die there three months later. His fame stands now far above detraction. In purely intellectual qualities other rulers of British India have surpassed him. He made a few mistakes. In the supreme crisis of India's fate he showed some diffidence and hesitation, but by level-headed coolness, by unremitting toil, and by a splendid tenacity he won his way through to victory. He had literally worked himself to death. In his absorbing devotion to his task, he denied himself both physical exercise and mental relaxation. Lord Elgin, his successor, records that when he told Canning of his intention to ask two or three of his subordinates to dinner daily that he might learn something of the problems of administration, the retiring Governor-General replied simply, 'I was always so tired by dinner time that I could not speak'.[1] Before his retirement he had, in spite of his cold and reserved manner, lived down his former unpopularity. Slowly and painfully he extorted all men's respect by his unswerving sense of justice, his selfless devotion to duty, the magnanimity and innate nobility of his character. The exacting claims of their high office proved fatal to both the Cannings, father and son alike, and it is fitting that all that is mortal of these two lofty and puissant spirits—the Prime Minister of England and the first Viceroy of British India—should now lie together in Westminster Abbey with their country's supremely honoured dead.

[1] *Letters and Journals of Lord Elgin*, by T. Walrond, C.B., London, 1872, p. 402.

CHAPTER II

LORD ELGIN AND LORD LAWRENCE. OUR RELATIONS WITH AFGHANISTAN

THE new Viceroy, Lord Elgin, had been in his undergraduate days at Christ Church, Oxford, a contemporary and friend of both Dalhousie and Canning. As Governor of Jamaica from 1842 to 1846, and Governor-General of Canada from 1846 to 1854, he had enjoyed wide experience of colonial administration. In both these positions, and in the former immediately, he had succeeded the great Indian statesman, Sir Charles (afterwards Lord) Metcalfe. Appointed in 1857 special envoy and plenipotentiary to China, at the request of Lord Canning but on his own responsibility he had diverted to India, on the outbreak of the Mutiny, troops destined for the Further East, and had conducted the peace negotiations after the Chinese War of 1860. He assumed office in Calcutta in 1862, succeeding in his own words 'to a great man and a great war, with a humble task to be humbly discharged'.[1] Time failed him to display his undoubted abilities in the field of Indian administration, for he died at the hill station of Dharmsala, after a little more than a year of office, in November 1863.

At the time of his death a great danger threatened on the north-west frontier, and the Governor-Generalship was offered to Sir John Lawrence, who had so wide and profound a knowledge of that district and its troublesome peoples. At Sitana on the spurs of the Hindu Kush range, north of

[1] *Letters and Journals of Lord Elgin*, by T. Walrond, C.B., London, 1872, p. 396.

Peshawar and west of the Indus, there had existed since the early part of the nineteenth century a curious colony of Muhammadan fanatics known as the Wahabis. They possessed a kind of recruiting dépôt or agency at Patna in Bengal, and their influence spread far and wide by secret channels throughout India. They formed a rallying point for all fugitives from justice, turbulent Pathans, Afridis, and every wild spirit with a grudge against British rule. They were raided by punitive expeditions in 1853 and 1858, and in the latter year were driven from Sitana, but re-established themselves at Malka in 1861, and again menaced the Punjab in 1863. In that year Sir Neville Chamberlain was sent to coerce them with a force of 6,000, but at the Ambela Pass he was confronted by an army of 15,000. For three weeks the advance was checked and the British force kept on the defensive. The Calcutta Council in alarm was contemplating the fatal course of recalling the expedition, but Sir William Denison, Governor of Madras and acting Viceroy, hastened to Calcutta and, on the advice of Sir Hugh Rose, the Commander-in-Chief, insisted on operations being continued. In December the Wahabis were defeated, and their stronghold Malka was destroyed—three weeks before Sir John Lawrence assumed office in India, in January 1864.

Since his retirement from the Punjab in February 1859, Sir John Lawrence had served as member of the Secretary of State's Council in the India Office, bearing modestly the honours and compliments lavished upon him as the 'saviour of India' and the 'organizer of victory'. In 1860 he had declined the governorship of Bombay. He was a strong, determined, and sagacious man, with a certain noble ruggedness and simplicity of soul, though his character, as Lord Dalhousie noticed, was not without the spur of an honourable ambition. He possessed less genius, culture, personal charm and distinction than his elder brother Henry, who was, in the judgement of Sir Richard Temple, 'one of the most gifted men whom this generation has seen in India', but he was looked upon as a safer and sounder administrator. He was masterful, somewhat obstinate in temperament, and exacting in his relations with his subordinates, though, if they did him good service, he loyally supported them. He had risen through every grade in the Company's service, and in his case a notable break was made in the tradition—observed since the time of Sir George Barlow—that no Indian civilian should be appointed to the highest post of all. It was long a matter of controversy whether, even in his case, the departure from the rule was justified, and though we may now answer that question unhesitatingly in the affirmative, it is perhaps true to say that by 1863 Lawrence had done his best work, and that his administration as Governor-General rather disappointed—the possibly excessive—expectations formed of it. In internal affairs great progress was made with all those material improvements, railways, canals, and public works, inaugurated by his master Dalhousie and interrupted by the catastrophe of the Mutiny, but there was a certain truth in the criticism that Lawrence had not sufficiently learnt the art of delegating work to his subordinates; that he required more detachment from routine, and was so immersed in details that the general supervision of the administration suffered. Assuredly he never spared himself, and he was accustomed to sit at his desk from 6 a.m. to 5.30 p.m. with only an interval of half an hour for breakfast. Even then he only desisted from his labours with the half-jesting apology that a man could not work at his best for more than eleven hours at a stretch. He sometimes encountered in his subordinates an independence of character and originality of mind to which he did less than justice, and there is a substratum of truth in the jibe of his brilliant and impulsive lieutenant, Sir Bartle Frere, the Governor of Bombay, that Lawrence had imperfect sympathies with any one under him who did not belong to the Punjab or to the county of Derry, or to Exeter Hall.[1] It is certain that some drastic reforms had to be made by his successor in the direction of economy and in the methods of working of many of the public departments. But if he somewhat disappointed expectations in one direction, he may be said to have exceeded them in another. Possibly his greatest success as Governor-General was won in that field of diplomacy and foreign policy where he might perhaps have been expected to fall short of the purview of a statesman.

His only annexation was effected after a short war with Bhutan, the wild forest-clad mountainous country on the steep southern slopes of the Himalayas, bounded on the north and east by Tibet, on the south by Eastern Bengal and Assam, and on the west by the British district of Darjeeling and the little native state of Sikkim, which is driven as a wedge between it and Nepal. British relations with the Bhutanese dated back to 1772 when, coming to the aid of the ruler of Cooch Behar, we drove them back from that principality. In 1783 we dispatched to Bhutan a commercial mission under Captain Turner which proved a failure. Our occupation of Assam in 1826 brought us into close relationship with Bhutan, and the people of that country were found to have raided and occupied the Duars or passes leading into Assam. Unsuccessful negotiations followed; at one time it was arranged that the Bhutanese should retain the passes and pay us tribute, while later on we acquired the Duars and gave them instead an annual subsidy; but the Bhutanese lived in a constant state of revolution and intestine strife with the result that their turbulent troops frequently raided the districts of Bengal and Assam at the base of their hills. The British protested against these forays but all attempts to come to a settlement failed. In the winter of 1863–4 the Bhutanese grossly

[1] *Life of Sir Bartle Frere*, by John Martineau, 1895, vol. i, p. 444.

insulted the Hon. Ashley Eden, an envoy sent by Lord Elgin, forcing him under compulsion to sign a humiliating treaty which surrendered to their control the Duars leading into Assam. The Indian government repudiated the treaty and demanded the release of all British subjects kidnapped during the preceding five years. No reply being received, the western Duars were annexed and the allowances hitherto paid for them were withheld. Our military leaders conducting frontier operations in a spirit of careless security were suddenly attacked in January 1865 and a British garrison was driven from Dewangiri with the loss of two guns. There was a vigorous outcry against this insult to British arms, but General Tombs quickly retrieved the position and peace was made in November. By its terms the Bhutanese surrendered eighteen Duars in return for a yearly subsidy. Lawrence was fiercely attacked by a party in India for granting such favourable conditions, but generosity to a vanquished enemy on the part of an imperial power, provided that generosity is not abused, is not only magnanimous but sound policy. In this case the lasting tranquillity that followed amply justified the Governor-General's moderation. The subsidy is so highly prized by the Bhutanese that our relations with them since that date have remained peaceful and cordial. Further, the territory surrendered by them (a strip 180 miles long and twenty to thirty broad) has proved a valuable acquisition and is now dotted with productive tea-gardens.

Sir John Lawrence had always been famous for supporting the cause of the Indian peasantry as opposed to his brother Henry, whose sympathies were rather with the aristocracy. It was therefore peculiarly fitting that the Punjab and Oudh Tenancy Acts of 1868 should fall within the period of his Governor-Generalship. In his advocacy of these measures he championed the cause of the ryot against a formidable coalition of the Indian landowners, the European planters, the journalists, the Secretary of State, and a majority of his own Council. The Punjab Act recognized occupancy rights in the case of all tenants who had held their land for a certain time, and the measure became, as a subsequent Lieutenant-Governor of Bengal declared, 'the bulwark and charter of a contented peasantry'. On the annexation of Oudh by Lord Dalhousie, the landed proprietors or Talukdars had been at first, as we have seen, rather harshly treated. Subsequently Lord Canning's proclamation, though it nominally threatened a wholesale confiscation, had promised a favourable consideration to all those who promptly submitted; this clause had been interpreted so generously that it is said about two-thirds of the rebels received back their estates under stronger titles than before the annexation. The aim of the British authorities probably was to raise up, or rather to revive, a great territorial aristocracy who would consider their interests closely bound up with the stability of the new settlement. But undoubtedly indulgence to the Talukdars had gone too far, and the Oudh Tenancy Act of 1868 attempted to rectify this defect. It enacted that less than one half per cent. of the total number of ryots should be granted occupancy rights in the soil at privileged rents, that cultivators whose rents were raised should be compensated for unexhausted improvements, and that the rent itself should only be increased after application to a court of law and equity. There was a loud outcry against this agrarian policy, and the Act dealing with Oudh was only passed in the teeth of strong opposition based on the allegation that faith had not been kept with the landowners, but Lawrence was supported by the weighty authority of Henry Maine, John and Richard Strachey in India and John Stuart Mill at home. John Strachey gave it as his deliberate view that 'whatever was accomplished was entirely due to the resolution of Lord Lawrence', and he considered that more might well have been done.

Sir John Lawrence had thus extended to the cultivators of Oudh and the Punjab the protection which Canning had given to the ryots of Bengal. 'No more useful or beneficent legislation', says a distinguished Indian economist and historian, 'was ever undertaken by the British Government in India . . . legislation which respected the great and protected the weak, and which was based on the unwritten customs and ancient rights of India.'[1]

Two severe famines visited India during Lawrence's period of office. The first in 1866 was most severe in Orissa, a division of Bengal extending south-west of Calcutta to the northern boundary line of the province of Madras. Though it occupied geographically an apparently favourable central position between two great presidencies of British India, it was in reality isolated to an extraordinary degree owing to its physical features and lack of natural means of communication. On the landward side it was separated from northern and central India by the almost impassable tangle of hills and jungle in which the plateau of Chota Nagpur ends; its seaboard, very badly provided with harbours, was almost unapproachable by ordinary craft for the greater part of the year. The river Mahanadi, in spite of its broad stream and imposing volume of waters, is practically useless for navigation and only potent for destruction through its violent inundations and shifting channels. Most of the roads at that time were impossible for wheeled traffic and only traversable by pack mules; the people as a whole were poor, indolent, backward, and feckless. In such a country the ravages of famine were particularly difficult to deal with. 'The inhabitants', said the Famine Commission Report, 'shut up between pathless jungles and an impracticable sea' were 'in the position of passengers in a ship without provisions'. From one to two millions are said to have perished, and the

[1] R. C. Dutt, *India in the Victorian Age*, 1904, p. 271.

government was undoubtedly caught unprepared. The fault lies chiefly at the door of Sir Cecil Beadon, the Lieutenant-Governor of Bengal, and his Council, who gave the most positive assurances that there was no real danger of scarcity. But Lawrence himself acknowledged, 'I might, and perhaps ought to have overruled them and insisted on prompt action; and I blame myself for not doing so'. The famine was followed by devastating floods, which inflicted terrible misery and privations upon the inhabitants of the low-lying lands of Orissa; 'that which the drought spared', wrote Lawrence, 'the floods drowned'. In the second famine in 1868–9, which affected Bundelkhand and Rajputana, remedial measures were taken earlier, and the principle was definitely laid down for the first time that the officers of the government were bound to take every available means to prevent deaths by starvation. The years 1862–6 were notable for Richard Temple's administration of the Central Provinces and the land settlement he carried out there for a term of thirty years.

The finances of India under Sir John Lawrence were in an unfavourable condition, but he had many difficulties with which to contend. In 1866 a great commercial crisis was brought about by special circumstances. The American civil war had caused an almost total cessation of the export of raw cotton owing to the blockade of the Southern ports by the fleet of the Northern states. As a result, the demand of Lancashire for the raw material required by her looms turned to India; so that the production of the Indian cotton districts in Berar, Nagpur, and the southern Maratha country was immensely stimulated. Fortunes were rapidly made. The value of land rose, and, as a settlement at that time happened to be in progress, the government in many districts increased the assessment. There was a glut of capital seeking investment, an era of inflation, of reckless speculation—and then the inevitable crash. The sudden prosperity proved a mushroom growth. The end of the American war opened the Southern ports once more and poured a great mass of long-staple cotton into the English markets; the artificial demand for the inferior short-staple cotton of India quickly ceased. Many great commercial houses, among them the famous firm of Overend and Gurney, were ruined, and the Banks of Agra and Bombay, the latter of which was under the supervision of government, suspended payment. Besides the stringency caused by this celebrated panic, the financial position was weakened by lavish state outlay. It is true that Lawrence, at the beginning of his period of office, was accused of niggardliness in cutting down the expenditure of Government House, but he found it difficult to resist the importunity of some of the ablest of his subordinates, Napier, Frere, and Rose, who were continually clamouring for money to be spent in the public service. Large sums, therefore, were disbursed on public works, irrigation schemes, and modern barracks for European troops—the last being a project in which Lawrence took a special and personal interest. In this he was not unmindful of the words addressed to him by Florence Nightingale when she heard he was to be Viceroy of India: 'In the midst of your pressure, pray think of us and of our sanitary things on which such millions of lives and health depend'.[1] Thus the normal annual expenditure rose from forty-five and three-quarters to fifty-four and a half millions. Lawrence also introduced into Indian finance the principle of raising money for reproductive works by loan instead of paying for them out of the ordinary revenue, and though that policy may be unobjectionable, if carefully controlled, his successors were afterwards called upon to insist on a severer definition of the term 'reproductive'. The general financial

[1] *Life of Lord Lawrence*, by R. Boswell Smith, 1885, vol. ii, p. 378.

result of his five years of office was a net deficit of two and a half millions.

We have now to deal with the most important question of Indian foreign policy, the problem of Afghanistan. The annexation of the Punjab had extended the British frontier up to the base of the Afghan mountains, but the boundary line was very variable and ill defined. From Baluchistan in the south to Chitral in the north there was, and to some extent still is, a zone of territory occupied by independent Pathan tribes, through which run the passes that debouch on to the plains of the Punjab. Down to the year 1893 these tribes nominally owned the sovereignty of the Amir of Afghanistan, though in reality they were almost completely out of his control. They were fierce, turbulent, and treacherous, always ready for plundering expeditions and raids over the frontier, and a constant source of embarrassment to the government of the Punjab. Punitive expeditions had been sent to chastise the tribesmen for violating the integrity of the British frontier, and owing to the good fighting qualities of the enemy and the mountainous nature of their country, large forces had to be employed. In 1863, as we have seen, an army of 6,000 was employed against the Wahabis, and in 1868 a force of 12,000 had to be dispatched to read the Pathans of the Black Mountains a lesson.

The conditions of the border therefore were obviously not entirely satisfactory, and it is not surprising that different schools of frontier defence were formed from time to time. The most extreme in one direction, though practically of little account, advocated a retirement to the line of the Indus. The supporters of the opposing view, who were somewhat loosely known as the 'Forward School', favoured the subjugation of the tribal zone and a scientific frontier conterminous with the Afghan boundary line. The more extreme members of this party did not shrink from advocating the partition of Afghanistan, should a favourable opportunity be offered, or even its complete conquest. Practically, of course, they had to be content with far less than this, and their policy was not altogether unfairly described at the time as 'locating expensive bodies of troops in dangerous localities beyond our frontier for the purpose of guarding against an enemy who is still separated from us by sixty-six miles of desert and mountain'. Lawrence's policy was to leave the tribes their independence and endeavour to win their esteem; in relation to Afghanistan he advocated 'friendship towards the actual rulers combined with rigid abstention from interference in domestic feuds'. There can be little doubt that on the whole his policy was wise and provident. It acted well, with such slight modifications as the course of events required, till 1878. Lord Lytton's reversal of it proved disastrous in every way, and after 1881 we practically returned to it till 1919, for although we guaranteed the inviolability of Afghanistan as a buffer state, we scrupulously abstained from all interference in Afghan internal affairs.

To consider Lawrence's policy a little more in detail. Dost Muhammad, the strong and able ruler, whose career, so far as it brought him into relation with British India, has been already related, died in 1863. A fierce struggle for the right to succeed him at once broke out between the most prominent of his sixteen sons. Sher Ali, the favourite of Dost Muhammad himself, maintained his position on the throne for about three years with great difficulty, and was then driven by his half-brother Afzal successively from Kabul in 1866 and from Kandahar in 1867 to take refuge in Herat his last stronghold. Afzal, however, died in October 1867, and his eldest son Abdur Rahman waiving his claims, he was succeeded by another brother Azim. In April 1868 Yakub Khan, Sher Ali's son, recaptured Kandahar, and Sher Ali himself, occupying Kabul in September, thus regained all the possessions of his late father. Abdur Rahman and Azim were defeated in January 1869; Azim fled for refuge to Persia, where he soon afterwards died; Abdur Rahman, reserved for a higher destiny, escaped to Tashkend, and lived for ten years in that country a pensionary on Russian bounty.

Sher Ali, having re-established himself, proved his title by the only credentials that Afghans recognize, a stern and effective rule. The civil war with its extraordinary vicissitudes had rendered the position of the Indian government extremely difficult. Lawrence moved by a wise instinct—how wise only after-events could show—was determined at all hazards not to embroil himself in the dynastic wars of Afghan princes. This course he adopted not only from prudential motives and his own reasoned conviction, but also from gratitude to the memory of Dost Muhammad, who in spite of many temptations had loyally refrained from embarrassing us in the Mutiny, and had once in conversation with Lawrence himself expressed an earnest wish that after his death his sons should be allowed to fight out the succession question for themselves. Lawrence's policy therefore was only to recognize the *de facto* ruler and has been described as 'assenting peaceably to the visible facts resultant from a neighbour's settlement of his own affairs after his own fashion';[1] but it was certainly disconcerting that the various candidates for the throne underwent such kaleidoscopic changes of fortune. In 1864 Lawrence recognized Sher Ali as Amir of Afghanistan. In 1866 Sher Ali was driven from Kabul and Afzal was recognized as ruler of that city, Sher Ali as lord of Kandahar and Herat. Soon afterwards Afzal captured Kandahar and the Indian government acknowledged the *fait accompli* and only gave its recognition to Sher Ali as master of Herat. Critics of the

[1] *Essays on the External Policy of India*, by J. W. S. Wyllie, ed. by (Sir) W. W. Hunter, London, 1875, p. 119.

policy of *laisser faire* could say with some truth that such action was a direct encouragement to successful rebellion, that British approval of an Afghan chieftain's claims swung automatically with the gale of superior force like the vane of a weather-cock, and that no ruler of Afghanistan could set much store by a recognition which was transferred so lightly from one rival to another.

Meanwhile Russia spreading southwards from central Asia was tending to converge on the northern frontiers of Afghanistan, though her outposts were as yet far distant. About 1864 her forces moving westward from Vernoe and eastward from Perovsk brought her into contact with Khokand, Bokhara, and Khiva, the three great Muhammadan khanates between the Caspian Sea and western China. The absorption of these weak and disorderly states into the then colossal fabric of the Russian Empire was obviously a mere matter of time, but the movement only became marked towards the end of Lawrence's period of office. Tashkend, a city of over 70,000 inhabitants, was annexed in 1865; General Kaufmann was appointed Governor-General of Turkestan in 1867; Samarkand, part of Bokhara, fell in 1868.

Upon this event Sir John Lawrence urged the home government to come to some definite agreement with Russia as to a line of demarcation between the spheres of influence of the two empires. If only that were done, he professed little fear from Russian expansion, to which he felt that Great Britain had, least of all nations, any right to object; rather she might frankly welcome Russia's civilizing influence on the central Asian peoples. Nor did he stand alone in this opinion; Sir Herbert Edwardes the great frontier official wrote, 'Can any one say that to substitute Russian rule for the anarchy of Khiva, the dark tyranny of Bokhara and the nomad barbarism of Khokand would be anything but a gain to mankind?' Indeed no open objection was ever made by Great Britain to the subjugation of these three khanates, though envoys from their rulers appealed to the Indian government for assistance.

As soon as Sher Ali in 1868 had firmly established his power, Lawrence made him a present of arms and £60,000 in money, but he frowned on any suggestion that he should commit himself further. Sir Henry Rawlinson, when member of the Secretary of State's Council, penned a famous minute dated July 20, 1868, in which he advised a more 'forward' policy, though one that was still moderate compared with later developments. He advocated the occupation of Quetta in northern Baluchistan commanding the Bolan Pass—a suggestion first put forward by General John Jacob in 1856—a close alliance with the Amir of Afghanistan, and the grant to him of an annual subsidy. To these suggestions Lawrence was altogether opposed, and he was supported by the ablest of his advisers in India, Maine, Temple, and Strachey. Apart from the fact that there was a direct conflict of military opinion as to whether the Bolan Pass could best be defended from the western or eastern end, Lawrence was convinced that any interference in Afghan affairs would lead to a rupture, and he had no belief in the policy of attempting to check Russia on the Oxus by quarrelling with Sher Ali. He declared it would be impolitic and unwise to lessen the difficulties of Russia, if she seriously thought of invading India, by meeting her half-way in a country notoriously unsuited to military operations and in the midst of a hostile or exasperated population. He believed our real security to lie in abstinence from entanglements in Afghanistan, in a compact and highly disciplined army stationed on our own border, in a careful management of our finances, and 'in the sense of security of title and possession which is gradually imbuing the principal chiefs and the native aristocracy'. Elsewhere he said truly enough that the first invaders of Afghanistan, whether British or Russian, would be received as foes, while the next would be hailed as friends and deliverers. It should be obvious from all this that Lawrence was very unfairly charged with neglecting the Russo-Afghan problem. His 'inactivity', whether 'masterly' or not, was reasoned and deliberate. Few now doubt that he was right. He 'lulled the wakeful Anglophobia of Russian Generals and disarmed their inconvenient propensity to meet supposed plots of ours in Afghanistan by counter-plots of their own in the same country'.[1] His policy, with such modifications as changing circumstances required, was accepted by Lord Mayo, Lord Northbrook, and five successive Secretaries of State. All the misfortunes and disasters which Lawrence prophesied were fulfilled almost to the letter, when Lord Salisbury and Lord Lytton in an evil hour for their reputations decided to reverse it.

[1] *Essays on the External Policy of India*, by J. W. S. Wyllie, ed. by (Sir) W. W. Hunter, p. 119.

CHAPTER III

LORD MAYO. RELATIONS WITH SHER ALI. FINANCIAL REFORM

SIR JOHN LAWRENCE retired in January 1869, and on his return to England was raised to the peerage by the title of Lord Lawrence of the Punjab and Grately. Disraeli appointed to succeed him the Earl of Mayo, who had three times held the office of Chief Secretary for Ireland in Conservative ministries. Mayo's abilities, though appreciated by the Prime Minister, a shrewd judge of character, were as yet unrecognized by the people, and the nomination was received with marked disfavour. The fall of the government before the Governor-Generalship was actually vacant afforded Gladstone, the new Liberal Premier, a valid technical plea for cancelling the appointment, and he was loudly urged to avail himself of it. But he declined to do so, and Lord Mayo soon justified both Disraeli's original choice and Gladstone's magnanimity in not interfering with it.

It had been arranged that Lord Lawrence before his departure should meet Sher Ali in conference, but the Amir was long detained by troubles in his unruly dominions and the late Governor-General had sailed from India before Sher Ali could leave Afghanistan. When at last the Afghan ruler came to Ambala in March 1869 he met there not the wearied veteran Lawrence but his young, vigorous, and buoyant successor. There was, however, no breach of continuity in policy, because the new Viceroy in regard to Afghan affairs unreservedly adopted his predecessor's standpoint. At the meeting Sher Ali showed himself eager to enter into much closer relations with the Indian government. He asked for a definite treaty, a fixed annual subsidy, assistance in arms and men whenever he should think needful to solicit it, an obligation on the part of the British to support his throne and dynasty, and the recognition of his favourite younger son, Abdulla Jan, as heir to the throne, instead of Yakub Khan, the elder son, who had helped so much in the past to restore him to the throne, but had since incurred his bitter enmity. These terms, however, went far beyond anything that Lord Mayo or the home government was prepared to concede. It is clear that they would dangerously have linked up British power and prestige in India with the fortunes of a notoriously unstable Oriental dynasty. Upon Lord Mayo was laid a difficult and delicate task. He was practically required to refuse all these proposals and yet retain, if possible, the friendship of Sher Ali. He succeeded mainly because of his diplomatic management of the interview, personal charm, and warm, hospitable, Irish manner, which quite won the heart of the Afghan chief.

While Lord Mayo told Sher Ali that under no circumstances would a British soldier cross his frontier to assist him in coercing rebellious subjects, and that no treaty binding us to give him or his dynasty unconditional support could even be considered, he gave him a written promise of moral support to be followed by gifts of money, arms, and ammunition whenever the British government deemed it desirable. Sher Ali was also informed that we should 'view with severe displeasure' any attempt to oust him from his throne. Exactly how much satisfaction he was expected to derive from this statement is perhaps not clear, but the important thing was that he was sent away on the whole contented, charmed with the geniality of the Viceroy, for whom he contracted a romantic friendship, and obviously much impressed by the pomp and pageantry of the Durbar and the military resources of the British power. On his return to his own country he made some earnest, though occasionally misguided, attempts to carry out certain reforms suggested to him by Lord Mayo, and his admiring emulation of all things British ranged from the appointment of a council of state of thirteen members to an order to the shoemakers of Kabul to make henceforward only English boots.

The Lawrence policy of non-interference in Afghanistan required in the view of its author to be supplemented by a clear understanding with Russia, and considerable injustice is done when this complementary aspect of it is left out of account. Lawrence indeed had not shrunk from declaring his opinion that a border line should be definitely fixed, and that an advance of Russia towards India beyond that line should entail upon her 'war in all parts of the world with England'. Some tentative efforts were now made to reach such an understanding. Lord Mayo was indeed no Russophobe; he thought that Russia was not sufficiently aware of our power; 'that we are established compact and strong whilst she is exactly the reverse'. Negotiations were entered into between the British Foreign Secretary, Lord Clarendon, and Prince Gortschakoff in Europe, and Douglas Forsyth was sent on a mission from Calcutta to St. Petersburg in 1869 to lay before the Russian authorities the views of the government of India. The result was that Russia agreed to acknowledge Sher Ali's sway south of the Oxus over his father's former possessions, provided that he respected the integrity of Bokhara north of that river. The northern frontier of Afghanistan in detail had still to be fixed, and this took some considerable time. The Russians in 1871 claimed that Badakshan formed no part of Afghanistan proper, but after negotiations they accepted the British line in 1873.

The understanding with Russia as to the integrity of Afghanistan was a most important step forward in central Asian politics, and, had it not been for later European complications, a difficult and dangerous question might have been finally settled. From about 1870 General Kaufmann, Governor of Russian Turkestan, began a correspondence with the Amir, and though his letters were mainly complimentary and harmless enough, many have thought that Great Britain might well have asked that they should be discontinued. The Indian government would have had good reason for doing so, since Russia had given a pledge that she would regard Afghanistan as outside her sphere of influence, and Sher Ali himself was only embarrassed by these communications which he invariably sent on to the Governor-General. Lord Mayo, however, instead of requesting the Russian officials to communicate with the ruler of Afghanistan only through the British government, assured the Amir that Kaufmann's letters were mere matters of courtesy, and deprecated his uneasiness.

In internal matters Lord Mayo was called upon to undertake the unpopular and thankless task of the financial reformer. The deficit left by his predecessor had to be met, and supported by Sir Richard Temple and the Strachey brothers he set himself resolutely to bring about an equilibrium in the finances. Drastic measures were taken. It was reluctantly decided to increase the salt duties in provinces where they had hitherto been lightly imposed; and the income tax was raised from one to two and a half and then to three per cent.—an expedient which was extremely unpopular even among economists, for at this time it was contrary to fiscal orthodoxy to employ direct taxation as a normal means of raising revenue. In this particular case the levy of the tax was said to have been harsh and unjust and the expense of collection unduly great. It was discovered that the great spending departments, through want of proper control, had been lavishing money unwisely and unprofitably, and annual reductions of expenditure amounting to over a million were forced upon them. These measures, which were avowedly designed to meet the temporary crisis, were followed by a permanent reorganization of the finances. The system hitherto in vogue had been that grants were made each year by the Governor-General in Council to the treasuries of the provincial governments. All monies were definitely ear-marked for special purposes and could be used for no other. If the authorities at Madras or Bombay saved money through increased efficiency in administration, they derived no benefit from their laudable economy, for they were expected to return the balance they had saved to the imperial treasury. Thus extreme centralization discouraged thrift and stereotyped administrative defects, for the provincial governments naturally put their demands as high as possible and spent all the money they could prevail upon the supreme government to allow them. In December 1870 an important reform was carried through, largely by the efforts and initiative of Richard and John Strachey. A fixed yearly grant which could be revised every five years was made to the various provincial governments, but within certain carefully defined limits the latter were given a free hand in allocating and spending their respective quotas.[1] Thus money saved in one department could be

[1] Some of the critics of British rule in India regard this reform of Lord Mayo's with disfavour on the ground that it caused an increase in the general burden of taxation. Each province, to augment its own revenues, now imposed new cesses mostly on land. Thus the state demand on the soil was increased; this, it was said, infringed in spirit the permanent settlement in Bengal, and in regard to other provinces broke the rule adopted in 1855 and 1864 of limiting assessment to one-half the rental. See R. C. Dutt's *India in the Victorian Age*, p. 257. But it may be pointed out that this practice of separating imperial from local taxation is almost universal in modern states, and the complaint that the total burden of taxation is thereby greatly increased, while at the same time the enhancement is disguised, has been raised in many countries besides India.

more profitably spent in another. The result of these reforms (afterwards considerably extended) was that the deficit of Lord Lawrence's rule was converted into a surplus for each of the four ensuing years, amounting in all to nearly six millions, while through better management, economy, and a stricter control the amount of revenue which had to be raised by taxation was actually reduced. One of Lord Mayo's financial ministers thus sums up his work, 'he found serious deficit and left substantial surplus. He found estimates habitually untrustworthy, he left them thoroughly worthy of confidence. He found accounts in arrears and statistics incomplete, he left them punctual and full.'

It was under Lord Mayo that the first general census of India was taken. He organized a statistical survey of the country and created a department of agriculture and commerce. In February 1872, after inspecting the convict settlements in the Andaman Islands, he was walking back to the landing-stage of Port Blair, where his steam yacht was moored, when a Pathan fanatic who had been following him in the twilight as he strode on a little ahead of his staff, leapt upon his back before the horrified escort could do anything and stabbed him to death. This wild and senseless crime put an end to a career which had signally refuted the ungenerous criticisms made on Lord Mayo's appointment. His Governor-Generalship had lasted but three years; the time was too short, and the problems with which he had to deal were hardly serious enough to test his capacity to the full, but there was every reason to believe that his statesmanship would have been equal to demands far higher than were actually made upon it. Succeeding as he did to a somewhat weary and war-worn veteran, he impressed all his subordinates by his immense energy and untiring powers of work. He was not content with the portfolio of the foreign department which a Governor-

General invariably retains in his own hands but added to it the onerous duties of the public works office. 'Enthusiasm', says Sir Richard Temple, 'pervaded his whole existence and was his distinguishing mark.' His winning manner and universal popularity were more than engaging personal attributes, they became imperial assets of great value. They won for him the real regard and willing co-operation of the protected chiefs, and enabled the complicated mechanism of Indian bureaucracy during his Viceroyalty to work with a minimum of friction and a maximum of efficiency.

CHAPTER IV

LORD NORTHBROOK. AFGHAN AFFAIRS

WHEN the sudden and terrible blow of Lord Mayo's assassination fell upon India, arrangements were promptly and quietly made to carry on the government. Until a successor to the murdered Viceroy should be appointed in England, Lord Napier of Merchistoun was sent for from Madras to act as Governor-General, and in the short time that elapsed before his arrival in Calcutta, Sir John Strachey held the reins of office. Gladstone selected as the new Viceroy, his Under-Secretary for War, Lord Northbrook, the head of the Baring family, whose character formed a curious contrast to the impulsive energy of his predecessor and the restless brilliance of his successor. He was a cautious and sound administrator who knew his own mind and possessed considerable independence of judgement. He was neither an eloquent speaker nor a fluent writer, and he practised a severe economy in that engrossing occupation of Indian rulers, the composition of elaborate minutes and state papers. A man of high character and kindly instincts, he was outwardly undemonstrative and in appearance rather unsympathetic. His policy deserves far more than that of Sir John Lawrence to be called a 'masterly inactivity'. 'My aim has been', he wrote in 1873, 'to take off taxes and stop unnecessary legislation',[1] and again eleven years later, 'the main object of my policy was to let things go quietly on—to give the land rest'.[2] He seems to have

[1] *Thomas George, Earl of Northbrook, a Memoir*, by Bernard Mallet, 1908, p. 69.
[2] *Idem*, p. 122.

held the view that the reforming energy of the Indian government since the Mutiny had rather outstripped the necessities of the case. One of his early acts, a very strong measure for a Governor-General recently arrived, was to veto a Bill which Sir George Campbell, the able Lieutenant-Governor of Bengal, had passed through the legislature of his province for the setting up of rural municipalities. In the domain of finance Lord Northbrook showed, on the testimony of Sir Richard Temple—a high authority—'an admirable mastery of finance, economic facts and statistics such as I have never seen surpassed in India, not even by such economists and financiers as Wilson or Laing'.[1] Except for one year of famine, 1873-4, India in his time was passing through a period of material prosperity due partly to the effects of Lord Mayo's fiscal reforms, partly to the stimulus to oversea trade given by the increased amount of shipping using the Suez Canal, which had been opened in 1869. At home in the decade after 1860 the establishment of the Free Trade principle was completed by the gradual removal of all those remaining import duties which might have a protective effect, and in India the favourable state of the finances enabled Northbrook to make great advances towards the same ideal in India. The Indian tariff down to 1860 contained ten per cent. *ad valorem* duties on all imports, and three per cent. on the majority of exports. The import dues had been already reduced to $7\frac{1}{2}$ per cent. under Sir John Lawrence in 1864, and Lord Northbrook in 1875 lowered the rate to 5 per cent. At the same time he abolished all export duties except those on oil, rice, indigo, and lac. The remission of the duty on wheat with the completion of the Indus valley railway was especially beneficial and made India a great wheat-exporting country. The home government naturally, in view of the economic theories prevalent at the time, pressed upon him a still wider

[1] Sir R. Temple, *Men and Events of my Time in India*, p. 396.

application of the Free Trade policy, but though Lord Northbrook was a convinced Free Trader, he was no *doctrinaire*, and he always maintained that the retention of a low general tariff upon imports for revenue purposes, though it might unavoidably involve slight protective effects, was necessary in the special conditions which prevailed in India. Accordingly, though he was willing to work 'on the lines of Gladstone', he admitted that it was 'at a very considerable distance'.[1] Towards the end of his period of office still stronger pressure was put upon him by the Conservative government of Disraeli to abolish even the five per cent. duty on Manchester cotton goods, but he sturdily refused to do so, on the ground that the Indian exchequer could not afford to surrender the revenue, and that it was politically unwise to give any plausible ground for the insinuation that the interests of Lancashire were to override those of India. In maintaining his point of view Lord Northbrook did not shrink from opposing the Conservative Secretary of State, Lord Salisbury, and protesting against the attempt of the home government to 'weaken the authority and hamper the action of the executive government of India'.[2] The chief point in which his financial operations lay open to criticism was his unconquerable dislike of the income tax. It had been reduced before Lord Mayo's death to one per cent. only, but even this was too high for Lord Northbrook, who removed it altogether. In selecting a remission of the income tax rather than a lowering of the salt duty, Northbrook was undoubtedly considering the interests of the European settler, the native trader and landowner, rather than that of the peasant, and he acted in opposition not only to the most expert Indian financiers, Sir Richard Temple and Sir John Strachey, but to the Duke of Argyll, Secretary of State for India, who wrote with some justice

[1] Mallet's *Northbrook*, p. 110.

[2] R. C. Dutt, *India in the Victorian Age*, p. 407.

and force, 'in the contest between a reform of the salt tax and the abolition of the income tax my feeling is that you have chosen to relieve the richer class, which is also the most powerful and the most clamorous'.[1] In all other respects he showed a determination to prevent if possible any undue pressure of taxation upon the Indian masses. 'The natives', he wrote in 1881, 'will be passively loyal to us—active loyalty we cannot expect—if we govern them justly and do not increase their taxes', and in 1881 he wrote to Lord Lytton 'I have always had my suspicions that the land revenue has been over assessed, and always treated with great suspicion the opinion of Sir John Strachey who was for screwing up the land revenue'.

In 1873–4 a famine was threatened in Bihar and part of Bengal in an area where the population was very dense. Lord Northbrook and Sir George Campbell being determined that the record of the Orissa famine of 1865 should not be repeated, large quantities of rice were purchased in Burma; the most elaborate means were taken regardless of cost to transport and distribute it, and relief works were everywhere established. The result was the very large expenditure of nearly six and a half millions on 'a famine of unusual brevity and of no exceptional severity'. But though some of the expenditure was regrettable, the government had erred on the right side, and Lord Northbrook's economy of the finances enabled the charges to be met out of revenue only.

The only other important event of Lord Northbrook's régime in India itself was the trial by commission of one of the most powerful of the ruling princes, Mulhar Rao, the Gaikwar of Baroda. There had been evidences of misgovernment in the state since 1870 when the Gaikwar succeeded. A commission of inquiry had reported in February 1874 that he had been guilty of ill-treating the

[1] Mallet's *Northbrook*, p. 67.

relations of his late brother, of the torture of women, and of the spoliation of merchants and bankers. He was given eighteen months to reform his administration, but the period of probation elapsed without any improvement making itself manifest; finally in 1875 he was put to trial on a charge of attempting to poison the British Resident, Colonel Phayre. The court consisted of two Indian princes, the Maharajas of Gwalior and Jaipur, the chief minister of the Nizam, Sir Dinkar Rao, and three British officers. The result was unfortunate, for while the English commissioners found him guilty, the Indian brought in verdicts of not guilty or not proven. Lord Salisbury, the Secretary of State, found his way out of a very delicate and difficult position by causing Lord Northbrook to proclaim the deposition of the Gaikwar, not on the finding of the commission, the particular charge there investigated being dropped, but on his gross misgovernment and notorious misconduct, of which the murder charge would have been in any case but the culminating point. In the whole business the government had not been very happily inspired; the abortive result of the trial might with a little imagination have been foreseen; as regards the deposition 'the right thing was done', says Lord Northbrook's biographer, 'but the manner of doing it was questionable'.[1] The deposed prince was promptly and secretly removed to Madras, and the threatened outbreak of popular feeling at Baroda was quieted by the immediate installation as Gaikwar of a child prince of the royal house, with Sir Madava Rao, a Maratha statesman, as chief minister. The British authorities thus clearly showed that there was to be no return to Dalhousie's annexation policy, while the prolonged minority of the new ruler enabled the administration of the country to be placed on a sound basis under the superintendence of British officers.

[1] Mallet's *Northbrook*, p. 97.

During the Viceroyalty of Lord Northbrook the central Asian problem was growing more acute owing to the steady advance of Russia towards the northern frontiers of Afghanistan. That advance was in great measure inevitable and was by no means so deliberate as it was thought to be at the time. Prince Gortschakoff pointed out in a famous minute in 1864 that his countrymen were drawn southwards in obedience to the same political law that had led the British armies northwards to the base of the Himalayas. All history teaches that a strong civilized power can hardly ever long maintain a stationary boundary line with loosely organized and semi-civilized peoples. The history of even a peaceful mercantile body like the East India Company, as we have seen, was one continual violation of the self-imposed canon that no new territories were to be acquired. Russia from time to time announced, as Great Britain had so often done in the past, that the limit of her pioneering activity was reached. These protests were generally uttered in good faith at the time, but as the weak central-Asian khanates disintegrated and dissolved into anarchy when they came into contact with her line of outposts, she was forced continually to push forward and occupy the positions they vacated, or see her own advanced frontier violated by plundering raids. But to many British statesmen and to Sher Ali on his uneasy throne the onward march of Russia seemed unscrupulous, premeditated, and fraught with sinister meaning. In 1869 the Russians established themselves at Krasnovodsk on the eastern coast of the Caspian. In June 1873 Khiva fell, and in the following month a conference was held between the Viceroy and an Afghan envoy at Simla. It did not do much to restore the Amir's waning confidence in the value of British support. Though he loyally acquiesced in it, he had been greatly disappointed in an award given by British arbitrators as to the frontier of the province of Seistan, in regard to which there had been a long-standing dispute between himself and the Shah of Persia. At the conference the Afghan envoy declared that the rapid advances made by the Russians in central Asia had greatly alarmed the Afghans, and that the Amir, placing no confidence in Russian assurances of peaceful intentions towards Afghanistan, pleaded for a closer alliance with Great Britain. Northbrook saw the reasonableness of his request, and asked permission of the Secretary of State to assure Sher Ali that 'if he unreservedly accepts and acts upon our advice in all external relations, we will help him with money, arms and troops, if necessary, to repel an unprovoked invasion; we to be the judge of the necessity'; but he was not given authority from the Cabinet to commit himself to more than a reiteration of Lord Mayo's rather vague promise of support in a letter to the Amir dated September 6, 1873. The envoy asked that the British should regard the Russians as enemies, if they committed any aggression on Afghan territory, and Lord Northbrook had great difficulty in explaining to him that, since Great Britain was at peace with Russia, aggression on her part could not be specifically mentioned 'as it implied an admission of the probability of such a contingency arising'. Sher Ali accepted a present of 5,000 rifles, though he refused a proffered sum of ten lacs of rupees.

In spite of the many serious disadvantages of an offensive and defensive alliance with a semi-barbarous power like that of Afghanistan, whose action in the future could not be guessed or controlled, it is nevertheless a matter of regret that at this opportunity a more binding agreement was not entered upon with Sher Ali. In 1869 the Amir had not been long enough on the throne to warrant a confident belief that he could maintain his position, but by 1873 he had shown himself to be a capable and, judged by Afghan standards, an enlightened ruler. He seems to have seen clearly that he would have eventually to enter into closer relations with one or other of the two European peoples whose armies were converging upon his isolated kingdom. He would gladly have kept both at arm's length, but of the two he deliberately and spontaneously gave the preference to Great Britain. A more binding agreement at this time, if the clauses of the treaty had been carefully drafted, would have implied, not a reversal of the Lawrence policy, but only a necessary modification of it to suit the altered circumstances of the case.

The Amir was disappointed and disheartened by the conference. Lord Northbrook was constitutionally unable to import into his manner the geniality which had won for his predecessor the strong personal regard of Sher Ali, and he soon afterwards gave the latter the most dire offence by addressing to him a dignified rebuke for treacherously arresting and imprisoning his eldest son Yakub Khan and proclaiming the younger, Abdulla Jan, as his heir. But though from this time onwards, probably to show his annoyance with the Viceroy, Sher Ali received with less reluctance the communications of Russian agents, there is no evidence to show that he regarded the approach of Russian troops to his frontiers with anything but feelings of the strongest aversion. By the exercise of ordinary care and tact he could probably have been induced to resume his old friendly attitude. Unfortunately in 1874 there was a change of government in England followed two years later by the arrival of a new Viceroy in India. If the Liberal Cabinet and Lord Northbrook to some extent erred in the direction of *laisser faire*, the Conservative ministry and Lord Lytton by their energetic interference fatally precipitated the development of the whole question at issue.

In March 1874 Disraeli became Prime Minister with the Marquis of Salisbury as Secretary of State for India. Both of these statesmen looked with apprehensive distrust upon Russian policy in Asia, and indeed they had some reason, as we have seen, to regard the existing state of our relations with Afghanistan as unsatisfactory. Had they insisted on a definite understanding from the foreign office at St. Petersburg that the integrity of the Amir's dominions should be guaranteed, and required Russian officers to desist from communications with Sher Ali, they would not only have been on strong ground but would incidentally have carried the Lawrence policy to its logical conclusion; for as recently as June 1873 Lord Northbrook's government had reaffirmed their adhesion to the principle of 'establishing a frank and clear understanding with Russia as to the relative position of British and Russian interests in Asia'. Unfortunately they chose to exert pressure at Kabul rather than at St. Petersburg. A minute of Sir Bartle Frere, member of the Secretary of State's council, had suggested that, in view of the critical position in Asia, it could no longer be considered a satisfactory arrangement that the only agent of the British government in Afghanistan should be an Indian Muhammadan. Lord Salisbury, adopting this opinion, suggested that Sher Ali should be asked to admit a British Resident within his country. Against this plan Lord Northbrook and the whole of his council earnestly protested. They pointed out that in 1869 and 1873 Sher Ali had expressed strong fears of Russian designs but had been told that his apprehensions had no basis of fact. His request for a defensive alliance had been firmly declined on the ground that such an alliance was unnecessary. He was now to learn that the British government had swung violently round to the view that the Russian peril was so serious as to require the presence of a British Resident in his country—a plan to which it was well known that he was irreconcilably opposed. 'I cannot agree', wrote Lord Northbrook to Lord Salisbury, 'with your suspicions about the Amir, they are not confirmed by anyone of authority here.' Unluckily the Secretary of State, in the words of Lord Cromer, 'was disposed to neglect, and, I also think, to underrate the value of the views of the Anglo-Indian officials'.[1] He merely repeated his suggestion, declaring that the government could not view with indifference the influence of Russian expansion 'upon the uncertain character of an Oriental chief whose ill-defined dominions are thus brought within a steadily narrowing circle between the conflicting pressures of two great military empires, one of which expostulates and remains passive whilst the other apologises and continues to move forward'. Lord Salisbury therefore still desired that a mission should be sent, and suggested that 'there would be many advantages in ostensibly directing it to some object of smaller political interest which it will not be difficult . . . to find or, if need be, to create'. The Viceroy, however, merely repeated his protest of dissent and soon afterwards resigned his office. The resignation was said to be due to private reasons, but however this may be, it is clear that Lord Northbrook could not have worked much longer with the Marquis of Salisbury. There had been already, as we have seen, serious friction between the two men on the tariff question, and the Viceroy was quite convinced of the unwisdom of the new Afghan policy which, as he pointed out, was a reversal of that 'advocated by Lord Canning . . . renewed by Lord Lawrence . . . ratified by Lord Mayo'. 'All the spirited foreign policy motions', he wrote in a private letter, 'come from Frere and Co. at home. Here we are very quiet and steady people.'[2] The difference between their points of view was fundamental. 'Lord Salisbury's brilliant and subtle intellect', says Mr. Mallet, 'his contempt for precedent, and a certain proneness in him to impulsive decisions presented a striking contrast to Lord Northbrook's caution and common sense, his reliance upon ascertained fact and experience, his power of steady and effective action.'[3]

[1] Mallet's *Northbrook*, p. 91.
[2] *Idem*, p. 99.
[3] *Idem*, p. 90.

With prophetic insight Lord Northbrook on the eve of his departure warned Lord Salisbury that to force Sher Ali to receive an agent against his will was likely 'to subject us to the risk of another unnecessary and costly war in Afghanistan before many years are over'.[1]

[1] Mallet's *Northbrook*, p. 105.

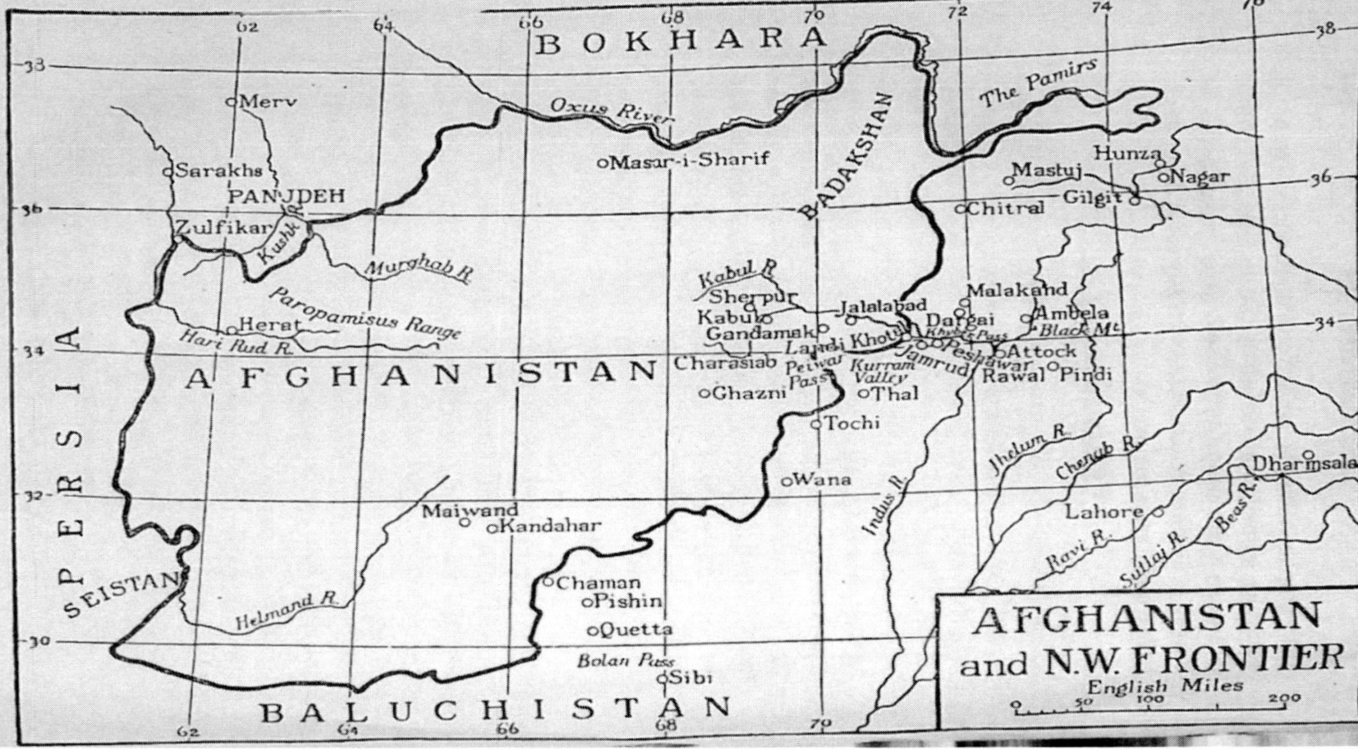
AFGHANISTAN
and N.W. FRONTIER
English Miles
BOKHARA
PERSIA
AFGHANISTAN
BALUCHISTAN
BADAKSHAN
SEISTAN
PANJDEH
Merv
Sarakhs
Zulfikar
Kushk R.
Murghab R.
Paropamisus Range
Herat
Hari Rud R.
Helmand R.
Oxus River
Masar-i-Sharif
The Pamirs
Hunza
Nagar
Mastuj
Gilgit
Chitral
Kabul R.
Sherpur
Kabul
Gandamak
Jalalabad
Charasiab
Ghazni
Peiwar Pass
Kurram Valley
Thal
Tochi
Wana
Malakand
Dargai
Ambela
Black Mt.
Khyber Pass
Jamrud
Peshawar
Attock
Rawal Pindi
Jhelum R.
Chenub R.
Indus R.
Ravi R.
Sutlej R.
Beas R.
Lahore
Dharmsala
Maiwand
Kandahar
Chaman
Pishin
Quetta
Bolan Pass
Sibi

CHAPTER V

LORD LYTTON'S POLICY IN AFGHANISTAN TO THE BEGINNING OF THE WAR

THE new Viceroy was Lord Lytton, son of Sir Edward Bulwer Lytton, the novelist. He was a man of great ability, a poet, essayist, and an eloquent speaker. As a member of the diplomatic service he had resided at many European courts, and exhibited in his general bearing and in his mental processes a certain unconventionality typical of the cosmopolitan traveller and the man of letters. 'He was born a Parisian', says his personal friend and political opponent, Lord Morley of Blackburn, 'with a pleasant touch of Bohemian added, and the Puritan and Philistine graces of Simla were repugnant to him.'[1] He came to India commissioned to inaugurate a new Afghan policy. The retirement of his predecessor and the vicissitudes of party government in England had thus by 1876 replaced Gladstone, the Duke of Argyll, and Lord Northbrook, as Premier, Secretary of State, and Viceroy respectively, by Disraeli, Lord Salisbury, and Lord Lytton, and there could hardly have been a more striking change in the personality of the men themselves or the ideas they represented. A strictly unaggressive attitude, non-interference carried perhaps to an extreme, and marked consideration for Afghan susceptibilities were replaced by a spirited foreign policy, imperialistic aims, and a subtle and provocative diplomacy. Under the guidance of the new governments in England

[1] Lord Morley's *Recollections*, vol. ii, p. 188.

and India we drifted within three years into the second Afghan war,[1] which to some extent in its inception, and still more in its course and conclusion, strangely recalled the disastrous campaigns of forty years before, proved, in contemporary opinion at any rate, the grave of Lord Lytton's reputation as a statesman, and, perhaps more than anything else, caused the downfall of the powerful Conservative ministry of 1874.

Lord Lytton, in his own words, brought out instructions for 'a more definite, equilateral and practical alliance' with Sher Ali, and he was empowered to offer the Amir most of the terms he had asked for in 1873, namely, a fixed and augmented subsidy, a recognition of his younger son, Abdulla Jan, as heir to the throne of Afghanistan, and a definite pledge 'by treaty or otherwise' of British support in case of foreign aggression. Unfortunately these terms were only to be granted if Sher Ali allowed a British Resident to be stationed at Herat. The stipulation was reasonable enough as a preliminary condition to a defensive alliance, but if Sher Ali chose to do without such an alliance we had no right to force a mission upon him or make his refusal to receive one a *casus belli*. Lord Lytton was given a very free hand in selecting the time and manner in which the new policy was to be carried out, and he was in fact mainly responsible for the calamitous series of events that followed. It is clear that Lord Salisbury, before he ceased to be Secretary of State, had begun to lag behind the eager promptings of the Viceroy, as was shown by his

[1] The main authorities used for this and the following chapter are first of all the Afghan Blue Books, from which most of the quotations are taken, viz. *Correspondence respecting the relations between the British government and that of Afghanistan since the accession of the Ameer Shere Ali Khan*, 1878; *Further Papers relating to the affairs of Afghanistan*, 1878, 1879, and 1881. Secondly, *The History of Lord Lytton's Indian Administration*, by Lady Betty Balfour, 1899; *England, India, and Afghanistan*, by F. Noyce, 1902; *The Second Afghan War*, by H. B. Hanna (two vols.), 1899–1904.

famous remark in Parliament that excessive dread of Russia might be mitigated by the study of large-scale maps.

Sher Ali was first asked to receive a complimentary mission, which was formally to announce to him the assumption by the Queen of the title 'Empress of India'. This he politely declined on the ground that it was unnecessary. At the same time the British native agent at Kabul reported, undoubtedly with the Amir's knowledge and permission, that among other reasons for the refusal was the fact that Sher Ali could not guarantee to protect a British envoy from the fanaticism of his subjects, and further that, if he permitted him to enter the country, he could not refuse the same privilege to the Russians. This was undoubtedly true, and the right course for the Indian government, if they still desired the Afghan alliance, would have been to grant him the terms offered without the objectionable condition attached to them. Lord Lytton, however, maintained that the reply of the Amir was couched in terms of 'contemptuous disregard' of British interests, and he warned him that 'he was isolating Afghanistan from the alliance and support of the British government'. Three members of the Viceroy's council, Sir William Muir, Sir Henry Norman, and Sir Arthur Hobhouse dissented from this view. They held that Sher Ali was acting within his rights in declining to receive the mission, and that the government was not dealing fairly with him in laying stress upon its temporary and complimentary character, when it was patent to all that its real object was to establish a permanent embassy in his country. In October it was arranged that Lord Lytton should have an interview at Simla with the British Muhammadan agent from Kabul, who was afterwards to return and communicate to Sher Ali the results of their conversation. It cannot be said that the meeting did much to improve matters, and the striking and picturesque phrases of Lord Lytton were under the circumstances more forcible than judicious. The agent was told that the position of Afghanistan between Russia and Great Britain resembled that 'of an earthen pipkin between two iron pots', that if Sher Ali remained our friend the military power of England 'could be spread around him as a ring of iron, and if he became our enemy, it could break him as a reed'.

At the end of 1876 a treaty was negotiated by Major (afterwards Sir) Robert Sandeman, the famous frontier officer, with the Khan of Kalat, which gave the British the right to occupy the long-coveted post of Quetta. The Khan claimed, but had lately proved unable to exercise, a general authority over the other chieftains of Baluchistan, the wide country bounded on the south by the Arabian Sea, on the west by Persia, on the east by Sind and the Punjab, and on the north by the dominions of Sher Ali. Quetta, a strategical position of great natural strength, with a climate peculiarly suited to Europeans, commanded the Bolan Pass, one of the gates of Afghanistan, and the Amir must naturally have looked upon the occupation of it as a preliminary step to a British advance upon Kandahar. He could hardly forget that Quetta was the base from which a British army had marched to the conquest of his country in the first Afghan war.

In January 1877 a conference was held at Peshawar between Sir Lewis Pelly and Seiad Nur Muhammad, the minister of Sher Ali, who had conducted the former negotiations with Lord Northbrook in 1873; the conference was without result, because the Afghan envoy steadily refused to concede the point that a British officer should reside in Afghanistan. Lord Lytton seems to have wilfully refused, or been quite unable, to understand that Sher Ali had the soundest reasons for his action. 'The British nation', said Seiad Nur Muhammad, 'is great and powerful, and the Afghan people cannot resist its power, but the people are self-willed and independent and prize their honour above life.' No Amir, if he desires to retain his throne, can afford to let it be supposed for a moment that he is in any sense controlled by a foreign state. The British Muhammadan agent at Kabul afterwards declared that the mere mistaken report that he was personally in favour of the coming of British officers to Kabul was as much as an order for his death. In our own time the able and powerful Amir, Abdur Rahman, though he had a genuine friendship and admiration for the British, to whom he owed his position, would never make the least concession on this point. The Afghans knew perfectly well that many of their administrative methods would not satisfy the tests of the British political officer. They dreaded the clear scrutiny of European eyes testing the semi-barbarous justice of the East by the humanitarian standards of the West. 'We mistrust you', said Seiad Nur Muhammad, 'and fear you will write all sorts of reports about us, which will some day be brought forward against us.' It is doubtful whether Sher Ali half understood the brilliantly phrased and closely reasoned letters and minutes that the indefatigable Viceroy launched at him. Lytton, indeed, with a strange lack of imagination for so imaginative a man, failed to make allowances for the necessary limitations of the Amir's knowledge or the doubts and suspicions that preyed on his mind. It was commonly reported in the bazaars at this time that Russia and England had agreed upon the partition of Afghanistan, and had sealed the unscrupulous compact by the marriage of the Duke of Edinburgh to a Russian princess. Lord Lytton's elaborate attempts in his dispatches to prove that, by sending an envoy at all, Sher Ali had given an 'anticipatory consent' to the admission of a Resident Officer, and that British relations with Afghanistan were still entirely governed by the treaty of 1855, Lord Mayo s famous letter and the assurances of Lord Northbrook having no binding force, gave a most unfortunate impression of disingenuous dealing. It is likely enough that from this point Sher Ali entered into closer relations with the Russian agents, though it is also plain that, had it been in his power, he would have avoided entanglements with either of the great European states. In March Seiad Nur Muhammad died at Peshawar. Lord Lytton very precipitately seized the opportunity to declare the conference at an end, in spite of the fact that a successor to the dead envoy was said to be on his way from Kabul with fresh instructions from Sher Ali. Communications with the Afghan court were now entirely suspended, though Lord Lytton by a manifesto assured the Afghan people in words that were often afterwards with good reason quoted against him, 'that so long as they are not excited by their ruler or others to acts of aggression upon the territories or friends of the British government, no British soldier will ever be permitted to enter Afghanistan uninvited'. In May the Viceroy gave his version of the negotiations in a long and brilliantly written dispatch which was afterwards severely and justly censured as an ingenious piece of special pleading rather than a state paper.

Up to that time no irretrievable step had been taken. There was much force in Lord Lytton's contention that our relations with Afghanistan, in view of the situation in central Asia, were unsatisfactory. It was a matter for regret that Sher Ali could not accept our point of view. But he was an independent prince, and however inconvenient it might be for our interests, we had no moral right whatever to forbid him to have relations with Russia or to force upon him an envoy of our own, and yet this was the course to which Lord Lytton ultimately committed himself and the British government. The old Lawrence policy was in truth based upon a generous recognition of the rights of small and weak states, the school of Lytton and his followers relied upon a cynical doctrine of political expediency. 'Chiefs like the Amir of Kabul and the Khan of Kalat', wrote Sir James Stephen, 'though not dependent upon us in the sense of any definite duties or allegiance to the Queen, must be dealt with on the understanding that they occupy a distinctly inferior position—their inferiority consisting mainly in this, that they are not to be permitted to follow a course of policy which exposes us to danger. . . . Relations . . . with these states are all determined by the fact that we are exceedingly powerful and highly civilised, and that they are comparatively weak and half barbarous.'

When the conference at Peshawar was over, Lytton turned his attention to the tribes of the north-west frontier, and plainly showed his eagerness to push his outposts nearer to Afghanistan through their territory. By a 'more or less confidential arrangement' with the Maharaja of Kashmir he established a British agency at Gilgit. Even his chosen instrument, Captain Cavagnari, warned him that such a policy would render a reconciliation with Sher Ali impossible, and Lord Lytton's daughter notes that he met with opposition from the old frontier officials 'who looked with suspicion upon any system of diplomacy which required secrecy and dexterity'. The truth is that the Viceroy's opponents regarded his policy as altogether too secret and dexterous, and would have preferred more of the straightforwardness which was formerly characteristic of Indian frontier policy. Lord Lytton indeed was now, on his own admission, working for the 'gradual disintegration and weakening of the Afghan power'.

But the ruin of Sher Ali, through the strange interplay of world forces, was finally brought about by disturbances in another continent. In 1876 the Serbians and Montenegrins rose in arms against the misgovernment of the Turk. In April of the following year, Russia, in sympathy with the insurgents, declared war upon Turkey, and in 1878 her armies crossed the Balkans. Disraeli, now Earl of Beaconsfield, holding that the interests of England demanded the integrity of the Ottoman empire, obtained from Parliament a grant of £6,000,000 for naval and military purposes, and ordered the Mediterranean squadron to pass the Dardanelles. The Russians were deterred by the British menace from attacking Constantinople, and in March 1878 concluded the treaty of San Stefano with the Sultan. But Russia's diplomatic success was neutralized by Great Britain. Lord Beaconsfield refused to recognize the treaty, called out the army reserves, occupied Cyprus with the permission of Turkey, and reinforced the Mediterranean squadron. War was only averted by the mediation of Germany. At a congress of the Powers at Berlin in June and July 1878 the treaty of San Stefano was modified in a manner unfavourable to Russia. The difference, however, between the terms of the treaties of San Stefano and Berlin proved of very doubtful advantage to Great Britain, and the Russian government was greatly irritated by Lord Beaconsfield's provocative and unfriendly attitude. During the height of the tension the Prime Minister had adopted the dramatic but useless course of bringing some Indian troops by the Suez Canal to Malta, and Russia naturally determined to afford the Indian government some outlet for its warlike energies nearer home.

On June 13, the opening day of the Berlin congress, General Stoletoff started from Tashkend for Kabul. The desperate attempts made by Sher Ali to stay his advance form in themselves a complete answer to Lytton's constantly repeated assertion that he was eagerly abetting Russian designs. Sher Ali appealed and protested; he repeated almost word for word to the Russian Governor-General of Turkestan the arguments which he had formerly used to the Viceroy of British India, and he offered, as he had done in the case of Lord Lytton, to send one of his own ministers to a conference at Tashkend. But his opposition was beaten down by the reply that Stoletoff could not now be recalled, and that the Tsar would hold Sher Ali responsible if any harm happened to him. The Russian government was in a position to put pressure upon the Amir from the fact that his nephew Abdur Rahman had long been a pensioner on their bounty. A significant hint was conveyed to Sher Ali that a dangerous rival to his throne might be put forward, if he proved obstinate. Sher Ali reluctantly yielded, and after his downfall papers at Kabul were found which showed that he now entered into a definite treaty with the Russian government for perpetual and permanent friendship and alliance between the two countries. On the news of the arrival of the Russian mission in Kabul, Lytton, after cabling home for, and receiving, the permission of the home government, determined to insist that Sher Ali should in like manner receive a British envoy on the ground that the only alternative would be a 'continued policy of complete inaction, difficult to maintain and very injurious to our position in India'. Sher Ali was to be required to enter into no negotiations with other states without permission, to concede our right to send British officers to Kabul for a conference with him whenever we saw adequate occasion, and to allow a permanent British agent to reside at Herat.

This whole procedure was a calamitous mistake. It was plain that Russia and not Afghanistan was responsible for the entry of the mission into Kabul, and it was she, if any one, as Lord Lawrence argued, who ought to have been called to account. After the signature of the treaty of Berlin, the continued residence of Stoletoff in the Afghan capital could reasonably be regarded as an unfriendly act, and the British ambassador at St. Petersburg should have been instructed to demand his recall. There is no doubt that the request would have been promptly granted, for, even as it was, Stoletoff at once left Kabul when he heard that the British intended to send a mission. Russia's action was solely designed as a counter-stroke to British policy in Europe, which had thwarted her in the hour of triumph. A golden bridge for a retreat from an untenable position was built by Stoletoff's retirement. The right course for the Viceroy was to assume that Sher Ali, as indeed he did, welcomed the Russians' withdrawal, and to attempt to win him back to friendship. Unfortunately Lord Lytton only looked upon the treaty of Berlin as having 'freed our hands and destroyed, at the same time, all hopes on his (Sher Ali's) part of complications to us, or active assistance to himself, from Russia'. A Muhammadan envoy was dispatched to Kabul on August 30 to announce the approach of the British mission. The Afridis of the Khyber Pass, who owed allegiance to the Amir, were bribed to allow the envoy and his escort to pass—an action to which Sher Ali had every right to object. The news of the death of Abdulla Jan, the Amir's favourite son, in August 1878, grief for whose loss is said for a time to have almost unhinged his reason, caused a little delay, but after a few days Sir Neville Chamberlain, the envoy selected by Lord Lytton, set out from Peshawar; an advance escort was met at Ali Masjid, a lonely post at the entrance of the pass, by an Afghan officer, who courteously but firmly intimated to the leader, Major Cavagnari, that he could not allow him to proceed without orders from Kabul. The British envoy having ascertained that the Afghans were prepared to use force, if he attempted to proceed, returned to Peshawar.

Lord Lytton declared that the mission had been 'forcibly repulsed'—a statement obviously at variance with the facts—and eagerly pressed the home government to sanction a declaration of war. But the Cabinet imposed a few weeks delay, and according to their requirements an ultimatum was sent on November 2 demanding from the Amir, if he wished to avoid the calamities of an invasion, a 'full and suitable apology' and his consent to a permanent British mission in Afghanistan. Hostilities were to commence, unless an answer were received by November 20. A belated reply reached the Viceroy on November 30, dated November 19, which, though it announced Sher Ali's acceptance of the mission, was declared to be inadequate as containing no apology. By that time moreover the war had begun, for Lord Lytton had set his forces in motion the day after the ultimatum expired.

Once more therefore Great Britain was committed to a war with Afghanistan. But at home the opposition to the policy was widespread and powerful. In Parliament, Gladstone in one of the weightiest of his public utterances condemned the Lytton policy in words unimpeachably true as a summary of the past, and strikingly prophetic as a forecast of the future—'We made war in error upon Afghanistan in 1838. To err is human and pardonable. But we have erred a second time on the same ground and with no better justification. . . . This error has been repeated in the face of every warning conceivable and imaginable, and in the face of an unequalled mass of authorities. It is proverbially said that history repeats itself, and there has rarely been an occasion in which there has been a nearer approach to identity than in the case of the present and the former wars. . . . May heaven avert the omen! May heaven avert a repetition of the calamity which befell our army in 1841.'

CHAPTER VI

THE SECOND AFGHAN WAR

On the declaration of war, November 21, the three great passes of Afghanistan were entered by British armies. Sir Samuel Browne threaded the Khyber, captured Ali Masjid and advanced to Jalalabad. Major-General (afterwards Lord) Roberts marched up the Kurram valley, and drove the enemy from the heights that command the Peiwar Pass, a position of great natural strength. The southernmost invading force under General Stewart marched from Quetta through the Bolan Pass upon Kandahar. There was little effective opposition. The whole Afghan people seemed sunk in sullen apathy. The wretched Sher Ali vainly endeavoured to get help from General Kaufmann, but that astute officer warned him, as a friend, to make his peace with the British, if they gave him the opportunity. In December the Amir fled into Russian Turkestan having first released his eldest son, Yakub Khan, from imprisonment and left him behind at Kabul to make the best terms he could with the invaders. Sher Ali renewed his appeals for assistance to Kaufmann, but the Russians only replied that to invade Afghanistan was at present beyond their power, and they gave him no encouragement when he expressed a desire to make his way to St. Petersburg and lay his wrongs before the Tsar. Nothing was done for him by Russia, though the Russian ambassador in London is said to have obtained a promise from the British government that the integrity of Afghanistan should be respected. On February 21 Sher Ali, worn out by physical disease and mental anxiety, died at Masar-i-Sharif. The story of his career is a rather mournful commentary on the consideration likely to be shown to a weak semi-barbarous eastern monarch when, unhappily for him, his territories form a possible point of contact between two powerful and expanding western empires. His lonely death in bitterness and exile is not an incident upon which either Russia, who had led him on by false and delusive hopes, or England, who had at first repelled and then coerced him, can look back with any feelings of satisfaction. Sher Ali was a man of considerable ability, who had proved himself competent to weld his unruly dominions into a single political entity, but he beat in vain against the ruthless ambitions and selfish interests of his powerful neighbours. The Cabinet decided to recognize Yakub Khan as his successor, though Lord Lytton would have preferred the disintegration of Afghanistan. He declared that the rulers of the country would always tend to prefer the 'ambitious, energetic and not over-scrupulous' government of Russia to 'alliance with a power so essentially pacific and sensitively scrupulous as our own'—a description which, it is to be feared, Sher Ali might have failed to recognize as particularly applicable to the British policy of Lord Lytton's own time.

In May 1879 a treaty was made at Gandamak with the new Amir, by which he agreed to conduct his foreign relations with other states in accordance with the advice and wishes of the British government, to countenance a permanent British Resident at Kabul with agents at Herat and other places on the frontier, and to assign the Kurram Pass to British control together with Pishin and Sibi, districts in the neighbourhood of the Bolan Pass. The British engaged to support him, at their discretion, with money, arms, and men against any foreign aggression, and to pay him an annual subsidy of six lakhs of rupees. The British troops were to be withdrawn from Afghanistan, except those stationed at Kandahar, which was not to be evacuated till the autumn. The treaty of Gandamak marked the apogee of Lord Lytton's Afghan policy. He claimed that it fully secured all the objects of the war, and Lord Beaconsfield added that, by it, we had attained 'a scientific and adequate frontier for our Indian empire'. But their triumph was short-lived. The Indian government had once more, by painful experience, to learn the lesson that directly any ruler of Afghanistan is supported by a foreign power he forfeits all the respect and allegiance of his fellow countrymen. How blind the Viceroy was to the real state of affairs may be seen from his statement that 'the Afghans will like and respect us all the more for the thrashing we have given Sher Ali'. A month after the time when these words were written the clouds were ominously gathering, and the fate of Burnes and Macnaghten was impending over Sir Louis Cavagnari, who, having entered Kabul as British Resident on July 24, was exhibiting in that position something of the same blindness to sinister signs of danger and the same fatal optimism as his predecessors.

On September 2 Cavagnari sent a telegram to the Viceroy containing the words 'All well'. The next day the mutinous and disorderly Afghan army rose, attacked the residency, and murdered the envoy with the whole of his escort. Yakub Khan was either powerless to intervene or in secret sympathy with the assassins; at any rate he made no useful effort to protect the embassy. The catastrophe was a terrible blow to the Viceroy. 'The web of policy', he wrote, 'so carefully and patiently woven, has been rudely shattered. . . . All that I was most anxious to avoid in the conduct of the late war and negotiations has now been brought about by the hand of fate.'[1] British forces were soon once again in motion. Sir Donald Stewart reoccupied Kandahar, General Roberts once more marched through the Kurram valley on Kabul, which he entered on October 12 after defeating the rebels at Charasiab, and inflicted

[1] *Personal and Literary Letters of . . . Earl of Lytton*, ed. by Lady Betty Balfour, vol. ii, p. 169 [1906].

severe punishment on those who were proved to have taken any part in the attack on the residency. Yakub Khan, dreading the reception he might meet with, had joined the British army before the entry into Kabul. He now abdicated his throne and threw himself upon British protection, declaring that he would rather be a grass-cutter in the English camp than ruler of Afghanistan. An inquiry was afterwards held into his conduct, and though he was acquitted of any complicity in the murder, he was pronounced to have been 'culpably indifferent' to the fate of the envoy, and was removed to India as a state prisoner. In any case it was felt to be impossible that he should ever be replaced upon the throne.

The Indian government had now to face a very difficult position. Afghanistan had practically relapsed into anarchy, and there was no government left with which to negotiate. In the winter there was fierce fighting round Kabul, and it was only with great difficulty that Roberts kept his communications with India open. Indeed, for ten days, December 14 to 24, those communications were cut. He was forced to abandon Kabul and the Bala Hissar, the famous citadel, and retire to defences at Sherpur, where he was besieged by 100,000 tribesmen. In the spring of 1880 Stewart, marching from Kandahar, defeated the rebels at Ahmad Khel and joined Roberts at Kabul. It was plain that the British were only in effective occupation of the comparatively small portion of Afghanistan east of a line drawn between these two cities. To conquer the whole country would have involved ruinous expense, and was impossible unless the forces hitherto employed were largely increased; while to retire without leaving some constituted authority in the country would be fatal to British prestige. It was finally decided on Lord Lytton's advice that western Afghanistan should be permanently severed from the rest of the country; the province of Kandahar was detached from Kabul and handed over to an independent chief, Sher Ali Khan, to whom the Indian government pledged itself to give military support in case of need. The difficulty still remained of dealing with Kabul and north-western Afghanistan, and it was finally solved in a very unexpected and, as it turned out, fortunate manner. 'We have found in Abdur Rahman', wrote Lord Lytton, 'a ram caught in the thicket'.[1] This man, the nephew of Sher Ali, son of that Afzal Khan who had reigned as Amir for seventeen months in 1866–7, suddenly appeared on the northern frontier. Since 1870 he had lived in banishment beyond the Oxus under Russian protection, and his patrons, with the obvious intention of embarrassing the British government, now furnished him with a small escort of armed men, and sent him to try his fortune in the land of his birth. Lord Lytton had already investigated, and reluctantly disallowed, the claims of many other candidates for the Afghan throne; he now took the exceedingly bold step of offering to give Abdur Rahman a free hand in north-western Afghanistan, and recognize him as Amir, if he proved acceptable to the people. This policy was described at the time as 'the greatest leap in the dark on record', and must indeed have seemed exceedingly hazardous, but it was fully justified by success. Abdur Rahman was one of the greatest Asiatics of his time, a man at once of penetrating shrewdness and of far-reaching vision. In his eleven years of brooding solitude as a pensionary upon Russian bounty, he had fathomed the political ideals and methods of his patrons, though he was always personally grateful to them for affording him an asylum in his exile. With remarkable insight he recognized that Great Britain, in spite of her dubious record in the past towards his country, was likely to be the truer friend to Afghan independence. But from the first he had to walk with the utmost wariness, and there was thus

[1] *Personal and Literary Letters of . . . Earl of Lytton*, ed. by Lady Betty Balfour, vol. ii, p. 202.

considerable danger that the British would (as indeed some of them often did) misunderstand his attitude. 'I was unable', he says in his remarkable memoirs, 'to show my friendship publicly to the extent that was necessary: because my people were ignorant and fanatical. If I showed any inclination towards the English, my people would call me an infidel for joining hands with infidels. . . .'[1] He was bound therefore, even while accepting our proposals, to give his countrymen no ground for suspecting that his power rested on the support of British bayonets, to treat us coldly and churlishly and make it appear as though concessions were extorted from, rather than granted by, us. Considering the universal detestation felt for us at the time and long afterwards by the Afghan people, Abdur Rahman's success in raising himself to the throne by our connivance and gradually winning over his subjects to acquiesce in our alliance and protection is one of the most remarkable political feats in modern Asian history.

But before this plan could be carried out Lord Lytton had resigned his office. In April 1880 the Conservative government had suffered a severe defeat in the general election. Gladstone succeeded Lord Beaconsfield as Prime Minister, and Lord Hartington replaced Lord Cranbrook (Lord Salisbury's successor) as Secretary of State for India. In normal cases no Viceroy would be expected to resign owing to a change of ministry in England, but the foreign and Indian policy of the Conservative government had met with unsparing criticism and severe condemnation both in Parliament and in the country, and Lord Hartington himself had described the Viceroy as 'the incarnation and the embodiment of an Indian policy which is everything an Indian policy should not be'. Accordingly Lord Lytton laid down his office when the verdict of the nation, as given at the polls, was known to him. It will be convenient here

[1] *The Life of Abdur Rahman, Amir of Afghanistan*, ed. by Mir Munshi Sultan Mahomed Khan, two vols., London. 1900, vol. ii, p. 117.

before dealing with the other measures of his administration to complete the story of the Afghan settlement. The policy of the Liberal government was outlined in Lord Hartington's dispatches of May and November 1880: 'it appears that as the result of two successful campaigns, of the employment of an enormous force, and of the expenditure of large sums of money, all that has yet been accomplished has been the disintegration of the state which it was desired to see strong, friendly and independent, the assumption of fresh and unwelcome liabilities in regard to one of its provinces and a condition of anarchy throughout the remainder of the country'. Therefore the government, 'sharing the opinions of some of the most eminent Indian statesmen of past and present times, and, up to a very recent date, of every minister of the Crown responsible for Indian policy', believed that the consequences of the recent interference in the internal affairs of Afghanistan 'have been precisely those which had been foreseen and apprehended by the opponents' of the Lytton policy. 'If the Afghans', added Lord Hartington, 'have ever been disposed to look with more friendship on either their Russian or Persian than their British neighbour, it is not an unnatural result of the fear for the loss of their freedom which our past policy has been calculated to inspire.' The aim of the Cabinet therefore was to return, as far as possible, to the position of affairs before the war, and Lord Ripon was sent out as Viceroy to bring about a peaceful settlement. Lord Lytton's policy in regard to the succession was accepted, and in July Abdur Rahman was formally recognized as Amir of Kabul. The only conditions attached to the recognition were that the Amir was to 'have no political relations with any foreign power except the English', and that the districts of Pishin and Sibi were to be retained in British hands; as long as Abdur Rahman observed the first condition, the British government would aid him to repel the 'unprovoked aggression' of any foreign power. The policy which had been the main motive for the war was definitely and explicitly given up, and Great Britain bound herself not to require the admission of an English Resident anywhere in Afghanistan. For the present Lord Ripon considered himself bound by the treaty with the ruler of Kandahar to maintain the severance of western from north-western Afghanistan; but he did so with reluctance and the course of events soon gave him an excuse for abandoning this—almost the sole remaining plank of the Lytton policy.

Since Herat at this time was under the control of Ayub Khan, a son of Sher Ali, Abdur Rahman had succeeded to a much-reduced kingdom. Three independent rulers at Kabul, Kandahar and Herat presaged troublous times, and war broke out before British troops had been withdrawn from the country. In June Ayub Khan marched from Herat on Kandahar, and at Maiwand won over a British force under General Burrows one of the most notable victories ever gained by oriental troops in conflict with a European army. The British had 914 men killed and were driven back in full retreat. The only redeeming feature of the battle from our point of view was the glorious conduct of 100 officers and men of the 66th regiment. Surrounded and hopelessly outnumbered they inflicted enormous loss upon the enemy, and held an isolated position till only eleven men were left. Then the survivors charged out of their cover and 'died with their faces to the foe fighting to the death'; 'history does not afford', runs the official dispatch, 'any grander or finer instance of gallantry and devotion to Queen and country'. Ayub Khan after his victory marched on to invest Kandahar, and Roberts was at once sent by Stewart from Kabul to relieve our ally according to the treaty. Roberts with 10,000 men accomplished his historic forced march of 313 miles in twenty days—a wonderful military feat—and completely defeated Ayub Khan at the battle of Kandahar. In spite of the sudden resumption of hostilities Stewart withdrew his forces from Kabul on the date originally fixed. Roberts remained at Kandahar for a few months, until in 1881 the government decided to evacuate it. Our pledge to support Sher Ali Khan was an embarrassing tie, but he was persuaded to abdicate and retire to India. Though the withdrawal from Kandahar was fiercely resisted by the advocates of the 'Forward' policy and was opposed by Lytton in an able speech in the House of Lords, it was justified by success. Abdur Rahman had never accepted with equanimity the partition of his ancestral kingdom, and it was the recovery of Kandahar that perhaps more than anything else won his fidelity to the British alliance. For a time, however, he seemed in imminent danger of losing not only his newly recovered possession but Kabul as well. When the British troops had departed, Ayub Khan marched again from Herat, occupied Kandahar and held it for several months. Abdur Rahman set out from Kabul to offer him battle. The Indian government watched events with great anxiety. The Amir had hitherto had little opportunity to display ability in the field, while his opponent came to meet him with all the prestige of Maiwand. Few thought that Abdur Rahman could prevail ; the relief was great when he won a complete victory near Kandahar in September. Ayub Khan fled into exile in Persia. Herat as well as Kandahar surrendered to the victor, who had once more consolidated together the territories of Dost Muhammad and Sher Ali, and henceforward governed his unruly subjects with great success.

Thus ended Lord Lytton's 'fancy prospect . . . painted on the blank wall of the future of bequeathing to India the supremacy of central Asia and the revenues of a first class power'.[1] Such imaginative political dreams are seldom realized ; they are characteristic of the visionary rather than the statesman. The famous words of Lord Beaconsfield's last public speech seem to show that even he, though

[1] *Letters*, vol. ii, p. 200.

late in the day, realized at last the lessons of the Afghan war: 'The key of India is not Merv or Herat or Kandahar. The key of India is London. The majesty and sovereignty, the spirit and vigour of your Parliaments, the inexhaustible resources of a free, an ingenious and a determined people, these are the keys of India.'[1]

[1] Since this chapter was in type, vol. vi of Mr. G. E. Buckle's *Life of Disraeli* has appeared. The hitherto unpublished letters and papers, there quoted, shed some new light upon the Afghan policy of the Conservative Government of 1874–80, deepen the responsibility of Lord Lytton for the war and show that, in the concluding stages, Ministers strongly disapproved of the unwise measures which precipitated the conflict. Both Beaconsfield and Salisbury, though in public they loyally supported their colleague, deprecated Lytton's haste in sending the Chamberlain Mission. In September 1878 the Prime Minister wrote to Lord Cranbrook, 'He (Lytton) was told to wait until we had received the answer from Russia to our remonstrance. I was very strong on this, having good reasons for my opinion. He disobeyed us. I was assured by Lord Salisbury that, under no circumstances, was the Khyber Pass to be attempted. Nothing would have induced me to consent to such a step. He was told to send the Mission by Kandahar. He has sent it by the Khyber. . . .' Beaconsfield admired Lytton's manifestoes and dispatches, and declared 'with Lytton's general policy I entirely agree. I have always been opposed to, and deplored, masterly inactivity', but he recognized that wider imperial interests required peace with Russia. Lytton's policy, he wrote to Salisbury in October, 'is perfectly fitted to a state of affairs in which Russia was our assailant; but Russia is not our assailant. She has sneaked out of her hostile position, with sincerity, in my mind, but scarcely with dignity, and if Lytton had only been quiet and obeyed my orders, I have no doubt that, under the advice of Russia, Sher Ali would have been equally prudent.' From Beaconsfield's report to the Queen of the Cabinet meeting of October 25 it is clear that the Government only entered on the war with the greatest reluctance. Lord Cairns, Sir Stafford Northcote, Cross, and Lord Salisbury were all against it, and the latter, writes the Prime Minister, 'said that the Viceroy was "forcing the hand of the Government", and had been doing so from the very first; he thought only of India and was dictating, by its means, the foreign policy of the Government in Europe and Turkey. He had twice disobeyed orders: first in acting on the Khyber Pass; secondly in sending the Mission contrary to the most express and repeated orders that he was not to do so, till we had received an expected dispatch from Russia. . . . He (Salisbury) spoke with great bitterness of the conduct of the Viceroy, and said that, unless curbed, he would bring about some terrible disaster.'

CHAPTER VII

INTERNAL ADMINISTRATION UNDER LORD LYTTON

THE chief event of Lord Lytton's Viceroyalty apart from the Afghan war was the appalling famine of 1876–8, the most severe on record as regards loss of life. It was terribly prolonged, lasting over two years and affecting most of southern India, Madras, Bombay, Hyderabad, and Mysore, and in the second year, parts of central India and the Punjab. The scourges of fever and cholera followed in its wake. It was impossible to stave off a calamity of this nature as the comparatively local scarcity of Bihar had been staved off by Lord Northbrook in 1874, nor could the Indian government contemplate an expenditure proportionately lavish over an area so much wider. The efforts to save life were made with a due—some critics said an excessive—regard to economy; 'speaking generally', says the writer in the *Imperial Gazetteer of India*, 'the administration of relief was as strict on this occasion as it had been lax in Bihar'. The Madras authorities at first embarked on an over-generous system of relief, but Lord Lytton sent Sir Richard Temple to report on their methods, and in the late summer himself visited the Presidency. His own view was that the lavish relief measures adopted there were not only more wasteful but actually less efficacious in saving life than the more economical system in Bombay. 'We are fighting', he wrote, 'a desperate battle with nature, and our line of battle has been completely broken at Madras.' Although a sum of eleven millions sterling was expended from the Indian treasury and charitable funds, more than five million people are said to have perished in British territory alone, two million acres of land were temporarily thrown out of cultivation, and the loss of land revenue to the exchequer was over £2,250,000.

It was henceforward decided that the Indian government should not, as in the past, deal with each famine empirically when it occurred, but that preventive and anticipatory measures should be taken. Two means to accomplish this end were adopted. A famine commission with General Richard Strachey as President conducted an exhaustive inquiry during 1878–80 into the whole question of famines and the granting of relief, and laid down careful regulations for future guidance. The main principle adopted was the finding of employment for the able-bodied on relief works at a wage sufficient to maintain health, and the giving of gratuitous help only to the impotent poor. Secondly it was decided henceforward to budget for an annual surplus of £1,500,000 over the ordinary revenue—which surplus was to be used partly for the reduction or avoidance of debt, so that the state might more easily bear the exceptional drain on her resources necessary in the periodical return of years of famine, partly for the construction of railways and canals through districts where drought was especially prevalent. The money was raised by a licence tax on trades and professions producing more than £200 a year and by new 'cesses' (or taxes) on land. Lord Lytton, says Mr. V. A. Smith, 'deserves high credit for sound views on famine policy, thoroughly thought out and expressed with forceful lucidity. The whole existing system of famine administration rests on the foundations well and truly laid by him.'

Lord Lytton's period of office was notable for the great fiscal reforms carried out by Sir John Strachey, who in 1876 left the lieutenant-governorship of the North-West Provinces at the Viceroy's request to become financial member of council. One of the most important sources of revenue in India is the salt tax. It had hitherto been levied at very different rates in different provinces, and to prevent smuggling from one province to another and the importation of untaxed salt from native states into British territory, an inland customs line made of impenetrable cactus hedge, wall, and ditch stretched across India from Attock on the Indus to the Mahanadi in the Deccan, a distance of 2,500 miles. It had to be patrolled by an army of revenue officers 12,000 in number; Indian finance ministers had long desired to abolish this fiscal anachronism, but to do so two things were necessary—the manufacture of salt in native states had to be controlled, and the salt tax in the various British provinces had to be equalized. Some preliminary steps in regard to the first of these measures had been already taken under Lord Mayo and Lord Northbrook by negotiations with the protected chiefs, and Lord Northbrook had been enabled to shorten the customs line at its southern end by 1,000 miles. Sir John Strachey now concluded agreements with other native states producing salt, by which in return for compensation they surrendered control of its manufacture. Though he could not sacrifice enough revenue to equalize the salt duties entirely, the variations were brought within so narrow a margin that it no longer paid to transport salt from one province to another, and the remaining 1,500 miles of the customs line were swept away.

Sir John Strachey made another important advance in the direction of establishing Free Trade in India. In the tariff of 1878 he abolished the duty on sugar levied at the inland customs line, and remitted import duties on twenty-nine commodities. The avowed desire of himself and the Viceroy was to make India one great free port open to the commerce of the world, and the only reason they did not go farther still in the realization of this aim was that the great strain put upon their resources by the Afghan war and the famine made any further sacrifice of revenue impossible. Controversy centred mainly round the five per cent. *ad valorem* import dues hitherto levied on cotton manufactured goods at Indian ports. The Lancashire manufacturers had long been clamouring for their abolition, and in July 1877 the House of Commons passed a resolution without a division that 'the duties now levied upon cotton manufactures imported into India, being protective in their nature, are contrary to sound commercial policy and ought to be repealed without delay as soon as the financial condition of India will permit'. In India, however, there was much popular, and some official, opposition to any modification of the duties. The majority of the Viceroy's council strongly opposed the change on the ground that it was not a fitting time to give up duties, which, they maintained, had no real protective effect at all. They regarded the proposal as 'one which has been adopted not in the interest of India, not even in the interest of England, but in the interest or the supposed interest of a political party, the leaders of which deem it necessary at any cost to retain the political support of the cotton manufacturers of Lancashire'.[1] But there can be little doubt that both the Cabinet and the Viceroy were honestly convinced (for orthodox political economy was then almost unchallenged) that there was no real conflict between Indian and English interests, and that both countries would ultimately benefit by the abolition, or at least the lowering, of the duties. Accordingly, in 1879, the duties were removed on the coarser kinds of cotton cloth, on which the protective nature of the impost had most effect. To carry this measure Lytton was obliged to use his constitutional right to override the majority of his council—the only instance of the exercise of this exceptional power in recent times. The great expansion in oversea trade following the abolition of the duties fully justified, at any rate from the

[1] Minute of Sir Alexander Arbuthnot, March 15, 1879.

purely economic point of view, the Free Trade policy. The passing of the Southern India Agricultural Relief Act in 1879, which curtailed the money-lender's power of distraining on his peasant debtor's holding, shows that the Viceroy and his Council were not mere *doctrinaires* in their general adherence to the policy of *laisser faire*.

In 1877, by giving the provincial governments a share in the revenues instead of a fixed grant from the imperial treasury, Sir John Strachey extended and developed the system of financial decentralization which had been begun in 1870 on his own and his brother's advice by Lord Mayo. Altogether his tenure of office as finance minister was a notable landmark in Indian fiscal history and it was only marred by one most unfortunate blunder. In May 1880, to quote the Viceroy, 'the tremendous discovery' was made that the war estimates, prepared by the Military, and accepted by the Financial Department, were utterly worthless and would be indefinitely exceeded. Lord Lytton foresaw much 'public scandal and reproach', and indeed at the time the government was accused by political opponents of intentional concealment and deception. But though the miscalculation was enormous—over twelve millions in excess of the estimates, the total charges being seventeen and a half millions instead of five—the error was due to a faulty system of account-keeping in the Military Department. At the same time it must be admitted that Sir John Strachey and the Viceroy, knowing how military operations had been prolonged, exhibited a rather confiding trust in the remarkably low figures supplied to them by their Military Accountant-General, and they can hardly be acquitted of a lack of vigilance in the matter. It was fortunate that Sir John Strachey's financial reforms and his step in the direction of Free Trade had so improved the Indian revenues that fifteen millions of the war charges—the proportion falling on the Indian exchequer—were paid for out of revenue. The balance of five millions was discharged by the imperial treasury, and in view of the fact that the war was mainly due to Lord Beaconsfield's opposition to Russia in Europe for reasons of general imperial policy, there was some reason in the contention that a larger proportionate share might have been discharged by the British government.

By the founding of the Statutory Civil Service in 1879 the Indian government made a rather belated attempt to give some reality to the promise of the Charter Act of 1833, reaffirmed by the royal proclamation of 1858, that no native of British India should be debarred, by reason of his nationality, from holding any place or office. The Act of 1853 had indeed formally opened the higher or covenanted civil service (so called because its members on appointment entered into a covenant not to trade or receive presents) to all subjects of the Crown, whether British or Indian, by a competitive examination. But as that examination was held in England, all but a very few Indian subjects were practically debarred from competing. It appeared therefore to the more liberal school of Indian statesmen that, in regard to the higher judicial and administrative posts, some 864 in number, the promises of the East India Company and the Crown were hardly being fulfilled. On the other hand, it was pointed out that a great preponderance of men of British origin was only found in the case of the highest posts; that it is always necessary this should be so; and that practically the whole of the much larger subordinate or uncovenanted civil service, which included in its upper grades positions of no mean importance and responsibility, was in the hands of native Indians. The more conservative school held that this fact was in itself a sufficient fulfilment of the promises of 1833 and 1858 and that, if more than this was meant, then that those promises had been too rashly given. In spite of this, attempts were made from time to time to bestow upon men of Indian origin a greater share in the covenanted civil service. Lord Lawrence introduced a short-lived system of scholarships to be won in India and held in Great Britain for three years. The next step was taken by the Duke of Argyll in 1870, who carried an Act of Parliament enabling the government in India, with the approval of the Secretary of State, to frame rules by which native Indians might be appointed to some of the posts hitherto held by members of the covenanted civil service, without the necessity of passing the examination in London. But the Duke of Argyll obviously approached the question with extreme caution, suggesting that Indian candidates should be selected mainly for judicial, and rarely, if at all, for executive posts. If the Secretary of State was lukewarm in his advocacy of the proposed change, the Indian government was decidedly cold, and though much correspondence ensued, the various rules framed were either disallowed by the home government or found to be practically useless. Lord Lytton's policy, as stated by himself, was 'Define more clearly the promises which have been given so vaguely and indeed so rashly. Cautiously circumscribe them, but then make them realities within their necessary limits.' In accordance with this theory, his government in 1878–9 produced the plan of the Statutory Civil Service. One-sixth of the posts hitherto held by the covenanted civil service, together with some of the most important in the uncovenanted service, were henceforward to be filled by men of Indian birth nominated by the local governments in India with the approval of the Viceroy in Council and the Secretary of State; the candidates were to serve two years of probation and to pass special tests before their final appointment. The authorities in India would have preferred to make the new scheme dependent upon the exclusion of Indian candidates from the competitive examination in London, but this suggestion was disallowed by the India Office. Native Indians had therefore henceforward not only a close service of their own but a legal right to fill as many places in the covenanted service as their abilities would enable them to win. The Statutory Civil Service in public estimation held a position mid-way between the covenanted and the uncovenanted or subordinate service, though its status was to be legally equivalent to that of the former. It was on the whole not a success. It failed to attract the higher classes and was mainly recruited from men who would normally have entered the subordinate service; accordingly eight years later, as we shall see, it was abolished.

In 1878 Lord Lytton passed his much-criticized Vernacular Press Act, which empowered a magistrate or collector to require the editor of a newspaper written in an oriental language either to enter into a bond to publish nothing likely to excite feelings of dissatisfaction against the government and antipathy between persons of different races, castes, and religions, or to submit his proofs to an officer appointed by government. Lord Lytton held that the seditious tone of the vernacular newspapers at that time rendered necessary some limitation to 'the exceptional tolerance' with which the government had hitherto regarded 'the occasional misuse of an instrument confided to unpractised hands', and he spoke of the liberty of the press as 'a privilege to be worthily earned and rationally enjoyed' rather than 'a fetish to be worshipped'. The opposition, which included three dissentient members of council, contended that the excesses of a few foolish journalists were not sufficient ground for repressive legislation; that the Indian government was showing itself too sensitive to attack; and that the differential treatment meted out to the English and vernacular press was highly invidious. There was much force in these criticisms, though the Viceroy tried to meet the last by pointing out that the distinction between vernacular and English papers was not necessarily, or altogether, one of race, because many papers edited by Indians were printed in English. The Act was in any case short lived, and was repealed by Lord Lytton's successor four years later.

No Viceroy in modern times has been subjected to fiercer criticism than Lord Lytton, and the reasons are not far to seek. His Afghan policy was condemned by the greatest Indian authorities in England, by the leaders of the Liberal party, and finally in no uncertain way by a majority of the nation. It was indeed a calamitous and unrighteous blunder, and on that head alone Lord Lytton's claims to statesmanship are justly forfeit. The great loss of life in the famine of 1878–80, the measures taken to limit the freedom of the press, the miscalculation in the estimates of the war charges, all these things naturally gave ground for criticism. Yet no one can read Lord Lytton's minutes and dispatches without realizing that he was a man of more than ordinary gifts. Though often hasty and impulsive, he brought some new and fruitful conceptions into the field of Indian politics. Many of his unrealized ideas only failed of realization because they were before their time. He advocated the introduction of a gold standard into the monetary system of India, and, had the change been made then, when the depreciation of silver was but beginning, India would have been saved great economic loss. He suggested the creation of a north-west frontier province under the direct control of the government of India instead of the lieutenant-governorship of the Punjab —a reform which was afterwards carried out in the time of Lord Curzon. He proposed the enrolment of an Indian peerage, and the formation of an Indian Privy Council of the ruling chiefs to consult with and advise the Viceroy. He tried to stop the tendency to pass too lenient sentences on Europeans who had assaulted their Indian servants. In a material and matter-of-fact generation he did not undervalue the effects of sentiment, pomp, and pageantry either on eastern or western minds, and his stately eloquence and striking presence effectively graced a great occasion. It is difficult now to understand the opposition and even ridicule aroused in England by the Royal Titles Bill, which conferred the title of Kaisar-i-Hind upon the sovereign of England. It stirred the personal loyalty of the great Indian princes, and without having the purely Muhammadan associations of the title *Padishah*, which would have alienated the Hindus, it suggested the vanished majesty of the Mughal empire and the political union of the Indian peoples beneath the sway of one great imperial throne. The opposition leaders in Parliament resisted the passage of the Bill on constitutional grounds, holding that the title of 'Queen' implied obedience to law, while that of 'Empress' signified the supremacy of force. 'We have seen him', said Lord Hartington, 'mimicking at Delhi the fallen state of the Mogul empire.' 'If it be true', said Gladstone, 'and it is true, that we have not been able to give India the benefits and blessings of free institutions, I leave it to the right honourable gentleman (Disraeli) to boast that he is about to place the fact solemnly on record .... I for one will not attempt to turn into glory that which, as far as it is true, I feel to be our weakness and our calamity.' Such language has to-day an unconvincing ring; it put an unneces sary construction on the meaning of the imperial title, was certainly unjust to the great achievements in social reform of Indian statesmen, and overlooked the fact that India is not altogether a congenial soil for the full development of mid-nineteenth-century Liberalism. Official opinion in India, though for different reasons, was not at first enthusiastic. Quiet unostentatious work, rather than outward show, is the honourable tradition of the civil service. When Lord Lytton proclaimed Queen Victoria Empress of India on January 1, 1877, in a durbar of unsurpassed magnificence, the famine was alreading casting the shadow of poverty and death over southern India, and many held that the hour was ill chosen for so gorgeous a pageant. But ceremonials of this nature can hardly be postponed, and the members of the civil service, as they stood in the great assembly on the famous Ridge, must have recognized that there was a measure of political wisdom in occasionally displaying to the ruling princes and their ministers not only the dry results of a sound administration but something of the might and splendour of that empire in which both British servants of the Crown and Indian rulers and statesmen occupied each his appointed place.

CHAPTER VIII

LORD RIPON AND THE ERA OF CONSTITUTIONAL REFORM

AFTER the settlement with Afghanistan, Lord Ripon was not called upon to deal with any other serious question of foreign policy. His own interest, like that of Lord William Bentinck, whose Indian career in many points resembled his own, lay in the field of political and social reform. Lord Ripon was indeed of a different stamp from the typical Viceroy, and in his whole political outlook was the very antithesis of his immediate predecessor. He was a true Liberal of the Gladstonian era, with a strong belief in the virtues of peace, *laisser faire*, and self-government. Hitherto the great material benefits conferred upon India had been almost entirely the work of an enlightened and disinterested bureaucracy, which was more concerned to labour for the people than to train them for political duties. This aspect of our Indian empire was in its early stages natural enough. 'The English nation in India', said Burke, 'is nothing but a seminary for the succession of officers. They are a nation of placemen. They are a republic, a commonwealth without a people. They are a state made up wholly of magistrates.' 'In India', said Sir Robert Montgomery in 1871, 'we set aside the people altogether; we devise and say that such a thing is a good thing to be done and we carry it out without asking them very much about it.' Among men of Indian race who had received an education on English lines there was growing up a strong and altogether natural desire to play a more active part in the administration of their country, and to introduce into the East those conceptions of constitutional and representative government with which their newly acquired western knowledge made them, in theory at any rate, acquainted.

With these aspirations Lord Ripon heartily sympathized, and he was determined to take some forward steps in the direction of liberalizing the Indian government. His views, as was natural, met with considerable opposition from a majority of officials, and whether the trend he gave to British policy in India was good or evil in its results is still regarded by many as an open question. To one party of Indian administrators, at any rate, he seemed to move too fast and too far, to put too unquestioning a trust in certain *doctrinaire* and *a priori* articles in the Liberal creed, to overlook the fact that western institutions, which require, even in the home of their origin, a long and painful experience for efficient working, rarely admit of being transplanted to eastern soil, and finally to have paid excessive attention to the aims of a small though clamorous section of society, which had little real sympathy with, or claims to represent, the great mass of the peoples of India.

But many Englishmen recognized that some advance in this direction was now inevitable. We ourselves had educated the rising generation—had inspired them with ideals and ambitions, and we could not stultify our own policy by keeping them in a permanent state of tutelage. Support sometimes came to Lord Ripon from quarters whence it might have been least expected. 'Men who really sympathise with the natives', wrote Lord Northbrook in 1880, 'do not grow on the hedges in the official hierarchy', and he declared in 1884 that the civil service 'with all their magnificent qualities have strongly ingrained in their minds, except some of the very best of them like M. Elphinstone and George Clerk of old and Aitchison, Lieutenant-Governor of the Punjab now, that no one but an

Englishman can do anything. . . . Ripon's main lines of policy in these respects have my cordial support.'[1] It need not, however, be assumed that those who honestly dissented from the new policy were swayed by any unworthy motives of jealousy or race hatred. Even in western lands the progress of a nation along the path of self-government is at first slow and halting, and the 'unforeseen tendencies of democracy' present many unlovely features. Lord Ripon's opponents were not prepared to look with equanimity on the sacrifice of efficiency, which to some extent was necessarily involved in handing over departments of administration from highly trained officials to nominated or elected boards, and they often imagined that Lord Ripon ignored this consequence of his policy. But he had not ignored it. He was prepared to face it. 'It is not primarily with a view to improvement in administration', ran the resolution, introducing one of his reforms, 'that this measure is put forward and supported. It is chiefly desirable as an instrument of political and popular education.' With the robust faith in democracy that was characteristic of him, he wished that Indians should learn even in the hard school of experience and disillusion the lessons of self-government and self-control.

We may now deal with Lord Ripon's policy more in detail under the headings of (i) Tariff and Revenue, (ii) the Decentralization of Administration and Financial Control, (iii) Freedom of the Press, (iv) Education, (v) the Protected States, (vi) Social Reforms.

In regard to the first of these points Lord Ripon was fortunate in his time. Financial circumstances were peculiarly favourable to experiments in internal reform. The great fiscal measures of Sir John Strachey now bore fruit, and there ensued four years of prosperity with an elastic and rising revenue. Surpluses instead of deficits became

[1] Mallet's *Northbrook*, p. 133.

normal features of Indian budgets. A few years later the conditions would have been less favourable, because famine, plague, the rapid fall of exchange, and increased military expenditure were destined to impose a severe strain upon the Indian exchequer. The Indian government seized the opportunity of favourable seasons to complete the Free Trade policy begun by Lord Northbrook and developed by Lord Lytton. In 1882 Major Evelyn Baring (afterwards Earl of Cromer), the finance minister, removed from the tariff all the five per cent. *ad valorem* import duties which could have any protective force. The only dues left were those on articles such as salt, wines and spirits, subject to internal excise, and one on ammunition and arms, retained for purely political reasons. In the same year the salt tax was lowered throughout India. But in one important point, that of land revenue, Lord Ripon was not able to carry his policy. In 1883, as we have seen (see p. 395), the home government had finally abandoned the proposal which had been before them for twenty years, of establishing a permanent settlement of the land revenues throughout India. Lord Ripon now suggested an alternative course, namely, that in districts, which had once been surveyed and assessed, the government should pledge itself to make no further enhancement except on the sole ground of a rise in prices. This compromise would have happily combined the ideal of comparative permanency with that of a certain incidence, while leaving to the government an open door for an increase of revenue if there was a general rise in prosperity. The moderate reform party in India has always deeply, and with good reason, regretted that it was not accepted by the Secretary of State.

The reforms under the second of our main headings, viz. the decentralization of administrative and financial control, were the most important of all and were those especially associated in the popular mind with Lord Ripon's administration. They are not very easy to summarize, but it may be said that by them the people were granted in matters of local and municipal administration a greater and more real share in the management and superintendence of their own affairs. A system of local boards or corporations was established, beginning with the unit of revenue administration known as the 'tahsil' or 'taluka'. These boards were entrusted with the management of such funds as the government of the province considered them capable of administering. To larger bodies was given the charge of public works, education, and similar public duties. Whereever possible the election by rate-payers of representatives to the corporations rather than their nomination by government was to be introduced. This was no new principle, popular election having been sanctioned in the municipal government of Bombay in 1872 and afterwards adopted in the other Presidency towns and elsewhere, but the practice was now greatly extended. The corporations of many towns were henceforward allowed to elect independent members as chairmen in place of the executive officer who had before this guided their deliberations. 'It was the policy of Lord Ripon's government', says Mr. R. Nathan, 'to substitute outside control for inside interference in municipal matters.'[1] Some control assuredly was, and still is, necessary. The proper working of free institutions is not to be learnt in a generation, and so, while municipalities are required to undertake some duties, encouraged to attempt others, and given certain financial powers and responsibilities, they are usually controlled by a district collector or commissioner of the division. The government in regard to municipalities retains powers of inspection, of providing for neglected duties, and even of suspension in case of gross default.

In the third place Lord Lytton's Vernacular Press Act

[1] *Imperial Gazetteer of India*, vol. iv, p. 289.

was removed from the statute book, and newspapers written in oriental languages were thus again allowed equal freedom with the rest of the Indian press in dealing with social and political questions, a freedom which later on was unhappily in some cases abused.

Fourthly, a commission of twenty members, under the presidency of Mr. (afterwards Sir) W. W. Hunter, inquired into the extent to which the principles of the Court of Directors' dispatch of 1854 had been carried out. The result was that regulations were laid down for the increase and improvement of primary and secondary schools, hitherto, in comparison with the universities, rather neglected by the state.

Fifthly, in the relations of the British government to native states, it was peculiarly fitting that it should fall to Lord Ripon to carry out by the 'rendition' of Mysore a notable act of grace to a Hindu dynasty, but the credit of this act belongs to Lord Lawrence and to Sir Stafford Northcote, who had determined on this policy in 1867. The actual administration of Mysore, it will be remembered, was sequestrated in 1831 by Lord William Bentinck owing to the misgovernment of the raja set upon the throne, as a minor, by Lord Wellesley in 1799. Lord William Bentinck afterwards came to believe that he had been to some extent misled by exaggerated reports of oppression in Mysore, but the Company declined to reverse the sequestration. The deposed raja died in 1867, and the British government then decided that his adopted son, as soon as he came of age, should be re-invested with the rule of Mysore. This event occurred in 1881, and he was installed with due ceremony by Lord Ripon, though very stringent regulations were made to prevent the country losing the benefits of British rule which it had enjoyed for half a century. All laws in force at the time were to be maintained and efficiently administered, no material change in the system of government was to be made without the consent of the Governor-General in Council, all settlements of land revenue were to be maintained, and the raja was to conform to such advice as the Governor-General might give him on details of administration.

Lastly, in social matters a modest beginning was made—not before it was necessary—of legislation to regulate and improve the conditions of labour in Indian factories. An act was passed in 1881 restricting the hours of employment of children between seven and twelve years of age to nine hours a day, requiring that dangerous machinery should be properly fenced, and appointing inspectors. In 1883 the Indian government found itself involved in terrible stress and turmoil arising from the delicate and difficult question of race distinction. By the criminal procedure code of 1873 it was enacted that no magistrate or sessions judge could try an European British subject unless he were himself of European birth, though in the Presidency towns this rule did not apply. By 1883 some of the Indian members of the covenanted civil service had risen by seniority to the stage when they would become magistrates or judges in the courts of sessions, and it was felt to be highly invidious that they should not possess the same rights as their European colleagues in the service. The Indian government accordingly determined to abolish 'judicial disqualifications based on race distinctions'. Mr. (now Sir) C. P. Ilbert prepared a Bill for this purpose. In spite of the fact that the change would have affected very few cases, and that no evil had resulted from Europeans appearing before Indian judges in the Presidency towns, a fierce and persistent agitation against the Bill immediately sprang up among Europeans in India. Indian opinion, as was natural, enthusiastically supported the proposed change. Deplorable bad feeling and animosity ensued between the contending parties. The reform was almost as much disliked by the rank and file of the civil service as by the non-official European residents in India. The Viceroy was subjected to something very like insult, and practically all intercourse ceased between him and those of his countrymen who were unconnected with the government. In the end the authorities were forced to bow before the storm, and agreed to a compromise which practically amounted to a surrender of the principle for which they were contending. It was decided that every European subject brought before a district magistrate or sessions judge (whether an Indian or European) could claim to be tried by a jury, half of whom were to be Europeans or Americans. As Indians could not make a similar claim, the privileged position of Europeans was still maintained, and the endeavour of the government to remove race distinctions was thus completely foiled. But if Lord Ripon had forfeited popularity among his countrymen he had at any rate won, by his championship of their cause, the enthusiastic devotion and support of men of Indian birth. On his resignation, in 1884, the route of his journey to Bombay was lined with acclaiming and admiring crowds, and his name has ever since been enshrined in the hearts of the nationalist party in India as the great champion of their cause on the Viceregal throne.

CHAPTER IX

LORD DUFFERIN. ENGLAND, RUSSIA, AND AFGHANISTAN. THE CONQUEST OF UPPER BURMA

LORD RIPON was succeeded by the Earl of Dufferin, whose long public career in politics and diplomacy gave him the best possible preliminary training for his high office. He had been Under-Secretary of State for India twenty years before (1864–6) when Sir John Lawrence was Viceroy; from 1872–8 he had been Governor-General of Canada; he had then become successively Ambassador at St. Petersburg and Constantinople, and special British Commissioner in Egypt. In the first of these diplomatic posts he was brought into close relation with Great Britain's chief rival in Asia, and in the other two he had an opportunity of studying the methods and policy of the first Muhammadan power in the world.

Lord Dufferin was one of the foremost diplomatists of his time, an eloquent and graceful speaker, and a man of great personal charm. He was therefore peculiarly well fitted to smooth away the exasperation and bitterness engendered by the controversy on the Ilbert Bill. He met the crisis with tact, a sense of humour, and a determination not to allow a question of social and personal rights to become a dangerous political issue. The turbulent waves of this unhappy tempest of race feeling gradually subsided before the suave and masterly inactivity of a Viceroy who was so thoroughly, in the best sense of the phrase, a man of the world. But Lord Dufferin was rather old for a Viceroy, he was not eager to attack new problems or initiate new policies, and he was content to keep a light hand on the reins of administration. He addressed himself to the tasks of his office with the ability and tolerance borne of his long political experience in many lands, but there is sometimes a hint of weariness in his attitude, and after four years had elapsed he asked to be relieved of his duties before the full period of his appointment had expired.

Questions of foreign policy again became prominent in his time, one on the north-western frontier and another on the extreme eastern boundary line.

Abdur Rahman since the cession of Kandahar had consolidated his power in Afghanistan at the cost of much hard fighting and had reduced his subjects to an unwonted condition of obedience and order. It was certainly as well both for the 'buffer' state itself and for the Indian empire that this process of consolidation should have been coming to completion just as the tidal waters of the Russian advance were breaking on the northern outposts of Afghanistan. In 1876 the khanate of Khokand had been finally incorporated into the Russian empire. In 1879 the Russian General Lomakin had suffered a serious defeat at the hands of the Tekke Turcomans, a warlike and virile race, but in 1881 they were vanquished and their territory annexed. In 1884 British dread of Russian designs, which had remained for some time in abeyance, was roused once more to activity by the fall of Merv, a town about 150 miles from the frontier of Afghanistan. A fictitious importance had always been attached to this place by politicians in England and much popular excitement was caused by its passing into Russian hands. In the end this proved advantageous both for India and Afghanistan, for it brought about a better understanding between Great Britain and Russia and the more accurate delimitation of the Afghan boundary line. At one time, however, there was the greatest possible danger of a calamitous sequel. Lord Ripon's government had already accepted a Russian proposal for a joint commission to demarcate the northern boundary of Afghanistan, and the first meeting of the commissioners, after much delay on the part of Russia, had taken place at Sarakhs on the Persian frontier in October, a month before Lord Dufferin had assumed office. The boundary line in dispute was that lying between the rivers Hari Rud and Oxus. The British commissioners under Sir Peter Lumsden, when they arrived, found the political atmosphere heavily charged with electricity. Both Russians and Afghans, recognizing that possession is nine points of the law, were unscrupulously endeavouring to occupy as much as they could of the debatable land, and were everywhere quietly pushing forward their outposts.

The chief dispute centred round Panjdeh, a village and district a hundred miles due south of Merv where the Murghab and Kushk rivers unite their waters. The whole position was complicated and difficult. The commissioners were subordinate to the Foreign Offices of London and St. Petersburg respectively, and neither the government of India nor the Russian Governor-General of Turkestan had direct control over them. The home government had not yet definitely made up their minds as to the lawful extent of the Afghan claims and were still negotiating with the Russian ambassador in London. To add to Lord Dufferin's anxieties, he had not only to maintain the interests of the Indian government but to act also for Abdur Rahman who, as Sir Alfred Lyall pertinently observes, 'could not be much blamed for the profound distrust with which he usually regarded the acts and motives of the two foreign states which were saving him the trouble of laying down his own frontier '.[1]

The Russian General Komaroff, a rough and hot-tempered

[1] Article, 'India under the Marquis of Dufferin', *Edinburgh Review*, January 1889.

soldier, found some Afghan troops already in possession of Panjdeh, which appears undoubtedly up to this time to have been looked upon as belonging to the Amir. He promptly ordered them to evacuate the place and on their refusal attacked them and drove them out with heavy loss. The position was now extremely critical. Russia, in order to support her claims, had been moving forces from Transcaspia towards Afghanistan, and since Herat was only about one hundred and twenty miles south of Panjdeh, the Indian government had been clearing the lines of communication on the north-west frontier and assembling an army corps at Quetta to march across the Amir's country to the relief of Herat in the event of war. There were present therefore all the materials for a serious conflagration, and it looked as though the two empires of Russia and Great Britain were at last destined to drift into that 'war in all parts of the world' which Lord Lawrence had presaged as the penalty for the violation of the Afghan frontier. Indeed when the news came of the outrage at Panjdeh hardly any responsible person in England at the time thought that the danger could be averted. Popular opinion was greatly inflamed against Russia, there was something approaching a panic on the stock exchange, the Conservative opposition were clamorous for strong action, and Gladstone, the Liberal Prime Minister, speaking of the situation as one of extreme gravity, asked for and readily obtained a vote of credit for eleven millions.

The disastrous issue of war was averted by the labours of diplomatists, the tact of Lord Dufferin, and, above all, by the shrewd common sense of Abdur Rahman. Most fortunately at the time of the collision the Amir was actually on a visit to Lord Dufferin at Rawal Pindi. The Afghan, as Sir Alfred Lyall points out, does not regard a border skirmish as a thing about which it is worth while to make unnecessary trouble. The Amir declared that he was not sure whether Panjdeh really did belong to him, nor did he particularly covet its possession. He would be content to waive his claims to the place in exchange for Zulfikar, which lay about eighty-five miles to the west. The coolness and imperturbability of Abdur Rahman saved the situation, and certainly conferred upon Great Britain some return for the subsidies she had paid him in the past. It is likely enough that the apparent nonchalance of the Amir veiled a very complete grasp of the whole question and a resolute determination to avoid at all costs war between England and Russia of which his own country would necessarily be the theatre. 'Afghanistan', he declared, 'was between two mill stones and it had been already ground to powder.' 'My country', he wrote afterwards in his Autobiography using different imagery, 'is like a poor goat on whom the lion and the bear have both fixed their eyes and without the protection and help of the Almighty Deliverer the victim cannot escape very long.'

Lord Dufferin was able therefore to telegraph home that there was no need to make a *casus belli* of Panjdeh, and that the Afghan boundary commission might resume its work. Accordingly, though Sir Peter Lumsden had been recalled, Sir West Ridgeway continued his labours. The joint commission after long negotiations agreed upon a frontier line from the Hari Rud over the spurs of the Paropamisus range to the low ground of the Oxus valley, but they were unable to come to a satisfactory understanding as to the exact point where the line should touch the Oxus. Accordingly Sir West Ridgeway, after visiting the Amir at Kabul and discussing the matter with Lord Dufferin at Simla, proceeded to England. Finally, after prolonged negotiations between Kabul, Simla, London, and St. Petersburg, the line of demarcation was settled by a protocol signed at St. Petersburg in July 1887. What had been accomplished was of very considerable importance. Sir West Ridgeway declared that by the new boundary the Amir did not lose a penny of revenue, a single subject, or an acre of land. The settlement of the frontier up to the line of the Oxus put definite limits to the Russian advance in the direction of Herat, which strategists have agreed to look upon, though why is not quite clear, as the key of India. Farther east in the direction of the Pamirs the Russian forward movement still continued until, as we shall see, another Anglo-Russian convention was signed in 1895. 'The boundary pillars', says Sir Alfred Lyall, 'now set up by British and Russian officers on the Hindu Kush and by the Oxus record the first deliberate and practical attempts made by the two European powers to stave off the contact of their incessantly expanding Asiatic empires.'

The war scare left enduring marks on the body politic of India. The hurried military preparations laid an extra burden of two millions on the Indian exchequer and were followed by a permanent increase in the strength of the army both native and European. When the crisis was most acute many of the native states spontaneously tendered their services to the government, and from their offer sprang in 1889 the Imperial Service Troops, that is to say, forces available for wars waged by the supreme government 'when placed at the disposal of the British government by their rulers'. They were recruited in the protected states, officered by Indians, and only inspected by British commanders.

Lord Dufferin's conference with the Amir of Afghanistan at Rawal Pindi in 1885 did much to strengthen the latter's goodwill to the British. Sir Alfred Lyall, who was present at the time, has given us a vivid portrait of the Afghan ruler, 'a short burly man dressed in black half-uniform coat decorated with two diamond stars, with long black boots and an astrachan cap; a prince of frank and even bluff yet courtly manners; quite at his ease amid a crowd of foreigners; speaking pleasantly of the first railway journey he had ever undertaken; a man of some humour in jokes, with a face occasionally crossed by a look of implacable severity—the look of Louis XI or Henry VIII—that is now never seen in civilised life'.

The personal charm and tact of the Viceroy exerted much the same influence over Abdur Rahman as that of Lord Mayo had done over his predecessor Sher Ali, but again it was made clear that the reigning Amir was just as determined as his predecessor had ever been to exclude, at all hazards, British troops and officers from Afghanistan. Lord Dufferin criticized the weakness of the fortifications of Herat and proposed to send English Royal Engineers to strengthen them; but against this suggestion Abdur Rahman was obdurate on the ground that the Afghans would at once imagine that their independence was being attacked, and that mischief would result. Fortunately Lord Dufferin showed greater readiness than Lord Lytton to appreciate the Afghan point of view, and he refrained from pressing his suggestion, recognizing that this intense jealousy for their national integrity would inspire the Afghans with bitter enmity against any people seeking to make their country a base for the invasion of India. Abdur Rahman left the conference gratified with the honours paid to him, impressed by the evidences of India's military strength, and with sentiments of warm friendship for the Viceroy.

On the eastern frontier of the Indian empire the conquest of Burma was completed. The first Burmese war in 1826 had resulted in the annexation of Arakan and Tenasserim, the second in 1852 in that of the province of Pegu. Upper Burma, now cut off from all access to the sea, had hitherto remained independent. The Burmese still refused to give any facilities for British trade within their country. In 1878 the accession to the throne of Thebaw, a cruel despot, and

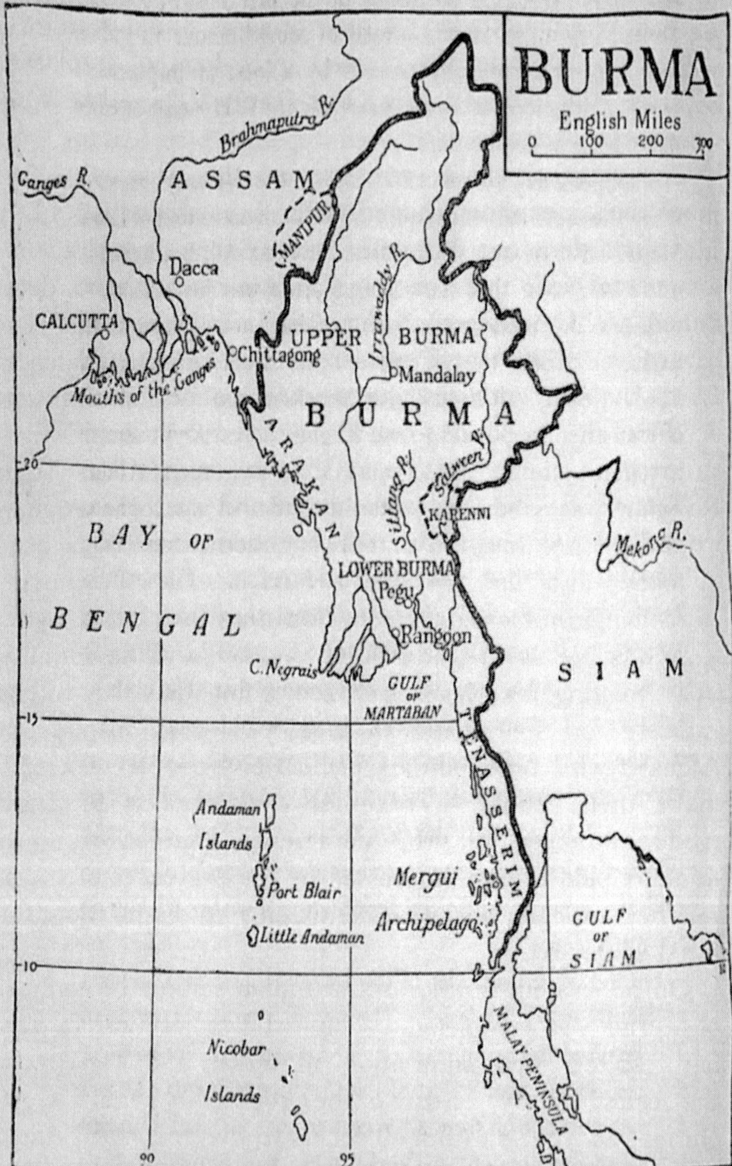

BURMA
English Miles
0 100 200 300
Brahmaputra R.
Ganges R.
ASSAM
MANIPUR
Dacca
CALCUTTA
Chittagong
Mouths of the Ganges
UPPER BURMA
Irrawaddy R.
Mandalay
BURMA
ARAKAN
Salween R.
Sittang R.
KARENNI
Mekong R.
BAY OF BENGAL
LOWER BURMA
Pegu
Rangoon
C. Negrais
GULF OF MARTABAN
SIAM
TENASSERIM
Andaman Islands
Port Blair
Little Andaman
Mergui Archipelago
GULF OF SIAM
MALAY PENINSULA
Nicobar Islands
20
15
10
90
95

his contemptuous treatment of the British envoy made it necessary to withdraw our representative in 1879. Negotiations for a renewed treaty in 1882 came to nothing, and British merchants in Rangoon and Lower Burma began to urge the annexation of Thebaw's dominions. But it is doubtful whether either the king's ill-treatment of his subjects or the importunity of the Rangoon traders would in themselves have moved the Indian government. Thebaw, however, began to negotiate commercial treaties with Germany, Italy, and especially with France, whose colonies in Indo-China approached his eastern frontier. This, though it seems impossible to question his right to do so, really brought upon him his doom. As the result of a Burmese mission to Paris in 1883, a French envoy proceeded to Mandalay in 1885. He made arrangements to establish a French bank in that city and, though the French government disclaimed all knowledge of his proceedings and recalled him, the government of India seized the opportunity afforded by the fact that the Burmese had imposed a heavy fine upon a British trading company to press matters to a crisis. Lord Dufferin insisted on a further inquiry. The King of Ava declined to reopen the case, whereupon an ultimatum was sent to him demanding that he should admit a British envoy at Mandalay, suspend proceedings against the company till the envoy arrived, have no external relations with foreign countries except on the advice of the Indian government, and grant the British the right to trade with the Chinese through his dominions. The Burmese government declined to accept these terms unless they were modified in certain particulars. Troops which had been already collected at Rangoon were now ordered to advance. General Prendergast invaded Upper Burma by a flotilla advancing up the Irrawaddy. The Burmese, who appear to have been taken completely by surprise, made hardly any resistance. The king surrendered unconditionally when the army approached his capital, and within ten days the first stage of the war was over. On January 1, 1886, Upper Burma, a country with an area rather larger than that of France and a population of four millions, was annexed by a curt proclamation, after the consideration and rejection of two alternative schemes, the first to set up a buffer state, the other to rule it through a British Resident.

But now began the real difficulty of the occupation. Isolated bands of armed men, taking refuge in the dense jungles which cover a great part of the country, maintained a harassing guerrilla warfare that often degenerated into mere brigandage and dacoity. Many British civil and military officers lost their lives. Considerable reinforcements had to be sent into the country, and desultory fighting went on for two years. Upper Burma was only subdued by establishing a system of small fortresses dotted all over the turbulent area, from which as a base, mobile columns operated. Gradually, under Sir Charles Bernard as Chief Commissioner, the settlement of the country was carried out. Skilled civil servants with wonderful celerity set up the machinery of British administration, political divisions were formed, roads, bridges, and railways were built, revenue assessments made, and laws promulgated.

In view of the tremendous difficulties of the task, the criticism passed in England on Lord Dufferin and the Indian government for the prolongation of military operations was certainly unfair; the justice of going to war at all might perhaps be more reasonably called in question. Indeed our action in annexing Burma involves a difficult problem of political casuistry. The whole procedure of the Indian government in the matter was high-handed and rather relentless. It may be conceded that Thebaw was a savage and unenlightened monarch, nor could it be reasonably denied that the bulk of the Burmese people were infinitely better off under the civilized régime of their new masters. It is also true that the Burmese had treated our traders with contumely, but it would be hypocrisy to maintain that the tyranny of the king or even the impediments he put in the way of British commerce would by themselves have brought about his downfall. 'If . . . the French proceedings', wrote Lord Dufferin before the war began, 'should eventuate in any serious attempt to forestall us in Upper Burma, I should not hesitate to annex the country.'[1] An impartial critic might hold that the French from Indo-China had at least as much right as the British from India to extend their influence over Burma, or even more, seeing that they came into the country at the express invitation of the king, who was, nominally at any rate, independent. But Great Britain rightly or wrongly considered that, having already conquered two-thirds of the Burmese country, she had a kind of latent right—a reversionary lien of annexation—to acquire the rest, rather than that it should pass under the sway of any other European state. The ethics of the relations between powerful western empires and weak eastern nations are admittedly difficult to disentangle, but it is to be feared that the abstract rights of semi-civilized countries receive scant recognition when great colonizing powers converge upon them.

The conquest of Burma involved some modification of India's diplomatic relations with the Chinese empire which claimed a vague suzerainty over that country. Although the claim was at this date merely formal, it could not be altogether ignored by the Indian Government. The circumstances of the time enabled a compromise to be effected. Tibet also owed allegiance to China, and Great Britain had just extracted from Pekin a very reluctant consent to the dispatch of a commercial mission to Lhasa. Now the

[1] *Life of the Marquis oj Dufferin and Ava*, by Sir Alfred Lyall, 398.

Tibetans themselves had shown very plainly that they intended, whether supported in their action by China or not, to oppose the entry of the mission into their country. A very awkward question therefore was settled in 1886—though to the bitter disappointment of those who had projected the Tibetan business—by an agreement now made with China that the mission should be abandoned on condition that the Chinese waived their claims to sovereignty over Burma and offered no objection to its annexation by Great Britain. There still remained, however, some little difficulty with the Tibetans. The road from India along which the mission was to have proceeded runs through Sikkim, a small independent state under British protection. The Tibetans, in order to bar the path to their country, had already marched into Sikkimese territory and fortified a port at Lingtu. All peaceful means to make them withdraw having failed, and China being either unwilling or unable to coerce them, they were driven back across their own frontier by British troops in 1888.

CHAPTER X

THE ADMINISTRATION OF LORD LANSDOWNE. THE FORWARD POLICY

In December 1888 the Marquis of Lansdowne took over the charge of the government of India. The most serious internal problem of his period of administration was the effect upon the currency system of the great world-decline in the value of silver. This decline was due primarily to the increased production of silver through the opening of new mines, which was one of the chief economic features of the latter part of the nineteenth century. A secondary cause was the demonetization of silver by Germany and the renunciation of bimetallism by the states of the Latin Union. Thus the silver coins, which circulated in most of the important countries of Europe, became henceforward token money only. Some curious economic results followed. None of the countries, whose currency was based upon a gold standard, suffered any appreciable loss. Countries with a silver standard but with few foreign liabilities to meet were affected to only a moderate extent. But silver-standard countries with heavy indebtedness to gold-standard countries were subjected to severe financial strain. India, of course, came under the last category. The bulk of her commercial and monetary dealings are with Great Britain; she is a debtor country in relation to her suzerain, and the balance of her indebtedness, which includes the charges on her public debt, interest on capital invested in India, pensions and India Office expenses, has to be discharged in gold. It is obvious that as the value of silver relative to that of gold declined, more rupees had to be paid for every pound sterling. The burden tended to become heavier in two ways; every year the rate of the fall of the rupee became accelerated, and owing to augmented imperial burdens following on the annexation of Burma and the growing expenditure on public works of all kinds, the amount of necessary remittances home steadily increased. Originally the value of the rupee was two shillings and threepence; for many years before 1873 it had remained constant at about two shillings. From that date, for the reasons given above, it began to fall, and after 1885, at a rapidly increasing rate. In 1890 the rupee was only worth one shilling and fourpence. The following year owing to special legislation in America there was a momentary rise, but in 1892 the value of the rupee touched bottom at one shilling and a penny.

It would not be easy to exaggerate the economic evils that resulted. The situation in 1894 meant that India through no fault of her own but owing to the interaction of economic world-forces had to pay almost fifty per cent. more than in 1873 to discharge a similar sum in London. It was calculated that in 1892, before the rupee stood at its lowest figure, six millions sterling more than would otherwise have been necessary had to be raised by taxation from the Indian peoples. The fluctuations of exchange produced unexpected deficits, and upset the forecasts of the most painstaking finance minister. They checked the flow of capital from Europe and paralysed commercial and mercantile transactions. The government was forced to restrict expenditure on necessary public works, and was naturally loath, even when prospects were apparently favourable, to remit taxation, which, through an unexpected drop in exchange, might afterwards have to be reimposed. Part of India's increased indebtedness was represented by an excess greater than normal of her exports over her imports, for none who study the phenomena of international trade will need to be told that the sums due from her were remitted to England in commodities rather than in bullion or specie. Twice as many goods valued in rupees had therefore to be sent to this country to discharge the same sum as expressed in sovereigns as before 1873. But such an artificial stimulus to her oversea trade only benefited one class, the producers of goods for exportation, while it reacted adversely on the general welfare of the community, who were being taxed that producers for export might enjoy this indirect bounty.

To meet their increasing obligations the government had recourse to further taxation. An income tax, which is always peculiarly unpopular in India, was reimposed, and the tax on salt which was both unpopular and, in the eyes of many, retrograde, was enhanced. Even these measures were mere palliatives, and the government warned the Secretary of State that, unless some more permanent remedy could be found, the condition of India would become financially bankrupt and politically dangerous. In 1892 the Indian government had proposed to the Cabinet that a fixed ratio between gold and silver should, if possible, be established by international agreement, or, if that expedient failed, that the Indian mints should be closed to the free coinage of silver with the view of ultimately introducing a gold standard. The International Monetary Conference met at Brussels in November and December 1892 and was attended by Indian representatives, but it separated without agreeing upon any solution. The home government, therefore, on the advice of a committee presided over by Lord Herschell adopted, with some modifications in detail, the second of the alternatives proposed to them, and in 1893 the Indian mints were closed to the unrestricted coinage of silver, gold coin or bullion being received in exchange for rupees at the rate of fifteen for a sovereign or an equivalent weight of metal. The rupee, however, still continued to fall till 1895 when, as we shall see, the decline was at last checked.

In 1890 a serious outbreak occurred in Manipur, a small independent hill state on the borders of Assam. An interregnum in the government was followed by a disputed succession. The anarchy reached such a pitch that the Viceroy determined to intervene on the ground that 'it is admittedly the right and duty of government to settle the successions in the protected states of India generally'. Quinton, the Chief Commissioner of Assam, was sent with an escort of four hundred men to investigate the causes of the revolution. An attempt to arrest the Senapati, or commander of the army, who had brought about the revolution and usurped the government, failed owing to the rising of the Manipuris. After some fighting the Chief Commissioner and three others were enticed to a conference and murdered under circumstances of the greatest treachery and brutality. The junior officers left in command of the escort lost courage and retreated to British territory, for which conduct they were afterwards cashiered. But the attacks of the Manipuris upon the frontiers of Eastern Bengal were repulsed, the capital was speedily occupied by British troops, and the murderers, including the Senapati himself, were executed. In spite of the provocation given, no annexation followed. The chieftainship was conferred upon a minor chosen from among the cadets of the royal house, and Manipur was administered during his nonage by a British political agent who took the opportunity of abolishing slavery in the state.

Another revolution occurred in a protected dependency at the very opposite extremity of India. In 1892 the Khan of Kalat, besides other cruelties, executed his Wazir together with the victim's father and son. The British government summoned him to Quetta to answer for his crimes, and with the assent of the Sirdars of Kalat forced him to resign, though they acknowledged his son as his successor.

The Viceroyalty of Lord Lansdowne was marked by a certain activity on the frontier lines of the Indian empire both to the north-east and the north-west, due to the fact that through the absorption of weaker states the great empires of England, Russia, France, and China were tending to converge upon a common centre. Russia's recent extension of her southern Asiatic railways, the advance of France in Indo-China to the line of the Mekong, and the British conquest of Upper Burma had drawn closer the web of international relations of all the powers affected. Their boundaries were not yet conterminous—they had not reached that stage of relative stability—but were in that transitional condition when the spark of political electricity seems most likely to generate explosive forces. It is the modern practice in the East for every great power to have extending outwards from the actual frontier a belt of territory defined by Lord Lansdowne as a 'sphere of influence, within which we shall not attempt to administer the country ourselves, but within which we shall not allow any aggression from without'. These spheres of influence beyond the actual boundary resemble the open ground round a fortress whence trees and buildings have been removed to prevent their affording cover to an enemy; the space is not occupied by the garrison, but it can be swept by their fire if necessary, and no foe would be allowed to establish himself there. So in these over-frontier regions the protecting power, while not interfering in the internal affairs of the people, reserves the right to remove an unfriendly government and to pass through its roads if need arise. The danger is that countries seldom remain permanently in the status of 'spheres of influence'. They tend naturally to be absorbed cither with their own consent or by coercion within the political boundary proper; when this happens, fresh spheres of influence are pushed forward till the outposts of empires advancing from opposite directions tend at last to meet, and form highly dangerous points of contact.

A good deal of work was done in Lord Lansdowne's time in extending and defining British Protectorates, especially on the north-eastern and eastern frontiers. Our influence and authority were spread out over Sikkim—the boundary between that country and Tibet being demarcated—the Lushais who inhabit the hill country north-east of Chittagong, the Chins a little farther east, the Shan states beyond the Irrawaddy, and Karenni, a native state on the eastern Burmese frontier.

On the north-western frontier things did not go so smoothly. Just as Lord Mayo had won the personal regard of the Amir Sher Ali, while a coolness sprang up under his successor Lord Northbrook, so the excellent relations with Abdur Rahman established by Lord Dufferin were not at first maintained with Lord Lansdowne. The great Afghan Amir never really wavered in his friendly attitude towards Great Britain, which was based on a shrewd conception of his own interests, but his feelings towards individual Viceroys varied from cordiality to coldness according as they exhibited a tendency to keep at a respectful distance from his frontier or to draw near to it.

Lord Lansdowne, with his somewhat austere standard of statesmanship and his colder and more reserved temperament, could not have been expected to win, as his predecessor had done, the private friendship of the Amir, and Abdur Rahman resented what he called the Viceroy's 'dictatorial' letters 'advising me upon matters of internal policy in the administration of my kingdom, and telling me how I ought to treat my subjects'. In fact, till the closing years of Lord Lansdowne's period of office there was a marked estrangement between the Afghan and Indian governments, due to the changed course of British foreign policy. There was, as has been already described, a belt of tribal territory, about 25,000 square miles in extent, between the British frontier and the Afghan boundary line. The tribes nominally owed allegiance to the Amir, who was very jealous of any interference with them, valuing their interposition as a screen between his country and the British lines. He had little control over them for good, though he found it easy, if he wished at any time to embarrass his powerful neighbours, to foment disturbances amongst them. They were always ready on the least encouragement to harry British trade routes and to raid across the frontier; while the Afghan government could always remain discreetly in the background, pleading a regretful incapacity to restrain their turbulent feudatories. The only method of redress open to the Indian government was a punitive expedition from time to time, followed by the destruction of offending villages and a retirement to its own borders. The Forward school had long clamoured for the extension of strategic railways, the definite settlement of an Afghan-British frontier, and the reduction to order of the whole tribal territory. The arguments against this proposal were the heavy cost which would be involved, the great extent of country to be subdued, and, most important of all, the certainty of permanently estranging Abdur Rahman. These considerations weighed heavily with the responsible authorities, who felt rightly that the Indian government should put up with many inconveniences rather than offend the feelings of so important an ally. Nevertheless, while Lord Roberts, who held that a policy of non-interference with the tribes was 'not altogether worthy of a great civilizing power', was Commander-in-Chief, some cautious steps were taken in the direction of the Forward policy, which caused great uneasiness to Abdur Rahman and were not always approved of even by military authorities. 'The border policy of late years', wrote Sir John Adye, 'has in many instances been too aggressive and regardless of the rights of the tribes.' A strategic railway was completed up to the Bolan Pass, and a general activity was evident along the frontier line from Quetta to Kashmir.

In Kashmir occurred some rather obscure movements and intrigues which have not hitherto been thoroughly elucidated. In 1885 a new Maharaja, Pratap Singh, had succeeded. In 1888 Plowden, the British Resident, was recalled by Lord Dufferin for a tendency to interfere too drastically in the internal affairs of the country. In 1889 Lord Lansdowne, acting on certain vague and indeterminate charges, which were never properly substantiated, took over the government of the country, entrusting it to a council under the control of the British Resident. The action seemed likely to lead to the annexation of Kashmir, and an alarm was raised in the House of Commons. The adjournment of the House was moved by Bradlaugh in July 1890, and a debate ensued. Whether as a result of the action of Parliament, or for some reasons unavowed, the Maharaja was restored in 1905, and no further attempt was made to control the administration in Kashmir.

In 1888 a mission under Mortimer Durand was on the point of starting for Afghanistan to attempt to remove the Amir's apprehensions and justify British policy, but was postponed owing to the rebellion of Ishak Khan, which detained Abdur Rahman for two years on the distant frontier of Afghan Turkestan. As a result the position became still more strained. The Amir looked with great distrust upon British activity in Gilgit, a frontier province of Kashmir. A British officer had been sent there in 1889 owing to a rather needless fear of Russian aggression. His presence was resented by the chiefs of Hunza and Nagar,

[1] *Indian Frontier Policy*, by General Sir John Adye, G.C.B., 1897, p. 58.

two small states owning a loose allegiance to Kashmir. They attacked Gilgit, but were defeated and punished. The real importance of Gilgit is that it gives direct communication with Chitral, a small state with an area rather larger than that of Wales and a population of about 80,000 hardy mountaineers, which commands the easiest and least elevated passes across the Hindu Kush. In 1892 the chief died, and his son only secured himself in the succession after some difficulty. This afforded a pretext for the sending of an English envoy, Dr. Robertson, who arrived in Chitral in 1893. Abdur Rahman looked with great distaste upon the gradual approach of the ubiquitous British agent and the pushing forward of railways to the very mouths of the passes leading into his country. The position was very critical, and Lord Lansdowne admitted that at this time 'all the conditions were calculated to lead to misconceptions and strained relations'. The statement is fully corroborated from the Afghan side, for Abdur Rahman declared that Afghanistan and Great Britain were brought to the very verge of war. Fortunately the crisis passed away, and before Lord Lansdowne laid down his office a satisfactory settlement was attained. In 1892 it had again been proposed to send a mission to Afghanistan, but in selecting Lord Roberts as the envoy an unfortunate blunder was made, for he had always been a prominent defender of the Forward policy, and the fact that he had played a great part in the Second Afghan War did not make the choice of the Indian government any the more tactful. The Amir, who had no intention of receiving Lord Roberts, played his cards astutely. He announced that owing to troubles in the Hazara country and the state of his health he could fix no date for receiving the mission. Having thus delayed matters till Lord Roberts had left India, he proclaimed himself ready to receive Sir Mortimer Durand, who was appointed envoy. The reception of this mission and the task it accomplished show how great a change had passed over the Afghan-Indian problem, and how thoroughly Abdur Rahman held his turbulent subjects in hand. Once more a British envoy entered the city with its sinister memories of his two predecessors, Burnes and Cavagnari, done to death. Durand proceeded without an escort, his protection being left solely to the troops of the Amir. He entered Kabul on October 2 and left it on November 16. Within that time all causes of friction with Abdur Rahman were investigated, a thoroughly satisfactory settlement of all disputed points was negotiated, and an important agreement signed. The Amir engaged for the future not to interfere with the Afridis, Waziris, and other frontier tribes. The boundary line where possible was to be demarcated by Afghan and British commissioners. Certain districts were ceded to Abdur Rahman, and in return he agreed not to interfere in Swat, Bajur, Dir, or Chitral, and gave up his claims to the railway station at Chaman. The Indian government promised to raise no objections to the purchase and importation by the Amir of munitions of war, and increased his subsidy from twelve to eighteen lacs of rupees. Cordial relations between the two governments were now completely restored. Abdur Rahman, declaring that his officials had been driven out of Waziristan and other places, and that the new Chaman railway station had been built on his territory without permission, prophesied—and with truth as the sequel proved—that war would some day break out in the tribal country. He summed up shrewdly the results of the mission by saying: 'Sir Mortimer Durand's mission reconciled matters by giving me some sort of compensation, and I am quite contented and satisfied that I have gained more than I have lost by British friendship. I merely mention these facts to show . . that though England does not want any piece of Afghanistan, still she never loses a chance of getting one—and this friend has taken more than Russia has.' Further, the Amir accepted an invitation to come to England, but was ultimately prevented by illness from carrying out his intention. His second son, Nasrullah Khan, was sent to represent him in 1895, but his visit proved a failure; Abdur Rahman was disappointed that his request to have a representative at the Court of St. James was not granted.

When Lord Lansdowne laid down his office in 1893 the viceroyalty was offered to Lord Cromer, who 'for private reasons' declined it. It was then accepted by Sir Henry Norman, the Governor of Queensland, but after the lapse of sixteen days he, too, asked to be relieved of the office, considering after reflection that his advanced years (he was sixty-five) rendered him unequal to so heavy a burden. The government appointed to succeed him Lord Elgin, the son of the Governor-General of 1862–3.

CHAPTER XI

MEASURES OF SOCIAL AND ADMINISTRATIVE REFORM, 1885-92. THE INDIAN NATIONAL CONGRESS

THE events of Lord Dufferin's and Lord Lansdowne's Viceroyalties which most vividly struck the popular imagination have been described in the preceding chapters. It will be convenient here to deal with certain measures of social and political reform, rather repellent in detail but of great intrinsic importance, which were passed about this time. Some of them were initiated by Lord Ripon, some were only carried to fulfilment by Lord Lansdowne, while others were inaugurated and completed under Lord Dufferin. So careful and deliberate is the working of the Indian legislature that few first-class measures in modern times can be classified as the work of any single administration. Questions settled by one Viceroy are often found on examination to have been raised, discussed, and partially solved by one or more of his predecessors.

In the field of social reform three great agrarian measures were passed in Lord Dufferin's Viceroyalty. The first of these was the Bengal Tenancy Bill of 1885, initiated and all but carried to completion by Lord Ripon, which further extended and amplified the provisions of the Bengal Rent Act of 1859. It gave the ryot greater security of tenure at judicial rents, put restrictions on the practice of indiscriminate eviction, and framed rules for the settlement on equitable principles of disputed questions between landowners and tenants. The government, indeed, in this Act dared to interfere with the operation of free competition when such competition subjected a defenceless peasantry too rigorously to the will of the landlords. Opponents maintained that the new law was an infringement of the Permanent Settlement of 1793, and that the Indian government was failing to keep its pledged word with the zamindars. But the Viceroy's answer was that both this measure and its predecessor, the Act of 1859, were only rather belated attempts to carry out the supplementary reforms which Cornwallis himself had intended to introduce. Later followed an Act dealing with Oudh, the ground for which also had been prepared by Lord Ripon. It afforded increased security to the tenants-at-will not protected by Lord Lawrence's Act of 1868, and gave them, if ejected, compensation for any improvements they had made within the preceding thirty years. Finally, in 1887 a Bill on the same lines was passed to define and protect the rights of cultivators in the Punjab.

Two important Acts, one relating to the economic and the other to the moral welfare of the people, were passed in Lord Lansdowne's time. The first was a factory Act, which amended and amplified the measure of 1881. The hours of employment for women were limited to eleven *per diem*. The minimum age for children was raised from seven to nine years and the maximum from twelve to fourteen. They were only to be employed for seven hours, and that in the day-time. All workers in a factory of any age or sex were to have a weekly holiday. Secondly, the Age of Consent Act raised the limit within which protection was given to young girls from ten to twelve years. As in the case of Lord William Bentinck's abolition of *Sati*, the cry was raised that the government's action was an infringement of the clause in the queen's proclamation of 1858 promising that the religious scruples of the Indian people should be respected. But Lord Lansdowne refused to be moved by such arguments, declaring that the pledges of the famous proclamation must be read with the reservation 'that in all cases where demands preferred in the name of religion would lead to practices inconsistent with individual safety and the public peace, and condemned by every system of law and morality in the world, it is religion and not morality which must give way'.

In 1885 the first session was held at Bombay of the Indian National Congress, an unofficial body of men representing the advanced party of Indian reformers. That party was the direct offspring of the higher education on western lines imparted by the Indian universities since the educational changes of 1854. It was nourished, as we have seen,[1] on the study of the Whig and Radical political philosophy of the eighteenth and nineteenth centuries. The quick intelligence of the more advanced Indian races, especially that of the Bengalis, applied the lessons thus acquired to the conditions of their own existence with a relentless logic that sometimes proved disconcerting to their instructors. Their avowed aim was the establishment in India of that democratic and constitutional system which, as existing in western lands, they had been called upon to contemplate as the highest stage of political evolution. The Congress itself crystallized into a permanent form the demonstrations organized to do honour to Lord Ripon on his retirement. Its members professed loyalty and friendliness to British rule, but they pressed for the introduction into India of representative institutions and a larger share for men of their race in the executive and legislative councils of the state.

The full significance of the first meeting of the Indian National Congress has only been revealed in our own time. It was easy then to point out the anomalies of its position and to expose the extravagance of some of its claims; to

[1] See Part I, p. 304.

deny, for instance, even its right to the title 'National', on the ground that its members, as Lord Lytton in one sense truly said, 'really represent nothing but the social anomaly of their own position'. They were drawn at first almost entirely from the small section of Indians who spoke English and had acquired a western education. They had very little claim to speak for the great mass of their fellow countrymen, the dumb millions of agriculturists whose one absorbing interest is the wresting of a decent livelihood from the soil, who work out their destiny under the paternal care of British collectors, on the plains. Again the attempt of the Congress to clothe national ideals, which are often feudal and aristocratic in nature, with the drapery of democratic aspirations, produces an effect which is bizarre and incongruous in the extreme. For a long time its activities were looked upon with disfavour by the greater part of the Muhammadan community and the ruling chiefs. Yet undoubtedly some movement of this nature was sooner or later inevitable, and is indeed the logical result of some of the best tendencies of British rule in India. The Congress party in the past has done valuable work in directing attention to genuine grievances. Many of its leaders have been men of moderation, ability, and true patriotism, and from this time onward year by year it gradually extended its influence and sway over the minds of the educated Indian classes.

Lord Dufferin recognized that the aspirations of the party or, at any rate, the more moderate section of it, were natural enough. It was as yet impossible to set up in India any system of democratic government on the English pattern, but not impossible to accept the suggestion of the Conference for the widening of the basis of the legislative councils both of the Viceroy and of the subordinate governments. Already in 1886 a legislative council similar to that existing in the three great Presidencies had been established in the North-west Provinces, now the United Provinces of Agra and Oudh; Lord Dufferin's suggestion, recalling that of Lord Lytton, was 'to give quickly and with a good will whatever it may be possible or desirable to accord; to announce that these concessions must be accepted as a final settlement of the Indian system for the next ten or fifteen years; and to forbid mass meetings and incendiary speechifying'. He declared indeed that he would feel it a relief if in settling administrative questions he 'could rely to a larger extent than at present upon the experience and counsels of Indian coadjutors'. Before he laid down his office his government suggested that new members, representing as far as possible different classes and interests, should be added to the legislative councils, that the Viceroy's council should annually discuss the budget submitted by the finance minister, and that the right of putting questions to the executive should be allowed to members of council as to the British House of Commons. This last reform, he declared, would both be a valuable concession to the reform party and give the government a recognized and constitutional means of justifying its policy. All these suggestions, with certain modifications in detail, were carried out in the time of his successor by Lord Cross's Indian Councils Act of 1892, which enlarged the legislative councils of the Indian governments. In the imperial council of the Viceroy the additional members were to be at least ten and at most sixteen, and not more than six were to be men holding official positions. The Act gave the Governor-General in Council the power to lay down conditions under which the members should be nominated so as to be representative of different classes and interests. In accordance with this provision it was decided to appoint ten non-official members; four selected by the provincial legislatures, one by the Calcutta Chamber of Commerce, while the remaining five were nominated by the Governor-General. The provincial legislatures of Madras and Bombay were also enlarged by twenty members each, not more than nine of whom were to be official. The non-official members were nominated by municipalities, university senates, and various trading associations. Thus the representative, if not the elective, principle was cautiously introduced into the councils, though as yet both in the Supreme and in the Provincial legislatures an official majority was guaranteed. The functions as well as the constitutions of the councils were enlarged. Up to this time the Viceroy's council had only the right to discuss the government's financial policy when fresh taxation was imposed. Hereafter, as Lord Dufferin had suggested, the budget was to be laid each year before the council and every member rising in turn could discuss and criticize it. The right of interpellation, i. e. of questioning the executive officers as to their administrative acts, was also granted under much the same kind of restrictions that are imposed in the British House of Commons.

These reforms, though they did not satisfy the extreme wing of the advanced party, constituted a notable step forward in the direction, if not of Indian self-government, yet of Indian participation in the highest administrative functions. Henceforward men of Indian birth sat at the same council board as the Viceroy and the executive ministers. Though they could not outvote the official majority if it was solidly arrayed against them, on all questions where there was a difference of opinion they could often determine the issue, for they formed usually about a third of the total council. In any case they had the right of expressing their opinions; their views were listened to with deference, and it was incumbent upon the Viceroy and his lieutenants to meet their criticisms.

The permanent Civil Service also underwent reorganization at this period. We have already seen that the statutory

Civil Service set up in Lord Lytton's time had disappointed expectations.[1] The Public Service commission, which sat in 1886–7 under the presidency of Sir Charles Aitchison, exhaustively considered the whole question, and its recommendations were carried out in 1891. The statutory Civil Service was abolished. Henceforward the civilian officers of the government were divided into three classes—the Imperial Indian Civil Service, the Provincial, and the Subordinate Service. The first was still to be recruited in England, but was open to Indians who made the journey to England and sat for the examination in London. The other two services were recruited in India almost altogether from Indians. Admission to the Provincial service was to be made in one of three ways: by examination, nomination by the Provincial governments, and promotion from the subordinate service. The members of the Imperial Civil Service held the majority of the most important posts; executive, administrative, and judicial offices of lesser but still considerable importance were filled by the officers of the Provincial service. To the subordinate service were allotted positions of minor importance. In 1893 the government of India was embarrassed by a rather unexpected Resolution of the House of Commons in favour of holding simultaneous civil service examinations in England and India. The local governments in India, with the exception of Madras, reported unfavourably on the proposed change. The Resolution was not followed by an Act and so remained merely an expression of the academic and pious opinion of the legislature in one of its impulsively Liberal moods.

[1] *Supra*, p. 459.

CHAPTER XII

FAMINE, PLAGUE, AND FRONTIER WARS. LORD ELGIN'S ADMINISTRATION

THE Viceroyalty of Lord Lansdowne to some extent closes an epoch. Under his rule the surface of the sea of Indian politics had been singularly unruffled. The only disturbing features were the steady fall in exchange and the cycle of deficits in the annual budgets—signs that the era of financial prosperity dating from Sir John Strachey's fiscal reforms was for the time at an end. India indeed was about to enter upon a period of toil and stress, of famine, plague, and harassing frontier wars—events which were destined to be followed by widespread social and political unrest, and ultimately by far-reaching constitutional changes. For two years Lord Elgin, Lord Lansdowne's successor, enjoyed comparative tranquillity, but at the end of that short respite he was confronted with difficulties which taxed every branch of the Indian administration. Lord Elgin was the head of an old and traditionally Liberal Scottish family. His reputation was that of a sound and cautious administrator, and it was unfortunate for him that he was called upon to deal with problems, which would have severely tried the ablest Governors-General, who have guided the destinies of India. Wisely, perhaps, he eschewed heroic measures, allowing himself for the most part to be ruled by the advice of his permanent officials. His administration came in for a full share of criticism, not all of it quite fair or generous. Some mistakes were made, some hesitation shown, and his grasp of the helm of state might perhaps have been at times a little firmer and more confident, but at least he held on his course through very stormy seas and suffered no shipwreck.

The state of the finances first claimed attention. The closing of the Indian mints to the free coinage of silver failed, as we have shown, to have any immediate effect, and chiefly through the continued fall in exchange the new Viceroy was confronted in his first budget with the prospect of a serious deficit. Drastic measures were called for and the Indian government reluctantly decided to reimpose the old general duty of five per cent. on all imports, cotton goods alone being excluded. As to this exception a fierce controversy naturally arose. The duties were imposed for revenue alone, and though most economists admitted that they must necessarily have some slight protective effect, protection for Indian commodities was certainly not the motive for imposing them. It was argued with some force that the cotton spinners of Lancashire ought to put up with the same disability as all other British manufacturers, and though it might be logical to force upon India a general policy of free imports, to except Manchester goods alone from a general revenue tariff was really to give them a kind of indirect protection. The truth of this was admitted by many Free Traders who would have strongly opposed the imposition of any duty on cotton goods when imports were generally free. At the end of the year the financial position was still so serious that cotton goods were included in the tariff, but as a corresponding countervailing excise duty was levied on the products of Indian mills, the Indian manufacturers, so far from being mollified, were the more exasperated. In 1896 after a long and heated controversy both the import and the excise duties were reduced from five, to three and a half, per cent. The perennial question of the interest of India *versus* the interest of Manchester was thus no nearer a permanent solution, but the monetary problem for a time, at least, was settled. It is true, as already mentioned, that the value of the rupee continued to fall till 1895 when it reached its lowest point at one shilling and a penny, but after that year (whether through the continued closing of the mints, the restrictions on the import of silver, or more general causes, is still a matter of dispute) it gradually rose to the value of one shilling and fourpence, the point at which the government proposed to maintain it, by introducing a gold standard at the rate of fifteen rupees to the sovereign.

In 1895 an important military administrative reform came into operation which the slow-moving machine of the Indian government had been maturing since 1879, a period of sixteen years. The change had received the approval of many Governors-General, and the details were worked out between the home and the Indian authorities under Lord Dufferin and Lord Lansdowne. In the old system there had been three Presidential armies under three Commanders-in-Chief, and just as the Commander-in-Chief of Bengal had been a member of the Viceroy's council, the Commanders-in-Chief of Bombay and Madras had been members of the councils of the two subordinate Presidencies. Henceforward there was to be a Commander-in-Chief of the whole Indian army, and under him four Lieutenant-Generals for the forces in Bengal, Bombay, Madras, and the North-west Provinces with the Punjab. What appears at first sight to have been a mere adjustment of administrative detail has a further interest as being the belated recognition of the unification of India under the conquering and absorbing power of Great Britain. The 'three army' system was an anachronistic survival recalling the fact that in the past each of the three Presidency towns was an outpost of British dominion in the eastern world surrounded by belts of hostile territory. From these three settlements the waves of British conquest had flooded out across the peninsula, till the territories of all the Presidencies were linked together. The Indian states that survived were encircled in the Pax Britannica, and Madras and Bombay now possessed no frontiers to defend, or hostile neighbours to overawe. Except for garrison and routine duty, troops in India were rarely needed except on the great arc of her continental boundary extending from the Baluchistan border to the eastern confines of Burma.

The year 1895 was also noteworthy for the report of the commission appointed by Act of Parliament in 1893 to inquire into the extent of opium consumption in India, its effects on the physique of the people, and the suggestion that the sale of the drug should be prohibited except for medicinal purposes. The preparation of opium in British India is a state monopoly, and a considerable revenue is derived from it. Government limits and regulates the cultivation of the poppy and maintains two factories at Ghazipur and Patna for the manufacture of the drug. The larger part of the product was exported to China, and the rest retained for Indian consumption. There had always been a party in England which strongly objected to this instance of state production as immoral, holding that the revenue derived from it should be sacrificed on ethical grounds, whatever the economic loss involved. They believed that the consumption of opium, whether by eating or smoking, was pernicious to health and degrading to the character, and considered that the Chinese in the 'opium war' of 1842 had been unrighteously coerced into allowing the importation of the drug against their will and in detriment to the best interests of their country. On the historical point the defenders of the government allege that when the Chinese in 1842 destroyed the opium chests they were actuated, not by any motive of preserving their countrymen from a degrading habit, but by a hatred of foreign trade and the erroneous economic belief that China was being drained of bullion to pay for an excess of imports over exports. The argument is not perhaps very convincing, and it may be maintained with some plausibility that war is a rather severe penalty to impose upon a nation for an honestly held, though mistaken, theory of international trade. The apologists of the government were on stronger ground when they contended that in the Treaty of Tientsin of 1858 China without any coercion voluntarily permitted the importation of opium. The commission reported that there had been much exaggeration as to the evil effects of consumption. They compared indulgence in it to indulgence in alcohol in western countries; of both commodities a temperate use was unobjectionable, and total prohibition was no more reasonable in one case than in the other. They declared that it was for China to take action if she desired to prohibit the importation of the drug, that the state control really ensured a considerable restriction of cultivation, since poppy cultivation was only allowed in definite areas, that Indian opium was the best and purest form of the drug procurable, and that the Chinese, if deprived of it, would only use larger quantities of their own home-grown supply, which was of a very inferior quality. Finally, turning from the ethical to the economic standpoint, the commissioners declared that the Indian exchequer could not afford as yet to surrender the revenue from opium. The report seems plain common sense to men of moderate opinions. Neither opium smoking nor drunkenness will ever be stamped out by government regulation, and prohibition would inevitably be followed by illicit production and smuggling on an extensive scale. The promoters of the anti-opium agitation of course were not satisfied, and were destined to win a further victory for their cause. By arrangement with the Chinese government a gradual decrease of the export trade on a progressive scale was guaranteed to begin from January 1908.

In 1896 the two scourges of famine and plague devastated the land. India had been free from famine for nearly twenty years, and this was the first occasion on which the famine code of 1883 was put to the test. The rains were deficient in 1895, and in 1896 they almost completely failed. The United and Central Provinces, Berar, some districts of Bengal, Madras and Bombay, Rajputana and Upper Burma passed beneath the desolating shadow of scarcity and drought. There were three-quarters of a million deaths in British territory alone, and in the spring of 1897 4,000,000 people were receiving relief. The cost to the state, including necessary remissions of revenue, amounted to more than five and a half millions sterling. The most scientific and successful work in combating the famine was done in the United Provinces (then known as the North-west Provinces), while in the Central Provinces, partly owing to the great difficulty of administering relief to the aboriginal tribes of that region, the record was comparatively one of failure.

An event of even more sinister import than the failure of the monsoons was the notification at Bombay in August 1896 of the first case of bubonic plague. Less terrible in its immediate effects, its ravages were destined to be ultimately far more permanent and devastating. The worst famines rarely last into the second year, and the kindly forces of nature with their wonderful recuperating power soon restore to parched lands and stricken peoples fertility and abundant sustenance. The deadly virus of plague infection advances by insidious steps, strengthening month by month its deadly grip upon paralysed cities and provinces. In spite of every effort of science and human forethought the tale of its victims continues. For a time it seems to recede, and the curve of the death-rate falls for reasons that are often as inexplicable as those that govern its rise; but even as hopes are being formed that plague will be driven from the shores of India, it begins once more to gain in intensity. Plague has now existed in India for twenty-two years, and at the present time (1918), though it appears to be waning, it still claims a considerable toll of victims every year. The history of this curse of humanity stretches far back into the past. It is supposed by some authorities to be the disease which appeared in Athens in 431 B.C., decimated the population of Attica crowded within the walls of the capital owing to the Peloponnesian war, slew in Pericles the greatest of Athenian statesmen, and was described with relentless realism and poignant art by the pen of Thucydides. It was the Black Death of the Middle Ages which passed westward across Europe in 1346–9, swept away at the most modest computation one-third of the population of England, revolutionized the social and economic aspect of society, and put an end to the condition of villeinage. It appeared again as the Great Plague of London in 1665, drove the 'Committees' of the Caroline East India Company from Leadenhall Street, caused Parliament and the Court to fly in terror from London to Oxford, and taxed all the pathos and descriptive power of Defoe. In every case the death-laden path of the scourge ran from East to West. After each expansive outbreak of destructive power it gradually and sullenly receded to its pestilential fastnesses in Asia, lingering longest in the Balkans and the coasts of Asia Minor where the border lands of two continents meet under the suzerainty of the Turk.

In certain crowded festering centres of the Chinese empire the plague never died out, though its explosive and travelling energy seemed to be exhausted. But in the closing years of the nineteenth century, after a long period of brooding quiescence in remote parts of Asia, it once more became charged with a baneful activity. In 1877–8 it appeared for a time in Eastern Europe at Astrakhan in Russia. In the early nineties it spread slowly across China, and, probably brought by infected rats on grain ships from Hong Kong, it broke out in Bombay in the autumn of 1896, rapidly spreading among the crowded and squalid tenement houses of the native quarter, and causing an exodus of the panic-stricken population. By February 1897 it was estimated that 400,000 of the inhabitants had fled from the city. The government were at once faced with a difficult and delicate problem—the extent to which it was possible in view of Indian prejudices and convictions to put into force the scientific counsels of perfection pressed upon them by their medical advisers. The doctors drew up plans for house-to-house visitation, disinfection, isolation hospitals, segregation camps, and inoculation, all of which were intensely distasteful to the Indian population with their caste regulations and their jealousy of any infringement of privacy in their home life. In 1897 an Indian civilian and a military officer who had been engaged on plague work were assassinated at Poona. In March 1898 serious riots broke out in Bombay. The vernacular press had conducted an unscrupulous campaign against the Indian government's precautionary measures, and as a result the law against seditious publications was made more effective—an expedient which, however necessary, only intensified popular feeling. Though the opposition to plague restrictions was based on ignorance and panic, it was for the most part sincere and genuine enough. In 1898 this fact was recognized by the government of India, and the more stringent rules recommended by the medical experts were abandoned for milder methods which, since they respected the prejudices of the people, actually produced better results. All hope of stamping out the plague promptly had perforce to be given up, and the efforts of the authorities were henceforward directed towards keeping it under control.

On the frontier the storm centre was the north-west. The history of our first relations with Chitral has already been related in Chapter XI. By the Durand agreement of 1893 that little hill state, with its capital of the same name, had been included in the British sphere of influence. The Indian government had long been eager to exert some control over the country, especially its external relations. A British agency was now established at Gilgit, in Kashmir territory, with an outpost in Chitral at Mastuj, whence the British political officer from time to time visited the capital. In January 1895 the Mehtar, or ruler, of Chitral was assassinated at the instigation of Sher Afzal, an ex-Mehtar, and Umra Khan, the ruler of Jhandol. When the revolution took place Dr. (afterwards Sir George) Robertson, the British agent at Gilgit, proceeded to Chitral. The rebellious chiefs ordered him to retire to Mastuj and on his refusal besieged him in the capital. The Indian government sent Sir R. Low with a force of 15,000 men to fight his way northwards through the Malakand Pass and the country of the Swatis, who rose to support the Chitralis. Chitral, however, was ultimately relieved from the eastward by Colonel Kelly, who performed a notable military feat in marching from Gilgit to the beleaguered town through 220 miles of barren and hostile territory, crossing on his route the Shandu Pass, more than 12,000 feet above sea level. The garrison of about 500 men at the time of their relief had held out gallantly for forty-six days. Although Lord Elgin advised the retention of Chitral, the Liberal government of Lord Rosebery considered with some reason that, apart from our own interests, we had had very little justification for interfering in the internal troubles of the state, and they therefore decided on the evacuation of the country. Before this resolve could be carried out, the Liberal ministry fell from power and the Unionist government of Lord Salisbury reversed their decision and authorized the construction of a military road from Chitral to the British frontier with garrisons to protect it.

Over the reversal of the policy of evacuation and the building of the famous road a fierce controversy arose in England, and when the widespread movement on the north-west frontier of India began in 1897 the Liberal party were naturally inclined to attribute the trouble amongst the tribes largely to the retention of Chitral. So far they were acting entirely within their rights; there was a good deal of truth in their statement as to the fact, and their own policy of withdrawal received the warm support of many civil and military officers. But the whole development of the controversy affords a good illustration of the manner in which the violence of party may distort and embitter an imperial problem. In 1897 Mr. Morley and Mr. Asquith spoilt a good case by declaring that Lord Salisbury's government had been guilty of 'a breach of faith'. They based this accusation on the ground that it had been decided to retain Chitral in spite of the fact that Sir R. Low, when advancing through the country in 1895, had issued a proclamation to the tribesmen that no permanent occupation of their territory was intended. The government's reply was that by opposing Low's advance the Swatis had rejected the offer contained in the proclamation, and that they and the other tribal leaders had afterwards voluntarily entered into friendly arrangements to make and guard the road. But the most conclusive answer to the charge of bad faith was made by Lord George Hamilton, the new Secretary of State for India, who was able to show that the late Liberal government itself, when Lord Elgin suggested the policy of retention, dealt with the question from first to last as a matter of expediency, and never, in public dispatches at any rate, mooted the point that to accept the Viceroy's proposal would have been to violate a pledge. Sir Henry Fowler, the Secretary of State in the late administration, was obviously embarrassed by the fact that the zeal of his colleagues had so far outrun their discretion, and he did his best to restate their charge in more moderate language, with the result that the controversy came to a rather lame conclusion.

It can hardly indeed be doubted that our incursion into Chitral politics was one of the reasons that produced the serious risings over the whole extent of tribal territory in 1897, but there were many other contributary causes. The tribesmen had always been intensely jealous of their independence, and they looked with growing alarm upon some of the manifestations of the Forward policy of the preceding decade—the construction of roads and railways up to the limits of their territory and the gradual but persistent pushing forwards of British outposts. The delimitation by British officers of the boundary line between their territory and Afghanistan almost inevitably suggested to their suspicious minds that the same line was ultimately intended to be the northern frontier of British India; nor would it be fair to disguise the fact that an extreme minority of the advocates of the Forward policy did in fact desire such a consummation. The mad Mullahs, or fanatical priests of Islam, were for ever preaching in fiery language a crusade against the infidel Christian power that was threatening to absorb all independent Muhammadan territory. Abdur Rahman himself had recently issued a theoretical treatise on the *jehad* or holy war against unbelievers as enjoined in the Koran. Popular platforms in England at this time abounded in rhetorical abuse of the Sultan of Turkey, the head of the Muhammadan faith, for his treatment of the Armenians—abuse which, however well deserved, roused to fury much latent anti-Christian feeling.

The north-west frontier war broke out in June 1897 with a treacherous attack on a political agent and his escort in the Tochi valley. In July the people of Swat launched fierce onslaughts on the British fortified posts at Chakdara and the Malakand, which had been maintained since the

Chitral expedition. In August the Mohmands who dwelt north of the Kabul river raided up to the outskirts of Peshawar. Risings followed of the Afridis south of the river and the Orakzais in the neighbourhood of the Khyber Pass. The Afridis besieged the fortified stations on the Samana Ridge, one of which made an heroic defence, the Sikh garrison dying to a man at their post. The British fortresses in the Khyber at Ali-Masjid and Landi Kotal were held for a time by loyal Afridi tribal levies, but they were fiercely attacked and driven out by their countrymen.

It was now clear that the whole Pathan country was seething with rebellion and formidable forces were massed to crush the movement. There were two distinct campaigns. The first was directed against the Mohmands. The Malakand field force under Sir Bindon Blood relieved Chakdara in August and carried the war into their territory in September. After fierce fighting in a difficult and barren country the Mohmands made their submission in January 1898. The second campaign was in the Tirah valley south-west of Peshawar, the country of the Afridis, hitherto practically unexplored by Europeans. Sir William Lockhart was in command of a force of about 35,000. In October the heights of Dargai were brilliantly stormed with the loss of 199 killed and wounded. The whole valley was traversed and the fortified villages were destroyed, but the Afridis fought with great courage and skill, everywhere waging a perpetual guerrilla warfare, harassing the line of march, and cutting off all stragglers. We suffered some of our severest losses in desperate rearguard actions when the troops were being withdrawn from the country by two routes in December 1897. But the enemy had learnt their lesson, and when threatened with another invasion in the spring of 1898 they made submission, paid the fines imposed upon them, and surrendered their arms. A notable feature of these campaigns was that Imperial service troops under Indian princes fought side by side with the British forces. Our losses in the war were about 300 killed and 900 wounded. The military operations were the severest test to which the British army in India had been subjected since the Mutiny, not even excepting the Afghan war of 1878.

CHAPTER XIII

THE FOREIGN POLICY OF LORD CURZON IN THE NORTH-WEST, AFGHANISTAN, AND PERSIA

IN January 1899 Lord Elgin was succeeded by Lord Scarsdale's eldest son, the Hon. George Nathaniel Curzon,[1] who had made so promising a start in Parliamentary and Ministerial life in England that some surprise was expressed at his leaving Westminster. He was now in his fortieth year and had served in Lord Salisbury's government as Under-Secretary both for India and for Foreign Affairs. At his own request he was elevated to an Irish peerage instead of one of the United Kingdom, in order that on his retirement, if he desired it, he might not be debarred from continuing his career in the House of Commons. It had been for long the dream of Lord Curzon's life that he might one day hold the great position to which he was now appointed, and he had trained and prepared himself for it by wide and frequent travel in both the nearer and the further East. He had already sailed four times to India, and had visited Ceylon, Afghanistan, China, Persia, Turkestan, Japan, and Korea. He had enjoyed personal intercourse with the rulers of the last four countries. He had given to the world three important books on Asian questions. No Viceroy not an ex-civil servant ever took up his office with so full and extensive a knowledge of the problems to be faced in India.

It is no reflection on the able and sound administrators

[1] For the chapter on Lord Curzon the author desires to acknowledge his obligations to that brilliant and fascinating book *India under Curzon and After*, by Mr. Lovat Fraser, London, 1911.

who preceded and followed him, to say that Lord Curzon's viceroyalty was destined to stand out with special prominence. For good or ill no Governor-General since Dalhousie so deeply impressed his personal mark upon the whole framework of Indian administration, or so widely attracted to himself and to Indian questions the attention of his fellow-countrymen. It is not meant by this that there were no reasonable grounds of dissent from some part of his policy or justification for criticism. Much of what he achieved has still to be tested by the supreme criterion of time, and this generation stands far too close to the events of his administration to pass anything like a final verdict, but even Lord Morley of Blackburn, who belongs to the very opposite school of political thought and tradition, has admitted that 'the old system (of Indian government) had never been worked with loftier and more benevolent purpose or with a more powerful arm than by the genius and indomitable labour of Lord Curzon'. Like all strong men Lord Curzon sometimes came into sharp collision with the wills of others. He challenged criticism and invited enmities. He was too outspoken and too honourably careless of consequences to be popular. Endowed himself with powers of work that seemed almost superhuman, he exacted toil in proportionate measure from his colleagues and subordinates. His vivid and ardent temperament sometimes made him advocate a good cause with unnecessary vehemence. His masterful nature was not altogether favourable to initiative and independence in others. His sense of humour was, perhaps, not so highly developed as his other great qualities. Undoubtedly he tried to do too much. He drove his reforming plough onward a little too rapidly, a little too relentlessly. As they breathlessly pursued his high conception of efficiency, men sometimes sighed for the deliberate restraint and wise tolerance of Viceroys like Lord Northbrook and Lord Dufferin. No statesman ever yet lacked an opposition, and Lord Curzon had plenty of opponents; so that, what seemed to kindly critics to be an altogether admirable devotion to the duties of his high office, appeared to unfriendly and jaundiced observers as 'the bounding exuberance of a vain-glorious personality'. But when all the facts are reviewed, and when all possible deductions are made, Lord Curzon's viceroyalty must surely stand out as great and notable, great in the roll of the tasks actually achieved, great in the lofty sense of duty invariably displayed, in the exacting labours unremittingly fulfilled, and great in the stately and impressive eloquence which defended his policy before the bar of public opinion.

Lord Curzon's external policy was mainly concerned with the north-west frontier tribes, with Afghanistan, with Persia, and with Tibet. Of these problems the settlement of the tribal country in the north-west first claimed his attention. The Tirah campaign, as we have seen, had been concluded in the spring of 1898, but a year later, when Lord Curzon assumed office, about 10,000 troops were still quartered beyond the British boundary line in Chitral, the Tochi valley, Landi Kotal and the Khyber Pass. In Parliament Lord Curzon had ably defended Lord Elgin's policy in regard to Chitral and the construction of the famous road from that town to Peshawar, and he had generally been regarded as one of the ablest exponents of the forward school. But in India he clearly showed that he had little sympathy with its extreme advocates. It was, of course, no longer a matter of practical politics to evacuate Chitral, Quetta, and the posts already occupied, but short of that, Lord Curzon deliberately reversed the trend of frontier policy of recent years. Large numbers of British troops were gradually withdrawn from the Khyber Pass, the Kurram valley, Waziristan, and the tribal country generally, though isolated posts like the Malakand and Dargai just over the border were retained and fortified. Their place was taken by tribal levies trained and commanded by British officers. Down to 1914, for instance, the whole of the Khyber Pass was held by the Afridis of the Khyber Rifles. Within our lines our forces were increased and concentrated; strategic railways were built up to Dargai, Jamrud, at the entrance to the Khyber Pass, and Thal, the gate of the Kurram valley. A determined attempt was made to regulate and limit the importation of arms and ammunition to the tribesmen, and generally speaking, the latter were taught that, while we would scrupulously respect their independence, we should not tolerate outrages upon our frontier. The best defence of this policy is the fact that, with the exception of the blockade of the Mahsud Waziris in 1901, the fierce conflicts of 1897–8 were followed by ten years of peace. 'If anybody', said Lord Curzon, in the House of Lords in 1908 after his retirement, 'had been disposed to doubt the success of the scheme of frontier policy which has now been in existence for ten years, his doubts must have been dispelled, and I hope that we shall now hear no more of the wild-cat schemes for advancing into tribal territories, annexing up to the border, and driving roads through the tribal country.'

Hitherto the north-west frontier districts had been subordinate to the lieutenant-governorship of the Punjab, and the government of India could only indirectly control them. This arrangement dated back to the time when the Punjab was itself regarded as a frontier province, and was administered by the famous school of district officers who were purposely left by the government a large amount of freedom and initiative. Their relations with the people were personal and intimate, and as long as their methods were justified by success, they suffered little interference from Calcutta or Simla. But, as the British boundary line shifted further to the north-west, most of the Punjab became as much subject to law and regulations as the old settled provinces. Lord Lytton, as we have seen, had already suggested that the frontier districts should be placed under officers directly controlled by the supreme government. but the projected reform, though considered by Lord Elgin and Lord George Hamilton, had remained in abeyance. In 1901 Lord Curzon carried it through. The trans-Indus districts of the Punjab were joined with the political charges of the Malakand, the Khyber, the Kurram, Tochi, and Wana to form a new North-West Frontier Province, with an area of 40,000 square miles, under a chief commissioner directly responsible to the government of India. At the same time, in order to avoid confusion the old North-West Provinces were renamed the 'United Provinces of Agra and Oudh'. The change, though now almost universally approved, was not effected without much friction and opposition at the time. Some of the Punjab officials were aggrieved at the curtailment of their powers, and were offended at Lord Curzon's strictures on the former frontier record of the Punjab government—strictures which, it may be confessed, were unnecessarily vigorous.

The peace secured along the north-west frontier did much to improve our relations with Abdur Rahman, which since the troubles of 1897–8 had inevitably been critical. The Amir, indeed, was in an extremely difficult position. Though he was accused by many Englishmen at the time of secretly fomenting the trouble from his side of the frontier, the charge was probably untrue. The tribesmen appealed to him, and the majority of his own turbulent subjects would have been only too pleased to plunge into the troubled waters. But Abdur Rahman succeeded, and it was no mean feat, in keeping them in hand. In a vigorous proclamation he ordered them to keep the peace, denied that the movement was a *jehad*, or holy war, and declared that when the right time for such a crusade occurred he would announce it and put himself at their head. In 1900 the Amir published his autobiography, a work of great interest. His point of view was naturally different from our own, but the very complaints he makes against British policy testify to the value he placed upon our alliance. He asserts that the policy of the government of India in relation to his country has too often been inconsistent and vacillating. Great Britain should give her ally more material and moral support against Russian aggression, and should take him more into her confidence. He ought to be allowed to annex the territories of the tribesmen, and to form a triple alliance with the two great Muhammadan powers of Turkey and Persia. This able and sagacious ruler died in September 1901, and perhaps the greatest testimony to his power was the fact that, against all the precedents of Afghan history, his son Habibullah was allowed to succeed peaceably, and no internecine civil war broke out between the numerous sons of the late Amir. Our relations with Habibullah, at first, were hardly as cordial as they had been with his father. The Indian government regarded the treaty with Abdur Rahman as personal to that ruler only, and desired that it should now be renewed. The new Amir, however, argued that the agreement was one between the two countries and that a renewal was unnecessary. For some years intercourse almost ceased between Afghanistan and the Indian government, and Habibullah refrained from drawing his subsidy. No doubt he had internal difficulties of his own, and it is at any rate in his favour that he succeeded in holding back his unruly subjects from serious depredations across the frontier. Three years later (November 1904) when Lord Curzon was in England, before he embarked on his extended period of office, Lord Ampthill, the acting Viceroy, sent Sir Louis Dane on a mission to Kabul. The mission, which remained at the Afghan capital from December 12, 1904 to March 29, 1905, was so far successful that better

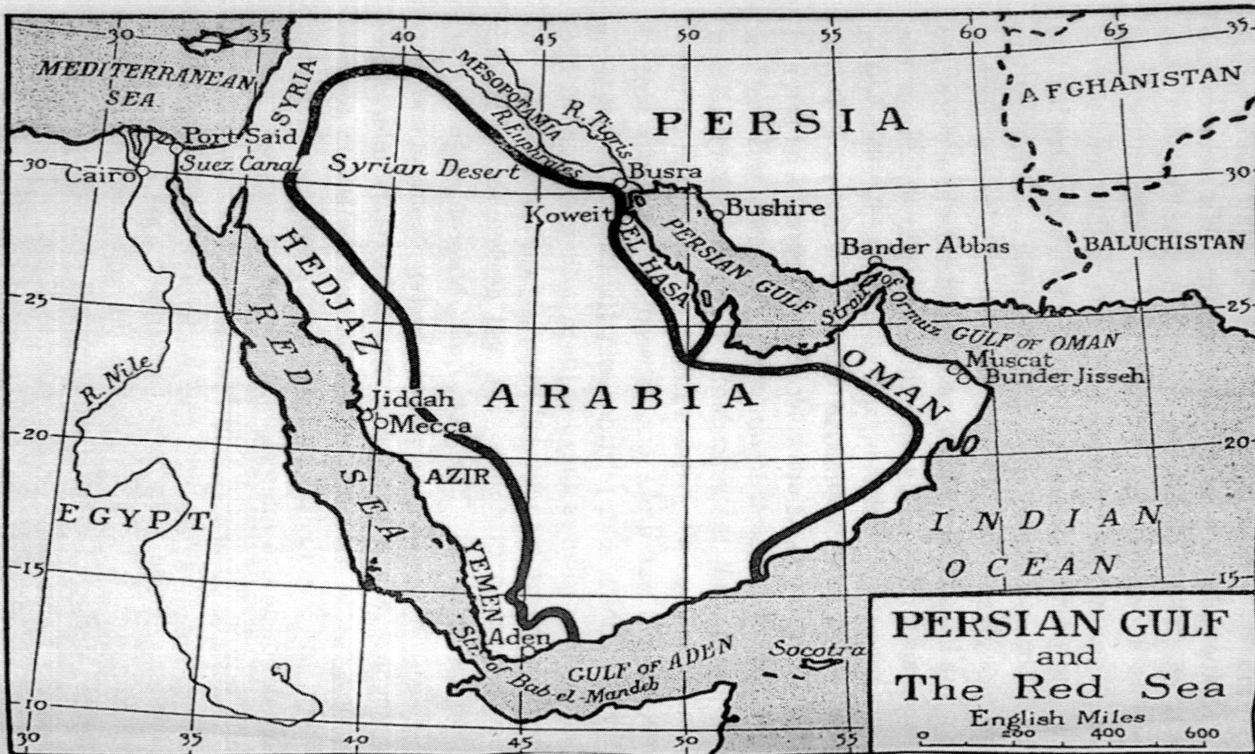
PERSIAN GULF
and
The Red Sea
English Miles
0 200 400 600
MEDITERRANEAN SEA
SYRIA
Port Said
Suez Canal
Cairo
Syrian Desert
MESOPOTAMIA
R. Tigris
R. Euphrates
PERSIA
AFGHANISTAN
BALUCHISTAN
Busra
Koweit
Bushire
Bander Abbas
EL HASA
PERSIAN GULF
Strait of Ormuz
GULF OF OMAN
Muscat
Bunder Jisseh
OMAN
ARABIA
HEDJAZ
Jiddah
Mecca
AZIR
YEMEN
Aden
Str. of Bab-el-Mandeb
GULF OF ADEN
Socotra
RED SEA
EGYPT
R. Nile
INDIAN OCEAN

relations were established with the Amir, but only at the price of concessions which, according to some critics, seriously impaired our credit and prestige. Habibullah certainly treated the envoy rather cavalierly and arrogantly claimed the title of 'His Majesty' for himself. In the end this claim was allowed, and his view of the treaty was accepted, whereupon he consented to draw the arrears of his subsidy.

Within the preceding twenty years Indian foreign policy had been increasingly concerned with the Middle East, and especially with the Persian Gulf. Great Britain's influence in that landlocked sea had always been of a unique character. It had steadily grown by prescriptive right, and till the end of the nineteenth century it was practically unchallenged because, with a wise prevision, no definite claims in regard to it had ever been put forward by British statesmen. The Gulf was one of the main areas of British exploration and commercial enterprise in the seventeenth century. We had cleared it of the piratical craft that once infested it, had patrolled and policed its waters, and since 1853 had kept it open to vessels sailing under every flag. The need of maintaining over the seas the route to India caused us to claim a general control over all the coastline eastwards from Aden to Baluchistan, though we have not questioned the sovereignty of independent Arabian tribes, the Ottoman government, the Sultan of Oman and the Shah of Persia over the territories along the shore. So, too, in the Gulf itself we have never desired to acquire land on either seaboard, but we will allow no other European nation to obtain territorial stations there. In time, as was inevitable, our attitude attracted the rather resentful attention of other powers. In 1892 a French statesman declared in the Chamber of Deputies that Great Britain's claim to keep order by herself in the Persian Gulf, and to be sovereign arbiter of all disputes between Arabian, Persian, and Turkish chiefs was 'exercised in a form European diplomacy had never recognized'. This statement, though it ignored actualities, had a certain literal truth about it, and for eleven years from this date France, Russia, Germany, and Turkey, by diplomatic activity in the Gulf and neighbouring waters appeared to be deliberately testing the validity of our unavowed claims. In 1898 the Sultan of Oman, in violation of a secret agreement with Great Britain of 1891 debarring him from alienating any part of his dominions to a European power, granted to the French a coaling-station at Bunder Jisseh, five miles south-east of Muscat, with the right to fortify it. In 1899 when this transaction became known, a small naval squadron was sent by Lord Curzon from Calcutta and, under threat of a bombardment of the Sultan's palace, the concession was revoked. In the negotiations that followed this drastic action, in London and Paris, the French accepted our view that a former treaty of 1862 precluded either country from acquiring any territory in the State of Oman. In 1900 a similar attempt of Russia to obtain a coaling-station on the northern shore of the entrance to the Gulf was quietly frustrated. At the head of the Gulf the ruler of Koweit (whose title is the 'Sheik Mubarak'), a town possessing a fine harbour, was supported by us against Turkey's persistent efforts to undermine his independence, and in 1899 we entered into an agreement with him that he should make no concessions to any foreign power with the result—a contingency we had foreseen—that he politely refused Germany's request in 1900 to grant her a site for the terminus of the Berlin to Bagdad railway. The only result of these tentative essays upon our position was that we were driven to formulate our claims explicitly; in May 1903, Lord Lansdowne, the British Foreign Secretary, announced to the world that we should regard the establishment of a naval base or of a fortified post in the Persian

Gulf by any other power 'as a very grave menace to British interests which we should certainly resist with all the means at our disposal'.

This famous declaration was rendered necessary not only by the incidents which we have described but by a far greater world movement, the disintegration and dissolution of the Persian empire. Though Great Britain still held in her hands the greater part of the trade with southern Persia, her influence in the country as a whole had in recent years steadily and inevitably declined. The appointment of Sir Henry Drummond Wolff as minister to Teheran in 1887 did a good deal to restore our waning prestige, but in the northern province of the Persian empire we naturally did not, and could not, compete with Russia. Since the downfall of the Turcomans, of Khiva, and Bokhara, the Russian frontier for about a thousand miles has marched with that of Persia. The construction of the Transcaspian railway, and the development of navigation on the Volga had, up to the outbreak of the European War of 1914, diverted most of the commerce of northern and central Persia into Russian hands. But Russian commercial policy at this time was still dominated by ideas of monopoly and restriction. The construction of railways in Persian territory was forbidden, and other measures for the improvement of the country were discouraged. Politically, as well as commercially, northern Persia tended to pass more and more under Russian control. The northern frontier was ill-defined and encroachment upon it in one form or another was easy. Teheran the capital was within a hundred miles of the Russian frontier, and the most formidable—perhaps the only formidable—force in the Persian army consisted of Persian Cossacks trained and commanded by Russian officers. There could have been little doubt at the time that but for British influence in southern Persia, the whole empire of the Shah would soon have been absorbed into the colossal dominions of the Tsar. Lord Curzon had for many years urged that attempts should be made to extend and develop that influence. His visit to the Gulf in 1903 —the sequel to Lord Lansdowne's famous pronouncement in the same year—the establishment of consulates in the ports and the internal trading centres, the Seistan mission of 1903–5 which, under Sir Henry McMahon, completed the work of Sir Frederic Goldsmith's boundary delimitation of 1872, and the projection of the Quetta to Nushki railway, with a view to opening up a trade route to Seistan, did much to further these projects. Lord Curzon's policy, which was also that of the Cabinet at home, has been attacked as too provocative, but in view of our long and unique services in keeping the peace in the Gulf, in surveying, lighting, buoying, and patrolling these pirate-infested waters the criticism is unreasonable. Lord Curzon found that there was a danger of our prestige as paramount power, which, even if unrecognized in the formal diplomacy of Europe, had been hallowed by long prescriptive right, crumbling away almost unnoticed amid the multiplicity of our imperial interests and distractions. His prompt yet carefully considered action repelled the insidious attempts of other powers to insinuate claims that would in the future have been embarrassing. He quietly but unmistakably proclaimed our intentions to the world, and on the shores of the Gulf itself displayed plain evidence to the nations dwelling there that the naval power of Great Britain extended even to their torrid, remote, and secluded waters its protecting and overshadowing arm.

CHAPTER XIV

THE EXPEDITION TO TIBET. 1904

Lord Curzon's policy in relation to the north-western frontier, Afghanistan, and the Persian Gulf, as we have seen, merits high praise, and the results achieved fully justified the line of action which he adopted. His treatment of the Tibetan problem is far more open to criticism, and the outcome of his activity in that quarter cannot be regarded as entirely satisfactory.

The central Asian tableland of Tibet stretches northward from the Himalayas; its western and southern frontier of about 1,000 miles marching with Kashmir, the Punjab, Garhwal, the United Provinces, Nepal, Sikkim, Bhutan, Eastern Bengal, and Upper Burma. It is bounded on the East by the Chinese empire and on the north by Eastern Turkestan. With an area in square mileage about equal to the combined territories of France and Germany it has a population of probably less than half that of London. The mean altitude of Tibet is far greater than that of any considerable country in the world. Lhasa, the capital, stands 12,900 feet above sea level. The town of Phari is built at a height of 15,000 feet—only about 800 feet lower than the summit of Mont Blanc. During Younghusband's expedition military operations at the Karo La were conducted at the stupendous elevation of between 18,000 and 19,000 feet. The vast Tibetan plateau sinking in places into shallow cup-like depressions and narrow valleys heaves up its crest in mountain ridges of 24,000 to 25,000 feet. A great part of the country is treeless waste covered with glaciers and eternal snows, and swept by bitter dust-laden winds, but the declivities and valleys are abundantly fertile and are clothed with luxuriant crops. Communications are naturally of supreme difficulty. Wheeled traffic is practically unknown. Trade routes pass over heights where men faint in the rarified atmosphere and grow dizzy with mountain sickness. The political, social, and religious genius of the people of Tibet sedulously seeks to strengthen still further the barriers which the forces of nature, sublime in their grandeur and ruthlessness, have built up round the country.

The faith of the Tibetans is Buddhism. The government is a monkish and aristocratic theocracy, at the head of which are the two great Lamas, that is Pontiffs or Abbots, known as the Dalai Lama of Lhasa and the Tashi Lama of the great monastery of Tashilhunpo near Shigatse, who are regarded as reincarnations of the Buddha in one or more of his various manifestations. As soon as either of these pontiffs dies, a successor is immediately appointed from infant children born about the time of his death. Till he comes of age, regency councils govern for him. In spiritual matters the Tashi Lama is theoretically superior, but political power has for many years practically centred in the hands of the Dalai Lama or rather the council that rules during his minority; it is a sinister fact that few Dalai Lamas in the past hundred years have outlived the period of their nonage, and the government therefore has consisted of a succession of ecclesiastical regencies. The Dalai Lama, or those that represent him, and the executive council are advised by the Tsong-du, or national assembly, mainly controlled by a few hereditary nobles and the abbots of three great monasteries at Lhasa. But Tibet since the early years of the eighteenth century has owned the suzerainty of China, and two Chinese officials called Ambans, i.e. Residents or Ambassadors or Viceroys (for they partake in some degree of the unctions of all three) reside at Lhasa and control the Tibetan government.

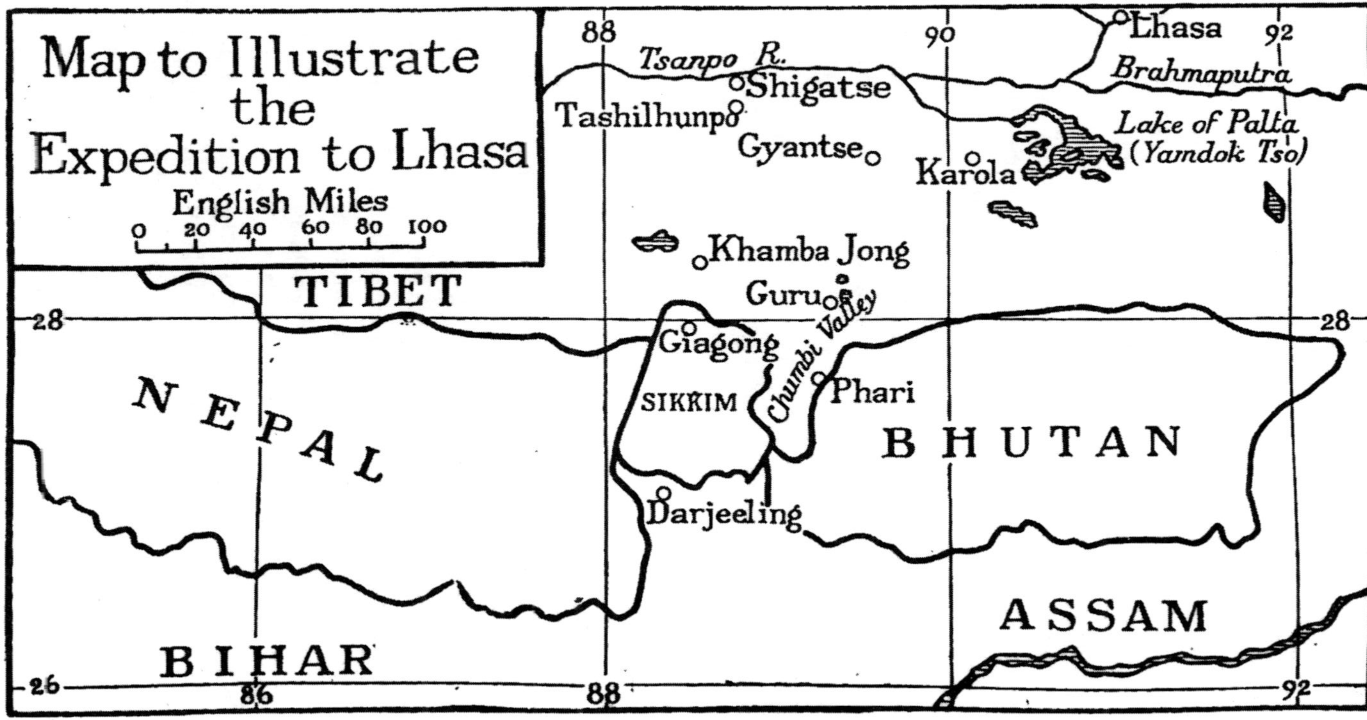
Map to Illustrate the Expedition to Lhasa
English Miles
0 20 40 60 80 100
TIBET
NEPAL
BIHAR
SIKKIM
BHUTAN
ASSAM
Lhasa
Brahmaputra
Tsanpo R.
Shigatse
Tashilhunpo
Gyantse
Karola
Lake of Palta
(Yamdok Tso)
Khamba Jong
Guru
Chumbi Valley
Giagong
Phari
Darjeeling
88
90
92
28
26
86

Though the country is undeveloped, entirely uninfluenced by western ideas of progress, and, in the words of Captain O'Connor who accompanied the expedition, 'oppressed by the most monstrous growth of monasticism and priestcraft which the world has ever seen', it has, from the point of view of the inhabitants, many redeeming features. The same observer records the fact that in spite of the arbitrary rule of the nobles and officials the country on the whole is well governed and the people well treated. 'They live simply and happily enough under a sort of patriarchal sway.' Though the monasteries lie everywhere like an incubus on the land, and drain away the resources of the soil, the fertility of the valleys in the comparatively small portion of Tibet which came under Captain O'Connor's observation, is such that 'the agriculturist has an easy time and little anxiety . . . the standard of comfort amongst the very poorest is high and indeed luxurious as compared with that of an Irish cottar'.

The history of British relations with Tibet dates back to 1774–5 when Warren Hastings sent a young and talented writer of the East India Company named George Bogle to visit the Tashi Lama of that period. He was kindly received and his report of his journey forms a valuable early source for our knowledge of Tibet. A second envoy, Samuel Turner, was dispatched in 1783 but found a colder welcome and less inclination on the part of the rulers of Tibet to open up trade with India. In 1811–12 Manning, an English free lance, actually succeeded in penetrating to Lhasa and visiting the child Dalai Lama of those days. In 1885–6, as we have seen, the consent of the Chinese was reluctantly given for a British commercial mission to Tibet, but in the end our prospects in that country were sacrificed to obtain the consent of the Chinese government to the annexation of Burma. In 1887 the Tibetans invaded the territory of the little protected state of Sikkim but were driven out with loss by General Graham the next year. In 1890 a convention was concluded between Great Britain and China which settled the Sikkim-Tibet boundary and appointed joint commissioners, who were to discuss the possibility of providing increased facilities for trade, and to settle the question of pasturage on the frontier, both the Tibetans and the people of Sikkim being accustomed at certain seasons of the year to drive their cattle over their neighbours' boundary. By 1893 the Commissioners entered into a more definite agreement and a trade mart was established at Yatung just over the Tibet-Sikkim frontier. But practically no real trade or intercourse resulted. The truth was, as a British frontier officer declared, that 'neither the Chinese nor the Tibetan rulers will ever assent to free intercourse with India except through fear of something which they may regard as a greater calamity'. In maintaining their isolation both parties made effective play with the curious dualism of the government. The Chinese politely regretted that the Tibetans, owing to 'their doltish feelings', refused to welcome British intercourse, the Tibetans declared they could do nothing without the authority of the Chinese who, so they averred, had even failed to inform them that a convention had been concluded.

Things remained for some time in this unsatisfactory state, and just about the time of Lord Curzon's accession to office two new conditions in the political aspect of Tibet made their appearance. In the first place, the control of the Ambans over the government was sensibly weakening; the Tibetans showed a strong desire to free themselves from Chinese sovereignty and to welcome the influence of Russia as a counterpoise. Secondly, the Dalai Lama unlike most of his predecessors had outlived the period of his minority, overthrown the regency government by a *coup d'état*, and had revealed himself as a ruler with considerable personal force, a strong will and headlong disposition. He was greatly influenced by a remarkable man who had risen to a high position in the administration of Tibet, Dorjieff, a Mongolian Buriat, and by birth a Russian subject. This man had been sent from Lhasa in 1898 to Russia to collect contributions for religious purposes from the numerous Buddhist subjects of the Tsar. He returned to Russia more than once within the next few years, and in 1900 and 1901 was received in audience by the Emperor. The Russian press hailed these events as heralding the spread of their country's influence in Tibet. It is likely enough that the initiative in this *rapprochement* came originally rather from Tibet than Russia. The Russian Foreign Minister assured the British ambassador in St. Petersburg that the visits of Dorjieff had no political significance, and certainly it would have been difficult for the Tsar to refuse to receive an envoy coming ostensibly on a religious mission. But the Indian government grew uneasy. They believed that Dorjieff, whatever the original purpose of his journeys, would be used to promote political aims, and would end by becoming practically a Russian agent in Tibet. As a matter of fact it appears that the Dalai Lama himself was the main convert to the new Russianizing policy. Dorjieff seems to have persuaded him that to fling off the onerous suzerainty of China it would be necessary to enter into closer relations with some other strong empire; the tremendous yet far distant might of Russia with her great number of Buddhist subjects was preferable to the power of Great Britain established so near the southern gates of Tibet, whose emissaries had long been endeavouring to penetrate the country for commercial purposes. The Tsong-du opposed the policy of the Lama, and, according to one theory the latter deliberately provoked aggression with India to force the hands of the national council and drive them into an agreement with Russia.

Lord Curzon eagerly pressed upon the home government the sending of a mission to Tibet. Complaints were to be made that the Tibetans had encroached upon the Sikkim frontier, established a customs post at Giagong, thrown down certain boundary pillars and walled off the only road leading from Tibet to Yatung. These detailed grievances were to be supported by the more general statement that the isolation of the Tibetan government 'is not compatible either with proximity to the territories of a great civilized power at whose hands the Tibetan government enjoys the fullest opportunities both for intercourse and trade, or with due respect for the treaty stipulations into which the Chinese government has entered on its behalf'. But the alleged reasons for the mission were flimsy, and it is certain that nothing would ever have been heard of them but for the recent visits of Dorjieff to Russia.

The home government was not in favour of any advance into Tibet. They pointed out that the country was politically subordinate to China, and that therefore the only proper course was to put pressure upon the authorities in Peking to bring the Tibetans to reason. Accordingly, in 1902, upon a report that an agreement had been concluded between Russia and China concerning Tibet, Lord Lansdowne informed the Russian ambassador that Lhasa was within a comparatively short distance of the northern frontier of India, while it was 1,000 miles distant from the Asiatic empire of Russia. We were more closely interested than Russia in Tibet and 'it followed that, should there be any display of Russian activity in that country, we should be obliged to reply by a display of activity not only equivalent to, but exceeding that made by Russia'. The British Minister at Peking had already informed the Chinese government that, should any agreement affecting the political status of Tibet be entered into by China with another power, the British government would be compelled to take steps for the protection of British interests. But Lord Curzon still believed in the existence of an agreement, if not a treaty, between St. Petersburg and Lhasa, and urged the home government to send a mission direct to Tibet. The Chinese suzerainty was a 'political affectation', and the diplomatic use made by the two countries of the dualism of the government was a 'solemn farce' which 'has been enacted with a frequency that seems never to deprive it of its attractions or its power to impose'. In the view of Lord Curzon and his supporters England could not afford to see Russia allied with the Tibetans and controlling their policy. No Russian invasion of India through Tibet was indeed possible, but Russia's career of conquest and absorption in Asia was then at its zenith, and her presence in Tibet would have ruined British prestige in the East. The Secretary of State, however, declaring that the dispatch of an expedition to Tibet while Great Britain and Russia were discussing matters would be most unsuitable, imposed delay. Meanwhile, the Russian ambassador assured the home government that there was no convention about Tibet nor any Russian agent in that country, though the Russians regarded Tibet as forming part of the Chinese empire, in the integrity of which country they took an interest.

The whole situation was complicated and difficult. We have the Indian government pressing a forward policy on the Cabinet; the Cabinet endeavouring to restrain the eagerness of a masterful Viceroy and anxious not to offend the susceptibilities of Russia; the British Minister at Peking trying to put pressure on the Chinese government; the Chinese, hating our interference altogether, unable to coerce the Tibetans and anxious to conceal their inability to do so from the British government; and finally Russia protesting that she had no political designs, but obviously uneasy at the prospect of British intervention in Tibet.

Lord Curzon next proposed that negotiations should be opened with China and Tibet at Khamba Jong, a place fifteen miles north of the Sikkim frontier, to impress upon both those governments the need of fulfilling their treaty obligations, and that if envoys did not appear there, the British commissioners should move forward to Shigatse or Gyantse. The home government, most weakly from their own point of view, allowed themselves to be squeezed. They reluctantly sanctioned the advance of a mission under Colonel (now Sir) F. E. Younghusband to Khamba Jong, and though they declined to accept Lord Curzon's proposal that we should insist on having a British agent at Gyantse or Lhasa, they had in fact embarked upon a course of operations which under the pressure of further demands was to lead them step by step to the occupation of Lhasa itself.

Colonel Younghusband reached Khamba Jong in July, but though the Chinese officials made their appearance, the Tibetans refused to come to a conference unless the mission should retire to the frontier. Colonel Younghusband himself admits that there was some force in their argument that the discussion should have taken place on, and not within, the Tibetan boundary, and that it would have been reasonable for us to assent to their demand. It certainly seems difficult to contest this, and Colonel Younghusband's own reason against doing as the Tibetans requested is the purely arbitrary statement, which events might or might not have proved true, that 'such negotiations would not in fact have led to any result'. This could only be proved by the issue, and we should at least have attempted to negotiate without first crossing the boundary line. There ensued a long deadlock, during which the Tibetans began to mass troops in the neighbourhood of Khamba Jong. The home government, on November 6, after pressure from the Indian authorities, sanctioned an advance to Gyantse on the understanding that as soon as reparation should be obtained a withdrawal should be effected. This decision was followed by a prompt protest from the Russian ambassador to Lord Lansdowne, the Secretary of State for Foreign Affairs, a protest which, in view of repeated British assurances on the subject of Tibet in the past, could certainly not be regarded as unnatural. Lord Lansdowne, however, countered the Russian objections by declaring that the British government had shown extraordinary self-restraint and avowing his belief that under similar provocation the Russians would long ago have been in Lhasa; at the same time he gave an assurance that Tibetan territory should neither be annexed nor permanently occupied.

The advance to Gyantse began in March 1904, and on the last day of the month came the collision with the miserably-armed and badly-led Tibetan troops at Guru, which inevitably presented such a pitiful aspect to the world, and caused a great outbreak of indignation in England among the opponents of Lord Curzon's policy. The Tibetans had ranged themselves across the path of the expedition, and refused to give way when ordered to do so. A few rounds from the British modern weapons of precision left 700 dead and wounded on the field, while only a few casualties, none of them fatal, were sustained by our troops. Gyantse was reached on April 11, but there, too, the Dalai Lama refused to negotiate, and the Cabinet now authorized a further march on Lhasa. More fighting was found to be necessary. An advance guard brilliantly defeated the Tibetans, who occupied a strong position in tremendous altitudes amid eternal snows at the Karo La pass, and a surprise attack on the mission camp in the rear on May 5 was beaten off. The Dalai Lama, now thoroughly alarmed, sent mission after mission to meet the British force with offers to negotiate, but Younghusband sternly refused to enter into *pourparlers* till he reached Lhasa. On August 3 the expedition entered the holy and mysterious city, the goal of so many vain endeavours in the past, marching through the famous gateway and looking up with wonder at the glittering Potala Palace of the Lamas raised high above the rest of the town on its escarpment of solid rock, with its tier upon tier of storied windows and golden roofs flashing in the sunlight. Three weeks before, the Dalai Lama, bitterly disappointed that no help was forthcoming from Russia, and convinced at last that nothing could stay the relentless advance of the men he had despised and flouted, had fled from his capital.

Younghusband now entered into negotiations with the Regent to whom the Dalai Lama before his flight had delegated his powers. The Chinese Resident proved courteous and obliging, in fact too much so for the taste of his government, which afterwards degraded him for what they regarded as excessive compliance to the mission. The Tonga Penlop (or Prime Minister) of Bhutan and the Nepal representative, who were present in Lhasa, gave the British valuable help, and did much to persuade the Regent to conclude the treaty. It was finally signed on September 7, and the expedition was able to start on its return journey sixteen days later. The treaty provided for the establishment of trade marts at Yatung, Gyantse, and Gartok, and the promotion and encouragement of commerce between India and Tibet. A British commercial agent was to be stationed at Gyantse, and he was empowered, if occasion demanded it, to proceed to Lhasa. The indemnity was fixed at 75 lakhs of rupees, and was to be paid off in annual instalments of one lakh. The Chumbi valley—that is, the wedge of Tibetan territory inserted between Bhutan and Sikkim—was to be occupied by British troops till the whole sum was paid off. Other provisions secured to Great Britain direct influence over the external policy of Tibet. No portion of Tibetan territory was to be alienated to any foreign power, nor was any agent of such power to be admitted into the country. No concessions for railways, roads, telegraphs, no mining or other rights, were to be granted to any foreign state or to the subjects thereof. If such concessions were granted, similar powers would at once be demanded by the British government.

But, in concluding such terms, Younghusband had undoubtedly exceeded his powers. The Secretary of State had laid it down that the indemnity was not to exceed an amount which it was believed would be within the power of the Tibetans to pay by instalments spread over three years, though Younghusband 'was to be guided by circumstances in the matter'. No resident was to be demanded at Gyantse, Lhasa, or elsewhere. The home government considered the Tibetan question from the wider standpoint of imperial policy, and were bound by the pledge recently given to Russia that so long as no other power endeavoured to intervene in the affairs of Tibet, Great Britain would not attempt either to annex it or establish a protectorate over it, or in any way control its internal administration. Colonel Younghusband, viewing the problem from the narrower and simpler standpoint of Indian policy, allowed himself to deviate from these instructions. It is true that the reasoned dispatch setting forth the grounds of the home government's policy did not reach him till after the treaty was signed, when undoubtedly it would have been very difficult—if not impossible—to reopen negotiations, but the telegraphic instructions he had previously received were perfectly clear and definite. In spite of this he convinced himself by some curious reasoning that the discretion granted to him to be governed by circumstances would cover the prolongation of our hold over the Chumbi valley from three years to seventy-five, and justify the provision for an agent at Gyantse because his business was commercial and not political. The Government of India defended Younghusband's action as showing a 'fearlessness of responsibility which it would be a grave mistake to discourage in any of their agents'. The fact that they sympathized strongly with his point of view will perhaps explain this euphemistic synonym for disobedience to orders, for it must be confessed that Lord Curzon's government had not appeared hitherto to welcome this kind of independence in their subordinates. On the other hand, the Secretary of State, Mr. St. John Brodrick, was very angry, as he had a right to be, at his instructions being disregarded. Clearly the proposed occupation of the Chumbi valley for seventy-five years would appear to the world a disingenuous evasion of the recent pledge to Russia. He therefore insisted on a revision of the treaty; the indemnity was reduced from 75 to 25 lakhs; it was agreed that after three annual instalments had been paid, provided the other terms of the treaty had been carried out, the Chumbi valley should be evacuated; finally, the condition which gave the British agent at Gyantse access to Lhasa was disallowed.

As regards the question of the justification for Lord Curzon's policy, it was noticed by Lord Rosebery in the House of Lords in 1904 that the situation of 1903 in regard to Tibet presented some rather sinister points of resemblance to that of 1878 in regard to Afghanistan. At both dates an independent state on our borders was showing a strong inclination to enter into relations with Russia. In both cases we had a very doubtful ethical or legal right to interfere, but in both too there existed a strong feeling, in many respects no doubt well justified, that our prestige would seriously suffer if we were excluded and Russia's representatives were admitted. Once more a vigorous forward policy was pressed on reluctant home authorities by the Indian government. Just as Lord Lytton desired the retention of a British agent at Kabul, so Lord Curzon was eager to keep a representative at Lhasa or Gyantse. There is even a somewhat striking resemblance between the vigorous and brilliantly-phrased dispatches of the two Viceroys. There was a tendency in 1903 as in 1878 to read into certain actions of our opponents more evidence of hostility than the facts warranted. For instance, it was stated that the Tibetans had usurped grazing rights on the Sikkim side of the border, but it was afterwards found that they were balanced by similar rights which had been ceded to the Sikkimese, and that this mutual arrangement was the one most convenient for both parties.

To one school of thought it appeared that Lord Curzon 'by his policy of persistence crushed a cleverly-veiled design', inimical to British imperial interests; to another he seemed to have embarked upon a course of unwarranted and disastrous interference with a weak and independent state. It is easy, of course, for the historian, in the illuminating wisdom that comes after the event, to point out that politically the results would have been more impressive if there had been no compromise between the two policies. Either Lord Curzon should have been allowed to pursue his path unhampered, or the Cabinet should have refused to sanction any interference at all. Within the next few years it seemed to some of those best acquainted with the East that 'China was the one power which has reaped solid advantages from the Tibet mission'. Chinese claims were developed into actual sovereignty. 'We have not extended our trade as we had hoped, and we have raised up for ourselves a new and disturbing situation on the north-east frontier of India.'

Whatever may be the political and ethical rights of the matter, the actual conception and conduct of the expedition were brilliantly successful. It has been rightly described as 'a triumph of organization and daring'; and indeed this sudden penetration of a little band of pioneers into the jealously-guarded seclusion and mysterious snow-clad solitudes of Tibet forms a fascinating episode in the unromantic annals of modern India.[1]

[1] The main authorities consulted for this chapter are: The Tibet Blue Book, i. e. *Papers relating to Tibet*, 1904, and *Further Papers relating to Tibet*, 1904 and 1905; *Lhasa and its Mysteries*, by L. A. Waddell, London, 1905; *Central Asia and Tibet*, by Sven Hedin, two vols., London, 1903; *Lhasa*, by Percival Landon, two vols., London, 1905; *India and Tibet*, by Sir Francis E. Younghusband, K.C.I.E., London, 1910; *The Unveiling of Lhasa*, by Edmund Candler.

CHAPTER XV

INTERNAL ADMINISTRATION UNDER LORD CURZON

In internal affairs Lord Curzon succeeded to a heritage of plague and famine. The drought of 1899–1900 was one of the most severe on record. It came before the country had fully recovered from the ravages of the visitation of 1896, and a simultaneous outbreak of cholera and malarial fever intensified the miseries of the famishing people. The scarcity extended over an area of 475,000 square miles with a population of 60 million souls. The provinces affected were the Punjab, Rajputana, Baroda, Bombay, the Central Provinces, Berar, Hyderabad, and Gujerat. One million people are said to have perished in British territory alone, and over six millions sterling were spent in relief. A commission presided over by Sir A. Macdonnell afterwards reported that the relief distributed was excessive, and that the excess was due to 'an imperfect enforcement of tests on relief works . . . a too ready admission to gratuitous relief and . . . a greater readiness on the people's part to accept relief owing to the demoralizing influences of the preceding famine'.

After 1900 India had for some time respite from severe famines. Plague, however, persisted and through the whole of Lord Curzon's viceroyalty increased in intensity. The most devoted efforts to combat its ravages proved in vain, and in the last year of his period of office the total number of deaths amounted to more than 900,000. In April 1900 serious riots occurred at Cawnpore, directed against the plague regulations. They were found on inquiry to have been deliberately planned, and seven of the ringleaders suffered the penalty of death.

At the end of the nineteenth century there was a marked improvement in the financial condition of India. The closing of the mints to the free coinage of silver began to show its effects, and the depression due to unstable exchange was relieved. From 1899 Indian budgets, instead of a dreary series of deficits, began to reveal handsome surpluses. It was therefore determined to carry to its logical conclusion the policy initiated in 1893. A commission at the India Office, appointed in May 1898, after an exhaustive examination of the question, reported in favour of making the British sovereign legal tender in India at the value of fifteen rupees, and an Act carrying the reform was passed in September 1899. Gold began to flow into India; the profits of the coinage of silver were set apart as a gold reserve fund, and by the time Lord Curzon laid down his office it amounted to about £9,000,000.

There are so many disturbing factors to be taken into account that monetary problems of this nature may not lightly be made the subject of confident assertion, but expert opinion seems generally agreed that (disregarding the entirely abnormal conditions brought about by the great war) the reform has had good practical results, and the lugubrious forecasts of those who opposed the closing of the mints appear not to have been realized. At the same time it is not easy in theory to justify the existing position in India. While gold is the standard of value, silver is still legal tender for sums of any amount, even though its intrinsic worth falls far below its exchange value, and no gold coinage has yet been issued by the Indian mints. The improvement in the finances made it possible to alleviate the distress of the population after the terrible famine of 1899–1900 by granting considerable remissions of taxation. In 1902 the provinces that had suffered most received back a million and a quarter of the land revenue, and within the next two years the salt tax was brought down to a lower point than it had reached since the Mutiny. One other fiscal measure of Lord Curzon's time deserves mention. The financial settlement as between the imperial and provincial government adopted by Lord Mayo (*see* p. 416) was revised, the quinquennial system was abolished, and the arrangement made permanent.

Internally Lord Curzon's period of office was made especially notable for a drastic overhauling of the whole machinery of administration. The Viceroy himself claimed that 'abuses had been swept away, anomalies remedied, the pace quickened and standards raised'. Certainly many departments of government were submitted to searching tests. The method adopted was a preliminary investigation conducted by a committee, followed by legislation carrying out the main recommendations of their report. Lord Curzon found a new use for an old administrative weapon: commissions were utilized not, as was so often the case in the past, to shelve inconvenient questions, but to survey the ground and clear the way for vigorous action. Changing circumstances and the lapse of time had made the traditional methods of the civil service sometimes ineffective and antiquated, sometimes actually mischievous. But the process of reform, however salutary, was not always popular. A few errors were inevitably made, some susceptibilities were ruffled, and many vested interests disturbed. Yet on the whole the results obtained were valuable and the necessity of the reforming process has now been generally recognized. One of the least admirable parts of the administration was the police service, largely staffed in its subordinate branches, and almost entirely manned, by

Indians. The commission that inquired into its condition was highly condemnatory, declaring it to be 'far from efficient . . . defective in training and organization . . . inadequately supervised . . . and generally regarded as corrupt and oppressive'. So severe indeed were the strictures of the commissioners that though the report was signed in 1903 it was withheld from publication till 1905. In that year a reform of the service was inaugurated and some important changes for the better were introduced, but it is still widely recognized that the Indian police system is far from satisfactory.

An important series of measures dealt with the ever-present problem of the land revenue, which is, naturally enough, from time to time subjected to searching criticism by the opponents of the government of India. The extreme presentment of the opposition case, as we have already indicated in Chapter I, is that the frequent occurrence of famine in recent times is due less to the failure of the rains than to the demands of the government upon the ryots, which leave them impoverished and resourceless in time of drought. No impartial or responsible judge can accept so exaggerated a statement. Lord Curzon's government, in the famous resolution on land revenue policy of 1902, pointed out that within seven years drought had inflicted upon the Central Provinces alone a financial loss equal to the whole land revenue for fifty years, so that no remissions could have made any appreciable difference; that though in recent years assessments have steadily diminished, a cycle of unfavourable seasons has resulted in an increasing number of famines, and that drought and scarcity have sometimes slightly affected highly assessed lands while they have fallen with devastating severity on districts more leniently treated. But not all the opponents of the Indian government commit themselves to such an extreme position, nor must we imagine that the easy refutation of the charge that land revenue causes famine exonerates the administration from all temperate criticism. There were undoubtedly plenty of defects to deplore and errors to amend. Land revenue administration, like most other government activities, tends to become too formal and mechanical in operation. In some provinces revenue has been rigorously collected in the past, though cultivators were impoverished. Settlement officers are naturally prone, as zealous state servants, to raise assessments, if they can, to benefit state revenues. Local governments have sometimes raised the settlement of their own officers. No impartial judge could deny that cases have occurred of serious over-assessment and a too rigid collection of government imposts.

In December 1900 eleven retired Indian civilians possessing records of distinguished service, of whom ten were British and one Indian, addressed a memorial to Lord George Hamilton, the Secretary of State. They quoted with approval the following words of Lord Salisbury written in 1875, 'So far as it is possible to change the Indian fiscal system, it is desirable that the cultivator should pay a smaller proportion of the whole national charge. It is not in itself a thrifty policy to draw the mass of revenue from the rural districts, where capital is scarce, sparing the towns, where it is often redundant and runs to waste and luxury.' Their suggestions were (i) That where land revenue is levied directly from the cultivators the demand should not exceed one-half of their net profit after disbursing the cost of cultivation; (ii) where it is derived from the landlords, it should not exceed one-half of the rental; (iii) that settlements should be for thirty years; (iv) that the only ground for enhancement in the cultivator's assessment should be increased value of the land due either to government irrigation works or a rise in prices; (v) that local taxation on land should in no case exceed a further ten per cent. To this memorial and to criticisms that appeared elsewhere the

Indian government replied in the Land Resolution of January 16, 1902, part of which has been quoted above, admitting that the question was 'one of the highest national importance, transcending the sphere of party or sectional controversy'. In dealing with the memorial, the weakest part of the government's answer was their attempt to meet the first two demands, which were moderate enough and might well have been conceded. Lord Curzon and his advisers declined to make any definite rule on the subject, though they showed that there was a growing tendency for the state share of the produce, both in the case of the cultivator and the landlord, to approximate to the fifty per cent. line and in some cases to fall below it. The reply to the third point was practically a cautious promise to do away in due course with shorter terms of settlement than thirty years. The fourth proposal was not approved. The reply to the fifth was the assertion that the limit of ten per cent. suggested was in fact nowhere exceeded.

Altogether the government went a considerable way to meet the memorialists, and this is plainly shown in the words of Mr. R. C. Dutt, the Indian representative, who thus summed up his view of the Resolution: 'Lord Curzon has approached the subject with a statesmanlike conviction of its importance. He has virtually affirmed the principle which we urged, that in temporarily settled estates held by landlords, the government revenue should generally be limited to one-half the actual rental. He has given us hopes that the rule of thirty years settlements, which we urged, will be extended to the Punjab and the Central Provinces, and he has also given us hopes that the pressure of local cesses will be mitigated. If to all this his Excellency had added some clear and workable limits to the government demand in *Ryotwari* tracts, and defined some intelligible and equitable grounds for enhancement of revenue in such tracts, the government Resolution would have given to millions of cultivators the assurance and protection they need so much.'[1]

The Land Resolution promised that the government would make a further advance in the direction of 'the progressive and graduated imposition of large enhancements' when they were justified, for they recognized that cases had occurred when 'a reduction of revenue was not granted till the troubles of the people had been aggravated by their efforts to provide the full fixed demand'. The new land policy was also to aim at greater elasticity in the revenue collection and a more general resort to reduction of assessment in cases of local deterioration.

To sum up, Lord Curzon endeavoured to remedy the abuses of the land revenue and ameliorate the whole condition of the Indian peasantry in four ways. He had already in 1900 passed the Punjab Land Alienation Act to free cultivators of the soil from eviction at the hands of money-lenders to whom they may have mortgaged their estates. Lands of an hereditary cultivator cannot henceforward be sold in execution of a decree. This Act is said to have saved the cultivators of the Punjab from wholesale alienation of their land, but to orthodox economists such a measure must appear both wrong in principle and likely to prove hazardous in operation; indeed its ultimate effects may turn out to be the very reverse of what was intended. Lord Curzon's other measures were less open to criticism. As we have seen, the Land Resolution of 1902 ordered that if the revenue were largely increased by a settlement it should be graduated, and, in the further Suspensions and Remissions Resolution of 1905, rules were laid down that the government demand should vary according to the character of the season. In the third place co-operative credit societies were founded to provide cultivators with capital at a low rate of

[1] It is only fair to say that Mr. R. C. Dutt seems afterwards rather to have qualified this favourable verdict.

interest, and finally an Inspector-General of Agriculture was appointed, and an Imperial Agricultural Department, with a research institute, laboratories, and experimental farms, was founded to encourage the application of scientific methods to Indian tillage.

In the army while Lord Kitchener was Commander-in-Chief the native regiments were re-armed, better guns were supplied to the artillery, and the whole transport service was reorganized. In 1901 the Imperial Cadet Corps was founded, consisting of young men of princely and noble families. The services of the Indian army were at this time employed for wider duties than the protection of India itself. Indians were employed against the Boxer insurgents in China and against the Mullah in Somaliland; while in South Africa troops from India helped to hold Ladysmith and to save Natal.

Largely increased expenditure was authorized on railways, and about six thousand miles of new lines were constructed. In regard to his irrigation policy it has been said of Lord Curzon that 'he only carried on . . . what others had done before him; but the special merit of his labours lay in the fact that he systematized the whole enterprise, prepared a clear and final programme which represented the utmost possible extension of the Indian irrigation system, arranged for its finance and for its steady prosecution, and incidentally silenced the foolish criticism which had been propagated without a check for years'.[1]

A new department of Commerce and Industry was established, presided over by a sixth member of the Viceroy's council. Lord Curzon's other activities included measures for preserving ancient buildings and monuments in India, and an attempt to put some check upon the elaborate system of minute and report writing, which he described as the most 'perfect and pernicious' in the world.

Lastly the thorny question of education was investigated

[1] Lovat Fraser, *India under Lord Curzon and After*, 1911, p. 304.

by a commission which, perhaps unfortunately, contained no Indian representative, and only one non-official member. Its report on the condition of Indian education, though cautiously worded, was on the whole disappointing. The theory of the pioneers in 1854 had been that education administered to the upper classes through the universities would 'filter down' to the lower social strata of the population. The commissioners considered that this sanguine hope had been largely falsified. Nor indeed could it be considered surprising if it were so. Even in western countries we know only too well how hard it is to maintain a high ideal of education, and how dissatisfied most nations are to-day with systems once considered, humanly speaking, near perfection. A university degree—designed to be a test of culture—was undoubtedly often looked upon by the clever quick-witted Bengali merely as an open sesame to a post in the Provincial Civil Service. But perhaps it is only fair to point out that many of those who pass this criticism seem to forget that a similar use of academic success for professional reasons is not entirely unknown even in this fortunate country. Indian universities were mere examining boards; they had tended to free themselves from state control, and they encouraged a system of 'cramming' which often produced the most lamentable effects when brought to bear upon the impressionable minds and imitative capacities of eastern peoples. The system of higher education in India, says an able critic, was 'mechanical, lifeless, perverted', and Lord Curzon himself declared with a great deal of truth, 'it has taught the people of India the catchwords of western civilization without inspiring them with its spirit or inculcating its sobriety'. Accordingly in 1904 the governing bodies of the universities were reorganized in the hope that they might be converted from mere examining boards to training institutions, and that the teaching staff, now given more power and scope, might work less with the purpose of mechanically turning out large numbers of graduates and more with the aim of establishing a sound system of education. But the changes were very unpopular with the Indian Reform party, who believed that they were made with the idea of undermining their influence. It is to a certain extent true to say that up to this time the party had supported Lord Curzon, but that they now turned against him. Indeed, first of all the education problem and secondly the Partition of Bengal revealed a fundamental divergence in the standpoints of the Viceroy and the *Intelligentsia.* Lord Curzon's aim was practical social reform, sound administration, and, above all, efficiency in method. He was impatient—perhaps sometimes too impatient—of incompetency and delay; he was loath to exchange counsels of perfection for a second best accommodated to the prejudices of the ruled. The interest of the National Congress Party was the fascinating pursuit of constitutional experiment, the application to Indian politics of all those western democratic creeds and party cries which they had so eagerly assimilated. The estrangement between the Viceroy and the Nationalist Party was the more to be regretted in that Lord Curzon undoubtedly had the welfare of the people at heart. It is only fair to record here that from the first he sternly set his face against any attempt to condone oppression or insulting treatment of Indians by men of European birth, and was ready in this cause to jeopardize his popularity with the army or the non-official British residents in India.

On New Year's Day 1903 Lord Curzon proclaimed King Edward VII Emperor of India at the Coronation Durbar held at Delhi, a pageant which in splendour surpassed even that of 1877. In April 1904 Lord Curzon, having served the normal period of the Viceregal office, was reappointed for a further term and sailed to England for a few months' rest, Lord Ampthill, the Governor of Madras, holding the reins of office during his absence. In December 1904 Lord Curzon returned to deal with two great problems which brought his extended period of office to an abrupt close amid heated controversies and embittered criticisms.

The first problem was the Partition of Bengal. There had long been a pressing need to lighten the duties of the Lieutenant-Governor of Bengal, his charge having grown to be a burden beyond the capabilities of any single man to bear. The population of the province was seventy-eight millions, almost twice that of the United Kingdom. One result of the impossible pressure of work upon the Lieutenant-Governor had been the unavoidable isolation of the districts of the province that lay east of the Ganges. That part of Bengal had been sadly neglected and formed a stagnant backwater in relation to the broad well-channelled river of British administration. The peasants suffered from the exactions of absentee landlords, and the police system was even worse than in other parts of India. Internal communications, in a country interlaced with broad estuaries, were bad, and a recent commission of inquiry had revealed an appalling condition of habitual outrage and undetected crime in the more remote districts, so that 'life and property on the rivers was unsafe to a degree which could not be tolerated by the government of any civilized country'.

There was abundant historical precedent for subdividing the province. The original Presidency of Fort William in Bengal had been lightened by the creation of the North-West Provinces in 1865 (since 1901 the United Provinces of Agra and Oudh) and by the placing of Assam under a separate High Commissioner in 1874. The Indian government now made up its mind that the time had come for a further partition of the province. There was no undue haste, as has been sometimes alleged, nor any particularly high-handed procedure. The policy was fully deliberated, many alternative schemes were considered, and the plans were modified from time to time in accordance with criticism from outside. Finally a new province of Eastern Bengal and Assam was constituted by amalgamating Assam and Chittagong with fifteen districts of old Bengal. The new province had an area of about 106,000 square miles and a population of about 31,000,000.

Before the reform was completed a fierce popular agitation flared out against the proposed change. The feeling aroused was no doubt partly genuine, but largely based upon a misunderstanding of the point at issue. But there can be no possible doubt, on an impartial view of the evidence, that the agitation was adroitly manipulated, often by questionable methods, by the literary and legal classes, whose vested interests in the Indian Press and the Calcutta Bar were considered to be threatened by the change. To pass so much of censure on the outcry does not of course imply for a moment, as is sometimes hastily assumed, that Indians are necessarily from their national character unfit for democratic government, or at any rate that they are more unfit than European peoples. Our own history affords abundant examples—for instance, Walpole's excise scheme in 1733—of salutary measures prevented by factious popular clamour. Everywhere in the world political agitations tend to assume in a free atmosphere an element of grotesque extravagance, and under western as well as under eastern skies the dry light of reason pales before the lurid glow of controversy and the storm-shot clouds of prejudice and party passion. To the government the Partition of Bengal was, in Lord Curzon's words, 'a mere readjustment of administrative boundaries', proposed with a view to the more efficient working of the imperial machine. To excited popular orators in Calcutta it meant the partition of a nation, an attempt to divide a homogeneous people, a deliberate and sinister attack upon the traditions, history, and even the language of the Bengalis. Not, of course, that all the opposition was attuned to this extravagant key. The more moderate party, supported by a section of Liberalism in England and a minority of the civil service, argued that, whatever the abstract merits of the scheme, it should have been abandoned when it was found to be repugnant to national sentiment. They did not, for that was clearly impossible, deny the need of some change. The solution they put forward was that Bengal, like Madras and Bombay, should be ruled by a Governor assisted by an executive council. Historically there was much to be said for this contention; the Charter Acts of 1833 and 1853 had actually authorized such a government, and the Act of 1853 had merely legalized the appointment of Lieutenant-Governors 'unless and until' this change could conveniently be made.

But their solution found no favour with the government, which replied that the Councils in Bombay and Madras were not designed to relieve the Governors of those presidencies of their work, but to supply the want of special Indian knowledge in distinguished public men appointed from outside the ranks of the civil service. Bengal, a province where there were many varieties of race and many problems which required firm handling and expert knowledge, was best controlled by a Lieutenant-Governor who had risen through every grade of the Indian administration. An executive council would only tie his hands and divide responsibility. Lord Curzon, in short, wished to weaken the executive as little as possible, while his opponents were eager to experiment in decentralization. But the Viceroy, unlike Walpole, was determined not to yield to popular clamour, which he believed to be partly unscrupulous and partly misinformed, and the partition was carried through in 1905. Was he wrong? Taking all the facts into consideration, I cannot think so. There seems little ground for supposing that the storm of opposition, which sprang up as suddenly as a squall upon landlocked waters, could have been foreseen. The Government was committed too far to draw back when the first indications of the hurricane were descried. Nothing is more fatal to a government than to create the impression that it will always yield to pressure. By doing so, it wins neither the gratitude of its opponents nor peace for itself. You cannot conduct a successful administration by a policy of continually selling the pass. Measures advanced to a certain stage must be carried through, or their authors stand forth as bankrupt in credit and prospects.

The second problem, which brought about Lord Curzon's retirement, was a disagreement with Lord Kitchener on the question of military administration. The matter in dispute is technical and difficult to explain, but a summary of it must be attempted. The existing system was as follows: The executive head of the army in India was the Commander-in-Chief, who could be, and in practice always was, appointed an extraordinary member of the Viceroy's council. There was, besides, an army administrative department in charge of an ordinary member of council, which kept closely in touch with the supreme government to an extent impossible to the Commander-in-Chief engaged in his manifold executive duties. This member of council was a soldier, but was not allowed during his term of office to hold any army command. He was the constitutional adviser of the Viceroy in military matters, and it was one of his duties to transmit to the Governor-General, with his own criticisms, all proposals on army administration made by the Commander-in-Chief. Lord Kitchener, who carried through in the military sphere much the same sort of salutary and drastic reforms as Lord Curzon himself achieved in civil government, who had moreover up till now received the Viceroy's cordial support, strongly objected to this rather cumbrous departmental machinery. It was, he declared, productive of 'enormous delay and endless discussion'. He advocated the creation of a single army department of which the Commander-in-Chief should be the head, and to which the whole business of military administration should be transferred. To this suggestion Lord Curzon and the rest of the council were unanimously opposed, holding that it would 'concentrate military authority in the hands of the Commander-in-Chief and subvert the supremacy of the civil power by depriving it of independent military advice'.

There seems on the face of it some reason for Lord Kitchener's dissatisfaction. Though the ordinary member of council of the time, Sir Edmond Elles, strongly dissented from Lord Kitchener's strictures, some delay and dislocation calculated to chafe an able and determined Commander-in-Chief must have been inevitable in the transmission of business through so complicated a system. Lord Kitchener maintained that in his suggested plan the supremacy of the civil power was left untouched, for it would still be possible for the Viceroy to accept or reject any proposals submitted, but he demanded that the head of the supreme government should be brought into closer relations with the head of the army, and he considered it highly undesirable that the proposals of the Commander-in-Chief 'should be criticized from a military point of view by the Military Member of Council, who must always necessarily be both junior in rank and inferior in military experience to the Commander-in-Chief'. Lord Curzon's answer to this in effect was that, unless he had some competent military authority to advise him, it would be difficult in practice for a civilian Viceroy to oppose a strong-willed Commander-in-Chief, and therefore a civil power would be too dependent on the head of the army. He pointed out also that the question was not entirely new—it had been considered before by Viceroys and Commanders-in-Chief in the past, but the experience of forty years, after periodical examinations of the problem, had always ended by deciding to retain the old system

Official opinion in India was almost entirely with Lord Curzon.

Such was the problem—a deadlock between high authorities in India—which the home government was called upon to solve. It seems, perhaps, obvious that the most satisfactory course would have been to come down decisively on one side or the other. But the Unionist government was now within sight of the breakers of dissolution; it was generally supposed, with some reason, that they were not anxious to go to the country with the resignation either of a brilliant Governor-General or a great and popular soldier upon their hands. They therefore attempted a compromise which was not very happily inspired. It barely satisfied Lord Kitchener, appeared to Lord Curzon merely to veil a surrender to his rival, and certainly seems to the plain man to diffuse darkness rather than light over a situation already sufficiently obscure. The Cabinet's solution was that the Commander-in-Chief should exclusively control the strictly military departments of army administration, and should alone have the right to speak in the Governor-General's council as an expert on military problems, but that subsidiary departments, not purely military, should be left in charge of another member of council known as the Military Supply Member. It was suggested that Sir Edmond Elles, as connected with the old system, should retire, and that Lord Curzon should propose another officer to be his successor, with the curtailed powers henceforward allotted to the office. Mr. Brodrick, the Secretary of State, was able to announce to the House of Commons that the compromise was accepted by both parties. But unhappily it soon became clear that Lord Curzon and Lord Kitchener, as was not perhaps altogether surprising, understood different things by the government's dispatch. Lord Curzon proposed Sir Edmund Barrow, but the home government declined his nomination for reasons that seemed sound in themselves and were entirely creditable to that distinguished officer. Mr. Brodrick then suggested, not very tactfully, that Lord Curzon should consult Lord Kitchener as to the officer to be selected. The dispatch was so unhappily worded that Lord Ripon—an impartial witness, as standing in Indian policy poles asunder from Lord Curzon—declared in the House of Lords that no such dispatch had been addressed to the Government of India since Lord Ellenborough sent to Lord Canning his famous letter on the affairs of Oudh. Lord Curzon, convinced now that the government were not prepared to allow him the kind of military adviser he desired, resigned his office in August 1905. The Cabinet asked him to withdraw his resignation, but he declined to do so.

Lord Curzon was succeeded by Lord Minto, the great-grandson of the first earl, who was Governor-General from 1807 to 1813. The new Viceroy had fought in Afghanistan under Lord Roberts in 1878 and had been Governor-General of Canada from 1898 to 1904.

It is no doubt too early yet to anticipate by conjecture Lord Curzon's final place in history. The present writer has not refrained from criticism where to the best of his judgement criticism seemed to be called for. Many judges, whose opinion is worthy of all respect, would carry that criticism much farther. It is probable enough that much of the unrest in India was due to the all-pervading rather restless energy of his ardent spirit, just as Lord Dalhousie's great governor-generalship had assuredly something to do with the cataclysm of the Mutiny. It is indeed an arguable position that the most successful rulers of men are those sedate, clear-eyed, disillusioned characters like Lord Northbrook or Lord Dufferin, who are content to guide circumspectly the ship of state, who distrust heroic policies, and do not believe that it is either desirable or possible for one man to mould to his will such a colossal organism as that of the imperial government of India. But as long as personal force, initiative, will, and eloquence are valued in politics, Lord Curzon will always stand out as a great figure. No man could set forth in more stately language the best aspect of Great Britain's rule in the East. 'I am not one of those', he said, 'who think that we have built a mere fragile plank between the East and the West which the roaring tides of Asia will presently sweep away . . . as the years roll by, the call seems to me more clear, the duty more imperative, the work more majestic, the goal more sublime . . . To me the message is carved in granite, it is hewn out of the rock of doom—that our work is righteous and that it shall endure.' And so while men may legitimately differ as to Lord Curzon's statesmanship and as to the ultimate effect of his general policy upon the destinies of the people he was called upon to govern, there can hardly be any question as to the high ideals that inspired him, or of the devotion to duty which, in the teeth of much ill-health, domestic sorrow, and physical pain, drove him on to the end of his course. His final speech in India, which ended with one of the noblest passages in modern oratory, summed up his conception of the Englishman's task in India. 'A hundred times in India have I said to myself, Oh that to every Englishman in this country, as he ends his work, might be truthfully applied the phrase: "Thou hast loved righteousness and hated iniquity." No man has, I believe, ever served India faithfully of whom that could not be said. All other triumphs are tinsel and sham. Perhaps there are few of us who make anything but a poor approximation to that ideal. But let it be our ideal all the same. To fight for the right, to abhor the imperfect, the unjust, or the mean, to swerve neither to the right hand nor to the left, to care nothing for flattery or applause, or odium or abuse—it is so easy to have any of them in India—never to let your enthusiasm be soured or your courage grow dim, but to remember that the Almighty has placed your hand on the greatest of His ploughs, in whose furrow the nations of the future are germinating and taking shape, to drive the blade a little forward in your time, and to feel that somewhere among these millions you have left a little justice or happiness or prosperity, a sense of manliness or moral dignity, a spring of patriotism, a dawn of intellectual enlightenment, or a stirring of duty, where it did not before exist—that is enough, that is the Englishman's justification in India. It is enough for his watchword while he is here, for his epitaph when he is gone. I have worked for no other aim. Let India be my judge.'

These proud and noble words formed the fitting conclusion to a great viceroyalty. They are valid as an *apologia* not only at the bar of Indian public opinion but before the higher court of the world and of time. Whatever errors, whatever failures—and both error and failure are inseparable from human agency—critics may detect in his six years of office, it cannot be doubted that when the cloud-belts of contemporary detraction have cleared away, Lord Curzon's name will stand amongst the foremost of those that make up the illustrious roll of the Governors-General of India.

CHAPTER XVI

THE MORLEY-MINTO REFORMS. THE ANGLO-RUSSIAN CONVENTION

THE departure of Lord Curzon marked a real epoch in Indian history. It synchronized with the advent to power in England of the most powerful Liberal and Radical government that had ever been successful at the polls. This event was destined to have profound and far-reaching effects upon the whole problem of British rule in India. It seemed indeed the irony of fate that, immediately after Lord Curzon, by indomitable labour, had renovated and strengthened the machinery of Indian administration, a party should succeed to power which was more concerned to apply conceptions of popular and constitutional government to our Eastern Empire than to pursue drastic reforming methods through the agency of an enlightened bureaucracy—a party which believed in freedom rather than in discipline, in autonomy rather than efficiency. The new Secretary of State, Mr. John Morley, was a man of strong personality, who, though he seemed to the 'impatient idealists' of his party to be unduly ready to compromise the hitherto unsuspected orthodoxy of his Liberalism, was determined to make his office a reality and to introduce constitutional reforms in India. Some former Secretaries of State might have been regarded merely as necessary links between the Cabinet and the Viceroys. Such was not Mr. Morley's conception of his position, and, even if he did not go so far as to regard the Governor-General as his 'agent' (though that designation was once employed by his under-secretary), yet he undoubtedly demanded a larger and more direct share in the administration than former Secretaries of State had been wont to claim. It is indeed inevitable that the viceroyalty of Lord Minto and Mr. Morley's rule at the India Office should be closely associated. They were appointed within a few weeks of one another. Lord Morley of Blackburn (he had been elevated to the peerage in 1908) resigned in October 1910 and Lord Minto left India a month later. Both Secretary of State and Viceroy in their co-operation depended less than most of their predecessors on the expert guidance and accumulated experience of their permanent officials, and, without prejudging the question of gain or loss to the country, it is certainly true that the famous Morley-Minto reforms 'were in the main the outcome of an exchange of views between two statesmen whose knowledge of India was obviously limited'.[1]

The time and manner of Lord Curzon's departure left some troublesome questions for his successors, and Lord Minto had embarrassments of his own to face arising from the fact that, though he had been sent to India by a Unionist government to support Lord Kitchener, he was called upon to work with a Liberal ministry, the sympathies of whose supporters, though against Lord Curzon in regard to the partition of Bengal, had been entirely with him in his disagreement with the Commander-in-Chief. The same question for a different reason had its difficulties for the Secretary of State. The English party system which suddenly transforms a free lance of opposition into a responsible minister of the Crown often plays strange tricks with men's endeavours to maintain political consistency. Mr. Morley had apparently burnt his boats in regard to the

[1] Sir Valentine Chirol in *The Times*. See also Mr. Lovat Fraser in the *Edinburgh Review* for January 1918: 'Lord Morley . . . whatever his virtues may have been, was certainly the most autocratic and the least constitutional Secretary of State ever seen in Whitehall.'

Curzon-Kitchener controversy by a declaration to his constituents just before he accepted the seals of office. 'Lord Curzon', he said, 'has been chased out of power by the military, and the Secretary of State (Mr. Brodrick) has sanctioned that operation. If there is one principle more than another that has been accepted in this country since the day when Charles I lost his head, it is this: that the civil power shall be supreme over the military power. That is what you will find at the India Office: that they have been guilty of this great dereliction, this great departure from those standard maxims of public administration which had been practically sacred in these islands ever since the days of the Civil War.' The still lingering echoes of these resounding periods did not make the position any the easier, and Mr. Morley's opponents waited with some natural curiosity and a certain cynical amusement to see how he would meet the situation. Strict logic should have led him to reverse the decision of his predecessor, but that would undoubtedly have meant the resignation both of the Viceroy and the Commander-in-Chief—a contingency that the new Cabinet could hardly have faced. Mr. Morley therefore decided with what grace he could muster to accept the *fait accompli* and not to reopen the question 'at the risk of an indefinite prolongation of fruitless and injurious controversy'. The Commander-in-Chief henceforward became an ordinary member of council and the army department was placed in his charge. The military supply department was created and was presided over by another member of council, but it proved an arrangement, in Lord Morley's words, 'good neither for administration nor for economy.' It was abolished in 1907, having rather expensively fulfilled its real, though unavowed, function of saving illustrious faces. In the end, therefore, Lord Kitchener's view prevailed, but twelve years later, in tragic circumstances and at a terrible crisis, Lord Curzon's position in the controversy was completely vindicated. In the intervening time the control of the government of India over military policy had seriously weakened. The concentration of executive and administrative power in the hands of one overworked Commander-in-Chief resulted in the breakdown of the transport and of the medical service in Mesopotamia during the great war. The commission of inquiry that followed passed a scathing condemnation on the Kitchener system and declared that it was impossible for the duties of Commander-in-Chief and military member to be adequately performed by any one man in time of war.

Mr. Morley also declined to reverse the Partition of Bengal. He declared his opinion that the policy of his predecessors had been mistaken in its methods, but added that it was a settled matter as far as he was concerned. The agitation, however, still continued, and led to an incident which brought much criticism and embarrassment upon the Indian government. An objectionable feature of the movement had been the participation of Bengali schoolboys in political meetings, often with the connivance of their teachers. Sir J. Bampfylde Fuller, the first Lieutenant-Governor of Eastern Bengal and Assam, addressed a circular to the educational department deprecating this practice, and threatening that the government would withdraw pecuniary aid from the schools where it was countenanced, and would recommend the Calcutta University to disaffiliate them. Two schools in the Patna district disregarded these orders, and sheltered the ringleaders among their scholars. Sir J. Bampfylde Fuller applied to the Calcutta University to disaffiliate the schools concerned, but was requested by the government of India to withdraw his application on the ground that it would result in an acrimonious debate in the senate of the university, which, in the excited condition of public feeling, would be highly undesirable. The Lieutenant-Governor thereupon tendered his resignation, unless the Indian government should reconsider their request, and his resignation was accepted. The incident was naturally regarded as a triumph for the opponents of the Partition, and Lord Curzon, in the House of Lords, declared that Fuller 'was sacrificed in the mistaken belief that it would pacify the agitators'. The reply of the Indian government was that they could not submit to the dictation of one of their own officials, but this hardly answered the charge that they were prepared to allow the schools to defy the Lieutenant-Governor, and Sir J. Bampfylde Fuller had many to sympathize with him.

In the foreign policy of the new Liberal government one of the most noteworthy achievements was the threefold convention between Great Britain and Russia concluded in 1907, relating to Tibet, Afghanistan, and Persia, which settled by peaceful diplomacy three long outstanding questions of Asian politics. In reviewing the external relations of India under Lord Minto's government it will perhaps be most convenient if, bearing this central fact in mind, we consider separately our relations with each of the three countries concerned, showing in due course how the agreement with Russia affected them.

Mr. Morley and Lord Minto took up the threads of the Tibetan question where their predecessors had dropped them. It was still requisite to gain the formal assent of China as suzerain of Tibet to the Treaty of Lhasa of 1904. The original intention was that she should sign a mere 'adhesion agreement', but this developed into a convention, concluded at Pekin in April 1906, which, besides confirming the Treaty of Lhasa, contained two other clauses. By the first, Great Britain bound herself neither to annex the country nor to interfere in its internal administration; by the second, China engaged to impose like restrictions on all other foreign powers. The second clause, though verbally a concession to Great Britain, was actually quite as much to the advantage of the Chinese as to ourselves, and certainly gave some colour to the contention of those who asserted that China secured all the advantages of our interference in Tibetan affairs. Throughout the whole course of the negotiations the Indian government, anxious to secure what fruits they could of Lord Curzon's policy, tried to insist on the *ipsissima verba* of the Treaty of Lhasa. The Secretary of State, on the other hand, was determined, and rightly, to withdraw from the whole entanglement as soon as possible, and in the end he prevailed. He therefore conceded the point, against the earnest representations of Simla, that the Chinese should pay the indemnity instead of the Tibetans, and should do so in three instalments instead of twenty-five. In 1908 the Chinese government asked that, the indemnity being paid, we should evacuate the Chumbi valley, according to our promise. Against this the Indian government protested on the ground that the Tibetans had not faithfully carried out their part of the Treaty in respect to the establishment of trade marts, and that by a withdrawal we were giving up the only guarantee we had for the fulfilment of the Treaty. But the Secretary of State, believing that for reasons of policy and expediency it was desirable that our occupation of the valley should terminate at once, disregarded the protest, and our troops were withdrawn in February 1908. In the meantime the convention between Great Britain and Russia of August 1907 had doubly barred the gates of Tibet against any further intrusion on the part of Europeans. Both powers agreed to respect the integrity of Tibetan territory, to abstain from any intervention in its internal administration, to treat with the government only through the Chinese, and to send no emissaries to Lhasa. In fact, Great Britain and Russia by this convention mutually agreed upon a self-denying ordinance in regard to Tibet. Two results, unexpected but perhaps inevitable, followed. The Dalai Lama was eventually deposed, and the whole control of the country passed into the hands of the Chinese Residents, who displayed a decidedly anti-British bias. In July 1908 the Dalai Lama was summoned to Pekin, and was there made so acutely to feel his inferiority that in 1910, after his return to Tibet, he appealed for help to the British government against the advance of Chinese troops on Lhasa. In February of that year he fled once more from his capital and crossed the Indian frontier to Darjeeling. The wheel had come full circle, and the traditional exclusiveness of the Tibetan was utterly broken down. The Tashi Lama had already crossed the Indian frontier in 1905–6 and been received in audience by the Prince of Wales and the Viceroy, and now the Dalai Lama himself, who had fled with horror from Lhasa in 1904 that his eyes might not even rest upon Europeans, visited the capital of British India and had an interview with Lord Minto. There he asked, but of course asked in vain, for help against the Chinese government, which in February had formally deposed him by an imperial decree. We were precluded now by our own action from giving him any aid, even had we desired to do so, and we could do nothing except address a mild and ineffective protest to the Chinese government. A new Dalai Lama was in due course found who was under the complete control of the Chinese Residents.

Mr. Morley's policy in regard to Tibet may be said to have skilfully settled a difficult question and to have disentangled us from a position that was full of danger. Opponents held that it amounted to a surrender of the aims of Lord Curzon's policy. But after all the main motive underlying Younghusband's expedition was to prevent the penetration of Tibet by Russian influence, and that end was secured by the convention of 1907. The pity is that the Russian and British governments could not have worked out such a solution in 1903. The whole trouble and expense of the expedition would then have been saved, Tibetan lives would not have been needlessly sacrificed at Guru, the Dalai Lama need not have been deposed, nor Tibet have passed under the despotic sway of China.

The Anglo-Russian Convention of 1907, so far as it affected Afghanistan, did little more than recognize the *status quo*. Great Britain disclaimed any intention of altering the political position there, and Russia, definitely acknowledging that Afghanistan lay outside her sphere of influence, agreed to act in all political relations with the Amir only through the British government, and to send no agents into the country. Equal commercial privileges were to be enjoyed both by British and Russian traders. From regard to the feelings of our ally it was stipulated that these arrangements were not to come into force till Great Britain was able to notify to Russia the Amir's assent to them. As a matter of fact, in spite of this precaution, Habibulla was affronted at this agreement between the two countries in regard to his dominions, and refused to give the convention his formal approval. This was the more to be regretted because he had paid a visit to England in the earlier part of the year, and seemed largely to have laid aside his former resentment against the British.

The convention in regard to Persia was more important than in the case of either Tibet or Afghanistan. It quite possibly prevented a disastrous war between England and Russia, and deserves to be ranked as one of the most notable diplomatic triumphs of the time. The disintegration of the Persian empire referred to in Chapter XIII was proceeding apace. During the period 1905–10 the condition of the country was rapidly lapsing into chaos. Persia's deplorable state was only intensified by the fact that western ideas of constitutionalism and popular government were germinating among her people, for the new wine of democracy proved too powerful a solvent for the old bottles of eastern autocracy. It was, therefore, a wise provision that inspired Great Britain and Russia to lay down certain definite rules circumscribing their position in regard to Persian territory, and defining their attitude towards the perilous situation created there.

The convention, though binding both Russia and Great Britain to respect the integrity and political independence of Persia, demarcated a Russian sphere of influence in northern Persia and a British sphere of influence in the south-eastern provinces. Each country agreed in regard to the other's sphere 'not to seek for herself or her own subjects or those of any other country any political or commercial concessions such as railway, banking, telegraph, roads, transport, or insurance', or to oppose the acquisition of such concessions by the other party to the agreement. The Russian sphere was bounded to the south by a line passing through Kasr-i-Shirin, Isfahan, Yezd, and Kakhk, the British by a northern boundary running from Bander Abbas through Kerman to Birjand. It was announced by Sir Edward Grey, the Foreign Secretary, that the Persian Gulf lay outside the scope of the convention, but that Russia had stated during the negotiations that she did not deny the special interests of Great Britain in the Gulf.

The convention was subjected to criticism, less for the general principle involved, though it is true that 'there is something amazingly cynical in the spirit in which western powers dispose of the heritage of other races',[1] as for the details of the bargain. One party declared that the Russian sphere of influence was too large and the British sphere too small, but as stated in Chapter XIII Russian penetration of northern Persia had proceeded very far, and there is no doubt that in this respect British statesmen, in the words of Sir J. D. Rees, 'had not so much given away advantages as accepted a position that had grown up'. The real justifica-

[1] Lovat Fraser, *India under Curzon and After*, p. 128.

tion for this fine piece of statesmanship is that it averted any serious trouble between Russia and Great Britain between the years 1907 and 1910 when Persia was in the throes of revolution and aflame with disorder—a situation affording innumerable opportunities for either side to intervene had there been no previous understanding.

In internal matters the agitation against the Partition of Bengal developed into a general political ferment throughout India. Indian unrest may, perhaps, be best characterized in the Secretary of State's own words. 'Of deeper moment', he wrote, 'loomed the vision of a wave of political unrest from various causes, partly superficial, partly fundamental, slowly sweeping over India. Revolutionary voices, some moderate, others extreme, grew articulate and shrill, and claims or aspirations for extending the share of peoples in their own government took more organized shape . . . Mechanical facility of communication between West and East improved almost from day to day, and made the transmission of sympathetic political currents more and more direct.'[1] This movement is the most momentous event of our time in Indian History. It is almost impossible to exaggerate its importance or the influence it is exerting on the whole problem of our position in the East. A brief analysis of the causes that produced it is, therefore, necessary.

The movement was part of a greater one. The continent of Asia was beginning in the world both of politics and of thought to rise from its old-world lethargy and free itself from the domination of Europeans. Japan had defeated the mighty armies of Russia. 'The reverberations of that victory', said Lord Curzon, 'have gone like a thunderclap through the whispering galleries of the East'. Western nations found both their material and spiritual weapons deftly turned against them, for the East, even in revolt, was imitative, and just as Japan vanquished Russia by modern

[1] Lord Morley's *Recollections*, vol. ii, p. 149.

weapons of precision so in Persia, India, and China the reform party modelled themselves on the most approved pattern of Western Liberalism, and derived their political armament from the political philosophy and literature of Europe.

Causes more particularly connected with India were first of all the high hopes excited by the advent to power of a great Radical majority at Westminster, many members of which were known to sympathize with the Indian 'Progressive' party. Secondly, there was the rapidly growing influence of the Indian National Congress and the gradual drawing together, at any rate in open political alliance, of the Hindu and Muhammadan leaders, although originally the Muhammadans had opposed the movement, and as lately as 1899 their chief representatives, under the presidency of Sir Amir Hassan, declared that the congress policy impeded the true political and moral progress of the country. Thirdly, there was no doubt a certain revolt against the vigorous efficient autocratic rule of Lord Curzon, which, rightly or wrongly, the Nationalist leaders considered to be reactionary in many of its aspects.

Like most progressive parties the Indian reformers contained a moderate and an extremist section. Men like the late R. C. Dutt, the late Mr. Gokhale, and Sir Satyendra Sinha maintained with moderation and great ability views which though advanced were inherently reasonable and logical. But the extremists by a revolutionary propaganda and inflammatory speeches embarked on a campaign which soon led to outrages and political assassinations. In April dangerous riots occurred at Lahore and Rawal Pindi. The position became so threatening that the government were compelled in the following month to issue an ordinance (later embodied in an Act) empowering local governments to 'proclaim' certain districts with the result that no public meetings could be held in them without seven days' notice being first given to the authorities, and to deport offenders under a Regulation of 1818. At the National Congress in December, held at Surat, the moderates and the extremists joined issue in a contest between two candidates for the chairmanship, the nominee of the latter being a man who had lately been deported for his share in the Punjab riots. The contest ended in a free fight and was adjourned *sine die*, but the moderate party immediately afterwards issued a manifesto that their goal was the attainment by constitutional and lawful means of the same position for India in the empire as that of Canada and the other self-governing colonies. Unfortunately in the next year, 1908, the seditious agitation continued and was accompanied by murderous attacks upon Europeans and others. On the earnest representations of the Indian government, and much against his will, the Secretary of State was obliged to sanction special legislation to meet the campaign of violence. Two Acts were passed making it a felony to manufacture or possess explosives or to incite to murder in the press, and later the Legislative Council sanctioned in a single sitting without opposition an Act conferring upon the courts summary jurisdiction in cases of seditious violence.

Nothing could well have been more inopportune than this outburst of political crime. Lord Morley and Lord Minto were honestly desirous of taking some decided steps in the direction of liberalizing Indian institutions, though the manifesto even of the moderate party was regarded by them as embodying a distant ideal at present quite unattainable. They had already begun to formulate reforms. The question was whether they were now to withhold their hand in view of what had occurred. They decided not to flinch in the course they had marked out. Lord Morley believed that the best way to draw the teeth of the extremists was to win the support of the moderate party by granting a real measure of reform. At the same time it was impossible to tolerate anarchy, and, therefore, the Indian government adopted that 'blended policy of repression and concession' to which it was easier to object than to suggest an alternative. The repression was certainly not excessive; indeed a high authority has declared that 'many innocent victims paid with their lives for the extraordinary supineness displayed in those first disastrous two years of Lord Minto's administration'.[1] The Secretary of State and the Viceroy suffered the usual fate of statesmen who adopt a moderate course, in being attacked from opposite sides as both revolutionary and reactionary. They persevered, however, with their policy, and so it came about that this year—so darkened by conspiracies and assassinations—witnessed at its close both the message of King Edward VII to the princes and peoples of India on the fiftieth anniversary of the assumption of government by the Crown, and the unfolding by Lord Morley in the House of Lords of plans intended to be the first step in the realization of the promised reforms. The message of November 2 began with a proud yet not unjustified claim for the recognition of Great Britain's services to India. 'Half a century is but a brief span in your long annals, yet this half century that ends to-day will stand amid the floods of your historic ages, a far shining landmark. The proclamation of the direct supremacy of the Crown sealed the unity of Indian government and opened a new era. The journey was arduous and the advance may have sometimes seemed slow; but the incorporation of many strangely diversified communities, and of some three hundred millions of the human race, under British guidance and control has proceeded steadfastly and without pause. We survey our labours of the past half century with clear gaze and good conscience.' After an enumeration of the benefits of British rule the message proceeded to a promise of further constitutional development. 'From the first, the principle of

[1] *Indian Unrest*, by Sir Valentine Chirol, 1910, p. 96.

representative institutions began to be gradually introduced, and the time has come when, in the judgement of my Viceroy and Governor-General and others of my counsellors, that principle may be prudently extended.' The Indian Councils Act which was a further development of Lord Cross's Act of 1892 (see Chap. XI, p. 498) was passed in February 1909. It provided for an increase in the numbers of the vice-regal and provincial Legislative Councils. The Executive Councils of Madras and Bombay were also to be enlarged and such councils were to be established in provinces ruled by Lieutenant-Governors. In the constitution of the Legislative Councils the principle of election was to be introduced side by side with that of nomination. The Act was mainly permissive in form, for almost everything depended on the actual Rules and Regulations which had still to be drawn up, and it has been rather appositely described as 'little more than a blank cheque drawn in favour of the Secretary of State, leaving in his hands the ultimate shape of the rules and regulations on which everything depended'.[1]

Unfortunately the Act had no effect as a check upon the anarchists. In February the Public Prosecutor of Bengal was shot dead by a Bengali student. In July Sir Curzon Wyllie was assassinated by a Punjabi at the Imperial Institute in London, and in December Jackson, a Bombay civilian, was murdered by a young Marathi Brahmin in an Indian theatre, while in the preceding month an attempt, fortunately unsuccessful, was made on the life of the Viceroy at Ahmadabad.

The Rules and Regulations defining the operation of the Act were published in November. They were too long and intricate to admit of an easily intelligible summary. The most elaborate arrangements were made for the representation in the legislative councils of various classes

[1] The Annual Register, 1909.

and minorities, for instance, of Muhammadans, landowners, the tea and jute industries, and Indian commerce. The Imperial Legislative Council was increased from twenty-one members to a maximum of sixty; the other legislative councils being generally rather more than doubled. In Madras and Bombay the members of the executive councils were increased in number from two to four. The Secretary of State supplemented these reforms by the striking innovation of appointing an Indian member to the Viceroy's Executive Council, other Indians to the Executive Councils of Bombay and Madras, and two to the Council at the India Office. Though in this way a great and notable advance was made, especially in the fact that an Indian sitting in the Viceroy's Cabinet was necessarily admitted to the most secret counsels of the government—a step in advance which was deprecated even by such stalwart Liberals as Lord Elgin and Lord Ripon—yet the Morley-Minto reforms failed to satisfy the National Congress Party, who had hoped that the whole of India would be divided into large popular constituencies. They criticized especially the principle of class representation on the ground that it created a distinction between the different classes of the community and made the fusion of their interests impossible. It is true that to satisfy these aims had at no time been the intention of the authors of the Act. 'If I were attempting', said Lord Morley in the House of Lords, 'to set up a parliamentary system in India, or, if it could be said that this chapter of reforms led directly or indirectly to the establishment of a parliamentary system in India, I for one would have nothing to do with it . . . If my existence, either officially or corporeally, were to be prolonged twenty times longer than either is likely to be, a parliamentary system in India is not at all the goal to which I would for a moment aspire'.

Yet the life of the *régime* based upon the Act of 1907 has

been but a decade, and it is now under criticism and revision. The Morley-Minto constitution turned out to be after all only a half-way house. The Montagu-Chelmsford Report of July 1918 condemned it as inadequate. 'Narrow franchises and indirect elections failed to encourage in members a sense of responsibility to the people generally, and made it impossible, except in special constituencies, for those who had votes to use them with perception and effect . . . while governments found themselves far more exposed to questions and criticism than hitherto, questions and criticism were uninformed by a real sense of responsibility, such as comes from the prospect of having to assume office in turn.' The general result was that 'Parliamentary usages have been initiated and adopted in the councils up to the point where they cause the maximum of friction, but short of that at which by having a real sanction behind them they begin to do good'. These views did not go unchallenged, and many considered that the Montagu-Chelmsford Report was misleading both in its estimate of what the Morley-Minto reforms had achieved and in its disbelief in their future. But there can be no clearer evidence of the rapidly accelerated pace of the Indian constitutional movement in our time than the fact that reforms, which in 1909 seemed even to many Indian politicians to exceed their utmost expectations, ten years later were regarded as merely a transitory and halting step on the path of progress.

CHAPTER XVII

THE CORONATION DURBAR. THE MONTAGU-CHELMSFORD REFORMS

LORD MINTO was succeeded by Sir Charles Hardinge, Permanent Under-Secretary for Foreign Affairs, who, on his elevation to the peerage, took the title of Lord Hardinge of Penshurst. In his period of office still further changes took place in the political state of Tibet owing to the outbreak of the revolution in China. In 1911 the Chinese garrison, deprived of all pay and supplies from Pekin, mutinied, plundered the treasury in Lhasa, and were finally expelled by the Tibetans. The Dalai Lama seized the opportunity to return to his capital after two years of exile. He entered into an understanding with the Chinese Resident that the latter should continue to reside in Lhasa, attended only by a bodyguard for his personal protection, and that he should no longer claim power over the general administration. Upon this a fresh decree was issued at Pekin restoring to the Lama all his old powers and privileges. In 1912 there were constant rumours that China was making preparations to reconquer the country. The British government made it clear to the Chinese authorities that, though they were willing to acknowledge the suzerainty of China over Tibet, they would strongly oppose the reduction of the country to the position of a mere province of the Chinese empire. A settlement of the question was made in 1913 and 1914 by a conference of Tibetan and Chinese delegates at Simla and Delhi, under the presidency of the Foreign Secretary to the government of India. The strange story of our dealings with Tibet and its ruler ends with the offer of the Dalai Lama to send us assistance in the Great War of 1914.

In Lord Hardinge's viceroyalty a delicate and difficult question of imperial politics came to the forefront, namely the attitude of the self-governing Colonies, and especially South Africa, towards Indian immigration. Asiatics were not welcomed in South Africa, and in 1913 the Union government passed a law limiting the facilities for immigration, and prohibiting them from trading, farming, or holding real property in the Orange Free State. The act naturally caused the deepest indignation in India; 'the people', says Sir Charles Roe, 'could not understand why the civil and political rights enjoyed by them so fully in India and in England should be denied to them in other parts of the empire, or why the government they had been accustomed to regard as all-powerful should tolerate a policy so opposed to its own principles. They could hardly be expected to realize how delicate and difficult is the task of interfering even by suggestion in the action of the self-governing colonies.'[1] In South Africa the Indian coolies adopted a policy of passive resistance. About 2,500 under the leadership of Mr. Gandhi marched into the Transvaal from Natal to assert their right to go from one province to another. Gandhi and other leaders were arrested. Strikes occurred in various parts of the country accompanied by some loss of life in collision with the military. Lord Hardinge won great popularity for the Indian government, but added something to the embarrassment of the Imperial Cabinet, by a strong speech at Madras in criticism of the South African Ministry. He protested against the position of Indians in South Africa, showed his sympathy for the passive resistance movement, and censured the Immigration Act as 'invidious and unjust'. He declared that the Union

[1] Annual Register.

Government of South Africa could only justify itself in the eyes of the world by appointing a Committee of Inquiry and allowing Indians to take part in it. Constitutional purists pointed out with some force that the imperial government was properly the only channel of communication between the different governments of the Empire, but the speech, notwithstanding much criticism, produced the desired effect. The South African government in the end appointed a commission, the Indian leaders were released from prison to prepare their case, and though at first they were inclined to boycott the commission, they ultimately appeared before it. An Act was passed, which, though it did not entirely satisfy Indian aspirations, was pronounced by Mr. Gandhi to be the Magna Carta of Indian liberty in South Africa.

South Africa at least admitted Asiatics under restrictions however hard. Canada and British Columbia declined to receive them at all. Certain Indian leaders, as a kind of concrete protest, chartered the steamship *Komagata Maru* to convey three hundred Indians, mostly Sikhs, to Vancouver. They were not allowed to enter the colony and were obliged after some trouble to return to Calcutta, where there was an unfortunate collision with the police on their disembarkation.

In May 1910 King George V, on the death of Edward VII, had succeeded to the throne of Great Britain. The Coronation in Westminster Abbey took place on June 22, 1911. The King had determined on the advice of his ministers to create an entirely new precedent by proceeding himself with the Queen to India at the close of the year, in order to preside at a great Coronation Durbar, and receive in person the homage both of the great officials of State and the protected Princes of the Indian Empire. In the absence of His Majesty four 'Counsellors of State' were appointed to transact the formal business of the throne, namely Prince Arthur of Connaught, the Archbishop of Canterbury, the

Lord Chancellor, and the Lord President of the Council, who happened at that time to be Lord Morley of Blackburn. All matters of high importance were communicated to the King daily by telegraph. As the King's suite included the Marquess of Crewe, the Secretary of State for India, the extraordinary spectacle was presented of the King-Emperor, the head of the India Office, and the occupant of the vice-regal throne being all on Indian soil together. The grand Durbar was held at Delhi on December 12 before a vast assembly of about 80,000 people. Certain imperial boons were announced including grants of land, a month's extra pay for soldiers and subordinate civil servants, the allotment of fifty lacs of rupees for the education of the people, and the declaration of the eligibility of Indians for the Victoria Cross. Then followed the announcement of changes of far greater magnitude, the secret of which had been extraordinarily well kept. These were the transference of the capital of India from Calcutta to Delhi, the creation of a Governor-in-Council for Bengal—a change associated with the reunion of Eastern Bengal with the old province, the creation of a new Lieutenant-Governorship of Bihar, Orissa, and Chota Nagpur, and the reduction of Assam once more to a Chief-Commissionership. These changes were striking and dramatic. The transfer of the capital had no doubt many theoretical and logical advantages; it was defended by the government on the ground that the consolidation of British rule in India and the development of the railway system made it no longer necessary for the seat of government to be upon the sea-board. The Viceroy henceforward would be increasingly concerned with matters of purely imperial interest, and the subordinate provincial governorships would become more autonomous in their administration. Delhi from its central position, and its historical associations was obviously the best fitted city in India for the capital of a quasi-federal empire. The reunion of

Bengal was said to be 'not a reversal of the partition but a rearrangement after experience'—a statement hardly consistent with the facts. The appointment of a Governor of Bengal, as we have seen, had long been a favourite notion with the advanced Indian party.

These political experiments were naturally submitted to criticism, and first of all the method of initiating them was called in question. The changes were ultimately to be enacted by Act of Parliament, but as their announcement had been put in the mouth of the King-Emperor speaking *ex cathedra* from his Indian throne, it was impossible for Parliament to go back upon them without fatally damaging the prestige of the Crown. The widely-held view that they should have been first submitted to Parliament was not unreasonable. If such momentous reforms could be carried by the executive on its own authority, it would be difficult to imagine any circumstances in which the legislature would have to be consulted. That this enhancement of the Prerogative was the work of a Liberal government, normally supposed to be jealous of any encroachment on Parliamentary privileges, only added to the embarrassment both of their supporters who were expected to acquiesce, and their opponents who would gladly have demurred. Economists objected to the cost of transforming Delhi into a capital adequate to the rather exacting needs of the imperial government. The expenditure was originally forecasted as £4,000,000, but revised estimates revealed the fact that the sum would probably amount to half as much again. To dethrone a great capital city is an invidious task. Round Calcutta had gathered all the most hallowed traditions of British India since the days of Job Charnock, and our national prejudices are little in sympathy with such dramatic strokes of constitutional experiment. It was held by many that the trouble aroused by the Partition had subsided, that it was a grave error to reopen the question, and finally that the government had made a concession to the agitators—always a doubtful policy—and what was worse, had gone out of their way to do so when such a step was in no sense necessary.

The outbreak of the European war in August 1914 revealed a deep and splendid loyalty to the British empire on the part of the princes and peoples of India, and although in the preceding year, during the Balkan war, the Moslem leaders had declared that Great Britain was committing a serious blunder in leaving Turkey to her fate, their loyalty to their suzerain did not quail even when Germany dragged the Porte into her alliance. Indian troops fought side by side with those of the self-governing colonies on the battle-fields of France, Flanders, Macedonia, Egypt, Palestine, and Mesopotamia. To the events of that world-wide conflict we cannot refer here. They are too recent, and too much obscured by controversy to be the fit subject of historical treatment. We can only briefly chronicle some of the political results which followed from the war, and indicate in outline the tremendous changes that are impending over the whole constitution of our Eastern empire. The supreme issues involved in the struggle dwarfed many questions that had aroused implacable passions in the past. One subordinate result of the war was the removal of the old Indian grievance (so often referred to in these pages) of the cotton duties, because, owing to the exigencies of war finance, the import duties on cotton goods were raised to the general level of seven and a half per cent. *ad valorem*, without any enhancement of the countervailing duty on the product of Indian mills. Protests from Manchester were not indeed wanting, but they went unregarded in the clash of arms. More important was the place allotted to India in the councils of the confederated and embattled empire. Two Indian representatives, the Maharaja of Bikanir and Sir Satyendra Sinha, took part together with Sir James Meston in the imperial war conference in London in the spring of

1917 and afterwards in the Peace Conference. In the reconstruction of the coalition government following the general election of 1918 Sir Satyendra Sinha was made Under-Secretary for India and elevated to the peerage under the title of Lord Sinha of Raipur.

These results, striking as they are, fall into insignificance when compared with other changes. On August 20, 1917, Mr. E. S. Montagu, the Secretary of State, made the most momentous announcement of British policy since the passing of India under the control of the Crown. He enunciated four principles for future guidance. The first was 'the increasing association of Indians in every branch of the administration'. The second, 'the gradual development of self-governing institutions with a view to the progressive realization of responsible government in India as an integral part of the British Empire'. The third laid it down 'that progress in this policy can only be achieved by successive stages', and the fourth, that the Home government in conjunction with the government of India 'on whom the responsibility lies for the welfare and advancement of the Indian people, must be judges of the time and measure of each advance, and they must be guided by the co-operation received from those on whom new opportunities of service will be thus conferred, and by the extent to which it is found that confidence can be reposed in their sense of responsibility'.

The difficulties in practice of implementing this declaration were very great. It involved the most extensive scheme of decentralization and devolution ever attempted, affecting as it did an empire with a population of over three hundred millions. This colossal task had to be undertaken in the last stages of a world-wide war, while it was still doubtful whether a cataclysmic defeat could be avoided. The details of measures had to be worked out between departments of an executive separated by thousands of miles of land

and sea. Unprecedented measures were employed. The Secretary of State proceeded to India to consult with Lord Chelmsford, who had succeeded Lord Hardinge as Governor-General in 1916. On his return a voluminous report was published, making proposals for reform. It was, for a government document, unconventionally philosophic in matter and picturesque in style, and was not to the taste of those accustomed to the neutral tone and matter-of-fact style of British state papers, nor, in spite of its eloquence and sincerity, can it be denied that, it seemed to distil a certain ethical and political unction.

After an analysis of failures in the past, the report advised that the legislatures should be granted responsibility:—'they must have real work to do: and they must have real people to call them to account for their doing of it.'[1] This of course implied a concession of the power to govern badly together with the duty of governing well, and the authors of the report squarely faced that fact:—'We believe that nationhood within the Empire represents something better than anything India has hitherto attained; that the placid, pathetic contentment of the masses is not the soil on which such Indian nationhood will grow, and that in deliberately disturbing it, we are working for her highest good.'[2] Criticism was invited, though it would clearly not be very acceptable if it assailed the main conclusions of the report.

Two committees under the chairmanship of Lord Southborough were sent to India to demarcate electorates and settle the lines of division between the 'reserved' and 'transferred' subject, of which more anon. A Bill was then drafted and was submitted, together with the reports of the two committees, to a joint committee of Lords and Commons presided over by Lord Selborne. This committee, perhaps

[1] *Report on Indian Constitutional Reforms* (Cd. 9109) p. 69.
[2] Ibid., p. 120.

somewhat cavalierly, rejected an alternative scheme put forward by a majority of the heads of the provincial governments in India, which, in the words of Sir Michael O'Dwyer, one of its chief promoters, aimed at the 'maintenance of a unitary government, the chief executive consisting of the governor, with an equal number of British and Indian colleagues, drawn respectively from the services and the elected assembly, and bound together by a joint responsibility to the Crown'.[1]

The measure was passed in December 1919. The provisions, supplemented by regulations made under the Act, established the following constitution :—

In the provincial governments an executive was set up with two sections (unofficially styled dyarchy) connected only by the fact that the Governor presided over both. One consisted of two to four members of Council appointed by the Crown, half normally to be Indians; it was ultimately responsible to the Secretary of State, and would handle certain matters called 'reserved subjects'. The other consisted of ministers appointed by the Governor from elected Indian members of the legislative Council and dealt with the 'transferred subjects'. The line of demarcation between reserved and transferred subjects was in effect that between the more and the less vital spheres of government :—'The transferred subjects should be those departments which afford most opportunity for local knowledge and social service, those on which Indians have shown themselves to be keenly interested, those in which the mistakes that occur, though serious, would not be irremediable, and those which stand most in need of development.' Ministers in charge of the transferred subjects held positions analogous to those of members of the British Cabinet. They were appointed by the Governor, as the latter by the Crown, but they retained office only as long as they kept the confidence of

[1] Sir Michael O'Dwyer, Letter to *The Times*, July 18, 1925.

the legislature and continued to be members of it. The line drawn between reserved and transferred subjects was not an arbitrary one; it was hoped that there would be a gradual transference of subjects from the first category to the second, until the distinction vanished and all departments were in the hands of ministers responsible to the legislatures.

The United Provinces, the Punjab, Bihar and Orissa, and later Burma (in 1923) and the North-West Frontier Province (in 1932) were each given a governor and council. The provincial legislative councils were largely increased, Bengal to 139 members, Madras to 127, and Bombay to 111. At least seventy per cent. of the members were to be elected. Communal electorates were constituted for Muhammadans, the Sikhs in the Punjab, Europeans, Anglo-Indians, and Indian Christians. The councils were given power to vote, and withhold supplies, but the Governor had power to demand grants for reserved subjects if he certified that the expenditure was essential. After four years the councils had the right to elect their own president.

In the Supreme Government there was no dyarchy, and the Governor-General was directly responsible to the Secretary of State and Parliament. The Executive Council was enlarged indefinitely. It was understood, though not actually ordered, that half should consist of men of Indian birth. The Indian legislature was entirely remodelled and made bi-cameral. The upper chamber, called the Council of State, was to be mainly a revising body. The majority of its 61 members were to be elected, so that the former official *bloc* no longer existed. The franchise was based on a high property qualification. The lower chamber, the Legislative Assembly, had 106 elected, and 40 nominated, members, of whom 25 were official. The franchise for the assembly was wider than for the council, and was granted to women. The period of the council was five, and of the assembly three, years. The Governor-General, in the event of a deadlock between the two houses, might summon a joint session. The assembly had a general control over finance, but the Governor-General could, at his discretion, authorize any expenditure which he considered essential for the safety or tranquillity of British India. In a similar way he was empowered, in the last resort, to ensure the passing of other bills as emergency measures.

After ten years, a commission was to be appointed by Parliament to inquire into the working of the constitution, and to report whether the degree of responsible government granted was to be extended, modified, or restricted. As soon as the royal consent was given, a proclamation established a Chamber of Princes (one of the unrealized dreams of Lord Lytton) as a deliberative and advisory body without executive authority, and granted an amnesty to political prisoners.

The general result of the legislative and executive reforms has been thus summed up by Dr. A. B. Keith:—'The Assembly . . . was made a more effective means of criticizing and holding the government within lines of action approved by Indian feeling. The executive, however, remained wholly free from direct authority of the legislature.'[1] It is noteworthy that the Bill was piloted through the House of Lords by an Indian, Lord Sinha.[2] When it had passed, he returned to India to become Governor of Bihar and Orissa. After a breakdown in health he was appointed in 1926 to the judicial committee of the Privy Council in England. His death in 1928 was a great loss to the British *raj* and to the peoples of India. The list of the great offices he held both in his own country and at the centre of the empire is a measure of the vast distance India has travelled in political evolution during the last thirty years.

Many judges, whose opinions were deserving of the highest respect, strongly dissented from the policy of the

[1] Dr. A. B. Keith, *A Constitutional History of India*, 1936, p. 263.
[2] *Supra*, pp. 579–80.

Bill. But it must in fairness be admitted that by implication Great Britain had been committed, by the whole trend of her policy since 1858, to advance on some such lines, while, since the historic declaration of August 20, 1917, she has been so pledged unreservedly. The policy had been deliberately adopted by a coalition government composed of representatives of all the great parties in the state. It was not seriously challenged by any prominent statesman. The declaration owed its final form to the draftmanship of Lord Curzon, himself the greatest living representative of the passing 'benevolent' autocracy. 'To reverse that policy', wrote Sir Valentine Chirol, 'would be regarded, and reasonably regarded, in India, as a breach of faith which would do more to shake the foundations of British rule than would the worst consequences which its gloomiest critics foresee from persistence in it.'[1] It was also widely felt that the generous and magnificent fidelity of the Indian peoples in the crisis of the Great War called for an equally generous trust from the suzerain power. But it would be folly to deny that the risks seemed to many to be, and in fact were, great. The dyarchy of the double executive was open to almost every theoretical objection that the armoury of political philosophy can supply.

The soil, too, for the sowing of the new seed was not altogether favourable. There were no doubt many thousands of loyal Indians prepared to give the new constitution a fair and honest trial, but there were also subversive forces working beneath the surface of society. The revelations of the Rowlatt Report,[2] issued in July 1918, proved beyond possibility of cavil the existence of a widespread and most dangerous revolutionary movement, which had originally been partly fostered and manipulated by men of extreme

[1] In the *Quarterly Review*, October 1918.

[2] *See* Sir Verney Lovett, *A History of the Indian Nationalist Movement*, 1920, chap. vii.

opinions living in France and the United States. Even the moderate progressive party were inclined to regard the reforms as incomplete. Yet they definitely engrafted upon the Indian system that Parliamentary government which only nine years before so staunch a Liberal as Lord Morley had visualized as an ideal scarcely capable of realization till many generations had passed. 'We have now', he wrote, 'as it were before us in that vast congeries of peoples we call India, a long slow march in uneven stages through all the centuries from the fifth to the twentieth.' No country, to which such words were applicable could be an easy subject for experiments in democracy. Behind the comparatively small but fast-growing band of western-educated Indians with their clamant demands for the self-determination, which we had taught them to revere, stood the silent millions of untaught peasants, whose interests we quite rightly dreaded to endanger. Dyarchy was felt to be the least concession we could make to the *intelligentsia* class; yet as Sir Reginald Craddock wrote with considerable truth—'it was all based on the assumption that a tiny novitiate of electors out of the vast masses of illiterate India, bristling with its racial feuds, its religious antagonisms, its castes, its social exclusions, its babel of tongues, its fierce communal controversies, would start functioning in response to a system absolutely alien to them, in the same way that the experienced electors of educated England to-day respond to a system which the people have gradually developed for themselves in the course of many centuries'.[1]

[1] Sir Reginald Craddock, *The Dilemma in India*. London, 1929, p. 173.

CHAPTER XVIII

DYARCHY AND NON-CO-OPERATION

To summarize the history of India from 1916 to the present time, on the limited scale suitable to this book, is no easy task. It is only possible here to deal with the outstanding events and main currents of the vast constitutional movement which is the predominant feature of the epoch, and it is open to any critic to aver that a different selection from facts embarrassingly abundant would justify quite another interpretation of them. That charge, however, must be risked, and the writer can only, as impartially as possible without a surrender of convictions, trace the course and analyse the causes of the development, as it presents itself to him, remembering always that he moves in an atmosphere heavy with the dust of conflict and shot with the fiery afterglow of controversies still sullenly smouldering.

These controversies were honest and sincere enough, for the cleavage of thought that produced them is one of those that strike down to the deepest foundations of political faith. To ignore, or omit the record of, them would be to present a misleadingly smooth and flattering view of intractable and disconcerting facts. Some regard the development since 1919 as—in the words of Lord Zetland—'an experiment in the domain of statecraft unparalleled in the annals of mankind'[1]—as the unique and altruistic effort of a sovereign nation to endow subject peoples with powers hitherto exercised in their behalf but not through their agency. Others honestly regard it as the ignoble surrender,

[1] *The New India.* Times Publishing Company, 1937, p. 7.

under constant political pressure, of a high imperial task, which Great Britain in a mood of faltering introspection has no longer the self-confidence to claim for herself—a dreary and futile attempt, by a series of desperate makeshifts, to placate the implacable and win a political gratitude which is everlastingly withheld from her.

No one can gainsay that the advance has been made at a rapidly accelerating pace.[1] India in a period of less than thirty years, that is since 1909, has passed through, as in a headlong constitutional cavalcade, changes the like of which were only consummated by Great Britain in five or six hundred years. It is only necessary to enumerate the stages marked by the Morley-Minto reforms (1909), the proclamation at the Delhi Durbar (1911), the Government of India Act (1912), the promise of responsible government (1917), the Montagu-Chelmsford report (1918), the Government of India Act (1919), Lord Irwin's pronouncement on dominion status (1929), the Simon Commission report (1930), the Round Table Conferences (1931–2), the White Paper (1933), the report of the Joint Select Committee (1934), the Government of India Act (1935), and finally the inauguration of provincial governments responsible to elected legislatures (1937). Great Britain, however, has been given little credit for this almost breathless rate of constitutional progress, and the aplomb with which Indian extremists invariably declare that they see no cause for thankfulness in concessions which exceed a thousandfold the most extravagant expectations of a few years before, extorts admiration at least by its hardihood. Truly, indeed, has it been said that 'the Indian *intelligentsia* exhibit the mentality of a traveller who is consumed with the desire to arrive at the end of a long and difficult journey. Every stage, no matter how essential, is a fresh grievance; any obstacle, no matter how inevitable,

[1] See *Moral and Material Progress and Condition of India, 1923–4*, p. 4.

an intolerable outrage; every advance, no matter how noteworthy, is ignored and forgotten in comparison with the distance which has yet to be painfully traversed'.[1]

We have, however, probably far more friends in India than we shall ever know—friends and well-wishers who dare not declare themselves. It has become an accepted convention, even with the parties least inimical to British suzerainty, that, unless they are to forfeit all popular support at the outset, they must never allow themselves to be startled into any expression of political gratitude; and that they can only agree to work reforms with the ultimate purpose—avowed at any rate, if not always intended—of overthrowing the constitution of which they form a part. It is not of course meant that this tendency is a special defect inherent only in Eastern psychology. It is equally characteristic of the mentality of Western pioneers. In the wide turning movements, made by democratic parties to outflank the strongholds of conservatism, the place of honour is always regarded as being on the extreme left of the line, and the more responsible and more vital armies of the pivot and the centre miss the sunlight of renown that gleams on the spearheads of the far-flung outposts. Indians, indeed, have been all too faithful students, not only of our faith in liberty, but of the questionable methods we have often employed to obtain it. We are, to adapt Edmund Burke's phrase, the unfittest people on earth to argue our fellow subjects back into acquiescent submission to paternal autocracy.

The Act of 1919, as we have seen, had established dyarchy—an ingenious scheme by which responsible government might be learnt in stages by progressive scholars in the school of constitutionalism, in the less before the more important departments, and in the provincial before the central sphere of administration. This form of government,

[1] *Moral and Material Progress and Condition of India, 1923–4*, p. 3.

however, never had perhaps any real friend except its sole begetter, Mr. Lionel Curtis. The authors of the Montagu-Chelmsford report only fell back upon it as a *pis aller*:—'Hybrid executives, limited responsibility, assemblies partly elected and partly nominated, divisions of functions, reservations general or particular, are devices that can have no permanent abiding place.' It was 'the best transitional mechanism' that appeared 'after a prolonged examination of alternatives'.[1] Herein, indeed, lurked the seeds of trouble. There have often no doubt been transitional periods in history, but they were only discovered to be such in the retrospective survey of historians. Successive stages in national development have generally been regarded as final by each generation in turn. The peculiarity about the decade 1919–29 is that it was a period required, so to speak, by statutory enactment, to contemplate self-consciously its own ephemeral nature, with the inevitable result that it was always hastening despairingly to a long-anticipated death-bed.

Quite apart from this, it must be acknowledged that the circumstances of the time would have made the working of the Act in any case supremely difficult. The aftermath of the war, its economic, social, and psychological effects, produced a general restlessness and discontent—as in other countries of the world—peculiarly unfavourable to political experiment; while permeating the whole texture of Indian life was the corrosion of communal bitterness—that 'abyss of unchained human passions', to quote Lord Irwin, 'which lies too often beneath the surface of habit and law'.[2]

Mr. Gandhi, uniting in his own person the culture of the West with the racial and religious instincts of the East, rallied many sections of Indian and even world opinion—

[1] *Report on Indian Constitutional Reforms*, Cd. 9109, p. 281.

[2] *Moral and Material Progress and Condition of India, 1927–8*, p. 17.

he had an enthusiastic following in the U.S.A.—against the government. Few can doubt his sincerity or his magnetic power. Mr. Jawaharlal Nehru, who is often at issue with him but regards him with a kind of despairing affection, writes :—'Reactionary or revolutionary, he has changed the face of India, given pride and character to a cringing and demoralized people, built up strength and consciousness in the masses, and made the Indian problem a world problem.'[1] Mr. Gandhi was aided not only by the extraordinary veneration felt for his character and services, but by his own acute political intuition and an efficient and astute organization. Few governments have been called upon to encounter in an adversary so formidable a union of the qualities of the mystic and the schemer. From that date till the present time (1938), though his opposition has passed through various stages of intensity or quiescence, the Indian government has never been able to leave him out of account. But his course is so incalculable, that he is often as great a problem to his supporters as his opponents. For if his policy of non-co-operation, civil disobedience, boycotts, and *hartals* (the enforced closing of shops as in times of public mourning) was directed against the government, his financial policy was often disliked by the Hindu mercantile class, his crusade on behalf of the untouchables alienated the most orthodox set of the Hindus (the *Mahasabha* party) and, curiously enough, was often resented by the very classes whose cause he was attempting to champion, while his insistence that every member of Congress should spin two hundred yards of cotton a month aroused but modified transports of enthusiasm in the hearts of the sophisticated politicians of the Congress party. As time went on, the stresses and strains set up by his personality caused splits and divisions in the nationalist ranks, while the embarrass-

[1] Jawaharlal Nehru, *An Autobiography*, John Lane, London, 1937, p. 406.

ments of his penitential fasts, like the rains of heaven, descended alike on the just and the unjust.

In 1919, then, Mr. Gandhi inaugurated the policy of non-co-operation which had brought him success and fame in South Africa. The pretext was the passing of an Act controlling the Press, providing for the trial of political offenders by judges without juries, and legalizing the internment of persons suspected of subversive aims. This measure was designed to implement the recommendations of the Rowlatt Committee on revolutionary propaganda. The Act was undoubtedly called for, if only temporarily, to maintain special powers granted to government by the Defence of India Act, which was about to lapse. The opposition was based on sentiment rather than on reason, for the most stringent clauses were limited in time, gave the government weaker powers than it had exercised under the Defence of India Act, and could only come into operation in conditions of peril carefully defined.

In March and April 1919 ominous disturbances broke out in Delhi, Gujarat, and the Punjab. Trouble in Afghanistan at the same time made the position still more precarious. On April 10 at Amritsar the mob rose, murdered four Europeans with horrible brutality, maltreated a lady missionary, leaving her for dead, and burnt to the ground banks and government buildings. The whole European community was in the gravest peril, and the civil authorities handed over the situation to the military. On April 13 a turbulent crowd in flat defiance of proclamations forbidding public meetings, assembled in a semi-enclosed space known as the Jallianwala Bagh. General Dyer marching thither with a tiny Indian force of fifty rifles and forty men armed with other weapons fired on the mob for ten minutes killing 379 and wounding 1,208. There can be no doubt that Dyer acted in good faith, having convinced himself that 'a determined and organized movement was in progress to submerge and destroy all the Europeans on the spot . . . and to carry the movement throughout the Punjab',[1] and the general opinion in Amritsar was that his action had saved the inhabitants from unspeakable horrors. But the large number of casualties naturally aroused strong criticism, and the episode was described in Parliament by Mr. Asquith as 'one of the worst outrages in the whole of our history'. A reasonable view is that, when every allowance is made for the terrible dangers that surrounded him, Dyer committed three disastrous errors of judgement, the first in not giving the crowd a final order to disperse before opening fire, the second in continuing to fire too long, the third, eight days later, in issuing the notorious 'crawling order'—that Indians traversing a certain street should do so on hands and knees. But he had passed through a terrible time of strain and anxiety[2] and had at least an arguable defence on the first two points.[3] He had good reason also to complain of the way in which he personally was treated. His conduct was at first approved by superior military authorities in India and the Lieutenant-Governor of the Punjab. He was given a higher command in the Afghan War, in which he did good service. Six months later a committee under Lord Hunter, a Scottish judge, was appointed to inquire into the troubled state of north-west India. They reported adversely on General Dyer's action at Amritsar on the ground that the duty of an officer on such an occasion was only to take measures necessary to save life and prevent the destruction of property, not to conceive it as incumbent upon him to strike terror into the province generally. The Government of India accepted this view, their considered opinion being that 'General Dyer acted beyond the necessity of the case, beyond what

[1] *Parliamentary Paper*, Cmd. 771.

[2] See Hansard, the fine speech of Lt.-General Sir Aylmer Hunter-Weston, July 8, 1920.

[3] *Parliamentary Paper*, Cmd. 771.

any reasonable man could have thought to be necessary, and that he did not act with as much humanity as the case permitted'. The Secretary of State also censured him, and the Commander-in-Chief required him to resign—an action upheld by the Army Council. Many thought he had been harshly dealt with, and subsequently the House of Lords and Mr. Justice McCardie in the famous case *O'Dwyer* v. *Nair* averred that his drastic action at the Jallianwala Bagh was justified and saved British rule in northern India. Whatever the final judgement of history may be, there can be no doubt that the episode at one time seemed to have opened up an unbridgeable gulf between the Indian and the British race.[1]

In the meantime, in an atmosphere thus unhappily suffused by race enmities, the first elections under the new constitution were held in October 1920. They were boycotted by the Congress party, but about two million voters, a third of the total electorate, went to the polls. Ministries were formed in the provinces, but, except in Madras, where the non-Brahmans secured enough seats to form a homogeneous cabinet, they had to be selected from various political groups. The Duke of Connaught opened the new central Indian legislature at Delhi on February 9, 1921, and read a gracious message from the King-Emperor:—'For years... patriotic and loyal Indians have dreamed of *swaraj* (Home Rule) for their Motherland. To-day you have the beginning of *swaraj* within my Empire and the widest scope and ample opportunity for progress to the liberty which my other Dominions enjoy.' Lord Chelmsford proclaimed that henceforward a guiding authority was to take the place of autocracy.

The new constitution on the whole may be said to have

[1] For the Amritsar tragedy see an admirable account in Sir Verney Lovett's *India* in the Nations of To-day series, London, 1923, chapters xxiv and xxv. See also Edward Thompson's *A Letter from India*, London, 1932, pp. 98–105.

worked better than could have been expected. This was partly due to the fact that, since the extremists held aloof, the moderates found themselves in a majority. Every effort was made by the permanent officials, as the Muddiman Committee reported, to make the administration both of the reserved and the transferred departments a success. The same policy of active good will was proved by the readiness of the Indian government to surrender many of the passes of British supremacy, which it had held so long. It allowed, for instance, a system of Protection to be set up, which but a few years before would have been stoutly resisted as detrimental to British interests, if not to the welfare of Indian consumers. The special privileges hitherto enjoyed by Europeans, when appearing before Indian Courts, were mostly abolished, and eight units of the army were set apart for Indianization in respect of their officers.

But in 1923 the *Swarajists* (a Congress Home Rule party under he leadership of Pandit Motilal Nehru) stood for election to the legislatures and, since they were largely successful, the prospects of dyarchy, which up till then had seemed to be fulfilling its function of training Indians in constitutional government, became at once overclouded. Amongst other events and tendencies, which also proved unfavourable to the hopes that had inspired the framers of the 1919 Act, the following may be enumerated:—the necessity forced upon the Governor-General, Lord Reading, of certifying Sir Basil Blackett's Act for doubling the salt tax—the only possible method of bringing to an end a series of annual deficits: the growing desire for the Indianization of the army coupled with the disinclination of the right kind of Indian youths to seek commissions: the grant to India of membership of the League of Nations, and a place at the Imperial Conferences of 1921 and 1923—a privilege which was meant to enhance her status both in her own eyes and in those of the world, but unhappily only made the Indian representatives feel keenly their inferiority to the Dominions when they found they could get little redress for the disabilities suffered by Indian emigrants to other parts of the Empire. There were besides, the riots caused by Mr. Gandhi's non-co-operation policy which marred the occasion of the Prince of Wales landing at Bombay in November 1921 and ultimately resulted in the trial and incarceration of Mr. Gandhi himself, after the dastardly murder by his misguided followers of twenty-one police-officers at Chauri-Chaura in February 1922 :[1]—the overthrow of dyarchy by extremist majorities in Bengal and the Central Provinces, resulting in the governors in these provinces being forced to take the administration into their own hands :—the ungenerous reception given to the report of the Lee Commission on the Indian services in 1923, though it approved of Indianization at an accelerated rate which seemed positively dangerous to civil servants of the older generation and clearly envisaged the gradual disappearance of the European element altogether except in the covenanted civil service, the police force, and in certain technical branches of public work such as engineering and irrigation :—finally a strong minority of Sir A. Muddiman's Committee on the working of the reforms, which reported in 1925, proclaimed that dyarchy was unworkable.

Another movement causing trouble to the government was the uneasiness of the Indian Moslems, first shown in 1919, as to the future of the Khilafat and the safety of the famous shrines of Islam, which were in jeopardy owing to the rash policy of the Ottoman Porte. The Muhammadan party were bitterly antagonized by that section of British and American opinion which was clamouring for the expulsion of

[1] Just before his imprisonment Gandhi in remorse for this untoward issue of a 'non-violent' policy called off the campaign of mass civil disobedience.

the Turks from Europe. Mr. Gandhi, not particular about the elements of opposition that he could bind together against the government, did not scruple to ally himself with the extremist Moslem leaders, the brothers Mohammad and Shauhat Ali. A singularly reckless and heartless scheme was set on foot of leading a *Hijrat* or migration of devout Muhammadans from India to Afghanistan which proved, as could easily have been foreseen, a disastrous failure. The road from Peshawar to Kabul was dotted with the graves of the hapless and misguided pilgrims. The Ali brothers finally called upon all Moslem sepoys to desert, and were imprisoned. The sting was very largely taken out of the Khilafat movement by the fact that Turkey was cutting herself adrift from her ancient moorings, and the Angora Assembly in 1924 exiled the last Khalif and abolished his office. The anomalous support given by Hindus to the movement had already been partly alienated by the rising in Malabar, in 1921–2, of the Moplahs, a fanatical Muhammadan tribe of Arab descent. Thousands of Hindus were cruelly massacred or forcibly converted to Islam. The baffling cross-currents of the troubled ocean of Indian politics were revealed by the fact that Mr. Gandhi gave a measure of support to the Moplahs, who were murdering and torturing his co-religionists, on condition that they proclaimed the doctrine of *swaraj*.

Yet, in spite of the acknowledged defects of dyarchy, certain lessons of constitutionalism were learnt, especially in those provinces where efforts were made to blur the distinction between reserved and transferred subjects and to make the dual executive in some way responsible for the administration. In the central government there can be no doubt whatever that the legislature with its majority of non-officials wielded great influence, for the official minority either through conviction or with a wise opportunism never opposed them except in matters which it deemed vital.

CHAPTER XIX

THE SIMON COMMISSION AND THE ROUND TABLE CONFERENCES

THE next stage in the constitutional problem was reached after the arrival of Lord Irwin as Governor-General in 1926. A man of high ideals, fine scholarship, and deep religious convictions, he showed such marked sympathy with the cause of Indian self-determination that he was often opposed by members of the political party (Conservative) to which he nominally belonged.

It will be remembered that the Act of 1919 had provided for the appointment of a commission of inquiry after the lapse of ten years, to decide whether the time had come for the next of those successive stages in the progressive realization of responsible government, of the advisability of which the British Cabinet and the Indian Government were to be the judges. There were, however, some people who declared, and perhaps not without reason, that the other condition attached to the promised advance, namely, co-operation rendered from Indians, had never come into existence at all.

Nevertheless, in reply to constant pressure, the Commission presided over by Sir John Simon was appointed in November 1927, two years before the full time. The seven members of it were all British. This was made a grievance both by the moderate nationalist party under Sir Tej Bahadur Sapru, and the more extreme section under Pandit Motilal Nehru. So high a constitutional authority as Dr. A. B. Keith seems to think that an avoidable blunder was committed, but only a body external to India could properly decide whether she was fit for a further step towards the goal of self-government. She was not yet independent and so could hardly with propriety be allowed to investigate her own case. Later it was announced that seven members of the Indian legislatures would be asked to co-operate and to issue a simultaneous report. The landing of the commission in Bombay on February 3, 1928, was made the occasion of *hartals*, strikes, and hostile demonstrations. The central Indian legislature remained obdurate in its attitude, but the provincial assemblies ultimately rendered assistance, while the depressed classes and other minorities willingly laid their grievances before the commission.

A campaign of outrage and assassination flared out in Bengal and the Punjab. Bitter industrial strikes inflicted grave economic loss. The government was forced to pass a public safety and a trade disputes act, and prosecuted in the courts twenty-nine agitators, of whom three were British. This step proved somewhat ineffective, for the trials were not concluded till five years had elapsed, and the sentences then tardily pronounced were afterwards either reduced or remitted by the Court of Appeal.

Lord Irwin became convinced that it was no longer feasible to maintain an irresponsible central government continuously enfiladed by the criticisms of an opposition which could never be challenged by the touchstone of office to make its criticisms good. He paid a hasty visit to England to confer with the new Labour Government, and returned to make on October 31, 1929, the momentous announcement that the natural issue of constitutional progress in India was the attainment of Dominion status and that, after the Simon Commission had reported, a round table conference would be held in London to hear representative Indian views before the bill was brought before

Parliament. Whatever may be thought about the statesmanship of this declaration, it seems a reasonable criticism that it should not have been made until the commission had concluded its labours. It left that unfortunate body in the air, and at the same time stole its thunder. In addition, the phrase 'Dominion status' was unhappily so ambiguous as to be capable of a variety of interpretations. Lord Irwin and the Cabinet seem to have used it in the sense in which it was employed in the preamble to the Act of 1919, as applicable to the constitution of a dependency enjoying responsible or autonomous government, whereas Indians immediately fastened upon the term the connotation made definite and explicit at the Colonial Conference of 1926, when it was defined as the status of 'autonomous communities within the British Empire, equal in status in no way subordinate one to another in any aspect of their domestic or external affairs, though united by a common allegiance to the Crown and freely associated as members of the British commonwealth of nations'. Clearly a whole sub-continent of manifold languages, warring faiths, and deep communal cleavages, where majority rule was impossible and reliance on the suzerain power for external defence inevitable, could not aspire to a status so defined.

When it became clear that no party in England was prepared to sanction any scheme of Dominion status which could be put into operation at once, the Congress meeting at Lahore authorized a new campaign of civil disobedience and passed a resolution, moved by Mr. Jawaharlal Nehru, that the goal of the Indian people was complete national independence.

The report of the Simon Commission was published in May 1930. It will always stand out as one of the greatest of Indian State papers. The impressive unanimity of the commissioners, who from their known party antecedents must clearly have sacrificed all but their deepest convictions to attain it, ought to have commended their sagacious and temperately worded conclusions to all men of good will. But the report was promptly assailed by the Indian extremists, who would equally have assailed any conceivable position that the commission might have adopted, while the British Government, as we have seen, had partly forestalled and ultimately side-tracked it, though some of its recommendations were afterwards adopted.

Briefly, the commissioners recommended that dyarchy should be abandoned in the provinces and responsible government made a reality, even the maintenance of law and order with all the other transferred subjects passing under the control of ministers responsible to the legislatures. In the central government, however, responsibility was not advised. This was not due to any lack of sympathy with the ideals of self-government, but to the inescapable difficulties of the actual position in India—difficulties from the existence of which both Indian patriotic leaders and British politicians were far too apt to avert their gaze. There were the communal dissensions making the majority rule, which is the *sine qua non* of a democratic government, a sheer impossibility. There was the question of defence, for not even the most violently patriotic of nationalist leaders could visualize with complacency long files of the British army marching from frontier-posts and garrison-towns to ports of embarkation for Europe. There was the necessity of finding a niche in an all-India constitution for the Indian Princes, whose point of view had been hitherto dangerously ignored. They were indeed out of agreement with either side in the main controversy. Determined not to acknowledge the suzerainty of Indian ministers responsible to popularly elected legislatures, they were far from being willing to regard themselves as mere princely supports and bulwarks of an imperial government with autocratic powers. They had long been restive under the tendency of the paramount power to supervise their internal affairs and whittle down, as they thought, their treaty rights. This attitude had dated especially from the very important pronouncement made by Lord Reading in 1925 on the claims put forward by the Nizam in relation to Berar, that in the internal affairs of his state, he stood on the same footing as the British Government in India, in regard to the internal affairs of British India. Lord Reading declared: 'The sovereignty of the British Crown is supreme in India, and therefore no ruler of an Indian state can justifiably claim to negotiate with the British Government on an equal footing. Its supremacy is not based only upon treaties and engagements but exists independently of them, and quite apart from its prerogatives in matters relating to foreign powers and policies, it is the right and duty of the British Government, while scrupulously respecting all treaties and engagements with the Indian states to preserve peace and good order throughout India.' And further:—'The varying degrees of internal sovereignty which the rulers enjoy are all subject to the due exercise by the paramount power of this responsibility.' The fiscal question also complicated the relation of the states to the British Government. It has been estimated that since the adoption of protection in 1921 the central government takes annually from the Indian states, who have practically no sea-board, £10,000,000 in custom dues levied solely in the interests of the population of British India.

The Simon commissioners realized that the rule of a government responsible only to the Secretary of State would not last for ever, and they looked forward to the conception of a Federation—though it was outside the terms of their reference to recommend it—which should unite the autonomously governed provinces of British India with the traditional monarchies of the Indian states, under the supervising and sympathetic control of the Crown. Part of the hostility of the nationalist leaders to the Simon report may well have been due, as Dr. Keith suggests, to its mild hint that autonomous government in an oriental environment need not necessarily be identical in every particular with its counterpart under occidental skies. They would have none of such a doctrine, for their 'views on these topics have throughout shown a remarkable lack of ingenuity and a determination slavishly to copy western models hardly compatible with the national spirit by which they are animated'.[1]

The publication of the Simon report did nothing to allay, it probably even intensified, the campaign of violence instigated by Congress agitators. An illegal movement for the manufacture of salt was inaugurated by Mr. Gandhi, who marched at the head of his followers from Ahmedabad to Dandi beach in April 1930. Commercial boycotts and the picketing of liquor shops were embarked on in the towns, and the non-payment of rent was advocated in country districts. Many serious riots took place, and the work of the police in quelling them was made very difficult by the unprecedented number of women who took part in them. In the North-West Frontier Province a 'red shirt' movement under a Pathan leader Abdul Ghaffar Khan, a queer amalgamation of Congress views and pan-Islamic sentiment, added a modern seditious tinge to the age-long tribal blood-feuds of the borderland.

The Indian Government was now forced, and not before it was time, to reassert its rapidly waning authority by press laws and other coercive measures empowering in certain cases detention of suspects in prison without trial, but it balanced this policy by strenuously endeavouring to proceed with its plan of conciliation and reform. Three round table conferences were held in London between representatives of all the British political parties on the one hand and all

[1] Dr. A. B. Keith, *A Constitutional History of India*, 1936, p. 294.

sections of Indian opinion except the Congress party on the other. The sessions took place November 16, 1930, to January 19, 1931, September 7 to December 1, 1931, November 17 to December 24, 1932. During the second session the Labour Government fell and was succeeded by the National Government, but the new Cabinet practically accepted the Indian policy of its predecessors.

The most surprising and momentous result of the round table conferences was the unexpected announcement by representatives of the Princes at the first session that the latter were in favour of a federation provided that responsibility was conferred upon the central government. The turn thus given to affairs at first won over both British and Indian parties in the conference. The Indian nationalists gladly made common cause with the Princes against irresponsible British control in the centre, and only later came to recognize that the Princes' main preoccupation was to ward off from their dominions the insidious virus of democracy. The British Government felt that to grant self-government to a federation to which the adhesion of the Princes would bring some element of tradition and sobriety, would be a very different thing from granting it to a popularly elected assembly of earnest but impatient idealists. On January 19, the concluding day of the first session, the Prime Minister announced that 'with the legislature constituted on a federal basis' the government 'would be prepared to recognize the principle of the responsibility of the executive to the legislature'.

Following this declaration, every effort was made by the Indian Government to conciliate the Congress party. The working committee of that body, which had been imprisoned, was released, and between February 17 and March 5 Lord Irwin had many interviews with Mr. Gandhi. Though some of the reactions to this unconventional course were not very happy, in that the Moslem party's fears of Hindu predominance in their disfavour were intensified, and many extremists believed that the government had yielded to pressure, yet an accord was made on March 4 between the Viceroy and the Mahatma by which it was agreed that civil disobedience was to cease, political prisoners except those condemned for outrages to be amnestied, and Mr. Gandhi to represent Congress in the next session of the conference in London.

The second session proved disappointing, for Mr. Gandhi was unhelpful and the Indian members were unable among themselves to reach any agreement on the communal question.

When Mr. Gandhi returned to India he found that under Lord Willingdon, the new Governor-General, the control over affairs which had been unduly relaxed, though from the highest motives, in Lord Irwin's time, had now been resumed. He was himself soon imprisoned, and the activities of Congress were declared illegal. This tardy re-establishment of authority was so successful that in three months the number of those detained in prison for civil disobedience fell from 34,458 to 4,683. The British government, to whom the task had been left by the contending Indian parties themselves, announced their award on the communal issue, as affecting representation in the legislatures. This award was supplemented and modified with the government's consent by the Poona Pact of September 1932 between Mr. Gandhi and the leaders of the untouchables. Mr. Gandhi forced this solution on his unwilling co-religionists by use of the weapon he had so often employed against the government—the threat of a fast to the death.

After the third session of the conference, November 17 to December 24, the government drew up a set of proposals for the reform of the Indian Government based on the agreed results, such as they were, of the round table conferences.

They were mainly approved by the Liberal party and a majority of the National Government's supporters, convinced that a bold and generous step forward was now essential, but opposed by a section of the Conservative party, who held that the toiling masses of the Indian people were wholly unused to, and unfitted for, democratic government, that it was hopeless to attempt to mollify Congress, now actually demanding complete independence, that already under Indian management many of the public services had sadly deteriorated, and finally that there would be a serious danger of anarchy when the police, who had shown heroic fortitude and loyalty through a time of searching trial, were subjected to the authority of autonomous provincial ministries.

Mr. Winston Churchill placed himself with gusto at the head of this recalcitrant party, who honestly believed that the proposals amounted to a surrender by Great Britain of her traditional task in India. It is likely that he was sincere enough, as most of his followers undoubtedly were, and his parliamentary and debating abilities were beyond all question, but, as is usually the case with his abounding personality, his slashing invectives and exuberant onslaughts gave a twist to the conduct of the case which probably did his cause little service and neutralized the quieter and more effective pleadings of experts like Sir Reginald Craddock.

The white paper was submitted to a joint select committee of both Houses of Parliament. Mr. Churchill and Lord Lloyd declined to serve on it (though the former gave evidence before it) on the ground, which had probably some foundation in fact, that it had been overweighted by the appointment of men already known to be in sympathy with the government's policy. The general opinion, however, was that they would have been better advised to take their places on the committee.

The joint select committee accepted the white paper,

but laid stress on the necessity of safeguards. The Government of India Act was passed on December 20, 1935. The chief modification made in its passage through Parliament was the surprising and rather unfortunate amendment introduced in the Lords, by which the election of members to the upper house of the Central Government was made direct instead of indirect, and transferred from the provincial legislative assemblies to unwieldly territorial constituencies. Thus there results the anomaly that in the upper house election is direct, and in the lower and theoretically more popular house it is indirect.

The government refused, with doubtful wisdom or consistency, to accede to the desire of the Liberal and Labour parties that the Act should re-affirm the famous preamble of the Act of 1919 declaring the ultimate goal to be dominion status.

Meanwhile neither communal riots nor murderous attacks on government officials ceased. The most terrible Hindu-Moslem outbreak was at Cawnpore in March 1931. The period 1930–3 was a black one for terrorist outrages, especially in Bengal. Within three years three district magistrates of Midnapore alone met their deaths at the hand of political assassins. It was found necessary under the special ordinances to detain in prison or under observation, without trial, a large number of suspects, many of them students and youths of impressionable age. Such a procedure is of course opposed to all normal principles of representative government, and offered nationalist orators an obvious opportunity for specious invective. But even democratic governments, as the guardians of freedom, are bound to defend their existence against subversive and fanatical minorities who endeavour by bomb or pistol to tear up the very foundations of liberty. Sir John Anderson, Governor of Bengal, happily survived a desperate attempt on his life by two young terrorists on May 8, 1934, at the

Lebong race meeting. He showed magnificent courage and coolness in facing his assailants, and with splendid magnanimity and by a happy and statesmanlike expedient did much to solve the problem of the *détenus*, as they were called, by establishing industrial camps and farm colonies in which the suspects could be trained in peaceful occupations against the day of their release.

CHAPTER XX

THE APPROACH TO FEDERALISM

THE Act of 1935 is so elaborate that only a brief summary can be given here. A great deal is involved in the momentous change from a unitary to a federal form of government, and in this case complications arose from the fact that the federation is formed not, as usual, by the coming together of a number of hitherto equally independent states each surrendering sovereign powers to a central government, but by a 'disparate'[1] union on the one hand of states surrendering quasi-independent powers and on the other of provinces of a unitary empire, receiving autonomy for the first time at the moment that they enter the federation.[2] For the provinces federation will be of course compulsory, but for the states it is voluntary, and at the present time (1938) no one knows how many of them, if any, will accept it. Even if, and when, they accept it, they only surrender such powers as are specified in each case by the instrument of accession, by which they enter the federation.

The date of the federation is to be proclaimed on an address from both Houses of Parliament when Indian rulers who have the right to fill not less than half of the 104 seats set apart for them in the Council of State, the upper house of the federal legislature, and having as

[1] See Dr. A. B. Keith, *A Constitutional History of India*, p. 320, and compare Jawaharlal Nehru, *An Autobiography*, p. 534.

[2] In dealing with the units of the federation for convenience it should be noted that by the states we mean henceforward the monarchal states of the Indian Princes and by provinces the local governments or presidencies of British India.

subjects not less than 39,490,956 persons, accede to it. As regards the federation itself a federal court is to be established to demarcate the spheres of the central and the provincial or state governments. The power to amend the constitution is vested in the imperial Parliament. The suzerainty of the Crown over those Indian states who may not choose to enter the federation (and over such powers of the other states as are not surrendered in their instruments of accession) is no longer to be administered by the Governor-General as such, but by 'the representative of the Crown in relations with the states'. This office normally, though not necessarily, will be conferred upon the Governor-General, but as King's representative, not as head of the federal government.

We will now briefly describe the executives and the legislatures first of the federation and then of the British Indian provinces:—

The federal executive. At the head of it is the Governor-General. He has, quite apart from his work as the representative of the Crown in its dealings with the Indian Princes, two distinct spheres of action:—In the first, which includes such matters as defence and external affairs, he is obliged to follow no one's advice, though he is aided by three councillors appointed by himself. In the second, he has a council of ministers responsible to the federal legislature, whose advice he would normally be bound to follow, though even here in some important matters, such as a menace to the peace of India, he can exercise his own discretion.

The responsibilities that fall upon the Governor-General are clearly in some ways heavier than they have ever been before, and some good judges have considered them too heavy a burden for any man to bear.[1] This would certainly

[1] See the letter of Lord Zetland in *The Times*, March 23, 1933, who has, however, probably modified those opinions since.

be true were it not that his discretionary and exceptional powers are never supposed to be exercised in normal times.

The federal legislature is bi-cameral and consists of an upper house, the Council of State, with 156 members for British India and 104 members for the Indian states. The British Indian members are directly elected on a high franchise with the exception of six nominated by the Governor-General to represent the interests of minority communities, women, and the depressed classes. The state representatives are to be appointed by the Princes.

The lower house, the Assembly, is to consist of 250 representatives for British India and a maximum of 125 for the states. Election to the Assembly is indirect either by the provincial assemblies, electoral colleges, chambers of commerce, societies of landowners, or labour organizations. In the states members again are appointed by the rulers.

The Council of State sits permanently, one-third of its members retiring every year. The Assembly sits for five years. When a bill has passed both houses, the Governor-General may assent to it, refuse his assent, or reserve it for consideration. A reserved bill drops, unless the Governor-General notifies the royal assent within twelve months. Certain items of federal revenue, for instance expenditure on defence, are to be determined independently of the vote of the legislature. Beyond all his other powers, the Governor-General is granted the right to legislate by ordinance in a crisis, and can in fact assume the powers of any federal authority except the federal court.

We now come to the provincial constitutions. In the realm of the executive, autonomous government is set up. The Governor acts in accordance with the advice of ministers responsible to the legislatures, though even here he possesses reserve powers only to be used in serious emergencies, and directly administers certain 'excluded areas' occupied by aboriginal populations.

The legislatures are bi-cameral in six of the provinces, and uni-cameral in five. As in the federal government, the upper chambers or Councils of State are permanent—a third of the members retiring each year, while the lower chambers or Assemblies last for five years. The number of seats for the different communities is settled by the British communal award of August 4, 1932, modified by the Poona Pact of September 25.

Aden and Burma, where there had been a serious rebellion December 1931–August 1932, under Jaya San, a former Buddhist monk turned quack doctor and fortune-teller, were detached from the Indian empire. As regards the Home government, the Secretary of State's Council of India dating from 1858 was abolished. Instead, he is to have from three to six advisers, whom he may consult individually or collectively as he thinks fit.

Until the Princes have accepted federation the old irresponsible central government continues side by side with responsible government in the provinces. Again, therefore, we have perforce a short period of transition, which however can hardly be avoided. Even if the Princes enter the federation—and unless they do so unanimously a very difficult situation will be created—it will still be open to Indians to say with a good deal of truth that a constitution which still reserves in emergencies such autocratic powers to the Governors and the Governor-General cannot be said to grant dominion status as that term is understood elsewhere in the Empire. An opponent of British rule puts it effectively though not very fairly when he says, 'We are provided with a car all brakes and no engines.'[1] The answer must be a regretful assent, coupled with the reminder that, in Dr. A. B. Keith's words, 'the

[1] Jawaharlal Nehru, *An Autobiography*, p. 581.

obstacles to dominion status were not created by the British government'.[1] They arise from communal cleavages and the inability of India as yet to undertake the burden of her own defence. 'The essence of responsible government . . . is the existence of a people sufficiently homogeneous to be governed by majority rule; where caste, race, religion intervene, majority government becomes difficult or impracticable.' As soon as the principle of safeguarding minorities has to be introduced 'the essence of responsible government is seriously if not fatally compromised'.[2]

[1] Dr. A. B. Keith, *A Constitutional History of India*, p. 471.
[2] Ibid., p. 473.

CHAPTER XXI

EXTERNAL RELATIONS, 1917–37

FOR some years after 1917 the whole of western and central Asia was exposed to great danger from Soviet Russia. The threefold agreement with the Russian empire in 1907[1] had for the time settled all outstanding questions with Great Britain, and in the Great War Russia was our ally, but with the fall of the Tsarist régime she relapsed for a time into anarchy. As soon as the power of the Soviet was established it proceeded to reconquer not only the outlying parts of the former Russian empire which had declared themselves independent but also the relapsed provinces of Khiva and Bokhara. The fall of these khanates left Persia and Afghanistan the only barriers between the Soviet's dominions and India, and Bolshevist propaganda has been assiduously employed to stir up trouble for the Indian government all along the North-West Frontier.

Fortunately our relations with Persia have remained friendly and the rulers of Afghanistan, as always, have shown themselves on the whole eager to pursue their independence of both the great empires that march with their frontiers. The Amir, Habibullah, who had rendered Great Britain invaluable service in the War by maintaining, in circumstances of the greatest difficulty, a friendly neutrality, was assassinated on February 20, 1919. In the struggle for the throne that ensued, Amanullah, one of his younger sons, succeeded in establishing his claim. Partly to stave off internal troubles, partly to fling a sop to the militarist party,

[1] *Supra*, pp. 564–7.

he embarked on the Third Afghan War in May 1919. He was however speedily defeated, for aeroplanes, wireless, and high explosives had robbed tribal warriors of their old advantages in guerrilla warfare. Jellalabad and Kabul itself were bombed. On August 8 the treaty of peace was signed by which the British Government prohibited henceforward the Afghans from importing arms or munitions through India, confiscated the arrears of the late Amir's subsidy, and made no grant to the new Amir. The British let it be known that they would no longer seek to control the relations of Afghanistan with foreign powers. The peace was followed by a new treaty, November 22, 1921, by which each nation agreed to respect the independence of the other. Further, the Amir was granted a privilege, which in former times Abdur Rahman had coveted in vain, that of having a British minister accredited to him at Kabul, and being represented by his own at the Court of St. James.

In the years following this peace, Amanullah embarked upon a programme of ambitious and sweeping reforms for which his country was unhappily not yet ripe. The introduction of secular education and a secular code of law bitterly antagonized the Mullahs or priestly party. In March 1924 a rebellion broke out in the southern provinces, and, to appease the malcontents, many of the new measures were cancelled. Amanullah, however, again soon pressed on with his westernizing policy, and visited Europe in 1927 to be everywhere fêted and honoured. But he had alienated the sympathies of the majority of his subjects, and was finally forced to abdicate in May 1929.

During the troubles, December 1928–February 1929, Kabul was cut off from communication with the outside world, but the Royal Air Force by a brilliant achievement brought away many Indian subjects and foreigners, and finally on February 25 the staff, women, and children of the Legation. 'In all they made eighty-six journeys from Peshawar to Kabul and back, and flew a distance of 28,000 miles. These evacuations were carried out at a height of 10,000 feet under every conceivable climatic difficulty in one of the severest winters on record.'[1]

The British Government observed the strictest neutrality in the Afghan civil war. For a time an illiterate bigot, Bacha-i-Saquo, usurped power, but he was eventually defeated by Nadir Shah, who re-established an ordered government. The new Amir abandoned the precipitate policy of Amanullah Khan, but obtained better results by a more cautious progress in the path of reform, and by wise conciliation of the Mullah party. His relations with us were most friendly, and his assassination on November 8, 1933, by an ignorant fanatic, was a calamity to both countries. The peaceful succession of his son, a youth of 19, was an eloquent testimony to the settled condition of the country.

The Third Afghan War, like a seismic disturbance, had sent out dangerous shock tremors through Baluchistan and all along the tribal areas of the North-West Frontier of India. There the position was already precarious, for the Curzon system (see *ante*, p. 517), which had worked well down to 1914, had broken down under the tremendous strains and impacts of the World War. The Pathans of the border were in a state of excitable unrest, and had immensely increased their store of modern weapons of precision. A new feature was their tendency to adopt as their own, grievances of the Indian Nationalist Party. There has been continual trouble with the tribes from 1918 onwards, but it is impossible to give the history of it in any detail here. The fiercest fighting was in 1919 against the Waziris. In 1925 the Mahsuds were attacked by the Royal Air Force, and in 1930–1 there was a serious rising of the Waziris, Mohmands, and Afridis. The Afridis in June 1931 actually raided up

[1] *Moral and Material Progress and Condition of India*, 1928–9, p. 276.

to the suburbs of Peshawar, and put forward demands for the release of Mr. Gandhi from prison and the repeal of the special ordinances in India—a demand illustrating the far-reaching effects of Congress intrigues.

The Curzon frontier policy has now been superseded by—or perhaps it would be fairer to say has developed into, for it is not in essence so very different—a new 'forward policy . . . not of military conquest but of civilization.'[1] Great high roads have been constructed through the hills of Waziristan, the main centre of tribal disturbances, the tribesmen themselves have been enrolled to police and control the country, and every effort has been made to display to the population the advantages of law and order and the benefits of trade and peaceful occupations.

[1] *Moral and Material Progress and Condition of India, 1930-1*, p. 14.

CHAPTER XXII

ECONOMIC AND SOCIAL CHANGES

THE fiscal and economic aspect of the Indian empire has greatly changed since the days of India's tutelage under a Free Trade paramount power. Things have been, and are being, done which must make the founders of the Manchester school turn in their orthodox graves. The gradual abandonment of Free Trade convictions by important sections of political opinion at home, and the necessity of allowing India, in her pursuit of ambitious policies of development and social reform, to raise a revenue by indirect taxation, since direct taxes were unsuitable to so poor a country and very expensive to levy, caused the British Government in 1919 to haul down the weather-beaten flag of fiscal orthodoxy so long kept flying by successive Viceroys and Secretaries of State, and to conclude a fiscal autonomous convention by which it engaged not to impose its own views on the Indian Government. This policy was reaffirmed on various occasions, and finally appears in the 1935 Government of India Act, which gives India full permission to set up a protective system even by the imposition of countervailing duties against British goods, though it is one of the reserved powers of the Governors and Governor-General to prohibit any duties designed rather to injure the United Kingdom than to further the economic interests of India.

While India still remains predominantly an agricultural country—seventy-one per cent. of her population being engaged on the land—her industrial development has been so rapid that she now takes a high place in the ranking list of the world's industrial states. She not only tends to produce her own steel, glass, cement, chemicals, and other commodities, but to convert her own raw products into manufactured or partly manufactured goods. India's isolation from Great Britain during the Great War obliged her to do for herself some things which she had hitherto relied on the enterprise of British capital and British labour to do for her. Both the central and the provincial governments on the advice of Sir Thomas Holland's Industrial Commission have decided to take a prominent part in the manufacturing and commercial development of the country. The Imperial Council of Agricultural Research (1934) applies a similar policy to the land. There has been a notable increase in the output of the extractive industries, especially of petroleum in Assam, and iron ore in Bihar and Orissa. Transport both by railway and road has been still further improved. The Indian Government has pressed on assiduously with its irrigation works, the great Lloyd barrage across the Indus at Sukkur in Sind which will eventually fertilize over five million acres of desert was completed in 1932. A new great harbour has been constructed at Vizagapatam and an old one enlarged at Cochin. The Indian Government has, indeed, in the words of a writer by no means excessively friendly to British rule, 'made famine impossible by an interrelation of transport and irrigation'.[1]

Social changes in India are even more epoch-making than those produced by economic developments. Some are due to scientific discoveries such as aviation and the radio, some to imponderable revolutions of the mind and the spirit. The new wine—new even in the West—of modern material and intellectual progress has been poured with a generous hand into the old wine skins of the East. Some of the

[1] Basil Mathews, *India Reveals Herself*, Oxford, 1937, p. 178.

changes are wholly to the good, as for instance the dying away of race prejudice, and the freer intercourse between Europeans and Indians. Some may appear dangerously premature, such as the partial breaking down of the age-long joint family system of the Hindus before another way of life has been fully evolved. But the change is clear for all to see. An India where viceroys annihilate time and distance in government planes, where the population of remote villages gather nightly round a communal loud-speaker, where women have broken through their immemorial trammels to sit side by side with men in legislative assemblies, and where illiterate masses throng into polling booths to deposit in different-coloured boxes voting papers distinguished by pictorial symbols for candidates of whom they know nothing in support of policies they cannot comprehend—this is indeed an India strangely different from the India of even twenty years ago.

Broadcasting stations have been set up in Delhi, the provincial capitals, and other important cities. Urdu, Marathi, Bengali, Gujerati, Tamil, and Telegu are the languages used at different centres, and at all there are at certain times programmes in English. Clearly the radio is a highly effective means of imparting instruction to a mostly illiterate population, and the government may through this most modern development of western science recapture that personal link between rulers and ruled which was the best characteristic both of Hindu and Mughal administration.

Nothing is more remarkable than the emancipation of women in the land of Purdah and child marriages. The vote was first granted in Madras in 1921. Under the new constitution 6,000,000 women will be enfranchised. Women are putting forward demands, such as a radical reform of the system of Hindu law, which are likely to bring them into collision sooner or later with the orthodox party even in Congress itself. They are inclined to agitate for ideal conditions in education and housing without much regard to sordid, if inescapable, questions of finance. They are thronging into the Universities to train for the medical and legal professions. In December 1925 the poetess, Mrs. Sarojini Naidu, presided over the National Congress.

The cinema is beginning to exert a strong influence, as in all other countries, partly elevating, partly degrading. Rapid travel, the commingling of different races, and great popular meetings have a certain disintegrating effect, though one very difficult to measure, upon the caste system. The motor omnibus too is now 'outstripping the train as a carrier of ferment into the peasant life of India. As the millions of Indian rats carry plague, so the thousands upon thousands of Indian 'buses . . . from the village to the city and back, carry the virus of modernism.'[1]

No one can foresee the harvest of the strange new forces, half tares, half wheat, germinating in the Indian soil. While a prophet like Gandhi is turning away from the satanic civilization of the West, preaching a Hindu revival and a return to medieval conceptions of economy, the younger leaders are eager for a completely scientific and secular view of life, and were in despair when the Mahatma proclaimed that the terrible earthquake in Behar of 1932 was a judgement for the sin of untouchability. At a time when Hindu-Moslem antagonism, intensified by the fact that since the communal award the votaries of different religions may be electors grouped in separate political constituencies, is peculiarly rife and deep-seated, the *intelligentsia* is growing more and more impatient of this Great Divide in the national life, declaring that it is merely a barrier between religious reactionaries, who deserve no sympathy, and that the whole communal question has been deliberately intensified by the British to weaken their opponents. Finally, at the very moment when the older

[1] Basil Mathews, *India Reveals Herself*, Oxford, 1937, p. 11.

type of Indian nationalist seems to be drawing near the goal of his ambition, Jawaharlal Nehru, the most brilliant of the younger men, derides the ideal even of dominion status, claims complete independence of Great Britain, and threatens a crusade for communism. Such a movement, though it would split the Congress party and drive large sections of Indian political thought into alliance with the moderate party, has clearly possibilities of the greatest peril among the millions of India's illiterates. Now that he has a vote, the Indian peasant, hitherto mainly the concern of the government and the district officer, has been discovered by the Congress politician, and he may prefer the glittering though unsubstantial bait of a communistic state after the Russian pattern, to the sober but more real benefit of Lord Linlithgow's policy of gradual agricultural reconstruction.

The great need for the solution of these insistent problems is that Englishman and Indian should each endeavour to understand better the attitude of the other. The Englishman, admitting, if he is honest, that he would never himself acquiesce in his own country in the rule of foreigners, however able, must acknowledge that the Indian Government in the past has been slow to recognize the inherent reasonableness of India's claim to manage her own affairs. The Indian, on the other hand, has been loth to give Great Britain the credit for her attempted abdication of imperial tasks, and has refused to understand how immensely the difficulties of devolution have been increased by the terrorist policy of assassination and outrage. Everlasting recrimination can never lead anywhere. Generosity is required from both sides alike: from those who are now called upon to divest themselves of powers which have on the whole been nobly wielded, and also from those who are asked still for a season to exercise their souls in patience till, by making a practical success of the reforms under the new Act, they prove their fitness for a dominion status as full as that enjoyed by the other great self-governing commonwealths under the British Crown.

If only co-operation and goodwill can take the place of rivalry and national antagonism, no two races are better fitted by natural endowment to work together and supplement each other's qualities. The Indian brings into the common stock his lively, adroit, mobile intelligence and his brilliant dialectical brain. The more stolid Englishman—too stupid perhaps alike in administration and war to know when he is beaten—contributes his practical sense and his capacity for getting things done. What fruitful results might not be achieved—and in fact already have been partly achieved—by such partners working in charity and unison! Englishmen no doubt have often in the past been tactless and arrogant, but Indians do not always understand that what seems to them to be incivility and pride is frequently only a lack of imaginative insight or a national shyness and reserve. There have been in the past, and will be in the future, many real and deep friendships between men of both races, for the charm of the Indian character, the grace and courtesy of Indian manners, the quick responsiveness of Indian minds, have often taken captive undemonstrative—but not necessarily unappreciative—British hearts. It must be the earnest prayer of all true friends both of India and Great Britain that under the new dispensation these happy relations may be extended from individuals to embrace the peoples and the governments of both countries.

INDEX

References to the new material on pages 580–623 are given either at the end of the entries in this index or in the additional index on pp. 668–9.

ADDITIONAL INDEX